C0-CZR-244

YOUR MASS AND YOUR LIFE

Nihil obstat : Fr. MARTIN M. DIETRICH, O.F.M.
Montreal, February 14th., 1960

Fr. BRENDAN CULLEN, O.F.M.
Montreal, February 14th., 1960

Imprimi potest : Fr. FULGENCE BOISVERT, O.F.M.
Minister provincialis
Montreal, February 18th., 1960

Imprimatur : † LAWRENCE P. WHELAN, V.G.
Auxiliary Bishop of Montreal
Montreal, February 29th., 1960

PRINTED IN CANADA

RICHER-MARIE BEAUBIEN, O.F.M.

Your Mass and Your Life

Translated by
ELLA-MARIE COOPER

•

FRANCISCAN EDITIONS
2080 Dorchester Street West,
MONTREAL 25

1960

By the Same Author

Corps mystique et modestie chrétienne (125 pp.)

(with questions and answers)

Loisirs (165 pp.)

(with questions and answers)

Le Troubadour d'Assise

(A life of St. Francis with 234 illustrations)

PREFACE

"SI SCIRES DONUM DEI." (John 4:10)

How many people understand what the Mass really is?

Many persons no longer scruple to miss Sunday Mass. Many attend Mass simply through force of habit, to conform to custom, for family and social reasons, or simply to avoid mortal sin.

"SI SCIRES DONUM DEI."

And how many people *live* their Mass?

No long observation of the faithful who attend Sunday Mass is required, to ascertain that the greater part are thinking of anything and everything else except what is taking place at the altar. And how many—once they have left the church—ever give another thought to their morning Mass?

If we would live the Mass, we must participate in it.

And if we would participate in the Mass, we must understand it.

If certain Catholics attend Mass only to avoid serious sin—if they have no love for the Mass—it is because they do not understand it; do not take part in it; do not live it. The Mass for them constitutes an exterior act of religion unlinked with life, a "church service" to which they go with resignation and of which they remain the indifferent witnesses and passive spectators.

These past few years, an effort has been made to further an understanding of the Mass on the part of the people. The means employed include popular missals, the dialogued Mass, the spoken choral Mass, study circles on the Mass, initiation to liturgical chant, and illustrated albums and films on the Mass. With a concern for better informed minds, an imposing array of books bearing on the multiple aspects of the Mass has been published. It has been said that the Mass is a "banquet", an "assembly", a "festival", an "offering", a "call to action", and so on.

All these points of view are genuine and capable of nurturing piety. Nonetheless, the most essential, the most important element, does not always appear.

"SI SCIRES DONUM DEI"

What then, is the Mass?

First and foremost, the Mass is a Sacrifice.

The Sacrifice of Christ and the Church. The Sacrifice of the Head and members of the Mystical Body.

Should we seek to know what Christ's Sacrifice really was, we would learn that our Divine Lord's Sacrifice consisted not alone in his martyrdom of a few hours on the Cross; but in his whole life of renunciation and obedience, of which Calvary was the glorious culmination.

This precise definition of Christ's Sacrifice is, perhaps, one of the most important that His Holiness, Pope Pius XII, has given in regard to the Mass, in his encyclical *Mediator Dei et hominum,* paragraph 17:

"Indeed, scarcely has 'the Word been made flesh' (John 1:14) than he manifests himself to the world in his priestly character; by making an act of submission to God the Father, which is to be life-long. 'Therefore, in coming into the world, he says, behold, I come to do your will, O God' (Heb. 10:5-7). This act is to be brought to its full perfection in a heroic manner in the bloody Sacrifice of the Cross: 'It is in this "will" that we have been sanctified through the offering of the body of Jesus Christ once for all' (Heb. 10:10). All Christ's activity among men had no other purpose. As a child, he is presented to the Lord in the Temple of Jerusalem. As a youth, he visits it anew. Later on, he will often return to instruct the people and to pray. Before inaugurating his public ministry, he fasts for forty days. By word and example, he exhorts us to pray, whether by day or by night. As Master of Truth, he 'enlightens every man', (John 1:9); that mortals may recognize the true immortal God, and not be 'among those who draw back unto destruction, but of those who have faith to the saving of the soul', (Heb. 1:39). As Shepherd, he has charge of his flock. He leads it into living pastures, and gives it a law to be observed: in order that none may turn aside from him, nor from the route mapped out by him; but that all may lead holy lives under his inspiration and guidance. At the Last Supper he celebrated the New Passover with pomp and solemn rite; and, thanks to the divine institution of the Eucharist, assures its permanence. The next day, uplifted between Heaven and earth, he offers his life in sacrifice for our salvation; and from his riven side, causes the Sacraments to flow, which distribute to men's souls the fruits of Redemption. In so doing, he has no other aim than his Father's glory, and man's greater sanctity."

So much for Christ's Sacrifice.

* * *

The Mass is likewise the sacrifice of the Church.
Where Christ is, there is the Church.
Where Christ is the victim, the Church is co-victim.
The Cross of Christ without our cross is not enough.

Does this mean that there are two sacrifices—that of the Cross and that of the Mass?

Not at all. There is only one Sacrifice of the whole Christ. It was as Head of the Mystical Body that Christ consented to die. He included us in his Sacrifice. All his life up to Calvary, he obeyed his Father in his own name and in ours. He satisfied "once for all", says St. Paul, "in offering up himself." (Heb. 7:27.)

There remains only for us to fulfill—each in his own life—the promises Christ made on our behalf. How? By becoming like him obedient unto death and uniting our daily immolations to his Sacrifice.

LIVING MY MASS means nothing less than filling my days with the same dispositions of offering and immolation that Christ had during his life and especially on Calvary.

Putting one's life into the Mass and the Mass into one's life, by accepting crosses, trials, sufferings and joys, uniting them to those of Christ offering himself to the Father, is the very essence of Christian spirituality. And it is this actual LIVING OF THE MASS that the author of this volume has undertaken to demonstrate in a historic, liturgical, ascetic, and mystic commentary on Christ's unique Sacrifice.

May every reader of this book come to comprehend the grandeur of God's gift!

"SI SCIRES DONUM DEI."

† Paul Emile Cardinal Leger,
Archbishop of Montreal.

FOREWORD

For the Catholic Christian, love has no trysting place more sure or more enriching than the Mass.

Participating in and living the Mass, is man's noblest task, and the finest response of his love to God's plea for that love.

When Jesus went up and down the highways and byways of Palestine, all types of human misery came to him; and he succoured all who came. The Mass brings Christ back in our midst with the same loving desire to come to our aid. In the Incarnation, he became one of us, that he might give fitting glory to the Blessed Trinity. He likewise wished to associate us in this concert of praise, by permitting us to offer ourselves with him to the Father by means of the Holy Sacrifice of the Mass; thus effecting our return toward Heaven, our eternal home.

Alas! Despite the numerous books written on the subject, the sublime rôle that every Christian is called upon to play in this unique drama, is but little known and poorly understood. This is due to the fact that books explaining the Mass are frequently either too theoretical and abstract; or else superficial, and devoid of an inner inspiration capable of touching the hearts they instruct.

The present volume attempts to remedy these deficiencies.

The book is addressed to all and sundry—to priests, religious and laity—because the Mass is for all of them.

We have particularly sought to be of use to those devout Catholics engaged in the lay apostolate and who like to group themselves in study clubs in order to increase their knowledge and their love.

Popular in scope, this study aims at being intelligible to the majority of readers. For this reason, we have avoided those theological and technical terms not generally familiar or readily accessible to the layman.

Not only has our aim been to enlighten the mind, but we have equally applied ourselves to touching the heart and moving the will to good. Hence, the numerous practical applications to be found at the close of each question.

The guiding motive on every page of this volume has been to show how—in the details of daily living—it is possible to LIVE ONE'S MASS. If the reader will but bear this motivation in mind, he will be able to explain many apparently superfluous digressions.

In order to make applications which would be practical for daily living, and to show the implications in our lives of a Mass that is "lived"; it has been necessary to bring out the aspect of interior sacrifice—the heart, so to speak, of the Mass.

We are happy to find in the teachings of His Holiness Pope Pius XII, a confirmation of this point of view. For in *Mediator Dei,* the Holy Father affirms that "if the liturgy be outward worship, it is PREEMINENTLY INNER ADORATION".

With regard to the prayers inserted in the text, we propose them to the private devotion of the faithful; having discovered in them substantial food for the soul.

Finally, we have added to this study of the Mass a supplement of the *Liturgical Year,* presented as a program of spiritual life. These pages are favourable to a more perfect comprehension of the Mass and foster a more perfect union with the prayer and life of the Church.

May Mary Immaculate, in this Marian Year, deign to bless our work and direct it toward souls thirsting for perfection. May she inspire the reader with the desire for an intense living of the Mass—centre of our lives, and bond of love uniting our obligations and duties.

Montreal, May, 1958

RICHER-MARIE BEAUBIEN, O.F.M.

TABLE OF CONTENTS

CHAPTER VI

THE FAMILY AND THE PRIESTHOOD

In order for a boy or girl to have the courage one day to say "Yes," to God, this "yes," in the majority of cases, must have been said by his parents before him— before his birth, and all through the formative years. It is Mary's "fiat" to the sacrifice asked of her.

Ordinarily, it is the mother who awakens her child's soul to things of God. "My first altar," once said a holy priest, "was my mother's knee!"

Education is of primary importance in the cultivation of a vocation; for vocations, like plants, are cultivated. It is God who sows the seed; but for the seed to come up, grow, and bear fruit, there must be a favourable soil and climate. If the soil be rocky (egotism), or choked with weeds (the passions), the seed will not sprout. Its existence will not even be suspected. The favourable climate is that of the true Christian family that prays together, where a taste for work, for faithfulness, for purity, and for generosity are developed. The priest perpetually sacrifices himself in the service of others. If he has not learned as a child to do without things, to share his toys, his cookies, and even his bread, he will not be able, later on, to share his faith with his brethren.

PROLOGUE

The ascent to the priesthood

The Ideal

A **priest!** . . .

"You are going to be My **priest!** "

A magic word, that, and mightier than all other words, because a boy heard it ever singing in his heart. Because the boy's parents may have heard it echoing in theirs. . . .

"I'm going to be a priest! "

This is the ideal that gleams on the horizon to the generous soul. An ideal that sometimes becomes mist-enshrouded where the road dips sharply, only to reappear brighter than before—like some mountain summit after the storm-clouds have passed!

This is the dream pursued, toward which the whole being tends—a dream that seems long-delayed! . . .

Finally, one day, after a slow ascent, secret and intimate. . . followed by a public ascension. . . the dream becomes true, becomes astounding reality! "Thou art a priest forever! "

The stages in the youth's formation have been passed in the years that lie behind—at the cost of great sacrifice.

The time for the final steps leading to God's altar has come.

Let us live them together.

The Tonsure

The priest is a chosen, a consecrated, man—taken out of the world, the better to serve the world.

The priest should no longer be occupied with things of earth, nor his heart engrossed by its "cumbering care."

The first step to the priesthood is a separation—of which the tonsure is a symbol.

The Pontiff clips a few locks of hair, and the young cleric himself elucidates the significance of this gesture: "Henceforth, in the eyes of all men, my only good shall be God alone".

In return, God gives him a fairer ornament—the snow-white surplice.

For the soul of the priest ought always to be adorned with innocence and holiness.

Porter—Lector

Everything surrounding the altar is holy.

The slightest function pertaining to it is clothed in inestimable dignity. Formerly, these minor offices were performed by clerics.

The Porter is the keeper of the temple. He it is who rings the church bell, opens the doors and watches that no intruder enters to trouble the congregation. The bishop confers this order on the cleric by presenting him with the keys. The cleric then locks a door of the church and rings a bell.

The Lector nurtures the piety of the faithful by reading to them the lessons contained in the Old Testament, and commented on by the Fathers. The conferring of the order of lector today is reduced to a touching of the lectionary, while the pontiff says a prayer.

Exorcist-Acolyte

Next is the exorcist who receives the power to drive out demons, placing the faithful out of reach of their malignity.

Then comes the acolyte whose duty it is to present the wine and water of the sacrifice and act as candle-bearer. The bishop causes him to touch a church candle and a cruet. Already the acolyte ascends the steps of the altar, and ought, by the dignity of his life. to serve as a light to the faithful.

These orders still subsist today. For, in addition to the function, they contain a symbol. And the grace conferred by the rite prepares the candidate gradually for the next steps leading to the priesthood.

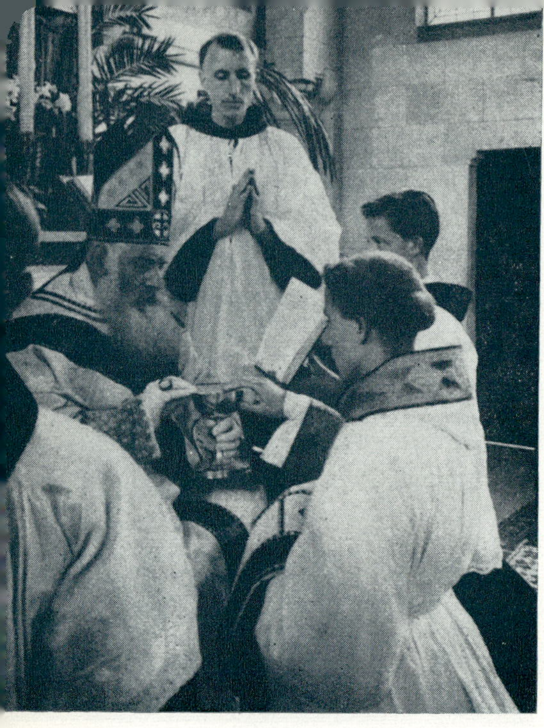

Subdeacon

This is the first of the **sacred** orders.

For the cleric who is not a religious, it is the definite and irrevocable engagement or step.

Before receiving the ordinands to this order, the bishop addresses to them a solemn, moving, invitation:

"You ought to consider with mature deliberation the redoubtable burden with which you, of your own free will, desire to be charged today. Up to this moment you have been free, capable of engaging yourself freely in the affairs of this world. But if you receive this order, you can no longer loose yourself from the bond which will bind you to God forever—to him whom to serve is to reign. . . . And you will remain irrevocably bound to the service of the Church. Reflect, then, while there is still time; and if you persist in your pious designs, then approach in the name of the Lord."

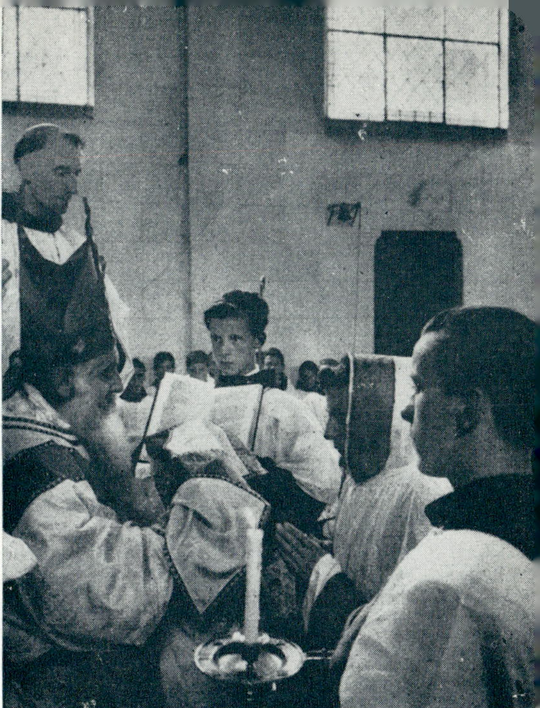

Subdeacon

Those who are willing, then, "take the step." . . .

Before presenting them with the chalice and paten, and the book of the Epistles, the bishop addresses them further:

"The subdeacon ought to prepare the water for the Holy Sacrifice and assist the deacon; offer with him the chalice and paten for the celebration of Mass; dispose the oblations of the faithful on the altar, and chant the Epistle.

"Apply yourselves to the fulfillment of these visible functions, to the accomplishment by your example of what they represent. The altar represents Jesus Christ. It is in him and through him that the oblations of the faithful are consecrated to God the Father. The sacred linens represent the members of Jesus Christ; namely, the faithful, with whom the Lord clothes himself as with a garment. It devolves upon you to present them the water of this celestial doctrine contained in the Epistles of the Apostles; which doctrine will purify them and render them worthy to adorn the altar of the Son of God."

Deacon

This is the last stage before the priesthood. This order confers the power to be the principal co-operator with the Priest at the altar and to preach the doctrine of Christ to the faithful.

In a long prologue addressed to the candidates for ordination, the bishop recalls the deacons or ministers of the Old Law: "Among the twelve tribes, God chose the tribe of Levi to guard the Tabernacle forever. . . . And so lofty was this dignity, that no man could perform the sacred functions, unless he belonged to this family.

"This is the origin of the deacon's reception of the name and functions of the Levite; for he is chosen to guard the Tabernacle, the Church of God."

Deacon

One after the other, the future deacons approach and kneel at the feet of the pontiff. Placing his right hand on the head of each, the latter prays this sublime prayer: "Receive the Holy Spirit. He will be thy strength." He then makes them touch the book of the Gospels.

For the deacon's mission is to preach. In his long monition at the beginning, the prelate, following up his somewhat veiled comparison, had said to them: "As the Levites bore the tabernacle of Yahweh on their shoulders through the burning desert, even so you are to bear the Church, the sum total of the faithful; and adorn it with a preaching that is wholly divine and by the perfection of your lives."

Priest

The soul is now ready to receive the final effusions of grace. Yesterday's boy has grown tall! One morning, pursuing his old dream, he enters the Church! Is it really true? Already?

The long years of formation flash rapidly through his memory. This is the blessed day of God's surprising gift. A priest! He is going to be a priest! In a few moments! He! But the fruitless years! His unworthiness, the misery of his human nature! He! Why should God's choice fall on him ?

"But since it is so, here am I, O Lord! You employ the workmen you desire, to teach us, in fine, that the work is not of us, for your instruments are unequal to the task."

Priest

In silence, the pontiff places his hands on the head of each ordinand; and the priests, in turn, do likewise.

And, majestic, the ritual continues, producing in this human being a mysterious transformation. . . Suddenly this voice becomes the voice which God himself will soon obey; which will speak with God's authority to men.

Another "Christ" is being created!

Like Christ, but through Christ's power, the Priest becomes a mediator between Heaven and earth; praying for men, offering for them the "pitiful" Victim of Calvary; making known God's will to men!

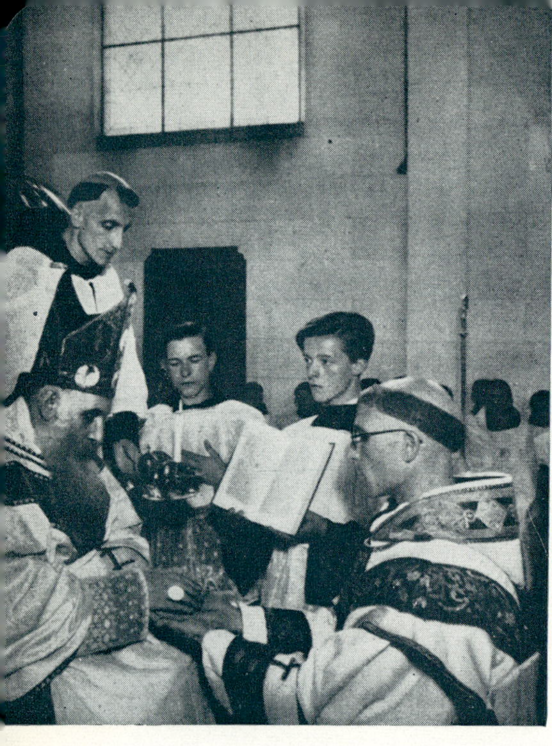

The Priestly Anointing

In the form of a cross, the prelate anoints the palms of the priest with the holy oils.

The hands of a priest!

Every morning you will hold aloft over the world the Host of man's Redemption.

You will pardon the guilty—those who suffer from the misery of sin. . .

Consecrated hands, what purity should be thine!

Hands that take away the ugliness of sin, what beauty should be thine!

Ah, surrender yourselves utterly to the holy anointing!

Let it be profoundly and eternally graven upon you.

So that never, never, shall anything defile it! . . .

O human hands, that are to bear God Almighty!

Christ's Prayer to his Priest

You are now a priest!

Behold the altar upon which I shall descend.

Even, as a boy, you saw it. Well you knew that the Mass would be your life's greatest act, the summit of each day—the Mass from which My Blood would flow over human souls!

You will see this altar always. . . The memory of it will incite you to ascend, O My priest—or to re-ascend, if you, unfortunately, have fallen. . . .

For My great desire is that your ascension should be constant; that with you may also ascend other men, your brothers.

My priests are the leaven of souls and the salt of the earth.

You are My priest forever! . . .

—John de Vaudemont

PRELIMINARIES

THE MASS:

Renunciation and choice

Those persons who apply themselves seriously to a study of the scope and meaning of the Mass, cannot help awakening in themselves a spirit of mortification, of subordination of the earthly to the heavenly, of absolute obedience to God's will and law. This is a necessity of the present hour, as is zeal for prayer. For many persons —among whom we observe with sorrow the presence of many Catholics—live as though their sole purpose in life were to establish an earthly paradise, with no thought being given to eternity or the hereafter.

—Pius XII

CHAPTER ONE

OBSERVATION - JUDGMENT - ACTION

The first thing to be considered before taking up our study of the Mass is the attitude of Catholics toward Sunday Mass.

OBSERVATION

1—Those among the faithful who attend Sunday Mass may be divided into three groups, corresponding to their degree of fervour. All three had their representatives on Calvary, during the Passion drama. Who are they?

1. *The enemies of God*: *Sinners.* This group forms the modern counterpart of the irreligious Scribes and Pharisees. In this category are those persons in the state of mortal sin who sometimes wind up an all-night bout of drinking, dancing, and offence to God, by dropping into church. Arriving after Mass has begun, they sit in the rear of the church, yawning their boredom—their provocative dress a scandal to others. Before Mass is over, they have already fled out the door.

2. *The indifferent, the slaves to routine, the shallow.* These persons may be compared to the Jews. This was a people who followed others like sheep: fickle, because deep, inner conviction was lacking—ready to join up with whatever crowd shouted the loudest. Yesterday it was Jesus they acclaimed—"Hosanna to the Son of David!" Today they are howling for His blood. "Let Him be crucified! Let Him be crucified!"

This was the group for whom Jesus prayed, "Father, forgive them for they do not know what they are doing!" [Luke 23:34. (Confraternity text.)]

Catholics of this breed attend all sorts of mundane events—political rallies, the movies, or the races—with considerably more promptness and enthusiasm than they put into their attendance at a religious ceremony. For these, Mass and sermon are always *too long.* That is why they come to Mass *late,* and why they leave *early!*

Still others make it a *deliberate point* to arrive some time after the hour set for Mass to begin, and parade up the full length of the middle aisle to the front of the church in order to show off their new clothes! For such, Mass affords a convenient occasion for staging a style show! Some business men make an act of bodily presence at Sunday Mass, because a reputation for piety helps their business. The customers are favourably impressed!... A young man may attend Mass merely to please his fiancée.

3. Finally, *the devout.* These are in the minority. Taking example from Mary, St. John and the Holy Women who suffered with Jesus at the foot of the Cross, these affectionate, compassionate individuals understand their Mass and live it intensely. They really share in the Saviour's sufferings. To be able to offer up Jesus Christ and themselves with Jesus Christ to God the Father, is for them an immense honour and grace; from which they allow no merely transient object to divert their attention. For these faithful, Mass and sermon are never too long—they experience no boredom in the presence of Jesus! For them, Sunday Mass is not enough. *They must have daily Mass too.*

2—Do many people habitually miss Sunday Mass?

The facts speak for themselves, and the facts are alarming! *People readily miss Sunday Mass, either through sheer negligence, or on the flimsiest of pretexts.* As if the keeping of the Commandments of God and the Church were something a man could take or leave at will!

For many city parishes, the church should be filled with worshippers at *all* the Masses. As a matter of fact, only at the late ten or eleven o'clock Masses are most of the pews filled up....

The decrease in church attendance is less evident in the country.... At the most, a few neighbours will notice that members of such and such a family no longer have any scruples about staying home comfortably on Sunday morning. In the summer it is: "What with spring ploughing and all the hard work on the farm, the poor horses are simply played out!" In the winter we hear, "The horses are all worn-out hauling those heavy logs!" So little is needed—once one lives out a little way from town—to squelch the indiscreet questioner!

All this does not prevent the same tired, "worn-out" horses, once noon has rung out from the church bell-tower, from breaking into a brisk trot in the direction of the hotel, the railroad station, and the restaurants; places where a man may idle away a few hours of time—lightening his purse at the same time he weights down his conscience!

The Curé of Ars used to say that a good Christian could always find something to do on a Sunday without resorting to servile work. Up to noon, the time could be spent thanking God for the graces with which one had been favoured during the week. From afternoon to evening, one could implore the graces one would need the coming week!

In the city, too many people "sleep in" until it is time to leave for Mass. Quite often, they decide to postpone their church-going a while longer.... If it is a nice day though, and doesn't rain, *maybe* they will—send the children!...

There is something ominous about a mentality like that. It is essential to seek out the *causes* and apply the *remedy.*

JUDGMENT

3—How explain the small number of those who hear Mass regularly?

The reasons are several:

1. *A sinful life*: Take a person who goes to confession once a year (when he bothers to go at all) to fulfill his Easter duty; after which he begins again to offend God seriously. A whole year passes without a fresh approach to the sacraments. The person will say to himself, "After all, one sin more or less isn't going to make much difference!"

2. *Loss of faith*: A sinful life leads to loss of faith. Now when a person no longer believes in the mysteries of our holy Faith, the next step is to abandon his religious practices altogether. The sheerest pretext now suffices to silence the not overly-tender conscience. For example, he can't go to Mass in the summer because his summer cottage is three or four miles from the church!... When one considers that the Holy Family walked three days to reach the Temple of Jerusalem, in order to

fulfill *their* religious obligations! (St. Luke, 2:46.) Some people (who have only themselves to blame) are certainly storing up plenty of trouble for themselves on the Day of Judgment.

3. *Saturday night parties*: Christian parents should never permit their children to attend or organize one of these interminable vigils, where drinking and dancing go on till the "wee small hours" of Sunday morning. Nobody, under similar circumstances, can hear Mass in a truly Christian manner. One simply does not give one's "leavings" to God!

4. *Ignorance about the Mass*: If attendance at Mass is such a boring affair for some people, it is because they do not understand their Mass. For a great many persons, the Mass represents some sort of bitter pill which Catholics are obliged (reluctantly) to swallow on Sundays to keep their souls alive! For Catholics like this, the Mass is meaningless: they are concerned only with the serious precept. Were the Church to withdraw the grave obligation of attending Mass on Sundays and Holy Days of obligation, our churches would suddenly be deserted, and attendance would drop to the level of the six other days of the week.

ACTION

4—How to remedy this sad state of affairs?

If *ignorance of the Mass*—and of this there can be no doubt—is the chief cause of this deplorable situation, the best remedy which we are able to suggest is the present volume—employing the question and answer method—which we propose as a basis for discussion in organized study groups: or in other groups which may be set up for this purpose.

The more numerous these Mass study groups, the wider will be the scope of your apostolate. For it is by the setting up of such Mass study cells that the masses will be reached.

But let each individual, first of all—before starting out for the conquest of others—begin by LIVING HIS MASS and so preach by the force of his example.

WHERE YOUR TREASURE IS, THERE WILL YOUR HEART ALSO BE

AT THE RACES

(Sunday, 1:50 P.M. Husband and wife are about to leave for the race track, two miles distant. The Man of the House has just donned his sports jacket. Milady is decked out in rose-coloured finery, diaphanously indiscreet.)

HE: "Hurry, Mary! You're going to make us both late for the first race!"
SHE: "How dreadful! I'm rushing so, I'm all out of breath!"

They enter the grounds.
SHE: "How long do the races last?
HE: "All afternoon, I hope!"

Opening preliminaries
(The couple sit down.)
SHE: (gayly): "These seats are what you might call roughing it! Oh, well, one must take the rough with the smooth!"
HE: "Anyway, it's better than standing!"

AT MASS

(Sunday, 9:50 A.M. The bell is ringing for ten o'clock Mass. The Man of the House is painstakingly knotting his tie. Milady is placing on her head (with a graceful gesture) an object resembling an inverted saucepan decked with flowers—VERY chic.)

SHE: "No matter how much I hurry, Darling, I'm always late!"

HE: "Take it easy, Dear! We'll make it in time for the Gospel!"

They enter the church.
HE: "Now we're in for a half hour of it!"
SHE: "Unless there's a sermon besides!"

The Kyrie
SHE *(in a whisper)*: "What hard, uncomfortable pews!"

HE *(voice equally low)*: "Yes, my back is broken!"

The pep-talk
HE: "Sh-h-h! Listen!"
SHE: "Probably has an important announcement to make!"

After the pep-talk
HE: "He's a whiz, that chap!"
SHE: "Always has something new to say!"

Tickets for the races
THE TICKET-VENDOR: "Seats, one dollar twenty! Standing room, fifty cents!"
HE *and* SHE together: "How cheap!"

End of the first race
(THE MAN OF THE HOUSE *is already keyed up to a high pitch of excitement.)*
SHE (suddenly): Did you remember to close the windows?"
No answer. (He didn't even hear her.)

The collection for the jockey fund
HE: "This is educational! I'm putting in a dollar, at least!"

The sermon
(The Man of the House dozes.... Milady, after listening to the sermon for a couple of minutes, has embarked on a serious study of women's hats.)

After the sermon
HE: "I knew all *that* before!"
SHE: "So did I!"

Collection in the pews
(MILADY, *under cover of flourishing a handkerchief under her nose, manages unobtrusively to slip a nickel into the basket.)*
SHE: "That adds up in time!"

The Offertory
(THE MAN OF THE HOUSE, *before relaxing, decides to relieve himself of a worry)*:
"Did you remember about the cakes?"
(His wife, slipping another bead through her fingers, nods.)

The collection for missions

HE: "Just another excuse for worming money out of people! You have to be a millionnaire around here!"

A crucial moment
(The Man of the House has just clambered atop a shaky tree stump for a better view.)
SHE: "Careful, Edgar! You'll tear your new suit!"
HE: "What if I do?"

After the final race
SHE: "Coming, Dear?"
HE: "I just want to take a look at the winners."

Summary
Q. Please give a definition of a horse race.
A. A vain spectacle.

The Elevation
"Don't kneel, Edgar! Remember your pants just came back from the cleaners!"
HE: "Right! Thanks for reminding me, Dear!"

At the final blessing
HE: "Come on, Mary! Let's go!"
SHE: "O.K. I guess the priest can finish without us!"

Summary
Q. Please define the Mass.
A. The redemption of a world by the Blood of a God!

O WORD, O CHRIST

•

How beautiful, how great you are! Who can know or understand you? O Jesus, make me know and love you!

Since you are the Light, let a ray of light shine in my poor soul, that I may see and understand you. Let me look on you, O Infinite Beauty! Soften the brilliance of your dazzling light, so that my eyes may bear to contemplate you and your perfections. Open my ears to your divine words, that I may hear your voice and meditate your teachings. Open my mind and intelligence, that your Word may find room in my heart and that I may taste and understand it.

Give me great faith, so that your words may be as so many lamps to enlighten me and lead me to you and make me follow you in the paths of charity and justice.

O Christ, O Word! You are my Lord, my one and only Master! I would listen to you and practice your Word, for I know that it comes from Heaven. I would listen to, meditate, and practice it; for in your Word lies life, joy, peace, and happiness.

Speak, for you are my Lord and Master. I would hear your voice.

(Prayer of Ven. Anthony Chevrier, Tertiary priest).

CHAPTER II

THE PLACE OF THE MASS IN THE DIVINE PLAN

5—If we are really to understand the Mass, we must know the place that it occupies in the divine plan. In your opinion, what is that place?

Our knowledge is too often limited to ascertaining the existence of a few isolated, unrelated facts. Hence, the perplexity and confusion of mind that often confronts us in the face of a comparatively clear and simple problem. *Many persons have an incredible faculty for raising a difficulty where no difficulty exists!*

Placed in its proper setting, however, an object assumes significance. Its meaning becomes luminous and clear.

For instance, show a small child a brick that you have previously plucked from a wall, or a red bean. (The kind you use for making soup.) Then ask yourself what idea the child is going to form of these two unrelated objects, detached from their settings. May he not, perhaps, consider the bean to be more important than the brick? Or else take the bean for a fragment of brick? Why not? Both objects are red and hard!

Now take the tot to the wall where you got the brick and put the brick back in the hole. Next go with him to a bean field and open a ripe bean pod in his presence. The child will soon comprehend. (No need to make a long speech.) All that was a mystery to him before, will become dazzlingly clear. How true it is that water becomes more limpid and clear when you go right back to its source.

So it is with the Mass.

For many the Mass is simply *another religious devotion;* somewhat longer than Benediction, but otherwise not much different. Vespers, Benediction, Mass—all are lumped together in their minds under the general title of "devotions"!

Pope Pius XII, in an address to the Sacred Council of Bishops on July 14, 1941, reminded them of the duty of pastors to exhort the faithful to regular and devout assistance at the Holy Sacrifice. The Holy Father deplored the fact that "a number of faithful" no longer have proper reverence for the Eucharistic Sacrifice; nor the eagerness of former times to have Mass offered for their own needs and for those of their departed. "On the contrary," added His Holiness, "many persons often do not hesitate to resort to less salutary practices."

In order to banish prevailing darkness and clarify our thinking, let us go back to the First Source of all things—the Trinity—and discover just where the Mass fits into God's plan.

Here we sound a warning to the reader not to be alarmed at the *abstract nature* of the subject to be treated! Persevere, follow this study through to the end, and you will be surprised—of this we are sure—at the very clear light that the Holy Spirit will give you on this dogma of our holy Faith.

The texts cited in response to this fifth question are from the pen of Fr. John Francis Motte, O.F.M.

A. The internal activity of the Blessed Trinity

The catechism teaches us that there are *three distinct Persons* in God—Father, Son, and Holy Spirit—possessing one identical divine nature.

God is love. The Father loves with infinite love. He gives himself as only God can give, *infinitely, totally.* He engenders his Son, also called the Word or second Person of the Trinity. To this Son, the Father communicates at each instant—for God is always in act—his nature, his perfections, his life.

Father and Son love each other with infinite, total love. They love each other and give themselves to each other. Their mutual love gives birth to a third Person, focal point of the personal charity of the Father and the personal charity of the Son. Thus Father and Son are united in a loving embrace, from which the Holy Spirit proceeds as from a single principle.

The Trinity—the Supreme Life of Love—is "perpetual exchange" —an eternal flame of charity.

And in this perfect union, even the appearance of egoism is excluded: either in the Father and the Son, or in the Holy Spirit himself. For, as St. Bonaventure says, Love, who is the Holy Spirit, does not proceed from the Father inasmuch as he loves himself; nor from the Son inasmuch as he loves himself; but proceeds from their mutual love for each other—he is a bond of love. He is the love whereby the lover tends toward the loved one.

Their reciprocal gift cannot be accused of egoism, such as is sometimes met with in married couples or between friends; for their interchange does not exclude, but is communicated to a third Person.

God's essential beatitude consists of this life which is both one and multiple.

B. The external activity of the Blessed Trinity

The Divine Family which the three Persons form in the unity of their nature, is perfectly happy. This communal life is *perfect,* and no new riches can be added to it. Nothing can be added to God, since in God nothing is lacking: he can neither acquire anything nor be increased. His goodness is self-sufficient, and is the source of all abundance.

Nevertheless, the Trinity, overflowing with joy and love, wills to find outside itself the most adequate possible praise; and to this end decrees first of all the Incarnation of the Son of God.

THE CREATION—GOD'S OUTGOING

In God's plan, it is not man who is the centre of the universe; but Jesus Christ, the Incarnate Word.

God created all things for Christ.

For the sake of Christ Jesus, in whom the Father already had "placed all his delight"; and for the sake of Mary, his Mother, "full of grace"; God decided to create man and the universe.

To this Son, in whom He is well pleased, friends were to be given—and so man was created. (The race of man represents the "friends of the Bridegroom" mentioned by our Lord in the Gospel.)

To this Son whom he loves, the Father will give a house and garden—and so the universe was created.

Man, created for Christ, is loved in him.

We thus form, as it were, a "wedding gift" from God the Father to Jesus Christ, the Bridegroom.

In Him, through Him, and for Him, we are pleasing to the heavenly Father. *Without Him we are nothing.* This last is very important for an understanding of the Mass. Our sacrifices are of value *only* through their being united with Christ's Sacrifice.

Since all have issued from the heart of God solely to give pleasure to Jesus, all then are brothers. Creation itself is our kin. "Ah, yes, the swallow twittering in flight; the humble, perfumed violet hiding itself; we can, we should, call them 'sister.' To do so is no mere literary fiction nor poet's fantasy; but a clear vision of reality, as was grasped by St. Francis of Assisi. The universe and I, what are we, if not a delicate thought of the Father toward his Divine Son?

"The creation, launched into existence by God's loving power, will forever have something unfinished about it, until that time when it shall return to the Source of its perfection; there to receive from that same Source its final perfection and beatitude in love.

"Thus the general plan of creation appears to us as an image and prolongation of the fecundity of the Most Blessed Trinity."

The chronological order of the plan is as follows:

Creation of the heavens
Preparation of the earth
Creation of minerals, vegetation, and animals
Creation of man

King though he may be of that creation predating his own existence; man, however, is not creation's final goal.

Man—simple link in a chain that must go back to God—paves the way for the coming of the Queen—of Mary, whose luminous humility God looked upon before the world was. Mary, God's jewel case, in which reposed He who upholds all things, Jesus Christ!

Christ is the centre of the universe. He is before all things:

"He is before all creatures." (Col. 1:17.)

"The first-born of every creature." (Col. 1:15.)

"In the beginning." (John 1:1.)

"In him. . . through him. . . unto him. . . all things!" (Col. 1:16, 17.)

All things are through Him. "Without him was made nothing that has been made." (John 1:3.) "Upholding all things by the word of his power." (Heb. 1:3.)

All things are in Him. "Blessed be the God and Father of our Lord, Jesus Christ; who has blessed us with every spiritual blessing on high in Christ, even as he chose us in him before the foundation of the world. (Eph. 1:3-4.)

All things are unto Him. "Whom he appointed heir of all things." (Heb. 1:2.) "I am the Alpha and Omega, the first and the last, the beginning and the end." (Apoc. 22:13.)

6—How can Christ be first in the thought of God, the Exemplar or Model of creation; and at the same time come to earth so long after the first man appeared on earth?

To understand this, let us make a comparison.

Suppose that you—here in Montreal—decide to go to Quebec City. The first thought that comes to mind is "Quebec." But before you arrive in Quebec, you must first take several steps. You must go by automobile or else buy a railroad ticket. You must pass through all the towns between here and Quebec, and the last place you will reach will be Quebec. That is why we say: *"That which is first in the order of intention, is last in the order of execution."*

7—What is meant by these expressions: "Through Him, with Him, and in Him?"

Let us make another comparison.

Here is an example. A rich father is about to give a cherished daughter in marriage. This father, because of his love for his daughter, has had a lovely cottage built for her in an enchanting corner of the country. He has completely furnished the cottage; and has even engaged servants, domestic help, and so on.

Here again, all these preparations—the result of the father's love for his daughter—may have been made far in advance of the wedding date. But they have been made solely in view of the marriage on which all these provisions hinge, toward which they converge.

Although the father is doing this purely because of his love for his daughter, the son-in-law will also share in the benefits. Why? Because of the latter's union with the cherished daughter. Except for this union, the father certainly would not have done anything for the young man; nor spent a penny on him.

With this example as a guide, it is easy to understand the meaning of expressions such as, "Through Him, with Him, and unto Him, we are made pleasing to God the Father."

To the degree that the marriage is a success and the young man pleases the girl, the father will feel affection for him and be favourably disposed toward him. The more the father-in-law sees his son-in-law trying to make his daughter happy, the more benefits will he shower upon him. As for the son-in-law, if he wants his father-in-law to do him a favour, or pardon him for some youthful prank, he will ask his young bride to intercede for him.

The practical application is not far to seek.

In the same degree in which we are united to our Lord and working for his interests, the heavenly Father loves us and pardons our sins "through Him"—through His intercession—and showers us with his blessings; even to the sharing in his divine life, and Heaven, the heritage of his Divine Son.

If God's love for Christ obtains for us the inestimable gift of life; Jesus' love for us obliges, as it were, his Father to extend his mercy and paternal solicitude toward us. It is this ardent affection of Christ for us—as we shall see later on—that saves us from the eternal loss of Heaven and from death-dealing sin.

MAN'S RETURN

Man, having come from God, must return to God: his Final End. "You have made us for you, O God," cried St. Augustine, "and our hearts are restless until they find rest in you!"

The creation—a work of sheer mercy, a stooping of the Creator toward the creature—returns to God, chanting a hymn of praise and thanksgiving. A feather from a bird, a ray of light, a finely modulated voice, a drop of water falling to earth, a hastening ant, a seed sprouting from the earth, the stars that whirl in the firmament with never a collision; all are directed by God to that magnificent end for which he has ordained them—man's pleasure, Christ's happiness, and finally, the glory of the Most Holy Trinity.

"All are yours, and you are Christ's, and Christ is God's." (I Cor. 3:23.)

Man looks; and the purity of his heart enables him to read God's message, inscribed in wondrous characters in the vast book of the universe. "Immediately, he perceives the sensation of an intense movement of life, pulsating throughout the entire universe. Man hears the prayer of all living creatures inviting him—as if a dumb man were to pluck him silently by the sleeve—to praise the God who gave them existence."

Man, mute with astonishment, observes that all this munificence is intended for him. He hears (as will hear many centuries later, St. Francis of Assisi) the voice of creation whispering to him, "O man, it was God who created me for you!" Man feels like a child in a Christian land who has just discovered—at the foot of the chimney—the profusion of gifts and toys left there for him by loving hands, in honour of the Saviour's birth. His poor heart, almost bursting with happiness at so many proofs of love, opens like an alabaster vase and breathes forth its perfume in an act of pure love and endless gratitude. And in this act of charity proceeding from man's heart and lips, the whole creation returns—*through him*—its thanks to God! For this was the admirable task entrusted to man: to be the intermediary (after Christ), the living link between creation and Creator; to be a priest, an authorized offerer of thanks.

THE BREAK IN THE HARMONY OF THE DIVINE PLAN—SIN

Alas, man is free to destroy God's harmonious plan! "Everything is in equilibrium, because everything tends toward God. All things cohere, because all things are submissive to the Author of life and being. But this adhesion to God is effected in a free act of love. The freedom with which man is adorned, gives to the entire creation an incomparable majesty. God thus receives a praise that is spontaneous. This very freedom, however, exposes the one enjoying it to immense peril. Let man but once refuse to spread forth his hands in a gesture of oblation, and the whole order of things falls apart."

But one day man, in a gesture of pride and egoism, rejected his priesthood. His rôle of mediator no longer satisfied him. Man "would be like God." Through his lips, Satan once more uttered his cry of rage, "I will not serve!"

By his refusal, man shattered the universe. For the universe rested on man as the arch on the keystone, or as the spider's web on the supporting filament, or as a house of cards on the bottom card.

The entire universe turned against man, its betrayer. In chorus, it hurled back into the teeth of man the cry that man had dared to address to God, "I will not serve!"

First of all, man's own body revolted. Man, terror-stricken, suddenly beheld within himself the unleashing of sinful passions. Henceforth, seven fetters, which theology is later to designate by the title of "Capital Sins," will shackle his formerly free impulses —Adam and Eve "perceive themselves to be naked."

Man is deeply stricken in the very harmony of his being: "I will multiply your sorrows and your conceptions; in sorrow shall you bring forth children."

Social discord now corresponds to inner imbalance. "You shall be under your husband's power, and he shall have dominion over you."

Looming up on the horizon, in addition to these "domestic squabbles," are quarrels between families, wars between city and city, between nation and nation, world war, revolution.

The animal kingdom, over which man formerly reigned, rises up in its turn. The earth itself refuses to co-operate with man. Only at the cost of a struggle, will man be able to wrest from it miserably a few meagre fruits: "Cursed is the earth in your work. Thorns and thistles shall it bring forth to you."

Man is broken, disoriented. Suffering is to be, henceforth, his earthly portion. "In the sweat of your face shall you eat bread.... In sorrow shall you bring forth children."

Man, created to be the friend of Christ, has gone astray in the disobedience of Adam. *Humanity, separated from Christ, is without form or beauty.* "The races of men, no longer unified by the life of Jesus, who made of them one body and rendered them —in him—pleasing to God; array themselves in opposite camps and tear one another to shreds. Separation from Christ unleashed inevitably hatred, blood, tears, death, and damnation. The world, through its own fault, now lives in fear.

Will God remain deaf, insensible, to the cry of his distressed creature? Will He punish or pardon?

Christ's intervention

At this tragic moment in the history of humanity, when the Blessed Trinity could have, conceivably, left us to shift for ourselves (i.e. left us in our state of hopeless misery); Jesus, listening only to his divine heart, intervened:

"Father, these men are for me the sign and expression of your love. They are my children—as this earth is already my garden. They are mine, for it was for my sake that you gave them life and being. Already, they have captivated my heart! Never will I abandon them! Since they are incapable of knowing my joy, I am determined to share their misery.

"Christ was to have come in glory; like the bridegroom, whose arrival on the wedding day is joyously awaited by the wedding guests. Now his coming will take place under the reign of Sin; in a body capable of being crushed by suffering; with a heart that affliction will overwhelm, but that only love can break! He will come to destroy sin; this 'wall of separation' between God and man—between man and man. He will reconcile in his blood Heaven and earth. He will unite the peoples."

The incarnation

"One day, in the long procession of men groping in the shadow of death, Christ appeared. To this poor, purblind race of ours, he revealed the Father's wondrous plan. 'The Father himself loves you. . . . He has not abandoned you. . . . I am your Saviour. . . . I am Life!' "

The redemption

It was bearing his Cross that he came—weighted down under the burden of our sins. He climbed Calvary's hill and reddened it with his blood. He was barbarously crucified on a Cross, and died between two thieves.

Let us look for a moment at our suffering Saviour. Taking place before our horrified gaze, is the drama that dominates the world. Christ was "made sin" for us, writes St. Paul!

The prophet Isaias paints for us a poignant portrait of Christ—his flesh torn and mangled because of us, and for love of us:

"So many there be that stand gazing in horror. Was ever a human form so mishandled, human beauty ever so defaced? . . . No stateliness here, no majesty, no beauty, as we gaze upon him, to win our hearts. Nay here is one despised, left out of all human reckoning; bowed with misery, and no stranger to weakness; how should we recognize that face? How should we take any account of him, a man so despised? . . . and all the while it was for our sins he was wounded, it was guilt of ours crushed him down; on him the punishment fell that brought us peace, by his bruises we were healed." {Knox.}

"On the high hill of Calvary, overlooking the world, a terrible struggle is taking place between *Love* and *Hate*—a struggle of unheard-of force. As a result of this fearsome combat, Hate dies in the blood of his immolated Victim. The last words of Christ are a shout of triumph: 'Father, it is consummated!' "

Love has conquered Hate!

"Life is now mistress of the world. From the height of the Cross, she dominates it. From this eminence, she will descend upon it as a refreshing shower. This is to be brought about through the instrumentality of the centurion, the blow from whose lance opened Jesus' heart: just as Magdalene's repentance broke an alabaster vase of precious nard over the Master's feet. And just as the whole house was filled with the fragrance of that perfume, so is the whole world enlivened by the life that escapes from this poor, torn body. From the opened side of this 'sleeping Man' the whole Church springs; just as several centuries before, Eve, the 'Mother of all living,' came forth from the opened side of the 'sleeping Adam.' "

Sin is now in full flight. A moment ago, an enormous tidal wave, made up of all the crimes of earth, had sought to engulf within its corrupt depths, Him who offered Himself as the Life of the World. Now, Life descends victorious from Calvary—an impetuous torrent of life—sweeping along with it everything in its path, driving back Sin to its ultimate retrenchments.

God's plan now unfolds in all its majesty—the return to the Father, to the Father's House.

How may we bring about this return?

By following Christ the Way, in what is to be henceforth his sorrowful way. "If anyone wishes to follow me, let him deny himself, take up his cross, and follow me." Integrated into Christ by Baptism, I (and not somebody else) ought to die to self, and live the life of Christ. "Christ died for all, in order that they who are alive may live no longer for themselves, but for him who died for them and rose again." (2 Cor. 5:15.)

With St. Paul we should say, "What is lacking of the sufferings of Christ, I fill up in my flesh for his body, which is the Church." (Col. 1:24.)

If our good works, sacrifices, and sufferings are to count for eternity and be pleasing to God, it is necessary for us (as we have seen above) to be united to Christ. It is *through Him, and with Him, and in Him* that we become recipients of God's loving-kindness and mercy.

Our union with Christ, our integration into his Mystical Body, is effected by the sacraments. It is by Baptism that we are introduced into Christ's mystical family. It is through Baptism that we receive divine life; become adopted sons of God the Father; brothers of Jesus Christ; temples of the Holy Spirit, and heirs of Heaven!

But how should we offer up—following our Lord's example—our adorations, thanksgivings, satisfactions, and petitions to God? How nourish the divine life within us?

By means of the Mass—the Sacrifice of the Mystical Body.

The holy sacrifice of the mass

Some two thousand years ago, the drama of Calvary took place.

"The Mass is not just a symbolic commemoration of the Sacrifice of the Cross. The Sacrifice of Golgotha has a grandeur all its own; situated in an immediate present, yet for all time—independent of time and space. It is the same Christ who died on the Cross, who is present. The whole assembly is united with his will to sacrifice; and, through Christ present, offers itself as a living victim. Holy Mass in thus a living, breathing reality—the reality of Golgotha." (Karl Adam, *The Spirit of Catholicism.*)

The Mass is, therefore, the means whereby we may become *the prolongation of Christ.*

Through the *offering* of ourselves *with* Christ

Through the *consecration* of ourselves *through* Christ
Through our *communion in* Christ
to the greater glory of the Blessed Trinity and the sanctification of our souls.

As Fr. J. Blondel so aptly puts it, the Mass reminds us at one and the same time of God's CONdescension toward man, and of man's AScension toward God!

For the Mass sums up the twin mysteries of the Incarnation and Redemption, at the same time that it applies to us their fruits. Crib and Cross manifest to mankind God's love for *all*: whereas the Mass stresses his love *for the individual.*

One ought, then, to look on the Mass as the sum total of man's ascensions toward God, because it presupposes and completes them. The sinner derives from it abundant graces of conversion. The just man finds fervour in it—outstripping himself from one Consecration to another. *Through the Mass, man offers to God praise that is worthy of him.*

This, then, is the place that the Mass occupies in God's plan. Like Christ, it is at the centre: as a sun to bring light and warmth, to transform and uplift all creation and bring it back to its Creator in a hymn of thanksgiving.

The Mass ought to occupy, not the first place in our lives (as if the Mass were some great personage), but ALL the place. We ought to:

★ Offer ourselves up, like Christ on the Cross.

★ Consecrate ourselves, "transubstantiate" ourselves—dying to our life of sin; to live, henceforth, the life of Christ.

★ Unite ourselves to Someone stronger than ourselves, communicating with Christ through reception of his Sacred Body, in order to identify ourselves ever more closely with him, so that—our bodily members belonging more to him than to us—we may be able to accomplish divine and supernatural works.

★ Render—through Christ—perfect praise to the august Trinity.

Such should be the constant concern of our earthly existence, and the prelude to our heavenly life in a blessed eternity.

A single Mass heard by a person during his lifetime, is more advantageous to him than a great number of Masses celebrated for him after death. (St. Ambrose)

CHAPTER III

SOME GENERAL NOTIONS ON THE SACRIFICE OF THE MASS

- **Offering Christ to the Father**

  Definition of Sacrifice
  Mass and Calvary—Resemblances and Differences
  Primary and Secondary Ends of Sacrifice
  Infinite and Finite Values of the Mass
  Fruits of the Mass

- **Offering ourselves with Christ**

  Explanation of "Living my Mass"
  Three Preparations for the Mass
  A Drama in which we are Actors
  Our Obligation to Participate in the Mass
  Necessary Dispositions for Profiting from the Mass

- **St. Francis of Assisi and the Mass**

  The Tertiary and the Mass

- **Meditation**

  Reflexions of a Christian

SOME GENERAL NOTIONS ON THE HOLY SACRIFICE OF THE MASS

OFFERING CHRIST TO THE FATHER

We have seen that Christ is the centre of religion and the universe. The creation, over which Christ reigns, is willed by God for his glory. *We are beings created solely for the praise and glory of God.*

8—How can such a frail, feeble creature as man offer acceptable praise to the Blessed Trinity?

In this way. The Word of God—the second Person of the Blessed Trinity—was incarnated, became one of us, and to each one of us gave something of himself; in such a way that we are enabled through him, with him, and in him, to fulfill our religious duties toward God—duties that may be summarized in two acts, as follows:

1. *Our continual offering of Jesus Christ to God the Father.*
2. *Our offering of ourselves with Him and like Him in complete self-surrender and self-sacrifice, so as to become one with Jesus Christ.*

For Christ alone can glorify God as he deserves. Christ, equal to the Father by his godhead, lowered himself to our level by the Incarnation. *As man,* Christ is able to bow before God and render him true adoration in humility, submission, and obedience. As God, Christ offers his Father homage of infinite worth.

It is the Incarnation that empowers us to offer God to God in the Person of Jesus Christ.

Hence, the grandeur and incomparable superiority of the Mass over all other acts of religion. How many Catholics painfully seek for some way of thanking God as he deserves, or of offering him fitting adoration! They make novenas, they give themselves over to numerous pious exercises; they make sacrifices, and sometimes painful sacrifices; yet they always suffer from their spiritual indigence and powerlessness. Their distress will persist for just so long as they seek to glorify God by their own merits.

It is in his Beloved *Son* that the Father is "well pleased." Why go elsewhere in search of a more "pleasing" offering?

9—Why so many Masses?

In order that the thought of offering him up to God the Father may be continually present to our minds, Christ has willed to re-present every instant the offering up of his Sacrifice. Every twenty-four hours, 350,000 Masses are celebrated—four Elevations a second! Every minute of the day I can say to myself, *"Jesus is offering himself right now!"*

But the Christ who thus offers himself in the Mass is not just "Jesus, the Son of Mary," but the total Christ—Christ complete, entire. That is, all the members of the Mystical Body offer themselves with Christ, their Head. Hence, the active rôle what we should play in the Mass.

Our Holy Father, Pope Pius XII, recalls this truth to us in his encyclical on the Mystical Body. "In it, the priest not only represents our Saviour, but the entire Mystical Body; and each of the faithful in particular. The faithful, themselves, moreover, united to the priest in a common will and prayer, offer up to the Eternal Father the Immaculate Lamb brought down on the altar by the voice of the priest. They offer him, by the hands of the same priest, as a most pleasing Victim of propitiation and praise; for the necessities of the whole Church. And just as the Divine Redeemer, dying on the Cross, offered himself as Head of the human race, to the Eternal Father; in the same way, in this 'clean oblation,' he not only offers himself as Head of the Church to the Heavenly Father, but in himself he also offers his mystical members; since all—even the most infirm and feeble—are contained in his loving heart."

10—What else does the Holy Father have to say on the subject in his encyclical, *Mediator Dei et hominum*, on the liturgy?

In paragraph 101 we read: "Renewed daily, the Holy Sacrifice reminds us that there is no salvation outside the Cross of our Lord Jesus Christ [Gal. 6:14]; and that God himself has ratified this Sacrifice from 'the rising to the going down of the sun.' [Mal. 1:11] to the end that the hymn of thanksgiving and glory owed by men to their Creator, may never cease; for man has a perpetual need of God's assistance—need also of the Redeemer's blood to blot out the sins that provoke God's justice."

11—We call the Mass the "Holy Sacrifice." Can you give a simple, clear definition of the word "sacrifice"?

A. Sacrifice in general

In current usage, the word "sacrifice" may be taken in two ways:

1. In the *active* sense—as an act of immolation.
2. In the *passive* sense—as the object immolated.

The passive sense presupposes the active sense.

The word "sacrifice" conveys the idea of something painful of privation, of self-denial, of a voluntary giving up of a cherished object.

Sacrifice also implies the idea of subordination to something else—of a choice.

In a word, one might define sacrifice as the act of giving up something I like very much, for something I like even better. (Thus a person may sacrifice his health to study.)

When a father gives up his fortune so that his children may have a good education, while he himself lives a life of privation; people say, "He is making great sacrifices for his children." When a soldier goes to war in defense of his country, risking his life and health, they say, "He is sacrificing himself for his country."

Note that this act of renunciation (the material element) is transient: it is made at the moment of decision or choice and is symbolized by the immolation of the victim.

The choice (formal element) is permanent, once the decision has been made and provided it is not withdrawn. This choice is symbolized by the sacrifice.

B. Religious oblation

The name of oblation is ordinarily given to an offering made to God. For instance, the poor widow who, for love of God, offered her last two mites in the temple, made a great sacrifice. (Mark 12:43.) During the Jewish Captivity, Tobias distributed all his fortune to indigent Jews for the love of God; and—at the risk of his life—buried his slain companions. Tobias thus made a great sacrifice to God. (Tob. 1.)

Consequently, in religious oblation the object renounced must be a good thing: the object preferred is God. The choice is motivated by love for God.

It is a preferential love. "He who loves father and mother more than me is not worthy of me. He who loves son or daughter more than me is not worthy of me." (Matt. 10:37.) "If anyone comes to me and does not hate his father and mother, wife and children, brothers and sisters, and his own life, too, he can be no disciple of mine." (Luke 14:26.) [Knox.[1]]

"Giving up creatures," means giving up all created things and my own self-surrender.

The sacrifice required by God hinges on these two points:

First, the giving up, out of love for God, of seeking my own pleasure, and of doing my own will.

Second, the preferring of God to all things outside myself. That is, I acknowledge that God is better than these things. Next, I prefer God to myself. This means that I believe that God's will is better, more lovable, than mine. I ought to consider God's excellence, as well as his sovereignty.

To sum up, religious oblation may be defined as the recognition of God's excellence or absolute goodness, as shown by my renunciation of all created things; and the recognition of his sovereignty, as demonstrated by my acceptance of his will in preference to mine.

Let us apply these principles to our Lord's Sacrifice.

12—In what does Christ's Sacrifice consist?

1. Our Lord's Sacrifice consists in his *complete self-renunciation* —an immolation that began with the first instant of his earthly existence and terminated on Calvary's Cross.

2. Our Lord's Sacrifice consists above all in the preferring of God's will to his own: a preference shown by his oblation, which persists eternally. This perfect love of Christ for his Father was stabilized by his death and will abide throughout eternity.

Death fixes us in the dispositions we have at the moment of dying. Our degree of charity at death will mark our degree of glory for eternity. After death there are no more successive acts. The set of our hearts at death remains as the final disposition of our wills. Our Lord, at the

[1] Unless otherwise indicated (as here), all Scripture citations are taken from the Confraternity text, published by St. Anthony's Guild, Paterson, N.J. The substitution of "you" and "your" for the archaic "thee" and "thou," anticipates this change in the forthcoming revised English Bible now underway by Catholic scholarship; and has been especially requested by the publishers. [Translator's note.]

moment of his death on the Cross, attained (so to speak) the climax of his love for his Father. In fact, Christ's life, from birth to death, was the manifestation of his great love for God.

And it is precisely these sublime dispositions of our Lord toward his Father at the moment of his death that are made actual in the Mass. Now do you see why the Mass is of such great value?

13—Demonstrate, by quoting the encyclical, *Mediator Dei*, that our Holy Father, Pope Pius XII, clearly defines the nature of Christ's Sacrifice; namely, Christ's continuous obedience to his Father from the first moment of his Incarnation.

The page from the *Mediator Dei* here cited is one of the most important. It tells us in what Christ's Sacrifice consists; and makes it clear to us, that following our Saviour's example, our participation in the Mass does not mean just a few acts of penance accomplished now and then during life; but extends to our whole existence: which should be wholly devoted to the glory of God.

The passages in question are paragraphs 22-25:

"Indeed, scarcely has 'the Word been made flesh' [John 1:14.], than he manifests himself to the world in his priestly character; by making an act of submission to God the Father that is to be life-long: 'Therefore, in coming into the world, He says, 'Behold, I come to do your will, O God.' [Heb. 10:5-7.] This act of submission is to be brought to its full perfection in a wonderful way in the bloody Sacrifice of the Cross: 'It is in this 'will' that we have been sanctified through the offering of the body of Jesus Christ once for all.' [Heb. 10:10.] All Christ's activity among men had no other purpose. As a child, he is presented to the Lord in the Temple of Jerusalem. As a youth, he goes again to the temple. Later on, he will often return to instruct the people and to pray. Before inaugurating his public ministry, he fasts for forty days. By word and example, he exhorts us to pray, whether by day or by night. As Master of Truth, he 'enlightens every man' [John 1:9,]; that mortals may recognize the true immortal God, and not be 'among those who draw back unto destruction, but of those who have faith to the saving of the soul.' [Heb. 10:39.] As Shepherd, he has charge of his flock. He leads it into living pastures, and gives it a law to be observed; in order that none may turn aside from him: but that all may lead holy lives under his inspiration and guidance. At the Last Supper he celebrated the New Passover with pomp and solemn rite; and, thanks to the divine institution of the Eucharist, assured its permanence. The next day, uplifted between Heaven and earth, he offers his life in sacrifice for our salvation; and from his riven side, causes the sacraments to flow that distribute to men's souls the fruits of the Redemption. In so doing, he has no other aim than his Father's glory and man's greater sanctity.

"Entering, then, into the place of eternal beatitude, he desires that the worship initiated and offered during his earthly life, may continue without interruption. For he will not leave the human race orphans, but will ever assist it by his continuous and powerful protection; making himself our Advocate in Heaven with the Father. [I John, 2:2.] He will assist it also by his Church, in which his divine presence is perpetuated from age to age; which he established as a 'pillar and mainstay of the truth' [I Tim. 3:15.], and dispenser of his grace; and which, by the Sacrifice of the Cross, he founded, consecrated, and confirmed forever."

14—Demonstrate, using Scripture references, that our Lord always did his Father's will; and that his Sacrifice began at birth and was consummated by his death.

Our Lord's whole life consisted in *the fulfillment of his Father's will.*

Christ, "in coming into the world," expressed the guiding motive of his whole earthly existence:

"Sacrifice and oblation you would not have,
but a body you have fitted to me:
In holocausts and sin-offerings you have
had no pleasure.
Then said I 'Behold, I come—
(in the head of the book it is written of me)—
to do your will, O God.' " [Heb. 10:5.]

This idea of always doing his Father's will presided over all his existence and directed all his activity. It was this thought that caused him to descend from Heaven, to be born in a stable at Bethlehem, to live in poverty at Nazareth, to exercise his ministry in Palestine, to die on Calvary, and ascend to Heaven again to the bosom of the Holy Trinity.

Already, at the age of twelve, Jesus tells his parents, who had been looking for him, the motives of his conduct. "Did you not know that I must be about my Father's business?" [Luke 2:49.]

The Father's will guided him in the choice of subjects for his instructions and sermons: "I do not do anything on my own authority, but speak as my Father has instructed me to speak." (John 8:28.) [Knox.] "I speak what I have seen with my Father." (John 8:38.) "It is not on my own authority that I have spoken; it was my Father who sent me, that commanded me what words I was to say, what message I was to utter." (John 12:49.) [Knox.]

Entirely in the service of his Father's will, Christ went to the last limits of renunciation to fulfill his mission. "Christ did not please himself," St. Paul tells us. (Rom. 15:3.)

He might have elected the continuous enjoyment of Mount Tabor's rapture; he might have reserved a considerable amount of time for silence and solitude, in order to have lived alone in the intimacy of the Trinity—but the Father's will had ordained otherwise. So Jesus walked up and down the length and breadth of Palestine; mixed with Publicans and sinners; with quite ordinary, often rather stupid people; since even the apostles were "without wits." (Matt. 15:16.) [Knox.] He lived in continual self-denial and poverty: "The Son of Man has nowhere to lay his head!" (Luke 9:58.) Jesus and his apostles often did not have enough to eat. "My food, said he, is to do the will of him who sent me, to accomplish his work." (John 4:34.)

Jesus never worked for himself: "I do not seek my own glory." (John 8:50.) "Knowing, then, that they meant to come and carry him off, so as to make a king of him, Jesus once again withdrew on the hillside, all alone." (John 6:15.) [Knox.] Jesus never worked a miracle on his own behalf: "Do you doubt that if I call my Father even now, he will send more than twelve legions of angels to my side?" (Matt. 26:53.) [Knox.]

Jesus was always forgetful of self. To the daughters of Jerusalem, he said: "It is not for me that you should weep, daughters of Jerusalem; you should weep for yourselves and your children." (Luke 23:38.) [Knox.] As if to say, "It is useless for you to shed tears because of my death. I am doing my Father's will. Weep rather for yourselves, for you are living in sin and not doing God's will."

Texts abound. We can choose only a few.

St. Paul, in his Epistle to the Romans, clearly explains that Christ's redeeming Sacrifice consisted in giving up his own will to do his Father's—that is, through obedience. "A multitude will become acceptable to God through one man's obedience; just as a multitude through one man's disobedience became guilty." (Rom. 5:19.) [Knox.]

It is during Christ's Passion that his constant desire to do his Father's will stands out most sharply. He it is who turns himself over to his torturers: "The world must be convinced that I love the Father, and act only as the Father has commanded me to act. Rise up, we must be going on our way." (John 14:31.) [Knox.] On Jesus' way to the Garden of Gethsemane, in a moment of supreme anguish, he directs his prayer toward Heaven: "My Father, if it is possible, let this chalice pass me by; only as your will is, not as mine is." (Matt. 26:39.) [Knox.] Had he not said before. "Shall I not drink the cup that my Father has given me?" (John 18:11.) And without a murmur, Christ indeed drinks the chalice to the dregs; reserving his pity for the sufferings of others, rather than for his own. Dying on the Cross, he gives us the Blessed Virgin for our Mother (John 19:26.); promises Heaven to the repentant thief; and pardons his executioners. (Luke 23:34.)

"Jesus was obedient to death, even to death on a cross" ... (Phil. 2:8), until that moment in which he could give back his will to him who had sent him, saying, "Father, into your hands I commend my spirit." (Luke 23:46); because "I have accomplished the work that you have given me to do" (John 17:4), and "all is consummated." (John 19:30.)

Here, in résumé, is our Lord's Sacrifice: a Sacrifice identical with the Mass; namely, the continual abandonment of his own will, preferring—even at the most crucial moments—his Father's will to his own.

"This is the way we should act, if we are to make of our lives a mass." "The kingdom of Heaven will not give entrance to every man who calls me, 'Master, Master'; only to the man who does the will of My Father who is in Heaven." (Matt. 7:21.) [Knox.] We shall have more to say about this later on.

The Mass! — Every day is Good Friday. Thus is realized the word of the prophet: "From the rising of the sun to the going down of the same, My name shall be great among the nations and in every place shall be offered a clean oblation." (Pascal).

15—The word "sacrifice" implies both inner adoration and exterior worship. How did Christ's Sacrifice express these two modes of worship?

1. INNER ADORATION [1]

It will be recalled, that the Samaritan woman at Jacob's well asked our Lord one day if it were at Jerusalem or on Mount Gerazim that men should offer true worship to God. Jesus replied, "The hour is coming, and is now here, when the true worshippers will worship the Father in spirit and in truth. For the Father also seeks such to worship him." (John 4:23.)

---

[1] Christ's Sacrifice is unique. It was effected once and for all on the Cross. It is not repeated, but continued. In what sense ?

The multiple controversies on this point do not seem to be fully resolved as yet. Nevertheless, there is no reason for omitting this question completely from our study of the Mass. The question itself is a fundamental point of doctrine, needful to know in order to comprehend the meaning of the Eucharistic Sacrifice. What, then, is the best method to follow ? We are suggesting a series of ideas that seem to us to be useful for grasping the connections linking the Mass to the last Supper, to the Cross, and to the life of Christ in glory.

Sacrifice is the outward expression of an inner attitude. Let us distinguish between these two aspects of the situation and see how both are realized in Christ's Sacrifice. On the Cross, Jesus is placed in a perfect interior act of obedience and love toward his Father, which he has expressed in the exterior act of his voluntary death. Christ entered into Heaven with this same attitude of perfect submission and perfect love, and he lives eternally in this gift of himself. Christ's interior sacrifice continues in an act identical with that whereby he offered himself on the Cross. The question as to whether this act is expressed in a special manner in Christ's life in glory, need not concern us here. At the Last Supper, however, Christ instituted the eucharistic ritual (which expressed the attitude of oblation) in which he becomes present under the species of bread and wine.

This ritual is reproduced in every Mass, but does not renew the exterior act of death. Nevertheless, the words of Consecration, pronounced by the priest over the separate species of bread and wine, express—in the imagery of death—the interior sacrifice that Christ realized on the Cross and in which he lives eternally.

More recent papal encyclicals, which take up and develop the doctrine of the Council of Trent, avoid the expression "renewal of the Sacrifice of the Cross" —too feeble to express the interior sacrifice; which is *not* renewed, because it endures eternally—too strong to express the exterior Sacrifice; since the death of Christ is not renewed, the eucharistic Christ being alive and glorious. Such expressions as "the Sacrifice re-presented" and "continued" or "Christ's Sacrifice in union with that of Christians, "seem more accurate."—Marcel Van Caster, S.J., *Lumen Vitae,* Vol. VII, p. 52, *Points vitaux dans l'enseignement de la messe* ("Vital Points in the Teaching of the Mass.")

To "worship in spirit" means to prefer God, by an act of the intelligence, to all earthly things. The Jewish sacrifices had become mere rites, external observances, which had lost all significance. Therefore, God was offended by them. "This people honours Me with its lips, but its heart is far from Me."

In Christ's Sacrifice, this inner adoration really exists. It is Christ's homage paid to his Father in the act of supreme love of his death on the Cross, in fulfillment of the Father's will. Our Lord, in the most crucial moment of his life, preferred his Father to himself and to all else beside. He therefore gave Him the greatest possible proof of love. "This is the greatest love a man can show, that he should lay down his life for his friends." [Knox.] Here again, one sees the grandeur of Christ's Sacrifice, and the glory that his offering gave to God.

2. Exterior worship

In Christ's Sacrifice, exterior worship is the gift of all his being, of all his life, as expressed by his death.

Christ's death on the Cross is thus the expression or outward manifestation of his preference, or love, for his Father.

ONE SACRIFICE

There are not two Sacrifices, one of the Cross, and one of the Mass. There is only one Sacrifice of Christ. "By a single offering He has completed His work, for all time in those whom He sanctifies," declares St. Paul. But how is this possible? How can the Mass be a "true Sacrifice," without conflicting with the *uniqueness* of Christ's Sacrifice?

The Mass is a Mystery; which brings down upon the altar the drama of Redemption, and communicates its effects without any duplication whatever.

The Mass *re-presents* the liturgy of the Last Supper and of the Sacrifice of the Cross. It is turned thereby toward the past, but toward a past that remains ever present; since Christ's death on the Cross is no mere historical event. He who thus dies on Calvary, is the Word of God. His death, apparently localized in time, transcends history. The risen Christ is no longer subject to death.

Just as the sun that illumines the earth, appears to revolve around it, but is, in reality, immovable; for it is the different regions of the earth that present themselves in succession to the light; so Christ, the Sun of Justice, appears to repeat his Sacrifice on the altar every morning; but is, in reality, immovable in his eternity. All the apparent repetition comes from the earth, from the Church; which daily, hourly, renews the liturgical gesture of the Last Supper; offers herself to the Saviour and renders him present on the altar; in order to receive the light and warmth emanating from his glorious wounds.

—Louis-Marie de Bazelaire,
Archbishop of Chambéry.

16—Is the Mass the same as Christ's Sacrifice on the Cross, or is it a different Sacrifice?

It is the same Sacrifice. Christ offered himself once for all. "We have been sanctified by an offering made once for all, the body of Jesus Christ." (Heb. 10:10.) [Knox.]

To understand this, we have only to go back to the concept of oblation, renunciation, and choice.

The renunciation is summarized by Christ's death accepted once and for all.

On Calvary, this act of renunciation was made once, and it passed.

But above all, our Lord's Sacrifice consists in this constant desire for his Father's will in preference to his own; and this preference remains eternally fixed in Heaven. Suffering passes—the fact of having suffered remains. . . .

It is the same thing for us when we renounce anything. The act of self-denial is, like all acts, temporary; but the disposition of the will to deny itself for a greater good remains just so long as we do not take it back. Death fixes us forever in the dispositions in which it finds us.

Christ's Sacrifice persists in Heaven, because the legacy of his life made on the Cross has never been cancelled. That which he gave was given for all time. . . . *Christ's immolation is eternal.* St. John, in his vision of Heaven, sees Jesus as "a Lamb standing upright, yet slain (as I thought) in sacrifice." (Apoc.) [Knox.]

This is understandable. *The purpose of our Lord's Sacrifice having been to glorify God, the act whereby he glorifies him must, of necessity, be eternal.*

When the priest brings Christ down upon the altar, he renders him present such as he is in Heaven; and he is in Heaven with the same loving dispositions that he had on Calvary at the moment of his death.

The Mass is, therefore, not a new Sacrifice by Christ; but the same Sacrifice actualized in the present. "We know that Christ, now he has risen from the dead, cannot die any more." (Rom. 6:9.) [Knox.]

The Mass is thus the perpetual prolongation of the Sacrifice made on the Cross.

Consequently, every Mass is the one immolation of Christ repeated in the Act of Oblation. By the same act of the will, Jesus offers at the Last Supper his death in the future; on Calvary his death in the present; in Heaven and on the altar his death in the past.

This special presence of Christ on the altar is peculiar to the Mass and demonstrates its grandeur.

When we celebrate the other mysteries of Christ's life, we merely commemorate them. There is no real renewal of the mystery on the day devoted to it. At Christmas, the Church recalls to our minds the Saviour's birth, but this birth does not really take place—is not actualized in the present. On Ascension Thursday, our Lord does not renew his ascent into Heaven. It is quite otherwise for the Mass. It is no simple symbolic representation, for the same Sacrifice that Christ accomplished on the Cross is made truly present in an unbloody manner on the altar.

17—What does His Holiness, Pope Pius XII, have to say on this subject in paragraph 90 of his encyclical, *Mediator Dei?*

He says: "Therefore, the Holy Sacrifice of the Altar is not a mere and simple commemoration of the sufferings and death of Jesus Christ, but a true Sacrifice in the proper sense of the word; whereby in a non-bloody immolation, the High Priest does the same thing that he did on the Cross: namely, offer himself to the Eternal Father as a most acceptable Victim. It is the same Victim. The One who now offers himself through the ministry of priests, is the same One who offered himself then on the Cross—only the mode of offering is different." [Council of Trent, Session 22, c.2.]

18—Does the Mass differ in any way from the Sacrifice of the Cross?

A. EXTERNALLY

We have seen that on the Cross, Christ expressed inner adoration toward his Father, by loving him more than the thing most precious to him—his own life. We find the same interior adoration in the Mass, since Christ's preferential love for his Father persists eternally.

The difference appears in the outward expression of Christ's inner sentiments. On the Cross, Christ manifests his love for his Father by his death in a bloody manner.

In the Mass, Christ offers himself to his Father in a *non*-bloody manner.

What sign, then, in the Mass gives outward expression to Christ's inner adoration? For the Mass, like the Sacraments, has a visible sign that signifies and actualizes the Sacrifice.

This sign is the separate Consecration of the bread and wine, representing the separation of our Lord's body and blood on the Cross. The active Consecration—that is, not yet accomplished, but in process of accomplishment—effectively signifies Christ's Sacrifice; since it renders present on the altar the same Sacrifice as that of Calvary.

Note that the Real Presence of Christ in the tabernacle is not, properly speaking, a sacrifice; since the exterior sign—the Consecration—is lacking. Where the exterior element is lacking, there can be no sacrifice.

B. BY THE MODE OF OFFERING

We have said that two things are needed to make a sacrifice:

1. Renunciation or immolation.
2. Preference, choice, oblation or offering.

Now on the Cross, as in the Mass, it is the same Victim that is immolated—our Lord. A difference exists, however, in the method or mode of oblation. In the Mass, it is still our Lord who offers himself as he did on Calvary, *but through the ministry of his priests.*

Nevertheless, the priest is merely Christ's representative. There is only one priest—Jesus Christ. But our Blessed Lord, in his great mercy, and in order to make us participate still more intimately in his Sacrifice, has self-imposed the condition whereby he cannot offer himself on the altar without his priests!

Thus, on the Cross, Christ offers himself *by* himself *in our name.*

In the Mass, it is the priest who, in the name of all the people, offers Christ *exteriorly.* For interiorly, it is always Christ who offers.

C. As to time and place

The Sacrifice of the Cross occurred at a given moment in a given spot on the earth. Christ offered his death in the present.

In the Mass, Christ offers himself *throughout the whole universe,* exactly as the prophet Malachias had prophesied, *and at each moment of the day and night.* He offers his death as an accomplished historical fact.

19—With regard to the resemblances and differences between the Sacrifice of the Mass and that of the Cross, quote the words of our Holy Father, Pius XII, in his encyclical, *Mediator Dei,* paragraphs 91 and 92.

He says: "It is the same Priest, Jesus Christ, but in whose holy person his sacred minister acts. This minister, from the priestly consecration that he has received, is assimilated to the Great High Priest, and enjoys the power of acting with the might and in the name of Christ himself." [Cf. St. Thomas, Summa Theol., III, q. 22, a. 4.] That is why in his priestly action, he lends, as it were, 'his tongue to Christ; he offers him his hand.' [St. John Chrysostom in Ioann, Hom. 86, 4.]

"It is the same Victim—the Divine Redeemer—in his human nature and with his true Body and Blood.

"The mode of offering is, however, different. On the Cross, Christ offered himself and his sufferings to God in their entirety; and the immolation of the Victim was effected by a bloody death freely accepted. On the altar, on the contrary—because of the glorified state of Christ's human nature—'death has no more power over him.' (Rom. 6:9.) [Knox.] Consequently, the shedding of blood is no longer possible. Nevertheless, Divine Wisdom has discovered an admirable means of showing forth the Redeemer's Sacrifice by external signs symbolic of death. Indeed, by the transubstantiation of the bread into the Body, and the wine into the Blood of our Lord, Christ's Body becomes actually and truly present; as likewise does his Blood; and the eucharistic species under which they appear are symbolic of the violent separation of his Body and Blood. Thus the real death on Calvary is recalled in every Holy Mass, for the separation of the symbols clearly indicates that Jesus Christ is present in the state of victim."

20—Demonstrate that the Mass constitutes a renewal of the Last Supper.

Our Lord's Sacrifice was especially manifested on two occasions:

1. In an unbloody manner in the intimacy of the Cenacle.
2. In a bloody manner in His Passion.

We have seen something of the resemblances and differences in the Sacrifice of the Cross and that of the Mass. Let us pause briefly to consider the resemblances of the Last Supper with those of the Mass.

The Upper Room	*The Mass*
I. PREPARATION	
Purification of the apostles	**The aspersions**
The washing of the feet	**The Confiteor**
II. INSTRUCTION	
Jesus' discourse	Epistle, Gospel, Sermon, Creed
III. OBLATION	
Jesus takes the bread, blesses it, and offers it to his Father. Likewise for the wine.	At the Offertory, the same words and gestures are renewed by the priest.
IV. CONSECRATION	
The same potent words are pronounced: "This is My Body. This My Blood."	

V. COMMUNION

Jesus distributes the Bread of Life to the apostles.	The priest, "another Christ," distributes the consecrated Hosts to the faithful.

VI. THANKSGIVING

Jesus with his apostles recites the thanksgiving hymn.	At the Postcommunion, the priest, in union with the people, gives thanks to God.

By means of this comparative table, we are better able to visualize the identity of the Mass with the Sacrifice that Christ offered to his Father more than nineteen centuries ago.

21—To whom is the Sacrifice of the Mass offered?

To GOD ALONE

Why to God alone?

1. Because the Mass is an act of adoration.

2. Because the dignity of Christ, Victim and Sacrificer, is infinite. Hence his offering can be addressed only to God.

3. Because an offering made to a creature would be idolatrous, since the end of sacrifice is to acknowledge God's pre-eminence and kingship over all creation.

Nevertheless, the Sacrifice of the Mass may be offered in honour of the angels and saints:

1. To thank God for the wonderful way in which he has rewarded their virtue.

2. To ask graces from God through their intercession or patronage.

3. To celebrate their virtues and their triumphs.

4. To stir us up to imitate them.

The custom of offering the Mass in honour of the saints is a very ancient one. In the early days of the Church, it was customary to gather round the tombs of the martyrs on the anniversaries of their deaths and have Mass celebrated to honour their memory.

22—For what four ends is the Sacrifice of the Mass offered?

We may distinguish between primary and secondary ends.

1. Primary ends: Praise and thanksgiving.
2. Secondary ends: Propitiation and petition.

Praise. The primary purpose of the Mass is to glorify God. When we give God first place in our lives, we acknowledge that God is:

1. A Being of infinite grandeur. (God beholds at his feet a God who is co-equal—abased, humiliated.)

2. A Being pre-eminently holy. (Jesus, the sole stainless Victim, is offered up to him.)

3. A Being who is First Cause and Final End of all things.

"When we attend Holy Mass, we offer God more honour than the angels and saints do in Heaven, for their homage is that of creatures; whereas in the Mass we offer Jesus Christ himself: a Victim who obtains for him infinite honour." (St. Alphonse.)

Thanksgiving. We have every reason for according God first place in our lives! Daily God showers down upon us a multitude of graces. Yet the great duty of gratitude is so often forgotten! We are deluged with divine gifts—gifts of nature, gifts of grace. We should understand these blessings better and be more grateful for them if the Lord had done less for us!... Now, "what shall I render unto the Lord for all his benefits"? All that we have comes from him. And all earthly goods are as nothing, in comparison with those "greater goods" that he has heaped upon us.... Here the Mass comes to our aid. By means of it, we are able to offer God a gift worthy of him—a God who is consubstantial with him. We offer him a thanksgiving of infinite worth—that of a God! For in the Mass it is Christ who thanks God on our behalf.

Propitiation or expiation. The Mass obtains for us the pardon of our sins. Jesus alone can obtain this pardon for us. Only a God can atone for the insult made to God. In fact, Jesus not only *can* render, but *wills* to render, God propitious to us. He is the Lamb of God that takes away the sins of the world. From the altar he cries to his Father as he did on the Cross, "Father, forgive them!" He affirms as he did at the

Last Supper: "This is my blood, shed for many, to the remission of sins."

Doubtless, in the Mass we are not redeemed anew, but the fruits of the Redemption are applied to us afresh by means of this non-bloody Sacrifice.

What a marvel of grace! We have so often offended God! Count, if you can, the number of your own transgressions; those of a parish, of a city, of a nation, of the whole world. The thought alone is dreadful. If the fire of Heaven's vengeance does not descend to destroy mankind today, as it did once for the cities of Sodom and Gomorrah, it is because the potent voice of the Lamb immolated on the altar demands not vengeance, but pardon! For in the Mass, Christ atones for us.

Again, how explain the fact that so few Catholics participate in the Holy Sacrifice?

Impetration or petition. During Mass we should implore the outpourings of divine grace. We are all beggars. From a supernatural point of view, we are incapable of producing the smallest act of virtue. Grace, then, is indispensable. How are we to obtain this supernatural help? Through the Mass.

The Holy Sacrifice renders glory to God. When we offer it, we show God reverence; and, in return, God showers down abundant graces and is propitious to us. God never lets himself be outdone in generosity. Remember the seven petitions of the Pater. The first three have to do with the glory of God, the last four with our personal concerns! Among men, the offering of one's respects to a person before begging a favour of him, is elementary. The God who has created us for his glory and our happiness, is likewise entitled to our respect. If we are reverent toward God, we may be assured that God will grant us every blessing. So much the more, since in the Mass it is the voice of Jesus that pleads for us—the only voice to which God listens! It is of faith that we can obtain nothing, except through the mediation of Christ. "Without me you can do nothing," in all that concerns your salvation. "No one can come to me unless he is enabled to do so by my Father." This mediation is mighty with God: "So that every request you make of the Father in my name may be granted you." "Ask, and you shall receive."

In the Mass we offer the Mediator ordained by God to solicit graces on our behalf. Here it is that Christ especially fulfills his mediatorial office. It is from the summit of the altar that God's voice speaks most plainly, "Ask, and you shall receive."

23—What does Pope Pius XII have to say about the fourfold end of the Mass in his encyclical, *Mediator Dei*, paragraphs 92-96?

"The first end of the Mass," says the Holy Father, "is *to glorify God.* "From the cradle to the grave, Jesus Christ was inflamed with zeal for God's glory. The offering of his blood ascended to Heaven from the Cross as a pleasing perfume; and in order that the chorus of praise may be unceasing, the members are joined to their Divine Head in the Eucharistic Sacrifice; and with him, united with the angels and archangels, 'cease not to repeat day by day,' crying out with one voice... [Roman Missal, Preface.] ascribing to God the Father Almighty... all honour and glory.' [Canon.]

"The second end is *to show fitting gratitude toward God.* The Divine Redeemer alone, as the Beloved Son of the Father, whose immense love he knows, can offer him a worthy hymn of thanksgiving. Such was his aim and purpose in 'giving thanks' [Mark 14:23.] at the Last Supper. And this aim and purpose did not cease when Christ hung on the Cross, nor does it cease in the Holy Sacrifice of the Altar; whose very meaning is 'giving thanks' or Eucharistic Action; for to do so is truly meet and just, right and availing unto salvation.' [Roman Missal, Preface.]

"In the third place, the Sacrifice proposes the purpose of *expiation,* of *propitiation,* and of *reconciliation.* Assuredly, none other than Christ could offer satisfaction to God for the sins of the human race. Hence, he desired to be immolated on the Cross; for 'he in his own person is the atonement made for our sins, and not only for ours, but for the sins of the whole world.' [1 John 2:2 (Knox).] In the same way. he offers himself daily on our altars for our redemption, that having been snatched from eternal damnation, we may be numbered among the flock of his elect. And this not only for these who are in this mortal life, but also for all those 'who have gone before us with the sign of faith and who sleep the sleep of peace.' [Roman Missal, Canon.] So that whether we live or die, 'we may not depart from the one and only Christ.' [St. Augustine, *On the Trinity,* Vol. XIII, c. 19.]

"Finally, in the fourth place, there is the end of *impetration.* Man, the prodigal son, has made but ill use of the substance received from his Heavenly Father, and has wasted it. Hence, he finds himself reduced to a state of deepest degradation and poverty. But Christ, from the summit of the Cross, 'not without a piercing cry, not without tears... offered prayer and entreaty... with such piety as won him a hearing. [Heb. 5:7 (Knox).] In like manner, he exercises the same efficacious mediation on our holy altars, to the end that we may be filled with every blessing and grace."

24—Does the Sacrifice of the Mass possess infinite value?

Yes and no!

Considered as Christ's Sacrifice, the Mass always achieves its full effect. For the merits of Christ, the Divine Victim, are infinite.

But the Mass is not Christ's Sacrifice alone. It is also that of the Church, of the whole Mystical Body; consequently of each one of us. As the Sacrifice of the Church—in the application of the fruits—the Mass is finite, limited. The merits of Christ are distributed to us in accordance with our dispositions, our sacrifices, and the glory we give to God.

From this, may be seen the importance of making our own personal oblation with the best possible dispositions.

25—What do we read in paragraphs 97-100 of the encyclical, *Mediator Dei*, with regard to the infinite value of the Mass?

"The Apostle to the Gentiles," says His Holiness, "in proclaiming the superabundant fullness and perfection of the Sacrifice of the Cross, declared that Christ, by one offering, had perfected forever those who are sanctified. [Heb. 10:4.] For the merits of this infinite and immeasurable Sacrifice are limitless; they extend universally to men of all time and of all places, because the God-Man is both Priest and Victim; because his immolation, like his obedience to God the Father, was perfect; and because he willed to die as the Head of the human race. 'Behold in what manner our Redemption—Christ hanged upon the tree. Behold at what a price it was purchased—he shed his blood. Our Redemption was bought with the blood of the Immaculate Lamb, with the blood of God's only Son.... The purchaser is Christ; the purchase price, his blood; the purchase, the universe.' [St. Augustine, *Discourse on Psalm 147,* No. 16.]

"The full effect of this purchase, however, was not attained at once. It was needful that Christ, after having redeemed the world at the costly price of himself, should enter into full and undisputed possession of men's souls. In a manner of speaking, one may say that Christ established on Calvary a pool of atonement and salvation, which he filled with his shed blood; but if men do not plunge into its depths and there cleanse their sin-stained souls, they can neither be purified nor saved.

"In order, then, for each sinner to be made white in the blood of the Lamb, it is necessary for Christians to associate their labours with those of Christ. If, generally speaking, one may say that Christ reconciled all mankind with his Father by means of his bloody death; he has nevertheless willed that in order to obtain the salutary fruits produced by him on the Cross, all should be led and brought to his Cross by the Sacraments; and chiefly, by the Eucharistic Sacrifice."

26—For whom may Mass be celebrated?

God always receives infinite praise from the Mass, even should the celebrant be unworthy of his high office; for it is Christ, who—in the Mass, as once on Calvary—is both Priest and Victim.

The Mass is offered to God alone; but for the advantage, profit, utility, and benefit of the Mystical Body of Christ.

The beneficiaries of the Mass are thus the members of the Mystical Body. As we shall see farther on in taking up the various parts of the Mass, the Mass includes the "Memento of the Living" and the "Memento of the Dead." We shall find there indicated the persons for whom Mass may be celebrated.

1. *The living.* These are the members of Christ's Mystical Body still on earth: consequently, each one of us.

Incidentally, a beautiful prayer formula for offering prayer for dying sinners is the following:

"My God, I offer you all the Masses that are being celebrated today for those sinners who are in their agony now and are to die today. May the Precious Blood of Jesus obtain mercy for them!"

2. *The dead. In other words, the souls in Purgatory.*

Charity demands that those members of the Mystical Body who have access to Christ's oblation, should not forget those members no longer able to offer the Holy Sacrifice. It devolves on us to see that the Church Suffering is not deprived of its greatest good: the Mass, which applies to it Christ's merits. If we would have Christians still on earth think of us, when we in our turn shall be in Purgatory; let us not forget the departed, who implore our prayers and Masses!

The merit of a charitable work depends on three factors: (1) The value of the work in question; (2) the effort involved; (3) the amount of charity with which the work is accomplished.

No work of mercy surpasses in value the gift of a Mass. If the cup of cold water is rewarded, of how much greater merit is Christ's infinite oblation applied to a human soul! No other offering or riches is comparable. If material or spiritual aid to a neighbour in need, draws down upon us Heaven's blessings, how much more meritorious still, the offering to a suffering member of the Mystical Body of the very immolation of Christ!

27—Do all members of the Mystical Body have an equal share in the fruits of the Mass?

It is customary to distinguish four fruits of the Mass:

1. A *general* fruit destined for all members of the Mystical Body.

2. A *special* fruit designed for all those assisting at the Sacrifice with suitable dispositions.

3. A *functional* fruit directed toward those persons for whose intentions the Mass is being offered.

4. A *personal* fruit designated for the priest celebrating the Holy Sacrifice.

Be it noted, however, that whatever may be our title for sharing in the fruits of the Mass, the profit we derive from the Mass will depend on the dispositions with which we hear it.

28—What do we mean when we say that the faithful offer Mass?

In *Mediator Dei,* paragraphs 114 and 115, His Holiness, Pius XII, defines the meaning of the word "offer" as follows:

"In order not to give rise to pernicious errors in this most important matter, it is necessary to determine the exact meaning of the word 'offer.' The unbloody immolation by means of which Christ is made present on the altar in the state of Victim, following the words of Consecration, is accomplished by the priest alone; as acting in the person of Christ, not as acting in the person of the people. Yet by virtue of the fact that the priest places the Divine Victim on the altar, he presents him to God the Father as an offering; to the glory of the Most Holy Trinity, and for the good of the whole Church. As for the oblation in this restricted sense, the people do take part in their fashion, and this in two ways; not only because they offer the Holy Sacrifice through the hands of the priest, but also because, in a manner, they offer it with him; and this participation causes the peoples' offering to be attached to the liturgical action itself.

"That the faithful do offer the Holy Sacrifice through the hands of the priest, stands out clearly from the fact that the minister of the altar represents Christ in his capacity as Head, offering in the name of all his members. That is why it may be affirmed with justice, that the universal Church presents through Christ the offering of the Victim. That the people offer at the same time as the priest, does not mean that the members of the Church accomplish the visible, liturgical rite in the same manner as the priest (a thing that devolves solely on God's delegated minister); but that the people unite their intentions of praise, petition, propitiation, and thanksgiving with the intentions of the priest, and even of the Great High Priest; in order to present them to God the Father in the same external rite of the priest offering the Victim. Indeed, the external rite of the Holy Sacrifice, should, of necessity—by its very nature—manifest this inner adoration. Now the Sacrifice of the New Law signifies that act of supreme homage, whereby the Chief Offerer, Christ—and with him and through him all members of his Mystical Body—offer to God due reverence and honour."

OFFERING MYSELF WITH CHRIST

29—What is the source of our obligation to offer ourselves in the Mass with Christ?

We have seen that the Mass is Christ's Sacrifice, that is, the Sacrifice of Calvary made present on the altar.

Now Christ's Sacrifice on the Cross was not an individual, but a social sacrifice. It was as Head of the Mystical Body that Christ consented to die. In offering and immolating himself on the Cross, he included us in his Sacrifice. Christ was obedient to his Father in his own name, and in ours. Our Lord had a right to include, to integrate us into his Sacrifice; because we belong to him, we are his members. He could require, therefore, that we should be obedient to his Father, as he himself was obedient.

On our Lord's side, the Sacrifice is *complete, of infinite merit.*

On *our* side, it is *incomplete, finite, limited in its application.*

We carry out this offering, this submission, or this immolation, with the passage of time; and also to the degree in which we do not draw back from immolating ourselves with Christ.

We understand better now St. Paul's words: "I rejoice now in the sufferings I bear for your sake; and what is lacking of the sufferings of Christ I fill up in my flesh for his body, which is the Church. (Col. 1:24.) Christ's sufferings are complete in the order of satisfaction and merit, but not in the order of appplication.

On *our* side, the Sacrifice of the whole Christ is incomplete. It will terminate with the death of the last member of the Mystical Body, who adds the last thing lacking to the Passion of Christ.

Consequently, our obligation to offer ourselves with Christ in the Mass comes from our membership in Christ's Mystical Body, into which we were introduced by Baptism.

"It is not surprising," writes the Holy Father in *Mediator Dei,* paragraph 110, "that Christians should be raised to this dignity. For by the bath of Baptism, Christians are made members of the Body of Christ-Priest; and by the 'character' which is, as it were, graven on their souls, are ordered to divine worship. They thus participate according to their condition in the priesthood of Christ himself."

A non-baptized person may be bodily present at Mass, and may even follow the ceremonies intelligently. Yet, in the full meaning of the term, he does not "assist" at Mass; for he who truly assists has to be offered with Christ. Now to be offered with Christ, one must first have been incorporated into Christ—be the prolongation of his life. Hence, the baptismal character comprises a union with Christ, a likeness by reason of which we share in his priesthood. And by virtue of our integration into Christ, we are enabled to be offered with him; and to share in the offering of his immolation, in his Sacrifice.

Not only is it permissable for us to be offered with Christ, but we are under obligation to offer ourselves with him—under pain of mutilating the total Christ! For the head alone is not the total Christ. In order for the Mystical Body to be complete, both head and members are needed. This is the whole Christ, as he was offered up to God on Calvary—as he is offered each day on our altars.

Father Plus, S.J., has written these beautiful lines on this subject:

"I am a part of Jesus Christ. That is why I can offer Christ to the Father, and why I ought to offer myself to the Father with Christ.

"How is it that it is permissable for me, a nonentity, to lay hold of Jesus Christ and offer him in homage to the Most High? How is it that for me to do so is not sacrilegious? It is because the Offerer and I are one!

"Why is it, that in offering Jesus Christ, it is prescribed that I should not separate my oblation from his? It is because the One being offered is the total Christ, and that in that total Christ I am included!

"The Saviour's holocaust comprises Jesus Christ in his entirety; that is to say, Christ and the multitude of the just of all ages, intimately bound to their Head, sharing his sufferings, and offering up a perpetual sacrifice.

"The Saviour's immolation—for he has so willed—is incomplete—*we must add ours*. The Cross of Christ, minus our cross, is not enough. Our Lord's merits were infinite; but in order for these merits to reach souls, our co-operation is needed. Christ effected the main part, but not all, of the task. It is up to each one of us to bring *his* contribution. The Saviour's work suffices only for him who completes it by adding his share.

"Our Lord has obligated himself to the mission of summing up all things in himself; but on each one of us devolves the task of supplying the few lines of text still required. In Christ is comprised the whole of redeemed and faithful humanity, the entire Church, the Communion of Saints. In Him who offers, as well as in what He offers, we are included.

"Christ, the High Priest, we as subordinate priests; Christ, the Chief Victim, we as co-victims! But Christ and we—total Priest, and total Victim!

"Christ's constant attitude toward his Father is to offer himself, and with himself, us. The constant attitude of the Christian toward Christ, is to offer up Christ, and himself with Christ."

30—What are the three principal parts or "peaks" of the Mass?

Many people fail to understand the Mass, because they become lost in the maze of its secondary details.

Before going on with our study, let us detach now the three principal parts from all those purely accidental ceremonies that prepare, accompany, or continue them.

These three parts are: (a) the *Offertory* or oblation; (b) the *Consecration* or immolation; (c) the *Communion* or reception.

These three parts belong together and are the indispensable elements of every sacrifice.

Every Mass demands an offering, a relinquishment, a renunciation.

Every offering calls for a consecration, an immolation, a choice.

Every consecration presupposes a communion—love calls for love, sacrifice for reception.

31—What is meant by this expression: "The Mass must be lived"?

We have seen that on Calvary, Christ included us in his Sacrifice by offering us together with himself to the Father.

We have likewise seen that the Mass is the means the Church has at her disposal for offering supreme homage to the Blessed Trinity.

The Mass is not Christ's Sacrifice alone, but that of the whole Mystical Body as well. If we are content to offer up our Lord's sufferings, there is no sacrifice on our part, but a petition ("Dear God, here are the sufferings of your Divine Son. In return, please grant me such and such a favour!")

If the Mass is to become *my* Mass, *my* sacrifice offered to God, if I am to offer the Blessed Trinity my infinitesimal portion of thanksgiving and praise, I must live the way Christ lived; in the same dispositions of denial of self and of placing God first, of obedience, of daily immolation. My sacrifice must be added to His!

Needless to say, our sacrifices alone are of little value—God looks upon them as so much dross. It is only when we offer them to him in union with Christ's Sacrifice that they become as gold. Just as the tiny drop of water that falls into the chalice becomes wine! As we remarked in question 7, it is "through Him" and "in Him" that our sacrifices acquire all their value.

Hence, the extreme importance of centering our lives on the Mass.

Our Sacrifice, our Mass, is in *two parts*:

1. The ritual offering in union with that of Christ in his name. I offer myself *completely,* and in advance, for the hours that lie ahead.

2. The second action—too often forgotten—is as important as the first. This consists in the carrying out of the offering, throughout the course of the day, in the midst of the series of actions that make up its warp and woof. This is what is known as LIVING MY MASS.

Everything does not end with the *Ite, missa est.* On the contrary, it is then that everything begins!...

For when a person has offered himself, *all* himself, with Christ, how is it possible for him to think, speak, and act as do those who have never offered themselves?...

Remember! God gives himself to the one giving himself (or herself), and God is not pleased with half gifts! God never lets himself be outdone in generosity. That is why, after giving ourselves to God through Christ, our Mass is completed by Communion; which gives God to us through Christ.

Here again we can, during the course of the day, communicate with Christ in the person of the beggar, of the sick man, of our neighbour in general—with whom Christ has been pleased to identify himself.

We shall deal with this question at greater length, when we take up the study of the Mass in detail.

32—What does the Holy Father have to say about this in his encyclical, *Mediator Dei*, paragraphs 99 and 102?

He writes: "To the end that their redemption and salvation, in that which concerns the individual and all generations... may be accomplished and made pleasing to God, it is essential that all men should individually come into vital contact with the Sacrifice of the Cross and thus share in the merits derived from it.

"It is therefore, necessary, that all Christians should esteem as a chief duty and supreme honour, their participation in the Eucharistic Sacrifice; and that, not in a passive and negligent manner, while thinking of other things; but with an attention and fervour intimately uniting them to the Great High Priest, in accordance with the Apostle's words: 'Have this mind in you which was also in Christ Jesus' [Phil. 2:5] offering with, and through him, and sanctifying ourselves in him."

33—What preparation should I bring to my Mass?

The celebration of a Mass is not just something that can be improvised on the spot; especially when one considers that the Mass is the greatest event in world history. A proper preparation should be threefold:

1. *Doctrinal preparation.* By means of reading, of listening to God's Word, and of study groups. Such preparation for Mass is most important and fruitful; because it shows us the prime value of the Mass and compels us to study the great dogmas of our Faith, for which the Mass serves as a rallying-point: The Trinity, the Incarnation, Redemption, grace and glory.

If many souls fail to progress, if instead of going forward, they continually go backward; it should be recognized that the principal cause of their spiritual anemia is to be found in their total or partial ignorance of the Mass—centre of their lives. Such souls scarcely suspect the existence of this admirable doctrine—small wonder that they neither live it, nor are nourished by it.

Let us rise up against this ignorance and apathy. Let us study these great truths and then share with others the knowledge that we acquire.

2. *Liturgical preparation.* The ceremonial of the Mass is of singular help in the understanding of the doctrine. The Church, always careful to adapt herself to the needs of popular piety, has multiplied the number of liturgical ceremonies; so as to present, under a simple form of imagery, the fundamental theology of the Sacrifice of the Mass.

We shall observe the part played by ritual when we study the Mass in detail.

3. *Ascetic preparation.* Of the three preparations, the ascetic (or that of the heart and will) is the most important. It should be the constant concern of my life. Its purpose is to conform me more and more to Christ. The more I am a victim, the more will my Mass profit me. For Christ, the Mass is the Sacrifice of utter self-abasement and self-surrender. We are members of Christ, so. . . .

There are several degrees of union with the Divine Victim:

THE STATE OF GRACE

First of all, is the importance of keeping in the state of grace. This is the first sacrifice.

As everyone knows, the maintaining of oneself in the state of sanctifying grace, calls for continual combat, for ceaseless vigilance.

"Let no one say," writes Fr. Grimaud on page 204 of his book, *Ma messe,* "that this first formation in us of 'the victim for the sacrifice' is of small merit. Who then is so ignorant of the effort it costs our poor fallen human nature to keep itself in the state of grace? The general obligations of the Christian life already are a repeated source of privations: regular prayer, Sunday Mass in preference to a pleasure trip, kneeling before the priest in the confessional, fasting and abstinence on the days set apart by the Church, setting oneself down 'for the record' as a practicing Catholic in a non-Catholic environment—just so many opportunities for those little sacrifices that pave the way of THE Sacrifice!

"How many mortifications are required to perform the duties of one's state in life: Married people know the courage and trust in Providence that are required in order never to offend God in the exercise of the duties and obligations imposed by marriage. Youth with a concern for chastity must shun the theatre, novels, and undesirable companions, and oppose a stubborn 'No!' to the solicitations of vice. When a young man or a young woman goes through the maelstrom of youth without having been cut off from Christ by mortal sin, does not such a young member of the Mystical Body offer an authentic preparation for the state of co-victim: permitting him (or her) to offer himself (or herself) with the Adorable Priest on the altar? Is not a young woman who chooses to walk through this modern world simply as a 'Christian virgin' the astonishment of all who know her? . . . Such a girl is modest in dress and demeanour, graced with womanly reserve. She shuns the dance floor, where she could 'shine' and make a public display of her beauty. Unostentatiously, yet deeply religious, she is helpful at home: showing herself ready and willing for the most distasteful tasks, charitably devoted to the sick and poor. . . . And what is society's verdict on this young lady? Admired by some, she is blamed by others. Why? For 'wasting her best years' by being—a Christian!"

34—What do we read on this subject in numbers 120 and 121 of the encyclical, *Mediator Dei*, written by His Holiness, Pius XII?

The Holy Father writes as follows:

"In order that the oblation whereby the faithful offer the Divine Victim to God in this Sacrifice may have its full effect, it is necessary that they should add something—their own immolation as victims. This immolation is not restricted to the liturgical Sacrifice. Since we are built on Christ as living stones, the Prince of the Apostles wishes us to become 'a holy priesthood, to offer up that spiritual sacrifice which God accepts through Jesus Christ.' [Peter 2:5. (Knox.)] And the Apostle Paul, speaking for all time, exhorts the faithful in these terms: 'And now, brethren, I appeal to you by God's mercies to offer up your bodies as a living sacrifice, consecrated to God and worthy of his acceptance; this is the worship due from you as rational creatures.' " [Rom. 12:1. (Knox.)]

Addressing himself to priests (whose dispositions should be espoused by the faithful), the Holy Father adds:

"When we are at the altar, our souls must be transformed. Every trace of sin must be completely destroyed. Whatever is capable through Christ of engendering supernatural life, must be vigorously restored and strengthened; so that we may form, together with the Immaculate Host, a victim acceptable to God."

THE ACCEPTANCE OF THE TRIALS PERMITTED BY PROVIDENCE

The *state of grace* is a requisite for offering Christ and for offering ourselves worthily in our Mass.

To profit fully from the Mass, the *state of sacrifice* is essential. We must accept the trials God sends. For how are we to become one with the Victim, unless we, too, are victims? When Jesus sees a growing desire for perfection in a soul, he makes it feel the weight of his Cross. That is what he said just a few years ago to a Visitation nun, Sister Louise Marguerite: "I will perfect in your heart the faculty to live and suffer, so that you may be able to understand and feel the sufferings of mine." Corresponding to this desire of Jesus, she wrote: "Lord, I want to go straight toward you! I will break with whatever holds me back. If it is my friends, I will leave them. If it something I have, I will give it away. If it is my heart, I will tear it out. If it is my body, let it be destroyed." It was this humble religious whom our Lord used as a channel for the overflowing abundance of his infinite love for priests.

Christ would increase in us if we would let him. Our Lord let himself be crucified on Calvary. On the altar he abandons himself in the hands of his priests. What a Model of detachment!

We should take the "Christian risk," have faith in Providence, surrender ourselves utterly to the divine will. Surrender of self! This means the great plunge into the divine Sea, the leap of the human soul into the depths of divine Love! Thenceforth, nothing on earth has power to trouble, disturb, or charm. Forever lost and submerged in the ineffable delights of the divine will, the soul wills all that God wills, and *as* he wills! To reach this point, one must—of all necessity—have lost his earthly "foothold," abandoned earth's security and support. He must have "laid hold on" God's plan of salvation, the way a drowning man "lays hold on" a plank extended to him—with both hands! Now to grasp an object with both hands, one must first "let go" of everything else one may be holding—*everything!* For this is the "pearl of great price" of the parable. Whoever would possess it, must first sell all that he has!

Voluntary penances

In addition to the sacrifices required for the preservation of the state of grace, besides the acceptance of the trials that God's Providence permits, one also prepares for Mass by voluntary penances. Not content with mere acceptance of what God is pleased to send in the way of mortification, one ought eagerly to seek out—always within the bounds of prudence and obedience, of course—all existing possibilities of reproducing within oneself the inner dispositions of Christ offering himself to his Father as a victim. It will not do to come to Mass empty-handed. That is tantamount to saying to our Lord, "Immolate yourself, dear Lord. Offer yourself up. That's *your* job! Only, please, dear Jesus, don't count on *me* to help!"

His Holiness, Pius XII, treats of this in number 102 of his encyclical, *Mediator Dei*:

"The words of the Apostle, 'Have in you the same mind that was in Christ Jesus,' requires of all Christians the taking upon themselves in some sort of the victim state; a complete submission to the precepts of the Gospel; a spontaneous and voluntary addiction to penance; and for each one the detestation and expiation of his sins. It requires that each, together with Christ, should die mystically on the Cross; so as to be able to make St. Paul's thought, 'With Christ I am nailed to the Cross,' [Gal. 2:19.] his own."

However, "nothing demands so much wisdom in its application," writes Fr. Grimaud, "as does the use of supplementary penances. One cannot recommend too strongly to our people, if they would avoid the perils of temerity, and often of pride, to undertake nothing in this line of mortification without having received the permission of an enlightened director.

"But what a field for voluntary privation still remains open to all those desirous of becoming 'Living sacrifices pleasing to God,' without detriment to health or the obligations of their state, without risk of being imprudent, and without the necessity of asking permission of their confessor! When Christians shall have sacrificed idle words—frivolous conversations—distractions in church—luxury in food—immodesty in dress—when they shall have given to the poor or to good works the abundant alms that their social status permits—when they shall have put themselves out to do a neighbour a service, to have consoled and encouraged him—when they shall have exercised the apostolate in accordance with their abilities and circumstances, by the teaching of catechism, by a charge accepted in a parish group, or in Catholic Press publicity. . . ." In other words, when Tertiaries shall have integrated the Rule into their lives, then they will have practiced a great number of voluntary penances; then they will have formed within themselves the "victim for the sacrifice"; then they will be ready each morning to "celebrate" their Mass!

35—Father Dutil has said that "the Mass is a drama in four acts": and that in this drama, Catholics are not merely "spectators," but "actors." Are you able to prove this?

Here we embark on the concrete and easiest part of the explanation of the Holy Sacrifice of the Mass.

The mass is a drama in which we are actors

Our Lord sometimes used parables to make himself better understood. Supposing we try a parable to explain the Mass!

To begin with, we recall that the Council of Trent declared that the best way to hear Mass is to offer it up to God, to meditate on the sufferings and death of Christ, and to receive Holy Communion.

We have said a word about the Offering, and we shall come back to it. Later on, we shall also discuss Holy Communion.

Let us pause here for a meditation on Christ's Passion, remembering, of course, that Christ in Glory is incapable of suffering. The parable:

The Mass may be compared to a drama whose scene is laid in a penitentiary. A criminal, guilty of numerous crimes, is about to mount the scaffold.... In the rear of the execution chamber, we see the criminal's family and a few friends; who—grief-stricken—address one another in low tones. They seem to be deliberating something.... Now the judge reads the death edict and gives orders to proceed with the execution.... The culprit shuffles toward the scaffold; when suddenly from the rear of the hall a young man steps forward, and cries out: "If it is a victim you want to satisfy for these crimes, then let me die! And let my young brother live!"

The judge accepts. The elder brother (the "big brother") is executed. The criminal is set free!

And that is not all! This poignant drama has been filmed in its entirety, and now every morning the redeemed one sees unfold before his eyes the scene of his liberation by his elder brother—whom he had so often outraged.... He sees his father and mother plunged into the depths of grief... the friends of the family sharing... in their hearts...

the sufferings of the noble victim, sacrificed for him. He sees all this and says to himself, "It is I who am the cause of so much suffering and of so great generosity!" . . . He then gives way to mixed feelings of repentance and love for the one who saved his life, and for those who took part in his ransom, or suffered because of him.

This daily enactment of his liberation, far from becoming tedious, affords him an occasion to make reparation and to grow in love—for the thing concerns him personally.

As you will have seen for yourselves, the application of the parable is not difficult.

The culprit condemned to death is all humanity. He is you and I. The case is ours.

The deliberations of the family at the beginning represent God the Father asking his Beloved Son to atone for the outrage and immolate himself on the Cross that I may live! Again, it is the Son who turns toward his Mother, Mary, to ask if she consents to become the Mother of the Crucified! (Adam had a woman as accomplice to his crime. By virtue of Mary's *fiat,* Christ will have a woman as Co-Redemptrix.)

The compassionate friends are the saints, who participated in Christ's sufferings by their generous acceptance of the trials with which their lives were strewn.

The elder brother of the parable saved only his brother's physical life. Christ, by the torments of his Cross, ransomed all mankind—including me! He reconciled me with God; assures me of his favour; permits me to praise him; and has prepared for me a blessed eternity.

And it is every day, in the Mass, that our "film of liberation" is shown. Film, did I say? And much more than a film! For it is the very drama of the Passion that takes place on the altar!

At each renewal by a priest of the words and actions of the Last Supper under the symbols of bread and wine, Christ becomes really present in his redemptive action with the same dispositions that he had on Calvary, of love toward his Father and of mercy toward us.

Alas, how often we, his friends, are conspicuous by our absence! Or if we do attend Mass, how often do we do so listlessly, with scattered thoughts!

No wonder that on the night of the Agony in the Garden, Jesus was sad, "even unto death"!

We are actors and not spectators

We are actors, for we have a rôle to play in the Mass. If we want a striking example of the difference that exists between a simple spectator and a genuine participant, let us imagine a political or patriotic rally, meeting to discuss the choice of a national flag—with or without the Union Jack! ! ! Here we have action and reaction galore—silent or expressed—between chairman and speakers; or the crowd which applauds, hoots, laughs, roars, stamps its feet, jostles its neighbour, etc.; while the curious or indifferent spectator, who has no part in the dispute, will be either "bored stiff," or content to be merely an onlooker.

The same thing holds good for those who have risked their money on the horses. Although the betters do not have the leading rôle (since that is played by the jockeys and their horses), it's the folks in the grandstand who get more excited and who shout louder than the ones on the track. Why? Because they have money on a horse!

Well, we are more than concerned about the Mass, for this is the drama of our redemption; because we must bring our share of praise and sacrifice, if we are to give to God the homage due him, and share in the merits of Jesus Christ.

We are permanent actors

For many persons, religion consists in giving God a half-hour every week, in order to satisfy the precept of the Mass.

"A Christian in church, and a pagan in the market place"!

These already have Christ's answer: "No man can serve two masters!"

Just as Christ's Sacrifice—obedience to his Father—continued from birth to death, so our rôle of actor ought to spread out over our whole life—ought to be our "job", our every-minute concern.

The Mass ought to enter into our life and our life into the Mass, like a sponge in water, and water in a sponge. Let us say in fine that the Mass is the biggest event in our life—and we ought to live it constantly.

To repeat. We are actors, and not just spectators. If, in addition to being present at an event, we take an active part in it; then we *really* get excited. Then we *really* have something to remember!

Everybody likes illustrations, so here are a few:

You are moving, and you are helping the movers. . . . It is raining. . . . You are going to live three flights up. . . . Now, just as you are getting ready to move in the piano by means of a pulley, the wet rope slips! The piano plunges from the third floor and lands with a crash on the pavement below! You will always remember the beautiful "philharmonic concert" that crash made! If you live to be ninety, you will still be telling your grandchildren about it.

Your house is on fire, and you are about to perish in the flames! A fireman rescues you in a swirl of billowing smoke!

After that, whenever you see a fire, you recall your harrowing experience in all its details.

You were drowning. Someone fished you out of the water, just as you were going down for the third time. Or maybe it was you who saved another's life! Either way, you were the hero or the victim of a near-tragedy. Memory need jogging?

You had a "steady date." You used to think about this boy all the time. You were "crazy" about him. You even dreamed about him at night! Well, one fine day he told you he no longer "cared"! Now he's dating another girl! Hard to forget, isn't it?

You joined the Army and saw some real action. Several men in your outfit fell at your side, and you came back wounded. Remember?

A play was put on in your school or parish hall, and you had a stellar rôle. You had lived your part for so long and played it so realistically that the audience actually shed tears! For you were "living" your rôle. And it is a psychological fact that this play in which you "starred" will influence your whole life.

* * *

Well then! The Mass is the event that ought to have the biggest impact on our life, and on all that we do: on our work, our leisure time, our rest, our joys and our sorrows—in fine, on *all* our life.

All these things should be gathered up by us all through the day and placed on the paten of tomorrow's Mass. For in the Drama, our "lines" call for this!

Whoever fails to center his life on the Mass, and comes to the Offertory with empty hands, has fluffed his rôle and ceased to be an actor. He has stopped offering up his share of praise to the Most Holy Trinity, and has also ceased to receive his blessings.

The Church requires not only our bodily presence at the Holy Sacrifice, but our co-operation with Christ in his immolation and offering. She desires us to form together and with Christ "one heart and soul"; to the end that Head and members of the Mystical Body may offer up to the Blessed Trinity in fellowship, perfect praise, and abundant and overflowing satisfaction and thanksgiving: thus obtaining God's reign in our hearts, and the many spiritual and temporal favours of which we stand in need.

As we see, the Mass is a social Sacrifice, a communal work; the sum total of the united efforts of all the members of the Mystical Body and their Head. Consequently, if one member plays his rôle badly, he hinders others as well. For example, a person who, instead of edifying his neighbour, scandalizes him. . . .

A drama in four acts

Nothing could be easier to prove!

Act I: The Mass of the Catechumens or Mass Prelude, from the Introït to the Offertory.

Act II: *The Offertory.* From the Oblation to the Sanctus.

Act III: *The Consecration.* From the Sanctus to the Pater Noster.

Act IV: *The Communion.* From the Pater Noster to the end of the Mass.

To stage this drama we need:

1. *A stage.* This is the altar with its raised platform, enabling the "audience" to see and hear what is taking place.

2. *A cast.* The visible "cast" is composed of the priest, the server, and all those who are offering the Mass along with the priest. (Our Lord, who plays the lead, is invisible.)

3. *A prompter.* This rôle belongs to all those who are present at Mass. For the rôle of the faithful at Mass is to offer up Christ and themselves with him to the Heavenly Father. The prayers and gestures of the priest are an invitation to this twofold oblation. Those who participate in the Holy Sacrifice, should follow the priest at the altar, inwardly reproducing his movements and gestures. They ought not only to follow him with their eyes, but repeat along with him the same words. That is why we say that they are "prompters" in this great drama. (Hence, the necessity of a good missal.)

It should be noted however, that a mere mumbling of the prayers of the Mass to oneself, without having brought one's share in the Sacrifice, means leaving out the main part altogether. For the Mass, as we know now, does not consist in prayers and formulas; but consists above all in the inner immolation of each Christian, united to that of his brothers and of Christ, to the glory of the Trinity.

That is why, even should you not know how to read, even should you not understand the words of the Mass, you can take part—and that actively—in the Holy Sacrifice; provided you bring your sacrifices to be offered along with Christ's Sacrifice. This is very important to remember: for it is the condition required for having your Mass bring about the constant ascension of your soul toward God.

36—When are we obliged to attend Mass?

Mass is obligatory under pain of mortal sin:

On all Sundays and Holy Days of obligation.

Mass is "obligatory" out of love for God:

If we have understood a little what the Mass is, we shall never miss it through our own fault. It will be for us a "duty of love" to participate as often as possible. The Mass should become our daily delight.

Just think! The Mass is the supreme act of religion; the one most pleasing to God and most profitable for us. "The prayer which we say during Mass, in union with the Divine Victim, possesses ineffable potency." So wrote St. Francis de Sales. "The thing that we are unable to obtain during Mass, will be obtained with difficulty at another time," adds St. John Chrysostom.

Nothing is of greater advantage for saint and sinner alike:

1. *For sinners.* Because sinners attending this divine Sacrifice, receive actual graces and illumination from God, and good impulses leading them to reflection and conversion; provided they are docile to the inspirations of grace.

2. *For "saints."* Because the righteous find in the Mass powerful assistance for persevering in sanctity, for making new progress in virtue, and for laying up a treasure of merit in Heaven. "Place your good works, prayers, fastings, and alms on one end of the scales, and a single Mass on the other, and you will see that the balance is not even; but that the scale bearing the Mass will go down." (St. Lawrence Justinian.)

37—How should Mass be heard in order to satisfy the precept?

1. *In full.* That is from beginning to end.

It is a venial sin to miss *voluntarily* a *non-essential* part of the Mass. For instance, from the beginning to the Offertory exclusively; or else everything after the Communion. Or, again, if one should miss at the same time everything before the Epistle and after the Communion.

It is a mortal sin to miss *voluntarily* an *essential* part of the Mass. For example: if a person were to omit everything before the Offertory and at the same time everything after the Communion; or, again, all of the Mass from the commencement to the Offertory exclusively; or else all the part of the Canon up to the Elevation; or from the Consecration to the Pater Noster; or else the Consecration alone.

Whoever misses through his own fault an important part of the Mass, is bound to make up this missing part at another Mass heard the same day.

Legitimate excuses. A person is excused from hearing Mass for a weighty or important motive (as would be the case of serious personal illness, or the risk to oneself or to others of spiritual or temporal injury being brought about by illness, distance from church, the duties of one's state in life, etc.). In such a case, the person should unite himself in mind and heart with the Masses being celebrated all over the world, and offer himself through Christ to the Most Holy Trinity.

2. *Physically.* This means my actual, bodily presence in the place where the Sacrifice is being offered. Thus, I may not satisfy my obli-

gation by following Mass on the radio or my television set. Why not? Because the obligation is one of exterior and social worship, entailing by its nature that the required act should be public. Celebrant and worshippers should form an ensemble, a congregation; in such a way as to enable one to follow the Mass at least in its main divisions.

3. *With devotion.* The ideal would be to possess the same interior dispositions as Our Lady had on Calvary—to be a "host with the Host," a victim with the Victim! Mary's greatest sacrifice was her consent to the death of her only Son, and what a Son! She did not try to drive back the executioners, the way St. Peter did in a gesture of natural compassion; for she knew that the Crucifixion was the Father's will for his Son. Mary simply conformed to that will! Standing at the foot of the Cross, she endured in her heart all that her Divine Son suffered in his flesh. That is how she became Co-Redemptrix with Christ. . . . If we accept our crosses as the expressed will of our Heavenly Father, we also, through the Mass, may become pleasing to God; and like Jesus and Mary, "saviours of souls."

We should show great reverence in our comportment during Mass. We should avoid all conversation, curiosity, or distractions.

We should observe modesty in dress. The church is not a place for staging a style show, still less for displaying unsuitable dress.

Always be punctual.

It is better to wait a few minutes for Mass to begin, than to arrive late. A woman who has invited guests for dinner, always finds it annoying to see them strolling in sometime after the soup has been served! The Church has her "etiquette" too, requiring that the faithful should not be distracted by latecomers.

We should cherish thoughts of love and faith in our hearts. Our Lord is sacrificing himself for the glory of his Father and for us. He is the Mediator between us and the Father. What confidence we should have in Christ's all-powerful mediation!

Knowledge of God's omnipotence ought to strengthen our trust in him. And how it should increase at the thought that our Heavenly Father, besides being all-powerful, loves us with boundless love! And who can doubt it? We have but to glance at a crucifix to find proof of God's incomprehensible love for men! Now Jesus is present during Mass with the same loving sentiments toward his Father and toward each one of us. How great our ingratitude, should our hearts remain cold and insensible!

38—What means does the Holy Father propose in numbers 127-129 of *Mediator Dei* for promoting participation in the Mass by the people?

"Therefore, they are deserving of praise," he writes, "who with a view to facilitating and making more fruitful for the Christian people participation in the Eucharistic Sacrifice, try to place in their hands the Roman Missal; so that the faithful, in union with the priest, may pray with him, using the same words and the very thoughts of the Church. Also deserving of praise are those who strive to make of the liturgy—even in its external expression—a holy Action, in which those present really take part. This participation may be accomplished in several ways. As, for example, when all the people, in accordance with the rubrics, either respond in a uniform manner to the words of the priest, or sing chants in keeping with the various parts of the Sacrifice; or when they do both. Or finally, in a Solemn Mass, when they sing the responses to the prayers of Christ's ministers and take part in the liturgical chant.

"These modes of participation in the Sacrifice are praiseworthy and commendable, when they carefully comply with the precepts of the Church and the norms for sacred ritual. Their chief end is the nourishing and fostering of the devotion of Christians, their intimate union with Christ and his visible minister, and the stimulation of those interior sentiments and dispositions by which our soul must be in conformity with the High Priest of the New Covenant. They show in an outward manner that the Sacrifice, according to its nature (it having been accomplished by the Mediator between God and man) [I Tim. 2:5] should be considered as the work of the whole Mystical Body of Christ. Nevertheless, these exercises are by no means necessary for the constitution of its public and communal character. Furthermore, the dialogued Mass cannot take the place of a Solemn Mass; which even though celebrated in the presence of the sacred ministers only, enjoys a peculiar dignity, owing to the majesty of the ritual and the pomp of the ceremony. This latter, however, assumes much more solemnity and grandeur, if—in accordance with the desire of the Church—a numerous and devout people are present."

The Steeple

●

Chaste outline against chaste skies,
Framed by verdant foliage.
Like some pure creature detached from earthy things,
The steeple soars straight and true toward Heaven.

In mystical flight to the Throne of God,
It seems to bear upward
The sighs, aspirations, and prayers of a people;
The chorus of praise that wells up in their bosoms,
In the alternate strophes of the bells in its tower,
As in turn they ring out and are mute.

Architectural splendour
Or esthetic failure,
The steeple remains
The proud confession of our faith
In the Invisible Guest of the Tabernacle!

Unfeeling no longer,
But with tender emotion,
Our gaze should more often be fixed on the steeple:
Beacon tower for the Christian at home or abroad,
And glad symbol of hope o'er his head!
Invitation to place above temporal cares
The one great eternal Concern!

ENVOI:

The pointing steeple, with imperious finger,
Forces our dull gaze heavenward.

Baie S.-Paul
Ric Photo

The Sheaf

That it may become food,
It awaits man's labour;
To be changed into bread,
Woman's diligence.
To become a wafer,
The zeal of a nun.
Trembling word of thy Priest,
To be thee, O Lord Jesus!
SUBLIMITY!

All that was needed to produce it
Was for a humble grain to perish in the earth—
Watered by the sweat of the sower.
See, it is now full of life
And offered to all human hunger.
FESTIVITY!

Why, on our generous soil,
Must so much wheat be wasted,
Or lie rotting in acquisitive silos;
While the scandal of the famished
Covers the earth like a pall?
While millions of unsatisfied mouths
Are as yet unassuaged with the Host?
MISERY!

Mother of goodness, Mother of Jesus,
Change our hard hearts into hearts of brothers.
Teach us the glory that comes with sharing
Our abundance with the starving.
Give both to them and to us
Eagerness for the Bread of the Strong!
SOLACE!

Jean Salem Photo

39—What warning does the Holy Father give in regard to these means? (Numbers 130, 131.)

"It is likewise to be noted that the attaching to these external things such importance that any should dare to assert their omission to be capable of preventing the holy Action from achieving its end, is to turn aside from right reason and let oneself be guided by erroneous notions.

"For many of the faithful are unable to use the Roman Missal, even when it is translated into their vernacular; nor are all capable of understanding correctly, liturgical rites and formulas. The talents, natures, and minds of men are so varied and different, that all cannot be directed and led in the same manner, by communal prayers, chants, and actions. Furthermore, the needs of souls and their tastes are not the same for all persons; and do not remain the same for each individual. Who, then, would dare to affirm—on the strength of such prejudice—that so many Christians are unable to take part in the Eucharistic Sacrifice and enjoy its benefits? But they may assuredly do so, in some other way that may be easier for them; as, for example, by devoutly meditating on the mysteries of Jesus Christ, or by performing other exercises of piety, or reciting other prayers; which though differing from the sacred ritual in form, nonetheless, correspond with it by their nature."

A PRAYER FOR CHRISTIAN YOUTH

•

Our Father who are in Heaven.

We would consecrate to you our youth, that we may prepare now for the unfailing loyalty of a lifetime.

Give us the grace and courage to keep our souls pure.

Strengthen in our hearts the will to live according to your will, to be at all times and in all places witnesses to the Truth that you have entrusted to us that it may shine in the world.

Give us an understanding of the Saviour's Sacrifice, so that we may be ready for every sacrifice you ask of us.

Make us worthy to be missionaries of your light, charity, and truth to our comrades ignorant of you.

Give us a feeling of brotherhood for all men in all classes of society, and in all nations, who seek for the reign of justice.

Give us the conquering faith of your Apostles, so that we may be worthy to be our Redeemer's brothers. Amen.

ST. FRANCIS OF ASSISI AND THE MASS

40—What did St. Francis of Assisi think of the Mass?

"St. Francis was on fire with love for the Sacrament of the Lord's Body to the very marrow of his bones," wrote Celano. "And he was struck with amazement in the face of this mercy full of charity, and more especially before this so merciful charity."

Celano does not exaggerate. St. Francis, whose spirituality sprang from a penetrating gaze on the body of Christ, whose loving longing for our love led to a Cross, was bound to make "the Lord's most Sacred Body" the core of his devotion.

While still a pleasure-loving youth, St. Francis had purchased costly vestments and other objects for the celebration of the Holy Sacrifice and given them in secret to priests and poor churches. All his life he continued his pious ministry, sending his friars throughout the world with precious vases, with host irons, or with altar linens made by Clare or her daughters.

It was during the celebration of Mass on the feast of St. Matthew the Apostle (February 24, 1208), and through the voice of the priest explaining the Gospel, that Francis received special light from Heaven and an intimation of the necessity of a changed life, and dimly glimpsed the vocation that was to be his.

When prevented by illness or some other circumstance from going to a church or oratory to hear Mass, St. Francis would ask one of his brother priests—Friar Benedict or another—to celebrate the Holy Sacrifice for him in private; because "sick though he was, he always wanted to have or hear Mass said, whenever it was possible to do so." [*Mirror of Perfection,* 6:87.] If even this consolation was denied him, he would have someone read the Gospel of the day in a Gospel-Book that had been copied by his express order. And he would say: "When I do not hear Mass, I pray and adore the Body of Christ by the look of the heart; just as in the Mass I see and adore him." [Note of Brother Leo in St. Francis' breviary, preserved in the Basilica of St. Clare. See also *Mirror of Perfection,* 12:117.]

Effortlessly, Francis poured out at the foot of the altar those effusions of love with which the memory of the Passion and death of Christ inspired him. He, more than all others, found in Holy Mass the authentic and official means of uniting his personal sacrifice to that of the beloved Master.

"Penetrated with the reverence that these dread mysteries deserve, he offered up all his members as a holocaust; and whenever he received the Immolated Lamb, he delivered his spirit over to those flames with which the altar of his heart was ever aglow." [II Celano, 152.]

Thus, "to let a day pass without hearing at least one Mass when one was able to do so, was in his eyes the proof of a grave indifference." [Idem.]

His writings

Of eight letters written by St. Francis which we possess, five are in great part—or even exclusively—devoted to the Eucharist:

The letter to all the faithful.

The letter to the General Chapter.

The letter to all clerics.

The letter to all superiors of the Order.

The letter to all leaders of the people.

In addition to these official letters, should be mentioned:

All his Rules, in which the Eucharist plays a leading rôle.

His testament.

His first admonition (the longest).

His thought

"We have living among us from the Son of God", wrote St. Francis, "his most sacred Word, and his most Sacred Body.

His living Body, his living Word! Here we have in a nutshell, the two parts of the Mass.

The Mass is Christ's Sacrifice. St. Francis places it in the very centre of the Christian religion. For a "plain man without learning," as St. Francis styled himself, he turns out to be a pretty deep theologian!

It is not necessary to recall here his reverence for and veneration of the Holy Scriptures—the Lord's living Word—for St. Francis was a living Gospel.

Communion

"The Precious Blood of the Son of God," he wrote, "has been for mankind the price of their redemption, a purifying bath, and the beverage that sustains their strength."

In the Eucharist, Christ draws us toward his Father with an irresistible impetus. "Lives" of St. Francis relate that the saint received Holy Communion often, and so piously that his devotion was communicated to others.

Dissemination of his doctrine

In the thirteenth century, St. Francis launched an immense eucharistic movement. Franciscans outstanding in this movement include St. Paschal Baylon, patron of eucharistic works and congresses, and Fr. Joseph Plantanida of Termo, who founded the Forty Hours Devotion.

41—What does the Rule and spirit of the Third Order require in respect to Holy Mass and Communion?

Clarifying the present text by the ancient, one finds that the Rule mentions the Holy Eucharist, either directly or indirectly, in five places:

1. "They shall approach the Sacraments of Penance and of the Holy Eucharist every month." (Chap. 2: art. 5.)

2. "Let those who can do so, attend Mass every day." (Chap. 2: art.11.)

3. "Let them attend the monthly meetings called by the Superior." (Text of the primitive Rule.)

4. "Let them contribute according to their means to a common fund, from which... provision may be made for the dignity of divine worship." (Chap. 2: art. 12.)

5. At the funeral of a deceased member, the Tertiaries shall assemble, and, having received Holy Communion, pray with fervent charity for the eternal rest of the deceased." (Chap. 2: art. 14.)

Monthly communion

Around 1883—that is, before the decree of St. Pius X on frequent Communion—the prescription of the Rule marked a considerable step forward in the customs of the Christian elite. Jansenism had alienated Catholics from the Sacraments, and monthly Communion was the practice of the most fervent.

To hold to the letter of this article today, would be to misunderstand it completely. The Tertiary ought to receive Holy Communion as often as the most fervent of Christians; that is, daily.

This article, moreover, should be interpreted in connection with the article concerning Holy Mass. (Chap. 2: art. 11.) Today the elite among the faithful, thank God, no longer think of the Mass apart from Communion; nor of Communion apart from the Mass. This being so, one merely rejoins the most venerable traditions of the primitive Church.

We should point out that in the primitive rules, reference to Communion (which was immediately linked with Confession) was followed by a pressing invitation to mutual concord.

Daily mass

This is an invitation to the fervent, therefore to all Tertiaries, since Tertiaries profess to tend toward perfection.

The Tertiary will participate in Holy Mass the way St. Francis did, namely:

By looking on the liturgical texts as Christ's living Word; and in seeking in them his directives for action, the orientation of his life, and a guide for thanksgiving.

By offering himself as a sacrifice and by renewing his profession.

By ratifying his participation in Christ's Sacrifice by means of an intense fraternal life.

By a loving fellowship with the Head and members of the Mystical Body.

The dignity of worship

We know with what reverence St. Francis surrounded the altar and all pertaining to it. He desires his children to be apostles of the "dignity of worship," by virtue of their living faith in the Real Presence.

"I beseech you, the more especially because it is not just something that concerns me... to venerate above all things the most Sacred Body and the most Sacred Blood of our Lord Jesus Christ. Let chalices, corporals, the furnishings of the altar, and everything used in the Holy Sacrifice be regarded as precious."

Hence, Tertiaries are to be, by every means in their power, apostles of eucharistic devotion, in their relations with the clergy and with the rest of the faithful.

Many Tertiaries have already understood their rôle, for a great number are members of nocturnal adoration groups; taking an active part in all eucharistic celebrations and in the work of vocations to the priesthood. Sewing groups have been set up in many fraternities for the making of altar linens and for the care of the poor: who are especially dear to Jesus Christ.

The monthly meeting

In the rules of 1221 and 1289, the monthly meeting consisted essentially in an active and fraternal participation in a High Mass. The text reads as follows:

"All the brothers and sisters of each place or city, shall assemble monthly in the church to attend Mass" (Rule of 1221.) "Every month... let them assemble in the church to attend High Mass." (Rule of 1289.)

The Rule brings out sharply that Holy Mass is the bond, the source, and the Sacrament of the fraternity.

The funeral of a deceased member

The Rule requires the Tertiary to pray especially during the Communion (common-union) for a departed brother. The Eucharist is thus seen as a charitable "meeting"—always renewable—with the departed.

It is clear that if the Tertiary is to resemble his spiritual Father, he must be devoted to the Eucharist. His life should be centered on the Mass. For is not the Holy Sacrifice a centre from which love streams; an offering, an immolation, a Communion, a thanksgiving?

So great a gift demands a return!

From now on, may every Tertiary, through the intercession of St. Francis, understand the significance of the divine mysteries of the altar; and so make of his life a pure oblation, a daily immolation, and a fervent communion with Jesus Christ, the Divine Victim!

In this way, every child of the Patriarch of Assisi may fearlessly offer a "sacrifice of sweet odour" to the adorable Trinity; and begin on earth the life of praise that he will lead in his heavenly home!

THE EUCHARIST and ST. FRANCIS

I. *St. Francis lived his thanksgiving. His life was a "eucharist."*

Everywhere and always St. Francis thanked God for all his goodness; and invited all living creatures, even those not endowed with reason, to show their gratitude toward him.

"Almighty God, most Sovereign and Most High! Holy and just Father! We thank you because you are God; for by your holy will, by your only Son, and in your Holy Spirit you have created both spiritual and corporal creatures."

(One should read here all of chapter 23 of the Franciscan Rule of 1221.)

The exquisite soul of Francis, sensitively aware of God's goodness, felt crushed.... How could he, "poor sinner," and with him his fellow man and all creatures, his brothers and sisters, ever offer truly pleasing praise to God? How? Through Jesus Christ our Lord!

"Because, miserable sinners that we all are, we are unworthy even to name You, we beseech You that our Lord Jesus Christ, Your Beloved Son, in whom You and the Holy Spirit, the Paraclete, take pleasure, may give You thanks in a way pleasing to You and to them—for Christ suffices for all things."

II. *St. Francis placed the supreme thanksgiving, the Eucharist, at the center of his life.*

St. Francis was quick to grasp that the Mass permits us to give perfect thanks to God.

His Words and Writings

Of the eight letters that we have of St. Francis, five are either chiefly or exclusively devoted to the Eucharist.

The notes that we have of his sermons as reported by witnesses of his life, always direct his hearers toward participation in the Eucharist.

"I entreat you all, Brothers, with deep respect and with all the affection of which I am capable, to show every veneration and honour to the most Holy Body and Blood of our Lord Jesus; by whom all that is in Heaven and on earth has been appeased and reconciled with God Almighty." (Letter to the General Chapter.)

"And the Father's will was that his blessed and glorious Son should, through his own blood, offer himself in sacrifice and as a victim on the altar of the Cross; not for himself (by whom all things have been made); but for our sins—leaving us an example, that we should follow in his steps.

"O admirable grandeur! The Master of the Universe, God himself and Son of God, humiliates himself to the point of concealing himself, for our salvation, under the frail appearance of bread! Brothers! Behold the humility of God and pour out your hearts before him! Humiliate yourselves in turn, that you may be exalted by him! Do not keep back any part of yourselves for yourselves; that he may possess you wholly, who has wholly given himself to you." (Letter to the General Chapter.)

His example

"Not to hear at least one Mass daily, unless prevented, would have seemed a serious imperfection to him. St. Francis received Holy Communion frequently, and so devoutly that his piety was transmitted to others. He accomplished this holiest of acts with great recollection, sacrificing all his members to God; and when he received the Immolated Lamb, he made the immolation of his soul in the fire always burning on the altar of his heart.

"Because France had a tender affection for the Body of Christ, he cherished that country, and desired to die there; because of the reverence people there showed for religion. He sent his friars throughout the world with costly ciboria; that they might enclose in a worthy place the price paid for our redemption, wherever they might find it not preserved in a befitting manner. He desired that one should show the greatest reverence for the hands of priests, who have received divine power to deal with such divine mysteries.

"Sometimes he went through the churches and villages of the Assisian region, announcing and preaching penance to men. He always used to carry a broom for cleaning the churches. For the Blessed was much afflicted, in entering a church, to find it dirty. Thus, when he had finished preaching to the people, he would gather together all the priests of the place.... He would speak to them, then... recalling especially to their minds the pains they should take that the churches, altars, and all objets used in the celebration of the sacred mysteries, be kept clean." (St. Francis of Assisi's life as related by his first companions, Chap. XV.)

THE RULE OF THE THIRD ORDER AND THE MASS

Practical applications

"Let those who can do so, attend Mass every day." (*Rule*: Chap. 2:11.)

"Let them contribute according to their means to a common fund, from which... provision may be made for the dignity of Divine Worship." (Chap. 2:12.)

"At the funeral of a deceased member—the Tertiaries shall assemble, and... having received Holy Communion, pray with fervent charity for the eternal rest of the deceased." (Chap. 2:14.)

"And devoutly say grace before and after meals." (Chap. 2:3.)

Does the Mass constitute for me the instrument for expressing gratitude for all goodness (joy and suffering), that the Good Lord has bestowed upon me?

I will gather up my whole life at the Offertory and lay it on the altar of sacrifice; to the end that, being purified by Christ, it may become a hymn of gratitude.

I will make of my thanksgiving a REAL THANKSGIVING. (Should I need help for this, I will make use of some of the liturgical prayers such as the "Canticle of the Three Hebrew Children," or one of its paraphrases, such as the "Canticle of Creation.")

Like St. Francis, Patron of Catholic Action, who "offered to God in Communion the sacrifice of all his members," I will surrender myself wholly to Christ, seeking only his good pleasure.

I will come to Mass with all those persons for whom I am responsible. I will consider Communion as my assignment to a mission.

When I attend Benediction, I will offer myself up together with Christ—the Eternally Immolated.

I will reverence the priest who gives me Christ's Sacred Body.

I will look upon the Lord's Body as constituting food for the feeble, rather than as being a reward for virtue!

During this day, I will prove by my every act that I consider as my brothers and sisters, all those who partook with me of the repast of the Lord. I will show a particular affection toward those whom our Lord has associated more closely to him in his life as victims.

When, during the day, I feel wearied, I will go to Jesus in the tabernacle (either by actual visit or by spiritual communion), and beg him for strength to continue my thanksgiving.

I will surround with reverence everything that touches the Lord's Body.

A Problem. . . a Solution

HIGH MASSES VERSUS LOW MASSES

We are often asked this question: "If I have five dollars, is it better to have a High Mass sung, or use the money for five Low Masses?"

The answer to Question 24 supplies the necessary elements for solving this problem.

Considered as Christ's Sacrifice, the Mass possesses infinite value.

Considered as the sacrifice of the Church or Mystical Body, the Mass is limited in the application of its fruits.

For the infinite merits of Christ are distributed to us in proportion to our sacrifices and interior dispositions.

Consequently, from the monetary point of view, there is no more advantage in "sacrificing" five dollars for a High Mass, than there is in distributing it among five Low Masses. My *sacrifice* is the same.

In a tract entitled "Déviations eucharistiques" ("Deviations from Eucharistic Truth"), Fr. Paul Belanger, S.J., elucidates the case and resolves the problem as follows:

The Church fixes for the use of the faithful an offering for a High Mass, and another for a Low Mass.

Now, should the offering be more or less concentrated on one or a few Masses, or more or less spread out over several? We shall attempt to answer this question.

The ideal Mass is the High Mass, especially the Solemn High Mass. As this is not always possible, the Church has long admitted of a simplified Mass—the Low Mass—for which at the same time she has simplified the stipend. (Since a Low Mass costs less to celebrate.) Such is the origin of the two Masses. As a result, the Church has never issued a formal statement as to the greater efficacy of the one or the other;

nor as to the relative value of concentrated or diversified offerings. So much for the "legal aspects" of the question!

It is legitimate for us, however, to straighten out a few twisted notions on the subject.

To begin with, let us say, generally speaking, that in the distribution of merit, God does not so much heed what we give away, as what we keep! Thus the "widow's mite" of the Temple, or the widow's votive candle in our churches, may be greater and more meritorious gifts than the dollars donated by the wealthy who keep back much more for their own ease and pleasure. Hence, the truly poor need not fear a longer stay in Purgatory, because of their inability to make large offerings. (I call "truly poor," those persons who must habitually do without the superfluous. Not those, who having first bought everything their hearts desired, then proceed to proclaim their poverty before God and the Church!)

These preliminaries are intended to remove from over the ear of the Deity the too official, administrative pencil, which some (by a too human digression) have placed there!

Since, after all, one must have some system in one's giving; the question remains pertinent—concentration, or diversification of the Mass offering? Once again, the Church's answer is ambiguous: "Whichever way seems better to you. You are free to choose."

You insist? Well then, here is a great principle in the theology of the Church; which, in lieu of a ruling, will serve to elucidate your choice.

What makes an act meritorious? Love! A dime given with great love, is much more meritorious than ten dollars given without love. One step of a Saint Thérèse taken out of love for the missions, is more meritorious than the steps of some other convalescent person, more or less distracted in her loving!

As a general rule, this esteem or love will manifest itself by more or less marked sacrifices in favour of the object loved. (This is doubtless the reason why one is prone to attribute the merit to the difficulty alone; while failing to stress the motive, love—alone capable of evaluating the difficulty accepted.)

Thus, the one of you who is willing to "sacrifice" a hundred dollars for this ring I am holding, instead of the fifty dollars the other is willing to pay, certainly has the more "esteem" or "love" for the ring.

As applied to Masses! One man might say, "I think a Mass is worth about fifty cents. Here's a hundred dollars. Put me down for two hundred Masses. Masses are like making camomile tea. You have to put in an awful lot to give it any strength." While another man might say, "Here's a hundred dollars for a Mass." Now which of these two men has a greater esteem for the Mass? Loves it more? Merits more?

The bishops have stabilized the Mass stipend.... And therein lies wisdom. This setting of norms is calculated to forestall all kinds of abuse, or of easily conceivable embarrassment. So, bringing our high and low bidders and their emulators down from hyperbole to discipline, let us simply conclude that an offering for one High Mass is better inspired than an offering for several Low Masses.

Well, now that *that* is settled, does this mean that our bishops would seek to set a ceiling on love? I do not think so! And if it is true that no one will look askance at the one who holds to the spreading over of his Masses and offerings; it is likewise true that no one will seek to prevent the concentration—even the intense concentration—of love on a single Mass.

The irreverent will find that this "theology of concentration" is also the most profitable for—priests! As a matter of fact, it *is* true that over and above being the most loving, this concentration is also the most liberal for—God, for his worship, for the maintenance of his priests; for the faithful, whose eternal salvation is dependent on this worship and on these priests; for the poor, unostentatiously sustained by the Church; for education. It is more amusing, however, is it not, to say, with that accent of anticlerical skulduggery, which is (strangely enough) almost never employed by fathers of large families—"for *priests*"!

To sum up, this solution is, from every point of view, the most generous and the most loving.

But it is a solution—that counsels, rather than commands.

If we do not attend weekday Mass when we are able, we deprive ourselves of graces which Jesus places at our disposal. One day Jesus appeared to a saint with his hands full of precious stones and said to her: "I ask only to distribute these, and no one comes for them."

Meditation

REFLEXIONS OF A CHRISTIAN

What is a Christian life, if not a "mass" that is celebrated daily "according to the rubrics"?

My life should be sealed with the sign of the cross. Just as the priest celebrates Mass before a crucifix, and can do so only before it; so only in the shadow of the Cross is the Christian's life a "holy sacrifice."

Every Christian life has its "Introït," for every day is a new beginning.... Let us set out then with renewed ardour and courage, and adorn our soul with all that a solemn introït is able to contribute to the day.

No Mass but has its Epistle and Gospel—no day void of all religious instruction can be called a day in which the Mass is lived. If my life is a "holy sacrifice," then its missal is the Gospel. I will use this missal daily; lest I become, through negligence, a Catholic who no longer knows what he does, or must do, to say his "mass."

Every Christian life must have its offertory. This is what takes place when the offering is brought to the altar to be immolated. If I give myself, it is that self may be sacrificed. An offertory calls for *consecration,* and consecration is the essence of sacrifice.

Many persons like the thought of being placed with all that they have in the chalice, mingled with the water and wine in the chalice. Like the priest, they stretch forth their hands over the offering, but on the condition of not becoming victims. And what kind of "celebrants" are these, unwilling to enter into the heart of the sacrifice?...

As for me, I will go on to my consecration and I will utter sincerely the sacramental words: "Dear God, here is my body that you gave me to be used in your service. Take it. May it live and die for your glory! Here is my blood, the blood that you put in my veins. Take it! Let it be compressed into my sweat, my tears, my prayers and all my work. It is yours to the last drop! Here is my insignificant person. You gave it to me when you made me a free being, responsible for my acts and capable of loving—to you I surrender it, together with my will."

Such is the consecration of the Christian's "mass"; to which the integral part, the *communion*, must be added. The host is consecrated at the altar to be eaten—a sacrifice is complete only when the victim becomes food. My sacrifice then shall be complete. And of what shall I complain? My neighbour "lives off" me; he consumes my strength, my time, my liberty, and my rest. He has a right to do so. He takes his communion where he sees there has been a consecration—nothing could be more logical.

My neighbour consumes and ruins my reputation, brushing aside my rights and the gratitude he owes me. He is wrong. His acts are like sacrilegious communions committed against me, but Jesus suffered in his person Communions more sacrilegious still. The Christian—like the victim of the altar—is made to be eaten and drunk. Let us leave it to God to distinguish among communicants; asking him to forgive those who prey on us more than they have the right.

If my sacrifice is celebrated "according to the rubrics," then it, too, will have its glorious *Ite, missa est*—"Depart, Christian soul!" This will be as if someone were to say, "Go, for your mass is finished. It has had its oblation, its consecration, its communion. No more shall you ascend the altar of your sacrifice, for you are about to ascend to Heaven. *Ite, missa est*. Amen!"

BRUSHWOOD

● The Mass is the point of union between God and man. Here it is especially that God is "linked up" with us.... Here it is that he pours forth upon us, not the vials of his just wrath, but the "vials" of his absent.... Let us, then, in a brotherly gesture, attend Mass in their

● The Mass is a grouping together of men: of labourers, employees, business men, housewives, students.... But so many Christians are absent.... Let us, then, in a brotherly gesture, attend Mass in their name—in the name of a dock worker, of a miner, of someone who is ill....

● The Mass is a grouping together around Christ—God and Man —the "Main Link" that nothing can break; eternally "welding" God to mankind.... Am I a link in this chain?... Does mortal sin separate me from Christ and hence from God?... Then let me re-form the chain by a sincere and perfect Confession.

● The Mass is a grouping together around the priest—man's representative before God, and God's representative before men. Once a young man who might have become a lawyer, a doctor, or a business man; he renounced all this that he might serve Christians. . Do I respect the priest?. . . Do I have a just concept of the sacrifices he has made in order to stand there, in my name, at the altar? . . .

● The Mass is a grouping together around a priest, who is a man, and therefore not perfect; and who commences the Mass by confessing aloud that he—like all men—is a sinner (Confiteor). . . . Whatever a priest may have said or done, let us realize that he remains a man who acknowledges his frailty at each Mass he celebrates. . . .

● The Mass is a "quiet zone," an isle for reflexion in the midst of life's turmoil. . . . An automobile driver takes his car in regularly for a check-up; an intelligent man checks up on his life. . . . I should participate in the Mass so as to get a firm grip on myself, determine my bearings, and regulate the human mechanism. . . .

● The Mass is a communal act, and not a private prayer to be bracketed up with other private prayers. . . . It is a public, official ceremony; wherein God receives homage not from just me, but from mankind. . . . I should take an active part in anything that tends to give to the Mass its social aspect: singing, praying aloud, mass dialogued with the priest, etc. . . .

● The Mass is the rendez-vous of Christ, come to deliver himself into our hands that we may offer him to his Father in the name of all humanity. . . . of Christ come to be made food for us, so that we may become united—with him, through him, and in him—to God. . . . In what other religion do we find a gesture that is simpler, richer in meaning?

● The Mass is Christ's Sacrifice. . . . I should not be astonished if the Mass becomes likewise a sacrifice for me—of my time, of my comfort, of my need for speech. . . . Trifles, these, compared to Christ's Sacrifice, compared to the long trek of Christians in the bush; compared to the mortal peril of those participating in a clandestine Mass in a concentration camp. . . .

● The Mass is the meeting-place of the sincere, who recognizing their proneness to act stupidly—in small things or in great—come to ask

God's forgiveness (only the Pharisees believed themselves to be perfect).... Certainly, I must not torture my conscience if nothing startling appears, but I should at least regret my past negligences....

● Again the Mass is the gathering-place of the grateful, come to thank God for all that they have received from him.... For instance, a student living comfortably at home, able to go on with his studies; when youths of his own age, more gifted than he, are obliged to work with their hands....

● The Mass is likewise the meeting-place of pallid "Christians" come to Mass to avoid thereby a nagging wife!... They have kept their religious knowledge at the infantile level, though they are strictly "adult" in all that pertains to the mundane and profane.... Is the Mass for me a half-hour of yawning boredom, my chin pillowed in my palm? ...

● The Mass is the meeting-place of too many "dolls," come to show off their finery; or who become furious at sight of a coveted costume on another girl's back! ... Much time has gone into the hair-do, the make-up, and manicure—and they arrive with an often dusty, not to say soiled, soul! ... The aim is to please the boys, and not God.... (Am I a "doll"? And to the boys: Do I know how to tell a "doll" from a girl whose religion is sound and whose first Love is God?)...

● The Mass is the meeting-place of too many youths who imagine they have lost all religious sense, because they no longer pray with the same spontaneity and affection they once knew.... No, a young man reasons more than a child and lacks a young girl's sentimentality. His life, moreover, is often a field of battle, of temptation, and also of defeat.... For him the Mass is often a more arid, more cerebral contact with Christ, who understands his inner turmoil...

A PRAYER FOR THOSE MAKING A SPIRITUAL RETREAT

Lord Jesus, who, in order to form your Apostles, drew them to the mountain solitude or within the walls of the Cenacle; inspire all souls today who wish to serve you with fidelity and zeal, with a desire for the closed retreat, so dear to your heart and to that of your Vicar on earth.

Our Lady of the Cenacle, Faithful Spouse of the Holy Spirit, and Universal Mediatrix of his gifts, grant to all those making a retreat pure faith, charitable zeal, and holiness of life. Amen.

CHAPTER IV

THE LITURGICAL FRAMEWORK

- Places where Mass may be celebrated
- Symbolism or signification of the Church
- Sacred vessels and liturgical vestments
- Positions and gestures—their meaning

Before taking up a detailed explanation of the different parts of the Mass, we shall say a few words concerning the liturgical setting in which the Holy Sacrifice unfolds: church, altar, sacred vessels, vestments, etc.

42—May Mass be celebrated anywhere?

According to Canon Law (C. 822) Holy Mass ought ordinarily to be celebrated in consecrated or blessed churches and oratories.

Permission to celebrate outside a church or oratory may be granted by the resident Bishop (or for a religious Order, by its major superior), provided that the Mass be said in a suitable place and on a consecrated stone (Mass may never be said in a bedroom); and that the permission be granted for a just and reasonable cause; in an extraordinary case, and for a limited period. (For instance, Scouts may obtain this permission for the duration of their stay in camp.)

HISTORIC NOTES

The apostles celebrated Holy Mass in private homes, on tables—for the Mass, like the Last Supper, is a meal. "My Body is real food," said Jesus, "and my Blood is real drink."

Mass may be celebrated outside a church; but it may not be celebrated without a table and this table is the altar.

When we go to Mass, we sit at a table with our brothers around the Head of the house.... Our altar rails are tables of brotherhood. It is as a family that we eat the Body of Christ, our Daily Bread....

In the era of the great persecutions, the Holy Sacrifice was celebrated in the catacombs over the tombs of martyrs. This is the origin of the form of a tomb still given to the altar today, and of the custom of placing the relics of martyrs in altars—a custom that also reminds us of our communion with the saints in Heaven.

It was for this same reason that churches were later built over the tombs of saints—as is St. Peter's Basilica in Rome—and that martyrs and illustrious Christians were interred in them.

This is also the source of the custom of chanting the "Requiem" at funerals in the presence of the deceased.

As in the subterranean passages, the early Christians needed torches for assisting at the Holy Sacrifice, the Church has preserved the use of candles on the altar during Holy Mass.

43—Show how our churches, by their location and exterior, invite to prayer.

Larger and more elevated than the surrounding houses, the church is usually built on an eminence. For it is the dwelling-place of the Most High, and lofty places particularly invite to prayer. There one is separated from the clamour of the world; and thereby brought nearer to God.

If churches are to be found in the centre of cities and towns (of which they are the fairest ornament), it is to recall to our minds that the Good Shepherd dwells in our midst by his Real Presence in the Blessed Sacrament. That is why the church is called "the house of God."

The church usually faces the East; because in it is worshipped Jesus Christ, the Sun of Justice.

The church has the form of a cross, because in it the Sacrifice of the Cross is renewed and the doctrine of the Crucified is preached.

44—Of what do the steeple and belfry remind us?

The church is surmounted by a steeple, whose spire, like a pointing finger, indicates Heaven and seems to say to us: "Mind the things that are on high." (Col. 3:1.)

The belfry contains the bells which summon us to divine worship or to prayer, and by their harmonious sounds enhance the solemnity of religious feasts.

Incidentally, St. Francis de Sales once observed that many Christians and church workers are like church bells. They invite others to church, but never go themselves! If by chance, we belong to this category of folk who urge others to do the good works they do not do themselves; then let us stop our "clangour" and start preaching by the force of our example.... Only then will our words find an echo in our neighbour's soul.

The tower in the belfry often contains a clock, which warns us to make good use of the hours of life—the hour of death will be too late. In eternity we shall reap as we have sown....

Finally, because Christ crucified reconciled Heaven and earth; we place a cross on the spire of the steeple. This cross makes clear to all who the Head of this house is.

45—What is the message of the church steps?

To him who has eyes to see and tongue to pray, who knows how to live recollected in the presence of God, the most ordinary objects—things a man can reach out and touch—have a richness and language all their own.... For example, steps! We climb an incredible number of them! Have you ever thought about the almost imperceptible change that takes place when we go up? It is not just my foot that ascends; my whole body and my soul arise as well! A moment's thought brings intimations of another ascent—this time, a spiritual one. Of the long climb toward the summit where our "ascension" ends—toward that blessed eternity where God himself constitutes the happiness of his elect.

How great my destiny! Let us always remember where the steps lead. Leaving below all useless baggage—the world and its futilities—let us "mount up as with wings" toward Him who is the Most High.

46—What is the symbolism or significance of the church door?

Often we have crossed its threshold, and each time it has spoken to us. Have you ever listened to the message of the church door?

Let us hear what it says first: "You are now leaving the exterior for the interior."

Let us be recollected for a moment, and try to comprehend the deep and symbolic language of the church door.... The "exterior" is the world with its beauty that allures, and also with its ugliness and tumult. The world resembles a vast market place, with people rushing hither and thither and elbowing one another. Far be from us the thought that in the world holiness is impossible. Nevertheless, certain conditions are requisite for sanctity.... The door, then, separates us from the world with its bustle and stir; and introduces us to the interior, where all is silence and recollection—to the sanctuary wherein dwells the Prisoner of Love! Assuredly, all things are God's handiwork; and he is to be met with in the tiniest of his creatures, for everywhere God beckons to us and invites us to think of him. But we all know that God reserves for himself especially consecrated places—just as he reserves for himself especially consecrated souls.... All, unfortunately, do not respond to his call; preferring the ephemeral pleasures of this world to the divine intimacies....

The door is placed, therefore, between the outside and the inside—between that which belongs to the world, and that which is vowed to God. The steps of the stairway have already prepared us to lift up our souls to the Lord—let us prove it by our lack of precipitation as we cross the threshold. Slowly opening the door, let us open our hearts to its language so rich in meaning: "Leave without whatever is not of God: frivolous thoughts, earth-bound desires, vain care, curiosity, worldly pleasures.... Purify yourselves, for you are entering God's house!"

And lest we forget this purification, the holy water font offers us holy water at the door.... Let us say, then, with St. Francis:

"Be praised, my Lord, through Sister Water,
For greatly useful, lowly, precious, chaste, is she."

Again, it is that souls may be purified before they enter God's house, that baptismal fonts are placed in the vestibules of churches.

47—What are the interior divisions of the church?

The interior of the church is divided into three parts:

1. The vestibule, where in ancient times the catechumens and penitents stood. It exhorts us to enter in a spirit of recollection.

2. The nave, which is like the ship in which the faithful must sail toward eternity's port; and in which they are saved, as in Noah's Ark, from eternal perdition.

3. The choir, or part reserved for priests and ministers of public worship.

48—What is the altar?

The altar is the stone table on which the Eucharist is offered. It is used for the Sacrifice and for the sacred meal.

There are two kinds of altars—fixed and portable.

Since the altar represents Christ, the altar stone must be a single slab; in order to represent the unity of Christ's person.

The surface of the altar is inscribed with five crosses. In a cavity in the centre of the altar stone, called the sepulchre, are placed relics of at least two saints; one of whom must have been a martyr.

The sepulchre also contains three grains of incense.

49—How is the altar covered?

The altar is covered with three white hempen or linen cloths.

Why? It is a question of suitability, of neatness, and of utility. It precludes all possibility of profanation of the Precious Blood, if the chalice were accidentally overturned. Again, these three white cloths recall the swaddling clothes of the Crib and the linens that enveloped Christ in the tomb.

A crucifix on the altar is essential. It recalls that the Sacrifice of Calvary becomes present in the Mass.

For a Low Mass, two beeswax candles are placed on the altar; for a sung Mass, four; for a High Mass, six; and seven if the celebrant is a bishop.

The candle has several meanings. It typifies Jesus Christ, the Light of the World; the wax symbolising his human nature; the flame, his divinity.

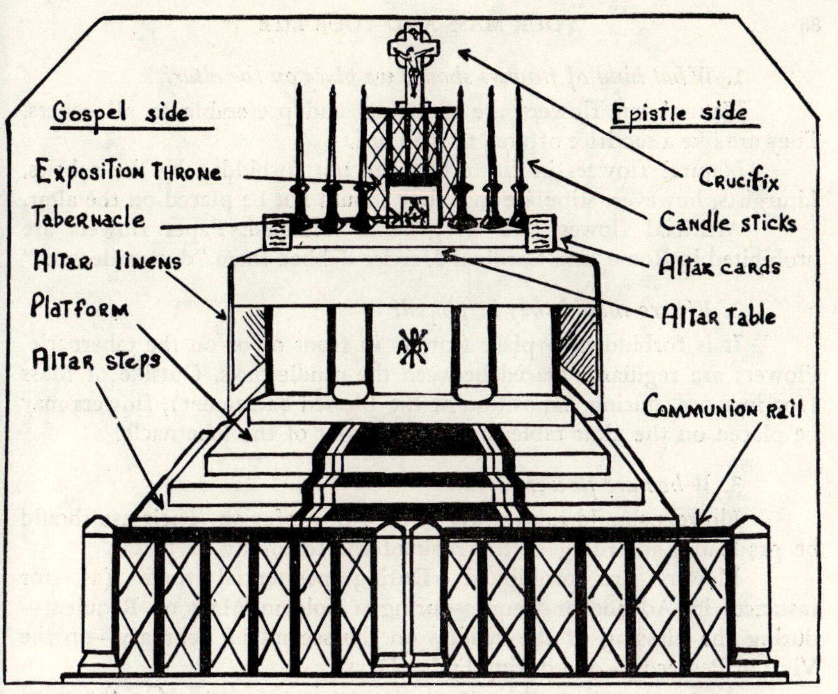

Again the candle symbolizes the soul of the Christian standing straight and pure before God. It gives light and warmth while consuming itself to the last moment of its earthly existence. . .

On the altar also are placed three cards called the altar cards (or canons), which bring to the priest's mind the prayers to be recited during Mass.

The tabernacle or tent is the place where the Blessed Sacrament is reserved.

Finally, there is the missal on its missal stand.

Without being the principal ornament, flowers on the altar are admissible.

Let us say a few words about floral decorations for the altar. These few remarks may be of interest to sacristans, and even to others. . .

1. *What kind of flowers should we place on the altar?*

Natural cut flowers are desirable, and preferable to all others. They are like a sacrifice offered to the Lord.

Natural flowers in flowerpots are not forbidden by the rubrics. Liturgists, however, stipulate that they should not be placed on the altar.

Artificial flowers are, in general, tolerated. Paper flowers are prohibited in Rome, and Cardinal Mercier dubbed them "dust-collectors."

2. *Where should they be placed?*

It is forbidden to place flowers in front of or on the tabernacle. Flowers are regularly placed between the candlesticks. Outside of Mass (for instance, during Exposition of the Blessed Sacrament), flowers may be placed on the altar table; but *not* in front of the tabernacle.

3. *When are flowers used?*

Flowers should not always be used in profusion. Their use should be graduated according to the rank of the solemnity or feast.

Flowers are prohibited: During penitential times (as, for instance, in Advent or Lent)—during a Solemn Mass of Requiem—during the blessing of the candles on the second of February—on the Vigil of Pentecost—and during Ember Days.

As an exception, the use of flowers is permitted: On the third Sunday of Advent—on the fourth Sunday of Lent—at the Mass of the Vigil of Christmas—at the Mass of Holy Thursday.

4. *How should flowers be arranged?*

With good taste and moderation. A too great abundance of flowers does not always serve to adorn.... One should take into consideration the setting, the lighting, the character of the feast, the way the flowers harmonize together, etc.

50—What is the purpose of the sanctuary lamp?

The custom of having a sanctuary lamp burning before the tabernacle does not go back to the beginnings of the Church, for the very good reason that the Blessed Sacrament was not then reserved in the tabernacle as it is today. Everything ended with the Mass. The Holy Eucharist for the sick was kept in private homes.

At first limited to Holy Thursday, as the Rule of St. Bernard recommends, use of the sanctuary lamp was extended toward the close of the twelfth century to all days of the year; especially in Jerusalem. During the course of the thirteenth century, this ruling was evidenced in Flanders, England, Germany, and later in Italy. We know that St. Francis used to beg oil for the upkeep of the sanctuary lamps of the churches of Assisi.

The official obligation dates from 1614.

The rôle of the sanctuary lamp is to remind us of the presence of Jesus and to represent us before the Blessed Sacrament. Doubtless, the Master prefers "living lamps" to candles, and we ought often to keep the Divine Host of our tabernacles company.... If only we loved God a little more, our churches and chapels would not be so deserted all day long.... Is it not true that when one loves a person, he often visits him?...

The sanctuary lamp typifies our soul. Its flame is like a living thing. Warm, luminous, ever in movement, ever seeking to rise higher, it is the image of our interior. Unceasingly, its flame is directed toward the heights. The merest breath causes it to waver, but it nevertheless continues to mount and to transmit the light and warmth it has received. Of itself this material light does not speak to God—it is for us to give it a voice expressive of our lives wholly given to God. We, too, despite our continual tendency to seek higher things, sometimes feel our high aspirations falter beneath the boisterous blasts of the world and its pleasures.... Always, however, we must seek to rise to the summit of perfection, to draw closer to God—Source of light and warmth—that we in turn may illumine, warm, and transfigure other souls, strayed from the path of duty.

Let us then often draw nigh to the tabernacle for a few moments of profound recollection. After this fruitful visit, let us calmly return to our appointed tasks; not without first having pointed to the flickering flame of the vigil lamp and whispering, "Lord, this lamp stands for my soul, which will never leave you."

51—Please name the sacred vessels used in divine worship.

1. The *chalice,* which has the form of a cup, is of gold or silver. The interior of the chalice is always of gold, out of reverence for the Precious Blood. (Fig. 10.)

2. The *paten* is a small round plate of the same material as the chalice, because it receives the host destined to become the Body of Christ. (Fig. 10.)

The chalice and paten do not receive an ordinary blessing, but are anointed with holy chrism.

3. The *ciborium* (from the Latin word, *cibus*: "food"), is a sacred vessel which contains the consecrated Hosts reserved in the tabernacle for the people's Communion. The ciborium consists of a goblet with a golden interior, and a lid surmounted by a cross. (Fig. 15.)

4. The *monstrance*, which resembles a sun, contains in its centre the lunula or lunette—a receptacle in which the large Host reposes during Exposition. (Fig. 16.)

The ciborium and monstrance are blessed.

52—Who may touch the sacred vessels?

The sacred vessels containing the sacred species may be touched only by priests and deacons, except in case of necessity (such as fire or the danger of profanation); in which case anyone may touch them.

The chalice and paten (and, before they have been cleansed, the purificator, pall, and corporal), may be touched only by clerics (at least, tonsured); and by lay persons, such as sacristans, who have custody of these objects.

However, the empty and purified ciborium, the lunula, the monstrance, the custodial, and the corporal used for Benediction of the Blessed Sacrament, are not subject to this ruling. Consequently, a simple lay person may touch them without sacrilege.

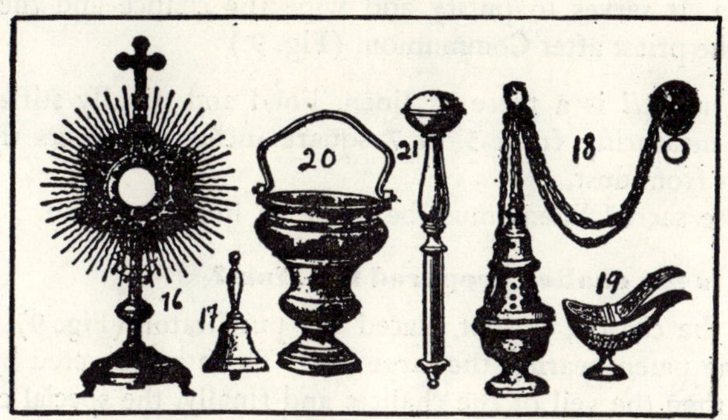

53—Please name the other liturgical vessels.

1. The *Communion paten* is a plate of gold metal, designed to receive the small particles of the Consecrated Host which sometimes fall during distribution of Holy Communion. This usage is not of recent date, as the Communion paten was employed in the Middle Ages.

2. The *cruets* are small flasks in which are contained the wine and water of the Mass. (Fig. 13.)

3. The *sanctus bell* is a small bell that is rung at the moment fixed by the rubrics, to permit the people to associate themselves more intimately with the principal parts of the Mass. (Fig. 17.)

4. The *censor* and the *incense boat* in which the incense is placed. (Figs. 18, 19.)

5. The *holy water pot* and *holy water sprinkler* for the aspersions. (Figs. 20, 21.)

54—Please name the sacred linens necessary for the celebration of Mass.

1. The *corporal.*[1] So called because the Body of Christ rests on it during Mass. It is a piece of linen about 15 inches square which the priest unfolds on the altar at the commencement of Mass, and on which he places the chalice. (Fig. 12.)

2. The *purificator* is a piece of linen about 14 inches long and 9 inches wide. It is triple folded, then measuring 14 inches long by three inches wide. It serves to purify and wipe the chalice and the lips and fingers of the priest after Communion. (Fig. 9.)

3. The *pall* is a piece of linen, lined and usually stiffened with cardboard, measuring from 5 to 7 square inches. It covers the chalice to protect it from dust.

These sacred linens must be made of linen or hemp.

55—How is the chalice prepared for Mass?

On the chalice, is first placed the purificator (Fig. 9), to which is added the paten bearing the large host. These are covered by the pall (Fig. 10), then the veil of the chalice; and finally, the special case called the burse, containing the corporal. (Fig. 11).

56—What is the origin of Mass vestments?

In the early days of Christianity, the vestments worn by the priest at Mass were those worn by laymen of the time, in their homes and on the street. Since that time, as we all know, fashions have changed. Yet the Church still uses her first vestments as precious heirlooms; carrying

---

[1] From the Latin *corpus*: "body." Trans. note.

us back through the ages to Christ at the Last Supper, thus affording us a vivid historical witness of the antiquity of the Mass.

These sacrificial vestments likewise have their own language. The priest is reminded that each vestment bears a relation to Christ and to the Sacrifice.

The priest is clothed from head to foot in symbolic garments. This should invite you to "put on" Christ in your spiritual life; divesting your entire self of selfishness and sinful habits—sacrificing everything to acquire the mentality and dispositions of Christ.

57—Please name the Mass vestments and their symbolic significance.

1. The *amice.* A piece of linen about the size of a small chawl. The priest touches it to his head, drops it over his shoulders, tucks it around his neck, and ties it around the waist. Formerly, it was a covering or hood to be worn outdoors. Indoors, it was lowered over the shoulders. (Fig. 1.)

Symbolism: It recalls the cloth used to blindfold Jesus when the soldiers struck and insulted him. It symbolizes our "helmet of salvation" (Eph. 6:17), touched to the head to protect us against idle and evil thoughts at Mass; tucked around the neck to restrain the tongue before and after Mass.

Prayer said by the priest while vesting: "Place, O Lord, the helmet of salvation on my head that I may resist the attacks of the Devil."

2. The *alb.* A full flowing robe reaching to the feet, completely enveloping the priest. (Fig. 2.)

Formerly, this was an ordinary outer garment worn in warm climates, and is still worn today in the Near East. In ancient Rome, it was a garment worn by those in places of authority.

Symbolism: The alb recalls the white robe Herod placed on Jesus in mockery. *Alb* comes from the Latin word, *albus,* meaning "white." The alb symbolizes the purity required of the priest and of all those who would assist worthily at Mass. The alb reminds us that our darkness must be changed into the light of Jesus.

Prayer said by the priest while vesting: "Make me white, O Lord, and purify my heart; so that being made white in the Blood of the Lamb, I may deserve an eternal reward."

3. The *cincture* or cord is a thick cord about 10 feet long with tasseled ends. The cincture secures the alb around the waist. (Fig. 3.)

Symbolism: The cincture recalls the cords that bound Jesus to the pillar when being scourged.

If the alb recalls purity, the cincture is symbolic of chastity; of girding ourselves for hard service; keeping the passions in check, so as to be pure and strong spiritually.

Prayer said by the priest while vesting: "Gird me, O Lord, with the cincture of purity, and extinguish in my heart the fire of concupiscence; so that, the virtue of continence and chastity always abiding in my heart, I may the better serve you."

4. The *maniple.* A band of cloth of the same colour as the stole and chasuble, worn on the left arm, about 4 inches wide by 30 inches long. (Fig. 4.)

Formerly, it was the custom in hot climates to wear such a cloth on the arm to wipe away both dust and perspiration.

In relation to the Passion, the maniple recalls the manacles with which the hands of Jesus were cruelly bound.

Symbolism: The maniple suggests wiping from the mind and heart all sloth or fear of labour.

Prayer that the priest recites while vesting: "May I deserve, O Lord, to carry this maniple of sorrow and penance, so that I may one day enjoy the reward of all my labours."

5. The *stole* is a long strip of cloth about 6 or 7 feet long and 3 or 4 inches wide, of the same material and colour as the chasuble. It is worn around the neck, and resting on the shoulders, crossed over the breast, and fastened in place by the ends of the cincture. (Fig. 5.)

Formerly, the stole was a sort of scarf worn crosswise; later, a badge of honour.

The stole reminds us of the Cross Christ carried on his shoulders.

Symbolism: The stole signifies our duty of uniting ourselves to God by accepting his will, bringing to mind our dignity of immortal beings in Christ's service.

Prayer to be said by the priest while vesting: "Restore unto me, O Lord, the stole of immortality which was lost through the sin of my first parents; and although unworthy to approach your sacred Mystery, may I nevertheless attain to joy eternal."

6. The *chasuble.* The outer vestment, covering nearly all the others; extending from the shoulders to the knees, with a large cross on the back. (Fig. 6.)

Formerly, it was used as a circular cape without sleeves, with a hole in the centre for the head to pass through; worn to protect against the weather. (The word chasuble comes from the Latin, *casula*—"a little house.")

The chasuble recalls the purple cloak thrown over the Saviour's shoulders, and the large cross on it represents the heavy burden imposed upon him.

Symbolism: The chasuble signifies the all-enveloping yoke of Christ's service, made sweet by his all-embracing love.

The prayer which the priest says while vesting: "O Lord, who has said, 'My yoke is sweet and my burden light,' grant that I may carry it so as to merit your grace. Amen."

7. The *surplice.* This is a white vestment, a shortened alb. It is used by the clergy and altar boys. (Fig. 8.)

8. The *biretta.* A three-corned black head covering (red for cardinals), which the priest wears in the sanctuary. (Fig. 7.)

58—Please name the colours of the Mass vestments and state their significance.

We usually distinguish five colours: white, red, violet, green, and black. (Gold brocade may be used in place of white, red, or green.) Rose is worn twice yearly: on the third Sunday of Advent and the fourth Sunday of Lent, because of the joy expressed by the Church on those days.

1. *White* is symbolic of joy, purity, light and glory.

It is used on all the feasts of Jesus, except those of his sufferings; on all feasts of Our Lady, of the angels, of All Saints, of Popes, Doctors, Confessors, and Virgins; and in general, of all saints not martyred.

Ripples

No word, no thought, no gesture here below
In this vast world, is meaningless
        or vain;
Each leaves its trail of joy
        or pain
In this world's wilderness.

What, then, tho thought or deed,
Or word thou utterest,
May seem but to fall into nothingness?

        Take heed! It is not so!
Each thought, each word, each deed of thine
Is like a stone one hurls into the deep;
Whose ripples, in ever-wid'ning circles, go
To distant shore or clime,
        For thine eternal happiness—
        Or thine eternal woe!

Ric Photo

Apple Blossoms

Fragile whiteness,
Floral splendour.
Who could dream of crushing you?

Should one have then
Less heed for souls
Made to God's own image?

Blessed be thou, O Lord God,
For the glory
Of nature that surrounds us,

Blessed be thou, O Lord God,
For the beauty
Of life that lies before us.

Make us reverent toward Thy creation,
In the visible and invisible worlds!

Ric Photo

2. *Red* is the colour of love, blood, and fire.

It is used on Pentecost Sunday and on the feasts of martyrs.

3. *Green* is the emblem of hope, the colour of springtime.

It is worn on the Sundays after the Epiphany and after Pentecost.

4. *Violet* symbolizes penance and faith.

It is worn during Advent and Lent, for Vigils, Days of Rogation and Ember Days, and for the administration of the Sacraments of Baptism, Penance, and Extreme Unction.

5. *Black* is the symbol of mourning.

It is worn on Good Friday and at Masses for the Dead.

Everything, you see, has a message for us. Even inanimate objects have a language for those who think and listen.

59—Show how the various postures and movements of worshippers (kneeling, standing, sitting) during Mass—and more especially, during High Mass, are conducive to devotion, to unity of Faith, to participation in the Holy Sacrifice, and to spiritual fellowship.

An interesting unsigned article appearing in "L'Ami du clergé" (the Priest's Friend) under date of May 27, 1948, supplies an excellent answer to this question:

At our daily Mass, we no longer want people "without minds or hearts": that is who bring their bodies to Mass through force of habit, but whose minds and hearts are elsewhere.

Nor do we want people "without eyes," (i.e. those who have eyes to see what the lady who came in late is wearing, but certainly not to see what is taking place at the altar!)

We no longer want those who have "lost their voices"! (Not alas, perhaps, for chattering with their neighbour; but certainly for the responses, for taking part in plain chant, or in a dialogued Mass.)

We do not want any more people "without ears"—the kind who take no interest in what Christ and his Apostles have to say to them in the Scripture lessons, nor in the prayer intentions of the congregation.

Finally, we do not want any more people "without missals"; who, rather than hold a missal or a few sheets of music, prefer to hold in their hands their hat, their handbag, their rosary, or—nothing at all!

Do you intelligent, fair-minded parishioners not agree?

But this morning I am going to add a new item to our "not wanted" list—just as definite as the others! We do not want any more people at our parish Mass "without bodies"! Now I expect this calls for a few words of explanation! It goes without saying (but it goes still better when you do say it) that my remarks today are *not* aimed at the aged, or the very tired!

I. The part my body plays when I hear Mass

1. God created us with bodies and souls that are substantially, or very intimately, united. Or to put it differently, the human composite is one. As a result, body and soul influence each other mutually. You see the proof of this every day. The person whose liver or stomach is out of order must be "handled with gloves." My intellectual labours are influenced by my aching molar! In like manner, my body may promote, or paralyze, my prayer. Doubtless, prayer is first of all an up-welling of the human spirit. Yet it is not my spirit or my mind alone which prays, but the whole man. This is an everyday experience for each one of us. The flesh is either a help or a hindrance to the spirit; according as it enters, or does not enter into the great activity of prayer.

If your bodily attitude before God is impeccably correct, if you have piously knelt and proudly made your sign of the cross, you feel at once that your prayer is off to a "flying start." And why is this so? *Because the physical has helped bring you closer to God.* By means of these simple gestures, your spirit has been given a "boost," sustained, stimulated, sometimes even firmly fixed.

On the contrary, if your gestures are mechanical or relaxed (i.e. a sign of the cross made as if you were shooing off flies, or making a hypnotic "pass" at the congregation), this means a "grounded" prayer—one that did not "take off." The reason, this time again? You were not bodily "attuned" to God; you were not on God's "beam." For prayer is action. Man must enter as a whole—body and soul—into the great work of prayer.

2. God is the Creator of Heaven and earth. The sun, stars, springs, flowers, trees, and animals, are all God's handiwork; which should sing, and does sing, God's glory. But how much more is the magnificent body of man, animated by an intelligent and free mind, the work of God! It belongs to him—your body belongs to God, not you. Then it should be in God's service. A far better offering than flowers or a candle, I must offer it to the Master, as I sing with the Scouts: "'I give you myself, O Lord,' all myself, body and soul, and I offer myself to you, not like a serf, but like a knight; by all my physical comportment, by all my bodily attitude in your house. Because in the deepest recesses of my heart I love you, there is a deep, imperative need to express my love with my body as well as my soul, in the presence of my brothers." Péguy wrote: "When St. Louis knelt on the flagstones of Notre-Dame, it was no spineless weakling, no limp rag, no trembling oriental slave, who knelt there. This was a Frenchman, and a man!" Likewise today, each one of us by his bearing and posture, proclaims to all and sundry the sincerity of his love, the depth of his conviction.

3. The Mass is not a private act; nor do I take part in it as an isolated individual. I have no right to do as I please during its celebration. The Mass is a communal act. It is the homage of a visible society to its God: it is the worship of the Church. It is the Mystical Body of Christ offering up its Head and offering itself to the Divine Majesty. It is my duty, then, as an individual member, to submit to the ritual and group discipline set up by this society, the Church of Christ.

You find this strange? But do you not take for granted a certain amount of ritual in your daily life? You respect the world's etiquette, its accepted rules and conventions. There is nothing wrong about that, either! A certain amount of "regulation" is necessary among civilized peoples. The invisible must needs enter into the visible. In this life the sign is indispensable. And would you not expect his Divine Majesty, Christ the King, to have his "court etiquette" too? Isn't that being just a wee bit illogical? Look at the celebrant. His gestures are regulated by the rubrics; that is, by a precise formula. His gestures and movements during the course of the Holy Sacrifice are made, not to satisfy some personal whim, but to conform to the rubrics. The faithful seated in the nave should likewise move in unison, really giving the impression of a parish that prays as one man—of prayer that is corporate action. In this way, together with Christ, they will render full homage to the Most Holy Trinity: praise that is perfect. Under such conditions, the Mass will have become the common task of that part of Christ's Mystical Body contained in this church—our Mass will have truly been a "celebration."

What an edifying spectacle Christians afforded in olden times, when in the primitive Church they took a tangible, active part in the various phases of the Mass! Yes, edifying indeed was this assembly that moved as one man. On the contrary, take a look today at the congregation during Sunday Mass. You will be mostly struck by the general attitude of indifference, abandon, lack of cohesion, individualism, of (let us say the word) anarchy, that is offered by this so-called "assembly," supposedly participating in communal action; but whose members stand, sit, or kneel in accordance with their fantasy, their fervour, their laziness, or their indifference.

It is time to change, and to learn how we should conduct ourselves at Mass. I should like to give you a few practical pointers that will help in forming an assembly united in posture and gesture—posture and gestures that will be inspired not by personal whim, but by the logical consequences of the sacred Action.

II. What are these postures?

Kneeling. This is the posture of adoration, of penitence, of supplication. Hence, one kneels for the prayers at the foot of the altar; and after the Sanctus to the very important "Amen" which concludes the Canon and precedes the Pater. Again we kneel after the Agnus Dei to prepare ourselves for Communion, up to the Communion antiphon. (Those who did not receive may sit down for the ablutions.) We kneel again to receive the priest's blessing. And that is all! (An exception being made for those without kneelers.) Be it noted that kneeling is by no means the most religious posture; the Nicean Council having banned it for the duration of the Paschal Season and for all Sundays in the year. Kneeling, in fact, may easily become the posture of individualism and self-sufficiency (particularly, when the person covers his face with his hands). Perfect for private devotion, kneeling is by no means the ideal posture for communal action.

This leads me to speak of *standing,* a position which some people believe is reserved for lackadaisical gentlemen or those concerned with the Sunday crease in their trousers. You are mistaken! Standing is the normal posture of an assembly. In former times, it was the normal posture for congregational prayer. Churches then were devoid of benches, pews, or kneelers; as is the case even today in the East and in the great Roman basilicas. Standing is the most virile, as well as the most fatiguing, posture. It is the posture of the free man, of the man who aspires to divine things. It is the posture of the Resurrection. Finally, the celebrant, or prayer leader, always stands. Why not the baptized co-celebrants in the nave?

Stand, therefore, when the priest enters and again when he leaves. *Stand* every time he addresses the people, intones a chant, or prays in their name. (Prayers, Postcommunion.) *Stand* for the Gospel and Creed (group affirmation of faith), and again for the Preface. (Solemn entry into the great prayer of thanksgiving.) *Sursum corda*—"Lift up your hearts!" This means my body should be lifted up as well!

Sitting is the natural posture when some one reads to you. (Epistle, Gradual, Alleluia, sermon.) It is admissible also for the people to sit down for the Kyrie and Gloria. It would be preferable, however, if the people stood whenever anything is chanted or sung. One sings so much better when one stands!

Getting up, sitting down, standing! It doesn't seem terribly important, this problem; and one that has little to do with the spiritual renewal of our country. Perhaps. But one problem *is* important—the attempt to re-form an assembly.

That this end may be achieved, let us attune—not only our hearts and voices—but also our bodies, to the rhythm of unified worship!

A PRAYER FOR MY CONFESSOR

O God, who has willed to give me in your servant to whom you have entrusted the care of my soul, a support for my frailty, a light in my darkness, a guide in the path of salvation, permit me to implore for him here an abundance of your grace; and all those virtues needed for sanctity in the priesthood. Grant him charity to support my misery, and wisdom to guide me. Increase your love in his heart, that he may help me love you more and more.

DIVISIONS OF THE MASS

The Mass Prelude

The Mass

A PRAYER FOR RECEPTIVITY OF SOUL

•

O Lord, deliver me from myself!

Break up this hardness, this crust of self-complacency which has formed on the surface of my soul.

Deliver me, O Lord, from the intellectual pride which paralyzes my curiosity.

Keep my spirit youthful and my mind open.

Grant me the amazement of the scholar.

No! Restore to me, rather, childhood's gift to wonderment.

Grant me new vision to read your Book of Creation in all its original splendour.

Grant me, O Lord, a receptive soul, an open heart, a hand always ready to clasp the hand of friendship.

Open my heart to all those needing love—from the dear old grandfather who awaits a show of affection, to Little Sister—so proud to be walking alongside Big Brother!

Help me to understand the man who needs only the affection to which he is entitled to help him to "expand."

Let me not pass by with indifference the lowly man who awaits but my expression of interest to open his closed heart.

May the eyes of my fellow man never meet mine without finding me ready to give of my time.

Lord, you alone can do it! open my heart!

Deliver me, O Lord, from self-satisfaction!

Deliver me from my so-called "virtues," which render me impervious to your grace.

Do not permit me to think of myself as "right-thinking," "honest," and "good," unless I participate in your purity and love.

Make my heart transparent as the heart of a child, my soul translucent to your light—a soul wherein grace penetrates through the wounds caused by sin.

Grant me, O Lord, a soul ready to serve, receptive to the plans of your Providence, a soul ready to accept from your hands suffering or joy; a soul which no reverse can dismay, nor summons take by surprise; and which will be ready to wing her flight toward you in that day when you shall call me within your all-enveloping beatitude. Amen. Alleluia.

JUST AS
THE PRIEST
RECEIVES
CHRIST
CORPORALLY AT THE ALTAR
SO MAN RECEIVES HIM
SPIRITUALLY IN THE SOUL
EVERY TIME HE ABSTAINS.
FOR LOVE
OF HIM,
FROM SOME
FAULT, BE
IT ONLY AN
IDLE WORD
OR VAGRANT
GLANCE.

ST. ALBERT THE GREAT

CHAPTER V

THE MASS PRELUDE

The soul is purified.

- Prayers at the foot of the altar
- Introït
- Kyrie
- Gloria
- Orations

The soul receives instruction

- Epistle
- Gradual and Alleluia
- Gospel and sermon
- Creed

COMMENTARY ON THE DIFFERENT PARTS OF THE MASS

60—Are you able to give a detailed division of the principal parts of the Mass?

As we know, the Mass comprises *two great divisions*: with their subdivisions. These two divisions are:

1. *The Mass Prelude*: from the commencement to the Offertory.
2. *The Mass proper*: from the Offertory to the end.

The different parts of the Mass may be grouped as follows:

The Mass Prelude		
	The soul is purified Preparation:	Prayers at the foot of the altar Introït Kyrie Gloria Orations
	The soul receives instruction Instruction:	Epistle Gradual and Alleluia Gospel and sermon Creed

Mass

- *The soul offers itself*
  Offertory:
  - Offertory
  - Oblation of the host
  - Mingling of the water and wine
  - Oblation of the chalice
  - Washing of hands
  - Prayer to the Holy Trinity
  - Orate Fratres
  - Secret
- *The soul is immolated*
  Consecration:
  - Preface
  - Sanctus
  - Canon
  - Te igitur
  - Memento of the living
  - Communicantes
  - Hanc igitur
  - Quam oblationem
  - Consecration of the host
  - Consecration of the chalice
  - Unde et memores
  - Supra quae propitio
  - Supplices to rogamus
  - Memento of the Dead
  - Nobis quoque peccatoribus
  - Per quem haec omnia
- *The soul is united*
  Communion:
  - Pater Noster
  - Libera nos, quaesumus
  - Haec commixtio
  - Agnus Dei
  - Communion prayers
  - Domine, non sum dignus
  - Quid retribuam
  - Reception of the Divine Victim
- *The soul gives thanks*
  Thanksgiving:
  - Ablutions
  - Communion verse
  - Postcommunion
  - Ite missa est
  - Placeat
  - Last blessing
  - Last Gospel

THE MASS PRELUDE

• WE SPEAK TO GOD • GOD SPEAKS TO US

61—What are the two main themes of the Mass of the Catechumens or Mass Prelude?

When we pointed out the three peaks of the Mass (cf. No 30), we put you on your guard against the danger of getting lost in the details of the ceremony and forgetting the essentials.

Just to make it easier for us to get our bearings, let us extract the central idea from this first group of ritual ceremonies.

The Mass Prelude (formerly called the Mass of the Catechumens) is primarily a preparation for the Sacrifice proper.

1. *Preparation of the heart*: humility, desire for purification, prayer.

2. *Preparation of the mind*: Eagerness to know Christian doctrine and the Gospel.

62—Are you able to recall in a few words the ceremony of the Mass of the Catechumens as it took place in the early days of the Church?

The meaning of several liturgical gestures would escape us without this "flash-back" to the history of the early days of the Church.

Let us go back, if you will, in retrospect, to the fifth century, the golden age of Christianity. In imagination, let us enter, during the first hours of Sunday morning, one of these venerable Roman basilicas, as the Bishop of Rome, the Pope—accompanied by his retinue of priests and deacons constituting the *presbyterium*—makes his solemn entry to the chant of the Introït.

The faithful are massed in the nave—the men on the right, the women on the left. They are separated from the clergy by a barrier that shuts off the choir. In the centre of this, is the altar—a bare, unadorned altar, a mere large flat table, the table of sacrifice—on which, facing the people, the Pope will celebrate the Mystery. On our left and right are the *ambos,* these being a sort of pulpit from which the readings will be made. The members of the *presbyterium* now take their places in the rear of the choir, and the Pope is seated on the *cathedra.*

It is in this very plain and simple setting that the ceremony is about to unfold.

Immediately following the Introït (or chant of entry), chants of supplication (or litanies, of which our Kyrie is a faint remembrance) burst forth. Then comes the mighty shout of praise to the Trinity, the Gloria. Then, turning toward the faithful, who are completely integrated with him, and who reply "Amen"; the Bishop recites the first prayer—the prayer over the assembly or *oratio super collectam*—hence its present name of Collect.

Now begin the readings and chants designed for the instruction of the faithful: readings taken from the Old Testament, or from St. Paul's "Letters" (our Epistle of today); then the chanting of the Gradual, followed by the Alleluia or Tract, executed much more rapidly than is the custom today, and in a language understood by the people: a factor giving them an instructive value to some extent lost today....

Finally, comes the solemn reading of the Gospel; surrounded by a stately and slow-moving ceremonial. For it is toward this reading that all others converge—it marks the high light of this part of the ceremony. For it is Jesus who speaks. And it is already a commencement of initiation into the Mystery.

All this, however, is by way of introduction and preparation. The Mass, properly speaking has yet to commence.

And it will not commence until after the Bishop's "homily" (which was placed here, and later, after the chanting of the Creed); until those who remain in the Basilica are those only, who really belong to the Church; those who constitute its living and visible body; the initiated, the faithful; in a word, the baptized. At this moment of the Mass, those who are still only catechumens or aspirants to Baptism and who have no right to participate in the Mystery, leave the church. The Mass, properly speaking, will not begin until after they have withdrawn.

Each individual in turn now approaches the altar with his gifts, and the Offertory, or ceremony of offering, takes place. During the chanting of a Psalm by the congregation, the gifts are collected and placed on tables; a part of these gifts being reserved for the Sacrifice. These constitute the "secreta." When this last preparatory ceremony is over, the Bishop goes up to the altar; where he recites the "Secret" prayer, and then embarks with the people upon an extraordinary dialogue; of which the clear, concise, and close-knit terminology is profoundly moving. This swift and dramatic exchange of words between officiant and people is to serve the former in a certain sense as a springboard, from which to "take off" in his great mystical ascent:

CELEBRANT: "The Lord be with you."
PEOPLE: "And with your spirit."
CELEBRANT: "Lift up your hearts!"
PEOPLE: "We have lifted them up unto the Lord."
CELEBRANT: "Let us give thanks to the Lord our God."
PEOPLE: "It is meet and just.
"It is truly meet and just, right and availing unto salvation. . . "

Let us pause here a moment. We have reached the threshold of the essential part of the Mass. The liturgy designates it under the mysterious name of "Canon," or Rule. Down through the ages, its text has remained the same. It constitutes the framework of the Mass. It makes us penetrate to the heart of the Mystery. Up to now, all has been but preparation. Now we are entering into the drama, the Action.

Better disposed through this backward glance at this very important preparation, let us henceforth consecrate our efforts on understanding more thoroughly the meaning of each liturgical word and gesture; so as to appreciate at their just value its hidden riches and so discover the best way to participate in or LIVE OUR MASS.

A PRAYER TO BE SAID BEFORE MASS

Eternal Father, I offer you the Sacrifice wherein your dear Son, Jesus, offered himself upon the Cross; and which he now renews upon this altar, to adore you and to render to you that honour which is your due, acknowledging your supreme dominion over all things, and their absolute dependence on you, who are our first beginning and our last end; to give thanks for countless benefits received; to appease your justice provoked to anger by so many sins, and to offer you worthy satisfaction for them; and finally to implore your grace and mercy for myself, for those who are in tribulation and distress, for all poor sinners, for the whole world, and for the blessed souls in Purgatory.

(**Enchiridion Indulgentiarum,** No. 68. An indulgence of 5 years for devoutly making this act of oblation at the beginning of Mass.

A plenary indulgence under the usual conditions (Confession, Communion, and visit to a church), if this devout act has been recited on all days of precept throughout a month, even at a Mass of obligation. (Prayer of St. Pius X.)

The soul is purified

63—Reread with attention the prayers that the priest recites at the foot of the altar and look for the spiritual meaning you can find in these prayers for daily living.

PRAYERS AT THE FOOT OF THE ALTAR

In nomine + Patris, et Filii, et Spiritus Sancti. Amen.

In + the Name of the Father and of the Son and of the Holy Ghost. Amen.

Ant. Introibo ad altare Dei.

Ant. I will go unto the altar of God.

℟. Ad Deum, qui laetificat juventutem meam.

℟. To God, who gives joy to my youth.

(PSALM 42:1-5.)

℣. Judica me, Deus, et discerne causam meam de gente non sancta: ab homine iniquo et doloso erue me.

Judge me, O God, and distinguish my cause from the nation that is not holy; deliver me from the unjust and deceitful man.

℟. Quia tu es, Deus, fortitudo mea:* quare me repulisti* et quare tristis incedo,* dum affligit me inimicus?

For you, O God, are my strength. Why have you cast me off, and why do I go sorrowful, whilst the enemy afflicts me?

℣. Emitte lucem tuam, et veritatem tuam: ipsa me deduxerunt, et adduxerunt in montem sanctum tuum et in tabernacula tua.

Send forth your light and your truth. They have conducted me, and brought me unto your holy hill, and into your tabernacles.

℟. Et introibo ad altare Dei:* ad Deum qui laetificat juventutem meam.

And I will go unto the altar of God, to God who gives joy to my youth.

℣. Confitebor tibi in cithara, Deus, Deus meus; quare tristis es, anima mea, et quare conturbas me?

To you, O Lord, my God, I will give praise on the harp. Why are you sad, O my soul, and why do you disquiet me?

℟. Spera in Deo* quoniam adhuc confitebor illi:* salutare vultus mei,* et Deus meus.

Hope in God, for I will still give praise to him, the salvation of my countenance, and my God.

℣. Gloria Patri, et Filio, et Spiritui sancto.	Glory be to the Father, and to the Son, and to the Holy Ghost.
℟. Sicut erat in principio,* et nunc et semper:* et in saecula* saeculorum. Amen.	As it was in the beginning. is now, and ever shall be, world without end. Amen.
Ant. Introibo ad altare Dei.	Ant. I will go unto the altar of God.
℟. Ad Deum qui laetificat juventutem meam.	℟. To God who gives joy to my youth.
℣. Adjutorium + nostrum in nomine Domini.	℣. Our help + is in the name of the Lord.
℟. Qui fecit caelum et terram.	℟. Who made Heaven and earth.

1. *The sign of the cross at the commencement of Mass*

Because the Christian ought to make the sign of the cross before starting anything of importance so as to ask God's help through the Cross, the Mass could not commence otherwise than with this sacred sign; particularly when it is a question of making present the Sacrifice of Calvary and of offering it to the praise of the Most Holy Trinity.

When we make the sign of the cross, let it be no mere sign or meaningless gesture; but a reminder of our glorious title of Christian—a gesture of praise to the august Trinity. This sacramental, moreover, is a powerful weapon against the Devil. . . .

2. The antiphon *Introibo ad altare Dei*

"I will go unto the altar of God,
To God who gives joy to my youth."

This ancient antiphon recalls the burning desire that ought to inflame our hearts at the thought of going up with the priest to God's altar, there to offer up the Body and Blood of Christ.

The server's response expresses the joy of those about to be reborn by Baptism, the catechumens. It likewise expresses our trust in God's goodness, which permits us to renew our spiritual strength through communion with the Divine Victim and to draw joy and happiness from their true source.

The word "youth" indicates here spiritual childhood, made up of simplicity and frankness, as opposed to the crafty, deceiving, and jealous "old man."

3. The Psalm *Judica me*

In order to understand this Psalm composed by David, we must recall under what circumstances the holy King wrote it.

The revolt of his son, Absalom, had obliged David to flee Jerusalem. Separated from God's Tabernacle, he is disconsolate. He envisions his situation as being a sign of divine wrath. Hence, he expresses his ardent desire to be delivered from his enemies and to return to the sanctuary to pray to God and offer him a sacrifice of thanksgiving. At the close, he experiences great hope, and his trust in God overflows. Thus this Psalm is filled with touching plaints, burning desires, joyous hope, happiness, and gladness.

We all have enemies: the world, the Devil and—ourselves.

Comprehending the perfect innocence we ought to have in order to offer up the Holy Sacrifice, and filled with trust in God's mercy; we ought to have a strong desire for great purity of conscience and should pray to be delivered from our enemies.

We shall next open our souls to the feelings of gladness with which the thought of a Sacrifice of infinite worth inspires us, and shall anticipate our gratitude by saying: "Lord, you are about to visit our souls and make them taste the sweetness of your presence. With the Cross of Jesus Christ we praise you! Why should we be afraid? The King of Heaven is our Saviour and our God!"

Bowing as we recite the Gloria, we shall adore the Blessed Trinity and renew before him the consecration of our whole being.

The priest repeats anew the *Introibo.*

Conscious of his frailty, he immediately adds: "However, it will not be by trusting in myself that I shall fill so sublime a ministry! It will be in the name of the Lord who made Heaven and earth—he alone is my stay and succour."

The words "who made Heaven and earth" give us a vivid feeling of God's power to help his minister. If God made the whole world out of nothing, he will likewise create pure hearts in priest and people; and make the priest worthy to offer the pure and spotless Host.

64—Is the Psalm *Judica me* recited at every Mass?

This Psalm is omitted at Masses for the Dead and during Passiontide, because of these words, "Why are you sad, O my soul?" The question would be pointless when, robed in garments of mourning, the Church mingles her prayers with the tears of her children; or when she celebrates the sorrowful memory of Christ's Passion.

4. *The Confiteor*

Confiteor Deo...

℟. Misereatur tui omnipotens Deus,* et, dimissis peccatis tuis,* perducat te ad vitam aeternam.

℣. Amen.

℟. Confiteor Deo omnipotenti* beatae Mariae semper Virgini,* beato Michaeli Archangelo,* beato Joanni Baptistae,* sanctis Apostolis Petro et Paulo,* omnibus Sanctis, et tibi, pater:* quia peccavi nimis cogitatione, verbo et opere:* mea culpa, mea culpa, mea maxima culpa.* Ideo precor* beatam Mariam semper Virginem, beatum Michaelem Archangelum,* beatum Joannem Baptistam, sanctos Apostolos Petrum et Paulum,* omnes Sanctos,* et te, Pater, orare pro me* ad Dominum Deum nostrum.

℣. Misereatur vestri omnipotens Deus, et, dimissis peccatis vestris, perducat vos ad vitam aeternam.

℟. Amen.

I confess to Almighty God....

May Almighty God have mercy on you, and forgive your sins, and bring you to life everlasting.

℣. Amen.

℟. I confess to Almighty God, to blessed Mary ever Virgin, to blessed Michael the Archangel, to blessed John the Baptist, to the Holy Apostles Peter and Paul, to all the Saints, and to you, Father, that I have sinned exceedingly in thought, word, and deed through my fault, through my fault, through my most grievous fault. Therefore, I beseech the blessed Mary ever Virgin, blessed Michael the Archangel, blessed John the Baptist, the Holy Apostles Peter and Paul, all the Saints, and you, Father, to pray to the Lord our God for me.

℣. May Almighty God have mercy upon you, and forgiving you your sins, bring you to life everlasting.

℟. Amen.

℣. Indulgentiam, + absolutionem, et remissionem peccatorum nostrorum tribuat nobis omnipotens et misericors Dominus.	℣. May the + Almighty and merciful Lord grant us pardon, absolution, and remission of our sins.
℟. Amen.	℟. Amen.

The priest still stands at the foot of the altar, as if to proclaim his unworthiness and the humility that is befitting God's presence.

And we? Do we always have this *reverence* and these sentiments when we enter the church to offer the Holy Sacrifice? Do we arrive in time to say the prayers at the foot of the altar with the priest? Do we take time for a pious genuflexion before taking our place in the pew? Think of the preparation the Church requires of her priests before they ascend the altar....

Bowing deeply, the priest now makes the avowal of his transgressions to God that he may obtain pardon for them. Nothing is more proper to evoke clemency than the frank acknowledgment of one's guilt and the contrite and humble avowal of one's unworthiness.

It is hard to humiliate oneself. It is terrifying to make one's accusation of guilt. Repentance, retraction, the frank admission that one has been in the wrong, making an apology, are things repugnant to our pride. This is normal. Confession is a surgical operation, and nobody enjoys being "chopped up." But what relief is brought to our anguished heart by this avowal of our misery! Confession is the surgeon's scalpel that lances the abscess, after which we are flooded with joy.

So that the faithful may have the generosity to make this accusation, the priest begins first. He prays for mercy, "because I have sinned exceedingly." And he implores the intercession of Mary, Refuge of Sinners; of blessed Michael the Archangel, the vanquisher of Lucifer; of blessed John the Baptist, the preacher of penance; of the Apostle Peter, who received power to forgive sin; of Paul, the great convert of Damascus... "and of you, brethren...."

So you ought to pray for the poor priest who stands there with all the weight of his flesh and spirit upon him, at the moment in which he is about to ascend the altar to celebrate the sacred mysteries. Accede to his invitation and beseech God in his favour through the recitation of the *Misereatur*.

Must the priest be the only one to plead for pardon? To humiliate himself?

No. As *all the faithful* should participate in the Holy Sacrifice and offer the Eucharistic Victim with the priest, so all should purify their souls of the thousand and one dust particles picked up in the way. It is for this reason that the server—who represents the people—recites the *Confiteor* after the priest.

At this moment in the Mass, have you thought to beg pardon for your sins and negligences? Have you considered what you may have to reproach yourself with since your last Mass?

This is the moment indicated for examining your conscience as a Christian, Tertiary, and apostle—for there is no Christian without an apostolate.

Our Lord himself invites us: "Therefore, if you are offering your gift at the altar, and there remember that your brother has anything against you, leave your gift before the altar and go first to be reconciled to your brother, and then come and offer your gift." (Matt. 5:23.)

Remember, the voice of discord drowns out the voice of prayer. What God looks for in our offerings is ourselves; with our hearts overflowing with charity, and not with animosity.... Holding a grudge in my heart while I offer sacrifice, is taking back with my left hand what I give with my right. So let us make a little review of our daily lives as Tertiaries or members of Catholic Action.

Have I observed my rule of life? (Have I one?)

Have my practices of devotion really been a means for nourishing my inner life?

Have I lacked charity in speaking of my neighbour?

Have I lent a helping hand to those around me when a helping hand was needed? (So many people suddenly "vanish" when something needs to be done!)

What victories have I scored over my selfishness, my pride, my vanity, my fondness for the limelight, and my penchant for talking about myself?

How about my Third Order Rule?... My Office of the twelve Our Fathers?... My spiritual reading?... The wearing of the scapular and cord, etc.?

What have I done for God since yesterday? Since Sunday?

How many weekday Masses have I missed, through negligence and sloth?

Have I tried to outstrip myself each day? To be better today than I was yesterday?... To be better tomorrow than I am today?...

What has been my apostolate since my last Mass?

During the Confiteor, I ought to remember to ask forgiveness not only for my own sins, but for those of my family... my school... my office... my factory... my fellow-workers... my parish... my home town... my country... the whole world!

Let us not fear to widen the scope of our apostolate; which ought to be universal, like the Mass now being celebrated....

We read in The *Imitation of Christ* that the priest ascends the altar with two crosses on his chasuble—one cross in front for his own sins; and one on his back, for the sins of others.

Christ was the first to bear the sins of the whole world: "He was made sin for us." And for us, he offered himself as an atoning Victim.

We, too, should take upon ourselves the sins of others; and offer ourselves likewise in atonement to obtain God's mercy for poor sinners. It takes a soul to save a soul. Someone must pay the price!

With strong faith and in complete self-surrender, let us say to the Lord: "Take me for him... for her... I must have this soul!... this family!...

In an emergency, let us ask our brother and sister lay apostles for help, and storm Heaven with our prayers.... Surely, our prayer will be heard, provided we persevere and sacrifice the thing that is hardest....

Remember, the price of a human soul comes high!

When the faithful have confessed their transgressions, and have asked forgiveness with the server through the Confiteor, the priest responds with the same formula: *Misereatur*.

The priest implores God's clemency for the people; just as the people, a moment ago, implored it for the priest: "May Almighty God forgive you"... "And may he forgive *you!"*... a touching exchange of supplication and ardent yearning.

After the prayer, *Indulgentiam,* the prayer in common begins. The priest no longer prays for himself, nor the congregation for themselves—his prayers and theirs are blended. He it is who pronounces

EXAMINATION OF CONSCIENCE

I agree, God said, that you should examine your conscience.
This is a fine thing to do, but it must not be over-done.
It is even recommended. That is well.
And not only is it recommended. It is commanded.
Therefore examination of conscience is an excellent thing.

So there you are in your bed! Now what is this that you call "examining your conscience"?

If it is to think about all the stupid things you have done during the day. If it is to call to mind all the day's stupidities,

With feeling of compunction (and perhaps I would not say of contrition). But at any rate, with a feeling of compunction that you offer me, that is also well. I accept your compunction. You are good people, well-meaning people.

But if your idea is to sift over and ruminate at night every unfruitful moment, all your feverish activity and bitterness of the day.

If what you want is to mull over again at night all your crabbed sins of the day.

If you want to keep a complete record of your sins,
Of all these stupidities and all these follies,

No! Let Me keep the Book of the Judgment! (It is not likely you stand to lose anything by it.)

And if your idea is to count up, calculate, compute like a notary and money-lender, like a collector of taxes,

You had better let Me attend to My work; and not try to do a job that doesn't need to be done!

Are your sins so precious that you must catalogue and classify them,
And register them, and line them up on stone tables,
And grave them, and count them, and calculate and compute them,
And compile them, and review them and go over them?...

Are you going to start in every night to bind up the miserable sheaves of your hideous sins of the day?

If it were merely to burn them, it would still be all out of proportion.

Why, your sins are not worth the bother!... You think too much about them, as it is!

You would do better to do some of your thinking about not committing them. While there is still time, my lad. Before you have committed them. You would do well to do a little more thinking then!

But when night comes, do not bind up these idle sheaves. (Since when did a farmer bind sheaves of darnel and cockleburs? It is sheaves of wheat, they bind, Friend!)

Do not draw up these lists and nomenclatures. It is just pride.
It is also just a long drawn-out process and a great deal of red tape.
When the pilgrim, guest, or traveller,
Has been wading through muddy roads for a long time;
He wipes off his feet before entering a church,
Before stepping over the threshold; because he is a cleanly person.
And mire from the roads must not sully the floor of the church.

But once he is done, once he has wiped off his boots before entering; he does not keep thinking about his feet.

Now that he is inside the church, he does not keep looking down at his feet to see if he wiped them off well.

He has no more heart, eyes nor voice, except for this altar where the Body of Christ, the memory of, and the waiting for the Body of Christ,
Are eternally significant.

PÉGUY

the formula in the name of all; once more beseeching the Divine Majesty to grant to this people and to himself full forgiveness, a complete remission of their sins.

Let us note in passing that it is to our advantage *to come to Mass on time!* In this way, we benefit from the precious prayers the priest sends up to Heaven, especially for those present at Mass. . . .

65—Why does the priest bow low during the Confiteor and why does he strike his breast thrice?

Surrounded by the faithful, the celebrant, bowing low like a criminal imploring pardon, is the figure of Jesus Christ followed by his disciples in the Garden of Olives; where he prayed for us with immense fervour and fell face down on the ground under the weight of our sins—the cause of his cruel suffering.

He bows *as a sign of confusion* and to symbolize the humility of the Saviour; who, being Innocence itself, willed to take on himself the sins of the whole world.

The breast is struck as a sign of sorrow and regret, following the Publican's example. It is struck thrice to indicate the three kinds of sin by which we offend God: *sins of thought, sins of word and deed, sins of omission.*

5. *The verses following the Confiteor*

Latin	English
℣. Deus, tu conversus vivificabis nos.	℣. You will turn again, O God, and give us life.
℟. Et plebs tua laetabitur in te,	℟. And your people shall rejoice in you.
℣. Ostende, nobis, Domine, misericordiam tuam.	℣. Show us, O Lord, your mercy.
℟. Et salutare tuum da nobis,	℟. And grant us your salvation.
℣. Domine, exaudi orationem meam.	℣. O Lord, hear my prayer.
℟. Et clamor meus ad te veniat.	℟. And let my cry come unto you.
℣. Dominus vobiscum.	℣. The Lord be with you.
℟. Et cum spiritu tuo.	℟. And with your spirit.

Here, in brief, is the meaning of the verses said by the priest with head bowed to show his submission to God.

Because of our sins, God is, as it were, turned away from us and irritated at us. But he will turn toward us when, through grace, we abide in his friendship.

The first verse, *Deus,* means then: "O God, vouchsafe to turn toward us, forgiving our sins which put an obstacle in the way of this greatly longed-for union; so will you give us life through sanctifying grace."

The faithful, God's people, beginning a new life, are filled with joy and sing hymns of thanksgiving to God.

In the following verses, the Church makes us say to God: "Permit us, O Lord, to experience your mercy in the remission of our sins; and grant us your grace in abundance by the gift on this altar of your salvation: Jesus your Son, the Saviour of the world."

And the priest, conscious of his unworthiness to ascend the altar, appeals anew to the Lord.

Do we all have like delicacy of conscience when we come to church to offer the holiest of sacrifices—the stainless Host—to the Blessed Trinity?

Do we think to shake from our soul the "soil of the road"—inconsiderateness, self-love, unrestrained looks and words, jealousy, vanity, human respect... ?

Next comes the *Dominus vobiscum!* May the Lord here present, Father, Son, and Holy Spirit, be in you—in each one of you—living tabernacles of Divinity! May he enlighten you and inflame you with his burning love!

The faithful reply to this wish of the celebrant, to this appeal for attention (wandering thoughts and distractions are so easy at prayer-time!), by a wish in no whit inferior to the *Dominus vobiscum.* They reply, *Et cum spiritu tuo!* That is, "May be the Lord be likewise in your priestly heart! We need priests—light of the world and salt of the earth—learned priests, priests on fire—burning with zeal for the salvation of souls and for God's glory.

Let us avail ourselves of this moment to pray hard for priests.... People ask many prayers of priests, *and only too often, people forget to pray for priests!* Let us think a bit of the great responsibility that is theirs, and then become victim souls for priests.

After the *Dominus vobiscum,* the celebrant adds, *Oremus.*

Note that this moment marks a new order of things. Priest and people no longer stand indiscriminately on the same level on the floor of the temple. For the sacrificer is about to leave the place proper to him as a man, and ascend the altar, where he will act as a priest. Before separating himself from the people, he salutes them: "The Lord be with you," immediately adding as in an ardent plea: "*Oremus.* Let us pray together! Do not leave me all alone to pray, to offer myself, to immolate myself, to receive Communion! ... *Let us pray together.... In oblation and in immolation, let us be united....*"

And the priest ascends to the altar.

66—What does the priest ask for in the two prayers he recites as he goes up to the altar?

Aufer a nobis

Aufer a nobis quaesumus, Domine, iniquitates nostras, ut ad Sancta sanctorum puris mereamur mentibus introire. Per Christum Dominum nostrum. Amen.

Take away from us our iniquities, we beseech you, O Lord; that being made pure in heart, we may be worthy to enter into the Holy of Holies, through Christ our Lord. Amen.

Oramus te...

Oramus te, Domine, per merita sanctorum tuorum, quorum reliquiae hic sunt, et omnium sanctorum: ut indulgere digneris omnia peccata mea. Amen.

We beseech you, O Lord, by the merits of your saints whose relics are here, and of all the saints, to vouchsafe to pardon all my sins. Amen.

In the prayer, *Aufer a nobis* the priest prays again for *purity of conscience* (but here for himself especially).

(You may make the same request for yourself.)

With the, *Oramus te,* the priest interests the saints in his cause; he unites their merits to his insufficiency and weakness. He makes them his intercessors with God that he may more surely be heard.

While saying this last prayer, the priest kisses the altar. The altar stone containing the relics of saints represents Christ, the total Christ; that is to say, all the faithful united to Christ—the whole Mystical Body. This ritual kiss—seemingly so unimportant a gesture—is nonetheless rich in symbol. It is a token of brotherly love given by the priest to Christ and to all members of the Mystical Body.

We are all united in this token of friendship, for the priest at the altar acts in our name.... Therefore, this pact of love made with Christ and with all our brothers in Christ, pledges us for this day... for this week.... Do we think of what this means? How can we (without betraying Christ) give our neighbour this token of friendship in the morning and hate him the rest of the day?...

Observe once more, how our Mass enters into our life and our life into our Mass.... Let us live our Mass with the utmost sincerity, and we shall soon achieve sanctity.

67—What is the significance of the incense used at a Solemn Mass?

Incense is the symbol of interior sacrifice and of prayer, especially, disinterested prayer; whose only desire is to rise up toward God like a song; for it is love, perfume, beauty.

The heart of a fervent Christian has already been compared to an incense burner, open at the top and closed at the bottom—opened to God and closed to the world. It sends up to the Blessed Trinity the incense of its purity and the fire of its love.

DAILY MASS

•

Attend Mass daily. This brings happiness to the day. All your duties are done better, and your soul is stronger for bearing the Christian's daily cross.... There we receive graces of repentance, of justification; there we receive help to avoid backsliding. We find there the sovereign means of practicing charity to others—applying to them, not our own feeble merits, but the infinite merits, the immense riches of Jesus Christ, which he places at our disposal. There we obtain the conversion of sinners. All Heaven finds in it a motive for joy, and the saints an increase of exterior glory.... Oh, if the souls in Purgatory could come back to this world, what would they not do to be present at Mass! If you yourself could comprehend its excellence, its advantages, its fruit, you would not let a single day pass without attending Mass.

Blessed PETER JULIAN EYMARD

68—What is the Introït?

Introït means "entrance."

In the primitive Church, the Pope, accompanied by the bishops, priests, and numerous ministers of public worship, set off in procession to celebrate the Holy Sacrifice of the Mass in the different basilicas of Rome—the stations of Rome. Chanting Psalms, the procession entered the church.

All that we have preserved of this today, is a brief passage from a text (the most frequently from the Holy Scriptures), together with a verse from one of the Psalms, followed by the Glory Be. The Introït is repeated, the better to engrave in men's minds the memory of God's mercy. Love never wearies of repeating the praises of the loved one.

The Introït symbolizes Christ's entry into Jerusalem, and the beginning of the drama of Calvary.

The Introït varies with each Mass and is characteristic of the feast being celebrated. Thus St. Francis of Assisi, distinguished by his great zeal for the Cross of Christ, has in the Introït of *his* Mass, these words of St. Paul: "God forbid that I should glory, save in the Cross of our Lord Jesus Christ."

The Introït, then, puts us in the tone of the solemnity.... Now to get the tone, remember, we must come to Mass on time!

69—What is expressed by the Kyrie?

Kyrie, eleison	Lord, have mercy on us.
Kyrie, eleison	Lord, have mercy on us.
Kyrie, eleison	Lord, have mercy on us.
Christe, eleison	Christ, have mercy on us.
Christe, eleison	Christ, have mercy on us.
Christe, eleison	Christ, have mercy on us.
Kyrie, eleison	Lord, have mercy on us.
Kyrie, eleison	Lord, have mercy on us.
Kyrie, eleison	Lord, have mercy on us.

Borrowed from the Greek, the *Kyrie* is an urgent supplication addressed to the Blessed Trinity to obtain help before offering the Holy Sacrifice.

The Kyrie contains *nine invocations,* designed to honour the three Persons of the Holy Trinity. The first three refer to the Father, the following three to the Son, and the last three to the Holy Spirit. Another purpose of this great number of invocations is to move Divine Justice more surely. God loves to be importuned!

The Kyrie is like a tocsin clamouring for God's help. "Let us cry out," writes one author, "three times for forgiveness of our past life; three times for help in the present; and three times for mercy in the future, that we may be saved."

Kyrie eleison—Lord, have mercy on us!

This cry recalls St. Francis' ardent prayer on Mount LaVerna a few moments before he received the stigmata: "O Lord, who are you?... and who am I, poor worm?" It is an acknowledgment of the greatness, omnipotence, and mercy of God—and of our nothingness.

In the measure that we humbly acknowledge our destitution, God will come to our aid.

Kyrie eleison. Lord have mercy on me! This was the humble, earnest prayer of the blind man of Jericho, who shouted these words with all his might as Jesus was passing by. It was the invocation repeated by the ten lepers to implore the Saviour's goodness. The Canaanite woman used it to obtain the healing of her daughter. And so on!

No supplication expresses more clearly the misery and need of our poor human nature. No other goes more surely to the Heart of Jesus, who is mercy incarnate. No other is more concise, nor expresses more vividly the ardour and vehemence of our desires and our absolute dependence on God.

Kyrie, eleison. Lord have mercy on us!

Mercy on our negligence... our selfishness... our weakness...

Mercy on our impatience... our harsh words... our jealousies!

Mercy on our pride, our vanity, our sensuality!

Mercy on our injustice, our criticisms, our detractions, our calumnies!

Mercy on our attachments, our resistance to grace!

Mercy on our suffering brothers and sisters!

Mercy on the coldness and ingratitude of our family. Of our country....

Mercy on those who are in their agony now and are to die today....

Mercy on those who hate, instead of loving, one another....

Mercy on your Church which is suffering persecution....

Mercy, Lord, mercy!

Thoughts such as these are suggested by the Kyrie.

70—What prayer does the priest recite after the Kyrie?

The Gloria, which is said or chanted on every feast day.

71—Is the Gloria said in every Mass? Why, or why not?

No, Since the Gloria is a *hymn of joy,* its recitation is not suitable on days of mourning or on penitential days.

The Gloria is therefore omitted:

On ferial days; that is, on weekdays when no feast is observed,

On the Sundays of Advent and Lent.

At certain Masses expressive of humiliation and penance; on the vigils of certain feasts; and, in general, at every Mass celebrated in violet vestments.

At Masses for the Dead, and at votive Masses (said by devotion outside the regular order of offices of the Church) except that of the Angels and of the Blessed Virgin on Saturday. (In these two cases, the Gloria is said.)

72—At what words does the celebrant bow his head during recitation of the Gloria, and why?

At the words, "We adore you"; "We give you thanks"; "Receive our prayer"; and the two times the name of Jesus is mentioned.

The purpose of all these inclinations is to intensify the meaning of these words and sentiments of reverence, honour, gratitude, trust, and love.

In addition, the Church permits a lesser inclination during Mass at the mention of the name of the Blessed Virgin, of the saint of the day, and of the reigning Pope.

73—What sentiments are expressed by the Gloria?

The Gloria has been given the name of "the Angelic Hymn," because its first words were sung by the angels in the fields of Bethlehem at the Saviour's birth: "Glory to God in the highest, and on earth peace to men of good will."

"The angels themselves," wrote Dom Guéranger, "gave the pitch; and Holy Church, led as she is by the same Holy Spirit, continued the angels' words."

This hymn, which begins with the heavenly song, may be divided into two parts:

1. The first part is a *thanksgiving* to God the Father Almighty.
2. The second part is a *supplication* to God the Son, our Lord Jesus Christ.

It concludes by *glorifying the Holy Trinity.*

Without being composed in verse form, the Gloria may be divided into strophes, readily formed of groups of rhythmic short invocations; welling up from a heart on fire, like ejaculatory prayers.

The following division brings out in sharp relief the symmetrical harmony of this beautiful prayer:

INTRODUCTION
(Double theme)

1. Gloria in excelsis Deo	1. Glory to God in the highest
2. Et in terra pax hominibus bonae voluntatis.	2. And on earth peace to men of good will

Part I
GLORY TO GOD

First strophe

a. Laudamus te Benedicimus te	a. We praise you We bless you
b. Adoramus te Glorificamus te	b. We adore you We glorify you
c. Gratias agimus tibi, propter magnam gloriam tuam	c. We give you thanks for your great glory

Second strophe

a. Domine Deus Rex caelestis Deus Pater omnipotens	a. O Lord God Heavenly King God the Father Almighty

b. Domine Fili Unigenite, Jesu Christe	b. O Lord Jesus Christ the only-begotten Son.
c. Domine Deus Agnus Dei Filius Patris	c. O Lord God, Lamb of God, Son of the Father

Part II

PEACE TO MEN

First strophe

a. Qui tollis peccata mundi, miserere nobis.	a. Who take away the sins of the world, have mercy on us.
b. Qui tollis peccati mundi, suscipe deprecationem nostram.	b. Who take away the sins of the world, receive our prayers.
c. Qui sedes ad dexteram Patris, miserere nobis.	c. Who sit at the right hand of the Father, have mercy on us.

Second strophe

a. Quoniam tu solus Sanctus, Tu solus Dominus Tu solus Altissimus	a. For you alone are holy! You alone are the Lord; You alone are most high.
b. Jesu Christe, Cum Sancto Spiritu, in gloria Dei Patris. Amen.	b. O Jesus Christ! together with the Holy Ghost, in the glory of God the Father. Amen.

The text presents no difficulty of interpretation.

You will have no doubt remarked that *the four ends of the Sacrifice of the Mass are to be found in the Gloria*:

1. *Adoration.* The first sentiment of the creature toward the Creator: "Glory to God... we adore you, we glorify you."

2. *Thanksgiving.* Recalling all the gifts received from God, "We give you thanks... God the Father Almighty."

3. *Propitiation.* A backward glance on our wretchedness, a thought about expiation for our sins: "God the Son.. have mercy on us."

4. *Petition.* Humble and trustful, for our countless needs: "You who take away sins. . . receive our prayers. Amen."

Created for God's glory, all mankind ought to send up to Heaven an uninterrupted concert of praise and love. Alas, sin has, as it were, frozen the lips of many sinners and paralyzed their voices; so that the echo of their songs no longer mingles with the harmonious hymns of the heavenly court. Let each one of us personally, during the Gloria, join our voices to those of our brothers and sisters in the whole world and glorify the Blessed Trinity for those creatures who refuse to give the glory that they owe.

74—Do you know the beautiful hymn composed by St. Francis of Assisi, Patron of Catholic Action, which singularly resembles the Gloria?

St. Francis of Assisi, God's Troubadour, loved to sing. Tramping along the Umbrian roads with Brother Leo, joyous of soul at the serene loveliness of the day and the beauty of creation, he used to sing "lauds," or in other words, songs of praise. These beautiful hymns, composed by himself, welled up spontaneously from his heart to his lips, because he was inundated and inebriated with joy, gratitude, and love!

When reading the question, many readers no doubt have thought of the "Canticle of Creation," also called, "The Canticle of the Sun." These persons are not altogether wrong. Personally, however, we are inclined to find a greater resemblance between the Canticle of Creation and the Preface of the Mass—as we shall see later on—rather than with the Gloria.

What is this song of St. Francis that has such a strong resemblance to the "Angelic Hymn"?

This is the story. According to the chroniclers, in September 1224, along toward the feast of the Finding of the Holy Cross and after the miracle of LaVerna (in which, in a loving embrace with Christ, he received the stigmata), St. Francis buried himself in a solitary spot, going over in memory and heart the ineffable vision of the Crucified Lord. As he felt the flames of love that consumed him grow in intensity, he felt a need to breathe forth in words the burning sentiments of his soul.

Then it was he said to Brother Leo, "God's little lamb," "Bring me paper and ink, for I would write down the words of God and his praises as I have conceived them in my heart." As soon as Brother Leo had brought him the piece of parchment for which he had asked, St. Francis wrote on it the song you will find indicated below. On the other side of this same parchment, he drew up, in his own hand, a special blessing for Friar Leo, his friend and companion; recommending him to keep it on his person till death. Here is the text of this precious blessing: "The Lord bless and keep you! May he show you his face and have mercy on you. May he lift up his countenance upon you and give you peace. God bless you, Brother Leo!" (Here you have a fine model for a Christmas wish!)

And finally, here is the text of "the divine praises" or "Gloria" of St. Francis of Assisi:

You are holy, O Lord; you alone work wonders.
You are mighty. You are great. You are the Most High!
You, omnipotent King, Holy Father, King of Heaven and earth.
You are the Lord God triune and one.
You are goodness, all goodness, supreme goodness, the Lord God, living and true.
You are charity and love.
You are wisdom.
You are humility.
You are patience.
You are security.
You are tranquility.
You are joy and gladness.
You are justice and temperance.
You are riches and our all-sufficiency.
You are beauty.
You are clemency.
You are our protector, guardian, and defender.
You are strength.
You are our refuge.
You are our hope.
You are our faith.
You are our great sweetness.
You are our eternal life, great and admirable Lord, God all-powerful, merciful Saviour.

Here we have a glimpse—in this lenghty hymn of praise and thanksgiving—of how a heart inflamed with love and gratitude is able to render perfect homage to God.

St. Francis, like St. John the Apostle, is of an affectionate nature. One looks in vain for any searching after literary effect, in his manner of speaking about God. It is rather a welling up from the heart, a violent clamour that cannot be contained but bursts forth in a hymn of sublime adoration. Here, St. Francis does not have creation before his eyes as in his Canticle of the Sun. It is of God alone that he sings, and of whom he proclaims all the attributes and perfections. First, of God in himself: his holiness, his Unity of nature in the Trinity of persons, his omnipotence, beauty, and life. Then God's perfections in relation to us: truth, joy, hope, Supreme Good, love, riches, goodness, and power. In a word, God is that unique and ineffable Being who fulfills our desires and gives all happiness and joy.

The Canticle of LaVerna concludes with the following prayer which we should make our own:

"O almighty, everlasting, just, and merciful God, for your own sake, grant us hapless ones to do what we know you desire, and to will whatever pleases you; so that purified, enlightened, and inwardly aflame with the fire of the Holy Spirit, we may follow in the footsteps of your dearly beloved Son, Jesus Christ our Lord; and attain unto you by your grace. You, the Most High, who in perfect Trinity and simple Unity, live and reign and are glorified, omnipotent God, forever and ever. Amen."

PRAYER FOR AN ENGAGED COUPLE

O God who has chosen us to found a Christian home, grant that we may prayerfully and chastely prepare ourselves for the worthy reception of the Sacrament of Marriage.

Help us, Dear Lord, to understand the seriousness of our vocation. Prepare us ever to love you faithfully; always to prefer your sovereign will to our own; to accept with equanimity the joys and burdens of married life; and to bring up in a Christian manner the children that your Providence may confide to our keeping.

May the home that we are soon to set up, be pleasing to you. May your name be sanctified in it, and your kingdom on earth extended; to the end that in you we may be united forever and ever. Amen.

THE KISSING OF THE ALTAR AND THE "DOMINUS VOBISCUM"

75—Immediately following the Gloria, the celebrant kisses the altar and turns toward the people to say, *Dominus vobiscum.* Can you explain the meaning of this gesture and short salutation?

The *"kissing of the altar"* and the *Dominus vobiscum* appear several times in the Mass, but we shall speak more particularly of them here.

The close connection between this liturgical gesture and this benevolent greeting forms one of the most touching symbols of Christian charity and the ineffable communications that Christ wishes to have with us through the Holy Sacrifice of the Mass. In order to comprehend its meaning and riches, we must first recall what has been said of the altar.

The altar represents Jesus Christ. Therefore, when the priest presses his lips to the altar, this kiss is for our Lord. He thereby expresses his love, and asks for His in return.

Frequently, that is, *eight times* during Mass, priest and people express this wish to each other: "The Lord be with you!" and, "The Lord be with your spirit!" The Church desires to show the celebrant thereby how much the presence and help of God are necessary for the fulfilling of his sublime functions.

It is moreover important to remark that the kiss of the altar immediately precedes the *Dominus vobiscum.* And for this reason: *The priest desires to pray in union with the people.* He thus renews and revivifies this union of which Jesus Christ is the principle and bond, by kissing the altar. He also desires to impart celestial goods to the people. Himself possessing nothing, he prays to Jesus for them, drawing them in abundance from his Sacred Heart that he may communicate them to those present. Have you ever noticed how the priest's hands rest on each side of the altar during the kiss; and how they are opened and spread wide during the *Dominus vobiscum,* as if to distribute God's love and grace to the people?

No wish could be more sincere! Then turning toward the congregation (his eyes lowered, lest he be distracted by thoughts of earth), he says: I desire with all my heart that "The Lord be with you!"

The language that he speaks is angelic—for has he not borrowed the very words used by the Archangel Gabriel when the latter saluted our Lady? What depth of expression, what power, are to be found in this wish of the priest! Since in this mysterious kissing of the altar, he breathes in, so to speak, the very love and spirit of Jesus, which he will in turn bestow upon the people—giving Jesus to each one spiritually.

The liturgical gesture is therefore rich in meaning. Each one will readily find in it inexhaustible food for his own devotion, even though it is repeated so frequently.

Is it possible to obtain from the Mass the spirit and love of Christ, and live as though one possessed nothing?

It is the duty of him who has received abundantly, to give abundantly.... Must Jesus always be the one to give? In a kiss between lovers, is it possible for only one person to take part? If there is any act for which reciprocity is required, it most certainly is the kiss; on the condition, of course, that the kiss owe its inspiration to a love that is deep and true. If that be true, how can we, without being traitors, give Jesus our kiss of love in the morning and offend him during the rest of the day?... And can we really love Jesus and not our neighbour also?

Let us ask ourselves if we are living our Mass!...

76—Do you know of any kisses of which mention is made in the Gospel, which might serve to foster our devotion?

1. The kiss of Mary Magdalene in the house of Simon the Pharisee. You remember how, kneeling close to our Lord, she kissed his feet, regretting her many sins. This is penitent love: an attitude befitting all of us, for we have all sinned.

2. Mary Magdalene's kiss, this time close to the Cross, when she clasped in her arms the feet of the crucified Saviour. This is *compassionate love,* which ought to inspire in us the thought that the Mass brings down on the altar the Sacrifice of Calvary.

3. The kiss of St. John at the Last Supper, when his head reposed on Jesus' heart. This is satisfied love. Presently, we, too, shall be privileged to be united with Jesus and even to receive him in our heart.... Let us taste now this happiness which angels envy us and which too many Christians, alas, refuse!

4. Mary's kiss at the foot of the Cross. This is Love that suffers for and with the Loved One. The Cross is sister to the altar. We must be victims with Christ and drink his cup of woe, if we are to drink one day from the cup of heavenly joys.

5. One might also add the kiss of the saints in Heaven. This is *Love triumphant,* which will be our portion in the Beatific Vision!

Thus the "kiss of the altar" and the *Dominus vobiscum* are images of Christian charity; which freely spends itself with no risk of impoverishment! The celebrant receives and bestows; but no sooner is his gift received by the people, when back it bounds to him! For the people return the priest's greeting with an expression of the most affectionate respect and perfect union: *"Et cum spiritu tuo!"* "And with your spirit!" That is, may the Lord illumine you, that you may become the "light of the world," and the "salt of the earth! . . . that you may make God's Word luminous to us!" Such is the wish that God's people make to the priest when they say to him: *"Et cum spiritu tuo!"*

All Catholics long for holy and truly enlightened priests. . . . *Instead of criticizing priests if they are not perfect, rather, let us pray for them that they may become so. . . .*

THE COLLECT

77—What is the meaning of the word "Collect" given to the prayer the celebrant recites in the Mass?

At the mention of the word "Collect," many people doubtless think of "collection." To tell the truth, they are not altogether wrong!

The word "collect" means a "gathering together," a "heaping together." One could also add "a collection," only here it does not mean of money! For at this point in the Mass the Church gathers up as it were in a pile all her children's needs, to present them to God and to plead for his help. In a certain sense, then, the Collect is a "collection of hearts."

78—With what word does the Collect begin, and why?

The Collect begins with the word, *Oremus,* meaning, "Let us pray." It is a *general invitation* to prayer in common, or communal prayer.

Formerly, the priest said, *"Oremus pro... pro..."* that is, "Let us pray for... and...." Here were indicated the intentions for which the Collect was being prayed. After each, the deacon would intone, *"Flectamus genua"*—"let us kneel," and the people would kneel down and pray for the intention until the deacon intoned the *Levate* or "Rise."

Then the priest would pronounce or chant a prayer summing up the needs and desires of the congregation (for the priest at the altar does not act as an individual, but *is a mediator between men and God);* and all the congregation replied "Amen!" As we know, we have kept something of this manner of praying in the Mass for the Ember Days and more especially in the services for Holy Week.

Note in passing how the hieratical and social character of the liturgical prayer is emphasized in these rites:

PRIEST:	"Oremus."	Let us pray.
DEACON:	"Flectamus genua."	Let us kneel.
SUBDEACON:	"Levate!"	Rise!
THE PEOPLE:	"Amen!"	So be it!

79—Is the word, "Amen," said by the congregation at the close of the Collect, binding on those who utter it?

Certainly. "Whoever says 'Amen,' teaches St. Augustine, signs, consents, confirms." On the part of the people, it means giving their full approbation, and attesting their solidarity, and their complete union with what the priest says or sings. Hence the importance of espousing the broad, deep, and "Catholic" intentions to be found in the orations of the Mass... and of pronouncing with all one's heart the word "Amen!"

St. Jerome tells us that the faithful of Rome pronounced their "Amen" so loudly and in such great numbers that it sounded like the roll of thunder!

80—What should we pray for when the celebrant says the Collect?

Have you thought about it?

Our prayer here ought to be universal and broad if we are to keep in line with liturgical tradition. *We must not just think of ourselves, or have too egoistic an outlook.* Those who understand the teaching about the Mystical Body do not fear lest they deprive themselves by praying for others, for they know that they will be the first to benefit from the good that their prayers obtain for others.

The first Christians set us an example in this, for their prayers were all-embracing and were directed toward all groups. "Our prayer is public and congregational"; wrote St. Cyprian in the third century, "and when we pray, we pray not for an individual alone, but for the people." And Origen, of the same period, completes the definition by saying, "We must pray for great and heavenly things, for ourselves and for all men, for our intimates and friends."

We should make our own the particular and general intentions which directed the piety of the first Christians.

What were these intentions?

Well, the faithful of the primitive Church prayed for:

The Catholic hierarchy: the Pope, bishops and priests, the emperor or heads of states, the faithful....

Catechumens, those possessed of the Devil, penitents....

The sick, the starving, captives, voyagers....

Heretics, schismatics, pagans, and Jews.

They requested for them:

Fidelity, the extension of God's kingdom, sanctity, and peace..

Enlightenment, deliverance from and pardon for sin..

Divine aid in all tribulation, conversion, and a return to the true Faith....

The first Christians intended to be charitable in their prayers. They thought much more about the general welfare of the whole Mystical Body, than of their own private and temporal concerns....

Their intentions, however, did not entirely exclude those personal and corporal goods normally useful in God's service; such as health, peace, security, healthful air, an abundance of the fruits of the earth, etc.

This universality of intention was sometimes expressed through the multiplicity of the Collects—three, five, or even seven of them. Remember that purely personal petitions found their normal place, not in the congregational prayer, but in the Mementos. We shall speak of this again when discussing these two parts of the Mass.

The Collect concludes the first subdivision of the Mass of the Catechumens: *The preparation, or the soul is purified.*

Before beginning the second subdivision, it is perhaps timely to point out that the Preparation for the Sacrifice consists entirely of supplications; whose admirable gradation will not have been overlooked by the devout. These supplications start off by seeking to make God favourably inclined toward us, by acknowledging our guilt and confessing our sins *(Judica me* and *Confiteor)*. Then, emboldened, we rap repeatedly at the door of Divine Mercy (the *Kyrie*). We go still farther, adding to our prayer praise and thanksgiving for this mercy, (the *Gloria)*. Finally, we describe in detail our needs and those of the Church —this is the object of the orations or "Collects."

PRAYER FOR A NURSE

•

Dear Lord, make me see you today and every day in the person of the sick. You it is, my Divine Master, whom I would serve, in caring for their needs.

Sometimes you conceal yourself under the guise of those patients who are hard to please, unreasonable, demanding. Help me ever to recognize you beneath these veils with which you so enshroud your sacred person. At such times I would say to you: "My sick Jesus, how sweet it is to serve you!" Jesus, impart to me this living faith, so that my task may never become monotonous; that I may find a joy that is ever new in caring for, in cherishing, my patients; in satisfying their every wish, and even, when possible, their whims and fancies!

Dear Suffering Ones — doubly dear to me, because I see Christ in you! . . . What a privilege to be called upon to serve you! Divine Saviour, make me appreciate the dignity of my beautiful vocation and understand its great responsibilities. Never permit me to dishonour it through neglect of duty, coldness, impatience, or rudeness to my patients.

Finally, dear Jesus, since you have willed to be my patient, be to me my Jesus most patient, supporting my short-comings and faults, see only my intention to please you, love you, and serve you in the person of the sick.

Lord, increase my faith, bless my efforts, and sanctify my work today and all the days of my life. Amen.

The soul receives instruction

81—What is the general idea of the second part of the Mass Prelude and what does it comprise?

We have seen that the first part deals with the preparation of the heart: *humility, a desire for purification, prayer.*

The main idea of the second part is the preparation of the mind, or, instruction.

After having been purified from attachment to sin and having prayed, the soul is disposed to receive enlightenment from the Holy Spirit and to feed on truth by placing itself in the school of the Prophets, of the Apostles (Epistle), and of Christ himself (Gospel), and to proclaim its faith in the truths revealed and taught by the Church (Creed).

This second part, then, contains the Epistle, Gradual, Alleluia, and sometimes a Sequence or Tract, the Gospel, sermon, and Creed.

THE EPISTLE

82—What is the Epistle?

The word "Epistle" means "letter." We ought to look on the Holy Scriptures as a "love letter" received from God himself; in which he tells us all that he has done for us, and teaches us what we ought to do to become holy and win Heaven.

Can you imagine a girl receiving a letter from her fiance and not reading it, or starting to read it and stopping before she gets to the end? Hardly! How is it then that there are so many Christians who are completely ignorant of the Scriptures or who do not take the trouble, to become acquainted with them? . . . Do we really love God? St. Jerome was right when he said, "To be ignorant of the Scriptures is to be ignorant of Christ! "

83—What is contained in the Epistle?

The Epistle sometimes contains an Old Testament passage, but more often it contains extracts from the letters sent by the apostles to new Christian communities. St. Paul, who alone wrote fourteen epistles, is the writer most often cited.

In the beginnings of the Church, the faithful met only to assist at the Holy Sacrifice. So it was during Mass that St. Paul's Epistles were read in accordance with his recommendation: "And when this letter has been read among you," wrote Paul to the Colossians, "see that it be read in the church of the Laodiceans also; and that you yourselves read the letter from Laodicea." (Col. 4:16.)

In conformity with St. Paul's instructions, the different epistles were read to the people as soon as they were received. They were then copied with great care and exchanged with a sister church.

It was a moving scene, this reading of St. Paul's letters, written sometimes from his prison!

A priest, almost always an aged priest, would hold—in a hand trembling from age or emotion—the precious papyrus on which the Apostle had penned the words the Holy Spirit had dictated. The mighty inspiration of the Preacher to the Gentiles was like a living presence in their midst. With what attention, with what eagerness, and in what silence, people listened! How faith was enlightened and the will made strong as they listened!

84—Why does the celebrant rest his hands on the missal when he reads the Epistle?

The Church wishes us to understand thereby that we should not only listen to the Holy Word, but also put it into practice.

85—What does the server say after the reading of the Epistle?

At the end of the Epistle, the server and the congregation also, give the response, *"Deo gratias"*—"Thanks be to God!" This was the formula formerly employed by the Bishop to terminate the reading of the Epistle. This formula was of frequent usage with the early Christians, and resounded triumphantly in their reunions and even in the midst of the arena where Christ's faithful witnesses endured martyrdom for him.

Thanking God ought to be our duty of every moment. We receive nothing except through him in the order of nature and of grace. His power and love have multiplied his benefits toward us.

Deo gratias! It is a cry of gratitude to God, Author of all good. From one end of the liturgy to the other this cry is reechoed, for the giving of thanks always and for all things is one of the principal ends of our eucharistic liturgy.

In passing, we might ask ourselves if the Mass constitutes for us an instrument of gratitude for all the goodness in the way of trial and joy that our Heavenly Father lavishes upon us with such loving discernment.

86—Do you know a practical method for making the Epistles of the Mass, and Holy Scripture in general, our own?

Just as we might say of the Gospel, it is the Holy Spirit who is the Author of the Bible. He it is who inspired the writers of the Old and New Testaments—he it is also who reveals the Bible's deep and hidden meaning. We all have need of his light. "Was not our heart burning within us," asked the disciples of Emmaus, "while he was speaking to us on the road and explaining the Scriptures to us?" (Luke 24:32.)

This light is obtained through prayer.

Other requirements are deep humility and a strong desire to meet Jesus, God's Gift. St. Augustine tells us that the humble penetrate the deep meaning of the Scriptures. . . and Jesus blessed his Heavenly Father for having hidden these things from the proud and for having revealed them to "the little ones"—the humble.

Finally, a strong spirit of faith is needed in order to believe the truths taught; and a great spirit of moral reform, in order to live up to one's beliefs.

For the Scriptures help their reader to know himself. Knowing himself, he should transform himself: renouncing the world's spirit, even at the risk of passing for a fool. A Christian ought to be "different". . . .

Benedict XV sums up this whole method in his encyclical, *Spiritus Paraclitus*: "Search the Bible solely with sentiments of devotion, of firm faith, of humility, and with a desire for your perfection."

Here is the testimony of a laywoman, Madeleine Chasle, taken from her fine book, *Une catholique devant la Bible* (A Catholic Looks at the Bible):

> After the Psalms, the Epistles of St. Paul were to become clear to me, thanks to the liturgy. Father Audollent's course had prepared me better to penetrate their meaning. Still, it was only after the self-imposed Sunday duty—of several years duration—of

placing the Epistle read at Mass in the setting of the whole letter, that I came to a better understanding of these great texts—so difficult at the start.

I would read a part, or even the whole, of the Epistle whose portion I had found in the missal. This rapid reading of an Epistle is of great help in arriving at a better grasp of the fundamental thoughts of the apostle. And then God no doubt took pity on me and my good will; for at last the day came when St. Paul appeared luminous, clear, and easy to grasp.

More advanced now in the life of intimacy with God, I discovered in these texts the revelation at once practical and profound of the mysteries: of sin and death; of Calvary and the Resurrection; of the Church's splendour. Dry formulas and definitions came alive—became for me fullness of truth.

Insatiable, I drew from these words of the apostle, the riches of God's grace. I realized the profound meaning of the divine adoption, of deliverance from the slavery of Satan, the world, and of self. I walked, according to St. Paul's expression, "in newness of life." (Rom. 6:4.)

87—May Catholics read the Bible?

We do not want to go into this question too deeply, so as not to get away from our subject. Let us simply say that the Church has never forbidden the reading of the Bible. On the contrary, she has encouraged the faithful to read the Scriptures, even daily.

St. John Chrysostom rose up with energy against those who thought Bible-reading was something reserved for monks. "The worst of it is," he exclaimed, "is that you think Bible-reading is just for monks! Why you need to read the Bible much more than they do!"

Another time he said to his flock: "Be always diligent in your Scripture reading.... Let each of you, when he returns home, take the Holy Scripture in his hands and search the meaning of its words."

St. Jerome counselled this program to a mother for her daughter: "Take care to have her study some Scripture passage every day.... Instead of silks and precious stones, let her cherish the divine manuscripts."

However, if the Church permits us to read the Bible, she does impose certain conditions. Why? *Because some Bibles are not orthodox.*

The Jehovah Witnesses and Protestants distribute among Catholic populations, profusely and free of charge, Bibles that are falsified and heretical; and therefore on the Index. English Bibles having the widest circulation are the King James Version and the recently published Standardized Version. All such versions of the Bible ought to be burned.

Why?

Because the Bible, especially the Old Testament, contains obscure passages and presents almost insurmountable difficulties to a layman.

For this reason, the Church, like a good mother who watches over the faith of her children, requires the faithful who wish to read the Scriptures *to procure a Catholic Bible;* that is a text bearing the imprimatur of the Apostolic See or of a contemporary bishop.

The Scripture text should, moreover, contain notes and commentaries taken from the Church Fathers or works of Catholic Biblical scholars.

Since the inspired books of the New Testament are easier to understand, beginners are usually counselled to prefer them to the Old.

And when a passage from the Holy Bible does not seem clear to you, there is no law against imitating St. Francis and getting "some light on the subject" from a priest or some well-known theologian.

88—What advice would you give to a lay person who would like to make an interesting and fruitful study of the Scriptures?

We would encourage him to go ahead, assuring him that this study will be most useful to him.

Here, in outline form, are a few suggestions for his study:

1. Read the whole Bible (a Catholic Bible with notes) right through, without stopping for difficult passages; so as to get an all-over concept of its contents.

2. Next read a general introduction to the Scriptures, by an easy-to-read author like Dougherty, LaGrange, or Grannon, or Pope's *Students' Aid to the Bible,* Gallagher's *Searching the Scriptures,* or Lattey's *First Notions of Holy Writ.*

3. Follow the rules of exegesis [exposition] and hermeneutics [interpretation and explanation].

4. Acquire a sufficient knowledge of biblical geography. Take the trouble to draw an outline map of Palestine—this will be most use-

ful for understanding the text. Study Jewish usages and customs by reading one or more of the best lives of Jesus Christ.

5. Pick a Book of the Bible that particularly interests you. As you know, the Bible contains seventy-three books: forty-six in the Old Testament and twenty-seven in the New. Read a special introduction for the book you have chosen; noting the book's purpose, how it came to be written; its principal divisions, and the linking up of main themes.

6. After each thoughtful reading, analyze the fundamental themes. Look for the connecting links, the way things tie up together.

7. Make a comparative study of texts. For example, make a four-column outline of the four Gospels.... Even though similar synoptic tables have already been published, making up your own table is always interesting and fruitful.

8. Make use (wherever possible) of the commentaries of the Doctors of the Church: particularly those of St. John Chrysostom, St. Jerome, and St. Augustine.

9. Jot down your own personal observations and keep them.

10. Note those verses that particularly strike you and memorize them.

11. Set up a goal for your Scripture reading. For instance, look up those places in the Bible where Jesus is mentioned as doing his Father's will... Jesus' concern for cleanliness and order, etc.

12. Read and study with your mind, but above all with your heart. Garner up those teachings useful for your own soul, and for those souls entrusted to you, who must be brought to God.

13. Never let a day pass without reading and reflecting on some Scriptural passage.

14. Take your subject for meditation, from time to time, from a Bible chapter.

15. Persevere, despite difficulties, in your study (for which your assiduous application will give you a taste). And remember! Obstacles were not made to overcome *us,* but to be overcome *by* us!

By a single Our Father prayed from the bottom of the heart, and with at least imperfect contrition, the venial sins of a day are expiated. How much more does one atone for one's sins by the Mass!

St. Augustine

GRADUAL — TRACT — ALLELUIA — SEQUENCE OR PROSE

89—Make a brief statement concerning each of those portions of the Mass which are interposed between the Epistle and Gospel: the Gradual, Tract, Alleluia, and Sequence.

In olden times, the reading of the Epistle was much longer than it is today. In addition, Old Testament passages were added. We still preserve a vestige of this ancient arrangement in the Masses for Ember Days.

By way of relaxation after these readings, the chanting of Psalms, or psalmody, was placed here. Formerly, these Psalms were chanted in their entirety. Later on, they were given a shortened form, which persists today in the Gradual, Tract, and Alleluia.

1. The *Gradual* is so named because it was sung during a High Mass as the deacon ascended the steps *(gradua)* of the ambo (a sort of pulpit), for the chanting of the Gospel.

2. The *Alleluia.* The Gradual is followed by two Alleluias, between which is inserted a verse from one of the Psalms. The Alleluia expresses joy and gratitude for the benefits which God has showered upon us and the saints. . . .

3. The *Tract.* From Septuagesima Sunday to Easter, the Alleluia and versicle are replaced by the Tract, which expresses the sadness felt by the Church at this season. (Tract comes from the past participle of a Latin verb meaning "to draw".)

4. The *Sequence.* For certain important feasts, the Church causes the Gradual to be followed by an anthem, whose theme is the mystery being celebrated that day. This anthem is called the Sequence or Prose, because originally the Sequence was written in prose. The Mass for the Dead likewise has its Sequence, the *Dies Irae;* commonly attributed to Thomas of Celano, the first biographer of St. Francis of Assisi.

MUNDA COR MEUM

90—What prayer does the priest say before reading the Gospel?

Let us observe again in the prayers that follow, the great concern of the Church to prepare the souls of priest and people for the important acts leading them on to the Oblation of the Holy Sacrifice.

This time *the Son of God himself will speak through the lips of the priest!*

The celebrant advances to the centre of the altar. There, hands joined before him, he raises his eyes toward Heaven; and lowers them again. Then, bowing low, he says the *Munda Cor Meum* to implore greater purity, and the *Jube, Domine, benedicere* to obtain Heaven's blessing. The following is the English translation of these two prayers:

Munda cor meum ac labia mea, omnipotens Deus, qui labia Isaïae prophetae calculo mundasti ignito: ita me tua grata miseratione dignare mundare, ut sanctum Evangelium tuum digne valeam nuntiare. Per Christum Dominum nostrum. Amen.	Cleanse my heart and my lips, O Almighty God, who cleansed with a burning coal the lips of the prophet Isaias; and vouchsafe in your loving kindness, so to purify me, that I may be enabled worthily to announce your Holy Gospel, through Christ our Lord. Amen.
Jube, Domine, benedicere.	Vouchsafe, O Lord, to bless me.
Dominus sit in corde meo et in labiis meis, ut digne et competenter annuntiem Evangelium suum. Amen.	The Lord be in my heart and on my lips, that I may worthily and becomingly announce his Gospel. Amen.

At solemn Masses, it is the deacon who recites the *Munda cor* and the *Jube, Domine, benedicere,* and the celebrant blesses him, this time saying: "The Lord be in your heart and on your lips, that you may worthily and becomingly announce his Gospel. In the name of the Father, and of the Son, and of the Holy Ghost. Amen."

91—What do we say during the *Munda cor Meum?*

Like the priest, *all the faithful ought to announce the Gospel;* and to announce it worthily, they, too, ought to say the *Munda cor*: "Purify my lips, and for greater sureness, Lord, speak through my lips.... As it is from the abundance of the heart the mouth speaks, purify my heart, too, especially; so that I may worthily announce your Gospel."

THE GOSPEL

92—Can you list some of the marks of honour given to the Gospel?

No other book has received so many honours as the Gospel! *This inspired Book* which contains the Good News of the Kingdom of Heaven, and on which men take solemn oaths, has been surrounded with the same veneration and treated with the same reverence as the Holy Eucharist itself! Here are a few interesting details:

1. In ancient times the Gospel was enclosed in the tabernacle with the Holy Eucharist.

2. Until the eleventh century, the Gospel was solemnly carried in procession. The Gospel Book (our missal) was placed with honours on a litter and borne by deacons—the crowd escorting it with banners. It was not until the eleventh century, in the flourishing monasteries of Normandy, that the first processions of the Blessed Sacrament were organized; which were finally to replace those of the Gospel.

3. The first Christians transcribed the Gospel and carried it on their person. After their death it was laid on their breast. One day, under the persecution of Diocletian, a judge ordered the Gospels of the martyrs consigned to the flames. "Cruel inquisitor," replied one of them, "even should you lay hold of all our Scriptures, so that there should remain no trace of them on earth, our sons have but to consult their hearts to find there graven the Word of God. Rend if you can, and destroy, this inner Gospel written in our souls."

4. At the reading of the Gospel, the whole Church stands! In olden days, the emperor laid down his crown, and knights drew their swords to affirm their readiness to shed their blood for the Gospel. Up to the "era of wigs" (Louis XIV), both men and women wore head-coverings in church; but at the reading of the Gospel all heads were bared.

"From the year 800 until the thirteenth century, they carried a traveller's staff to church to lean on during the ceremonies. It was not until later that the use of chairs and pews was introduced into the churches. But at the chanting of the Gospel, all laid down their staffs." (Cf. Croegaert: *The Rites and Prayers of the Holy Sacrifice of the Mass,* p. 220.)

5. The Gospel is the only book that is incensed; after receiving another mark of reverence, the inclination. It is incensed three times like the Blessed Sacrament.

6. The Gospel is the only book to be given a kiss.

7. The Gospel is the only book that is accompanied by lights. "In all the churches of the East," St. Jerome tells us, "although the sun already shines in the heavens, we light candles; certainly not to dissipate darkness, but to show our joy." These candles seem to say to us, "Do not trust too much to your feeble reason. Let yourselves be guided by the light of the Gospel!"

8. In olden times, the Gospel was richly adorned with purple and gold, decked with gems, and ornamented with artistically tooled engravings. Both text and cover of the volume were richly illuminated. It was kept in a costly case, wrapped in silk, and deposited on cushions. During the Middle Ages, on special feast days, it was placed as an ornament on the altar, along with the crucifix and chalice.

93—Why does the Church honour the Gospel so highly?

Because the Gospel is Jesus Christ speaking to us! The Gospel contains the core of Christ's teachings! The least word of the Gospel is as a precious particle of the Consecrated Host, and should be received with the same reverence with which we receive the Holy Eucharist. The words of the Gospel are inseparable from the Host. For the Gospel is Jesus Christ, the Word of God, in the form of words; while the Host is Jesus Christ, the Word of God, under the appearances of bread.

Our Lord speaks to us through his priests. Hence, whoever hears Christ's representative, receives Jesus Christ, receives Holy Communion.

Thus we have no need to be envious of the contemporaries of Jesus; for many of those who saw and heard him, failed to believe in him. Many among them even persecuted him and put him to death. For it is not words as such that save. Reduced to their material reality —to sounds—they are useless: "It is the spirit that gives life." *The Gospel will save us in the measure that we live the Gospel.*

94—Why does the priest or deacon make the sign of the cross over the missal, and a threefold sign of the cross at the beginning of the Gospel?

Before reading the sacred text, the priest uses his thumb to make the sign of the cross on the book, his forehead, lips, and over his heart:

1. *On the book,* to distinguish the Gospels from the writings of the prophets or apostles—for here are the very words of the crucified Christ.

2. *On his forehead,* that he may be preserved from all distractions, vain or perverse thoughts.

3. *On his lips,* to consecrate them to proclaiming the Good News.

4. *Over his heart,* that he may keep the words of Christ in his heart, in imitation of the Blessed Virgin, for loving meditation.

All those present should make the sign of the cross together.

95—What are our obligations as regards the Gospel?

In speaking of the Epistle, we indicated what our interior sentiments should be toward the Scriptures. We have just seen the great veneration shown by the Church for the sacred text. Now we must live up to our knowledge. We should make it a point to become familiar with God's Word and feed upon it daily. In this way, we shall increasingly prove the truth of Christ's own promise: "He, however, who drinks of the water that I shall give him, shall never thirst"—for anything else.

For Christ gives himself under the species of his divine Word, just as he gives himself under the accidents of bread and wine. The words of Christ are "spirit and life," just as the Eucharist is the Bread of Life.

We should strive, therefore, to become as it were one with God's Word, to convert it so to speak into our substance. St. Augustine shows us St. Ambrose returning home wearied from public life, a prey to a sort of spiritual hunger, which he hastens to assuage by going over—in a secluded chamber in his home—the beloved pages of the Holy Book. In a meeting of Christians where Deacon Lazarus was reading God's Word, St. Augustine, overpowered by strong emotion, suddenly begged for the Book. "I, too, want to read!" he exclaimed. "I would rather put you in contact with God's Word than embarrass you with my poor words."

For the Gospel is Jesus, the Good Samaritan who binds up and heals the wounds of the soul, robbed and left beaten on Life's highway. None has quaffed the pure and sparkling waters of this source without having assuaged the burning fever of his soul's unrest. It is within its pages that his spirit finds peace, joy, and the light that calms and refreshes. When one listens to the words of Jesus, when one reads his life, he feels himself growing better. Virtue, so attractively portrayed in its immortal parables, appears less arid; duty, as seen in the adorable face of the Master, less austere. Like St. Francis, one becomes enamoured of Christ's ideals and longs to follow him in sacrifice. What an educator is the Gospel! What a lever for raising the moral standard! How its force is felt in families where parental authority rests on the authority of this book! That is why the Bible used to be read in every Christian home. Many Protestants who have remained faithful to this custom, have, through it, found the true Faith....

96—How is the Gospel thwarted?

It is a naturalistic life lived according to this world's maxims that makes us look on the Gospel's teachings as something impossible to follow. People prefer walking down the broad and easy way, to following the steep and narrow path leading to perfection. Critical minds devoid of faith would destroy the Gospel; and always find ways of arranging things to make them fit into their purely naturalistic lives, solely swayed by human motives.

Father Chevrier was right when he wrote: "Human reasoning thwarts the Gospel's action and nullifies all that is lofty, grand, and spiritual in the precepts and counsels of our Lord: notably in whatever concerns poverty, detachment, charity, self-denial, mortification, and penance.

"So when men find the one, so rare upon earth, who has the Spirit of God, how they seek him out! How they come in search of this spirit, of these counsels from on high! Men feel then as if they were in God's presence, as if Heaven had come on earth. This spirit is rare; and yet it depends on each one of us to possess it, by filling ourselves with the Gospel and putting its precepts into practice."

97—What practical resolutions should we make as regards the Gospel?

There are *four ways* to restore the Gospel to its rightful place in the world:

1. Let every Christian family *possess a New Testament* and read it, at least in the evening, after family prayers. Let this reading be longer in the long winter evenings.

2. *Let it be read and studied in all our schools*: primary, secondary, and high. It should everywhere be accorded first place in Christian education. It should be studied more than grammar and arithmetic!

3. Let there be a short reading from it in churches at every meeting of the faithful: Mass, catechism, confraternities, fraternities, etc., with a word of practical explanation.

4. In every parish, let there be a little group of Christians more thoroughly instructed in the Gospel. They could meet in study groups every week or every month to study the Gospel with a priest; and they will be for the parish something of what the Apostles of Jesus Christ were for the whole world, after they had been evangelized by him: *saviours of men, flaming torches, and saints!*

98—Are you able to show how St. Francis of Assisi, Patron of Catholic Action, was not content with following the Gospel; but wanted to go further and become a "living Gospel?

The humanity of Jesus Christ is the centre of Christian life; St. Francis truly centered his life on it. The Christian life has its Code —the example of Jesus Christ contained in the Gospel. For St. Francis, the Gospel was to be the rule of life which he would always have before his eyes: with the precepts, counsels, and examples of Christ.

For several years after what is termed his "conversion," Francis sought the road to follow. It was only at the Mass for the Feast of St. Matthew (which we believe occurred on the 24th of February, 1208), that St. Francis had the complete revelation of what God expected of him. St. Francis assisted at Mass that day. At the Gospel (which is not the same today), St. Francis heard the priest reading Jesus' instructions to his disciples whom he was sending forth to preach: "Do not provide gold or silver or copper to fill your purses, nor a wallet for the journey, no second coat, no spare shoes or staff... and preach as you go. . . . When you enter this house, wish it well. . . ." [Knox.] Francis had the impression that this was addressed to him personally. After Mass, he looked up the priest and had him reread and explain this Gospel passage. Then he declared, "This is what I want! This is what I am going to do from now on!" At once, he took off his shoes, cloak, and belt. Over his great grey smock he passed a cord, and set forth to preach. From then on, he wished to lead "the life of the Gospel."

This "Gospel life" is the one recommended by the Saviour to the Apostles—the precepts and counsels. From that moment St. Francis was prepared to observe the Gospel in its fullness. In his testament, he declares: "The Most High himself revealed to me that I was to live according to the Gospel."

Assuredly, all the saints have willed to observe the Gospel. But here is something new. St. Francis proposes taking the whole Gospel—precepts and counsels—as his "life rule." The founders of Orders who preceded St. Francis did not have this idea. Benedictines, Augustinians, and Carthusians, naturally accept all the Gospel precepts; as for the counsels, they adopt those applicable to the contemplative life or to manual labour; adding to them poverty, chastity, and perfect obedience. They do not concentrate on those counsels concerning the apostolic life. But Francis takes everything—precepts and counsels, counsels aiming at the salvation of the individual by means of poverty, chastity, obedience, contemplation, and manual labour; but also counsels concerning the apostolic life—and of this whole he intends to make his life rule, with nothing omitted and nothing added.

Generosity in accepting

We are often checked in the way of perfection because we do not look closely enough at Jesus, lest he ask of us that certain "something" we do not want to do. . . or give up.

When St. Francis had seized upon a truth, he let himself be seized upon by *it*. It saturated, shaped, transformed him, became incarnate in him. He *became* the living truth that he had meditated and absorbed and he followed it unswervingly to the end.

Celano tells us that St. Francis, "illumined by the rays of eternal light, thoroughly understood the Scriptures. His chaste intelligence sounded the depths of the mysteries, and his love enabled him to penetrate to the interior of those things which the science of the masters knows only from without. He sometimes read in the sacred volume, and what his mind had once grasped remained graven in indelible characters in his heart. His memory served him in lieu of books, and he never forgot the word his ears had heard; for his heart ruminated it continually and devoutly. This manner of learning and reading, said he, is fruitful—it is futile to skim through a thousand treatises. He held him to be a true philosopher, who puts nothing ahead of the desire for life eternal.

"One day that the priest of San Damiano gave him the explanation of a Gospel text, St. Francis hastened to put these salutary words into practice; not wishing to delay a single moment to carry out what he had just heard."

Again Celano emphasizes: "It was necessary for Francis to correspond to the evangelical vocation—he who was to become the "minister of the Gospel."

He was not one of those who remain deaf to the words of the Gospel; but entrusting to his memory all he heard, he endeavoured to fulfill it to the letter.

"To the letter," indeed, insofar as the Church does not adjudge excessive; for Francis, thanks to his devotion to the Church and his care to receive from her his interpretation of the Gospel, avoided an excessive literalism. Perhaps it should be added that he owed it also to a power of intuition which prevented him from being hypnotized by some particular passage or aspect of the Gospel, and which always made him see the "Gospel teaching as a whole."

Generosity in practice

Here are a few examples. The Gospel says: *"Give to him who asks."* It is only a counsel, but Francis practiced it—he gave whatever was asked of him. The Gospel says, "If anyone take your tunic, let him have your cloak as well." It is only a counsel, but Francis kept it. The Gospel says, "Eat what is set before you." It is a counsel addressed to the Apostles and disciples who were sent forth. Francis observed this counsel to the letter. When he received hospitality in the homes of laymen on days of abstinence for religious, if these laymen offered him meat, Francis would eat it. Oh, not *much* meat! That is something else again!

Again the Gospel says, "When you enter a house, say, 'Peace to this house!' " This is another counsel our Lord addresses to the Apostles and disciples sent out on missions. Francis observed it to the letter; and not just when he entering a house, but on the road, in the street, or in a field. To every man he met, Francis gave this greeting: "The Lord give you peace!"

A few incidents from St. Francis' life bring out this "constant care to keep the Gospel." For instance, there is the story of the friar who wanted to have his own Psalter. This friar having already obtained one from the Minister General, contrary to the lessons and example of Francis, wanted likewise to obtain permission from the Saint. So one night when he was alone with him, he broached the question. The Saint did not reply. The friar insisted. Francis finally replied, "I do not want to give up the Gospel we have promised to keep, for the sake of your books."

Then there is the story of the mother of one of the friars who went to the Portiuncula to beg alms. There was nothing to give her. Francis noticed a copy of the New Testament used for community reading. "Give this book to our mother," said Francis to Peter of Catano. "It is better to lose the book of the Gospel while following the Gospel teachings, than to keep the Gospel book while violating its teachings.

So Francis "made the whole Gospel the rule of his life." It was also the whole Gospel that he was to give as a rule to his Order—the Friars Minor were to be Men of the Gospel. When Bernard of Quintavalle and Peter of Catano came and offered themselves as companions to St. Francis, he said to them, "This is an important matter. Let us consult our Lord Jesus Christ about it."

The three companions went to hear Mass at the Church of St. Mary of the Bishopric. After Mass, Francis asked a priest to open the missal at random. Three times the book opened at the recommendations of the Saviour to the disciples sent forth to preach. "Brothers," cried Francis, "this is the life and rule for us and for all who may want to join our company." *The Legend of the Three Companions* notes, "Starting from that moment, they began to live together according to the Gospel."

When he had eleven companions, Francis drew up a brief rule for himself "composed almost entirely of extracts from the Gospel." He went to Rome with his companions to ask Pope Innocent III to approve this rule. He had several interviews with Cardinal John of St. Paul. To every objection of the Cardinal as to the difficulty of reconciling complete poverty (even of the Order) with preaching, Francis always opposed this answer: *"I am called to live according to the Gospel."* The Cardinal went to the Pope. "I have found," said he, "a man who wants to live according to the Gospel, and follow it to the letter."

The other cardinals likewise raised objections: "This rule, above human strength, is impossible to keep!"

"Take care!" cried Cardinal John of St. Paul. "Since this Rule is taken entirely from the Gospel, saying that it is impossible to keep, amounts to saying that no one can practice the Gospel. And that would be blasphemy!"

This argument made Rome decide to approve the first Rule.

When in 1221 the Order had grown like a mushroom, the need was felt for a Rule that would be more detailed and more precise. Francis drew up such a Rule in the same spirit as the first. Acting on his orders, Caesar of Spira showed, by comparing texts, that every precept of this second Rule corresponded to some passage from the Gospel. The Rule began: "This is the life according to the Gospel of Jesus Christ, that Brother Francis begged our Lord Honorius III to grant him." Here is the first article: "The Rule and life of the Friars Minor is to live in obedience, chastity, and without personal possessions, and *to follow the doctrine and footsteps of our Lord Jesus Christ."* And here are the final words of this Rule: "Let us keep, therefore, the words, the life, the doctrine, and the Holy Gospel of Him who deigned to pray to his Father for us."

This second Rule raised a storm of protest. Francis withdrew to Fonte Colombo to draw up the Third Rule, that of 1223. This time again, he made sure that everything—from one end to the other—conformed to the Gospel. This Rule began: "The life and Rule of the Friars Minor is to observe the Holy Gospel of our Lord Jesus Christ," and it ended with these words: "We have promised to observe the Holy Gospel of our Lord Jesus Christ."

One day, St. Francis saw himself in a dream distributing crumbs to a famished crowd. But no matter how many crumbs he distributed, the people were still hungry. A voice said to him, "Make a host from these crumbs and give it to the people." He obeyed, and thus everyone had enough to satisfy his hunger. It was then revealed to him that the crumbs were the words of the Gospel and that the host was his Rule. This he himself affirmed: "The Rule is the gist of the Gospel." And he it was who dubbed the Friars Minor, "Men of the Gospel."

The ideal of the Friars Minor was the same for Poor Clares —to make the Gospel in its entirety their rule of life. The whole Rule of 1224, which St. Francis wrote for them, is contained in this sentence: "You have chosen a life in conformity with the perfection of the Holy Gospel."

Finally, it was St. Francis' intention for members of the Third Order "likewise" to base their life of observance, if not on the counsels, at least on the precepts of the Gospel; and to "imitate as closely as possible in the world the evangelical life of the Friars Minor and of the Poor Ladies."

From the thirteenth century on, this Gospel base was considered the characteristic feature of the sons of St. Francis. A Minister General of the Dominicans, Father Hubert of Romans, commented, "Blessed Francis wanted the Friars Minor to keep the Gospel in all its perfection: not in just the easy things but in those that are hard, such as turning the other cheek to the man who has just hit you on the one." James of Vitry, speaking of the sons of St. Francis he came across in Egypt, Asia Minor, and Italy, made the same observation: "They apply themselves to observe not only the precepts, but follow the counsels of the Gospel very closely; striving to live in every way the apostolic life."

On this point, are we true children of St. Francis?

LIVING THE GOSPEL

We can see that Francis was not satisfied with following the Gospel. He fed on the Gospel, was transformed into the Gospel, became a living Gospel!

There is a shade of difference between "following" the Gospel and "living" the Gospel.

Following the Gospel, means accepting only those parts that please.

Living the Gospel, means becoming what the Gospel is, means accepting the whole Gospel... Thus, St. Paul was not content with following Christ. He went further. He became clothed with Christ to the point that he could say. "It is no longer I that live, but Christ lives in me." Likewise, St. Francis of Assisi, first a follower, soon became a living Gospel. He became Christ even in his flesh by his glorious stigmata!

How can I live the Gospel?

By becoming as it were "clothed with Christ" and placing myself docilely and wholly at his service.

Or to be more specific, by doing always what our Lord would do if he were in my place and in my state of life.

Let me ask myself, for instance, if I am using my mind to think the thoughts Jesus would think if he were in my place? . . . my heart to love the things Jesus would love? . . . my will to want the things Jesus would want? . . . my imagination to imagine the things Jesus would imagine? . . . my eyes to see the things Jesus would see? . . . my ears to hear the things Jesus would hear? . . . my feet to go where Jesus would go if he were in my place?

THE DIVINE WORD

•

The sermon is like a sacrament—
The priest a ciborium pulsing with Life!
The Word that he sows as a host without spot.
Which the heart eagerly embraces.
Just as beneath the appearance of bread,
God is found in the Word which instructs and makes holy;
There is Holy Communion as well of the Word,
When the priest serves the food divine.
Be still, then, my soul, and savour in silence
This nourishing bread of God's wond'rous sowing;
Designed to produce in you fruit of high sanctity!
Meditate at length on the words that the Master
Purposely placed on the lips of his priest—
For in this bread is the taste of eternity!

M. of L.

SERMON

99—Does it really make much difference if I don't pay any attention to the sermon, or if I deliberately go to an early Mass because I know there won't be a sermon?

It makes a big difference, and many people have compromised their eternal salvation because they neglected to listen to the Word of God. A man without religious instruction is a man without religion, and hence without moral principles. . . .

Let us listen to the strong words of St. Augustine on the subject: "The man or woman who, during a sermon, allows the Word of God to fall unheeded, sins just as much as a person receiving Communion who would carelessly let the Host fall on the ground."

Indeed, we should receive God's Word with the same dispositions with which we receive the Holy Eucharist.

Have you ever noticed that in most churches the pulpit has the form of a ciborium? This may serve as a reminder that Jesus is to be found in his spoken Word, as well as in his consecrated Host.

The necessity of preaching is such that (Baptism excepted), it is more important than the sacraments! "How many people," remarked the holy Curé of Ars, "have gone to Heaven without ever having received the Sacrament of the Eucharist, or that of Extreme Unction, or of Confirmation. But as for the Word of God, as soon as we have reached the age for instruction, it is as difficult for us to be saved without it as it is to be saved without Baptism."

The reason for this is very simple. Our Lord said, "He who believes and is baptized shall be saved." Faith then is required, and St. Paul tells us that faith comes from the preaching of God's Word: *Fides ex auditu.*

Now to make an *act of faith,* the virtue of faith infused into us by Baptism, is insufficient. It is not enough to have eyes to see with: there must be an object to see. That is why a baptized baby brought up by pagans possesses the virtue of faith, but is incapable of making an act of faith.

To produce an act of faith, there must be a truth to believe. Now we ourselves cannot discover this truth—that would not be faith. This truth must be presented to us by another. Now for this transmission of truths to be believed, the ordinary means employed by the Church is that of preachers.

Thus it is essential to listen to the sermon in order to strengthen and increase our faith.

We will go further. Preaching is more necessary than prayer! This is why. No preaching, no faith; no faith, no prayer; no prayer, no salvation. Or to put it in another way: if no one tells me that God loves me, I shall not know it and shall be unable to believe it. Not believing in his love, I cannot hope either for the forgiveness of my sins, or for the reward of Heaven. Therefore it is useless for me to pray and make sacrifices. And if I do not believe in this love, and do not trust in it, I shall never love God in return. Therefore, without preaching, faith, hope, and charity are impossible for me.

That is why the saints attached such great importance to preaching, that they placed it above the works of charity.

St. Paul did not baptize. He left this to other disciples. "For Christ," says he, "did not send me to baptize, but to preach the Gospel. . . ." (I Cor. 1:17.) He adds that he is not free to choose: "For even if I preach the Gospel, I have therein no ground for boasting, since I am under constraint. For woe to me if I do not preach the Gospel!" (I Cor. 9:16.) St. Paul was not afraid of long sermons. At Troas, he prolonged his address until midnight. (Acts 20:8.)

St. Chrysostom enjoyed a frugal meal—eating very little, and always alone—so as to have more time and a clearer mind for preaching his immortal homilies.

St. Vincent de Paul taught his Sisters of Charity that they ought to prefer a spiritual conference to vespers. (Of course, it's better to attend both!)

These holy persons had understood that without faith it is impossible to please God, "for he who comes to God must believe that God exists and is a rewarder to those that seek him." (Heb. 11:6.)

No one should be surprised, therefore, that when our Lord sent his apostles throughout the world to preach the Gospel, he should have commanded them first of all: "Go and make disciples of all nations. . ."

100—If preaching is so important, how does it seem to have so little effect?

Of itself, the Word of God always works, unless there are obstacles put in its way!

Listen to the words of Isaias: "Once fallen from the sky, does rain or snow return to it? Nay, it refreshes earth, soaking into it and making it fruitful... So it is with the word by these lips of mine once uttered" (for when the preacher preaches, it is God who speaks); "it will not come back, an empty echo... all my will it carries out, speeds on its errand." (Is. 55:10.) {Knox.}

Proof is not lacking. God said: "Let there be light, and there was light." (Gen. 1:3.) He commanded the sea, "and there came a great calm." (Mark 4:39.) "Lord, that I may see!" cried the blind man of Jericho. And Jesus said to him. "Go your way, your faith has saved you." And at once he received his sight. (Mark 10:51-52.) Jesus said: "This is my body, this is my blood," and at once the bread and wine were changed into his body and blood, etc.

The efficacy of this divine Word again appears in a striking manner in the account of the first two sermons of St. Peter. (Acts 2:4.) "Now they who received," (note the expression, "received") Peter's word, "were baptized, and there were added that day about three thousand souls." (Acts 2:41.) At his second sermon: "And many of those who had heard the Word (Peter's discourse) believed, and the number of the men came to be five thousand." (Acts 4:4.)

This divine Word which converted the pagan world and is still taught today, is no less powerful. "If it produces less effect," commented the saintly Curé of Ars, "it is because we do not listen to it." Or if we do listen, our hearts may not be in the proper dispositions to profit from it. Several of these dispositions are enumerated in the Gospel in our Lord's explanation of the Parable of the Sower. (Matt. 13.) These may be summarized as: (a) Eagerness for God's Word; (b) Great humility and a great spirit of faith; (c) A detached and mortified state; (d) Courage for putting the Word into practice.

Our Lord said to his first priests, "He who hears you, hears me." Therefore, a priest in the pulpit is as an open ciborium; and his preaching is a sort of "general communion" in which our Lord—Truth and Life—is distributed to all.

Whether the preacher preaches well or not so well, should not enter into our appreciation of the sermon. Let us simply say that every sermon contains something prepared by Jesus for the spiritual advancement of every soul. If we listen to God's Word without having the fixed determination to become better by what we hear, we shall go home worse than before. For we shall have made but ill use of God's grace, and God will demand a reckoning for his Word that we have heard, without putting it into practice. By this Word neglected we shall be judged on the last day. . . .

A WORKING GIRL'S OFFERTORY

•

Deign, Lord, this work of my hands to make blest—
This task I accomplish at thy behest.
Like balm on earth's toilers may it descend.
(At threshold of day let my prayer ascend.)
That this new day of thy glory may sing,
And here below more of eternity bring,
Lord, I unite my poor offertory
To that of the altar—for thy glory.
I offer my youth, my heart, and my soul,
Yesterday's weakness with tomorrow's goal;
I offer the love thine own love requires.
(Lord, thou alone canst assuage my desires.)
Let each moment, Lord, thy presence within
Shine out to others and keep me from sin.
For I am a monstrance—bearer of three—
True guest of my soul, thou invisibly.
If thou hide thy face from me on life's way,
Give me strength to accept and courage to pray;
That I may thus rescue some straying soul
Plunged in the darkness and far from the goal.
O give to the worker, Dear God, I pray,
More of peace and joy and beauty today;
And grant that faithfully I may fulfill,
With heart full of love, thy most holy will.

(By a young girl of the J.O.C.F.
Jeunesse ouvrière catholique française).

What Will You Be, Little Boy?

Of what is he thinking,
That can so beguile—
With cherry lips parted
In the birth of a smile?

What glimpse of the future
Is seen in that look,
Which turns from the picture
In his favourite book?

Small hearts have their secrets,
And dreams of an hour;
Other dreams will yet come,
With their mystical power,

Wish grows to fulfillment,
And poem to prose,
And dream to vocation,
As the little boy grows!

Vocation? State? Calling?
(He's scarcely more tall
Than the book that he holds!
Why then mention of "call"?

To duty, to virtue—
Though waiting seem long—
Small heart must be guided:
Lest small heart should go wrong!

One must keep oneself pure
To reach a high goal.
A "calling" is made sure
By the watch o'er one's soul!

Starting tomorrow?
No! Now! Starting now!

In this life of mystery,
Little Boy, what will you be?

Ric Photo

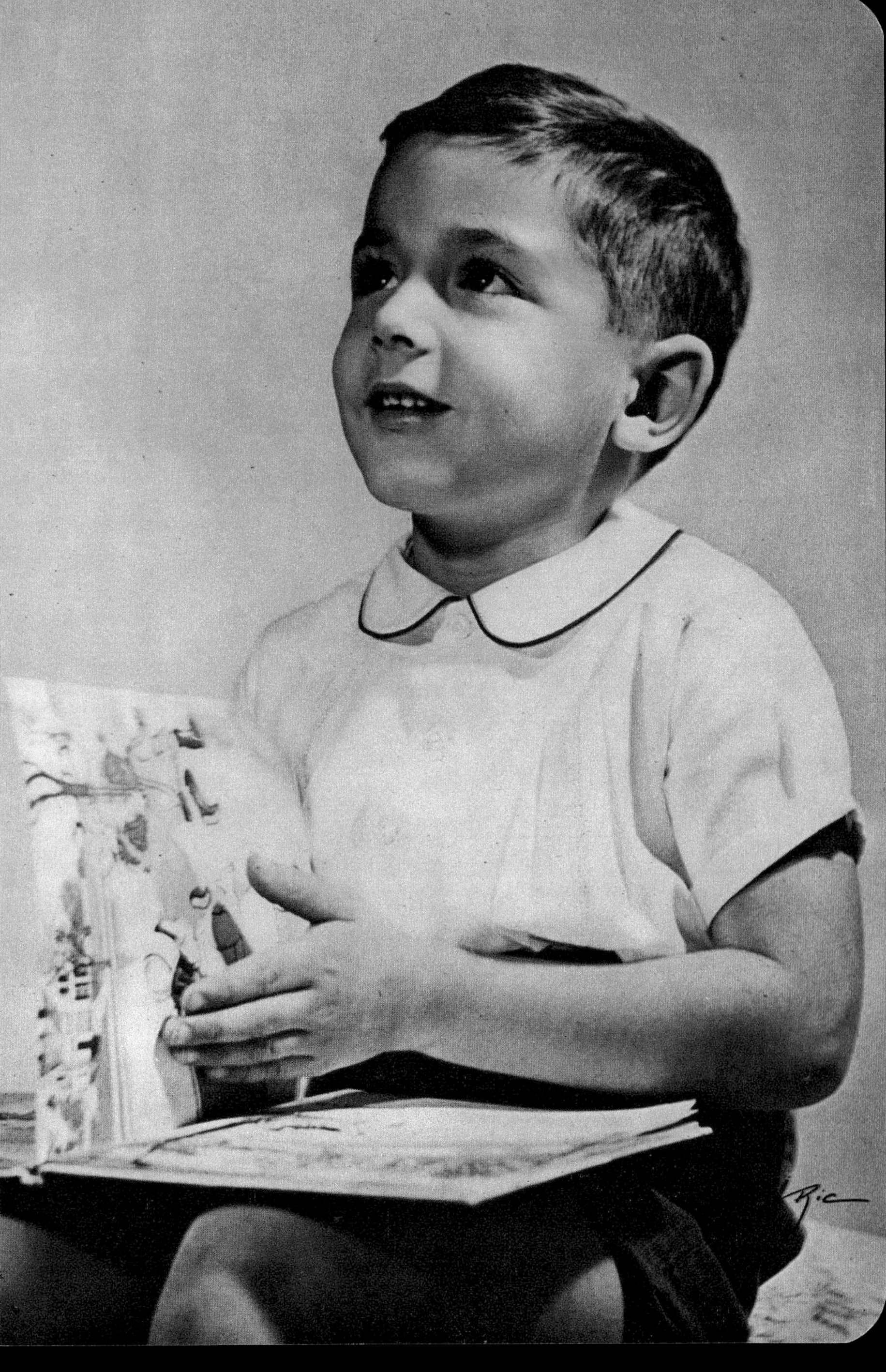

Woman with a Rosary

●

Thoughtfully she tells her beads,
Like Mary, full of grace,
Whom with each "Ave" she salutes,
The grave pray-er "ponders in her heart"
Many things.

Her life has known the joys of Life's morning,
Love, maternity, gifts divine.
The Joyful Mysteries.

Next came Life's noon-tide
Opening the door to affliction,
Separations, sickness, sorrows, solitude,
And their train.
The Sorrowful Mysteries.

Now it is evening.
Christian when happiness gilded her days,
Christian still after the blows of disaster,
Henceforth, it is all that matters.
This it is that approaches her soul
To the Queen of the Rosary.
To Her, so pure in Her joys—
So holy in sorrow—
So eager to welcome to Heaven
The "good and faithful servants" of Her Son!
The Glorious Mysteries.

Ric Photo

THE CREED

101—What does the celebrant recite after the Gospel or Sermon?

He recites or chants the Creed, also called the "Nicene Creed."

The *Creed* is a sign, a *password.* It serves as a mark of identification for those who belong to Christ's Church. A sign was required of the first Christians to distinguish them from the pagans. "Give me the countersign," one would say to them. And all had to recite the Creed, under penalty of being dismissed from the assembly of the faithful. In the Catacombs, the Creed served as a password.

In the beginning, the Creed was not written, but transmitted orally. It was taught to those about to be admitted to Baptism. In this way, it was very difficult for unbelievers to infiltrate into the assembly during Mass.

102—Were the catechumens present for the Creed?

No. To begin with, we must remember that the Creed was not said during Mass in the early days of the Church. It was introduced in some rare places about the sixth century, and it was not until long after that its recitation became universal on certain days.

In order to understand fully the meaning of the recitation or chanting of the Creed, let us transport ourselves for a moment to an assembly of faithful in the first centuries of the Church.

The bishop has just finished explaining in his homily, the Gospel of the day. As he descends from the pulpit, the deacon calls out from the choir loft: "*Sancta sanctis!* Holy things for the holy! Let the unworthy depart!"

And now a great rustling sound is heard in the crowd. Those unbelievers whom curiosity or piety had drawn to hear the Word of God; catechumens under instruction who had not yet received Baptism; public penitents not yet solemnly reconciled with the Church, leave the holy place. There remain only the faithful, the "saints," according to St. Paul's expression—those worthy of participating in the sacred mysteries.

It is the *Ite, missa est catechumenorum,* or the dismissal of the catechumens.

The Mass, properly speaking, or the Sacrifice, is about to begin.

Again, let us note the insistence of the Church for great purity on the part of all those who unite with the priest in the offering of the Holy Sacrifice.

If in our days, all the unworthy, all those in mortal sin, were invited to leave at the Offertory, we should be astonished at the sight of so many empty pews!

Why this strange anomaly? Because people no longer live in accordance with their faith, according to their Creed!

The Creed was inserted in this portion of the Mass because it affords a preparation to the Oblation of the Sacred Victim.

The Word of God has just been heard—the Epistle, Gospel, and sermon. The time has come to testify publicly and aloud to our acceptance of the truths revealed and taught.

103—Does the Catholic Church have many creeds?

There is only one Creed, for there is only one Gospel. Truth is one. We all believe in the same dogmas revealed and taught.

However, though we have only one Creed, the Church utilizes three formulas of faith all containing the same truths: abridged in the Apostles' Creed; more detailed (to refute errors) in the Nicene Creed chanted in the Mass; and in the Athanasian Symbol, recited on Trinity Sunday in the Breviary.

104—What are the three great divisions of the Nicene Creed which is sung or recited during Mass?

The Creed is composed of *three distinct parts*:

The first is concerned with the Father and the work of creation.
The second, with the Son and the work of Redemption.
The third, with the Holy Spirit and the work of sanctification.

The following is the text of the Creed as it is found in the Mass:

CREDO in unum Deum,* Patrem omnipotentem,* factorem caeli et terrae, visibilium omnium, et invisibilium.*	I believe in one God, the Father Almighty, Maker of Heaven and earth, and of all things visible and invisible.

Et in unum Dominum Jesum Christum, Filium Dei unigenitum. Et ex Patre natum* ante omnia saecula.* Deum de Deo, lumen de lumine, Deum verum de Deo vero.* Genitum, non factum, consubstantialem Patri: per quem omnia facta sunt.* Qui propter nos homines,* et propter nostram salutem descendit de caelis.* Et incarnatus est de Spiritu Sancto* ex Maria Virgine: ET HOMO FACTUS EST.* Crucifixus etiam pro nobis: sub Pontio Pilato passus et sepultus est.* Et resurrexit tertia die,* secundum Scripturas.* Et ascendit in caelum: sedet ad dexteram Patris. Et iterum venturus est cum gloria* judicare vivos, et mortuos: cujus regni non erit finis.*

Et in Spiritum Sanctum,* Dominum, et vivificantem; qui ex Patre, Filioque procedit. Qui cum Patre, et Filio* simul adoratur, et conglorificatur: qui locutus est per Prophetas.* Et unam, sanctam, catholicam et apostolicam Ecclesiam.* Confiteor unum baptisma in remissionem peccatorum.* Et expecto resurrectionem mortuorum. Et vitam + venturi saeculi. Amen.

And in one Lord, Jesus Christ, the only-begotten Son of God. Born of the Father before all ages. God of God, light of light, true God of true God. Begotten, not made, consubstantial with the Father, by whom all things were made. Who for us men, and for our salvation came down from Heaven.

And was made flesh by the Holy Ghost, of the Virgin Mary, AND WAS MADE MAN.

He was crucified also for us, suffered under Pontius Pilate and was buried. And the third day he rose again according to the Scriptures and ascended into Heaven, and sits at the right hand of the Father.

And he shall come again with glory, to judge the living and the dead, and his kingdom shall have no end.

And I believe in the Holy Ghost, the Lord and Giver of life, who proceeds from the Father and the Son. Who, together with the Father and the Son, is adored and glorified, who spoke by the prophets; and in one holy, Catholic, and Apostolic Church. I confess one Baptism for the remission of sins. And I expect the resurrection of the dead. And the life of the world to come. Amen.

105—When is the Creed said in the Mass?

The Creed is said: on every first-class feast, every Sunday, on every feast of our Lord and our Lady, on the principal feasts of the Apostles and Evangelists, on the feast of a Doctor of the Universal Church, throughout the octave of the feasts of Christmas, Easter, and Pentecost; and in solemn votive Masses.

106—When is the Creed omitted?

The Creed is omitted: in the Mass of a martyr, of a virgin, of a widow, of a confessor, in a simple votive Mass, in a Mass of requiem.

107—What do the postures and gestures of the celebrant at the Creed suggest to us?

If, since the start of this study, we have called your attention several times to the gestures of the priest at the holy altar; *it is because they have a language which fosters our devotion.*

Christianity is essentially an "incarnation" of God—God made man, and assuming a body like ours. This makes clear why our holy Religion is not just a dogma, but something to live—an extended incarnation of the life of God in us.

Hence, the great reverence shown by the Church for the human body—endowed as it is with intellectual and sense faculties—and the care she has always taken to have it take part in the worship man offers to God. This is the "raison d'être" of all Catholic liturgy; of the use of sign and symbol; of the expressive gesture used during Mass and in the Sacraments. All these signs and symbols are intended by the Church to awaken in us the spirit of faith—thus facilitating our "collaboration" in God's sanctifying action.

Let us note each of the priest's gestures during the Creed:

The celebrant, standing at the middle of the altar and facing the crucifix, commences the Creed. Just as in the recitation of the Gloria, he elevates, extends, and then joins his hands, as he says, *"in unum Deum."* This gesture is the outward sign of the elevation of his mind and heart toward God. It attests the assent of his mind, and his whole-hearted love for the truths outlined in the Creed.

The celebrant bows his head at the words, *Deum, Jesum Christum,* and *simul adoratur;* in order to show his reverence for Father,

Son, and Holy Spirit. The devout faithful will not fail to attest in the same way their faith in the divinity of the three Divine Persons.

He genuflects at the words: *Et incarnatus est... et homo factus est* to adore the Son of God, abased in his Incarnation. The congregation should do likewise.

At the end of the Creed he crosses himself, for it is through Christ's Cross that we look forward to resurrection and eternal life.

108—What meaning should the Creed have for us twentieth century Christians?

The Creed should afford us *an opportunity for making an Act of Faith.*

Have you ever made an Act of Faith not only in the Creed as a whole, but in each of the articles it contains?

Are you convinced that all these articles of the Creed ought to have an influence on your whole life: at church, at home, on the street, in the factory, at the office, at social gatherings, in your hours of leisure?

Our actions are coloured by our faith.

Too many Christians, alas, praise Jesus Christ with their mouths and disparage him in their hearts!... On how many lips does the Creed become nothing but irony!

We have no need to go to Russia to find atheists and the godless!...

Think of the:

Catholics in name only: who go to church only on great occasions, and who traditionally fulfill their Easter Duty without changing anything in their lives! They go to Confession, but with no interior conversion.

Surface Catholics: who no longer have any idea of God. Their "catholicity" is all on the *out*side—God is far from their hearts! They act from purely natural, human, interested motives....

Routine Catholics: who practice their religion without understanding and without thought. They have been accustomed since childhood to hear Mass every Sunday—so they go to Mass. Why? It's a family custom!...

Superstitious Catholics: who fulfill their religious duties to keep from having bad luck! People of this ilk put much faith in fortunetellers and in dubious pet devotions! . . .

Selfish Catholics: who possess the Truth, and do nothing to give it to others. The word "apostolate" is not in their vocabulary. These are "settled" folk; who feel very comfortable, ensconced in their easy chairs by the fireside, playing cards with their little "clique"; and indulging in candid criticism of priests and of those who try to bring the "ignorant unwashed masses" back to God. . . .

Negative Catholics: whose sole ambition is to avoid mortal sin; and who consider religion as a code of prohibitions and sanctions. These people, tainted still with Jansenism, are the bane of the joyous. . . .

Part time Catholics: who are "Catholics in church and pagans in the market place." At home, in business, in society, in their leisure time, their religious awareness is side tracked, making them a scandal to those who do not share our beliefs, perhaps just because of the senseless conduct of these self-styled "Catholics" . . . .

But before looking around at our neighbour, let us see if we ourselves do not fit into one of these categories. . . .

In fact, before trying to change those around us, before striving to put God back into the hearts of these soft and spineless Christians, it might be better to transform ourselves first; and to become REAL RED BLOODED CATHOLICS—not only "alive" but life-giving!

For how many are these complaints of our Lord only too true:

You call Me MASTER,
yet you heed Me not;
You call Me LIGHT,
yet you see Me not;
You call Me WAY,
yet you walk not after Me;
You call Me LIFE,
yet you desire Me not;
You call Me WISE,
yet you listen to Me not;
You call Me BEAUTY,
yet you love Me not;

You call Me RICH,
yet you pray to Me not;
You call Me ETERNAL,
yet you seek Me not;
You call Me GOOD,
yet you trust in Me not;
You call Me GREAT,
yet you honor Me not;
You call Me MIGHTY,
yet you serve Me not;
You call Me JUST,
yet you feer Me not;
If, then, you are damned,
reproach Me not.

This attitude reminds us of the passage in the Gospel wherein the Master gives us a charitable warning that the Kingdom of Heaven is not for those who say, "Lord, Lord," but rather for those who live in accordance with their faith and who do the will of their Father who is in Heaven.

To act otherwise would draw down upon us the vehement rebuke of Christ to the Pharisees: "Whited sepulchres. . . full of all uncleanness! The outside of the cup gleams, but the contents are disgusting!" Or again, the sorrowful complaint of the Divine Master: "This people honours me with its lips, but its heart is far from me."

Saying the Creed then (if one is upright and sincere) implies the *complete acceptance of Christ's teachings;* and hence, should bring about a change in one's way of life. . . ought to disturb one a little!

The mere fact of saying, "I believe in God," is binding on me, and involves my whole existence! It spells a complete program—God's plan that I accept; his Commandments, his Gospel, his Church, his Cross, his friends, the saints, and their demands. . . .

His enemies (the world, the vitiated flesh, and the Devil) become my enemies, and I must treat them as such. They will give no quarter.

Once one has said sincerely, "I believe in God," he has taken his stand for God against whatever is opposed to him. For a man is either for or against—there is no middle course. God will not suffer in his service people who are neither fish nor fowl. We must not content ourselves with being half-Christians!

He is not a true Christian, and therefore does not really profess who:

Gives alms with one hand and robs his fellow man with the other....

Carries his rosary in one pocket and a courtesan's address in the other....

Claims to be a "practising Catholic," but does not mean to miss an outing because of Sunday Mass....

Believes in God's mercy, but not in his justice....

Eats Christ's Body in the morning and sinks his teeth into his neighbour's reputation in the evening....

Raises his hand with equal ease to make the sign of the cross and to swear to a false oath....

Believes himself to be humble while aspiring to the highest places and honours....

Recites in the Our Father, "Forgive us our trespasses as we forgive"—and yet holds a persistent grudge in his heart....

Claims to love Jesus, but detests his neighbour....

Makes sure of having a bottle of holy water in the house—and likewise a few bottles of brandy....

Accepts the Church as his Mother, but does not obey her priests....

Acknowledges the grandeur of the Sacrament of Marriage, but has more confidence in human methods than in the Creator's designs....

Wants to eat, drink, sleep, amuse himself, have a good time, get rich, deprive himself of nothing, and—go to Heaven!...

You can add to the list!

People who fall into this category of amphibious Christians who mix religion and worldliness; who excuse their every weakness with reasons that have long been moth-eaten; who call evil good and good evil; ought to either change their lives or stop reciting their Creed. "For if you divide your life," affirms St. Augustine, "giving one part to the Devil and the other to the Lord; the Lord will reject the whole."

God has no use for divided hearts—it must be all or nothing with him. "If you are not with Me, you are against Me."

How many people live in the Christian religion without comprehending its essence!

Ask, if you will, the Catholics you know in what their "catholicity" consists. Many of them will reply: "I was baptized a Catholic. I go to Mass. I don't eat meat on Friday. I go to Communion. . . .

If you insist, "Is that all?" a few will exclaim, "Of course, that's all! What *more* is there to do?"

To this, Christ might reply: "In addition, you must have a Christian mentality. You must not wear your Christianity like a coat to be donned or doffed on certain days; but bear it in your heart as a source of living inspiration for everything you do."

Too many persons would seem to have drawn up in advance a sort of "moral budget"—so much for the world, so much for God. "Dear God, I give you this: my Mass, prayers, rosary, and alms. The rest I keep for myself!"

Such division is not God's idea. He wants the whole undivided Christian, with no strings attached. God would appear not to see the gifts that come to him from grudge-filled, lying, selfish hearts. . . .

Of what good are our works, if our soul does not breathe forth the warm, rich tones of unalloyed purity?

In our day, alas, many persons who would not like to think that they are against Christ, are certainly not for him!

They declare themselves to be reverent admirers of Jesus, but lack the courage to accept him as he is, with *all* his doctrines, *all* his demands, and *all* his rights.

Hence, this prevalent half-Christianity, these modern lives which are but a travesty and parody of Christian life; with a progressive watering-down of duty.

Hence, those incomplete Catholics, who pay homage to Christ in their private lives; but who seem to deny him the moment they set foot upon the domain of public life.

Hence, those Catholics who make furtive signs of the cross; and then, trembling before the audacity of evil, betray justice, and embrace iniquity.

Hence, those degenerate Catholics, so weak when faced with religious and social duty—those rich people, devoid of pity for the destitute, business men who take better care of their machines than they do of their employees; masters who are harsh to their servants.

Hence, those inexplicable Christians who strive to justify such impossible combinations as:

Dancing and Lent...

Late parties and Holy Communion in the morning...

The prayer book and the latest spicy novel...

The pleasures of marriage without its responsibilities...

Holy intentions and vicious impulses...

The result: an easy, and hence unrecognizable, Christianity. "Heaven," said the Master, "is for the violent" (i.e. against self).

In sincere hearts the Master's voice still echoes, especially in hours of strong illumination and faith. "If you really want to be with Me," he says, "then give up your unwholesome greed, your senseless pride, your unslaked selfishness. Give up your own tastes and worldly desires—this is a task for the strong! Do not think that some day you will be able to rest on your oars, in the pleasant conviction that you have acquired perfection. No, you must continue to climb so as to merit more every day!"

Again the Creed ought to make us think of the terrible controversies which the Church has weathered, in order to preserve intact the sacred deposit of faith!

What gratitude we should feel toward our holy Mother the Church, who has suffered so much that she might remain the guardian of Truth! For this simple word, *Consubstantialem Patri*—consubstantial with the Father"—which we chant so peacefully in the Mass, what heroic struggles did she not sustain! For this short passage, Athanasias, Hilary, and how many others, endured persecution, calumny, exile, and death! It is fraught with their sufferings, and their heroism!

And we! To defend the Creed, our faith in Christ, would we be willing to die? Let us think it over seriously, especially if human respect has won so many victories over our faith in the past—particularly if a sly smile is enough to keep us from showing that we are real Christians... particularly if our conduct has been modeled on what everyone else has been doing!

Tertiaries of St. Francis! Do you realize that you are followers of the "Little Poor Man," whose one great desire was that he might die for his Catholic faith and for the love of Jesus? Have you considered that the first thing required by your Third Order Rule for admission is "fidelity to the Catholic faith"? Are you conscientiously keeping this point in your Rule? . . .

May the Creed of your Mass help you to make any necessary adjustments. . . .

Let us profit by the Creed of our Mass to strengthen our faith; to confirm our convictions; and to make our daily lives coincide with our beliefs.

When we know how to harmonize the Christian doctrine, that we accept when saying the Creed, with the sum total of our attitudes and actions; then we shall be ready to go on to the Offertory of our Mass; because we shall have ceased to be "honorary Christians" and become true disciples of Christ and of Christ's Gospel.

With the Creed, the Mass of the Catechumens, or the preparation for the Sacrifice proper, is concluded.

This preparation of mind and heart is thus most important for profiting as fully as possible from the fruits of the Mass. Let us never omit it except for a serious reason, and let us strive to be penetrated with its mentality and spirit; so that our lives may be saturated with it.

O God, should my flesh and my imagination know doubt, I will believe with my reason and will. I do not ask you to move mountains. Small though my faith may be, because it is true and sincere, vouchsafe, O Lord, to accept it. Do not break the bruised reed nor quench the smoking wick. . . . I believe, O Lord, but increase my faith.

Where shall I go, Good Master? You have words of everlasting life!

A generous soul is ready to sacrifice certain advantages of modern comfort, the better to love God and neighbour. Such a one will give up the idea of having new modern furniture, so as to assist a poor family. Another will give up his comfortable home to become a missionary; another will give up her jewels, dresses, and ornaments in the service of Christ. And you?

CHAPTER VI

THE MASS

I. Panoramic view

II. Offertory

III. Consecration

IV. Communion

V. Thanksgiving

VI. Conclusion

THE MASS

• WE GIVE TO GOD • GOD GIVES TO US

1. PANORAMIC VIEW

109—What are the three principal parts of the Mass?

As we have already said, the Mass contains three principal parts: *the Offertory, the Consecration,* and the *Communion.*

These three parts are clearly indicated by the words and gestures of our Lord at the Last Supper:

Jesus took the bread... and the wine: Offering.
He gave thanks and blessed: Consecration.
He broke... and gave to all: Communion.

As the Mass ought to have first place in the life of a Christian, we should not be satisfied with an external and superficial knowledge; but should constantly seek to go deeper into this mystery, so as to live it and glorify the glorious Trinity, more perfectly.

To this end, let us ask the Holy Spirit for light. Let us never miss Mass through our own fault and let us be eager to study about the Mass.

110—Can you give a panoramic or bird's eye view of the three most important moments of the Mass?

In order not to lose our bearings, it is always good to outline our study plan.

As we saw at the start, the Mass recalls God's action concerning man, and man's ascent toward God. (*See* Q. 5.)

Having come from God, we must return to God.

The Way is Christ, and the Christ of our Mass.

Celebrating Mass, then, is giving again to believers the Sacrifice of the Cross, by bringing Jesus Christ down on the altar with the same sublime dispositions of love that he had for his Father when he was crucified in fulfillment of his will.

Therefore, in the Mass, our Lord comes to place himself at our disposal; so that we may offer him, and ourselves with him, to the glory of the Trinity.

The life of Christ, the Mass, and our own life follow the same movement in three-part rhythm:

I. *Offertory*: the up-beat
II. *Consecration*: the down-beat
III. *Communion*: the outward movement

I. The up-beat

A. *The life of Christ*

1. Christ's look toward his Father to glorify him. "Behold I come. . . to do your will, O God." (Heb. 10:7.)

B. *The Mass*

1. The Offertory with its characteristic prayers.

a. *Suscipe, Sancte Pater*—Receive, O Holy Father. . . this. . . Host, which I, your unworthy servant. . . .

b. *Deus qui humanae substantiae*—a prayer of union with the Son, for it is through him alone that we are able to ascend. He is the divine "Elevator." The tiny drop of water represents our human nature assumed by the Word; the wine, Christ's divinity. The union of this drop of water with the wine symbolizes the union of the human and the divine—the ascent of the creature toward the Most High. . . .

c. *Offerimus tibi calicem. . . ut cum odore suavitatis ascendat*: The ascent should be swift and direct, like that of a light and fragrant perfume. Man's spirit, ever more disengaged from matter, should soar like a column of incense. . . .

d. *Veni Sanctificator omnipotens*: An appeal to the Holy Spirit to impart to us the power of his sanctifying inspiration—for we must start from the depths.

e. *Suscipe, Sancta Trinitas*: Receive, O Holy Trinity. . . . Our eyes fixed on Heaven, we present you these offerings, fully cognizant of our misery.

C. *Our own life*:

The first movement of our lives ought to be one of adoration, of glorification of the Trinity.

Life is an ascension. But how do we ascend?

1. Look up. Do not insist on looking down, on letting ourselves become fascinated by non-essentials, details, passing things. When one has a task to accomplish—and we all have the noble task of working for God's glory and our own sanctification; and this not just individually, but together—it is useless to stop and look at the defects and shortcomings of our fellow-workers and ourselves. In that way lies paralysis of all ascent; not only of our own, but assuredly, that of our associates.

2. Forget self. Think first of the goal and not of self. We are undertaking great things; a task that surpasses us, and that is seemingly impossible to nature. Do not reason about your "inability." When faced with a hard task, we must throw ourselves into it, become lost in it, like the tiny drop of water in the wine of the chalice. We must rely on God's help. Otherwise, we begin to figure and calculate, then to back up, and finally, to fall. . . .

II. The down-beat

A. *The life of Christ*

1. Christ's sacrificial look at himself. Christ's whole life was that of a victim, of a holocaust for mankind's redemption. "The measure that began with the Incarnation, had its down-beat in Christ's Passion and death; wherein the Sacrifice proper took place."

B. *The Mass*

1. The Consecration with its prayers and gestures.

a. *Te igitur clementissime Pater*: We call the Father's merciful attention to earth.

b. *In primis*: We pray the Father to look at the whole earth; at his Church, the Pope, our Bishop, all Christians, and all our intentions.

c. *Memento.* We beseech God graciously to receive this offering *(hanc oblationem)*—the homage of our misery. May it become the Body and Blood of his Beloved Son!

d. *This is My Body; this is My Blood.* Christ comes down on the altar.

e. *Unde et memores*: We recall the incredible self-abasement of Jesus from the Incarnation to the Redemption.

f. *Supra quae... Respicere*: It is henceforth without fear that we call God's attention from Heaven to earth—the Divine Victim reposes on the altar.

g. *Supplices te*: A prayer to beseech God to send his Holy Angel to bear the Victim on high and place him at the Father's feet.

C. *Our own life*

A book has been written on the "fruitfulness of sacrifice." All fruitfulness is based on immolation. "Unless the grain of wheat fall into the ground and die, it remains alone...." The fruitful life consists in the immolation of self for a cause, for a great ideal, for the fulfillment of the duty of one's state of life. For this cause, for this ideal, for this duty, I endure everything and give all my substance—it is herein that all my joy of living consists. This means to act logically with the impulse received at Baptism and with the *Hoc est Corpus Meum* of the Mass. It means to translate into living speech the words that my lips have pronounced. How do I do this?

a. Love humility and self-abasement. In time of trial or humiliation, I must stand firm. After having looked up, I must look down. Every true life must needs be seasoned with humiliations and abasements. Being a true disciple of Christ means to drink of the same cup of ignominy and unjust treatment. Whoever gives himself over to the work of his own sanctification or that of his brothers ought to expect this. Whoever does not accept them, does not love this work; it is not his life work; he has not wholly given himself to it.

b. Suppress all murmuring. A victim does not murmur. Murmuring, like pride, is a false note in my life. Murmuring pushes a man upstairs at the very time he ought to be going downstairs. From the spiritual point of view, it means that I am out of step with life.

c. Briefly, to come back to the ideas stated on the subject of sacrifice, we must give up those things pleasing to us, especially self (Offertory), in order to prefer God (Consecration). The Offertory is an act of detachment. We give God the thing we love most—emptying our hearts to make room for Love. The Consecration is God—the Object preferred—giving himself to the soul, coming to fill the empty place left by our renunciation or detachment. Let us note that this preferring of God, based on renunciation, ought to be continuous in our life. This is what living our Mass means! All that we have to do is to look at Christ's life to be convinced. Christ always gave up his own will to do his Father's will. Jesus' whole life in this world was as a solemn Mass because of the incessant vision he had of his Passion. The cross is what awaits us if God destines us for great things.

III. THE OUTWARD MOVEMENT

A. *The life of Christ*

1. Christ's sanctifying look toward men.

Jesus' life was both contemplative and active, a life of prayer and of apostleship. Though Jesus lived thirty years in seclusion, yet all his life he was the Shepherd worried over his sheep. The three years of his public life were spent in ministering to the souls he came to redeem at the cost of his Precious Blood, that their return to the Father's House might be hastened. Jesus left his place of retreat to search for the lost sheep.

B. *The Mass*

1. The Communion. Jesus leaves the altar to give himself, and to give himself to all. He gives of his Person; bringing God's love to men, provided that men do not shut him out of their lives. Christ enters the human soul in three ways: peace, truth, and charity. This is what we pray for in the Communion prayers.

a. *Pater Noster*: We implore peace of soul as we pray "Forgive us our trespasses. . . . Deliver us from evil."

b. *Agnus Dei*: May the most pure Lamb take pity on our misery and give us peace.

c. *Domine Jesu Christe*: We pray God to look, not upon our sins, but on the faith of his Church. . . . May he grant it peace and unity! Further on, we add: "Make me always adhere to your Commandments and never suffer me to be separated from you. . . ."

d. *Sanguis Domini*: May the Blood of our Lord keep my soul unto life everlasting. It is the clinging of the soul to God, the consummation of charity.

C. *Our own life*

We shall likewise find in our life this third movement which goes from the interior to the exterior—a movement proceeding from

Love and culminating in the apostolate. We cannot give what we do not have. This involves, then, establishing the primacy of the contemplative life and inclining it to flower into action. First the Third Order, then Catholic Action.

For we have within us two opposing needs which make themselves continuously felt. Our soul swings between concentration and expansion—between the interior life and the apostolate. This alternative movement appears in the surge of the tide which brings back the wave that it has hurled afar. . . . Or again, it is the tree which plunges its roots deeply into the soil that its trunk may soar aloft. Observe that the obscure work of the roots is of prime importance, and if we destroy it, we destroy the fruit and the leaves. Soon the whole tree dies.

An apostolate, therefore, to be supernaturally fruitful, requires:

1. *An intense interior life,* a life concentrated on the heart of Jesus, that inexhaustible Source of love. "He loved me," wrote St. Paul, "and gave himself up for me." (Eph. 5:2.) This is the key word: "Loves—gives!" Two "beats" that are really one, so much does the first necessitate the second. Love never rests till it has given everything, itself included! Now the Eucharist is the very fountain-head of charity, the source of Christian energy, the reservoir of the apostolate. . . .

2. *A peaceful life.* The interior life will enable us to know ourselves and to rectify anything in our conduct opposed to Christ. For breadth and scope of vision in accomplishment, purity is required. "Blessed are the pure in heart, for they shall see God." The Holy Eucharist will give me this supernatural insight. . . .

3. *An enlightened life*, that is, a life of faith clinging to Christ in utter trust. The apostle ought to be the "light of the world"; he ought to shine by his faith; by his convictions embodied in his life and in all that he says and does.

4. *A unifying, kindly life.* If I am to go to others, I must be charitably disposed toward them. "Where there is no love," says St. John of the Cross, "sow love, and you will harvest love." We must avoid everything that leads to misunderstanding. Without mutual trust and charity, we cannot have fellowship with anyone. The highest unifying principle, the Eucharist, will bring about this fusion of souls if we nourish our souls with it—I was going to say "daily." . . . Oh, if we only understood! . . . If only we loved Him more!

111—In order to have an exact concept of the Offertory, a "flash-back" to the ritual ceremonies as they took place at the beginning of Christianity, would be of great help to us. Can you give us a description?

For about the first ten centuries, assistance at the Holy Sacrifice of the Mass entailed an active and material participation in the Offertory by means of the congregational offering of the elements of the Sacrifice —the bread and wine brought to the altar by the faithful.

Marked with the sacred seal of Baptism; made partakers in a certain fashion in Christ's priestly power; deputized to the authentic and official worship of the Church—the Holy Sacrifice of the Mass— the faithful were of a mind to exercise their mandate, their power, and their rights as regenerated Christians—they co-offered. The whole assembly without exception took part in the offering: the Pope, the clergy, the faithful, both men and women.

For the faithful, "hearing Mass" was interpreted as a most active participation.

Hearing Mass or offering one's bread amounted to the same thing.

The non-offerer was not considered to have been associated in the Sacrifice.

The axiom of the Jewish Law: "You shall not appear before me empty-handed," (Ex. 23:15 and Deut. 16:16) was likewise a law for Christians.

Observe again that the faithful by their offerings assured to the Mass the indispensable elements—the bread and wine destined to become our Lord's Body and Blood.

OFFERING

Dear God, in union with my guardian angel and all the saints, I want to take part in every Mass now being celebrated, or to be celebrated this day and this coming night in the whole world.

In union with the Divine Victim, I want to offer myself continually day and night as a living host for the glory of God, the salvation of souls, and the preservation of priestly and religious vocations.

To this same end, I desire that my every heartbeat may be an act of reparation; each movement of my body, an act of gratitude; each sigh, an act of love.

It is my intention to offer the last Mass to be said before midnight in reparation for all my past negligences, and in thanksgiving for all favours received.

THE OFFERTORY PROCESSION

After the celebrant had read the Offertory, the faithful, bearing candles and bringing their offerings or oblations, marched in procession to the choir. First to be offered were the bread and wine, of which a part was destined for the Holy Sacrifice and the people's Communion; then beeswax, milk, honey, oil, and even money, for the upkeep of the church and the subsistence of its ministers. A portion of the offerings also went to the poor, and to widows and orphans. . . .

During the Offertory procession, the people chanted Psalms or appropriate liturgical selections, and also recited prayers.

Right now, let us try to make some practical applications.

To begin with, the Mass that the priest is celebrating is likewise YOUR Mass.

Why? Not only because you benefit along with him, *but because you are privileged to offer it up with him.*

Now offering the Mass is a priestly function. You then are in a certain sense "priests" too! Doubtless you have not received the priestly character; but by your Baptism you became members of the Mystical Body of which Christ—the Priest of the New Testament—is the Head. By the very fact, you participate in the priestly power of Christ, you are "priests" spiritually.

For this reason St. Peter called Christians "a royal priesthood, a holy nation," and St. Ambrose told the faithful of Milan: "All children of the Church are priests. At Baptism they receive the anointing with holy oil that makes them share in the priesthood. The 'host' that they offer to God is wholly spiritual—themselves."

Rejoice, then, fervent Christians! Although you did not receive the Sacrament of Holy Orders, giving you power to consecrate the bread and wine of the Mass; you *can* offer, in union with Christ's Sacrifice, a spiritual "mass," a living sacrifice; which is not unrelated to nor without resemblance to the Mass the priest offers at the altar.

This unique "mass," YOUR "mass," which began with your Baptism; which is life-long; and which, because you are immortal, will never end; contains the three principal parts of a sacrifice—the Offertory, the Consecration, and the Communion. (This will appear more clearly as we study the Mass in detail.)

"Hearing Mass and offering one's bread," we said above, "amount to the same thing."

We might have written with equal truth, "Hearing Mass and offering oneself, amount to the same thing."

Why? Because bread is an indispensable element in life. Bread is "the staff of life." He who takes away my bread takes away my life. Those Christians who offered their bread, offered by that very fact their lives—they made of themselves a living offering.

And the richer the personal dispositions of the offerer in living faith, in reverence, in adoration, in love for God, the more generous the offering. We know that it is not the gift that brings pleasure, but the way in which it is given.

And we? Have we thought about what we are going to offer God in our next Mass? . . . Or are we of the number of those who never have anything to offer. . . but who are always the first to receive?

With what interior dispositions do we offer? . . . . To begin with, do we have charity in our hearts, charity toward our neighbour? . . . or are we holding a grudge, a feeling of hatred that keeps us from forgiving? . . .

Have we sufficient faith to realize what purity is required on the part of the offerer, when we know that our offerings are to be united to that of Christ himself? . . .

And do we really understand in what a sublime Action we are involved when we participate in the Holy Sacrifice of the Mass? . . . Have we ever thought that it is possible for us to increase the sanctity of the Church? (The holier the members of a society, the holier the society!) Have we ever thought about using the Mass to this end? . . .

When you offer a gift, you can consider:

1. The object presented, or the gift in itself.

2. The presentation of the object, the act by which it is presented. However humble the object presented, the more generous, loving, and thoughtful, this act is, the more pleasure it will give. Thus, a magnificent jewel, grudgingly given, may please as an object; but the act of its presentation will leave a painful impression.

In applying these principles to the Mass, we must distinguish:

1. The object offered (which, here, is twofold):

a. Jesus' love for his Father when he died on the Cross. This object is infinitely pleasing in itself—it is not this object which concerns us here.

b. Our love for God, as expressed by our sanctified lives, and offered in union with Christ's Sacrifice. Here, the object will be more or less pleasing to God, according as we give ourselves more or less fully to his service.

2. The presentation of these objects, the act whereby we offer them to God. The more holy this act of offering, the more pleasing will it be to God; the more will it move his heart; the better will it assure an abundance of his graces; the more fruitful will it be. Consequently, the holier our dispositions when we present our offerings to God, the more pleasing will our Mass be to God and the more profitable to us.

112—For what are "Mass stipends" or "Mass offerings" used? Why take up a collection during Mass?

Before going on with our detailed study of the Mass, let us touch on the question of Mass stipends. Far from taking us away from our subject, this question—dealt with here—will clear it up and complete it.

If, during the first ten centuries of the Church, the faithful themselves brought the elements of the Sacrifice in order to share in its fruits; the time came when the faithful, desirous of having the Holy Sacrifice celebrated for their own intentions, did not always have on hand the requisite oblations in nature—that is, the bread and the wine.

What happened then? Imperceptibly, and for practical reasons, the faithful substituted for these oblations of bread and wine their equivalent in coins or other material values; which were no less true oblations or offerings for the Sacrifice.

Already, in the fourth century, we find such an example. St. Epiphanus (+ 403) cites the case of a Jew who was secretly baptized on his deathbed by the Bishop of Tiberias and initiated into the sacred mysteries of the Eucharist. After the ceremony, he handed the Bishop a great quantity of gold; saying to him, "Offer for me."

But it is especially with the start of the tenth century that examples are rife. To mention only one, here is one related by the author of the life of St. Mathilda. "The Empress," he writes, "let no day pass without presenting her oblation of bread and wine to the priest at Mass for the safety and welfare of the entire Church—she never went to the altar empty-handed. Now the death of her husband, Henry the Fowler, the Emperor, taking her by surprise, in place of the ordinary oblations, she offered the priest two gold bracelets; asking him to celebrate Mass for the deceased."

Bread and money thus became interchangeable; to the point that the bread took the form of a coin, and the coins became an oblation just like the bread.

People "offered" or "sacrificed" gold and silver, just as they offered bread and wine.

With this oblatory money, the priest procured the bread and wine of the oblation as convenient. The money oblation was changed—as it is still changed today—into the oblation of bread and wine.

So to come back to our initial question—*for what are Mass stipends used?*—we must reply (if the foregoing has been grasped), that the money given to the priest for the celebration of a Mass in no way constitutes a "salary" or "fee" paid to the priest in exchange for his services—quit with the saying of a Mass. Still less is this money the "price" of a Eucharistic Sacrifice; but constitutes an object, the matter of oblation, the equivalent of the bread and wine; exchangeable for these elements of the Sacrifice. *Therefore this stipend is destined, not to the priest, but to God.*

Thus understood, these monetary oblations are just as noble as the ancient offerings of bread and wine. Such is the significance of the stipend or *stipendium,* or pecuniary offering, entrusted to the celebrant by the parishioner for the former to offer up for his intentions the Holy Sacrifice of the Eucharist.

And since the pecuniary offering replaces the oblation of bread, that which was said of the first should be said of the second—namely, that in presenting their coin, their monetary oblation for the celebration of the Sacrifice, the faithful present or offer their own lives—themselves.

Had you thought of it this way?

This ancient concept of the Mass offerings shows us, then, that the money placed by the faithful in the hands of the priest does not constitute a "fee" paid to him; but an object, a deposit entrusted to him, replacing the antique oblation of bread and wine and designed to be offered in sacrifice—in a word, it is an offering made to God.

From this, we may draw three conclusions.

1. The dignity of the priest is thus enhanced. He becomes one, not hired or paid by men, but by God.

2. The rôle of the faithful increases, for they are restored to their native condition of a holy and priestly race; qualified by their Baptism to offer God those gifts to be consecrated to him by the ministery of the priest, clothed in the priesthood of Jesus Christ.

3. Finally, this pecuniary transaction in Masses is ennobled; which otherwise risks lending itself to the horrible language so frequently heard today: "How much does a Mass cost?" "What is the price of a Mass?" "I'm paying for a Mass." As if with all the gold in the world one could pay for the Body and Blood of Christ!

(See page 75 of this volume for a further doctrinal treatment.)

113—Why take up a collection during Mass?

This question is of the same type as the preceding. The same thing may be said of the collection as has been said of the offerings of bread or wine or of Mass stipends.

As soon as the celebrant has read the Offertory, a basket or plate is passed to the people for them to put in their monetary offering. The money replaces the ancient oblations of bread and wine that all the faithful—not that we said *all* the faithful—brought to the altar so as to take an active part in the Holy Sacrifice and to benefit from it.

We can also say here that when the people drop their gift into the basket, they should do so with the intention of offering themselves in union with Christ's Oblation.

Do we, today, have this *high concept of the collection?* . . . Or does not the taking up of a collection rather furnish the pretext for impatience and for cutting comments about priests?

Yet, "what have you that you did not receive?" If everything you have belongs to God, why become annoyed when God reclaims his property? Especially, when you consider that God repays a hundredfold everything done for him.

Let us think, too, of the importance of having the right dispositions for profiting from our gifts and for pleasing God. . . . Instead of giving grudgingly and grumblingly when the basket comes round, we would do better to give nothing—and keep still!

Another point to envision is the priest's right to receive from the people—in exchange for his services in the spiritual order—those things necessary for his sustenance and support.

This was, moreover, the practice in the first centuries of the Church; and still is the practice wherever the Faith is really alive.

"For this reason," teaches St. Thomas, "the abundant oblation which the people offered to God, reverted from God to the priests, not only for their own use, but also that they might be faithfully employed; disbursing a portion for divine worship, a portion for their own upkeep, for as St. Paul says, 'those who serve the altar have their share of the altar,' (I Cor. 9:13) and finally, a portion for the support of the poor." [IIa IIae, Q. 86, art. 2.]

In the pages that follow, we shall continue to study in detail the riches of doctrine and life contained in the Offertory of the Mass.

OFFERTORY

•

If you have naught else to present to the Lord, then offer him your toil and your pains.

Much effort by many men has been spent that this small morsel of bread might repose there on the paten.

If your hands are empty and your throat grief-parched, then offer your wounded heart and all that you have suffered.

That the wine might be poured into the chalice, was it not first necessary for the grape clusters to be crushed and the wheat flailed?

If you have nothing within you to offer, save bitterness and sin, the distress that is to live, and all human anguish,

Then let your hands lift toward Heaven even these piteous things (which the Divine Mercy received beforehand at the Last Supper).

And should even the strength to implore and to offer be lacking, though all within you be but the sensible loss of God's presence and the sense of abandon,

Accept, then, in silence that Another should bear your burden, and yourself with your burden; that Offering and Offertory may be one.

II. THE OFFERTORY

The Soul is offered

- The Offertory
- The Oblation of the Host
- The Mingling of the water and wine
- The Oblation of the chalice
- The Lavabo
- Prayer to the Holy Trinity
- The Orate Fratres
- The Secret

The Offertory

114—What thought and what sentiments are suggested by the Offertory of the Mass?

With the Offertory we enter into the Sacrifice proper. We must integrate ourselves here into Christ's Sacrifice so as to be acceptable to our Heavenly Father.

Here begins in a still more tangible fashion *our real participation in the Mass.*

We have said that Christ is the centre of the universe, the only Mediator between God, his Father, and creatures. His mission is to glorify the Most Holy Trinity and to bring all creatures to do the same. His gesture of offering thus extends to the entire creation; which he gathers up in himself in the Mass—the tiny drop of water in the chalice —that he may offer it to God. But Jesus will take us with him only if we freely make him the offering of self with the intention of being hosts—that is, victims—with him.

Remember that refusing to be an offering and host would be—according to the strong words of Bossuet—to "mutilate Jesus Christ."... Members of the Mystical Body, we ought to adopt the same dispositions and attitudes as the Head, who is Christ crucified out of love for his Father.

What should I do at the Offertory?

Place my soul in the atmosphere of Christ's Sacrifice.

Adopt a state of soul in conformity with my great rôle as associate in Christ's Passion.

ON THE PATEN

When I placed my host on the paten, alongside those of my brothers and sisters, I felt that I was not alone. I understood what it meant to belong to the great Christian Brotherhood, and my duty of joining in the common oblation by the total offering of self.

That I may join in more fully; enter into, really integrate myself into the great Sacrifice of your Mystical Body; it is my intention, Dear Lord, to offer you my joys (the melody of heart and lips); my work, my troubles, my apostolic efforts, my successes and failures, my temptations, my good resolutions and my victories, my parents, friends, and fellow-workers, especially N—. I particularly offer you those things that are mine, that I did NOT receive from you, and for which I implore your pardon—my sins, failings, human misery, and frailty...

Dear Lord, penetrate all this with your merciful love. Please make all these poor things, by integrating them into your Sacrifice, count for eternity.

Tomorrow I will come to you again.

Unite myself with the priest... with the Church... with Christ.. who offer... and who offer up themselves....

Sacrifice myself; that is, offer my entire life to be immolated with Christ....

Offer the Body and Blood of Christ, augmented with my body and blood—and that of the whole Mystical Body.

I ought to convince myself once again that a Catholic does not "assist" at Mass; he *participates in it.*

If I bring only a *passive attitude* to Mass; if I am content to look, to listen, to dream... I am not playing my rôle; I am a dead weight, and because of me the drama is poorly played.... I am leaving to the celebrant an action in which he ought to feel all the faithful present, living, and active behind him.

My part will be *congregational.* The Mass is a drama—a drama presupposes several actors. I am not alone in this church where Mass is being celebrated. At least the priest is present besides me, and there is the whole Church of God in oblation with Christ.... Usually, there are other faithful present. At this time, other Masses are being celebrated in neighbouring churches, in other lands, in the whole world....

Each one has his offering to make.... Is each one then to make it alone? As an individual?

No, this is not the mind of the Church. "Bear one another's burdens," wrote St. Paul. Let us offer them together, then, through the divine Burden-bearer. Indifference toward others in our offering would not be Christian. Christ loves all his members; and I cannot pray in his spirit if I exclude them from my prayer and offering as if they did not exist. "Think of me, and I will think of you," said our Lord to St. Catherine of Siena. "Think of mine, and I will think of you," we might transpose it, for Jesus is in his own.

Further on, we will go into the details of our offering.

The Offertory is the starting-point of the Sacrifice.

The priest now presents the bread and wine to God and places them on the altar, with the fixed intention of having God transform and accept them. And this in such a way, that this bread and this wine are as it were in a state of expectancy—the bread to become Christ's Body, the wine, his Blood. When they shall have been thus changed, they will ascend in homage to God and will be of use to men.

The Offertory is doubtless and first of all a presenting of the wine to God with this twofold intent. It is, moreover, a presenting of myself to God; a placing myself before him in a voluntary state of expectancy, of a change to be wrought; and within, an expectancy of my divinisation.

Observe that this gesture of offering should not be a mere exterior ceremony; nor beautiful words murmured by my lips, in which my heart has no part.... If the Mass does not sanctify the souls of those who take part, could it not be precisely because those taking part have not put their whole life into it?...

Here, more than anywhere else, we may truthfully say that "keeping myself for myself, means depriving myself of God."

It follows, then, that all I offer at Mass becomes God's property for him to do with as he pleases....

Already, you can see where this leads!

My offering, then, will call for much self-denial.... When I offer myself in the morning at my Mass, I should—all day, all week—immolate my tastes and preferences, my egoistical self, and conform to the tastes, preferences, and will of Christ himself!

I ought to count myself fortunate, if every day I can unite something of myself to Jesus—and unite it irrevocably!

Besides, I need this union to make easier for my weakness the renunciation imposed by the total offering of self. By uniting my offering to Jesus' Cross, I make it supernatural and divine. All my Mass ought to fasten me to the Cross, give me a passionate love for it—like Francis of Assisi, who was nailed to Christ's Cross to the point of being crucified with Christ!

I ought to be a man "offered," "given," "consumed," in the service of God and my neighbour. My very Baptism should make me a victim with Jesus.

Who would have thought that the Offertory of the Mass was fraught with such high consequence?

Doubtless, I find all this frightening, and before the grandeur of this total death, I feel my weakness. And yet—as we shall see farther on—it is in the Sacrifice itself I shall find strength and courage.

Now I ought to bear this in mind: *I shall sanctify myself and others only through the Cross.* "Unless the grain of wheat fall into the ground and die, it bears no fruit." The Cross, rather *my* cross, will not be that of my own choosing; it will be the one willed by God and which will very often run counter to my views! But could I refuse anything now to God? . . . Now that I have just offered myself to him together with his Divine Son? . . . Now that I no longer belong to myself? . . . Now that Jesus gives himself every day to me and for me without stint; placing his Sacrifice daily at my disposal, so that I may add mine to be received by the Most Holy Trinity? . . . .

No, I cannot refuse Him anything. . . . And it is fully and freely that I will say with the celebrant, *Suscipe*—"Take everything."

It depends on me whether my "host" is to be complete, and constitute a total homage to God's infinite majesty. . . .

Whoever continues loyally, under the eye of God, to the end of the sign of the Offertory, lays down his heart—foundation of all the rest, our Lord said—his whole being, his job, his good works past and future, this whole day, this whole week, the efforts and sufferings of others, that they may be inwardly permeated and transformed by the divine; and that all may be pleasing to God and useful to one's neighbour.

At this point in the Sacrifice, it is probably better for me to close my missal and open my heart to the amazing drama now taking place on the altar. On the altar, where the priest is engaged in offering up to the august Trinity—alongside the Spotless Host—us "little hosts," who form with Christ an immense Host, a single Victim!

THE WORKER'S PRAYER TO SAINT JOSEPH

Glorious Saint Joseph, pattern of all who are devoted to toil, obtain for me the grace to toil in the spirit of penance, in order thereby to atone for my many sins; to toil conscientiously, putting devotion to duty before my own inclinations; to labour with thanksgiving and joy, deeming it an honour to employ and to develop, by my labour, the gifts I have received from Almighty God; to work with order, peace, moderation and patience, without ever shrinking from weariness and difficulties; to work above all with a pure intention and with detachment from self, having always before my eyes the hour of death and the accounting which I must then render of time ill-spent, of talents unemployed, of good undone, and of my empty pride in success, which is so fatal to the work of God. All for Jesus, all through Mary, all in imitation of you, O Patriarch Joseph! This shall be my motto in life and in death. Amen.

(PRECES ET PIA OPERA: 440. An indulgence of 500 days. Pius X. Rescript in his own hand.)

Behind the Clouds the Sun is Always Shining

●

Black storm-clouds scud threateningly by;
    Thick darkness has scattered light;
Terrified, ignorant, foolish folk
    Proclaim a perpetual night!

But **somewhere** the sun still is bright,
    And soon he will reappear;
And golden gleams from his glorious beams
    Will banish the midnight fear.

Tho Sun of the Soul seem to hide—
    Thick darkness enshroud the soul—
(Shaking her faith, grieving her heart,
    Till she almost forgets her high goal;)

Away with such puerile despair!
    Deep anguish and needless plight!
But swift-footed, run to greet our Sun—
    With burning love and delight!

Ric Photo

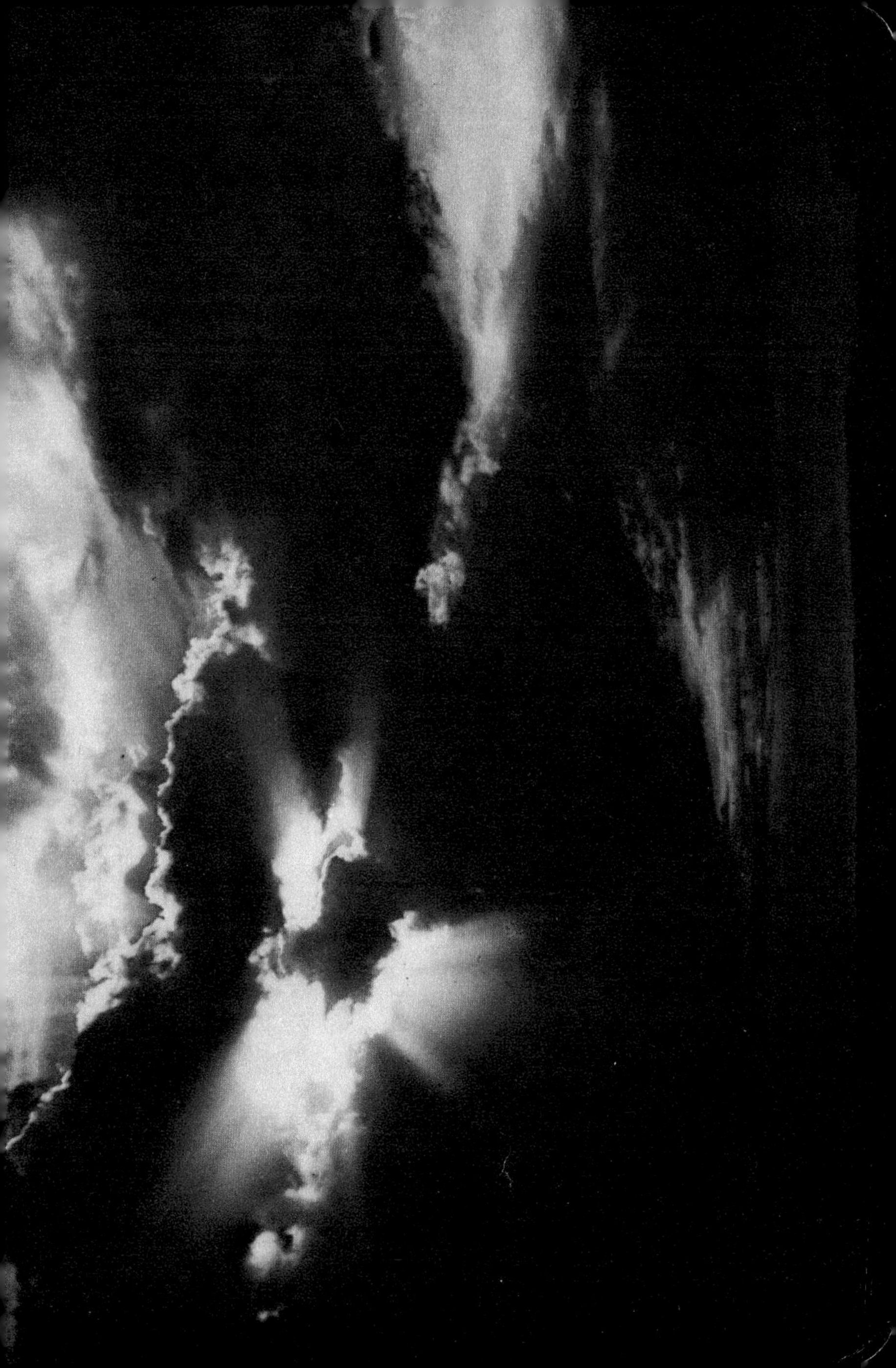

Whirlpool

The human soul is unstable as water.
A breath, a trifle, a leaf that is turned,
Suffice to disquiet and to disturb.

On peaceful paths,
Tranquility enters softly.
This calm is brief. The unforseen is life.

Ever seized upon anew by the ancient misery,
The soul passes from amazement to anger—
And knows not how to taste the joy of the Lord.

Forgetful that sadness is accomplice of pride,
The subconscious abandons itself to self-torture.
Round and round go the whirling thoughts in sadistic
delight.

(Though full well it knows that this tender compliance
Banishes afar off the God who is peace.)
The soul tortures itself—and God waits.

Holy Virgin, hasten the day,
When rising above Life's jolts and jars,
I find my happiness in Christ's peace!

Niagara River Rapids
Ric Photo

The Offering of the Bread

115—From what sort of bread is the host made? What does the Church wish to teach us thereby?

The host of the Mass is formed from the purest of wheat, and is unleavened; that is, made without yeast.

This has a symbolic significance.

Leaven typifies whatever is impure, bad, and not in accord with the Christian spirit.

Therefore, the host of the Mass must be immaculate, spotless.

Now (as we have said in question 111) by virtue of your Baptism, you participate in the action of the priest and have the privilege of offering Mass with him.... *You should also celebrate YOUR Mass like the priest....* Now your Mass is your life, begun at Baptism and continuing into eternity—your life offered with Christ's life on the altar.

To say Mass, the priest needs a host.

You, too, in order to celebrate your mystic Mass, need a host. But where are you to get it? Listen to St. Augustine as he says to you: "Do not seek *without,* the host you need; this host is to be found within." St. Paul completes the clarification by saying: "I exhort you... to present your bodies as a sacrifice... holy, pleasing to God." (Rom. 12:1.)

So you have your host—yourself—but it should have some resemblance to that of the priest.

We have just seen what purity the Church requires for the host of the Mass. You ought then to rid yourself from every trace of this sorry leaven that defiles body and soul....

Every morning, ask yourself if you are ready to celebrate YOUR Mass.... If your body is fit to be a living host, "holy and acceptable to God"?...

Ask yourself if you always respect your body so as to be able to offer it to the Blessed Trinity every moment of your life?... For YOUR Mass should not last a mere half-hour only.... It should be an uninterrupted offering even into eternity!...

Ask yourselves again if you are helping others to respect their bodies—their host—or if you are not rather, by your immodesty, your audacity, your flirting with evil... like the leaven that defiles both body and soul... and by that very fact, keeping others from celebrating THEIR Mass, and so depriving God of the praise due to him?...

Look within, in mind, will, and heart, in your feelings, for the thing that is too natural, too human, that is not altogether worthy of a true Christian; and then tear it out; destroy it! Every day, divest yourself of whatever is unchristian; purify, sanctify yourself. Every day, become more spiritual, purer, holier. Then your host will resemble the priest's and become a little less unworthy of being offered with it....

116—Describe the priest's gestures when offering the host.

After reading the antiphon called the "Offertory," the priest removes the veil and pall covering the Chalice; takes in his hands the paten on which the whole host reposes and raises his eyes a moment toward the crucifix. Then, fixing his gaze on the host, he recites the prayer, *Suscipe*—"Receive, Holy Father." Before placing the host on the corporal, he makes the sign of the cross with the paten.

117—The celebrant offers God the entire host.... Is there not another lesson for us here?

Yes, there is. The priest keeps back nothing. It is the *entire* host that he offers to God.

You, too, must offer up self as your "host." Take your whole self, witholding nothing, and offer yourself to God.

Take your body with all its senses, your soul with all its faculties, your mind with all its thoughts, your will with all its willing and desiring, your heart with all its affections; take your daily life with its work, its struggles, its sufferings, and efforts; take your prayers and all your good deeds and say to God: "Dear Lord, all this I offer you. It is all yours!"

Let us consecrate to God
Our humble lives, our modest arts.
On the paten with the Host
Let us offer him our hearts.

This oblation of self will be joyous, if generous and complete.... The Rich Young Man of the Gospel went away sad because he was unwilling to offer God all his riches, when God asked them of him....

"Who gives less than all, is grieved that he gives at all.
All sharing here below is heart-breaking or heart-rending.
If it is but half of my heart that I give,
Then it is my whole heart I deliver to martyrdom.
But if I give fully, not counting the cost,
It is filled with light and joy.
Love is all-engulfing—it will have *all* its prey.
Love's suffering knows no pain."

Let us not be like Cain, who offered the Lord only what was most vile—the leavings.... But let us, like Abel, offer the best that we have—the best of our heart, whatever we love most.... Let us offer God a *whole* host. Let us offer him all that we are and do—keeping back nothing. *Let God do with us what he will....*

118—Why is the bread on the paten called a "host"?

Because this bread is destined—by virtue of the Consecration—to become the Body of Christ: Victim, or true Host of the Sacrifice.

Since we ourselves are the host of our mystical Mass, it follows that once we have offered ourselves, we must consent to accept our glorious rôle as victim—and this to the end of our life, helping Jesus to bear his redeeming Cross, weighted down with the fearsome burden of every crime, of all human ingratitude—thus filling up in our flesh—for the world's salvation—whatever is lacking in the Passion of Christ.

PRAYER OF THE YOUNG CATHOLIC WORKER

Lord Jesus, who were a worker like us, grant me and my fellow-workers, and all workers' families, to work with you, to think like you, to pray through you, to work with you, to give you my strength and my time. May your Kingdom come in factory and workshop, in the office, at home, on the street, on earth as in Heaven.

May you be everywhere better known, loved, and served. Deliver us forever from injustice and envy, from all evil; and from all sin.

May the souls of all workers in danger remain in your grace, or promptly recover it, if lost.

And by your mercy, may the souls of workers fallen on the worker's field of honour rest in peace. Amen.

119—Are there degrees to this offering of self at Mass?

Certainly. We spoke a while back of the "'total gift," of the "complete offering." It now remains to be specific, by adding: "Within the limits of our state of life."

The offering of a soul consecrated to God by the vows of religion will doubtless be much superior in degree to the offering of a husband or wife, because their hearts are shared.... Speaking of the excellency of celibacy, St. Paul observed: "So a woman who is free of wedlock, or a virgin, is concerned with the Lord's claim, intent on holiness, bodily and spiritual; whereas the married woman is concerned with the world's claim, asking how she is to please her husband." (I Cor. 7:34.) [Knox.]

If the life of every Christian must be marked with the "seal of sacrifice," the life of every consecrated soul must be marked with the "seal of holocaust. . . ."

Do you see the difference?

Sacrifice may have several degrees in the matter and form of the gift.... A holocaust has only one degree, which is totality—the entire oblation of self until death! This is Love's augmented offering!

The Tertiary, by his profession, is held to a more generous offering of self than is the ordinary Christian.. . just because he has received more and promised more....

It is certain that we shall give to God in the measure that we love him, and we shall love him in the measure that we know his love for us.... The crucifix is still the most revealing book.... Our Lord on the Cross shows us his Divine Heart, wounded for love of us.

The love of God is demanding. The more we give him, the more he asks.... The more Jesus asks of us, the more he desires to give us.... His Divine Heart begs for our love simply because it overflows with love! He asks us for our tiny, cold, and selfish hearts, so as to put in their place his own big, generous Heart, burning with love for us!

"I am relying on you," He tells us, at once adding. "You can rely on Me!"

How is it possible that such an invitation still meets with resistance?

These are the exigencies of divine love which frighten many souls and keep them back from the total gift of self. They still do not love the

Master enough, who by his death on the Cross made it impossible for us *not* to love him! . . .

Starting today, let us always try to die a little bit more to self; so as not to impede the work of grace within us, and thus hinder God from taking full possession of our hearts. Yes, let us strive to diminish the share of self, and increase God's share. Let us take great care to purify our intentions, so that our acts may lose none of their merits. We know that if at the day's close, the share of self is 40—30—20—10—0, God's share will be 60—70—80—90—100, and we shall have attained totality in giving.

Let us ask ourselves this question here: "What is God suggesting that I offer him right now?" . . . What act? . . . What sacrifice? . . . "

Then, unhesitatingly, place all on the paten, that we may become hosts by the completest possible immolation of our tastes, opinions, and will. . . .

120—What are "hosts for priests"?

We call "hosts for priests" those generous souls who pray, sacrifice, and immolate themselves for the sanctification of priests and the fruitfulness of their ministry.

After the priesthood itself, could there be a more beautiful vocation?

A source of greater merit?

It has been well said: "Working on priests is working on multipliers," or again, as St. Thérèse of the Child Jesus put it, "It is doing business wholesale"!

For the priest is not saved alone, and alas, is not lost alone. The priest will enter Heaven with an innumerable number of elect; or he will fall into Hell followed by a multitude of lost souls, who will forever be his shame and confusion.

"Contributing to the vocation and sanctification of just one priest, means snatching souls from Hell and working toward the salvation of an entire population." "Making a holy priest," said Msgr. de Ségur, "means saving thousands of souls."

"Making good priests," declared St. Vincent de Paul, "means working at a masterpiece, beyond which one can think of nothing greater or more important! Oh, what a great thing it is to be a good priest! What conversions may he not obtain! What the pastor may be, so are the people."

We hear many criticisms today about priests.... *If instead of criticizing, we prayed for them to become saints,* don't you think it would be better?

You no doubt have a high idea of the priesthood, and when you meet a priest, you expect to meet a saint. You are quite right. Every priest ought to be a saint. Unfortunately, this is not the case. The priest has his faults, a fallen nature like your own, and temptations perhaps greater than yours.... The Devil works harder to ruin one priest than he does to ruin a hundred laymen; for well he knows that the priest who saves his soul will save many other souls; and that the priest who loses his soul will drag down many other souls with him in his fall.

All these considerations, of course, do not justify the weaknesses of certain unfortunate priests.... But be sure of one thing. Criticizing them is not the way to make saints of them. Instead, you will draw down upon yourselves the curse of God; you will scandalize your hearers; and perhaps fall yourselves into greater faults....

Let us pray for them, then, and pray to God for holy priests. Not just good priests, but holy priests. Do not be afraid of asking too much of God—this does him honour. He is not like men, but is rich *and* generous.

It is to the advantage of the faithful to pray for the sanctification of the clergy, for they are first to benefit from them.

A holy priest makes the people fervent.
A fervent priest makes the people good.
A good priest makes the people mediocre.
A mediocre priest makes the people bad.
A bad priest makes the peoples impious.

Hence, the heavy responsibility of the priesthood. The priest says to himself, "I am the yeast which ought to make the dough rise! I am the salt, and must answer for whatever around me has lost its strength. I am the beam; and if the building crashes, God is going to ask *me* why! I am the lighthouse God has set up to shine in the darkness; and if so many unfortunate souls are lost, perhaps it is because of my ineptness—because I am night in the night, instead of Christ's burning lamp....

Generous readers who read these lines, can you still hesitate a single instant to become "hosts for priests"? Can you refuse to priests this assistance they expect of you?... This sublime vocation may be embraced not only by religious but also by all laymen.

That was why on August 3, 1908, St. Pius X was able to write: "We rejoice at the thought that a large number of faithful of every condition, are preoccupied with the welfare of the clergy and of the Church, uniting themselves to Us; and it is no less pleasing to Us to learn that there are many generous souls, not only in the cloister, but likewise in the world; who, in an uninterrupted oblation, present themselves as victims to God to this end."

Monsignor Ambroise Leblanc, O.F.M., has written a booklet entitled: *Hosties Sacerdotales;* from which we extract a couple of pages, the better to show their rôle and practice.

"The more you are hosts, the more they will be priests"! And naturally, a soul will say to herself, "The less I am a host, the less they will be priests"! This pertinent reflexion is no less an incentive to sacrifice and heroism. If priests are "less priests," the glory they will give to God will be less; souls saved will be fewer; the number of the damned will be greater. Who would dare assume such a responsibility?

A soul who has understood the rôle of host, can no longer refuse anything to God. For priests she prays; for priests she sacrifices herself; for priests, she would even despoil herself of all her merits in order to enrich them. Like St. Catherine of Siena, like St. Teresa of Avila, or St. Thérèse of the Child Jesus, this soul makes the sanctification of the souls of priests the constant object of all her efforts. She lets no opportunity slip by.

Misunderstood, she does not complain. She offers her sufferings to God. May she merit for priests the grace to understand souls! So many souls who are misunderstood, thus fail to give their full measure!

Does she suffer from insomnia? She is almost happy.

One day I visited a young shut-in twenty-two years old, bedfast from a form of rheumatism declared incurable by the doctors. Her livid features told a tale of sleepless nights.

"You didn't sleep much, child," I remarked.

"Very little, Father!... But I found the night so short! I thought of the missionaries in distant lands for whom I had resolved to suffer. . . . It seemed to me as if my illness would do them good, and I felt so happy!"

Criticism and calumny apparently leave her unmoved. Not so! A delicate soul, she suffers. Yet, she does not ask God to remove this chalice. She drinks it in silence. She desires to preserve priests from whatever might cast discredit on their ministry. To merit this benefit, she is ready to sacrifice her reputation. If a priest has the misfortune to forget his priestly dignity, prayers and sacrifices are redoubled. She is inconsolable. Gladly would she wash this stain away with her blood; and just so long as it still remains, she will cover it with her royal mantle of charity.

She accords herself no rest. She is ready for every task. Is it given her to choose? She reserves for herself the most painful and humble task. To hear her tell it, she is *never* tired! What is the secret of her energy? She hopes to merit needed strength for priests. Is it not to such souls that certain priests owe their long and fruithful careers?

Suffering fails to daunt her. She cheerfully confronts it. She forbids herself all complaint, but keeps smiling. Her sufferings—if God wills to accept them—will preserve the precious health of priests. How many souls even offer up their lives for priests! I understand them. They could not sacrifice themselves for a more noble cause."

St. Thérèse of the Child Jesus made this reply one day to her nurse who gently chided her—with her feeble strength—for walking in the garden. "I am walking," she answered with a smile, "for a missionary who can go no further."

Let us listen to her once more in these touching lines addressed to her sister: "In the brief moments still remaining to us, let us not

PRAYER FOR A LAY APOSTLE

O Lord Jesus, who created the Apostles; grant to me and to all my companions, to work with you, to live in you, to give you my strength and my time.

Give me the strength joyfully to radiate a fully Christian life; at home, at work, on the street, in my dealings with my neighbour. Let me remember that I am responsible for souls. Make me worthy to be a missionary of your light, and an apostle of peace and joy, to youth forgetful of you.

Through your mercy, may all lay apostles who love you; who work and suffer to extend your reign; merit to enjoy with you, our Leader, a blessed eternity. Amen.

waste time, but save souls. I know that Jesus asks us to quench his thirst by giving him souls, especially souls of priests. . . . Yes, let us pray for priests. Let our lives be devoted to them." On the eve of her profession, she declared, "I came to Carmel to save souls and to pray for priests."

For her, it is a conviction. Whoever does not pray, does not immolate himself for priests, cannot flatter himself that he loves God.

"To live by love, this is, O Divine Master,
To beg of thee to pour thy sacred fire
Into the chosen, holy soul of this, thy priest.
Make him more pure than Heaven's seraphim!
Protect thy Church immortal—I beg of thee—
Each moment of the day.
Her child, I immolate myself for her.
I live by love!"

Elsewhere, Little Thérèse had chanted her prayer:

"I would have the soul of a priest
Resemble an angel in Heaven.
I would have him born again
Before he ascends thine altar!"

She has no illusions. Such miracles are the fruit of ardent prayer and of long immolation. Thus she adds:

"That this miracle may take place,
Many souls burning with love,
Day and night, near the tabernacle,
Must immolate themselves."

It is plain that this rôle of *host for priests* is simply sublime! Should you wish from now on to be counted among this army of generous souls, devoted to the cause of the priesthood, you will find below a truly inspired prayer written by Sister Louise Marguerite Claret de la Touche, and dictated by Jesus himself. For the Sacred Heart made—between 1900-1915—several revelations to this fervent Visitation sister, concerning the sanctification of priests. In particular, he asked her to found the League for Priests, whose purpose is to obtain abundant graces for Catholic priests, and to group priests with a view to a more successful collaboration in the expansion of the reign of Infinite Love—the Sacred

Heart himself! Here is the prayer, which we urge you to say daily, if possible. In return, the Sacred Heart will give you, as he did to Sister Louise Marguerite, the soul of a priest!

A Prayer to Jesus, the Eternal High Priest

O Jesus, eternal High Priest, divine Sacrificer, you who in an unspeakable burst of love for men, your brothers, caused the Christian priesthood to spring forth from your Sacred Heart, vouchsafe to pour forth upon your priests continual living streams of infinite love.

Live in them, transform them into yourself. Make them by your grace, fit instruments of your mercy. Act in them and through them, and grant that they may become wholly one with you by their faithful imitation of your virtues; and, in your name and by the strength of your spirit, may they do the works which you accomplished for the salvation of the world.

Divine Redeemer of souls, behold how great is the multitude of those who still sleep in the darkness of error; reckon up the number of those unfaithful sheep who stray to the edge of the precipice; consider the throngs of the poor, the hungry, the ignorant and feeble, who groan in their abandoned condition.

Return to us in the person of your priests; truly live again in them; act through them and pass once more through the world, teaching, comforting, sacrificing, and renewing the sacred bonds of love between the Heart of Jesus and the heart of man. Amen. (December, 1903.)

On those days when you are "snowed under" by extra work, you may use in place of the preceding, the following prayer, shorter (but equally efficacious) for the sanctification of priests.

A prayer for priests

O Jesus, live in your priest! Transform him into you. Make him by your grace, the instrument of your mercy. Act in and through him. Cause him to be clothed with you by the faithful imitation of the adorable virtues of your Sacred Heart. Make him a saviour of souls and a saint. Amen.

121—What prayer is said by the priest when he offers the host? Are you able to explain its meaning?

The celebrant takes the paten with the host; raises his eyes to Heaven as a mediator; then lowers them to the host as a sinner. He places his heart, together with the hearts of all those present and of all Christians everywhere, on the paten; that he may receive them back again, no longer in their present form; but renewed, changed, transformed, as soon the host will be. He then says the *Suscipe*:

Suscipe, sancte Pater, omnipotens, aeterne Deus, hanc immaculatam hostiam, quam ego indignus famulus tuus offero tibi Deo meo, vivo et vero, pro innumerabilibus peccatis, et offensionibus, et negligentiis meis, et pro omnibus circumstantibus, sed et pro omnibus fidelibus christianis, vivis atque defunctis: ut mihi et illis proficiat ad salutem in vitam aeternam. Amen.	Receive, O Holy Father, Almighty and Eternal God, this spotless host, which I, your unworthy servant, offer you, my living and true God, for my countless sins, offenses, and negligences; for all here present and for all faithful Christians, whether living or dead, that it may be profitable for my own and their salvation unto life everlasting. Amen.

This prayer clearly shows us to whom and for whom the Mass is offered.

Let us try to get the substance of it with a paraphrase:

Suscipe. "Receive." Take, lay hold of, everything. . . . Here I am, do what you please with me. . . . I belong to you utterly—my life, my family, my possessions—everything!

Sancte Pater, omnipotens aeterne Deus. "Holy Father, Almighty and Eternal God." O God, it is rather you who draw me, than I who give. . . . Holy Father, like Jesus, I too, your lowly creature, give you this name. Because you are all-powerful, you alone are able to answer the prayer we are about to offer. Eternal, you alone have a right to this Sacrifice.

Hanc immaculatam hostiam. "This Spotless Host." In this host, I already glimpse by faith the transformation about to take place, and call it "Spotless." Doubtless, when they come from our hands, these proffered gifts are human, earthly things. But at their terminal point, in

God's hands, they become heavenly; i.e., nothing less than the Body and Blood of Jesus Christ, under the subsisting accidents of bread and wine. Note that from our point of view, the offering, Consecration, and Communion appear to us as three successive acts—our feeble and finite minds being incapable of envisaging as a whole, the thing God sees in an eternal present. For God, Offering, Consecration, and Communion form a single action, a single whole. The denominations "past," "present," and "future" are expressive solely of the relations existing among creatures; and not of those of creatures with God.

Immaculate Host! Spotless Host! What purity should be mine in order to offer myself with Jesus!... Alas, I am far from this perfection, and I confess my unworthiness to God. This unworthiness is more keenly felt in proportion as I understand our good God better, and that I more fully grasp the dignity of my priesthood... of my Baptism... of my obligation to conform myself to the Divine Host....

Quam ego indignus famulus tuus. "Which I, your unworthy servant." This "self" of the sinner, this egoistical "I," wherein is comprised so much that is base, so much that is cowardly, so much of malice... this proud "I," so absurdly pleased with what it is, possesses, and does; which outside itself sees only mediocrity and nullity.... This jealous, tyrannical "I," whose motto is "Everything for me, and nothing for others." This susceptible, suspicious "I," itself the author of its sufferings; who envisions itself surrounded by people busily engaged in raising up difficulties that exist only in its own imagination—a word, a gesture, a trifle, are enough to arouse its suspicions.... And it is just this poor "I," convinced of its unworthiness (but still more of God's mercy); who comes to offer up the Spotless Lamb, and itself with him.

Offero tibi Deo meo, vivo et vero. "I offer this Host to you, my living and true God." What worlds lie between these two words, "I," and "God." Despite the infinite disproportion existing between the unworthy servant that I am, and you, my living and true God, the innumerable proofs of your merciful pursuit of your defiled and guilty creature, embolden me to offer you this Host. I offer it to you, living God and Source of life; as guilty humanity lavishes its incense on the vain "real life" idols of money, the flesh, and this world's fleeting honours.... I offer it to you, the only true God and Master of Truth; the while mankind prefers those masters who charm them and deceive....

Pro innumerabilibus peccatis, et offensionibus, et negligentiis meis. "For my countless sins, offences, and negligences." This is the ledger of my life.... Here, as in the *Confiteor,* I can plumb the depths of humility, without discouragement.... The sight of my sins is well calculated to increase my gratitude. Being perhaps more sinful than others, I feel that I have a greater share in the divine redemption—that I have been more loved.... This is the consolation repentance brings. There where the offence has abounded, grace has abounded yet more.... I love to feel this weakness which renders my Jesus more needful.... I was lost without him; I seem to belong doubly to him now....

Let us examine each clause separately:

"For my sins." I offer you the Host for my willful, deliberate sins: the despising of the divine friendship, the denial of the divine authority, the continual resistance to grace, the systematic pitting of my pride-swollen ego against Him who is my Master and Father, the Principle and Law of my being and activity; the repeated falls due to a lack of sincere contrition, the discouragements harboured through lack of deep faith and love, the undying resentments....

"For my offences." I offer you the Host for my offences: for this lack of courtesy, these wounded feelings, these thorns pressed by my fingers into a human heart—these "wounds of friendship," which though they may not take on the malice of actual sin, are nonetheless keenly felt by a Friend whose tender love surrounds me on all sides.... My offences: the long forgetfulness of God's presence, self-complacency over advantages, success, or praise, whose honour should revert to God; negligence in the Master's service, stemming from routine and loss of zeal; careless speech, degenerating into thoughtless, uncharitable criticism; loosing the bond of charity, the while it troubles my recollection....

"For my negligences." I offer you the Host for my negligences: for the half-hearted efforts, the lack of courage, the despicable boundary lines drawn between the thing that is permitted, and the thing that is out-and-out sin; the prolonged periods of tepidity, the zeal slowed down, and the effort taken to dampen down—short of absolute betrayal—Duty's stern demands. In brief, all the miserable alloying of base lead to the pure gold of charity!...

The prophet does not exaggerate when he affirms the heartbreaking reality: "The sinner drinks down iniquity like water." Still

"Happy fault, which merited so great a Redeemer." So sings the Church with great joy when celebrating the New Passover.

Pro omnibus circumstantibus. "For all those present." Though an unworthy creature, I, too, ought to offer the Host for others. I offer it then, first of all, for those present with me; who join their offering to mine and to yours. Here is seen the importance and advantage of participating body and soul in the Mass, since the congregation is counted among the first to benefit.

Pro omnibus fidelibus christianis, vivis atque defunctis. "For all faithful Christians, whether living or dead." And then the offering is extended to all the members of the Mystical Body of Christ, even to the souls in Purgatory.... The Church, like a good mother, thinks of all her children!... And we? Do we sometimes think of others?... Each one of my Masses, then, has a universal repercussion; it is going to bring grace to all the faithful, relief to all the souls in Purgatory!

Ut mihi et illis proficiat ad salutem in vitam aeternam. "That it may be profitable for my own and their salvation unto life everlasting." For all, for myself and for them, I make the essential request: "salvation and life everlasting"—final union with Christ. These words are short, but they say the one thing needful, the end of every life—God and eternal happiness!

122—When the priest offers the host, he recites the prayer, *Suscipe*, wherein he indicates the intentions for which he celebrates. Have we, too, thought to express our intentions here?

Like the celebrant, at this moment of the Offertory, *list your intentions,* saying something like this to God:

Lord, I offer myself to you in a spirit of sacrifice to expiate the sins of my past life, my offences, and all my negligences....

Lord, I offer myself to you as the living host of my family. I want to be sacrificed so that my parents, friends, and all those most in need may be sanctified, blessed, and saved.

Lord, I offer myself to you as the living host of this work (Third Order, Catholic Action, etc.) in which I am interested and to which I am devoting myself—I want to be sacrificed that this work may live and prosper.

Lord, I offer myself to you as the living host of your priests. I want to be sacrificed so as to come to the assistance of your ministers —so that their priesthood may be holy and fruitful.

Lord, I offer myself as the living host of poor sinners; particularly those for whom I feel antipathy or indifference. I want to be sacrificed in order to be associated in Christ's Redemption—to make reparation, atone, and merit in union with him.

Lord, I offer myself as the living host of your holy will. I want to be sacrificed so that I may become holy; so that I may go on to the end of my vocation of "host"; so that I may carry out all my mission; so that I may fulfill all your plans for my life.

Lord, I offer myself to you as the living host of your Love! I want to be sacrificed so that your name may be hallowed, your Kingdom come, your will be done, and you yourself better glorified and loved.

If you do this, your apostolate will be wide in scope and will bear fruit. More than ever before, the world has need of holy and generous souls, who, as "living hosts," are dedicated to immolation and sacrifice. Ally yourself, then, to these consecrated souls united to Christ crucified. Men will never know the supernatural, sanctifying, and fruitful ministry, which, in the secret of your immolation, you will exercise around you. But God who knows all, will give you an eternal reward.

These few intentions suggested by the prayer, *Suscipe,* of the Offertory, make no pretense at completeness. You can add your personal petitions to them; but whatever you add, your offering is never finished. At every moment of the day and night, you ought to complete and renew it in such a way that your life becomes a continual oblation. If you do this, you can truly say that your Mass is your life and your life is your Mass.

AN ACT OF OFFERING

Sister Mary Elizabeth of the Trinity, a contemplative of the Assumption, who died a holy death at Sceaux, France, at the age of twenty-seven; wrote down on the day of her first vows the following devout act of offering, which we would encourage you to make your own:

"Dear God, I unite to the Sacrifice that Jesus offers you on this altar, this oblation that I make to you of my whole being. Poor little drop of water that I am, pour me into the chalice that I may be lost therein; and so that your Beloved Son alone may live in me. May I be with Jesus, and like him, a host of praise to your glory alone—to you who are our Father, the Father of Jesus and my Father. My offering is not worthy; but look only on the superabundant merits of Him who has chosen me for his spouse, and receive from His hands the offering I make to you with so much joy.

"Jesus, my Beloved, my Spouse, I give myself to you; I will all; I accept all; I ask of you only one thing—yourself! You it is whom I want—you alone. I give up all things to cling only to you. Deliver me from myself. Teach me to immolate myself like you in silence, to unite my prayers and sufferings to yours, and to the great intentions of your Heart—the Church, the Pope, the Assumption, priests, sinners, the souls in Purgatory, and the whole world.

"Holy Spirit, set me on fire with love; unite me to my Spouse—you who are the bond between Father and Son—may we be two in one flesh. Draw me within, so that I may sing the eternal Sanctus in the heaven of my soul by a continual adoration. Never permit me to take myself back again. Defend me against myself; make me docile and faithful like Mary, my Mother and my model. Amen."

The Mingling of the Water and the Wine

123—What does the celebrant do after offering the host?

The priest goes to the Epistle side of the altar, wipes the chalice with the purificator; then holding the chalice in his left hand, receives the cruet of wine and pours some into the chalice. He then makes the sign of the cross over the cruet containing the water; and as he says the prayer, *Deus qui humanae...* he lets fall a few drops into the chalice.

124—What is represented by: (1) the wine? (2) the water? and (3) the mingling of water and wine?

1. The wine is the figure or symbol of Jesus Christ, more especially of his divinity.

2. The drop of water has several meanings:

a. *It recalls the Last Supper.* The Jews had a custom of diluting their wine with water. Jesus of course conformed to this custom.

b. It recalls the blood and water that sprang from the heart of Jesus Christ, when pierced by the lance.

c. It represents our *human nature* wounded by original sin and inclined to evil.

d. Finally, it is the symbol of the Church or Mystical Body, and signifies the *daily participation* of Christian people in the Passion of Jesus Christ.

(St. Bernard offers us a suggestive comparison between the water and the wine. He compares the water to the fear of God, and the wine to charity.)

3. The mingling of the water and wine typifies the union of Christ and his Church—the union of my sacrifices to Christ's Sacrifice.

This last is the traditional teaching. Observe what St. Cyprian (+258) says: "The wine is the symbol of Christ's blood, the water, of Christians. When the water is mingled with the wine in the chalice, the people are united to Christ. And the commingling of water and wine is such that they cannot thenceforth be separated. So it is of the union of Christ and the Church."

St. Cyprian pushes this symbolism still further: "We cannot offer the water alone, just as one cannot offer the wine alone. For if one were to offer only wine, the blood of Christ would be present without us; while, if there were only water, the people would be present without Christ. But when the two are mingled and confounded in intimate union, then the spiritual and celestial Sacrament is realized."

Thus, offering wine alone, would be to offer Christ without ourselves.

Offering water alone, would be offering ourselves without Christ.

And since in the Holy Sacrifice, Christ, the Head of the Mystical Body, integrates his members into his oblation, a little water must be added to the wine.

The faithful are not only co-offerers, but are truly *co-offered* with Christ.

Every morning, when they participate in the oblation of the Mass, those present pour into the chalice of Christ's Sacrifice—like the tiny drop of water lost in the wine—the sum total of the sacrifices that their fidelity to grace demands of each one in the course of the day.

125—Show how this mingling of the water and wine at Mass illustrates in a striking manner how our lives are enriched when they are added to Christ's life. Demonstrate also how the more we offer, the richer we grow.

We have said that the tiny drop of water represents human nature wounded by sin. Left to himself, there is no folly, sin, crime, or infamy of which man is not capable. But with the help of grace, the soul can master the rebellious flesh and achieve great sanctity.

Water of itself has neither colour, strength, taste, nor flavour.

Added to the wine, the tiny drop of water is absorbed by the abundance and generosity of the wine; indicative of the superabundance of the Redemption, and the infinite generosity of Jesus in applying it to us. That is why the priest adds to the wine the little drop of water of our unworthiness, misery, and weakness; so that it may be sustained, perfected, and sanctified by its union with the bounteous and divine wine that makes virgins.

As this water is commingled with the wine, and presently, absorbed by it, will be transformed into the Blood of Christ; in the same way, I should lose myself in Christ's divinity, if I wish to be perpetually united to him; and enter in a certain manner into the Holy Trinity, by reason of my union with the Eternal Son—becoming fully integrated into him.

Now our lives, activities, and sacrifices, taken by themselves, are of little worth. To use another metaphor, they are like lead alongside our Lord's Sacrifice, the Mass, which is pure gold.

Imagine, for a moment, that I have a magic wand that can turn into gold all the lead it touches. Now because you are all my friends, I announce that I am going to change into gold all the lead you bring me. If you bring me a small quantity of lead, you will receive a small quantity of gold; but if you bring me a large amount of lead, you will go away with a large amount of gold!

Were this to happen, how many would refuse my invitation?... or would be satisfied to bring me just a small amount of lead?

How is it that at Mass, there are so few faithful who come to offer their small sacrifices—however insignificant they appear to be—for Jesus to transform, transfigure, and by the Consecration, make them count for eternity? Why are our churches so deserted?

And yet the Mass is the only way to make our lives full and complete and pleasing to God. Christ, the "Divine Elevator," is the only Mediator between God and man, and the only One in whom the Father is well pleased. So it will be only by losing ourselves in Him, and offering ourselves with Him and through Him that we shall succeed. Without Him we can do nothing for Heaven.

THE MORE WE OFFER, THE RICHER WE GROW!

We just gave a little demonstration of this when we talked about the lead changed into shining gold bars, whose size would depend on the amount of lead brought.

Here is another example that illustrates this truth clearly, so much the more so because it is taken from the Gospel—the water changed into wine.

The story of the Wedding of Cana is too well known to be recounted here. Let us retain, then, the simple words: "Fill the jars with water. And they filled them to the brim."

What does the Master teach us in this brief passage?

Jesus asks us here for *our co-operation*. It is not God's way to "do it all alone." He asks us to bring him the part that depends on *us. He* will see to the rest!

Is water all that we have? Then let us bring water!

Do we have anything more? Something more precious? Then let us bring that. But let us never be content with merely folding our arms when we ask for God's intervention; especially when it has to do with something so important as our sanctification!

God gives his grace in abundance. It is only fair that we should give him our best efforts.

At the Wedding of Cana, the servants worked with a will. As everybody knows, there was no running water or plumbing in the Jewish homes of this period. The well may have been far from the village. It certainly must have taken more than one trip to the well to fill the jars. . . . If *we* had been in the place of the servants, *we* might have said after one or two trips: "That's enough. They're half full (or two-thirds full) now. Let's quit. . . . Anyway, this doesn't make sense! Here these folks are out of wine, and he makes us fill these jars with water!"

Think what the servants would have missed, if they *had* reasoned like that!

(But how many graces do *we* miss by dampening down our generosity and zeal in the service of God and our neighbour!)

The servants had only water, but their very poverty brought out God's infinite riches.

The same thing applies to us. Let us have no illusions. That which is ours to pour into eternity's jars, is insipid and worthless: a few good intentions, a few desires for perfection, a few charitable actions—the whole miserable mixture often spoiled by our too human views about it. When at life's close, we look back on the past, we are filled with foreboding at never having poured into the divine amphora anything less insipid and less significant than these....

Yet, even though we had, like the servants, discharged our duty to the end; filled our "jars" up to the brim; kept on till we could do no more; even then the Good Master would repeat the charitable warning he gave to his apostles: "When you have done all that was commanded you, you are to say, 'We are servants and worthless: it was our duty to do what we have done.'" [Knox.]

Alas, how seldom are our "jars" full! Through carelessness, selfishness, and greed; through sensuality and indolence, perhaps through fear that if we do *too* well, the Master will ask of us something harder, more fatiguing (it's the willing horse that does all the work, you know); we have watered down our service and kept for ourselves the talent that belonged to the Lord. We have said to ourselves, "After all, God does not ask us to do more than is strictly required, and keep the counsels." It is true that there is a difference between a Commandment and a counsel.... Jesus did not tell the servants to fill the jars to the brim—he left it to them to understand all that he wanted. But our specious wisdom, our niggardliness, our clever quibblings, are, in the last analysis, nothing but a series of shameful acts of selfishness, of futile evasions of duty; which enslave us and keep us from pouring into our lives their full maximum of faithfulness and generosity....

Because we have been unwilling to be wholeheartedly in the Master's service, like children who love with their whole heart, run with both legs, and shed all their tears; because we have claimed to behave like men (which often means like beings diminished by calculated self-interest); we have deprived ourselves of the happiness that comes from duty well done and from the total offering of self—and we have diminished the gifts that the Lord was disposed to give us.

The more we offer, the richer we grow.

Lord, that I may offer you an oblation pleasing to you and profitable for me (for in your goodness you have willed that we should be unable to work at increasing our merits without augmenting your glory, nor contribute to augmenting your glory without increasing our merits); I want to fill my mind with light—as much as it can hold—my will to the brim with strong love, my memory with wholesome thoughts and everlasting hopes, and devote all my energy to the daily task—in a word, to fulfill my humble, drab, and humdrum duty, to serve you as you deserve to be served, and to love my neighbour with my whole soul, heart, and strength.

You need hearts filled to overflowing, that you overwhelm with your gifts; for all the water poured into the jars of Cana was transformed by you into a bounteous and miraculous wine; so that it was this wine that the servants would have wasted, had they poured in less water. Make me understand your action, and bring me conviction that whatever I fail to give you, I lose. Remind me then that I ought to, together with the tiny drop of water that falls in the chalice, give myself to you wholly with all my treasures. On my vapid virtues may your grace descend, transforming the whole into eternal worth.

126—Why does the priest bless the tiny drop of water before adding it to the wine?

Because the tiny drop of water represents us, we shall never be pure enough and holy enough to unite ourselves to Jesus himself. That is why the priest blesses the water before adding it to the wine.

Have you noticed that the priest at a Mass for the Dead does not bless the water? This is why. The faithful for whom one prays are irrevocably sanctified—their degree of merit cannot be increased.

In allusion to this symbolism, Cardinal Mercier wrote:

"I am the tiny drop of water absorbed by the wine of the Mass, and the wine of the Mass becomes the Blood of the God-Man. And the God-Man is substantially united to the Most Holy Trinity. The tiny drop of water is carried away into the river of life of the Holy Trinity.

"Will it ever be pure enough, limpid enough, this tiny drop of water destined to participate in the Holy Sacrifice of the Mass?"

Let each one check up on himself here....

127—What does the priest say as he mingles the water with the wine in the chalice?

The priest recites this beautiful prayer which you will understand better now:

Deus, qui humanae substantiae dignitatem mirabiliter condidisti, et mirabilius reformasti: da nobis per hujus aquae et vini mysterium, ejus divinitatis esse consortes, qui humanitatis nostrae fieri dignatus est particeps, Jesus Christus Filius tuus Dominus noster: Qui tecum vivit et regnat in unitate Spiritus Sancti Deus: per omnia saecula saeculorum. Amen.	O God, who so wonderfully gave a dignity to human nature, and did more wonderfully restore it; grant by the mystery signified in the mingling of this water and wine, that we may partake of his Divinity who did partake of our humanity; namely, Jesus Christ your Son, our Lord, who lives and reigns with you in the unity of the Holy Spirit world without end. Amen.

O member of Christ, be cognizant of your dignity! Remember that you are created in the image of God. If Adam defaced it, Christ restored it. Having shared in divinity, never let your life sink back to its former level.

128—Can you show how the symbolism of the bread and wine preaches to us of our union to Christ and our brothers—the unity of the Mystical Body?

The bread and wine, substantially changed by the words of Christ at the Consecration, are richly significant. Their symbolism has been thoroughly explored from every angle.... It lends itself to numerous moral applications, as we have already seen and shall continue to see.

Bread is formed from many grains of milled wheat.... Wine is the product of many crushed grapes; in such a way, that once the bread is baked (has passed through fire), once the wine has fermented and reached the right stage, the grains and grapes no longer appear as such. We see only bread and wine.

Likewise, we have said above of the tiny drop of water dissolved in the wine, that it is transformed into wine, assuming its colour, taste, and nature; so that, the water having disappeared, we see only wine.

So it is with us. Once we are united to Christ, either by means of the Holy Eucharist, or by the offering of our whole life—of all our sacrifices in union with Christ's Sacrifice—we should no longer appear as men, but as "gods"; according to the strong expression of St. Paul, who added (logically enough): "It is no longer I that live, but Christ who lives in me."

The same holds true of the reciprocal union of the faithful. They should no longer be "isolated in common"; but form a sole body, of which Christ is the Head.

Observe that before the wheat can become fine, white bread, it must first be milled, crushed, and pass through the fire.... And before grapes can become wine, they must be crushed in a wine press.... This should serve to remind us that our union with Christ and our brothers is to be effected by suffering, by renunciation of the things we love most, by obedience for love of God.... We must be "crushed" and "baked" in the fires of tribulation and suffering.

Moreover, since the head cannot be separated from the members; Christ who is the head, having suffered, it is fitting that the members should likewise suffer.

Jesus died to give us life.... We, in turn, transmit that life by dying every day to self, so that we may rise with him. "Unless the grain of wheat fall into the ground and die, it remains alone." (John 12:24.) How many times have we proved this to be true! If our action failed to bear fruit, if our voice awakened no echo, if we "remained alone," was it not because Self was not yet dead?

Let us then die daily to self.... Let us become fair white hosts in the service of the pure and spotless Host.

129—Isn't it gloomy to speak of the Mass in connection with death?

No. Even though the Mass recalls the death of the God-Man, who was scourged, crowned with thorns, and crucified in great agony; the Church calls Christ's Passion, the "Blessed Passion."

There is a lesson in this for us. Christianity is not a religion of death but *of life.* If the Gospel invites us to die to self, let us beware of retaining only this part of its teaching. Let us follow the Divine Master's thought through to the end, so as to rise to a new life!

The sufferings of the Christian are not without hope, but are mingled with Christ's sufferings like the drop of water at the Offertory with the wine; and so they become glorious, redeeming, and blessed sufferings—sufferings with a meaning: sufferings with consolation already felt, and therefore joyous sufferings!

The Mass associates us with Christ's Passion, and also with his Resurrection. Every Mass is a "little Easter." Accepting to suffer and die with Christ, is to be already joyfully risen with him!

130—The tiny drop of water that falls into the chalice at Mass represents our life, our activity, our whole day with all its joys and sorrows. . . . In order for our offering to be as complete as possible, let us try to list the things we can put into the chalice of our daily or weekly Mass. In a word, how do we "live" our Mass?

If we lay so much stress and dwell so on this portion of the Mass, it is in order to bring out its extreme importance and value. Our sanctification depends on our offering. The more we offer, the more our lives will be enriched. This has been sufficiently shown above.

The Good Lord desires our offerings to be copious and complete, because his desire to sanctify us and make us happy is simply immense!

How are we to correspond with this ardent desire of God?

Many persons do not know what to offer. . . . Others are rather vague about it, and still others are content to offer their lives in the aggregate.

This state of affairs is not to be wondered at; for the most practical writers who have attempted to popularize the Mass for the people, have dealt in vague generalities. . . . Now generalities have seldom awakened slumbering souls emmeshed in routine, or shaken deeply-rooted prejudices!

Writers repeat to satiety that people must "live their Mass"—only they forget to tell how!

Now, before getting down to brass tacks, let us say right now that our offerings will be pleasing to God, if we are *in the state of grace* when we offer them. This is elementary.

Next, the more virtuous and perfect our acts, the more will they be pleasing and acceptable to God. It should come natural to Tertiaries to place in the chalice offerings pleasing to the Lord; since their profession pledges them to tend toward perfection in the tiniest details of their life and activity.

Therefore, since imperfect acts cannot please God, let us eliminate them from our lives. Let us think nothing, like nothing, desire nothing, want nothing, listen to nothing, say nothing, and do nothing, that we cannot offer up in our next Mass! Let us banish from our lives those thoughts, affections, desires, sights, sounds, words, and actions, that would not be pleasing to God.

It is true that all this is on the negative side. It is essential, however, to get rid of the evil in our lives before we can dream of putting any good into them.

And even when we have succeeded in filling our lives with good actions, we shall still have accomplished nothing worthwhile, until we have offered these good works in union with Christ's Sacrifice brought down on our altars. Isolated from the Mass, my life has no more value than the tiny drop of water which has not yet fallen into the chalice. Hence, the extreme importance of participating in the Mass—and of bringing to it all that we are, have, and do.

Let us see now how we are to LIVE OUR MASS; i.e. how we are to extract from our day of toil or suffering the precious ore that it contains, and which should be lovingly offered to God in union with Christ's Sacrifice.

When the priest pours the tiny drop of water into the chalice, let us offer ourselves in advance and entirely for the coming hours. Let us "lose" ourselves in God like a little drop of water in the ocean! Let us ask God to permit this drop of water to be our soul, ourself, or whatever good we have done or will do; "so that we may partake of his divinity, who did will to partake of our humanity!"

Finally (and this part is likewise very important), we shall live this offering in detail during the course of the day, in the series of acts which make up its warp and woof. We shall be LIVING our Mass!

LIVING MY MASS, then, means mingling generously with the wine (soon to be changed into the Blood of Jesus Christ) the tiny drop of water of:

A. All that I am:
  my body
  my intelligence
  my heart
  my will

B. All that I possess:
  material goods
  intellectual goods
  spiritual goods

C. All that I do:
  my activity, my apostolate

Going into the details of these practical applications, LIVING MY MASS, means offering the tiny drop of water of:

A. All that I am

1. *My body*:

Sick or well, as it pleases God....

Loaded down with infirmity, crushed under the burden of toil, fatigue, and the weather, or—standing up to daily toil and the inclemencies of the weather!

Temple of the Holy Spirit, ciborium of divinity, tabernacle in which dwells the Blessed Trinity, and hence, worthy of my reverence.

To LIVE MY MASS, I ought constantly to adorn this body with modesty... subject it to the strict discipline of chastity by:

Making it not an instrument of sensual and culpable pleasure... nor an idol for my vanity... but the instrument of sanctifying toil, of an activity favourable to my spiritual progress, of a penance that makes continuous reparation for the disorder wrought by sin....

Submitting it in keeping with its strength to the laws of *fast* and *abstinence*....

Mortifying it in its tendency to laziness, avoiding the too comfortable position. (Passing up that easy chair.)...

Making it strong and manly by compelling it to rise early, jumping out of bed at a fixed hour, so that it can carry (daily, if possible) my soul to Mass.... (To carry out this point, "Brother Ass," ought to go to bed early!)

Dominating its nerves, by mastering its impressions, "learning to like" that squeak or noise that grates on my nerves.

Caring for it when it is ill, *but forbidding it to break out in continual complaint....* The more selfish the person, the more he complains.... Broadcasting our little ills to everyone, is a good way to increase our sufferings and to make others miserable....

Mortifying its sense of taste, by not eating a single meal without imposing some little privation on it, unseen by others.... By not eating too eagerly of a favourite dish.... By not eating between meals unless necessary.... By refusing all alcoholic beverages....

Mortifying its eyes, by my custody of them, especially in the presence of persons of the opposite sex... on the street... in the company of others... in front of newstands, movie theatres, indecent billboards.... By not looking at immoral books or magazines, or at condemned films....

Preparing it for death, by making it die daily to the things it loves....

2. *My intellect*:

Intuitive, penetrating, subtle, keen, well-balanced, cultivated, or —limited, dull, deficient, dim, uncultivated.

Supernaturalized, or still imbued with the spirit of the world....

To LIVE MY MASS, I will work every day at developing my God-given talents; and so that my offering may be more abundant and more pleasing to Him, I will root out in me:

The spirit of pride, by the sincere acknowledgment that the good in me comes from God, and by always guarding against attributing the glory to myself... By avoiding talk about myself... my family... my work....

The spirit of conceit, by not believing myself superior to others.... By avoiding arrogant or insolent attitudes....

The spirit of independence, by submitting myself to established authority... to my parents... to my boss... to my superiors.... By ridding myself of the habit of always wanting to give orders... to run things... to lead....

The demanding spirit. Peremptoriness always has its source in pride.... There are persons who are never satisfied and are always demanding something or other—everyone must be at their beck and call.... They do not care whom they disturb, and they cannot wait a minute.... I will work then at being demanding toward myself and indulgent toward others.... I will not ask for special privileges or favours....

The argumentative, stubborn spirit, by ceasing my systematic opposition to the ideas of others, unless faith or morals are at stake.... Even then, I will go at it peacefully and calmly.

The lying, hypocritical spirit, by not trying to appear better than I am, nor to conceal my faults.... By doing my work as perfectly when I am alone, as when others see me....

The spirit of jealousy, by rejoicing at the success of others and trying to make them happy.... By rooting out in me the ambition for honours, for high places, and titles...

The spirit of luxury and vanity, by living in the spirit of the Third Order, being content with simple and modest furniture, clothing, and adornment.... By not making a show of those I possess.... By giving up all affectation in speech, words, tone, gesture, and mannerisms.

The spirit of murmuring, by submitting to God's will as manifested by persons in my environment, superiors, and providential happenings, and by imposing a penance on myself every time I have indulged in criticism or been lacking in charity....

The spirit of revenge, by forgiving.... This is likewise the condition required for God's forgiveness.... By speaking well of the person whose name I have blackened out of rancour.... apologizing to him... praying for him....

The spirit of anger, by refraining from speech or action when angry.... By working to acquire humility and patience....

It is not enough to tear down; I must build up, so that the chalice of my Mass will be full to overflowing.... I will strive then during my day to practice:

The spirit of humility, by:

Always seeking to decrease so that Christ may increase in me....

Remaining silent under attack....

Never excusing myself, even when I reason to do so....

Loving the last place and eschewing honours (without, however, refusing a charge imposed upon me)....

Frankly acknowledging myself to be in the wrong, with a "Yes, I was wrong," or "I made a mistake....

Patiently supporting my neighbour's faults....

Ascribing good intentions to others....

Seeking first to remove the beam out of my own eye, before taking the speck out of my neighbour's eye....

Not criticizing anyone....

Showing myself gentle and patient toward all....

Suppressing my movements of impatience and outburts of temper....

Learning to listen and to let others have the limelight... and not complaining about anyone or anything....

Not giving way to a love for finery and the desire to be noticed....

Not wasting time on vanity or spending hours at my dressing table....

Being agreeable to those I might have cause to envy....

Assuming ignorance of something I know, so as to give others the pleasure of telling it to me....

Never rereading a letter that has flattered my self-love....

Asking advice of an equal and even of an inferior....

Avoiding arguments....

Adapting myself to the opinion of others in things of little importance....

Rendering service to people of humble condition....

Giving heartfelt thanks to those having the kindness to point out my faults and try to correct me of them....

Confessing my sins sincerely and without excusing them....

The spirit of faith, by:

Believing firmly every article in my Creed...

Believing in Providence...

Not murmuring against God. . . .

Accepting trials as a gain, in the persuasion that they are permitted by God for my greater good. . . .

Seeing God hidden in my neighbour. . . in my confessor. . . in preachers. . . .

Not believing in current superstitions or in fortune tellers. . . .

Believing, but not credulous, I am going to try to understand why I believe; so that I may become the more convinced, a "fanatic" at defending my Creed—with at least as much tenacity as the Jehovah Witnesses and Communists put into tearing it down. . . .

I will study my "penny catechism," that I may have forgotten. . . .

I will be a believer in church, on the street, at the shop, at the office, at home, in my relations with others. . . .

Like a true Tertiary, I will fight against this current of apostasy, in which the sheep-like crowds are swept away. . . .

I will study my holy religion, so that I may defend it against falsehood and error. . . .

Without human respect, I shall not fear to show my displeasure at extremes in style. . . .

I will have the courage to oppose the commission of evil in my presence, and I shall insist on being treated with respect. . . .

I will advise a boy or a girl not to date those of another religion, for the marriages that follow upon mixed dating are disastrous for the faith and happiness of the couple involved and their children. . . .

I will not attend nonsectarian schools, Protestant clubs like the YMCA or YWCA, or atheistic clubs. . . .

I will combat the evils of the press and bad books. . . .

In a word, I will be a Christian in mind and heart, "at all times and in all places. . . ."

The spirit of perfection, by:

Doing perfectly whatever I do. . . .

Seeking to acquire knowledge, to develop my intellect, and form my judgment—not to dazzle others, or to become proud, but the better to serve and glorify God. . . . I will thus realize my profession in the Third Order; like the convert machinist who understood his Mass and who wrote to a friend: "A piston well made is a beautiful thing. I am always glad when I finish one. I offer it up to God—it is *my* host."

Whether it be in scrubbing floors, dusting, sewing, preparing meals, caring for the sick, educating children, writing, singing, playing, working at the office, or cultivating the soil; in class, at shop or factory, or my construction job, wherever I am and whatever I do, I will do it perfectly; so as to be able to put it into the chalice of my next Mass.

And in order to nourish my intellect on faith, humility, and perfection, every day I am going to read, reread, and meditate the Gospel and put it unhesitatingly and unswervingly into practice.

3. *My heart*:

Good, generous, devoted, loving, big, tender, sensitive, grateful, or—mean, stingy, selfish, inhuman, cold, hard, unfeeling, indifferent, ungrateful. . . .

In order to LIVE MY MASS with the heart that I have, and that I am going to strive to perfect so as to give it entirely to God; I will detach it from three things that enslave it—riches, creatures, and myself—and at the same time I will attach it to God, my ALL!

I will detach my heart from riches:

How?

By avoiding falling into avarice. The miserly person often excuses himself by saying that he is simply exercising prudence and economy. Of course, it is a good thing to be economical, but let us not exaggerate economy to the point of distrusting Providence and refusing to give needed assistance to the poor and to the Lord's work.

By eschewing luxury and unnecessary expense. . . .

By avoiding all excess in my clothing and dress. . . .

By loving the humble, the outcasts, the penniless, despised of the rich. . . .

By being content with what is strictly necessary, in imitation of Christ's poverty, and to bear some resemblance to St. Francis of Assisi, patron of Catholic Action. . . .

I will detach my heart from persons:

By keeping watch over my affections from their beginning. . . .

By a ruthless, even relentless, breaking off of forbidden affections.

By not permitting myself any inordinate natural affection. We know that natural love can degenerate into passion when one thinks too frequently of the same person; when one continually seeks his company; when one finds it hard not to be with that person; when one worries too much about what he is doing; when thoughts, and outer tokens of friendship, such as letters, telephone calls, visits, etc., are too frequent; when one feels jealous if that person is more interested or equally interested in someone other than ourselves; when just thinking about it brings temptations, stirs up emotions, etc.

By loving everybody in God and for God. . . .

By praying wholeheartedly for those persons to whom I am "allergic", and by doing them a favour with a smile. . . .

By never needlessly going out of my way to meet someone for whom I feel an exaggerated affection. . . but rather going with those whom I find less likeable. (Our Lord was accused of associating with the poor and humble. . . .)

By never questioning a third person about another of whom I am fond. . . .

By waiting a while before opening letters awaited with impatience. . . and by destroying them after I have read them. . . .

By accepting the bereavements sent by God. . . .

By giving away or burning "souvenirs" or those objects to which I am most attached. . . .

Finally, I will detach my heart from myself!

My "self" is an egoist, a coward, a pleasure-seeker, a lazybones, an ambitious, undisciplined individual. . . .

I will immolate Self by—

Forgetting Self to think of others. . . .

Not refusing suffering and self-sacrifice. . . . At sight of my crucifix, I will cry with St. Thomas in an outburst of love: "Let us go, too, and be killed along with Him." (John 11:16.) [Knox.]

Shaking off sloth; for instance, by going to Mass daily. (Since I was able to do so during Lent, why not the rest of the year?)

The result of the death of Self is the substitution of Jesus' life for our own; but this substitution can only be realized by making of one's heart an altar of sacrifice on which, at every moment, one immolates for God's glory and his love, something of self. It is a hard job that requires special, loving, generous souls for its success. For if bodily death is ordinarily preceded by a painful agony, one dies to Self only by passing through a moral agony still more painful. If a mysterious force would seem to intervene to separate soul and body; a divine force is needed to root out Self, which clings so fiercely to our poor human nature. Though a few hours or a few days suffice to complete the death-agony of a human life, the death-pangs of Self are of long duration. Self dies but slowly, gradually. It would be truer to say that Self never really dies at all.... Far from discouraging us, however, this ought to stimulate us by the thought that we shall always have some worthwhile sacrifices to bring to our daily Mass to be mingled with the wine of the chalice.

4. *My Will*:

Resolute, virile, tenacious, persevering, disciplined; or, hesitant, weak, fickle, wavering, stubborn, undisciplined....

That I may LIVE MY MASS, I will train myself every day to strengthen my will. *I will practice self-mastery,* so that I may become more submissive to God's will as manifested by those in authority over me: parents, teachers, superiors, the Church, the Government, providential happenings.... So that I may serve God better, I will discipline my will:

By promptly suppressing every impatient impulse...

By voluntarily giving in to the wishes of others—without, however, ever consenting to evil—for we are speaking here of things good or indifferent in themselves....

By moderating my desire to "have what I want when I want it." ...

By breaking off a bad habit promptly....

By submitting myself to the yoke of a rule of life.... of a diet prescribed by the doctor....

By practicing pleasantness, even when it hurts!

By being constant and persevering in the accomplishment of the duties of my state in life... by finishing one job before tackling another....

By being faithful to my meditation period, even in times of aridity....

By never acting on impulses, but going straight toward the thing that is hard to do....

By being on time for an appointment....

By keeping my word, etc.

Obedience, submission, the giving up of my own will—these constitute the shortest road to perfection. This is the road our Lord himself followed from his birth to his death on the Cross. "If anyone would come after me, let him take up his cross and follow me," these are still the words of the Divine Master to us.

LIVING MY MASS, means offering the tiny drop of water:

B. Of all that I possess

1. *Material goods*:

It is simply a question of placing in the service of others (insofar as possible, naturally) all that God has lent me in the way of talents and goods.

2. *Intellectual goods*:

I will offer my acquired knowledge—my experience, the capacities I have developed—and will use them to benefit others; teaching them, interesting them, etc.

3. *Spiritual goods*:

I will always correspond with the graces God has placed at my disposal. I will develop all the latent virtues of my soul. I will never frustrate the Word of God, but will cultivate the soil that it may bear fruit a hundredfold. I will share my merits and prayers with those souls most in need of them, etc.

LIVING MY MASS, means offering the tiny drop of water:

C. Of all that I can do—my Apostolate

Once I have given all that I am and possess, the next thing is to go on to the very end in the gift of self: to be an apostle, to work at the conquest of souls and bring them back to God.

So that nothing may be lost of the sufferings of others, I will place in the tiny drop of water of my Mass, the sufferings of those who do not offer them; I will offer the toil and trouble of those who suffer without loving—and I will ask for them the grace of conversion.

"That's easy enough so far! But me, an 'apostle,' Father? That's fine for young people—for good mixers and good talkers—great! But for a 'timid soul' like me, and at my age? Never!"

There, in a nutshell, is the opinion of thousands of good Catholics; who think that to be apostles, they must do something hard and heroic, like saving a drowning man at the risk of their lives, or spending three or four nights a week attending interminable meetings! That is one way, but it is not the only way. (In fact, I would call it the exceptional way.)

The apostolate takes a thousand forms and is adaptable to all ages and conditions. While it is certain that the apostolate will rarely demand anything startling of you, it will call for those small services that come up a thousand times a day. (Note that it is harder to help my neighbour in all circumstances, when he is confronted by some small daily difficulty, than once in a lifetime when he is in danger of death! Is not greater sensitivity and more heart required to be touched by a small hurt, to the point of putting myself out to relieve it?)

Convinced, therefore, that I can still add to my offering the fruits of an every-minute apostolate—for every minute I can make somebody happy—I will endeavour then according to the case to—

Leave an exciting story to run an urgent errand (without being asked), to be of help to Mother or a neighbour....

Take the trouble to place a footstool under the feet of a cranky maiden aunt, who won't so much as say "Thank you." ...

Lend my brand-new "bike" to the classmate I dislike, because it will help him get home quicker in the rain.... Or just lend it to him, if for no other reason than that he is "dying" to ride it! (Sometimes this "bike" could be a jewel, a tool, a game, a coin, and so on.)

Give my neighbour or a beggar a piece (the whole box would be better still) of the chocolate candy that tasted so good....

When I feel like taking refuge in my room, because everybody is nursing a grouch, I will stay where I am, and crack a joke to restore the good humour of the family or group—like St. Francis in his Perugian prison!...

Play cards (even though I detest cards) to amuse my aged parents....

Prepare a special surprise for someone on his birthday or anniversary....

Placing my apostolate in the chalice of MY MASS so as to fill it to overflowing, does not mean helping my neighbour or pleasing him just once a day, or whenever an occasion to do so occurs; but it means being on the lookout for such occasions, so as not to let any of them slip by! Hunting for them! Creating them! And from the time I get up in the morning till I go to bed at night, accumulating joy to give to others and to offer up to God!

And how much joy I can give in a day! The more joys I look for, the more I am surprised to find! . . . Every day, as I grow more observing, more thoughtful, these joys will continue to grow. . . .

By making a habit of acting in this way, I shall see many things to which the egoist is blind. I shall think to—

Adjust the pillows under an invalid's head to make him comfortable. . . .

Shut off an unpleasant draft. . . .

Amuse a child and divert an elderly person. . . .

Look cheerful, keep smiling; look for the least in everything (without my neighbour being aware of it). If others are comfortable, it matters little if I am uncomfortable. Say with St. Francis de Sales, "I am never so comfortable, as when I am uncomfortable!"

Offer with spontaneity, delicacy, and generosity, that which is asked of me. . . .

"Guess" that one person is cold, another hungry, and that still another "thirsts" to be understood! . . .

To keep this list within limits, let us stop here the enumeration of the things we can offer at our Mass. . . . If some repetition has crept in, so much the better! It will sink in more! The list could have been prolonged indefinitely. . . . Let each one finish it for himself, in accordance with the needs of his environment and of his state in life.

But, at least, let us say no more about "not knowing what to offer at the Offertory"!

Observe in passing what a wonderful life is led by the person willing to **LIVE HIS MASS**, and so become a **DISSEMINATOR OF JOY!**

For we all have our hands full of precious joy-seeds—why not scatter them broadcast everywhere?

To do so, of course, requires a great love of God and neighbour, as well as much generosity of soul. Let us have no illusions. If we live such a generous life, centered in **OUR MASS**, we shall have friends—and not all of them disinterested friends! . . .

For the person choosing this path, "the sky is the limit" ! . . .

If we give voluntarily of our ideas, our time, our strength, our rest, our liberty, our practical experience, and our money (if we have any), soon people will be coming to ask for—our ideas, our time, our strength, our rest, our liberty, and—our money! Soon they will be no longer content with *asking;* they will *demand* these things of us!...

People will use and abuse us....

Does it matter? If we are asked for, it is a sign that we are needed; and in giving, we enrich ourselves and add something to the chalice of OUR DAILY MASS....

Look at our Lord. He came to give his life as an example to men. And one day, men *took* his life....

"He who would save his life will lose it; but he who loses it will save it."

This, in a nutshell, is what may be contained in the tiny drop of water that falls into the chalice of OUR MASS—all to be transfigured and take on a divine value at the Consecration.

Now that the chalice of OUR MASS is filled to overflowing, let us offer it up to the glorious Trinity.

Before going on to the next question, let us forestall one objection. For a few timorous souls may have felt slightly dizzy after going over the long list of suggestions we drew up in answer to the last question: "How to LIVE our Mass"!

These little souls in swaddling clothes (baby pink or baby blue) must have exclaimed to themselves: "*I* could never do that!"

Be calm, Little Souls! You don't have to do it all in one day! Nor even try to do everything; but just do your utmost, as circumstances permit. In this way, your generosity will grow gradually; and the thing that "in the beginning appeared overwhelming and bitter," will—as St. Francis said—"be changed into sweetness for body and soul." The Poverello was speaking from experience when he wrote these words in his testament; for he himself had known that "feeling of sweetness" after kissing a repulsive leper—a veritable decaying corpse—for whom he had felt an instinctive repugnance.

In passing, let us never complain at God's exigencies; and let us not be content with a mediocre piety.... Holiness! Perfection! This is the sole idea worthy of a Christian, of a Tertiary. Let us rejoice when a sermon or a book invites us to the heights.... We—due to lack of faith or generosity—can resist grace; but grace itself is never lacking.... It depends, therefore, on us if we wish to succeed.

What can one obtain from soldiers to whom one never proposes anything heroic? . . . Do you not think that we shall suffer at the Last Judgment, when we realize what we might have been; and see that we have passed up true glory? . . . for eternity?

No! This shall not happen to us! Our hearts must be on fire! Yes, on fire! Let us not be of the number of those souls lagging along Life's way, content with mediocrity; seeking to fulfill the duties of their state in life with the least effort possible; who, lacking zeal for the ascent, would prevent others—more generous than they—from soaring toward the summits of perfection. . . . Let us not fall into this category of souls; who, instead of being victims of divine love, are victims of their own passions, their self-love, their susceptibility, their independence, or their egotism. . . .

Let us hasten to atone for all these infidelities and failings; not by sheer strength, but by sheer love!

PRAYER OF THE CHRISTIAN SERVANT

O God, grant me the grace to take pleasure in being a servant; and to accept my lot without murmuring, as the condition you have imposed on us all in sending us into this world. If we do not serve one another, then we do not serve God; for life is made up of mutual service. The happiest are those who serve their neighbour without wages, for love of you. But we poor servants must win the bread that you did not give us at birth. It may be that we are more pleasing in your eyes because of this, if we understand our condition; for in addition to the toil, we have the humiliation of the wages we are obliged to receive to serve those whom often we love.

We are of all homes, and homes can close their doors to us.

We are of all families, and all families can reject us.

We bring up children as if they were our own; and when we have reared them, they do not consider us as their mothers.

We take care of our master's property, and the property we have taken care of for them, goes to others.

We become attached to the house, tree, well, and dog in the yard—and house, tree, well, and dog are taken from us at our master's pleasure. The dog dies, and we may not mourn!

Kinsmen without kinfolk, members of the household but not of the family, daughters without mothers, and mothers without children, hearts that give without being accepted—such is the lot of servants before you!

Vouchsafe, O Lord, for me to know the duties, difficulties, and consolations of my state; and after being a good servant of men here below, to be in Heaven above the joyous servant of the Perfect Master!

LAMARTINE
(Geneviève, CXXIII)

THE OFFERING OF THE CHALICE

131—What does the priest do and say at the Offering of the chalice? What lessons are there in this for us?

After placing the tiny drop of water in the chalice, the priest comes back to the centre of the altar; raises the chalice to eye level; and looks up to heaven as he did a few moments earlier at the oblation of the bread. Only, this time, he does not immediately lower his eyes. His confidence would seem to be greater; since—by the mingling of the water and wine—he feels more intimately united to Jesus Christ.

As he raises the chalice toward Heaven, the celebrant recites the *Offerimus*:

Offerimus tibi, Domine, calicem salutaris, tuam deprecantes clementiam: ut in conspectu divinae majestatis tuae, pro nostra, et totius mundi salute, cum odore suavitatis ascendat. Amen.	We offer unto you, O Lord, the chalice of salvation; beseeching your clemency that it may ascend in the odour of sweetness before your Divine Majesty, for our salvation, and for that of the whole world. Amen.

In contradistinction to the offering of the host, the priest speaks here in the name of all the faithful. He no longer says, "*I* offer," but "*We* offer." The formula is in the plural to remind us once more that the Sacrifice of the Mass is a communal sacrifice. From now on, moreover, the people, now purified by the blessing of the water, can unite with the celebrant in offering the chalice.

Let us see how this truly universal prayer is to be understood:

"*Offerimus tibi, Domine*—We offer unto you, O Lord," We, your servants here present and your whole Church.

"*Calicem salutaris*—the chalice of salvation." This chalice that we already look on as if it were filled with Christ's Blood.

"*Tuam deprecantes clementiam*—beseeching your clemency." Begging you, O merciful God, not to look upon our indigence, our sins, and unworthiness; but only on your infinite mercy....

"*Ut in conspectu divinae majestatis tuae, pro nostra et totius mundi salute, cum odore suavitatis ascendat.*" We implore you to cause this offering to ascend to the throne of your Majesty; and to vouchsafe to accept it in the odour of sweetness, of atonement, and of reconciliation; for the salvation of our souls, and for the salvation of the whole world!

In order to say this admirable missionary prayer, one must have a great soul and a generous heart. . . . We pray here not for a particular soul, but for the salvation of every soul in the entire world. Our prayer should draw no other boundary line than that of Christ's Sacrifice. Moreover, are we not reminded of this by the sign of the cross that the celebrant makes with the chalice, before placing it on the corporal and covering it with the pall? Taking a lesson from the Divine Master who, on the Cross, extended his Sacrifice to the whole human race, let us pray with the Church for the salvation of the souls of the whole world—*totius mundi salute*—consequently, for heretics, pagans, and Jews, as well as for the faithful already united to Christ.

Would this not be the moment for us to commend to our Heavenly Father the conquest it is our ambition to make?

THE PERSONAL OBLATION OF PRIEST AND PEOPLE

132—The members of the Mystical Body are offered at Mass together with Christ. What should be their dispositions for their offering to be acceptable and pleasing to God?

Christ, Head of the Mystical Body, is not separated from his members. He offers Himself, and He offers them. So priest and people, after presenting the bread and wine at the altar, must bring their own immolation. The prayer, *In spiritu humilitatis*—humbled in mind—suggests the necessary dispositions—deep humility and sincere contrition for their sins:

In spiritu humilitatis, et in animo contrito suscipiamur a te, Domine: et sic fiat sacrificium nostrum in conspectu tuo hodie, ut placeat tibi, Domine Deus.

Humbled of mind, and contrite of heart, may we find favour with you, O Lord; and may the sacrifice we this day offer up, be well pleasing to you, who are our Lord and our God.

The priest recites this prayer while inclining moderately. It is the word *humilitas* (from *humus*—"earth") that suggests the bodily inclination. This attitude recalls that of Jesus in the Garden of Olives; when he was covered with confusion and crushed at the sight of our sins, whose weight he bore.

At this moment in the Mass, the Church places on the lips of the priest the magnificent prayer of the three youths in the fiery furnace.

If those present only fully appreciated the meaning of these words and entered into the sentiments expressed!

To this end, let us recall here the memorable circumstances in which they were said for the first time.

The place was Babylon. Faithful to their God, Ananias, Misael, and Azarias had not been willing to fall down and worship the golden image of King Nabuchodonosor. So they were bound with chains and thrown into a huge furnace. They walked there amidst the flames, praising God; and Azarias prayed in a loud voice:

"Blessed are you, Lord God of our fathers! In this land of idolatry, the sacrifices prescribed by the law of Moses are not offered up to you! But we offer ourselves as victims of expiation, to obtain mercy for our own sins and those of our people."

And he continued:

"But oh, accept us! For it is with contrite hearts and humble minds that we offer ourselves to you! Look kindly on the sacrifice we offer you today!" (Dan. 3:39.)

The priest speaks the same way at the altar in our name.

What a lesson! We say the same words that the three Hebrew youths sang in the furnace—but do we share their sentiments?

Unable to offer to the Lord the sacrifices of the Mosaic law—sheep and rams—they offered themselves with contrite hearts and humble minds.

And we? We who may never have endured so much as a pin-prick to defend Christ's interests, should consider that this is the moment to offer ourselves up body and soul as a "living sacrifice, acceptable to God," according to St. Paul's precept. (Rom. 12:1.)

And do we have this *humble mind,* which ought to be the sign and seal of our apostolate?

We have already encountered several times—and we shall again during our Mass—receive these calls to humility, to the recognition of our nothingness. . . . For we shall never have a really down-to-earth feeling for, nor a clear enough conviction of, the basic need for humility.

Every day in our daily Mass, this lesson is repeated; because we forget all too easily. Our apostolate, our position, age, success, the esteem with which we are surrounded, and our dominant "I," can all make us forget our total dependence on God. . . .

O God, the sole disposition capable of making our offering into a "sacrifice of sweet odour," is that of deepest humility, of a heart broken and crushed with repentance.

Dear Heavenly Father, we acknowledge and confess that without you we are nothing; are worth nothing; are incapable of nothing; deserve nothing; and what is incomparably worse, we are sinners! We have trampled underfoot your most precious gifts; we have been ungrateful. Yet with your grace (which we implore), we accept to be treated as we deserve. Give us not just any kind of humility and repentance, but make it true and real; that is, the spirit of humility and contrition; the spirit of repentance that transformed sinners into saints—like Mary Magdelene, like St. Peter after his denial, and like so many others, who once having been sinners, became holy. . . .

O Good Father, clothe our souls with this "humble mind," with the spirit of true repentance; so that the Sacrifice we offer you today may deserve to find favour with you.

To help us in acquiring this spirit of humility, let us say together and repeat it often and with conviction:

THE LITANY OF HUMILITY

O Jesus, meek and humble of heart, make my heart like unto yours.

From my own will, O Lord, deliver me.
From the desire to be esteemed, O Lord, deliver me.
From the desire to be loved, O Lord, deliver me.
From the desire to be sought out, O Lord, deliver me.
From the desire to be honoured, O Lord, deliver me.
From the desire to be praised, O Lord, deliver me.
From the desire to be preferred to others, O Lord, deliver me.
From the desire to be consulted, O Lord, deliver me.
From the desire to be approved, O Lord, deliver me.
From the desire for special consideration, O Lord, deliver me.
From the desire to be understood, O Lord, deliver me.

From the desire to be visited, O Lord, deliver me.
From the fear of being humiliated, O Lord, deliver me.
From the fear of being despised, O Lord, deliver me.
From the fear of being rebuffed, O Lord, deliver me.
From the fear of being slandered, O Lord, deliver me.
From the fear of being forgotten, O Lord, deliver me.
From the fear of being laughed at, O Lord, deliver me.
From the fear of being insulted, O Lord, deliver me.
From the fear of being distrusted, O Lord, deliver me.
From the fear of being forsaken, O Lord, deliver me.
From the fear of being rejected, O Lord, deliver me.

That others may be loved more than I, grant me, O Lord, to desire!

That others may be esteemed more than I, grant me, O Lord, to desire!

That others may increase in popularity and I decrease, grant me, O Lord, to desire!

That others may be used and I put aside, grant me, O Lord, to desire!

That others may be praised and I forgotten, grant me, O Lord, to desire!

That others may be preferred in all things, grant me, O Lord, ever to desire!

That others may be holier than I (provided I am as holy as I can be), grant me, O Lord, to desire!

Because I am poor and unknown, I rejoice, O Lord.

Because I am deprived of natural perfections of body or mind, I rejoice, O Lord.

Because nobody thinks of me, I rejoice, O Lord.

Because men employ me at the most humble tasks, I rejoice, O Lord.

Because they do not even use me at all, I rejoice, O Lord.

Because no one ever asks my advice, I rejoice, O Lord.

Because no one has any confidence in me, I rejoice, O Lord.

Because I am left at the lowest place, I rejoice, O Lord.

Because no one ever pays me a compliment, I rejoice, O Lord.

Because I am blamed in season and out of season, I rejoice, O Lord.

"Blessed are they who suffer persecution for justice's sake, for theirs is the kingdom of Heaven!"

THE INVOCATION TO THE HOLY SPIRIT

133—What prayer concludes this first part of the Offertory? What is its meaning?

A prayer to the Holy Spirit is about to crown the offering of the bread, of the wine, and the offering of the faithful.

Here again we are about to grasp a deep, but too little understood, dogma.

When the Son of God willed to become incarnate in the womb of the Blessed Virgin Mary, the Holy Spirit himself overshadowed her and formed the body which was to be offered on the Cross. In the Mass, the Church expects a similar miracle from the Holy Spirit. Here is the prayer:

Veni, Sanctificator, omnipotens aeterne Deus, et bene + dic hoc sacrificium, tuo sancto nomini praeparatum.	Come, O Sanctifier, Almighty and Eternal God, and bless + this Sacrifice prepared for the glory of your holy name.

"Come, O Sanctifier!" exclaims the priest, raising his hands, in a circular motion and joining them, as he raises and lowers his eyes.

"Almighty and Eternal God," who have adorned Heaven and earth, who have enlightened patriarchs and prophets; who are the Author of Mary's humility; who have sanctified the apostles and saints of every age—come and deign to sanctify our souls as well!

"Bless this Sacrifice prepared for the glory of your holy name." At these words, the priest makes the sign of the cross over the chalice and host.

Make this modest sacrifice that we have just prepared for the honour and glory of your holy name, worthy of being offered up to You. To this end, grant us the blessing that you caused to descend on the apostles—the blessing which gives the soul the grace to live peacefully in self-abasement, in humility, in suffering, in the acceptance of the divine will; the blessing which, in a word, makes the life of the Christian a continual sacrifice offered up to the Holy Trinity.

134—Why does the priest thus invoke the Holy Spirit at the approach of the Consecration?

Every act of the Godhead—Father, Son, and Holy Spirit—accomplished outside itself, is, of course, common to the three Persons; but when these are acts of love, they are especially attributed to the Holy Spirit, who is the substantial love of Father and Son.

The Sanctifying Spirit—"a devouring flame"—will consume the substance of the bread and wine at the moment of Consecration; he it is also who must destroy whatever is earthly and blameworthy in our souls....

As Creative Spirit, the Holy Spirit will—under the subsisting species of bread and wine—render present the Body and Blood of the Saviour; as he once did in Mary—as he will do in each of our souls....

As Unifying Spirit—the living link between the Head and members of the Mystical Body—it is he who will unite us more closely to Christ; so that we may be offered up with the Divine Victim and accepted in the odour of sweetness....

This is what priest and people should expect of the Holy Spirit—prodigies of love like the transubstantiation soon to take place on the altar, and the divinization to be effected in every heart!

So it is with reason that the people, like the priest, ought to long for the coming of the Holy Spirit; and lovingly pray: "Come, O Sanctifier!"

135—What should be our attitude toward the Holy Spirit?

1. *We should be convinced of the necessity of his co-operation for our sanctification, and for the success of our apostolate.*

Prior to Pentecost, all the essential elements of the Church were already in existence: doctrine, preachers, sacraments, a hierarchy; but all was in a state of suspense—like a great and powerful organism awaiting the breath of life that would set it in motion. The Holy Spirit came, and everything sprang into life and movement. And if the stormy winds of persecution blow against the Church, history teaches us that by the inspiration of the Holy Spirit, saints are raised up who cleanse the Augean stables; restore to the true Faith its unconquerable vigour; and stir up the burning furnace of love in the heart of Christ's Spouse, the Church.

"That which the soul does for the members of the human body," wrote St. Augustine, "the Holy Spirit does for the whole Church."

He it is who has established the Pope, bishops, and priests to rule the Church of God. He it is who spoke by the prophets. . . . He it is who aids the Church and keeps her from ever erring in the interpretation of revealed truths. The Church always promulgates her laws in the name of the Holy Spirit.

Just as Jesus Christ was made incarnate and offered himself by the Holy Spirit; so does he desire his Eucharistic Sacrifice to be produced and offered by the same Spirit, who is also the Guest of our souls.

2. *We ought to glorify the Holy Spirit, who dwells in us as in a temple*:

By thinking of Him, by having recourse to Him, by invoking Him by means of fervent aspirations. "*Veni, Pater pauperum*—Come, O Father of the poor." And poor we are indeed! (The worst poverty would be to believe ourselves rich.) "*Veni, Consolator optime*—You of all Comforters the best." Come and save me from paralyzing gloom; lift me up again from my repeated falls. . . .

3. *We ought to obey Him with docility*:

We should let the Holy Spirit act in us—permit him to instill within our souls a modicum of illumination, order, and peace. . . . We should be docile to the leadings of his grace—to the actual graces which ever and anon urge us to greater straightforwardness with Christ; to the breaking off of a sinful habit, some culpable attachment, the little watering down of duty. . . .

Under the direction of this Spirit of light and love, why should I not succeed in overcoming my mistakes, as soon as they are pointed out to me? . . . Why should I not pick myself up every time I drift into a perilous state of tepidity, or after a more or less serious slip? . . . Why should I not fulfill my daily task? . . . Or carry my cross daily without complaint? . . .

And if I do not, is not the cause my resistance to His pleadings? . . .

Once more, at this point of the Mass, let us beseech the Spirit of Love to transform and transfigure our souls; just as at the Consecration,

He will change the bread and wine into the Body and Blood of Christ.

In reparation for our ingratitude or insensibility, let us often make (with the intention of living up to it) the following act of consecration:

CONSECRATION TO THE HOLY SPIRIT

O Holy Spirit, kneeling before your Divine Majesty, in the presence of Heaven and earth, I adore the effulgence of your purity, the inalterable integrity of your justice, and the power of your love. I offer myself to you body and soul, O Eternal Spirit of God!

You are the light and strength of my soul—through you I live, think, and act. To you I cling; to you I give myself; and I supplicate your mercy to watch over my weakness.

May I never sin against you, nor grieve you by my resistance to grace. Rule my thoughts. Cause me ever to hear your voice and obey your gentle inspirations.

I supplicate you, Adorable Spirit, to keep me from all sin; but should I fall, grant me forgiveness. Give me the grace to say to you in all places: "Speak Lord, for your servant is listening."

Spirit of Wisdom, preside over all my thoughts, words, and deeds, from this hour to the hour of my death; and give me wisdom in the ways of God.

Spirit of Intelligence, enlighten and teach me.

Spirit of Counsel, guide my inexperience.

Spirit of Fortitude, strengthen my weakness.

Spirit of Knowledge, dissipate my ignorance.

Spirit of Piety, make me persevere in the right path.

Spirit of Fear, deliver me from all evil.

Spirit of Peace, give me peace of soul.

Divine Spirit, make me faithful in God's service; give me the strength to act at all times with kindness and good will; mildness and faithfulness; patience and charity; longsuffering and joy.

Holy Spirit, sanctify my body and my senses; and make use of my being as a docile instrument for doing your will.

Adorable presence of the Holy Spirit in my soul, illumine me with your divine light; impress in me the beauty of truth; and by the superabundance of your grace, form my soul in the mould of sanctity. Amen.

THE INCENSING OF THE ALTAR

136—At solemn Masses, the priest here incenses the altar. What prayer does he recite?

The censer typifies Christ's human nature; and also (as we saw in Q. 67) every Christian worthy of the name. The fire figures the Holy Spirit who inflamed the heart of Jesus, and will likewise fill our hearts with the flames of his love. For is not a true Christian composed of soul and body and—the Holy Spirit?

The incense which the fire consumes, and whose smoke ascends to Heaven, is an admirable symbol of the operation of the Holy Spirit in the Saviour's person and in the souls of all those present.

If we are fully to comprehend the meaning of these liturgical ceremonies, we must recall here an important point in Catholic doctrine.

It was the Holy Spirit who caused our Lord to make the acts of love which he produced for our salvation. He drove him into the desert to do penance; he incited him to preach the Gospel to the poor; he decided him to accept death so as to become our ransom; he placed on his lips the prayers that the God-Man addressed to his Father in the night watches. . . .

It is the same Spirit who acts on the soul of the Christian by his movements, which we call "actual graces," He is at one and the same time the Source of our good works, and the divine ferment which supernaturalizes them. He prays for us with "unutterable groanings."

These truths being present to our minds, let us now see how the fire, as it consumes the incense, causes the smoke to ascend above the altar. May our prayer united to that of Christ, and the perfume of our good works united to the Holy Sacrifice, likewise ascend toward God!

Let us carefully follow the order of each of these ceremonies. At solemn Masses, the priest blesses the incense, saying:

Per intercessionem beati Michaelis Archangeli stantis a dextris Altaris incensi, et omnium electorum suorum, incensum istud dignetur Dominus bene + dicere, et in odorem suavitatis accipere. Per Christum Dominum nostrum. Amen.	By the intercession of Blessed Michael the Archangel standing at the right of the altar of incense, and of all his elect, may the Lord deign to bless this incense and receive it in the odour of sweetness. Through Jesus Christ our Lord. Amen.

He incenses the bread and wine, saying:

Incensum istud a te benedictum, ascendat ad te Domine, et descendat super nos misericordia tua.	May this incense blessed by you, O Lord, ascend toward you; and may your mercy descend on us.

He incenses the altar, saying:

Dirigatur, Domine, oratio mea, sicut incensum in conspectu tuo: elevatio manuum mearum sacrificium vespertinum. Pone, Domine, custodiam ori meo, et ostium circumstantiae labiis meis: ut non declinet cor meum in verba malitiae, ad excusandas excusationes in peccatis.	May my prayer ascend, O Lord, like incense in your sight. May the lifting up of my hands be pleasing to you, like the evening sacrifice. Place, O Lord, a watch before my mouth, and guard the door of my lips; that I may avoid sinful speech and vain excuses for my sins.

He hands the censer to the deacon, saying:

Ascendat in nobis Dominus ignem sui amoris, et flammam aeternae caritatis. Amen.	May the Lord enkindle in us the fire of his love, and the flame of eternal charity. Amen.

137—What is the significance of these words and gestures?

The priest first swings the censer several times over the bread and wine.

Remember that we are offered up with this bread and wine presently to become the Body and Blood of Christ. This smoking incense is the offering of the Head and his members. It is the sacrifice of the total Christ—Christ and us—as he was offered to his Father by the Holy Spirit. Therefore, it is the offering up of our prayers, of our spiritual works, of the sum total of the operation of the Holy Spirit in our souls.

To make this teaching stand out still more sharply, every one of those merged in the oblation of the Mass is to be thus incensed.

The bread and wine are incensed first, and immediately afterward, the altar.

The altar represents Jesus Christ; but the bread and wine, soon to be transubstantiated into his Body and Blood, represent it still more perfectly. Just as the incense ascends toward God, so will Jesus soon present to his Father, together with his Body and Blood, the infinite merits of his Passion and death.

The celebrant is next incensed.

Then the clergy in the choir, and finally the faithful. May their works and desires likewise ascend like incense toward the throne of the Father and be pleasing unto him!

So much for the gestures. The words that the celebrant then pronounces are no less expressive. Each might well become a subject of meditation for our devotion. Let us be content to glean a few grains from the abundant harvest here offered us by the liturgy.

The priest beseeches the Lord to bless this incense "by the intercession of Michael the Archangel and of all his elect."

He invokes here the angel that St. John saw standing before the altar of the Most High. "And another angel came and stood before the altar, having a golden censer; and there was given him much incense, that he might offer it with the prayers of all the saints upon the golden altar which is before the throne. And with the prayers of the saints there went up before God from the angel's hand the smoke of the incense." (Apoc. 8:3.)

Is not this the very scene at which we are present at this moment of the Mass?

While incensing the bread and wine which are on the altar, the celebrant says this prayer, whose words make this ceremony appear in a new light:

"May this incense blessed by you, O Lord, ascend toward you; and may your mercy descend on us!"

There is no doubt about it. This blessed incense has the effect of a sacramental. It "ascends" toward Heaven to make God's blessings "descend." That is why the priest always blesses the incense—even before the Blessed Sacrament exposed—when he places it in the censer. He omits this blessing only when he is to incense the Blessed Sacrament alone. The incense is then employed as a symbol and not as a sacramental.

Remember that this sacramental will not produce its effects without our co-operation. The incense will cause God's blessings to descend on you only if it is accompanied by your desires and prayers. Here again, it is better to look at the altar than at your missal. . . .

These clouds of smoke rising toward the vaulted ceilings of our churches, or diffused in our humble sanctuaries, symbolize the power of prayer—and especially of liturgical prayer—made in common.

Descending from the altar where Christ is being immolated, and spreading over the hierarchy of the priesthood and over the people, they recall the union existing between the heads and the members—the unity of the Church, Christ's Mystical Body.

Returning the censer to the deacon, the celebrant clearly expresses the meaning of the incensing and the sentiments that this ritual should awaken in every heart:

"May the Lord enkindle in us the fire of his love, and the flame of eternal charity!"

If we have dwelt somewhat on the ceremonies of the incensing, it was to make you appreciate the High Mass better, and prefer it to the Low Mass.

AN APOSTLE'S PRAYER

•

O God, never let a soul leave me without having been united to you, without having been strengthened in virtue, inflamed with your love, encouraged and consoled; without having tasted the meekness and goodness of your Heart and the sweetness and delight of serving you.

May souls see in me Jesus alone, the gentle Saviour; Jesus, all goodness; Jesus with his heart open, Jesus with his arms outstretched, saying, "Come to Me, all of you."

May my soul, as well as my lips, smile at everyone!

May your Word, dear God, inspire my humble thoughts and give them the fruitfulness of your Precious Blood.

May nothing human infiltrate into the apostolate of the souls you have entrusted to me, but may I love them with your Great Divine Heart —even to suffering and death!

None but You! You alone! For me, failure, disappointment, and the unknown; but for You consolation and gratitude.

O Holy Trinity, dwell within my soul by your grace; sanctify me; sanctify all souls you place in my path today. Amen.

THE LAVABO

138—Why does the priest wash his hands at this point in the Mass?

There is a very natural explanation for this ceremony. After receiving the offerings of bread, wine, beeswax, olive oil, fruits, honey, and so on, and handling the censer; the priest may have at one time needed to purify his hands. So washing the hands was a most practical thing to do. Now-a-days this ceremony possesses mostly a symbolic value.

At a High Mass (because of the use of incense) the celebrant washes both hands. At a Low or private Mass, the fingers only (i.e., the thumbs and forefingers), are washed at the Consecration. He then dries them with a white linen cloth called the purificator.

139—What does this ceremony of washing the hands signify?

The ablutions during the celebration of Mass are performed *out* of *reverence for the holy mysteries.* And this for two reasons. First, it is customary not to touch precious objects without first washing the hands. (And what is more precious than the Blessed Sacrament?)

Next, this ceremony has a purely spiritual significance. The washing of the fingers signifies the purification of our venial faults. To approach the Lord, our hearts should be free not only from serious sin; but from the smallest stain.

Hence, the necessity of arousing in our hearts sentiments of perfect contrition; and of renewing those sentiments we had during the recitation of the Confiteor.

140—What prayer does the priest recite during the Lavabo, and what does it mean?

The celebrant recites the 25th Psalm:

Lavabo inter innocentes manus meas: et circumdabo altare tuum Domine:	I wash my hands in innocence; and I walk around your altar, O Lord.
Ut audiam vocem laudis, et enarrem universa mirabilia tua.	That I may proclaim aloud your praise, and recount all your wondrous deeds.
Domine, dilexi decorem domus tuae, et locum habitationis gloriae tuae.	O Lord, I love the house where you dwell and the dwelling place of your glory.

Ne perdas cum impiis, Deus animam meam, et cum viris sanguinum vitam meam:	Snatch not away my soul with sinners, nor my life with murderers.
In quorum manibus iniquitates sunt: dextera eorum repleta est muneribus.	On whose hands is crime, and whose right hand is full of bribes.
Ego autem in innocentia mea ingressus sum: redime me, et miserere mei.	But I walk in my innocence: deliver me and be gracious to me.
Pes meus stetit in directo: in ecclesiis benedicam te, Domine.	My foot stands on level ground, in the assemblies I will bless the Lord.
Gloria Patri et Filio, etc.	Glory be to the Father, etc.

As will have been seen, this Psalm expresses clearly—with a sort of candour and happy confidence—the joy of both priest and parishioner who are about to offer up the Divine Sacrifice; their tranquility of soul and the gladness they feel at being in the Lord's House among those souls most detached from the defilements of the world; and, one might well say (employing a somewhat more ambitious formula), among the "spiritual elite."

But let us not forget that it is God's grace that has kept our feet from straying from the path of justice (or that brought us back to it, if we chanced to stumble or fall).... And it is likewise through his grace that we hope to keep in that path today and all the days of our life; so that we may one day go to bless him, together with all the saints of God throughout endless ages.... We should do well to plead often for this grace.

THE PRIEST'S PRAYER

O Lord Jesus, Eternal Priest, keep me, your priest, within the shelter of your Sacred Heart, where nothing may touch me. Keep unstained my anointed hands, which daily touch your Sacred Body. Keep unsullied my lips, daily purpled with your Precious Blood. Keep pure and unearthly my heart, sealed with the sublime mark of your glorious Priesthood. Let your holy love be my bulwark against the world's contagion. Bless all my labours. May the souls to whom I minister be my joy and consolation here; and my everlasting crown hereafter. Amen.

PRAYER TO THE HOLY TRINITY

141—What does the priest do after the lavabo?

Returning to the middle of the altar, the celebrant raises his eyes to Heaven toward the crucifix; then, with a humble and recollected attitude, lowers them toward the oblation. With his hands joined on the edge of the altar, he renews the act of offering in these words:

Suscipe, Sancta Trinitas, hanc oblationem, quam tibi offerimus ob memoriam passionis, resurrectionis et ascensionis Jesu Christi Domini nostri: et in honorem beatae Mariae semper Virginis, et beati Joannis Baptistae, et sanctorum Apostolorum Petri et Pauli, et istorum, et omnium Sanctorum: ut illis proficiat ad honorem, nobis autem ad salutem: et illi pro nobis intercedere dignentur in caelis, quorum memoriam agimus in terris. Per eumdem Christum Dominum nostrum. Amen.	Receive, O Holy Trinity, this Oblation offered up by us to you in memory of the Passion, Resurrection, and Ascension of our Lord Jesus Christ, and in honour of blessed Mary, ever a Virgin, of blessed John the Baptist, of the holy apostles Peter and Paul, of these, and of all the saints, that it may avail to their honour and to our salvation; and may they, whose memory we celebrate on earth, vouchsafe to intercede for us in Heaven. Through the same Christ our Lord. Amen.

142—Of what does this prayer to the Holy Trinity consist?

This prayer, *Suscipe, sancta Trinitas,* has not always belonged in the Mass. It appeared for the first time in the ninth century in France and gradually was introduced into the universal Church.

It is a formula of offering, a repetition of the *Suscipe, Sancte Pater,* and of the *Offerimus;* with which it formerly was interchangeable

The prayer may be divided as follows:

Part One, comprising the *invocation,* includes the supplication addressed to God ("Receive, O Holy Trinity"), the mention of the offering ("this oblation offered up by us to You"); next, the remembrance of the mysteries of Christ, and of the saints.

Part Two, immediately linked to the preceding, implores for the blessed and for the faithful *the realization of the effects of the offering*

It then beseeches the intercession of the saints in favour of those celebrating the Holy Sacrifice of the Mass.

An outline could be made as follows:

A. *Invocation*

1. Supplication to the Holy Trinity
2. Remembrances
   a. Of the mysteries of Christ
   b. Of certain saints in particular
   c. Of all the saints

B. *Supplication*

1. Direct:
   a. For the saints
   b. For the faithful
2. Indirect: Intercession of the saints.

This prayer is addressed to the Holy Trinity, to the three Divine Persons, beseeching them to accept the offering made to them. For while Christ offered himself to his Father, the end of the Sacrifice is not to one Person alone, but to God; that is, to all three Persons.

By oblation *(hanc oblationem)* is meant here, first of all, the bread and wine; but also the things they stand for—the spiritual offering of the Church, and the personal gift of each individual.

The *Suscipe, Sancta Trinitas,* is no mere formula; but is intimately linked with the Consecration, for which it serves as the preparation. It is completely oriented toward the Eucharistic Sacrifice. The mention that is made of the Passion, Resurrection, and Ascension, is not, however, a duplication of the *Unde et memores* (that we shall discuss later on); for the latter accomplishes the eucharistic mystery, which the former prepares.

The offering of the Holy Sacrifice is addressed to God alone; and it is to him also that are offered the bread and wine which serve as matter for the Sacrament. But Mass may also be offered in honour of the saints.

It is fitting to mention a few of the saints for whom a greater devotion is felt; those with whom one is on more intimate terms (for instance, one's patron saint); and, especially, those saints more closely connected with the life of Christ.

The list is headed by the Blessed Virgin, who participated so fully in the offering up of the bloody Sacrifice of her Son. From Bethlehem to Calvary, she prepared the Mass.

No devotion should be dearer or more precious to us than devotion to Mary, especially that Marian devotion which is connected with our Mass. All of this proves once more that the Mass is a centre to which we may refer everything else.

After Mary comes the Precursor, St. John the Baptist, whose evangelical rôle is so considerable and has merited him a choice place in the liturgy. Marvellous in his birth accompanied by prodigies, and in his life of solitude and penance; he is no less so in his preaching and death. He is a model of purity. It was for his defense of chastity that he died a martyr, beheaded. He is particularly the model of apostles. His mission is to bring souls to Jesus, the Lamb of God who takes away the sins of the world. John the Baptist was a man who practiced self-effacement. It was not toward his own person that he drew men. On the contrary, he told his disciples to go to Jesus—detaching themselves from him.... This was true humility. John wanted to decrease, that Christ might increase.

Alongside the Precursor, it was fitting that the apostles Peter and Paul should find a place. They are the first depositaries of authority, the first priests of the new law.

St. Peter, with his ardour, his faith, his love, his authority, his falls and repentance, always brings us back to the sentiment of Catholic unity. The devotion we should feel for him is devotion to the hierarchy. For in Peter we see the head of the Church, the "gentle earthly Christ." Our attachment to him is an attachment to unity, to the rock of the Church, to infallible doctrine—and the Pope appears to us as the prolongation, the "incarnation," of Peter.

St. Paul—he of the fiery soul—should fascinate us.... To him it is we owe the grasp of the rich doctrine of our integration into Christ, to form within the Church a Mystical Body; with Christ as the Head and each of us as members. St. Paul, in his immortal Epistles, shows us the unity in the faith of our beliefs and morals. St. Paul is the herald of the burning love of Christ and the Church, of intimate union with Christ, and with one's brothers in Christ. Nothing in him is narrow. He expands, but without excess. He loves order; he knows what is fitting; he desires all to be done with decorum. He is another model for everyone of us.

The other saints here mentioned are those whose relics repose in the altar stone, and those commemorated in the Mass of the day.

In the second part of this prayer, we beseech God that this oblation made to him may procure glory to the saints. True, only their accidental glory is added to, but this glorification is very real.

But because this Sacrifice has above all a redemptive value; the priest, conjointly with his prayer for the honour of the saints, prays for the salvation of the people. While the material offering and the spiritual oblation which it expresses, already possess a sacrifical value; the material offering would have no power for salvation, were it not united to that of Christ; if it were not to be absorbed, transformed, consecrated, by that of Christ, which alone obtains our salvation.

Lastly, the priest entreats that the saints, whose glory is augmented by the honour rendered them in the celebration of Mass; may deign in return to intercede for us with God.

It is scarcely necessary to insist on the value of this prayer formula, and upon the dispositions required of both celebrant and participants. For, in addition to possessing the sacramental character common to all liturgical formulas, it is a prayer of preparation for the Sacrifice itself.

For this reason, it should be said by the priest and followed by the people with fervent devotion; in a spirit of sacrifice, of filial abandon, and of total self-surrender; while awaiting the transformation to be wrought by the Consecration.

To imbue us more deeply with the sentiments with which we should be animated with respect to the Trinity, let us often meditate on the following beautiful prayer composed by a Carmelite nun, Sister Elizabeth of the Trinity:

PRAYER TO THE MOST HOLY TRINITY

O God, adorable Trinity, help me to forget self utterly and fix my abode in you, immobile and calm as if my soul already were in eternity! Let nothing trouble my peace, nor cause me to depart from you, Immutable God; but may every moment plunge me deeper into your mysterious depths.

Tranquillize my soul. Make of it your Heaven, your beloved dwelling-place and the place of your repose. May I never allow you to dwell there alone, but always give you my undivided company—with living faith, wholly adoring, entirely abandoned to your creative action.

O my Beloved Jesus, crucified for love, I would be the loving bride of your Heart! Would that I could inundate you with glory, love you enough to die of that love! But I realize my powerlessness and implore you to clothe me with yourself; to identify my soul with all the movements of your soul; to enravish and permeate my soul, and yourself live in me; so that my life may be but the reflection of your life. Come to me as a Restorer and Saviour.

O Eternal Word, Word of my God, I want to spend my life listening to you. I want to become docile, that I may learn of you. Then in all dark nights of the soul, in all times of aridity and powerlessness, I would fix my gaze ever on you; and dwell in your marvellous light. O my Beloved Day-Star, draw me within your orbit so surely that I may never depart from you.

O consuming Fire, Spirit of Love, penetrate my very soul, that it may become as an incarnation of the Word; that I may be to him as another human nature, in which the divine mystery may be renewed. Father, incline toward your humble creature. Cover me with the shadow of your wing. Behold in me only your Beloved Son, in whom you are well pleased.

O my Triune God, my All, my Beatitude, Infinite Solitude, Immensity in which I lose myself; I abandon myself to you as a victim. Lose yourself in me, that I may become lost in you; until that day when I shall contemplate in your light, the abyss of your greatness.

A PRAYER FOR A BOY SCOUT OR A GIRL GUIDE

•

Lord Jesus, teach us to be generous.
To serve you as you deserve to be served.
To give without counting the cost.
To battle, and not mind the bruises.
To work, and not seek for repose.
To spend ourselves without thought of any other reward save that of knowing that we do your holy will. Amen.

ORATE, FRATRES

143—What appeal does the priest then address to the people?

After the *Suscipe,* the celebrant kisses the altar and then turns toward the congregation. Then extending his arms, and again joining his hands, he invites the faithful to redoubled prayers; saying, *"Orate, Fratres*—Brothers, pray!"

Orate, fratres, ut meum ac vestrum sacrificium acceptabile fiat apud Deum Patrem omnipotentem.	Brothers, pray that my sacrifice and yours may be acceptable to God, the Father Almighty.

Through the mouth of the server, the congregation replies:

Suscipiat Dominus sacrificium de manibus tuis,* ad laudem et gloriam nominis sui, ad utilitatem quoque nostram,* totiusque Ecclesiae suae sanctae.	May the Lord receive this sacrifice at your hands, to the praise and glory of his name, to our own benefit, and to that of all his Holy Church.

And the priest says in a low voice, "Amen."

With these words, *"Orate, Fratres,"* the priest takes leave, as it were, of the people, whom he will not see again until after he has consummated the Sacrifice. During all this time, he will not turn again toward the people; even when he says, *"Dominus vobiscum,"* though ordinarily, salutations are made only when looking at the persons saluted. Wholly given up to the great mystery about to take place, the priest continues to face the altar.

In the preceding prayer, the *Suscipe,* the priest had begged the assistance of the glorious members of the Mystical Body. Now he requests the co-operation of the whole congregation. He would even seem to issue an order, for the verb is in the imperative: *"Orate*—Pray!"

This appeal to prayer is easy to grasp.

For it will be recalled that in the Latin Church, from its origin to the ninth century, the people brought their offerings to the sanctuary. This coming and going might well have caused some distraction. So, when everyone had returned to his place, the priest would turn toward the congregation; inviting them to recollection with the words: "Brothers, pray!"

Even today this invitation to prayer is practical. Although the offering is not made in the same way as formerly; the closer we come to the Sacrifice, the more necessary do prayer and recollection become.

The celebrant invites the people to prayer for still another reason. He is convinced that nothing can be accomplished without prayer. "Without me," said Jesus, "you can do nothing." The priest also knows himself to be "another Christ" through the power of Infinite Love, and he feels his own powerlessness (overhelmed as he is by blessings) to thank God properly. Thus he pleads, "Brothers, pray!"

Again, he thinks of the future. It was for others he was made a priest. He knows that the fruitfulness of his priestly ministry depends on the prayers and sacrifices of the faithful, united to his prayers and sacrifice.... That is why the priest always adds: "Brothers, pray!"

The faithful should likewise pray and thank God for the immense graces they have received (and especially for....)

The celebrant is not satisfied with saying, "Pray," but adds, "Brothers!" He calls those present by the sweet name of "brother." For, present at the Mass, there should be only brothers and sisters. St. Paul in his Epistles addressed the Christians in this manner. So it is that the priest in the pulpit still addresses them in his Sunday sermon.

At this moment, especially, the appellation of "brother," should have its full force. At the moment of offering up the Holy Sacrifice, more than at any other time, grudges, bitterness, rivalries between individuals, families, and class, should vanish; giving place to brotherly love.... We should treat our neighbour as a brother, forgiving his frailties and faults.... Knowledge of the world, of its narrowness, malice, and selfishness, might sometimes tend to dishearten and disgust us; or inspire us with regrettable feelings of ill-will, disdain, or anger. Jesus, who understood human nature perfectly, had none of these sentiments. He was respectful and kind toward the fallen. He always saw in every man a brother to save, to form to his likeness....

Such should likewise be our dispositions—to see ourselves surrounded by "other Christs"; members of his Mystical Body, beloved brethren. That this love is sometimes difficult to achieve, none will deny! Sometimes it will clash violently with our self-love and selfishness.... Such love also calls for great self-denial—but it is indispensable.

Jesus did not recoil before the kiss of Judas. What is more, he called the traitor, "Friend"!...

"It is by this sign," Jesus told his disciples, "that men will know that you really are my disciples, if you love one another as I have loved you."

Can those who see our actions under certain circumstances, truly recognize us as disciples of the Master?

"That my sacrifice and yours." Once again, the Mass appears as the Sacrifice of the whole Mystical Body. The Mass is not Christ's concern alone, nor that of the priest alone; but the concern of all the faithful, and of the Church. Something would be lacking in the Mass, if the people did not offer the Divine Victim with the priest! Here is the tangible evidence of how strongly the Church desires to impress on us that by virtue of our Baptism, we have all been integrated into Christ—priest and people united in a common offering.

"May be acceptable to God the Father Almighty." Why does the priest request our prayers that God may vouchsafe to accept the proffered Sacrifice? Does not God *always* accept his Beloved Son, in whom he is well pleased? The reason is ever the same. It is because we offer ourselves as victims with Christ, and *we* are not certain of being "acceptable" to the Divine Majesty!...

144—What is the meaning of the response of the *Orate, Fratres,* the *Suscipiat?*

Let us now take up the words uttered by the server in the name of the people, in response to the invitation of the celebrant to pray.

That we may better understand these words, let us consider the following:

The old law had various kinds of sacrifices: the *holocaust,* or sacrifice of praise, to acknowledge God's sovereign majesty, and thank him for his blessings; the *impetratory* sacrifice, to implore God's help; the *expiatory* sacrifice, for the remission of sin; and the *propitiatory* sacrifice for the remission of the penalty. Every day, several of these sacrifices were offered to the Lord in the Temple of Jerusalem. The immolated victims were animals, and the Scriptures attest that these sacrifices were pleasing to God. They were agreeable to him because they were symbolic announcements of the Sacrifice of Jesus Christ, the Lamb of God.

Well then! Supposing you had immolated with your own hands all the victims sacrificed from the beginning of the world up to the time of our Lord. You would doubtless have given immense satisfaction to God, and paid him great homage. I venture to say, however, that you will honour the Divine Majesty more by saying the response to the *Orate, Fratres,* with a heart deeply penetrated by its sentiments.

Let us weigh carefully these words which the server says in your name:

"May the Lord receive the Sacrifice" (the only Sacrifice now acceptable to God).

"At your hands." From the consecrated hands of the priest, which thus become instruments of grace.

"May he receive it.... to the praise and glory of his name!" Here is the principal purpose of the Sacrifice—to adore God and thank him. This is why we say that it is a worship of latria and a Eucharist. It is more than all the ancient holocausts rolled into one. Nothing more than these two words, clearly explained and clearly grasped, give an exact understanding of Holy Mass; which ought to be the praise and glory of God, the recognition and praise of his sovereignty and Kingship.

"To our own benefit, and to that of all His Holy Church." Here is the other end that we propose to ourselves—that it may be useful to us who are here present; for the remission of sin, the penalty due to sin, and for obtaining grace. That it may be useful also to all those members of the Church who are not present.... Our sacrifice is thus impetratory, expiatory, and propitiatory.

If we make this response to the *Orate, Fratres* with thoughtful conviction, we shall be integrated voluntarily and actively into a Sacrifice whose value surpasses all those offered hitherto.

"Amen," replies the priest. "I am reassured. You are united with me. We are going to pray together—let the divine concert continue without interruption!"

And he withdraws into the silence of the "Secret."

The Beloved

●

Scattering a thousand graces
He passed swiftly through this wood,
He did but glance upon it—
And behold it clothed in beauty.

ST. JOHN OF THE CROSS.

Three Rivers

Ric Photo

Foot-prints in the Snow — Foot-prints Snow-covered

Foot-prints in the snow—the traces of feet in its feathery whiteness.
Thus in passing over a human life, a human mind, conscience, or heart,
An impression is left. Its kind? But that depends on who passes!
If he be good, the impression he leaves is one of goodness—If evil, impression of evil.
Defiled, a stain... Small feet, small impression...
Giant feet—prints that are wide and long...
All depends on the passer—prints made by blood-stained feet, traces of soot!...
What impression have we left on the lives of others
Whom our lives momentarily have touched?
The question is problematic and grave. Look behind you and decide.
Yes, the foot-prints are still there! Are they pure white,
My friend, or blood-red now, blackened, defiled, the souls that we have touched?
Foot-prints in the snow—our influence on others. The impression of our lives on theirs.
Snow over the foot-prints. Effacement, Burial.
Of the print made in passing by the passer-by!
Thus on, and in us, of God's grace the trace is left.
Easy to recognize. Delicate and forever fair.
Only other influences can cover over and blot out God's foot-prints:
Doubt, sin, scandal, falsehood—
A form of impure snow that in insidious flakes
Falls down upon the soul that once was sanctified!
One would say that God had never passed!
Sometimes it is others who cover over, obliterate God's foot-prints.
Sometimes it is we who blot them out in others!
Thereby to pose a new, twofold and still graver problem.
Our snow—covering God's foot-prints in others—
Their snow, covering them in us!

Ric Photo

SECRET

145—What is the Secret?

The name *Secret* is given to the prayer or prayers which the celebrant recites in a low voice, immediately after the *Orate, Fratres.*

Together with the Collect and Postcommunion (of which we shall speak later on), the Secret is one of the principal Mass prayers.

The name *Secret* is variously explained. The word itself comes from a Latin verb meaning "to separate." Thus Father Herwegen thinks that the word *ecclesia* should be added: *ecclesia secreta,* as distinct from *ecclesia collecta* (or the entire assembly before the dismissal of the catechumens). The *Secreta* would thus be the prayer of offering of the elite of the congregation.

It may be, however; that *Secreta* refers to the offerings or *oblata*: those separated from secular use for the Consecration (bread and wine) and so distinguished from those offerings simply to be blessed. (Honey, beeswax, oil, etc.)

146—What is contained in the "Secret"? How does it end?

The most ancient among the Secrets mention offerings made by the faithful, and imply an Offertory. More recent Secrets deal with the sacrificial action that follows. Nearly all beseech God to receive favourably the gifts on the altar, to prepare them for use in the approaching solemn Oblation of Christ; and by his grace dispose us to be offered up as "acceptable hosts."

The celebrant concludes the Secret and the commemorations which eventually came to be added to it, with the words: *"Per omnia saecula saeculorum"*—world without end. While saying them, he raises his voice.

This prayer conclusion is not (as it sometimes said) the beginning of the Preface. If the rubrics stipulate that the priest's voice should be raised, it is merely that the people (who are to reply "Amen") should be notified.

This "amen" forms a fitting conclusion for the part of the Mass termed the Offertory—the soul offering itself with Christ. By this "amen" the people approve what has been said and done.

This oblation of self together with Christ is preparatory to the immolation which will confirm it. The supreme moment of the Sacrifice approaches. The liturgical action becomes more reflective, more moving.

III. THE CONSECRATION

The soul is immolated

- The Preface
- The Sanctus
- Te igitur
- Memento of the living
- Communicantes
- Hanc igitur
- Quam oblationem
- Consecration
- Consecration of the Host.
- Consecration of the chalice
- Unde et memores
- Supra quae propitio
- Supplices te rogamus
- Memento of the Dead
- Nobis quoque peccatoribus
- End of the Canon
- Per quem haec omnia

147—What marks the beginning of the second part of the Mass of the Faithful, and its conclusion?

Part II of the Mass of the Faithful *begins with the Preface and ends with the Pater, inclusively.* This part—the most important—is composed of the prayers and action which precede, accompany, and follow the climax of the Mass, the Consecration.

The Preface

148—What is the Preface of the Mass?

The beginning of the eucharistic thanksgiving is called the Preface.

The Preface is a solemn prayer of thanksgiving, whose majestic air contrasts with the style of the prayers of offering which precede it. It is intoned by the priest alone, acting as spokesman for the congregation. It starts off with a dialogue as a distinguishing feature. The Preface is a prayer full of verve, vibrant with enthusiasm at thought of the One who is to come.

We all, however humble, ought to play our part in this great concert of love and praise sung by all creation (in Heaven and on earth); to the glory of God's infinite majesty.

149—How many Prefaces are contained in the Roman Missal?

The modern Roman Missal contains fifteen Prefaces, as follows: Christmas—Epiphany—Lent—of the Cross—Easter—Ascension—Pentecost—Trinity—Sacred Heart—Christ the King—The Blessed Virgin—St. Joseph—The Apostles—Common Preface—the Dead.

Several dioceses and religious Orders have prefaces proper to certain special feasts. Thus, the Romano-Seraphic Missal of the Franciscans contains three additional prefaces for the feasts of St. Francis, St. Dominic, and St. Clare.

In olden times, Prefaces were much more numerous than today. For example, the Leonine Sacramentary used in the seventh century contained 267 Prefaces! Each saint had his own Preface.

Two Prefaces that we should personally like to see restored to our Missals are those of St. John the Baptist and of Advent.

As a matter of fact, we know that according to the liturgical protocol as indicated by the Litany of the Saints, St. John the Baptist has precedence over St. Joseph.

But the holy Precursor does not have a Preface of his own!

Likewise, all the cycles of the liturgical year except Advent have their proper Prefaces.

150—Are there other Prefaces besides those in the Mass?

Yes. The solemn thanksgiving of the Eucharistic Sacrifice has become the model for several formulas of Sacraments and sacramentals in the liturgy.

A. Sacraments.

The typical Preface of the Mass with its introductory dialogue is found in the liturgy for the sacraments of:

1. *Baptism.* (Consecration of the baptismal font.)
2. *Confirmation.* (Consecration of Holy Chrism.)
3. *Penance.* (Public reconciliation of penitents.)
4. *Ordination.* (Of priests and deacons, Consecration of Bishops.)
5. *Extreme Unction.* (In certain annexed rites, concerning visitation of the sick.)
6. *Marriage.* (As in the *Ritual of Sanctorius* for the nuptial blessing.)

B. Sacramentals:

Besides the Sacraments, the Preface and its dialogue enter into the ritual of several sacramentals:

1. The blessing of candles, ashes, and palms.
2. The blessing of the paschal candle.

3. The dedication of churches and the consecration of altars.
4. The blessing and reconciliation of profaned cemeteries.
5. The consecration and coronation of emperors, kings, and queens.
6. The blessing of Abbots and Abbesses.
7. The consecration of Virgins.

151—How is the Preface divided?

The Preface is divided as follows:

1. The introductory dialogue
2. The beginning of the Preface
3. The body or Preface proper
4. The conclusion

152—What does each of these parts contain?

a. The introduction is composed of three versicles with their responses:

Dominus vobiscum.	The Lord be with you.
Et cum spiritu tuo.	And with your spirit.
Sursum corda.	Lift up your hearts!
Habemus ad Dominum.	We have lifted them up unto the Lord.
Gratias agamus Domino Deo nostro.	Let us give thanks to the Lord our God.
Dignum et justum est.	It is meet and just.

b. The beginning of the Preface never varies.

Vere dignum et justum est, aequum et salutare, nos tibi semper et ubique gratias agere:	It is truly meet and just, right, and availing unto salvation, that we should at all times and in all places give thanks to you, O
Domine, sancte Pater, omnipotens aeterne Deus, per Christum Dominum nostrum.	Lord, Holy Father, Almighty Everlasting God. Through Jesus Christ our Lord.

c. The body of the Preface varies according to the mystery or feast being celebrated.

The body of the Preface develops the reason for the thanksgiving: "It is truly meet and just, right and availing unto salvation, that we should always and in all places praise the Lord, because...."

Christmas: "For by the mystery of the Incarnate Word, the new light of your glory has shone into our minds; so that henceforth knowing God in a visible manner, we may be rapt in love for those things that are invisible...."

Epiphany: "For your only Begotten Son, appearing to us garbed in mortal flesh, restored us by the new splendour of his immortality...."

Passiontide: "(Eternal God)" who has placed the salvation of the world in the tree of the Cross, that where death had appeared, life might spring up; and that by the wood of the Cross might be conquered he who once triumphed by the wood...."

Easter: "But to praise you more gloriously than ever in this night wherein Christ our Passover was sacrificed for us. For this is the true Lamb who takes away the sins of the world; who by dying destroyed death and restored life by his resurrection...."

Pentecost: "Who, ascending above the heavens, and being seated at your right hand, sheds abroad on the children of adoption the Holy Spirit whom he had promised...."

We could do likewise with the other Prefaces of the liturgical year. In each, we might easily find a subject for meditation; and develop the rich theme of the particular feast or period of the liturgical cycle.

d. *The Conclusion.* Almost always the same. (At least, as to the ideas expressed.) It is a mingling of celestial and earthly voices in the praise of God's majesty:

Per quem (Christum) majestatem tuam laudant Angeli, adorant Dominationes, tremunt Potestates, Caeli, caelorumque Virtutes, ac beata Seraphim, socia exultatione concelebrant.	Through whom (Christ) the Angels praise your majesty, the Dominations adore, the Powers reverence, the Heavens and the Virtues of Heaven and the blessed Seraphim celebrate in common exultation.

Cum quibus et nostras voces ut admitti jubeas, deprecamur, supplici confessione dicentes. . .	Deign, O Lord, to permit our voices to join with theirs in saying. . .

Now that we are familiar with the structure of the Preface, it remains for us to get from it the substance we shall need for nourishing our spiritual life, and for a fuller LIVING OF OUR MASS.

153—What does the priest do at the Preface?

When the priest comes to the words, *per omnia saecula saeculorum,* concluding the last *Secret,* he lowers both hands on the altar; and in this position says, *"Dominus vobiscum."* At the *Sursum corda,* he raises his hands and holds them extended at shoulder height, with the palms facing each other. At the *Gratias agamus Domino,* he rejoins his hands; and at the *Deo nostro,* looks upon the crucifix and bows his head. At the response, *"Dignum et justum est,"* he again holds his hands raised and extended as before.

These gestures of the priest are most expressive: imparting a greater force and eloquence to his words.

154—Please explain the introductory words of the Preface.

"Dominus vobiscum—the Lord be with you!" says the priest to the people; without, however, turning toward them again: so as not to be distracted from the sublime mystery, whose coming draws on apace. You will note how appropriately the wish comes at the beginning of the Preface. This is the moment for increased fervour, and for asking God to be more intimately present in our souls.

"Et cum spiritu tuo—and with your spirit," replies the congregation. The people implore the Lord to vouchsafe to bless the mind and heart of their representative at the altar.

"Sursum corda—Lift up your hearts!" But this time, the *Dominus vobiscum* is not enough! Before commencing the Great Action, this vile earth must be more fully left behind; so that the heart may be lifted up to God. Then it is, that, joining word to expressive gesture, the priest raises his hands toward Heaven; and in this position, prays, *"Sursum corda!"* Lift up your hearts! Have both feet on the ground, but your head in Heaven! Away, then, with sordid, mundane, earth-born thoughts, unruly affections and aversions. Look upward! *Sursum!*

Plain Christians, soldiers of Catholic Action, Tertiaries, priests, all! Earth-bound hearts are not for you! Your hearts must be great hearts, noble hearts, hearts which have left the lowlands to soar in the heights. Heights of divine love, of brotherly love: Heights of contemplation and prayer, of apostolic zeal! Heights of imitation of Jesus! Heights of sacrifice! Every Mass can impart to us a new impetus for action, help us to rise higher, to remain in the heights.... Every day of our lives, let us—at each day's start—repeat a real *Sursum corda;* and then make a genuine effort to remain all day long *ad Dominum*—in the Lord!

"*Habemus ad Dominum*—We have lifted them up unto the Lord," replies the congregation (who, if it is a High Mass, is standing). Here, let us take care to attune our hearts to our lips!... Let us recall that our hearts can be truly "lifted up" toward God, only from that moment when they shall have tossed outside the ballast of passion and of earthly preoccupations.

"*Gratias agamus Domino Deo nostro*—Let us give thanks to the Lord our God," prays the priest; joining his hands in the attitude of prayer and looking up toward Heaven. The dominant note of the Preface is Thanksgiving—the rest serving only to develop this *gratias agamus.*

"*Dignum et justum est*—It is meet and just," the people reply.

And "the people" are all those present. They are you, they are I! Therefore, let us never forget to join our voices to those of "the people." Let our gratitude burst forth! For the moment approaches, when, in the words of the Council of Trent, "God is about to shower down on the altar all the riches of his love for us." God, with all his wisdom, could find nothing more moving than this to offer us. Infinitely rich, he had nothing more precious to give us. Infinitely powerful, he could conceive of nothing greater for us, than the Sacrifice soon to become present on the altar!

A SCOUT LEADER'S PRAYER

Lord Jesus, who despite my weakness, have chosen me as leader and guardian of my brothers (or of my sisters), may I by word and example illumine their march on the pathways of your law, and may I learn to show them your divine footsteps in the nature that you have created, teach them what I should teach, and lead my troop step by step to you, my God, in that "camp" of joy and repose wherein you have "pitched" your "tent" and ours for all eternity. Amen.

155—Please give a brief summary of the words of the Preface.

"Vere dignum et justum est, aequum et salutare, nos tibi. . . . It is truly meet and just, right, and availing unto salvation to. . . give you thanks" . . . . Note how the celebrant adds to the people's response. Our hearts would indeed be ungrateful, were they to remain cold in the face of such great blessings: *It is truly meet. . . to thank you, O Lord!* Our hearts ought to sing their gratitude to such a Benefactor—it is "meet" to do so! Our hearts ought to pay their tribute of praise to the Blessed Trinity—it is "just" to do so. And by virtue of this action, we are assured of receiving new favours—it is therefore "availing unto salvation."

"Semper et ubique—at all times and in all places." God never takes a holiday. Nor should we! It is "at all times and in all places" that we should praise and thank him. Not just in church; not just when we are on our knees in the morning, and again at night, to "say our prayers"; but on the street, on the street car, the train, the bus, the boat, the plane; in shops, in the office, at the factory, on the farm, in class, in college, on the tennis court, at a party—and even at the movies! Should you find this latter place not ideal for lifting up your heart toward God, then stay away from the movies! For it is "at all times and in all places" that it is "meet and just" to thank God. *Semper et ubique!* Everywhere and always!

"Per Christum Dominum nostrum—through Jesus Christ our Lord." It is true, in the strong words of Pascal, that "Christ's Passion persists to the end of time" in the members of his Mystical Body. It is true that every moment of the day and night is "Mass time." The Consecration is continuous—so then is also the *Eucharist,* or Giving of Thanks. "But how," you exclaim, "are we, with so many things to do, in our bustling, breathless, modern life, going to 'thank God at all times and in all places?' "

The answer is, "Through Jesus Christ, our Lord"!

Knowing full well that we are not able to sing hymns of praise all day long to the Lord; nor to have sublime prayers ever on our lips (especially when our small brood is assailing us from all quarters, or we have some engrossing work to do that takes up all our time!), the Divine Master has taken upon himself the task of our thanksgiving; willing to be our Mediator before his Father in Heaven. In order to come to our aid, our Lord offers himself at every instant of the day; thus making up for our insufficiency, by sending up to Heaven infinite thanksgiving—alone worthy of Infinite Majesty. Since we are unable always to express our thanks to God, and since it is impossible to reach our Heavenly Father without first passing through Christ; with what sincerity should we not, at the Preface, ask our Lord to accept our work, our life of busy activity or of suffering—all our actions—that all may be transformed into a song of gratitude to the glory of God.

"*Per quem Majestatem tuam laudant angeli*. . . . By whom (Christ) the angels praise your Majesty." Here the words of the Preface transport us right into Heaven, and there show us a scene of incomparable grandeur—the entire celestial court ranged round Jesus Christ, united with him to adore God and praise his glory. What a magnificent spectacle is afforded by the sight of these nine choirs, divided into three orders:

I. Angels—Archangels—Virtues.
II. Powers—Principalities—Dominions.
III. Thrones—Cherubim—Seraphim.

Yes, it is Jesus who inspires the inhabitants of Heaven—the most sublime celestial powers, the blessed seraphim—with these transports and ardours with which they burst forth into a chorus of praise at the foot of your throne, O Holy Trinity, in loving adoration and ecstasy, truly worthy of your divine majesty, your goodness, and infinite mercy. How beautiful Heaven is! How is it possible that men, for the gratification of sinful passions, or through their refusal to obey the divine law; risk losing it forever? . . .

Note in passing, that the angels and all the celestial spirits have no superior advantages over us when it comes to praising God. For the Choirmaster over all in this celestial concert is Christ, our only Mediator; whose members, through his Mystical Body, we are! Therefore, apart from Christ, the angels are no better able with their orchestra (than we with our poor instruments) to praise God in keeping with his dignity. . . . If Christ does not come to bring unity among us mediocre musicians, our "concert" will become an uproarious din; and will degenerate into another war (like the one just ended), because men willed to do without Christ, their King!

Let us never forget that without Christ no good can be accomplished. But *with* him! . . .

"Cum quibus et nostras voces... that our voices may join in their song." Have you caught these words of the priest at this point in the Preface? Here is what the priest asks for in your name: "Vouchsafe, O Lord, to permit us to join our voices to the voices of the Angels, so that we may humbly say with them, '*Sanctus!* Holy! Holy! Holy!' "

What an honour, and also what audacity! We, with the Angels!

They, who are pure—and we, who are sinful.

They, who are always attentive—and we, who are nearly always distracted.

They, who are burning with love—and we, who are cold and indifferent!

What a stimulus for our zeal! The angels and saints of Heaven (directed by the God-Man), blending their voices as one!... Henceforth, we should never lose sight of Christ, so that we may follow his directives; and sing our parts in this heavenly hymn in unison with the celestial choir!... Those who have the sad habit of swearing, should hasten to attune their voices to those of the angels—or run the risk of being unable any longer to LIVE their Mass!

A number will perhaps wish to withdraw from this choir, pretexting their "weak" or "untrained" voices. No, that will not do! In this great chorus which covers Heaven and earth, every man's note must be heard.

Whether you are a soprano, tenor, bass, alto, or contralto; whatever your character or temperament; you have your small part to play in this great concert of gratitude to God—Author of all good.

Naturally, each individual will make use of the instrument or talent which he has received and developed.... The whistle of a locomotive, the horn of a taxi, the whir of an engine, the blacksmith's hammer, the swish of the housewife's broom, the clatter of typewriter keys—all enter into the great rhythm; and when offered up with a pure heart, become harmonious to the divine ear.

Another thing! We talk of the "union of earth and Heaven." This does not mean a solo, where someone stands up in our midst and sings for the purpose of making himself (or herself) admired—or detested!!! No, in this great concert, the centre of interest is not you, but God! In the exact measure that you DEcrease, he will INcrease. This means no more "rugged individualism," but union; a communion of voices blended in a single hymn of praise!

Hence, when we give voice to our gratitude to God, let us stop putting ourselves forward; and instead, exert every effort to put God first. That we may do this, let us unite ourselves closely with Christ; and in him, to all his members on earth and in Heaven: to his Mystical Body, the saints in Heaven, the saints on earth, the Pope, bishops, priests, consecrated souls, the members of the three Franciscan Orders—who are our brothers and sisters—and together let us sing with our whole heart, *Sanctus!* So shall our song become a veritable prayer.

Sanctus

156—What does the celebrant recite after the Preface?

After the Preface, the priest recites the Sanctus.

Sanctus, Sanctus, Sanctus, Dominus Deus Sabaoth,	Holy, Holy, Holy, Lord God of Hosts;
Pleni sunt caeli et terra gloria tua.	The heavens and the earth are full of your glory.
Hosanna in excelsis.	Hosanna in the highest.
Benedictus qui venit in nomine Domini.	Blessed in He who comes in the name of the Lord.
Hosanna in excelsis.	Hosanna in the highest.

157—Is the Sanctus part of the Preface?

The Sanctus is incorporated into the Preface. It is joined to the final part of the Preface, of which it is the natural complement.

158—Why is the "Sanctus" sometimes called the "Seraphic Hymn"?

For the reason that the words of the Sanctus are taken from a passage in the Book of Isaias; an Old Testament prophet who had the following vision:

> In the year of king Ozias' death, I had a vision. I saw the Lord sitting on a throne that towered high above me, the skirts of his robe filling the temple. Above it rose the figures of the seraphim, each of them six-winged; with two wings they veiled God's face, with two his feet, and the other two kept them poised in flight.

And ever the same cry passed between them, Holy, holy, holy is the Lord God of hosts; all the earth is full of his glory. (Is. 6:1-3.) [Knox.]

So the Sanctus is called the "Seraphic hymn," because it is sung by seraphim. (St. Francis, too, was called "seraphic," because he loved Christ and sang his praises with the flaming ardour of a seraph.)

159—Can you give a brief commentary on the Sanctus?

When the celebrant has formulated this request in the name of the people, to unite our voices with those of the angels, he inclines moderately and rejoins his hands (which up to that time had been extended at his sides, shoulder level.)

Then, as if weighed down by the grandeur of his functions, as well as by the sentiment of his unworthiness, he slightly lowers his voice and recites the Sanctus.

Holy, holy, holy! Why repeat thrice the word "holy?" St. Ambrose replies: "The threefold acclamation expresses God's unity and the Trinity of the Divine Persons. The seraphim do not sing the word, 'holy' once only, so as not to indicate a sort of solitary Deity. They do not sing it twice only, so as not to exclude the Holy Spirit. They do not say it in the plural, because there are not several Gods. They repeat it thrice, and thrice in an identical manner; so that the hymn may help us to understand the distinction and equality of the Divine Persons, as well as their unity of nature." By our proclamation of the holiness of the One Triune God, we glorify his infinite purity and sanctifying power; from which our own sanctity derives. "O God, thrice holy!" we might exclaim, "of all Sanctifiers best, who by your grace blot out our crimes and stains; purify our hearts by contrition and repentance; so that we may ever approach you."

It may be noted here that the Apostle St. John, transported in spirit to Heaven, saw and heard, as Isaias did, the angels surrounding God's throne and chanting day and night without ceasing, this same hymn: "Holy, holy, holy, the Lord God Almighty, who was, and who is, and who is coming!" (Apoc. 4:8.)

"*Deus sabaoth*—Lord God of Hosts." In acclaiming the Lord here as "Lord God of Hosts," we do not mean the military forces of this world, but the angelic militia mentioned by Daniel the prophet :"A thousand

thousand they were that waited on his bidding, and for every one of these, a thousand others were standing there before him." (Dan. 7:10.) [Knox.] We recognize God's sovereign dominion over all earthly and heavenly powers; and affirm his authority over the angelic hosts who precipitated Lucifer and his henchmen into the pit of Hell and protect men from Satan's hordes.

"*Pleni sunt caeli et terra gloria tua*—the heavens and earth are full of your glory." We praise and glorify the Creator, whose attributes shine forth in all that is in Heaven and on earth: the heavens with their countless suns; the earth, chosen despite its small size, to manifest the marvels of his infinite mercy; to be watered with the blood of Christ and to become the dwelling-place of the Holy Eucharist!

"*Hosanna in excelsis!*—Hosanna in the highest!" "Hosanna" is an Hebraic acclamation, borrowed from the 118th Psalm; and meaning, "Aid us," or "Save us." It corresponds roughly to "Hurrah!" The joy of the crowds on Palm Sunday vibrates through this hymn. (Mark 11:10.)

"*Benedictus qui venit in nomine Domini*—Blessed is he who comes in the name of the Lord. "Yes, Blessed be Jesus, our Saviour! He is about to descend among us! Soon he will be on the altar.... Let us rejoice and be glad like the Hebrews who went to Jerusalem to see Christ make his triumphal entry.... Like them, let us shout "Hosanna!"

160—Can you draw a comparison between the Preface and the Sanctus on the one hand; and the "Canticle of Creation" composed by St. Francis of Assisi, Patron of Catholic Action, on the other?

It has been said of St. Francis when he prayed, that it was not a man praying, but prayer made man!... Prayer incarnate!

The following lines will surely help us to understand this statement by St. Francis' first biographer, and will give us a working model of eucharistic prayer or the prayer of thanksgiving—quite in tone with the Preface.

"The Canticle of Creation" (improperly called "The Canticle of the Sun") is a hymn of praise and gratitude to God for the blessings of creation. The circumstances of its composition are as follows.

St. Francis was ill at St. Damiano, in the summer of 1225, therefore, some months before the great miracle of La Verna where he received the stigmata.

Worn out by his austerities, consumed by the seraphic ardour which inflamed him, St. Francis suffered cruelly besides from an eye disease contracted in Egypt during the mission tour he conducted there, with a view to converting the sultan and his subjects. This malady was further aggravated by the incessant tears he shed before the crucifix, over the sins and ingratitude of mankind. "Love is not loved!" he wept. "Help me to make men love this Love who is not loved!"

The physicians were powerless to effect a cure; and to relieve the dreadful pain a little, St. Clare had a little cell made of reeds prepared in the garden, where Francis could withdraw and rest a little. It was there that he received the visits from "sister mice," which added to his tortures. . . .

One night when the torturing pain was worse than usual, and St. Francis was almost blind, his soul, pressed on all sides, purified by pain, and as if disengaged from matter, uttered its plaintive prayer to God; imploring patience to support his sufferings. God replied that by this suffering, St. Francis would gain the Kingdom of Heaven. Then, rapt in ecstasy, and adoring God's sovereignty, Francis submitted to God's rigours. And as St. Francis consented never more to see with his mortal eyes the light of day, and the beauties of nature he had so admired, he began, in a welling up of fervour, adoration, and gratitude, to celebrate their praises; causing to mount up to the Creator his hymn of the glory and blessings of creation. Here are the words that fell from his lips:

Most high, almighty, and good Lord,
Yours is the praise, the glory, honour, blessing all.
To you, Most High, alone of right do they belong.
And no mortal man is fit to mention you.
Be praised, my Lord, of all your creature world,
And first of all Sir Brother Sun.
Who brings the day, and light you give to us through him,
And beautiful is he, agleam with mighty splendour:
Of you, Most High, he gives us indication.
Be praised, my Lord, through Sisters Moon and Stars:
In the heavens you formed them, bright and fair and precious.
Be praised, my Lord, through Brother Wind,
Through Air, cloudy, and clear, and every kind of weather

By which you give your creatures sustenance.
Be praised, my Lord through Sister Water,
For greatly useful, lowly, precious, chaste is she.
Be praised, my Lord, through Brother Fire,
Through whom you brighten up the night.
And fair he is, and gay, and vigorous, and strong.
Be praised, O Lord, through our Sister, Mother Earth,
For she sustains and guides our life.
And yields us divers fruits, with tinted flowers and grass;
Praise and bless my Lord, and thank him too,
And serve him all, in great humility.

St. Francis later made two additions to the first seven strophes of the Canticle of Creation; one of them at Assisi, when he returned, almost dying, to his home town.

St. Francis wanted to see Assisi once more before he died. His friars carried him to Bishop Guido who, nineteen years before, had received his vow of perfect poverty; after Francis had, in his presence, given back to his father, Bernadone, the clothing he had received from him. There the saint learned that the podesta, or mayor of the city, and the bishop, were at loggerheads. The bishop had laid the magistrate under interdict, and the latter had outlawed the prelate.

The inhabitants of Assisi took up the cudgel for one faction or the other, and the peace of the city was troubled. When Francis learned this, he preached no sermon and reprimanded no one; but requested the magistrate to come to the square in front of the bishop's palace with his partisans, and he asked the bishop to be present also.

When all those invited had come together, two Friars Minor, whom Francis had instructed beforehand, intoned the Canticle of Creation, while the other friars joined their hands in prayer. They chanted the seven strophes in alternate choirs. Then, after the seventh, they chanted an eighth stanza which Francis had composed for the occasion; and which went as follows:

"Be praised, my Lord, through those who pardon give for love of you.
And bear infirmity and tribulation.
Blessed are they who suffer it in peace,
For by you, Most High, they shall be crowned."

Meanwhile, Francis prayed God to reconcile the adversaries.

Scarcely had the last word been sung, when the podesta knelt at the bishop's feet and implored his pardon; himself pardoned the bishop; and protested his obedience for the sake of our Lord, and of Francis his servant. The bishop raised up the kneeling magistrate, embraced him, and in his turn, implored forgiveness.

Once more, meekness had vanquished wrath and Francis had brought peace among men.

The holy poet composed the ninth and last stanza the same year, a few weeks before his death. (Probably, at the beginning of the month of September, 1226, at Foligno, where he had been taken to see his doctor.) Francis asked the physician if death were near. At first, the doctor declined to give his opinion; but at Francis' insistence, he replied that his patient would probably live until the end of September or the beginning of October. After a moment of silence and recollection, Francis raised his eyes and hands toward Heaven and began to chant softly:

"Be praised, my Lord, through our Sister, Death of Body,
From whom no man among the living can escape.
Woe to those who in mortal sin will die;
Blessed are those whom she will find in your most holy graces,
For the second death will do no harm to them."

161—What sentiments are expressed by St. Francis in his beautiful "Canticle of Creation"?

St. Francis had no other purpose than to express the sentiments of his soul: Adoration of the Creator, admiration for his works, and gratitude for his blessings. (Note these ends are the same as those of the Mass.)

St. Francis praises God. Why? Because God's works are beautiful and good. Which works? The most outstanding, for Francis could not give a detailed list of all things created. So he named those things that directly strike the senses: The sun, moon, stars, wind, air, water, fire, earth. As their spokesman, he calls on them to bow down in worship before their Creator and Lord.

In the Preface, we asked our Lord for permission to unite our voices to those of the angels. For St. Francis, this is not enough. He must give a still wider scope to his praise. So that everything may be included in his hymn, he calls upon all creation. He himself will play the rôle of mediator between Christ and inanimate creatures.

The first strophe of his canticle is like an introduction. It states this general truth; "God alone is praiseworthy. To him redound all honour and glory!" All the rest of the poem will be a development of this theme first expressed, whose import is so elevated; and at the same time, so profound. . . .

Glory is whatever I can imagine that is most magnificent and highest, and God is glory. . . . His glory fills all creation, from the highest to the lowest of creatures, surpassing and penetrating all things! Before this Infinite Being, all-glorious, all-beautiful, and all-great, my soul cannot remain insensible. In an ectasy of grateful love, it must needs break forth in a paean of admiration and joy!

God ought to be praised for the blessings enumerated in the first six stanzas of the "Canticle of Creation."

1. For our Brother Sun, who is God's image. He is good, for he gives us the day and the light. He is beautiful, for he is resplendent and radiant—he transforms all creation. So is it with Christ, the Sun of Sanctity. He transfigures those souls who dwell beneath his radiance.

2. For our Sisters, the Moon and Stars, who are bright and fair.

3. For the Wind (Breath of the Holy Spirit), for the air, which nourishes all creatures; and likewise for the Seasons, which pass in succession with their splendour and charm. (Here let us consider how our whole life should be subject to the influence of the Holy Spirit, who inspires our actions and prayers.)

4. For our Sister Water, who pleases us by her virtues; for she is lowly and chaste. (An invitation to humility, and to cleanness of body and soul.) We must be chaste in thought, word, and deed. And (St. Francis continues) for our Sister Water for her qualities, for she is useful and precious. (She cleanses and invigorates our tired, stiff bodies. And how well she quenches our thirst!) The water of Baptism produces similar effects in the soul. It washes away sin and regenerates the soul with the grace of divine adoption—a "fountain of living water," which unceasingly quenches its thirst.

5. For our Brother Fire, who complements the sun by illuminating darkness; and whose attributes are beauty, gaiety, vigour, and strength.

For the delectation of Scouts and Guides, here are a few reflexions which could serve as a meditation around the camp fire:

FIRE AND THE HOLY SPIRIT

The visible manifestation of the taking possession of our souls by the Holy Spirit on our Confirmation Day—our "Pentecost."

"Be praised, my Lord," cried St. Francis, "for Brother Fire, through whom you brighten up the night." It was through tongues of fire that the Holy Spirit illumined the minds of the Apostles on the Day of Pentecost, and illumined our minds on our Confirmation Day. (Gift of light.)

"... and fair he is, and gay." A call for true Beauty and true Joy that lift the soul up to God under the breath of the Holy Spirit, making it mount upward like a flame! Again, fire purifies as it burns. Let us, too, be "flames"; mounting upward toward Heaven, the home of true joy.

"And vigorous and strong." The gift of fortitude, which made of the hitherto timid apostles hardy witnesses of Christ, even to martyrdom. We, too, received this same gift of fortitude at Confirmation; enabling us to be—like the apostles—witnesses of Christ in our environment.

The fire dies down, but continues to smoulder a long time under the ashes: the image of Christian hope—a brand that continues to catch fire, despite death's certainty. (The fire going out.) For this virtue implants a seed-germ of immortality in our regenerated bodies.

The flame which draws inward as it dies, invites us to spiritual withdrawal (examination of conscience), to communion with the impressive silence of the night and nature. (The recollection period of our night prayers.)

May the Holy Spirit vouchsafe to rekindle more vividly in our souls tomorrow morning, the fire of his love, left smouldering through the night!

6. Finally, for the common mother of men, animals and plants, the Earth; charged by God to sustain creatures, to bring forth plants, fruits, and flowers and to nourish all living things.

Thus in these seven strophes or stanzas, St. Francis of Assisi becomes the poet of creation; which, through him, sings the Creator's glory.

The eighth stanza (the one St. Francis composed to reconcile the bishop of Assisi and the magistrate), is by its form, a laud; and while it does not celebrate the exterior works of God; it nonetheless praises God's action on the world, especially in the spiritual world of souls:

"Praised be God for his mercy and for those who pardon, for God will reward them."

After an elapse of thirteen centuries, St. Francis, most perfect copy of Christ, repeated the words of the Master in his third Beatitude: "Blessed are the merciful, for they shall obtain mercy."

The ninth stanza is the only one that St. Francis composed for his own intentions. In it he praises God for death—for approaching bodily dissolution. It is his swan song, his farewell to earth. It is at the same time his hymn of hope; for, "those whom death shall discover in the state of grace, united to God's will, shall not be hurt by the second death" (i.e. Eternal death or Hell).

The Canticle of Creation ends with a brief conclusion, wherein Francis, addressing his friars and all men generally, invites them to praise and bless God and humbly serve him.

"Praise and bless my Lord, and thank him too, and all serve him in great humility."

This is the lesson of the whole Canticle.

St. Francis wrote his Canticle of Creation in prose. Later on, he charged Brother Pacific—dubbed the "king of verse"—to recast the words in a more classic rhythm; so that the friars could recite or sing them.

Closer to our own times, the great admirer of St. Francis and founder of the St. Vincent de Paul Society, Frederick Ozanam, likewise versified the Canticle of Creation; and Fr. R. Thinot set it to music with an air in the Gregorian mode. Thus harmonized, this sublime anthem is sung at meetings of Franciscan fraternities in the twentieth century; just as it was among the brothers of the thirteenth century.

162—Can you recall a Psalm of David in which the same thought is expressed?

In the 148th Psalm, the holy king David likewise calls on all creation to glorify its Creator, and in a mighty voice cries out:

Praise Him, sun and moon, praise Him all you twinkling stars!

Praise Him, highest heavens, and waters that are above the heavens! . . .

Fire, hail, snow and fog, stormy winds that do His bidding... mountains and all hills... wild beasts... reptiles and winged birds... praise the name of the Lord.... A theme of praise for all His faithful, the children of Israel, a people near unto Him. [From the new translation of the Psalms by Fr. Joseph B. Frey.]

We find this prayer of praise again on the lips of three Hebrew youths, Ananias, Misael, and Azarias; of whom we have already spoken. (Question 132.) Thrown into the furnace heated by Nabuchodonosor "seven times more than it was accustomed to be heated," the three Hebrew youths walked amidst the flames, which had miraculously become harmless, and sang the Lord's praises.

In their hymn, they called upon all living creatures—from the pure spirits, the angels in Heaven, to the most humble of beings, wild and domestic animals, whales and fish—to bless, praise, and exalt the Lord forever and ever.

Of the same sublime poetic and religious inspiration, the Canticle of Creation, written by St. Francis, adds something to the hymn of the three Hebrew youths in the fiery furnace. God's Troubadour is not content with merely naming the creatures he calls upon to adore their Creator; but he proclaims the usefulness and virtues of each, which commend them to our attention. Again, to the somewhat formal and arid inspiration of antiquity, the Poet of Assisi adds an evangelical, pleasing, and delicate note—in a word, a Christian and chivalrous character. Since he courteously calls the sun, "*Sir* Sun"; and gives it, as well as the air and wind, the name of "Brother"; while to the moon, stars, water, and earth, he gives the names of "Sister" and "Mother"!

163—Now that you have studied the Preface, Sanctus, and "Canticle of Creation," are you able to define a hymn of praise?

At the beginning of this study—in question 5—we saw God's imposing plan for Creation; all in this plan being ordained *to the glorification of the Blessed Trinity.*

Man, an intelligent creature, is the intermediary—the living link —between creation and Creator. After contemplating the universe and hearing the prayer of unreasoning creatures praising God in their own way, man feels the need of lending them his heart and lips to send up a more perfect thanksgiving to the God of all goodness.

The prayer of praise, then, consists in a contemplation, in an opening of one's eyes and a perceiving of the interrelationship existing between creature and Creator; and in a making use of the knowledge acquired to thank God—or cause him to be thanked.

This is what St. Francis did when he called on the birds to praise God and give him thanks. In his book, *The Perfect Joy of St. Francis,* Felix Timmermans tells us the story of this in a charming way. It will not be taking us far afield from our theme to introduce this citation here:

(The period is that in which St. Francis was wondering whether he should lead the contemplative or the active life. After receiving Heaven's reply from the lips of Clare and Sylvester, commanding him to preach, Francis, filled with joy, took two brothers with him, Angelo and Masseo.)

> They could not keep up with him; for Francis, in his enthusiastic desire to preach, had sped on ahead. Suddenly sensing the beauty of life, he burst into song. His soul thrilled at thought of the clouds, the green grass, beasts and men, earth, sun, and stars—all come from God's hand, like wealth that cannot be contained. All penetrated with God's Spirit. God everywhere, and we moving in him!
>
> "Brothers! Brothers!" he cried, throwing open his arms toward all that he saw and all that he did not see. "We are all brothers! Let us serve our Father!" So they arrived at the route of Bevagna, in the valley.
>
> What was going on there, around those solitary trees? A thousand different birds, and thousands more coming, large and small, perching, hopping, flying. Birds by the armful, flocks of birds, flights of birds, birds tossed into the air like so many grains of wheat! Warbles, chirps, carolings, tremolos and trills—the skies vibrated with them!
>
> As St. Francis came nearer, the birds sang and whistled more loudly, seemed to grow in number, clustered thick in the trees, on the greensward and in the air. The two friars who had just emerged into the clearing farther back, joined their hands. And when all

at once they saw the birds begin to fly around St. Francis' head, they said softly to each other, "It is in his honour!" And they stood there, some little distance off, from respect. Francis was surprised to see so many birds together. Known varieties like the heron with its long beak and long neck, nightingales, starlings, kinglets, the robin, and its friend the lark, the pigeon, and the humble sparrow; and also unknown varieties; some of them so beautiful that no man could have found a name for them. There were rose-coloured birds, blue birds, speckled birds, birds whose plumage had the pearly lustre of shells, or else had golden glints in it, or the shimmer of red and green lights. Some there were like the rose-flush of dawn, like mother-of-pearl, like rich brocade, like flames, like silk, like threads of silver. Beauteous of form and line, with collars and caps and crests. Curly plumes, wavy plumes. Tails, sombre as an evening sky, or delicate as the frost-flowers on the window pane. A vision of colours and hues, with the sun above all to make all scintillate and sparkle. Each bird had its own peculiar call, cry, and song; and all fluttered and flew around Francis, who trembled with happiness.

"This is not because of me," thought he, "but for love of God!"

His heart was moved, and his tongue uttered soft sounds. He raised his hands, wishing to say a few words to the birds. Suddenly those thousands of birds became motionless and mute and settled down about him in a circle. The small birds slipped in among the large, even to the first row. The trees were thick-covered with birds—not a leaf was to be seen. Every bough was as if wrapped in silk, in down, in garnet stones of the most coruscant.... A few tiny birds perched on Francis' shoulders, on his outstretched arms, and even in the folds of his habit!

Listen! He is speaking to them!" whispered Friar Masseo, who had begun to weep softly. And they listened.

"Dear little birds, my brothers! Praise and give thanks to God, who is your Father and mine! For we are the work of his hands—his love surrounds us and moves us. See how he concerns himself with you! He preserved you in Noah's Ark. He has given you leisure time and the joy of flight, for whenever and wherever you will—all space is yours. He has given you warm plumage, thick coats against rain and snow; and your children receive them without your having to spin and sew. And how beautifully are you clad—like flowers and the rainbow! God feeds you. You find your food prepared for you on trees, in meadow-lands, along the shores of streams, by fountains, and in the streets. He has given you clefts in the rock, haymows, poplar trees, and tiled roofs in which to build your nests. He has given to each of you a song and a voice with which you may call your brothers and speak to them, with which you may praise God and bless him. Do you see now, how God cares for you and preserves your lives? So do not be ungrateful! Remain simple and poor, as an example to men and to the Friars Minor; and do not weary of glorifying your Father with enthusiasm and zeal. For your song is your prayer. So sing, brother birds, sing!"

And then the birds with their tiny beaks half-open, began again to whistle and sing, each according to its nature; nodding their little heads to show that this sermon was much to their liking. And Francis, seeing this, was filled with gratitude and joy.

In the background, the Brothers—on their knees— contemplated the marvel. They saw Francis give his blessing to the birds. Suddenly there was a great whir of wings! Like the jet of water from a fountain, all the birds flew higher and higher into the heavens; and dispersed in the form of a cross toward the four winds.

"O Lord, thank you! Thank you!" cried Francis, and running up to his Friars, he exclaimed.

"Come! Let us go forth and preach! If even the birds listen to us, then why not men?"

That was the way St. Francis prayed!

Everything in the divine plan harmonizes: People, things, minds, vocations, places. Everything fits together, dovetails together. Each is made for the other, like the pieces in an immense jigsaw puzzle. Each detail contributes to the whole, and the absence of the smallest piece destroys the beauty of the picture.

To the extent that we become detached and disengaged from matter, we shall have a clearer view of things; because we shall have acquired a little of God's simplicity. Creation will then no longer appear to us like a jumble of bewildering, unrelated things, which chance has hurtled helter-skelter into space, but we shall grasp the reigning harmony—the part which each should play in bringing about the Great Return and glorifying God.

Praying is a becoming aware of God's presence in creation. It is the recognition of his fatherhood over all creatures, and the treating of them as brothers.

The more we see and take into consideration—as in a single comprehensive glance—this ramification of links or relations, which, through Christ binds the Creation to God—down through the Trinity—Christ—Mary—the Angels—the Saints—the members of the Mystical Body—those not yet incorporated into it—friends—enemies—demons—animals—plants—minerals, and all else that exists—the larger will loom the importance and place of prayer in our lives.

Obviously, if all things cohere in God (and of this there can be no doubt); then the smallest most infinitesimal creature—the tiniest amoeba—forms a point of contact with God! So here is another definition for you! Prayer is essentially contacting God through his creation!

But you knew all this before? The penny catechism taught it when it answered your question, "Where is God? with the word, "God is everywhere"?

The trouble is, we forget!

As a matter of fact, how many persons say to us, "I can't be always taking time off from my work to pray!" (As if prayer were something extraneous that was superadded to life. As if it were necessary to flee somewhere, or withdraw from one's environment in order to pray!)...

On the contrary, we must make use of our surroundings to pray! Our life and activity should unfold in an atmosphere of prayer. Our every breath should be a prayer! Such is the way to put into practice the dictum of St. Paul: "Whether you eat or drink, or do anything else; do all for the glory of God."

Who has not heard, or perhaps let drop, a remark like this anent a person more given over to "pious practices" than to the "practice" of the crucifying duty of one's state in life: "Instead of spending all day in church, she'd do better looking after her children!"

Far from being an escape, prayer—true prayer—is a more profound attachment to persons and things, to reality, to duty; in fine, to God.

Prayer means the recognition of the relations God has set up between himself and the universe. Conscience and my Catholic Faith make clear what these relations are. If I am to pray well, I must take them into consideration.

When we speak of "profound attachment to persons and things," our meaning must be clearly understood. We are on the road leading back to the Father's House. Having come from God, we must return to God. We are not isolated individuals; but living, responsible members of the immense family that has sprung from the heart of God. Consequently, that man prays, who in his conduct, movements, actions, and thoughts, takes into consideration his position with regard to God and creatures; and constantly works to bring God's creation back to him. Praying, means laying hold of creatures, not for ourselves, but that we might, through Christ, attach them to God.

It's easier to understand now why a mother who leaves her house for long hours of "devotion" in church (while her children, left to themselves, stray from God, with great risk to their souls); is far from praying—even though she has "said" several rosaries and "made" an equal number of novenas!

164—Please give a few Gospel passages which demonstrate how Jesus kept in constant "contact" with his Heavenly Father, through means of creatures; and in which he thereby teaches us how we can always pray.

We have said that prayer was "contacting" God. Now Christ, who always maintained conscious contact with God, never ceased to pray.

He always perceived his Father everywhere present, everywhere active. He saluted creation coming from the divine, omnipotent, all-loving hand of God:

"My Father makes his sun to rise on the good and on the evil. . ."
"My Father sends rain. . . ."
"My Father clothes the lilies of the field. . . ."
"My Father feeds the birds. . . ."

"My Father has counted the very hairs of your head. Not one of them shall fall to the ground without his permission. . . ." etc.

Christ Jesus was always about his Father's business—He saw it everywhere.

Continuously he perceived in persons, events, and things, the presence, action, and love of God.

This constant vision of the divine goodness and omnipotence laid hold of him completely, and totally he devoted himself to his Father's service.

He abased himself, adored, praised, supplicated, and prayed.

Constantly, he gave thanks and offered himself to his Father.

"My food is to do the will of my Father." (*See* No. 12.)

"I give you thanks, Father, because you have revealed these things to the humble. . . ."

Before acting, Jesus thanked God, the Giver of all good; before the multiplication of the loaves, the raising of Lazarus, the Institution of the Holy Eucharist, etc.

It has been said with reason that Jesus Christ is the Father's "Religious"; that is, the One who is always united or "bound" * to His Father, or again, the one who binds all creation to his Father.

Although Jesus prayed to his Father through his contacts with the created universe, providential happenings, or the performance of the duties of his state in life; he nevertheless devoted a special time to prayer. Once he had ministered to the bodies and souls of men, or taken care of the necessities of life, he became absorbed in prayer. How many times have the Evangelists noted in their accounts: "And Jesus passed the night in prayer."

In Jesus' life, then, we find prayer and the practice of prayer.

This prayer life covered his whole earthly existence.

It is his Sacrifice, which began with his birth and ended with his death on Calvary. Jesus constantly lived his Sacrifice; just as we should constantly live our Mass, and so render glory to God and thank him "at all times and in all places."

As to the form these prayers took—the expression of his prayer life—the Evangelists tell us little.

---

* Because *religious* comes from two Latin words meaning "to bind things" . . . [Trans. Note.]

Every Sabbath, in the synagogue, Jesus (like all good Jews) alternately listened to and chanted the prophecies and Psalms:

"And he came to Nazareth where he had been brought up; and according to his custom, he entered the synagogue on the Sabbath and stood up to read." (Luke 4:16.)

Again there is this typical passage in which Jesus teaches us the most beautiful of prayer formulas, the Our Father!

"Once, when he had found a place to pray in, one of his disciples said to him, after his prayer was over, 'Lord, teach us how to pray, as John did for his disciples.' And he told them. "When you pray, you are to say, Father, hallowed be your Name." (Luke 11:1) [Knox.]

So should it be in our lives. It is the Preface which recalls all this to us: "It is truly meet and just, right and availing unto salvation, that we should at all times and in all places, give you thanks."

As a result, let those surrounding us, providential happenings (joys, and sorrows, sickness and loss, success and failure. . .), and the duties of our state in life, all be means for drawing us closer to God; for lifting up our hearts and minds toward him, in acts of praise and thanksgiving.

Let us be drawn on high toward the only Ideal worth our giving ourselves up to wholly, until death. (For our Sister, Bodily Death, be praised, O Lord!) and let us bring with us—as fruits of a life wholly devoted to prayer and works of apostolic zeal—the largest possible number of souls.

A FARM LAD'S PRAYER

Lord Jesus, who willed to live thirty years of our peaceful and laborious life in a small and humble hamlet, grant us to work with you, to pray with you, to love in you, our family, our village, and all our brother farmers.

Deliver us forever from the fear of human respect, from faintheartedness, from all evil, and from all sin.

May your divine life dwell and be radiant in our souls.

May your grace help us to work in peace for the union of all in our village.

Strengthen in the hearts of all militants the will to rechristianize their brothers.

Place in the hearts of our sister farmers the true spirit of Christian womanhood. Unite us in common ideals, and grant us to found homes that will people our beloved country with true Christians and your Heaven with saints. Amen.

OUR TWO PRAYERS

There are two ways to understand the word "prayer": the way Christ understood it when he said, "But when you pray, go into your room, and closing your door, pray to your Father in secret; and your Father who sees in secret, will reward you." (Matt. 6:6.) The other way is to live the way one should and offer up one's whole life. And neither of these two prayers will work without the other.

We must learn to go often into our "room" and close the "door." Learn to place ourselves alone before God; so that there is nothing in the world but God, and us before him—"God and myself," as Newman put it. We must learn to empty ourselves completely of past and future; forgetting for a time our most pressing cares, our most necessary occupations, our dearest friendships and affections. We must place ourselves before God thus completely stripped, and tell him that we love him; so that this relation of love of which his Holy Spirit is the true source, may so enlarge and transfigure us that this love will be reflected in and give life to our relations with others.

There will be days and hours when we shall not be able to go into our "room" and close the "door"; but we should not be slaves of time; and our prayer, to be true, need not be long. "But in praying, do not multiply words, as the Gentiles do, for they think that by saying a great deal, they will be heard. So do not be like them, for your Father knows what you need before you ask him." (Matt. 6: 7,8.) It matters little whether this look of supplication and love toward God lasts long—whether it takes few or many of our minutes—what IS important, is that this look should exist in our life: as frequently and as intensely as possible.

For we are living in a real world, with both feet planted squarely on the ground, in the thick of humanity; and we CANNOT spend our lives in prayer. And that is why our prayer—if it be really motivated by love—takes on another form, just as beautiful as the first. For it is the very enthusiasm with which we live, the very zest we put into each of our acts in the present, that builds our prayer. What else does the worker who "loves his job" do, if not to pray and adore the Source of all love? A surgeon operating on a patient cannot—must not—be thinking of the perfections of God as he wields the scalpel. We are feeble and finite beings, and our attention cannot be omnipresent. To do his job lovingly and well, our surgeon must have his mind on what he is doing. It is enough that he knows himself to be in God's hands; that he has a "right intention"; that before acting, he has offered God his work and his life.

We are like travellers going toward a star. If we would go straight toward the star, it is enough to know where the star is. We should then look down at our feet, so as not to stumble against the obstacles in the way. So shall we walk, with our eyes on the ground, but our feet marching toward the goal. (While a quick upward glance now and then enables us to keep our bearings.)

Thus it is that we need—each sustaining the other—both forms of prayer. Were we to look only at the earth, we should forget the direction of our goal. While were we merely to scan the heavens, we should not be able to discern the road leading to our star; and we should soon weary of the inexorable rough places in the road.

A WORKER'S PRAYER TO CHRIST

I worked hard yesterday, Lord—not like a saint, you know, but like the poor man I am. For life is no "picnic." We keep going, but we grumble (at least, inside.) We do someone a favor, but not always with a smile....

So this morning, I come to bring this to you—to you, my Big Brother—to buy Heaven with for me and mine, and to purchase the conversion of souls. But, frankly, I'm not very proud of my "money." No, my poor human work, so humanly done, cannot "buy" infinity.

That is why, Lord Jesus, I want very simply, to make you a little proposition! You have suffered, too; you have toiled; you bled and died. And you offer this every day to our Heavenly Father in the Mass.

If you are willing, I'll go to this Mass and I'll put what I have to offer in with your offering. And we'll be so united at that moment, that you can present my efforts as if they were yours; and it will be as though it were you who toiled yesterday.

And everything that Christians all over the earth have suffered, all that they do, and all that they hope, the Mass is going to blend this in with your offering, like the drop of water placed in the chalice, which is so mingled with the wine that it practically IS wine. And you will accept this sacrifice, dear Heavenly Father; and your life in the Church will increase.

—H. GODIN, priest

•

A PRAYER OF THE SICK WHO WILL NOT BE CURED

Our Father who are in Heaven, hear the prayer of your sick who will not be cured.

Lord, it is your will for me to fill up in my flesh whatever is lacking to the sufferings of my Jesus. Since you do not will to remove this chalice from me—which contains nothing of earth—then fill it with the goods of Heaven alone!

May it contain your blessed will for me. Give me the grace to comprehend its mysterious taste, and to use it wisely.

Cause my sufferings to make me better, and advance your kingdom in and around me. Father, if you do not will to remove these sufferings from my body, your will be done... your will be done... your will be done...

I wish to see you through my tears, recognize you in my sufferings; love you and help you to be loved by all those sick in soul and body.

I bless you, Father, because in you my sufferings are not in vain. I bless you, the Son, for teaching me by your Passion the value of suffering. I bless you, Holy Spirit, because you mingle my pains with those of my Jesus, to offer them in holocaust to the thrice holy God.

Holy Trinity, I beseech you, to let nothing be lost of what I can merit of recompense before you, on earth as in Heaven, by suffering as you desire me to suffer. Amen.

•

Silence and Solitude

The granite walls—
Jealous guardians of silence—
Have imprisoned the lake.

In this inviolate enclosure,
So profound is the peace of the wave,
And so crystalline clear the waters,
That they mirror the sky.

Who would have Christ in his soul,
Must erect in its recesses
A strong barrier of solitude:
Blocking all issues
Whence calm may escape,
Or anxiety enter!
Shutting out the vain tumult of the world,
Its confusion and clamour—
That nothing may trouble
The manifestation of his Presence.

Lake Minnewaka

Canadian Rockies

Ric Photo

The Little Gardener

With the grave mien of an Ursuline nun,
    This gardener fair works out in the sun;
Arranging the blooms with little girl grace—
    Lest leaf or small petal be out of place.

Fresh as a rose there (and scarcely more tall)
    With elfin-like pose, she stands by the wall;
With pride in her art, and joyous of heart—
    She does it "like Dad"—she's playing a part!

Lord, I implore you, Life's harshness may be
    Unable to mar the beauty we see!
Preserve the fair bloom of innocent charm.
    Immaculate keep her, free from all harm.

In your own garden, protect this pure rose
    From all baneful dusts and all evil foes—
From all icy blasts that kill and destroy
    A soul meant to bloom immortal in joy!

Ric Photo

165—To help in acquiring the habit of the prayer of praise and thanksgiving, can you recall some incidents from the life of St. Francis in which he "contacted" God through his creation?

One day two Negroes were talking together. One of these Negroes knew how to read, and the other did not.

"What are you looking at in this paper?" asked the illiterate one of his more learned companion.

"Oh, if you only knew how interesting it is!" the latter replied. "There are people talking in this paper! You can hear with your eyes!"

In the world of nature as well, there are persons and things that "speak" to us, and that we can "hear" with the ears of our soul. Too often, though, we are found among those who do not know how to read or listen!

As for the initiated, however—those who know how to see and understand—these read everywhere sublime, entrancing things. They read and hear the words of Nature's heaped-up marvels—the song of creation.

And from having read and heard, they understand. They understand how little it matters whether one is great or small, strong or weak, famous or unknown. They understand that the important thing for each is to be in the place where God meant him to be; perfect in the way God meant him to be perfect.

And having seen, heard, and understood, they thank God and praise him.

EVENSONG

O Jesus, my love, love of my life's sunset, gladden me with the sight of you at the hour of my departure.

O my Jesus of eventide, make me sleep peacefully in you and taste of that blessed rest which you have prepared for them that love you.

By one look from your eyes so pure, so winsome, show me the road leading to eternal life.

O my Love, be for me an eventide so fair that my soul will feel only joy in bidding a fond farewell to my body; and may my spirit at last returning to you, take refuge under the shadow of your wing.

Say to me then, in your clear and melodious voice, "Behold the Bridegroom comes! I have come to take you to eternity's wedding feast."

—SAINT GERTRUDE

Among those who have thus seen, heard, understood, thanked, and praised the Most High; St. Francis of Assisi, Patron of Catholic Action, seems to have succeeded most.

We have already recalled a few episodes in the life of St. Francis. We shall point out a few others. But it is St. Francis' whole life that should be cited!

These few incidents from the life of the Saint of Assisi, will help us to comprehend the spirit of the Preface; and better live our Mass, Eucharistic Sacrifice, or Thanksgiving.

We shall give a summary here of a magnificent chapter on "St. Francis and nature," taken from the book, *L'idéal de S. François d'Assise,* written by Fr. Hilary of Lucerne, O.F.M. Cap.

In St. Francis the love of nature took on a singular tenderness and warmth. Joy-intoxicated, Francis tramped through the countryside: admiring the charm of mountain and valley, the beauty of living things, and the redoubtable power of the elements.

St. Francis united in his person all the qualities of an attentive observer and delicate friend of nature: the pure look of the child, the fresh imagination and exquisite sensibility of the poet, the supernatural joy and divine charity of the saint. It was this last quality especially, which was the chief source of the joys he found in Nature and of his love for her.

All his dealings with nature were essentially religious. They had God for their beginning and end, and may be summed up in these words: From Creator to creature; from creature to Creator.

A. From creator to creature

It is not in the advantages to be reaped from nature, nor in the character of St. Francis, that we are to look for the underlying motives of his love for nature; but in his ardent love for God. *The Mirror of Perfection* puts it this way: "Blessed Francis, absorbed in his love for God, perfectly discerned God's goodness; not only in his soul—already adorned with all the virtues in their perfection—but also in all creatures. For this reason, he had a special and deep affection for them."

Possessed and penetrated by the thought that he was a child of God, he considered other creatures as belonging to the Heavenly Father's big family. In each of them he admired the wisdom, power, and goodness of the Creator. Merely to look at the sun, moon, and stars, or at creatures, great or small, filled him with unspeakable joy.

And because all alike had come from the Father's hand, Francis acknowledged with all a close kinship—they became his "brothers" and "sisters." Small they might appear to be, of little worth, contemptible; yet his heart penetrated their secrets; discovered their intimate essence; discerned God's mark. And from his lips these words fell, "My brother and sister in God—in him who is Maker and Father of us all!"

Francis did not stop with words (which were, after all, merely the expression of a profound conviction and of genuine feeling); but his heart overflowed with good will, not only for men in need, but for unreasoning brutes and the entire animate and inanimate creation, as well.

Thus did he embrace the universe in the bonds of a blissful harmony, similar to that existing between man and nature at the dawn of creation. His appeal to love resounded throughout all nature—and Nature's voice returned his loving accents.

Francis included all creation in a sacred hitherto unheard-of love; speaking to it of God and exhorting it to praise him. Did Francis but see a flower-filled field, he began preaching to the flowers as though they were endowed with reason—calling on them to praise the Lord. With the most sincere simplicity, he exhorted harvest fields and grapevines, rocks and forests, beautiful country sites, running water, verdant gardens, earth and fire, air and winds, to love God and willingly obey him.

Those animals which had been the object of special benevolence on the part of the Creator, were to show more gratitude toward God and be submissive to him.

Here are a few examples taken from among many:

1. *Sister Swallows*

One day, Francis came to the hamlet of Alviano to preach the Word of God. Having ascended a hillock where he could be seen of all, he requested silence. The crowd become silent; but a group of swallows which nested in the locality, twittered and made a great din. The Saint, unable to make himself heard, addressed the chatterboxes: "Sister Swallows, it is my turn now to speak, for you have talked long enough! Listen to God's Word; keep quiet; and do not move until I have finished talking about the Lord." To the surprise of all present, the little birds stopped twittering at once and did not move until the sermon was over.

2. *Brother Pheasant.*

A gentleman of the county of Siena sent a pheasant to Blessed Francis, who was ill. The latter accepted it with joy; not because he desired to eat it; but because, seeing such birds, he was accustomed to rejoice out of love for the Creator. He said to the pheasant, "Blessed be our Creator, Brother Pheasant." Then, addressing his Friars: "We shall see now if Brother Pheasant wants to stay with us; or if he prefers to go back to his familiar haunts, which are more suitable for him." On the Saint's order then, a friar took the bird and carried it a long way off to a vineyard. But the bird flew straight back to the Father's cell. Then Francis had the bird carried still farther away. Again, with unbelievable tenacity, the bird returned to the cell door; forcing its way in by passing under the habits of the friars who stood on the threshold. The Saint gave orders for the bird to be well fed, and began to stroke it and speak softly to it.

3. *Brother Falcon—alarm clock!*

Blessed Francis had withdrawn into a deserted spot, where he concluded a close pact of friendship with a falcon who had a nest there. Regularly every night, the bird would warn the Saint that is was time to rise; so that he might—following his custom—pay homage to God. Francis was most grateful to it for this great solicitude, which kept him from sleeping too long. But when Francis was worn out and weary from particularly violent pain, the falcon would take pity on him, and not indicate the hour to rise so punctually. As if the bird had received instructions from God, it was not heard until near dawn; when its voice sounding softly took the place of a bell.

4. *Sister Cicada*

Near the saint's cell at the Portiuncula, a cicada had set up housekeeping in a fig tree and often chirped with its accustomed sweetness. One day, the blessed Father, stretching out his hand toward the tiny insect, called to it kindly, "Sister Cicada, come here!" As if the insect had been endowed with reason, it came at once and lighted on his hand. Then he said, "Sing, Sister Cicada, and joyfully praise the God who made you!" Obeying on the spot, the insect began to chirp; and kept on chirping (the saint chiming in), until he ordered it to repair to its accustomed nook. The insect stayed eight whole days, as if it had been fastened there. When the saint came down from his cell, he always took it in his hand; enjoining it to "sing." And it always obeyed with alacrity! At last, the Saint said to his companions, "We shall now give Sister Cicada, who has cheered us so long with her song, her freedom." So dismissed, the cicada at once flew off and was never more seen in those parts.

5. *Brother Fishes*

Francis showed the same affectionate kindness toward fish; and whenever he had a chance, he would put fish that had been caught back into the water, counselling them not to let themselves be caught a second time!

Since everyone knows the story of the wolf of Gubbio, it would be useless to recall it here. It would also take too long to recount the adventures of St. Francis with a young hare and a wild rabbit....

The very elements seemed attracted by the loveable charm of our saint. In time of need, and at his behest, the miracle of the multiplication of the loaves was renewed; water was changed into wine; a living spring welled up from a rock; and fire lost its power to harm.

6. *Brother Fire*

It was at Fonte Colombo, near Rieti, during the time when Francis' eye ailment obliged him to undergo a cruel operation. The surgeon presented himself, armed with a cauterising iron which he placed in the fire and heated white-hot. The Saint, to comfort his body (which shuddered before the torture), addressed the fire in these terms: "Brother Fire, among all fair things, the Most High has created you beautiful, useful, and strong. Be kind to me in this hour! Be courteous, for I have ever cherished you in the Lord. I pray the Lord who created you to temper your ardour; so that you will burn me gently, and I shall be able to bear you."

His prayer ended, he made the sign of the cross over the flame and remained intrepid. The physician seized the white-hot iron. The friars, overcome by pity, fled. The saint, joyous and full of gladness, awaited the operation. With a crackling sound, the iron buried itself into his tender flesh, searing him from ear to eyebrow. And when the friars (whom fear had scattered) came back, he said to them with a smile, "Fearful ones, faint hearts, why did you run away? I tell you truthfully that I felt neither burning of fire nor any pain." Then, turning toward the doctor, he said, "If the flesh is not seared enough, you may do it again."

The astounded doctor exclaimed, "I tell you, brothers, I have seen strange things today." And the biographer, Thomas of Celano, adds: "I believe that he had returned to the state of pristine innocence—this man for whom cruel creatures became gentle at his will."

"Truly," he says elsewhere, "It was wonderful to see unreasoning creatures realize the affectionate interest that Francis felt for them; and divine his tender love for them." . . . All living creatures tried to return the love the Saint showed for them and correspond to his attentions by their gratitude. They smiled at his caresses, carried out his requests, obeyed his orders." It was the reward of his life of virtue.

St. Bonaventure speaks the same language:

"Francis had attained to such a high degree of purity, that his flesh was submissive to the spirit, and the spirit to God, in admirable accord. Thus, by the Lord's will, the creature, obedient to its Author, submitted in a marvellous manner to the will and command of his servant."

B. From Creature to Creator

Just as God's love inclined Francis toward creation, *so creation led him to God.*

Here especially does *the Mass Preface* come into play!

St. Francis proved the truth of the words of the Psalmist: "O Lord God, how glorious is your name in the earth."

At every moment, he learned how right St. Paul was when he said that God's power and divinity, though invisible, were clearly seen in "the things that are made": whose existence and perfections proclaim the infinite perfection of the Creator. (Rom. 1:20.) Every creature caused him to take another step forward on the road to Heaven. In each work of nature, he glorified its eternal Author. For St. Francis, the universe mirrored God's goodness. Francis thrilled with joy in the presence of God's handiwork. Before this ravishing spectacle, he saw and contemplated the living Reason and First Cause of all things.

In all beauty, he recognized the supreme Beauty. All things cried out to him: "The Hand that made us is divine!" Thanks to the marks and footprints imprinted in nature, he followed the Beloved everywhere; and all things served him as a ladder on which to ascend to God's throne.

Francis surrounded with the most tender affection, and loved to contemplate, those creatures in which he found a symbolic likeness to the Son of God. They served as a continual stimulus to show himself Christ's Perfect Knight. And to Francis, nothing else on earth was so important.

1. *Brother Fire Once More*

Christ gave himself to be the Light of the World. "It is fire that I have come to spread over the earth, and what better wish can I have than that it should be kindled?" (Luke 12:49.) [Knox.]

Even without this thought, light and fire are so beautiful and so useful in themselves, that they certainly appear as reflections of the beauty and liberality of God. Hence, among all inferior and insensate creatures, Francis evinced a particular affection for "Brother Fire," because of its beauty and utility; and he never wished to impede its action. He would leave torches, lamps, and candles burning; not wishing to extinguish with his hand, a light symbolic of the Eternal Light.

One day when Francis was seated near the hearth, his habit caught fire. One of the Friars ran forward to put the fire out; but Francis said, "No, dear Brother. Let us not harm Brother Fire." He would not let a friar fling a still smouldering log or smoking firebrand from one corner to another of the fireplace, as was commonly done; but insisted that the log be carefully placed on the ground, out of reverence for Him whose creature it was.

2. *Water*

Jesus called himself the Living Water, the Fountain of Water springing up into life eternal. He chose water as the symbol of the soul's purification, and it is through water that the rite of Holy Baptism is administered. Thus, after fire, Francis particularly loved Sister Water; and when he washed his hands, he did so in a place where the water would not be trodden underfoot.

3. *Stone*

In the Scriptures, Christ called himself the "Stone," the "Rock."

(I Cor. 10:4.) Francis remembered this, and walked as gently as possible on stone, out of reverence for his Master. If he had to recite the verse of the Psalm, "He set my feet upon a rock" (Ps. 39:2), he would say instead, out of reverence, "You have lifted me up on my feet." For Francis did not want to "stand" on the rock, which to him symbolized the Saviour.

4. *Wood*

Christ died on the wood of the Cross, and one reads in the Bible: "A tree has hope. If it is cut, it grows green again, and fresh branches spring from it." (Job 14:7.) So when the friars went to the wood to gather branches, Francis forbade them to cut down the whole tree, so as to permit—thanks to this precaution—young shoots to spring up and live.

5. *Flowers*

It is written of Christ that he is "the Flower of the Field and the Lily of the Valleys." (Cant. 2:1.) The flowers are as a vestige from the flowery carpet of the Garden of Eden! Imagine the pleasure Francis took in admiring their beauty, in considering the elegance of their form, in inhaling their fragrant perfume! But at once his thoughts turned toward the beauty of this other Flower, which flowered in the Spring in all its glory, from the "root" of Jesse (Is. 11:1); and whose perfume restores life to countless myriads of dead.

That is why St. Francis recommended to Brother gardener not to plant vegetables everywhere, but to leave a band of uncultivated ground around the garden. In this way, the vegetables by their green colour, and the flowers by their beauty, would proclaim in their season the beauty of the Father of all things.

St. Francis caused a border to be reserved in the garden for sweet-scented flowering herbs; so that those who saw them might think of Him who eternally is all heavenly grace and sweetness.

6. *The Earthworm*

The holy King David, in one of his Psalms (21:7), puts this complaint on the Saviour's lips. "I am a worm and no man." For Francis, this was a sufficient motive for loving earthworms. He used to pick them up when he found them in the road and tenderly carry them to another place, lest they be crushed by the feet of the passers by.

7. *Bees*

The sight of bees delighted him. Bees seemed to him like a pale reflection of God's infinite wisdom. He loudly proclaimed that the ingeniousness of their labours, and the sureness of their instinct, glorified God; and he often spent a day singing their praises. Fearing for them the rigorous cold of winter, he had honey or rich wine placed in the hives.

8. *Lambs*

St. Francis showed a marked preference for lambs, because Jesus is "the Lamb of God who takes away the sin of the world" (John 1:29); and because these animals bring to mind the meekness and humility of the Divine Redeemer.

At the friary of San Verecondo, a little lamb was cruelly bitten and finally killed by a vicious sow. When Francis learned it, he was moved to pity; for he thought of the Immaculate Lamb of God. He wept at the death of the little lamb and exclaimed aloud before them all: "Alas! little lamb, my brother! Poor innocent beast, you are a salutary symbol for men! Cursed be the impious brute that killed you! Let none—man or beast—eat of his flesh." Remarkably enough, the malicious sow immediately fell ill; and after three days of torment was stricken down by death, the Avenger. The carcass was thrown into the friary moat, where it remained a long time. It become dry as a board and did not serve as food to any living creature.

One day when Francis was crossing the Marches of Ancona, he met a goatherd in the field who was guarding goats and rams. Now also in the flock there was a timid little ewe-lamb, peacefully grazing. On seeing her, the Blessed Francis stopped short; and sorrowful of heart, and sighing deeply, said to Friar Paul, who accompanied him: "Do you see this lamb quietly walking among the goats and rams? Our Lord walked that way, quietly and humbly, among the Pharisees. So I beg you, my son, out of charity for him, to have pity, as I do, on this poor little lamb. We'll buy it and take it away from these goats and rams."

Brother Paul, admiring Francis' sorrow, began to moan with him. But since they had nothing but the coarse tunics they were wearing, they stood there in perplexity as to how to go about the rescue. But by great good luck, a rich merchant chanced to pass that way, and gave them the required sum. So they led Sister Sheep to the episcopal city of

Osimo; where Francis spoke at length on the parable of the sheep, and of Jesus Christ, the Lamb of God.

Another time, Francis was again walking gayly along the Marches of Ancona, accompanied by a friar; when he met a man who was going to sell at the market two lambs, trussed up and suspended from his shoulder. Moved at the sound of their bleating, Blessed Francis went up to them and caressed them with tender compassion, as a mother does when her child cries. "Why are you torturing my brother lambs," he asked the man, "by tying them up and letting them hang down that way?"

"I am taking them to market to sell them, for I need the money."

"What will they do with the lambs there?"

"The people that buy them will kill them and eat them."

"No! No! They musn't! Take this cloak I have on, and give me the lambs!"

The man lost no time in turning over the lambs for the cloak, which paid him handsomely. But the Saint was in a quandary. He asked himself what he was going to do with the lambs. After taking counsel of his companion, Francis gave the lambs back to the merchant to raise; making him promise never to harm them or sell them; but to keep them, feed them, and take good care of them.

Similar scenes were often repeated in the life of the Seraphic Francis of Assisi.

Theology sees in the devout contemplation of the works of nature, no less than in the contemplation of eternal truths, *a means and a guide to the contemplative life.* Of this true mysticism of nature, Francis was past master. A glance at the universe, and at all that which lives, moves, breathes, glistens, and gleams within it; sufficed to inspire his devotion. Creation's thousandfold repeated *Sursum Corda* greeted his every footstep and filled him with gratitude, praise, and love of God.

His own uninterrupted *Sursum Corda* was sung to the heart of creation. If creation led Francis to God, Francis, for his part, brought creation, so to speak, to the Creator—exhorting it to love and praise him.

We can make no better summary of this combination of prayer and action comprising the Franciscan spirit, than by citing this extract from *The Franciscan Message to the World* by Father Gemelli, O.F.M.

"St. Francis brought back action and prayer—the active, and the contemplative, life—to the same level. Within his soul, action was always converted into prayer, and prayer into action. The originality of Francis lies not so much in his having set up a mixed (contemplative and active) life, as already taught by other saints; as in the establishment of a life of supernatural action in the world —a life not content merely to unite prayer to action; but in which prayer and action are but two aspects of the soul's aspiration toward God. . . . To act supernaturally in the very heart of reality, however tempting or repugnant that reality may be"; to be joyful, to sing, to praise and to thank God in spite of everything and for everything—this is the Franciscan spirit!

Such is likewise the meaning of the Preface.

166—Why does the altar boy ring the bell at the Sanctus?

According to a decree of the Sacred Congregation of Rites (October 25, 1922), this ringing of the sanctuary bell constitutes:

1. A signal which warns the people of the approaching Consecration.

2. A manifestation of joy.

3. A profession of faith in the imminent presence of Christ in the Eucharist.

4. A token of union with the angelic choirs in common adoration and praise.

Ever since the Middle Ages, it has been customary at the Sanctus to ring briefly an outer bell of rather small dimensions, known as the "Sanctus bell." The purpose of this bell is to notify those prevented from attending Mass, to unite themselves in spirit with the Sacrifice about to be accomplished on the altar.

167—What do you know of the use of the "sanctus candle" during a private Mass?

In a Low or private Mass, just before the Elevation, the acolyte lights a special candle and places it on the Epistle side of the altar. He extinguishes it after the Communion of the priest and faithful. This practice (which today is not obligatory) persists in many places, notably among religious Orders.

This lighted candle indicates the imminent arrival, and presence, of the Eucharistic Christ and pays homage to him.

Toward the conclusion of the Preface in a High Mass, the acolytes (or candle bearers) light and bear two, or preferably four, candles in honour of the coming Consecration.

The Canon

168—What is the Canon?

The word "Canon" is of Greek origin; and signifies "rule," or something fixed that never changes.

The Canon consists of the *central part of the Mass,* from the Sanctus to the Pater Noster. It is made up of virtually invariable formulas, which the priest must follow with great exactitude.

The priest recites the major portion of these prayers with his arms extended, as Christ on the Cross.

169—Why does the missal have a large picture of the Crucifixion at the beginning of the Canon?

In ancient missals the letter *T* of the *Te igitur,* was not illustrated, as it is at present, by a reproduction of the Crucified Saviour. The letter, somewhat enlarged, served merely to recall the two transversal bars of the Cross. Gradually, artists came to ornament the initial. The design went on enlarging, finally to wind up with a representation of the Calvary scene. It then became necessary to detach the picture from the text and reserve for it an entire page of the missal. Today, every complete missal carries a reproduction of the crucifix at the beginning of the Canon.

Nothing could be more evocative at the start of the essential part of the Mass, than this pictorial representation of Christ's Sacrifice, soon to become present on the altar.

In certain souls accustomed to living their Mass, a similar crescendo may be seen. From the very beginning, Christ on the Cross has had his place in their lives. But ALL the page was not his! Gradually, they have come to understand that Christ must increase; and the "initial" with its two cross-bars has so spread over the rest, that the other letters have disappeared. It will not do to speak to *them* any more of "half-sacrifices." For such as these, the sacrifice must be total!

Does not this enthusiastic and complete gift recall the generous gesture of St. Francis of Assisi, when, kneeling before the stone of Mt. Alverna, he meditated on the bloody drama of Calvary; and, plunged in the depths of divine love, uttered this burning prayer to Christ? :

"O Jesus Christ, my Saviour! I beg you to grant me two graces before my death! Make me feel—as much as may be possible—in soul and body, O my sweet Saviour, the intimate suffering of your cruel Passion! And may I also experience—as much as is possible for a creature—this excessive love which inflamed you, the Son of God, and made you willing to suffer joyously for us sinners, so many horrible torments!"

We all know what happened to Francis of Assisi, Patron of Catholic Action.

Persevering in this ardent prayer, and prolonging his meditation on the sufferings of Christ on the Cross, so prodigiously did the fervour of devotion grow within him that love and compassion transformed him into another Christ!

ALVERNA

Down the road Saint Francis came.
    Love constrainéd. Hear his cries:
"Love is not loved!" (Hence his sighs,
    In love's frenzy, soul aflame!)
    Sad and solitary, he
    Now has scaled his calvary—
    Alverna is Golgotha!

Francis praying in the night,
    Now beholds a shining light!
To humble friar, all bathed in tears,
    Heaven opens, Christ appears—
Crucified! (Saint Francis weeps.)

O'er him soars the Seraphin,
    Marked with suff'ring wrought by sin;
Bright rays from the Crucified
    Pierce his hands, his feet, his side.
    On fire with love and mystery,
    The Saint now falls in ecstasy—
    Friar and Crucified are one! . . .

God returns to Heaven above,
    Francis remains—a flame of love!—
The peace of Heaven in his soul.
    For he has reached the mystic's goal—
Himself a living crucifix!

Rev. Fr. Felix-M. Cramoisan, O.F.M.

(Translated on the Feast of the Stigmata, 1954)

Jesus, the Divine Lover, whose Heart, in the matter of loving has never been wanting to any man; wishing to lift Francis to the level of his own supreme love, thought to transform him, and make him the living portrait of himself. Make him indeed, almost himself!

"You love me, Francis, you love me madly," Jesus seems to say to him. "Love calls for love, and with it all that love contains of suffering and of joy.... You, then, shall receive in your flesh and in your heart, my lot of suffering and of love!"

Suddenly, the heavens are opened, and in a halo of white light, Christ Crucified appears in the form of a Seraph with six luminous wings!

Uplifted from earth by an irresistible force, Francis stretches forth his arms toward Jesus. And Jesus stretches his toward Francis!...

Soon locked in a powerful embrace, the limbs of Francis are lovingly pressed to the Crucified Saviour. As if with flaming darts, five bleeding wounds are hollowed out in Francis' quivering flesh! And from the heart of the Seraph of Assisi, love exhales like fumes from an incense burner!... and the dazzling whiteness of his countenance is mutely expressive at one and the same time of anguish and of ecstasy, of suffering and of serenity!

What a model of seraphic love!

To resemble Jesus to the point of identifying oneself with him in his sufferings, even to the reproduction in one's flesh, of the Cross and of all that the Cross stands for, such is the ardent desire which should enflame the heart of every Christian who would LIVE HIS MASS all the way to the Consecration!

And this should be the ambition (a senseless dream indeed, were it not divine!) of every friend of St. Francis!

170—The Mass recalls Calvary and the Last Supper. Are you able, at this stage in our study, to give a brief account of Christ's Passion; so as to enter more readily into the spirit of the Holy Sacrifice?

We know that the four ends of the Mass are *adoration, thanksgiving, propitiation,* and *petition.*

In our study of the Preface, we spent some time on thanksgiving.

Here, we should like to say a word about *propitiation.*

"Never attend Mass," wrote Bossuet, "without transporting yourself in spirit to that sorrowful night wherein our Saviour endured for us his cruel Passion and death. We shall thus acquire fitting sentiments. It is for this reason that St. Paul, in relating the institution of the Holy Eucharist, places this fearsome sight before our eyes."

Now the first and principal sentiment that the Passion requires of us—and from which all others flow as from there source—is the sentiment of contrition.

For the Passion is the most perfect act of atonement and redemption. *Its purpose is to make reparation and to destroy sin.*

Had we not sinned, the Incarnation doubtless would have brought us a Model, a Master, and a Friend. But it would have been a glorious Christ; and not a Messiah, humiliated and suffering unto death. Sin was the sole cause of the Passion and death of Christ.

Between sin and Jesus Christ—or in the imagery of the Church, between Death and Life (for sin is death, and Jesus Christ is Life)—there was a titanic duel. Sin's blows rained thick and fast on Jesus. He was, the Scriptures tell us, "bruised for our transgressions."

But Jesus conquered sin and destroyed it. Dying, he gave us life.

Jesus' greatest suffering during his Passion come to him from sin. Now sin has three roots:

1. Pride, which affects the soul.
2. Sensuality, having to do with the body.
3. Covetousness, dealing with men and external things.

1. *Jesus extirpated pride during his Passion, by a humility that went the limit.*

Behold him in Gethsemani: first kneeling, then prostrate, with face to the ground, pleading for mercy, imploring pardon, confessing his weakness, appealing for assistance; until an angel came to console him.

Behold him before the tribunals—outraged, publicly disgraced, treated like the vilest of criminals.

Behold him at grips with the soldiers. They mock him, insult him, spit upon him, buffet him, make sport of him as of one undeserving of pity.

Behold him on Calvary—"a by-word to all, the laughing-stock of the rabble," hanged between two thieves.

Behold him in the sepulchre—underground, lifeless, having become Death's Victim. . . .

See if you can say, then, that it were possible for God, the Incarnate Word, the All-Powerful, the Everlasting God, the Infinite One to descend more deeply into ignominy, self-abasement, and humiliation.

Could he have done more to vanquish and uproot our pride? "O human pride," cries Bossuet, "come here and perish!"

2. *Jesus conquered and extirpated sensuality by delivering his flesh and members to atrocious torture.*

Behold him stumbling, faint and covered with blood, in the Garden of Olives.

Behold him writhing with pain under the scourges and thongs that tear his flesh to shreds as the blood streams down.

Listen to the deep sighs, the groans, the cries, that despite his superhuman courage, pain wrings from him.

Behold the thorns, pressing down upon his brow, and inundating it with blood.

Behold him carrying his Cross, crushed beneath the burden; and when he falls, blood-reddening the road to Calvary.

Try to imagine a little what the pain must have been, when they rudely tore off his tunic, which adhered to his wounds. The latter open again, causing additional suffering. The blood escapes afresh; reddening his whole body, which steadily grows weaker.

Behold him brutally stretched out on the Cross. Listen to the blows of the hammer. See the nails enter into his feet, into his hands—the blood spurting over his executioners.

Behold him hanging on the Cross, his body torn, mangled, desiccated; on fire with burning thirst—pain at its paroxysm. . . .

Then try to say that the Immortal One, "the Holy and Just One," could have suffered more in his body, in his senses, in his flesh, to conquer and extirpate our sensuality; and all the sins which our miserable bodies—with our permission—cause us to commit.

If we thought more about our sins as being not so much stains on our souls, as wounds in the body of Jesus, perhaps the haste with which we fall into the same sins again, might lessen. . . . Alas! When people receive the Sacrament of Penance, they think much more about searching for their sins, than they do about stirring up within themselves sentiments of contrition. . . .

3. *Finally, Jesus conquered and eradicated covetousness, by pushing privation and poverty to their utmost limits.*

Christ detached himself from all this world's goods, and from all creatures. He permitted his disciples, his beloved apostles, his intimate friends, to abandon, betray, and deny him. . . .

Moreover, he willed to deprive himself of those spiritual and material consolations which we seek so much, and of which we are so avid; to the point that we are plunged into discouragement when they are lacking. He accepted on the part of his Father, rejection, withdrawal, abandonment; to be delivered up—forsaken and alone—to the most cruel and incomprehensible of sufferings. . . .

Try to form some idea in your own mind of these profound mysteries of suffering and love—about which we can do little better than lisp—and then ask yourself if God, the Sovereign Master of all things, possibly could have more completely stripped himself or made himself more miserable or poorer; in order to atone for man's cupidity, and his senseless and disordered attachment to this world's goods; which are the cause of so many sins and of so many crimes. . . .

Contrition, humility, mortification, detachment—such were the dispositions of Jesus during his Passion; and it is these dispositions of generous love for his Father that are brought down on the altar.

Such are also the dispositions we should have, if we would really LIVE our Mass.

Let us strive to understand sin as God sees it, and as Jesus saw it, i.e., as the one, supreme evil, the only enemy, and irreconcilable adversary of God and the soul.

Let us detest and repudiate sin. Not in a spurt of passing and ficticious sentimentality; not in the artificial exaltation of a moment; but with deep conviction; with firm and solid sentiments; with a resolute, indomitable will.

If we are sincere, we shall become better from one Confession to another. . . . If this is not the case with us, then let us ask ourselves what kind of contrition we have. . . .

171—How can the Mass renew the Sacrifice of the Cross, since the resurrected Christ can no longer suffer in his human nature?

Though Christ is no longer capable of suffering IN HIS OWN HUMAN NATURE, which since his Resurrection is glorified in Heaven; he is still able to suffer in OUR HUMAN NATURE.

He *cannot* renew Calvary in his *physical* body; but he *can* renew it in his *Mystical* Body, which is the Church. And the Church is you and I!

This was the thought expressed by St. Paul when he wrote: "What is lacking to the sufferings of Christ, I fill up in my flesh *for his Body, which is the Church!"*

Our Lord then, *can* realize anew the Sacrifice of the Cross; *if* we offer him our body and blood so definitively that Christ can—just as if it were his own body—offer himself again to his Heavenly Father for the increase of his Mystical Body, the Church.

After we have made reparation for our own sins, we should—in imitation of the Saviour—take upon ourselves to atone for the sins of others: the sins of our loved ones (brothers, sisters, parents, children), of our friends, of our enemies, of our employes; and especially, of all those who are to die today. Every day 144,000 persons die!

Our Lord is relying on us! We must not disappoint him! How often has he complained bitterly of the malice and indifference of souls!

This is what he said one day to St. Margaret Mary:

"The ingratitude of men affects me more deeply than all that I suffered in my Passion. If men would but love me even a little in return, I would esteem all that I have suffered for them as a very little thing. I would be willing—were that possible—to suffer even more for them. But for all my eagerness to do them good, they show only coldness and disdain. You, at least, give me this joy; to make up for their ingratitude insofar as you are capable.

"I have come to you that you may pluck these thorns, with which an unfaithful spouse has pierced my Head....

"Behold this Heart which has so loved men... My Divine Heart loves men so passionately, that it is unable longer to contain the flames of its ardent charity. I must lavish them on others...."

So Jesus, Divine Beggar of love, goes through the world in search of CHRISTIANS who will consent to become *"other Christs"!*

Particularly with the approach of the Consecration, our Lord speaks to us in words something like these: "Francis, Clare, John, Helen, and *YOU!* Give me your body! Give me your soul! Give me *all* of you! I cannot suffer any more. I endured to the utmost the sufferings of my physical body; but my Passion must still be perfected in my Mystical Body; of which you are a part. The Mass is the time when each of you can fulfill to the letter, my injunction to take up your cross and follow me."

"Let me live in your stead," pleads Jesus to us once more. "Let me be your substitute; for by you, and in you, I would continue my ardent love for my Father, and I would save souls!"

To the whole human race, he cries: "I thirst!" I thirst with love for all those souls I would snatch from the jaws of Hell! I have a special thirst for the burning love of souls who are generous and ready for anything—souls who will abandon themselves to me in utter trust; and leave me free to satisfy in and through them, my infinite passion of divine love!... I thirst for the love of my priests, of my religious both men and women, of consecrated, faithful souls...."

Can we remain deaf to this anguished appeal of our beloved Saviour?

Of each one of us, his members, Jesus demands our whole being —our body and soul with all its powers—that he may assimilate it, appropriate it, and live in us his life of love toward his beloved Father and toward all men, his brothers; whom he has redeemed with his Precious Blood.

Jesus wishes to accomplish in us a kind of "transubstantiation," similar to that of the altar wherein the bread is changed into himself!

Jesus' thirty-three years of earthly life were all too short for him. In his unslaked love, he wishes to love, toil, pray, and suffer still more. In the beautiful expression of Sister Elizabeth of the Trinity, he asks of us an "extra human nature."

"Son," Jesus says to us, "give me your heart, so that through and in that heart, united to your life, I may love—rather, that *we* may love, our Heavenly Father ardently! Give me your lips, that together we may sing his praise! Give me your mind, your eyes, your hands, your whole being! My will is to live in and through you, as it were a second life;

a life all of love, which will be as the prolongation and complement of my life in Palestine."

Can anyone still say, "No"?

172—How are we to correspond to our Lord's desire for us to carry on his Sacrifice and his redemptive life on earth?

How? It is all very simple. *All that we have to do is to reproduce in our lives the sentiments and generous life of the Saviour!* . . .

Like our Divine Lord, let us try to be humble and lowly; to place ourselves in the "last place." Let us blush with shame at the thought of all our transgressions, and of all the sins of the world; since if we would co-operate in the redemptive work of Christ, we must take it upon ourselves to atone for others. . . .

Let us enter, too, into Jesus' spirit of mortification; accepting the sufferings, infirmities, illnesses, and all the physical and spiritual pains it shall please God to send us. . . .

Finally, let us detach ourselves from this world's goods; looking upon them as so much dust, ready to sacrifice them in the measure that God may ask of us. . . .

An end to these vague "religious feelings," to the feeble prayers interrupted by incessant distractions, to the search for sensible impressions which flatter the imagination, with little profit to the soul. In their place, let our hearts be profoundly penetrated with the Saviour's holy dispositions.

Let us sometimes lay aside our books; closing them that our hearts may be opened, that they may be penetrated and saturated with the Saviour's contrition, with his humility, mortification, and spiritual divesture of self.

Then during this holy and precious half-hour, instead of turning aside from our ordinary cares, from our struggles, trials and tribulations, let us look them all in the face!

Let us contemplate an imminent humiliation; the cross that must be borne; the trial destined to overwhelm us anew beneath its crushing weight. Then, looking on this burden of our daily life—no longer as it is in itself, but as seen through the humiliations, sufferings, and abandonment of Christ—let us love it and determine to carry it to the end!

Then taking up again our daily task, when this burden, this cross, these nails, these thorns, the lash of the scourge, again confront us; we shall not become (as too frequently happens) impatient, nervous, and irritable. But like Christ on the Cross, like Christ on the altar, we shall be meek, patient, strong, and heroic. We shall give over our hands, feet, head, body and soul—our whole being—to the sorrows and crucifixions of the day. And toward those persons who will pierce our heart, we shall know neither gall nor bitterness; but only kindness and good will.

The spirit of Jesus which we shall have received every morning at the holy altar, from Calvary, will fill and penetrate our souls with peace, serenity, spiritual unction and joy, goodness, pleasantness, kindliness, self-denial and devotion—and all the virtues of Jesus will overflow from our hearts aflame with love!...

When this happens, we shall really lead exemplary lives and be of real assistance to all those dear to us.... In our work, we shall have light, insight, prudence, simplicity, power, and an influence which will not come from ourselves, but from God....

We shall be so good, that souls will feel themselves grow better in our presence. And all that we do will be blessed of God, because we shall have done it in the spirit of Jesus; with which we shall have been filled during the Holy Sacrifice of the Mass....

Oh, if we but LIVED our Mass, how beautiful this world would be!

173—To be still more specific, what must we do to become victims with the Victim of Calvary?

"Without shedding of blood, there is no redemption." So wrote St. Paul.

Calm yourselves! The "blood" St. Paul is talking about, does not necessarily have to be that flowing in your veins! The phrase has particularly to do with those sacrifices self-imposed in the constant and firm flight from sin... in the prompt accomplishment of the Commandments of God and the Church... in the preservation of true patience in the midst of trial, and in the face of all kinds of obstacles... in the humbling and often thankless task of the conquest of souls!

Let us list a few examples:

To be "all things to all men"—with a smile!...

Never to reply, or excuse oneself when falsely accused....

To suffer humiliation in silence for another....

To desire nothing; to be always satisfied....

Not to be attached to anything or anyone except God. (My God, my All!)

To make at least one sacrifice every day....

To be silent, when the heart bleeds. To take refuge in the Heart of Jesus....

To be prompt to pardon... with no resentful after thoughts....

Everything for others; nothing for self....

To be the joy and consolation of others....

Not to feel sad when one is forgotten or "left out"....

To give way in a discussion....

To give spontaneously a cherished object to the person who admires it....

Never to talk about oneself or one's family....

To ride rough-shod over human respect....

To live by faith... to count more on God's grace than on one's own strength....

Never to make others suffer from that which one cannot stand oneself....

Never to judge another unfavourably....

To excuse the shortcomings of others...Not to laugh at them....

Never to say or write anything that would cause pain to others....

Insofar as is possible, to be where one ought to be, doing the thing one ought to be doing....

Not to take anything in bad part....

Not to "throw our weight around"....

Not to order harshly, but request politely....

Never to look down on an inferior....

Never to refuse a proffered reconciliation....

To try oneself to bring about this reconciliation....

To treat one's neighbour the way one would treat Christ....

To deny oneself for him. To give, if necessary, one's life for him....

Do not forget that our hearts are altars on which Jesus daily immolates himself for us. Consequently, we should be not only apostles, but martyrs, of love.

Our hearts are tabernacles wherein God dwells, and wherein we may continually adore him by doing everything we do with the greatest possible love.... Doing good is not enough—the good that we do must be well done.

Our hearts are living ciboria, from which we desire to communicate the Spirit of God to every soul that comes to us....

Our hearts are monstrances, which ought to—through our kindness, charity, meekness, and patience—let Jesus show through to all.

We shall furthermore carry on the suffering and redemptive life of Christ by our acceptance of the trials God's providence permits, in a spirit of faith and conformity to God's will.

For a wife, this will mean the patience shown toward a husband who drinks, who is hard to please, brutal, unfaithful.... For a husband, it will be the forbearance shown toward a wife who is jealous, frivolous, indiscreet, over-sensitive, unwell....

It will mean the acceptance of the total or partial loss of one's fortune... of one's reputation....

It will mean for each one of us the generous accomplishment of the duties of one's state in life taken up again every morning in the home, at the office, at the factory or at school, at the hospital among the sick, or working with children....

It will mean the resignation—or better still, the conformity—of the grief-stricken to God's holy will... when a friend betrays... when a loved one is ungrateful... over a rebellious, wayward child... at the absence from home of a dear one....

It will mean the prudence and generosity required to safeguard chastity... the violence that must be done to self to maintain the state of sanctifying grace.... It will mean silence in the face of ridicule and insult, of false accusation....

It will mean the forced inaction, powerlessness, and suffering of illness or infirmity, accepted with a smile for love of God and to save souls. So many conversions depend on our sacrifices!

It will mean the anguish felt by the father unemployed or unable to work; and by that same token, unable to provide for the needs of his family....

It will mean the suffering of those living in surroundings or a home where understanding and love are lacking. . . .

Or it will mean the sometimes bitter regret felt by so many young men and young women at their inability to fulfill their dream of vocation (the priesthood, religious life, marriage) . . . . These young people who understand the price of suffering and who accept their cross; know that their lives are more fruitful and rich in the fruits of salvation, than if they were to realize their youthful dreams outside of God's will. This was the truth grasped by Mr. Girard, martyrized by twenty-two years of illness. In his ascent toward the priesthood, he was obliged to stop at the subdiaconate! To a confrere who pitied him for not having been able to become a priest, he made this sublime response:

"I would rather be the host, and have Jesus be the priest; than be the priest and have Jesus be my host!" [i.e. "Victim".]

These few examples—taken from among many—will help to put us in the spirit of the Consecration; which commemorates the immolation of the Son of God for the redemption of sinful humanity. All of us have some suffering to undergo. Hence, all of us are able to cooperate in the sublime task of saving souls and glorifying God in union with Christ in the Holy Sacrifice of the Mass.

PRAYER OF A MOTHER-TO-BE

O Jesus, it is true, then, that I am to have the joy of giving a little Christian to the Church!

You who so loved little children when you were here on earth, especially bless the child you are entrusting to our keeping, and that we consecrated to you as soon as we had the happiness to expect one.

Dear Jesus, I give you my baby—may he be more yours than mine! Look on him already as your beloved child; prepare his little soul and adorn it, that it may be a worthy tabernacle of the Holy Spirit.

Sanctify me, so that I may sanctify him; and together with his dad, may our souls be sanctified. Increase your life in me, so that my baby may benefit from the overflowing abundance from his mother's soul.

Vouchsafe to accept and sanctify the little discomforts, present and future, which I offer you as a future mother.

Holy angel of my baby, lead him to the baptismal font at his entrance into this world. Preserve him from all harm now; and later, from all that could stain his soul.

O Mary, be his mother even now, and protect him ever!

St. Joseph, watch over him as you watched over Jesus!

Te Igitur

174—What is the first prayer of the Canon?

The *Te Igitur.*

Te igitur, clementissime Pater, per Jesum Christum Filium tuum Dominum nostrum, supplices rogamus ac petimus uti accepta habeas et benedicas haec + dona, haec + munera, haec + sancta sacrificia illibata; in primis quae tibi offerimus pro Ecclesia sancta tua catholica, quam pacificare, custodire, adunare et regere digneris toto orbe terrarum, una cum famulo tuo Papa nostro N., et Antistite nostro N., et omnibus orthodoxis atque catholicae et apostolicae fidei cultoribus.

Therefore, we humbly pray and beseech you, most merciful Father, through Jesus Christ, your Son, our Lord, to receive and to bless these + gifts, these + presents, these + holy unspotted sacrifices, which we offer up to you, in the first place, for your Holy Catholic Church, that it may please you to grant her peace, to guard, unite and guide her throughout the world, as also for your servant N., our Pope, and N., our Bishop, and for all who are orthodox in belief and who profess the Catholic and Apostolic Faith.

Before commencing this prayer, the celebrant extends his hands, raises and joins them before his breast. At the same time, he raises his eyes to the cross and immediately lowers them. He then bows profoundly, and rests his joined hands on the edge of the altar.

It is clear that the priest is addressing God, but his prayer is one of supplication. The position of his hands indicates his great desire for his prayer to be heard.

In this bodily attitude, he begins the *Te igitur.*

The priest kisses the altar, then rises to bless the oblations. At each of the words, "gifts," "presents," and "sacrifices," he makes the sign of the cross over the bread and wine. After this, you will observe that he continues his prayer with his arms extended at his sides, as Moses was accustomed to do when praying on the mountain.

175—What does the priest ask for in the first part of this prayer?

The priest implores the "most merciful Father," through his Son, Jesus Christ, to "receive and bless" the gifts he offers him and over which the priest makes the sign of the cross three times; so that they may be sanctified and less unworthy of being changed into the Body and Blood of the Saviour. Another purpose of these signs of the cross is to sanctify those participating in the Sacrifice. For it must not be forgotten, that at the Offertory, our hearts and intentions were together placed on the altar.

This supplication of the celebrant is a humble and trustful prayer. The priest raises his eyes and hands toward heaven; then bowing profoundly, kisses the altar in token of reverence and love.... Let us unite ourselves to him, trying to have the same interior dispositions.

176—For whom does the priest pray in the second part of the "Te igitur"?

For the Church

When we speak of "the Church," we often have the impression of not being understood! But the Church is you. It is I! It is the teaching Church (the Pope, bishops, priests), and the Church taught (the faithful). As we shall see, no one is overlooked!

We sometimes speak of the five "Mementos" of the Mass. We should not—at first sight—be too astonished at their number. To consider it at close range, we see surrounding the Consecration—before and after, on five different occasions—the whole of creation crying out (as the Good Thief once did) to the Lord lifted up above it: "Lord, remember us." *(Memento!)* Did, our Lord not say: "When I shall be lifted up above the earth, I shall draw all men to me"? At the Canon, these words of Christ are particularly pertinent.

Two of the five Mementos have always borne this title; while the three others are variously styled. Here, we shall be content merely to name all five; coming back to them again as they occur in the Canon.

1. The "Memento" of the Catholic hierarchy: the Pope, bishops, priests, *(Te igitur.)*

2. The "Memento" of those dear to us, of those for whom the Mass is being celebrated, and of all those from far and near who surround the altar.

3. The "Memento" of the Church Triumphant: the Blessed Virgin, the apostles, the first martyrs, the saints, the angels who sing with us at the Sanctus. *(Communicantes.)*

4. The "Memento" of the souls suffering in Purgatory. (No prayers for the souls in Hell! They have lost everything forever!)

5. The "Memento" for ourselves. "To us. . .sinners!" *(Nobis quoque peccatoribus.)*

We have said that the priest prays *first of all for the Church.*

"Your Holy and Catholic Church," says he to God, "the one that you set up and sanctified by the Blood of your Son; the one that is his Mystical Body, extending throughout the universe. . . ."

With what fervour and compassion we should pray for the Church Militant, which St. Bridget saw one day under the figure of a horribly suffering body; all covered with sores, mutilated, wounded, sick. . . . The thing that causes the greatest suffering to the Saints is the sad state of the Church Militant; in whose bosom so many souls live in a state of deadly indifference; whose holy religion is so persecuted in her members, in her clergy, in her religious Orders. . . . The Church Militant, we repeat, established in a world in which godlessness, working through the medium of press, radio, movies, TV, immodest styles, and drink; wreaks such fearful havoc in human souls. . . .

Freemasonry, Communism, the Jehovah Witnesses, and nonsectarian clubs, are leagued against her in a vain attempt to destroy her. . . .

Unfortunately, the Church is, in addition, wounded by those of her own members who are at sword's point; who bear life-long grudges; who go so far as to seek revenge in bloody brawls and fratricidal wars. . . .

Doubtless, the majority of Catholics do not go to these extremes. But how many there are who wound their neighbour and sully his reputation with their tongues! Who scandalize and murder souls by their immoral conversations and their immodest dress! . . Do such Catholics realize that when they thus wound the members of the Church, they cause her heart to bleed? . . . For it must not be forgotten that the Church is a prolongation of the Body of Christ; which latter will achieve its full plenitude only in Heaven—at the end of the world—with the entry of the last saint into Heaven.

177—What do we ask for the Church in the *Te igitur*?

We ask for four things, which are expressed by the four verbs of the *Te Igitur*: *Pacificare,* for peace; *custodire,* for protection; *adunare,* for unity; *regere,* for direction.

1. *Pacificare—Peace.* The Gospel must be preached to all nations to the uttermost parts of the earth. Now if persecution provides a providential means of purification for Christians, it nonetheless retards the work of expansion and conquest.... That is why we ask God to grant to the Church intervals of peace, so that she may continue the spread of the Gospel throughout the world.

"O God," we shall pray, "grant peace to your Church. Deliver her from persecutions, revolutions, and wars which prevent the salvation of so many souls; and which bring with them increased living costs, famine, massacre, and ruin."

2. *Custodire.* External peace is not the greatest of these needs of the Church.... It may even become an occasion of relaxation. So let us ask God to protect the Church by preserving her children from the dangers which too easy a life brings....

"O God, guard as the apple of your eye all the members of your holy Church. Preserve them from the temptations of the world, the flesh, and the Devil. Convert the wicked. Grant your grace and assistance to the dying...."

3. *Adunare.* Still other perils lie in wait for the Church—the spirit of pride and disunion in her own ranks. Schisms and heresies may attack her unity—that union for which Jesus prayed at length in such poignant terms at the Last Supper, a few hours before his death: "Father, that they may be one, as we are one!"

O God, receive and reunite all the Churches now dispersed in the fog and chill of division; in Canada, the United States, France, England, Italy, Russia, Germany, Belgium, Australia, the South Sea Islands, China, Japan, Peru....

Oh, how many times You have willed, and we have not been willing!... Yet it was that there might be one flock and one Shepherd that You gave us all Your blood—and all Your Masses!

O God, preserve in your Church the unity of spirit and belief. Deliver her from the divisions that build up a wall of separation between the children of a common Mother; convert schismatics, Protestants, and heretics; and bring them back to the centre of unity. Unite us all to Christ through sanctifying grace, and to each other by charity and love; so that henceforth we may be one in soul and body!

4. *Regere.* Unity of the Church will be impossible *unless all Christians* together *recognize Christ's Kingship.* He alone must be our guide. Therefore, we must stay united to those leaders whom he himself has placed at the head of his Church. In this way, the hierarchy and the faithful will be in perfect accord.

That is why the Canon has us offer the Holy Sacrifice for the Holy Father, for our Bishop, and then, after having named the leaders of Christianity, the liturgy envisages the totality of the faithful—all those who hold the one true Faith.

At this place in the Mass, let us offer up our own prayers for the Holy Father. *Papa nostro,* he is a father to us. We should be glad that this passage in the Canon furnishes us with an occasion to pray for him; to renew our union with him; to feel ourselves in full communion of mind and heart with him. We owe him obedience, perfect submission, and reverence; but perhaps still more do we owe him our affection, love, and devotion.... Think of the weight of responsibility resting on his shoulders! Let us resolve to read and meditate his encyclicals, speeches, and messages and put them into practice.

It is eminently fitting, that alongside the Holy Father we should place him who in our diocese represents him and likewise commands in Christ's name—the Bishop of our diocese.

To him we owe deep affection and respect. He has a right to our fidelity. We should assist him by our prayers and assistance in the task entrusted to him, without ourselves adding to his difficulties. We should loyally collaborate with him without self-seeking, self-interest, or self-love.

The faithful are bound to their Bishop by their parish priest and his assistants.... To these also we should renew in all our Masses, our promise of obedience and reverence, our will to serve them, and defend them against evil tongues.... And finally, we ought to pray for them.

O God, direct over all the face of the earth the minds and hearts of the members of your Church. Give strength and docility to the sheep, and energy and prudence to the shepherds. Give to all obedience and union with your servant, the Supreme Pontiff, your earthly representative; together with the Bishop of our diocese, who is directly delegated among us by the Supreme Pontiff; and with our pastor and those priests who represent the Bishop in our parish.

Grant that the faithful be submissive to their pastors.

Grant that pastors be submissive to their bishop.

Grant that bishops be submissive to the Pope.

Grant that the Pope be submissive to Christ, so that the great family of souls may be worthy to be integrated into Jesus Christ for all eternity.

In this solemn moment, let us not permit our hearts to shrink to the dimensions of our petty personal concerns; but let us enlarge them to take in all Christianity. Let our hearts in this hour be truly "catholic" hearts, vast as the universe, sensitive hearts, vibrating to the needs of the whole world, to all human misery.

Memento of the Living

178—What is the second prayer of the Canon, and for whom does the priest pray?

This is the "Memento for the Church Militant." (or Second Remembrance.)

Memento, Domine, famulorum famularumque tuarum N. et N., et omnium circumstantium quorum tibi fides cognita est et nota devotio: pro quibus tibi offerimus, vel qui tibi offerunt hoc sacrificium laudis, pro se suisque omnibus, pro redemptione animarum suarum, pro spe salutis et incolumitatis suae, tibique reddunt vota sua aeterno Deo, vivo et vero.	Remember, O Lord, your servants, N. and N. and all here present whose faith and devotion are known to you, for whom we offer, or who offer up to you, this sacrifice of praise, for themselves, their families, and their friends, for the salvation of their souls, and the health and welfare they hope for, and who now pay their vows to you, God Eternal, living and true.

Scarcely has the priest pronounced the first words when he joins his hands, slightly bows his head, and lowers his eyes.

What does he do in this attitude?

He thinks of the living members of the Church, to whom he especially wishes to apply the fruits of the Holy Sacrifice *(See* Q.27); and again makes brief mention of them before God.

He first commends to God the person who is having the Mass said for himself or his special intention.

He prays for his own intentions.

He mentions those who have expressed a desire for remembrance at the altar: Peter, Paul, Raymond, Angela, Frances, Theresa, Claude, etc.

He recommends those to whom he is most closely linked by the claims of justice, gratitude, or blood: Parents, friends, benefactors, penitents, those souls whom he spiritually guides, the poor of the parish, the dying, etc.

Incidentally, how fortunate the person whose son or whose friend is a priest who mentions him every day at God's altar; who intercedes for him! What a source of grace and consolation for a family!

This is the way it was understood by a certain generous Catholic who was paying a seminarian's board. One day the latter came to thank his benefactor, who at once said to him: "Oh, don't thank me! I shall be only too happy if, when you are a priest, you will mention my name just once in the Holy Sacrifice."

Once more he extends his hands and continues his prayer.

He makes a special mention of the faithful present at his Mass. (Unfortunately, their number is small.) And he asks God to take into consideration—in applying the fruits of the Mass to them—the "devotion" of each. It is up to us to be properly disposed.

At the hour of death, how we shall regret having missed a single Mass through sheer neglect or sloth!... Or again, having spent those solemn moments saying prayers bearing no relation to the Holy Sacrifice! For instance, it is a good thing to say my Rosary; but praying it during Mass, means that I understand nothing about what is taking place on the altar.

It is interesting to recall here what the Memento consisted of at the beginning of Christianity. We know that in the Missal, after the phrase, "Remember, Lord, your servants," we have the letters N. and N.

Now history tells us that from the time of the Fathers of the Church, certain person's names were mentioned at this moment. The deacon went toward the *ambo* (a sort of pulpit) and read the names inscribed on a sort of loose-leaf notebook, consisting of two tablets joined by a hinge, so that they could be folded together. (Hence, their name of "diptych"—twofold.)

These diptychs were used to list the intentions proposed to the piety of those present. One of the tablets contained the names of living, the other of deceased, persons. When the deacon had finished reading, the priest continued with the regular prayers.

It was inevitable that this list of names inscribed on the diptychs should tend to become rather long. The recommendation of the living was particularly popular, because of the honour involved. But this reading risked flattering human vanity. Already at this period—the fifth century—St. Jerome spoke out against the abuse of having those who had got rich dishonestly set down as "donors." This public mention, then, of those persons for whom the Holy Sacrifice was offered, speedily dropped out of use.

Today (as we saw above), the ancient public enumeration is replaced by a few moments of silence; during which the priest commends to God those intentions for which the Mass is being offered.

In order not to prolong the Mass indefinitely, the priest thinks beforehand (either the night before or a few minutes before he says Mass), about those persons for whom he is to apply the fruits of his Mass.

Why not do the same thing yourself?

179—What does the priest ask for in this petition? What do we ask for?

The first thing the priest begs of God for the people for whom he says Mass, is not riches, honour, and pleasure; but that the Sacrifice may serve *for the remission of their sins and for the salvation of their souls.*

This is what we should pray for first.

Next, alongside the universal prayer which we sent up to God for the entire Church a moment ago, we are entitled to pray for the intention of those persons having a special right to our remembrance. In fact, the Memento was instituted for this very purpose! (Here each one should formulate his personal intentions.)

A few suggestions follow:

"Dear Lord, please remember John, Charles, Edward, Lucy, Susan,

Elaine, Louise, etc., my parents, my family. Make us love one another. . . .

My fiancé, my girl friend. . . .

My fellow workers, especially N. . . . who has fallen away from the Faith, who is far from you. . . . Please bring him (or her) back to the Faith! . . .

Marilyn, who is ill. . . Paul, who is dying. . .

Poor Roger, who has taken to drink. . . our poor Helen who took the wrong path in a wicked world. . . .

My Third Order fraternity, my Scout troop, the Sodality, the League of the Sacred Heart, the Altar Society, the Seminary Guild, the Holy Name Society, the Knights of Columbus, etc. . . .

My examinations, this undertaking, this operation, this lawsuit, the coming "blessed event," my vocation, my apostolate. . . .

The apartment I have been hunting for so long! Not to mention a good husband! And a job! . . .

Dear Lord, Please remember:

The Government, and all those in authority over us. . . .

The sick who grow impatient and discouraged. . . .

The prisoners who are sad and unhappy. . . .

Travellers, the lost, the shipwrecked, missionaries. . . .

Sinners who wander on the brink of the precipice. . . .

Those who do not love, who do not forgive—who hate. . . .

Souls who are scrupulous or obstinate. . . .

Fervent souls, desirous of tending toward perfection. . . .

Especially, remember the dying!

It is commonly admitted that on an average 51 million men die every year, which breaks down into:

About 140,000 a day.

Some 5,820 an hour.

Around 97 a minute.

The Grim Reaper mows down, then, eight people every five seconds:

Desiring us to remember especially those who die and appear before God every day, St. Pius X exhorted priests to remember the dying in all their Masses. On the 26th of October, 1907, he even conceded an indulgence of 100 days to priests and faithful who, during the Mass (which they hear or celebrate), recommend to God the sinners of the whole world "who are then in their agony and are to die that day."

Here is an indulgenced prayer for the dying:

O most merciful Jesus, lover of souls, I beseech you, by the agony of your Most Sacred Heart, and by the sorrows of your Immaculate Mother, wash in your Blood the sinners of the whole world who are in their agony now and who are to die today. Amen.

Heart of Jesus, once yourself in agony, have mercy on the dying.

(An indulgence of 300 days. A plenary indulgence under the usual conditions (Confession, Communion, and visit) if this prayer is said with devotion thrice daily at three distinct times.)

We shall die too, perhaps soon.... Let us say by way of preparation:

O Jesus, while adoring your last breath, I beseech you to receive mine. Being uncertain whether I shall have command of my senses when I depart from this world, I offer you even now my last agony and all the sorrow of my passing. Since you are my Father and my Saviour, I give back my soul into your hands. Grant that the last beat of my heart may be a beat of pure love for you. Amen.

To conclude these brief considerations on the Memento, let us never forget the power of prayer, and of these Mementos made to our Lord in the course of the Holy Sacrifice.

"The thing that you did not receive during Holy Mass," wrote St. John Chrysostom, "will be obtained with difficulty at another moment."

A single Mass well heard can made you a saint! Think of the Good Thief—a highwayman. He truly assisted at the first Mass said on Calvary.... He participated in it personally by his sufferings.... He uttered a few earnest words: "Lord, remember me!" (Memento!)

And in that instant, he was transformed, canonized, and merited an eternity of happiness in Heaven! He took his place in that sublime legion of the saints, from which his sins had hitherto excluded him!

That day, Jesus clearly showed us the "value" of *just one Mass;* and demonstrated the importance the Mass should have in our eyes.

Some day—perhaps before long—when we shall see all that God in his love has packed into the august drama of the altar, we shall exclaim: "If I had only known!"...

Now that we *do* know a little, why not start—this very day—to LIVE OUR MASS?

Communicantes

180—What is the third prayer of the Canon, and what is expressed by it?

This prayer is the *Communicantes* or Memento of the Church Triumphant.

Communicantes, et memoriam venerantes, in primis gloriosae semper Virginis Mariae genetricis Dei et Domini nostri Jesu Christi; sed et beatorum apostolorum ac martyrum tuorum Petri et Pauli, Andreae, Jacobi, Joannis, Thomae, Jacobi, Philippi, Bartholomaei, Matthaei, Simonis, et Thaddaei, Lini, Cleti, Clementis, Xysti, Cornelii, Cypriani, Laurentii, Chrysogoni, Joannis et Pauli, Cosmae et Damiani, et omnium sanctorum tuorum quorum meritis precibusque concedas, ut in omnibus protectionis tuae muniamur auxilio: Per eumdem Christum Dominum nostrum. Amen.

Praying in union with, and venerating the memory, first, of the glorious Mary, ever a Virgin, Mother of Jesus Christ, our God and our Lord; likewise of your blessed apostles and martyrs, Peter and Paul, Andrew, James, John, Thomas, Philip, Bartholomew, Matthew, Simon and Thaddeus; of Linus, Cletus, Clement, Xystus, Cornelius, Cyprian, Lawrence, Chrysogonus, John and Paul, Cosmas and Damian, and of all your saints: for the sake of whose merits and prayers, grant that in all things we may be defended by the help of your protection, through the same Christ our Lord. Amen.

The word *Communicantes* with which this prayer begins, means "We who are in communion with all the members of the Church." It is the affirmation of the profound unity of the Mystical Body—and of the communion of saints.

Completely penetrated with these profound mysteries, the priest breaks through the too narrow circle of terrestrial preoccupations which enclosed him a moment, and directs his gaze toward Heaven. He there salutes "glorious Mary, ever a Virgin," the blessed apostles, the illustrious martyrs of the primitive Church, all the Saints, and calls them all together around the altar; that they may assist by their powerful intercession in the great Action about to take place.

With such associates, we may rest assured that our oblation will be favourably received in its entirety, and for each individual!

181—Give some brief facts concerning the Saints mentioned in the *Communicantes*.

First of all, the list evokes the name of Mary, with her glorious title of "Mother of God," bestowed on her by the ecumenical Council of Ephesus (A.D. 431.).

It is fitting that Our Lady should head the list. She plays a special rôle in the work of redemption, in the establishment of the Mystical Body of Christ.

In these few words are summarized all Mary's glories and privileges.

She is the *"Virgin"*—immaculate in her Conception—the one Creature who is all pure, without stain, ever untouched by sin.

She is *"full of grace"*—the channel through whom we receive from Christ the graces we need.

To her virginity, to her Immaculate Conception, to this abundance of graces, is joined her fundamental privilege—source of all the rest—her divine maternity. Mary brought forth the God-Man! This incomprehensible dignity, raising her above all creatures and giving her an extraordinary position, is her most glorious title; a title which the Church vigorously defended against heretics, and which contains the sum and substance of what Mary really is—the Mother of God!

She is most certainly the Mother of Jesus. She is the Mother of the Mediator and is likewise Co-Mediatrix with him. She is the Mother of the Redeemer and is Co-Redemptrix with her Son. It follows that she is also our Mother. She brought forth the Head of the Mystical Body; and hence also the members who are inseparable from their Head.

In these few concepts lies the groundwork of our devotion to Mary, of our confidence in her goodness, her mildness, and her powerful intercession.

It is understandable that after Jesus, Mary should have first place in our devotion. There are Catholics who greet Mary and who venerate her, but from afar. They leave her out of their lives, seeming to say to her: "Now that you have given us Jesus, everything's fine! We don't need you any more to go to him. . . ." Others would deem a childlike cult to Mary undignified. "A woman's devotion," they remark disparagingly." May Mary protect them!

But we know that Mary is indispensable to us!

In the Incarnation of the Word, Mary's rôle was essential. Without her "fiat," we should not have had Jesus. It was because Mary consented to become the Mother of Christ, that Jesus was incarnated. It is plain that devotion to Mary is not something "tacked on" to our piety —something to take or leave. Except for her, Jesus would not have become our Brother.

In the Passion, Mary becomes the Co-Redemptrix of the human race. Standing close to the bloody Cross, she immolates her divine Son; uniting the blood of her mother-heart to the divine blood which falls on Calvary to redeem the universe! There, too, she pronounces a "fiat" —one replete with sorrow and heartbreak!

We can understand, then, Mary's power over the Heart of her Divine Son; and the intensity of her love for us! The holy Curé of Ars had reason to say that the hearts of all mothers taken together are like an icicle, alongside the heart of the Blessed Mother! . . . "She is so beautiful," said St. Bernadette Soubirous, "that whoever once sees her, can hardly wait to die, so as to see her agin!"

Likewise, we ought to understand better Mary's rôle in the Mass. It is through Mary that we have the sacramental and mystical Body of Christ—Mary has a share in our Sacrifice. We can never know enough about Mary, or love her enough. With heart and soul formed for Jesus, Mary has a right to our complete trust—to all our love and devotion. During Mass, let us think of how she adopts us at the altar, just as she adopted us on Calvary. And so, the more we show ourselves her children, the more will Mary show herself our Mother!

Let us pause once more to contemplate the greatness of the Blessed Virgin, by showing how her life resembles that of the priest; and how it is with reason that we should think of her, as the time for the Consecration nears.

The following considerations are from the pen of Sr. Louise-Marguerite de la Touche, a nun of the Visitation, to whom our Lord appeared between the years 1902 to 1915. [See. *Au Service de Jésus Prêtre,* T. II, p. 191.] She writes:

Mary's whole life unrolled before me, as so many phases of the priesthood.

When as a tiny child, the Blessed Virgin made the offering of her virginity to God, she took, as it were, the decisive step of the subdiaconate. She offered to Love—in the first bloom of her innocence—this first Sacrifice of self.

The day of the Incarnation, when the Holy Spirit overshadowed her, and Love endowed her with his own virtue of fruitfulness; she received through the divine anointing, the sublime character of Mother of God. In the same way the priest at his ordination is marked by the Spirit of Love with the priestly character—indelible and divine.

Like the priest, Mary received at the Incarnation the power to sacrifice Jesus; the right to touch his Sacred Body; the duty to show him to the world—to give him to souls. Like the priest, she received the mission to reveal the Truth; to forgive sinners (not by herself, but by her power over the Heart of her Son); to console the suffering; to offer Jesus in Sacrifice and herself with him; in fine, to be a living link of merciful love between the Heart of God and the heart of man.

After that, Mary remained nine months in the contemplation of Love's mysteries; thus preparing herself for the first oblation of her Son.

Jesus came into the world. At that moment when for the first time he became visible to her eyes, Mary took him in her virginal arms; and, lifting him up, offered him to God. Who can comprehend the grandeur and ineffable sweetness of this first Mass offered up by Mary in the silence of the stable, in this serene night wherein the angels sang the Gloria! Who can comprehend the infinite worth of the Sacrifice, whose frail and delicate Victim was the Word made flesh, infinite Love; and whose virginal sacrificer had hands so pure, a heart so ardent, a soul so lofty and so close to God! . . .

Every day, at the hour of the morning sacrifice, Mary Immaculate took the Divine Lamb in this way in her innocent arms

> and lifted him up as a divine oblation to Heaven. And when Jesus had grown so that Mary no longer could lift him, she drew him to her heart; and in a chaste and loving embrace offered up Love's Victim to God the Father on the golden paten of her virginal heart.
>
> After thirty years of this daily sacrifice, the Virgin Mother followed her Divine Son in his apostolic career. . . and with him climbed Mount Calvary; where, with him still, she consummated her sacrifice.

(It should be understood, of course, that we have no intention of implying by the foregoing, that Our Lady was ever vested with the character of the priesthood, the way a priest is.)

After Mary, the *holy apostles* have their special place in the Canon.

St. Paul is mentioned after St. Peter. The two apostles are always inseparably linked. (St. Matthias, who was not directly chosen by our Lord, is omitted; so that the sacred number of twelve may not be surpassed.)

To the twelve apostles correspond the twelve martyrs.

Linus, Cletus and Clement, martyr popes, are the first three successors of St. Peter in Rome. Saints Xystus and Cornelius are two other martyred popes. Next comes a bishop, St. Cyprian; and a deacon, St. Lawrence, who enjoyed great celebrity in Rome, where the people venerated him almost equally with the Apostles Peter and Paul. "As Jerusalem was made famous by Stephen, so Rome was made famous by Lawrence from the rising to the setting sun." So writes St. Leo in one of his homilies. St. Lawrence was the poor man's friend. . . .

Next come five lay martyrs: SS. Chrysogonus, John and Paul, who died around A.D. 362, SS. Cosmas and Damian, two famous doctors originally from Syria. They cared for the sick—without a fee!

"It has been justly pointed out," writes Father Plus, "that this list must be very old; because it contains only the names of martyrs. In the beginning, only martyrs were canonized; that is, officially admitted to the honours of public cult. It was only after the era of persecution that bishops, ascetics, and virgins were declared to be saints—their mortified lives serving, perhaps, as an equivalent martyrdom. These, like the martyrs, 'confessed' the worth of faith in Christ."

So that none will be forgotten (it would take a little while to name all the saints!), the *Communicantes* closes with a comprehensive mention of "all the saints"—*et omnium sanctorum.*

It is thus all Heaven that comes down to assist at Mass and to unite their supplications, prayers, and thanksgivings to those that Jesus will soon come to address on the altar to his Father.

Let us join our supplications to theirs.

Hanc Igitur

182—What is the fourth prayer of the Canon and what does it mean?

It is the *Hanc igitur*, a prayer in which we beseech God for the Consecration.

Hanc igitur oblationem servitutis nostrae, sed et cunctae familiae tuae, quaesumus, Domine, ut placatus accipias, diesque nostros in tua pace disponas, atque ab aeterna damnatione nos eripi, et in electorum tuorum jubeas grege numerari. Per Christum Dominum nostrum. Amen.	Therefore, we beseech you, O Lord, graciously to receive this oblation which we your servants, and your whole family, offer up to you. Dispose our days in your peace, command that we be saved from eternal damnation and numbered among the flock of your elect, through Christ our Lord. Amen.

This is the conclusion. This prayer takes up again the initial theme of the Canon—the theme of oblation. We ask God to accept our offerings and to transform them into the Body of Christ.

In the preceding prayers, the concern for the interests of the Church Militant and the invocation of the Church Triumphant, have turned away our attention to some extent from the offerings of the Sacrifice.

In the *Hanc igitur,* the priest comes back to this theme; with confidence increased by the recalling of the dogma of the communion of saints.

Peace, solicited several times since the beginning of Mass, is here insistently demanded before the Consecration; for peace was solemnly promised by the Saviour a few hours before his Passion: "Peace I leave with you, my peace I give to you, not as the world gives do I give to you." (John 14:27.) For the peace of God consists in the possession of sanctifying grace and not in the enjoyment of the pleasures of sense.... It consists in the possession of those goods which no enemy—not even death—can take away from us!

The prayer next begs God to save us from the supreme evil, eternal damnation, and give us lasting happiness. We ask God that he will cause us to "walk in the way of the righteous"—of the Saints—so that we may be with them forever. We ask it through Christ our Lord, who will soon be present on the altar for the glory of God and for our sanctification.

183—What does the priest do when he recites the *Hanc igitur*, and why?

As the celebrant recites this prayer, he extends his hands, joined, and with palms down, over the chalice and the host.

We know that in the Old Testament, the high priest placed his hands on the head of the sacrificial victim—the scapegoat—to attest that he was placing all the sins of the people on the animal and substituting it for the guilty people.

Making the same gesture over the bread and wine which are to be changed into the Body and Blood of Christ, the celebrant recalls to us that the Divine Victim has been laden with all the sins of the entire world; according to these words of the Psalmist: "The reproaches of those who reproach you have fallen on me." (Ps. 68:10.) And of Isaias (53:6.): "The Lord laid on him the iniquities of us all."

Let us remember—at this moment in the Mass—that we are placing our transgressions on the Sacred Victim who willed to accept their burden and responsibility; to expiate their penalty by his death and Cross; and so pay all our debt to God.

If we reflected, that by our sins we bear down with all our weight on the Divine Victim; is it not true that we should not be in such a hurry to commit them?...

Let us—at this moment in the Mass—protest with all our hearts that we do not wish, through ill will, to render useless this renewal of Christ's Passion. And what is more, the *Hanc igitur* ought to be an eloquent invitation for us to unite our immolation to that of Christ.

184—Why does the server ring the bell at this point?

The ringing of the bell by the altar boy announces the approach of the Consecration. This is the place where those who did not budge for the Sanctus, finally decide to kneel! Msgr. de Ségur wittily calls the second bell the "lazy man's bell"!

Needless to say, this quip is not aimed at those who are feeble or ill!

Quam oblationem

185—What is the fifth prayer of the Canon and what does it mean?

It is the *Quam oblationem.*

Quam oblationem, tu, Deus, in omnibus quaesumus, bene + dictam, adscrip + tam, ra + tam, rationabilem, acceptabilemque facere digneris: ut nobis + Corpus, et + Sanguis fiat dilectissimi Filii tui Domini nostri Jesu Christi.	Vouchsafe, we beseech you, O God, to make this oblation in all things + blessed, + approved, + ratified, reasonable and acceptable, so that it may become for us the Body + and Blood + of your most Beloved Son, Jesus Christ our Lord.

AN ACT OF LOVE

"My God I love you and accept your holy will."

The love of God is to the life of the soul what health is to the life of the body.

A scratch endured with 10 ounces of love for God, is worth more than the martyrdom of a St. Lawrence endured with only 9 ounces. Every act of love brings with it:

1. **The remission of venial sin.**
2. **An increase in God's glory.**
3. **A thrill of joy in Heaven.**
4. **The multiplication of grace in and around us.**
5. **An alleviation of the suffering of the souls in Purgatory.**
6. **A delay in the punishment of sinners on earth.**
7. **The reparation of countless blasphemies.**

Imprimatur: Albert Valois, V.G.
Montreal, Nov. 14, 1953.

It is a prayer still *more solemn* than the preceding. It is addressed to God the Father, to obtain the transubstantiation, or changing of the bread and wine into the Body and Blood of Christ.

We are nearing the sublime peak of the Mass, in which God is about to operate *the greatest of all miracles;* in which the mystery ennobling our earth above all other planets, is about to take place.

At this moment, the sacred liturgy places upon the lips of the priest a prayer unlike any other. Up to this point, the celebrant has either implored God to accept the Victim he is about to present to him, or else he has prayed for the sanctification of the members, who are being offered up together with him.

But the prayer, *Quam oblationem,* has a different aim. It refers to the act of Consecration itself.

The priest declares that the words he is about to utter, will not be a simple narration of what Jesus did on the eve of his last day of earthly life; that he will not speak as one deputized by the Church; but that his words will be sacramental words. He will say these words in the name of Jesus; he will lend the Saviour his lips. These words will produce the same miracle that they produced the first time, when they were uttered in the Cenacle.

There is another thing to notice in this short prayer.

When Jesus was born in Bethlehem, he was born for us. "A Child is born to us, he is given to us," exclaimed the prophet Isaias in anticipation. (Is. 9:6.) And the angels, announcing the birth of the Son of God to the Shepherds, said to them: "A Saviour has been born for you." (Luke 2:11.) [Knox.] Again, when Christ died on Calvary, it was for us: "*Crucifixus etiam pro nobis*—Crucified for us," we chant in the Creed.

Now it is still *"for us,"* that we pray that the bread and wine may become the Body and Blood of Christ; that the God-Man, as Victim, places himself at our disposal that we may offer him to this Father, as belonging to us, with all that he is and all that he accomplishes on the altar. Let us not forget this last sentence. We shall have occasion to speak of it again in No. 186.

If the Blessed Virgin were suddenly to appear to you, and, placing her Divine Child in your arms, were to say to you, "I am furnishing you the means to fulfill all your obligations to God"; with what joy would you not lift the Child Jesus up toward Heaven in adoration, thanksgiving, and supplication to your Creator and Father!

In this prayer, the Church asks just that—and the Church will be heard!

Jesus is coming down on the altar for us! To bring us with him back to the Father!

Jesus is always the "Blessed" of his Father. It depends only on us to be so also by resembling him!

He is always "acceptable" and "pleasing" to God. With Jesus' help, we may be so, too!

He is always a "spiritual and pleasing Host" offered to God. He comes to help us to resemble him by reproducing his life in our own!

If we accept the rôle of victim with him, our offering will be pleasing to the Father for Jesus' sake and for the sake of the faithful who have become identified with the Divine Saviour.

As the celebrant sends up this plea—so far-reaching in its consequences—the words come slowly, almost haltingly, from his lips: as if he felt himself incapable of expressing all that he expects from the Divine Goodness and from the generosity of the faithful. . . . Five times he makes the sign of the cross; thrice over the bread and wine together, then separately and successively over the bread and the wine.

Let us not be surprised at this. These as yet profane, inanimate substances, cannot be sanctified too much. *And we* (whom they symbolize and represent) *surely stand in need—in this solemn moment—of a fresh effusion of grace!*

From this moment on, the priest disappears, and he who remains is Jesus!

Father Mateo relates an extraordinary incident in his retreats—something experienced by himself, and which marvellously illustrates what happens in the Mass.

One day he was celebrating Holy Mass for a deceased person. The family of the departed had invited friends and a small number of acquaintances. This is how an individual who might be qualified as a "free-thinker" came to be present, and in one of the front pews. In fact, the gentleman in question, a Freemason, believed in neither God nor Devil. He had come only to please the family.

As soon as Mass started, this person showed signs of irritation and boredom. His annoying attitude soon settled into one of open disdain and sarcasm.

His whole bearing took on an air of mockery and scorn. In truth, the unhappy man was unable to contain the hatred he felt toward the Catholic religion. Inside a Catholic Church, he was about as comfortable as a fish out of water. His fanatical attitude—to the astonishment and scandal of the congregation—lasted up to the Consecration.

But with the Consecration, an abrupt change took place in him. He lost all countenance. First, intrigued by what had just taken place at the altar, his gaze became fixed. He was astounded at what he saw!

What was the matter with him? What had happened?

He appeared to be in a fever of excitement. He became fearful, tormented, looked around.... He was terribly perturbed.... He began to weep!... And not realizing what he was doing or why, with great, shaking sobs, he fell to his knees!... Again he looked—and again, horribly worried, and trembling.... And this lasted to the time of Communion.

Needless to say, the witnesses of this unaccustomed scene were extremely puzzled at his actions.... But none dared question the man.

Scarcely was Mass over, when the poor man hastened to the sacristy; where the priest was just removing his vestments.

Panting, trembling with ill-suppressed emotion, the man asked brusquely. "Are you the priest who just said Mass?"

"Yes. May I help you?"

"What did you do? Father, what did you *do* out there?"

"What did I do! You a Catholic, and you don't know what the priest does at the altar when he says Mass?"

"Catholic? If you want to call it that! I *was* a Catholic once—more or less!"

"And did you never learn what happens at the altar when a priest says Mass?"

Briefly, then, Father reviewed how the Holy Sacrifice of the Mass reproduces and prolongs in a mystical, but real manner, the bloody Sacrifice of Calvary.... How Christ, the Eternal Priest, and at the same time the Most Holy Victim nailed to the Cross, is still the same Eternal

Priest; concealed in the ministerial priest. How it is the same Victim who is mystically immolated on our altars. . . .

Without waiting for more, the gentleman exclaimed, "Father, that's *it!* That's exactly what I saw a moment ago with my own eyes! I can hardly believe it!

"There was a certain moment in your Mass, when *you* suddenly disappeared! In your place I saw a Man of majestic appearance, in a most lamentable state... suffering horribly... his features livid... blood streaming from His hands, which were extended on a Cross. Blood flowing from His side, as well... into that cup you call a chalice!... Yes, that is what I saw just now!... Father, I'm all upset!... "

To conclude, let us ask ourselves, if this is the scene we look upon with the eyes of faith, when we are present at the Holy Sacrifice?

Perhaps, we are sometimes tempted to exclaim with the doubting disciple, "Lord, show me your hands and your feet, and I will believe!"

A famous theologian of the twelfth century, Hugh of St. Victor, had a great desire to see Jesus in the Mass. One day the Child Jesus appeared to him. Hugh was overjoyed. Then he heard these words: "Hugh, you have lost much merit!" And the vision vanished.

May this example teach us not to yield to the same temptation!

Let us say rather with the father of the epileptic boy, "Lord, I do believe. Help my unbelief." (Mark 9:24). Then will our Lord be able to say of us: "Blessed are they who have not seen, and yet have believed." (John 20:29.)

Now the Consecration is about to commence. . . . Let us be recollected. And let us stir up our faith!... Jesus is *very* near!

The silence which should reign from the commencement of the Canon, becomes, if possible, more profound. For there is "a time to sing and a time to be silent." (Choirmasters please take note!)

At three o'clock on Good Friday afternoon, the Catholic world is asked to suspend its work for a minute of silence, in commemoration of that solemn moment when Jesus breathed his last for us on the Cross. Now this event is renewed every day during the few precious and solemn minutes of the Consecration. . . . If all choir singers would respect at least this brief moment in the Mass, how grateful we priests would be!

The Consecration

186—What is the Consecration?

It is that most solemn moment in the Mass in which Jesus comes down on the altar! It is the act whereby he becomes present.

"In this sublime instant," said the holy Curé of Ars, "were a priest to have the full realization of what he actually does, he would die of amazement, of unworthiness, and—of love!"

Here it is that our meagre offerings placed on the paten and in the chalice, acquire eternal worth!

In popular speech, the term "Consecration" is given to this most divine operation of the changing of the bread and wine into the Body and Blood of our Lord. But theology, with its more rigid vocabulary, has given precision and completion to the sense of the word, *consecration,* by creating the term, *transubstantiation.*

In the religious sense, "to consecrate" means "to set aside, to devote," and implies the idea of a complete immolation.

To *consecrate,* is to withdraw a person or object from secular use or secular surroundings, in order to devote him or it to a distinctly religious use; and to make of him or it, the exclusive property of God.

This consecration necessarily entails the duty to reverence, honour, and surround with a protective barrier, the objects, goods, and persons thus marked with the seal of divine ownership.

No one would dare touch unauthorized the sacred vessels, much less make use of them for profane purposes.... It is passing strange that people should show so much more reverence for sacred vessels than for sacred persons—priests and religious—treated so cavalierly and so lightly criticized by "good Catholics."

Transubstantiation is more than a consecration. Transubstantiation is the miraculous and total change of a substance into a new substance; which exists under the appearances of the first substance. In other words, it is the change of the substance of the bread and wine into the substance of the Body and Blood of our Lord; who lives under the appearances (or "accidents") of the bread and wine.

We discussed earlier (Q. 11 and ff.) the concept of sacrifice. We said that the act of the separate consecrations of the bread and wine, which represent the separation of the Body and Blood of Christ on the

Cross, is the exterior sign expressive of the Sacrifice of Jesus, dying on Calvary out of love for his Father.

It would be impossible to stress too strongly this doubtless more difficult, but extremely important, point.

This point is important to remember: the ritual of Consecration renders the Sacrifice of the Cross sacramentally present in the liturgy of the Mass.

In a general way, the faithful understand well, and highly appreciate the Eucharist considered as a Sacrament; namely, in the form of Communion, when given to them in all its divinising effulgence; as food for the soul, solace along life's way, and Real Presence in the tabernacle....

Very few know, however (and as a result, very few prize), the Eucharist enough as a Sacrifice—as something primordially given to God; as offered to him in the Mass to adore and glorify him.

This regrettable gap in Catholic education brings in its train the most fatal consequences in the practical organization of the piety of the faithful.... Many people attend Mass for the sole purpose of receiving Communion. Others prefer Benediction of the Blessed Sacrament to Mass, and so on....

Let us remember, then, that the Eucharist is both a *Sacrifice* and a *Sacrament*. As offered (given to God) in the Mass, the Eucharist is a Sacrifice. Received as food (given to man) in Communion, it is a Sacrament.

A sacrifice does not consist purely and simply in a victim. The victim is the matter, not the whole, of the sacrifice. Sacrifice is before aught else an ACTION, an act which consists in the oblation of a victim (act of oblation).

In the Mass, then, the rite of Consecration truly brings us the Sacrifice of Calvary; not only the Victim who was once offered there, but also the ACT OF OBLATION by which, on Good Friday, Christ offered himself to his Father for the glorification of the Trinity and the salvation of the world.

It is an ACT that has no parallel, oriented as it is toward the glory of the Father, and the redemption of the world: this ACT OF OBLATION actualized at the Consecration, with the incomparable potency of adoration, and all that effulgence of glory, which, once for all, Christ incorporated into it.

Spanning two milleniums of time, this unique ACT OF OBLATION, becomes contemporaneous, is placed within our reach; so that we, in turn, in our time, may appropriate it, may unite ourselves to it, may actively participate in it: applying all the energy of mind and spirit, with all the faith, reverence, charity, and devotion of which we are capable. So, through Christ, "with him and in him," we shall offer again as ours, the same pure, holy, and spotless Host—once a bloody oblation; but today glorified beneath the sacramental veils—the sacred Bread of life eternal, the chalice of eternal salvation.

So does the Mass constitute a "divine proposition," in which is centralized and culminated all Christ's priestly adoration; thus placed within our reach and made available to us. Truly, THE HOLY SACRIFICE OF THE MASS IS THE HIGHEST FORM OF WORSHIP THERE IS!

First of all, the Sacrifice of the Mass is directed toward the Father and ascends toward him as an odour of sweetness.

To repeat, this primarily sacrificial, oblational, and ascending aspect of the Mass—this ACT OF OBLATION of Christ present on the altar during Holy Mass—has been lost sight of only too often.

By some strange aberration, the highest institution, the one giving greatest glory to God, has been wrenched from its setting; turned upside down; and made to apply EXCLUSIVELY TO OURSELVES. We have totally confiscated it for our utilitarian ends—for our "spiritual profit"—with the inevitable and incalculable disaster which such an offense against the glory due to God must inevitably bring in its train.

The end-result has been, for many of the faithful, the rise of regrettable deviations in the concept and practice of the Eucharistic cult.

Stripped of the concept of an ACT OF OBLATION by the Great High Priest of Calvary, the Mass appears as a sort of pious "exercise"; wherein the priest "exercises" his power to change bread and wine into Christ's Body and Blood; as a rite conducive of Communions, as a ceremony designed to assure us consecrated Hosts to replenish our ciboria and adorn our monstrances!

And to cap it all—as the direct consequence of implacable logic—we have the highest form of eucharistic worship—the Holy Sacrifice of the Mass—reduced to nothing more than a ritual preparatory to

Communion! To a ceremony whose purpose is to give us the object of our eucharistic devotion; to wit, Communion with which to nourish our souls, and the Divine "Prisoner of the Tabernacle" for us to visit!

Let us have no illusions on the subject. Such errors are not without unfortunate consequences.

By our violation of the established order, by our exaltation of Communion and adoration of the Blessed Sacrament, to the detriment of the Holy Sacrifice, we have, far from enriching these venerable forms of eucharistic piety in the minds of the laity, to a great extent, impoverished and depleted them.

When we tore Communion out of its proper place in the general economy of the Sacrifice of the Mass—from its subordinate rôle of a full participation in the sacrificial oblation—we thereby deprived it of its primordial rôle: that of assuming the communicant into the oblatory ascent of the sacrificial Victim; having as its purpose, (1) to bring about the return to the Father (Review Q. 5), and (2) to unite the communicant intimately with the priestly and supreme adoration of the Great Offerer; to bring to its fullest the glory given to God by active participation in the oblation.

Is not the very word host—meaning victim—significant?

Public worship of the Blessed Sacrament is not (as are the Sacrifice of the Mass itself and Communion) of divine, but of ecclesiastical, institution.

It was by way of reaction against the heresies of Tanchelm, Berengarius, and later on, of Luther (who alike, following various systems, denied the Real Presence), that the Latin Church in the eleventh century organized the public cult of the Consecrated Host.

These more recent forms of eucharistic worship, such as adoration of the Blessed Sacrament, solemn eucharistic processions, etc. are highly venerable, and from the point of view of popularizing the dogma of the Real Presence (especially since the rise of these heresies), of great importance. An attack on them would be an act of sacrilege. But whatever may be the practical utility of these forms, considered alongside something instituted by Christ, they are accidental, secondary; while from the standpoint of cultural content, they are of subordinate importance.

For there can be no question of comparison between a short Low Mass in which the very Sacrifice of our Redemption is brought down upon the altar; in which Christ, the Great High Priest, compresses all his energy of adoration and love to the glory of God the Father, all his effulgence of life and sanctification for us; and a Benediction of the Blessed Sacrament, or a eucharistic procession, however solemn; in which we poor sinners shower the Sacred Host with our poor, human adoration, which (however fervent it may be) falls so far wide of the mark. (See Croegart: *Les rites et les prières du S. Sacrifice de la messe.)*

THE CONSECRATION OF THE BREAD

187—What does the priest do and say at the Consecration of the bread?

Let us follow attentively every gesture of the priest at this most solemn moment of the Mass.

The priest wipes the tips of his thumbs and fore-fingers on the corporal to purify them, before touching the host, presently to become the Lord's Body. With these same fingers, consecrated the day of his ordination, he holds the host in front of him. He then elevates his eyes toward heaven. Thus did our Lord at the Last Supper.

He next—still like our Lord—bows his head slightly in thanksgiving. Then, holding the host in his left hand, he makes the sign of the cross over it with his right; in imitation of Jesus, who likewise blessed the bread at this moment in which he was about to give us this great proof of his love.

He then rests both forearms on the altar; and inclining his head, slowly pronounces the words of Consecration. After saying them, he genuflects, rises, and holding the Sacred Host—which has become the true Body of the Saviour—in his consecrated fingers (the other fingers being extended and joined together); he elevates it as high as possible; always keeping his eyes fixed upon it, and presents it to the adoration of the people.

At this moment the bell in the belfry rings out; inviting the parish to adore the Lord who has descended amidst his people. The altar boy rings the sanctuary bell, to announce to those present that the great miracle has taken place. Jesus, the Incarnate Word, the God-Man, the Saviour of the world, the Crucified One of Calvary, and Heaven's glorious King; is really and truly present on the altar.... Let us adore him.

The priest replaces the Sacred Host on the corporal, and again genuflects in adoration. He then rises and proceeds to the Consecration of the chalice.

The following are the exact words which the priest pronounces at the Consecration of the bread: •

Qui, pridie, quam pateretur, accepit panem in sanctas ac venerabiles manus suas, et elevatis oculis in caelum ad te Deum, Patrem suum omnipotentem, tibi gratias agens, bene+dixit, fregit, deditque discipulis suis, dicens: Accipite, et manducate ex hoc omnes: HOC EST ENIM CORPUS MEUM.	Who the day before He suffered, took bread into His holy and venerable hands, and having lifted up His eyes to Heaven to you, God, His Almighty Father, giving thanks to you, + blessed it, broke it, and gave it to His disciples, saying: All of you take and eat of this, FOR THIS IS MY BODY!

188—Please comment on these words of the Consecration of the bread.

We have now reached that point, that supreme moment in the Mass, in which Christ becomes present with the same sublime, loving dispositions which he had for his Father at the moment wherein he sacrificed his life on the Cross to accomplish the divine will!

"He who the day before He suffered." With the first words, the Cross is recalled. Nothing great is accomplished without the Cross.... Remember this! Thus it was "on the day before He suffered"; that is, when Jesus was on the verge of sweating blood to atone for our sins, of being betrayed by Judas, denied by Peter, buffeted before Caiphas, and scourged by Pilate; who after having acknowledged and declared his innocence, condemned him to death! Again, it was when Jesus was about to climb Mount Calvary laden with his heavy Cross; there to be savagely crucified and die like a criminal; it was in this moment, when our Lord saw clearly all these frightful torments, that he willed to accomplish the most sublime gift of His love—a gift for whose giving he had so ardently yearned!

Hard of heart or light of mind must he be indeed, who can remain cold, indifferent, or deaf, in the face of reiterated appeals to attend Mass even on weekdays: even at the cost of great sacrifice! .. Did *He* not suffer "unto death" for us on the Cross?

Let us continue our commentary:

He "took bread into His holy and venerable hands." The bread purposely chosen to be given as food to our souls, is about to change into *Jesus!* It is *Jesus* whom the priest will soon hold in his hands!

And "having lifted up His eyes, to Heaven, to you, God, His Almighty Father, giving thanks to you." In this moment, Jesus gave thanks to his Father with infinite gratitude, for permitting him to institute the Holy Eucharist; the marvel of marvels, the ineffable proof of love, through whose means our Lord is able really to remain with his Church till the end of time. By virtue of the priesthood which he was to institute on this same night of the Last Supper, Jesus would be able to descend on every altar where there was a priest to offer the Holy Sacrifice. Through his priests, he could give himself to souls and thus impart to them divine life. He would be able to satisfy his love by becoming in the tabernacle the pleasing Companion of our exile. In the monstrance, as in the tabernacle, he could be the Great Lover of Souls; drawing them to his feet, there to console them, to inflame them with love, to give them patience in trial, resignation, humility, and the strength to suffer in silence.... He could exercise his power and kingship by drawing to the lowly Host the adoration and homage of princes and kings, the small and great of the earth. He could be glorified in the midst of the silence and solitude of cloisters; and amidst the darkness of night by the chosen souls who would come—while sinners rush to their pleasures—to pay homage, give thanks, make reparation, and supplicate. Finally, he would be able to become the Sun of his Church; since it is toward the Eucharist—Sacrifice and Sacrament—that all other sacraments converge. For it is to house the Eucharist that men rear aloft the most splendid and magnificent basilicas; and it is by, with, and in, the Eucharist, that Jesus Christ pays glory and honour to the Blessed Trinity; even to the end of the world....

Such were some of the motives which consoled our Lord in this sublime hour, and caused him to "give thanks" to his Father.

How Jesus loved us! Think of all these mysteries especially prepared for each of us, on the very eve of his death!

If only we profited by all this!... Sad to say, unfortunately, the Eucharist, Jesus, the Mass, no longer interest us! Poor Jesus!

"He blessed it, broke it, and gave it to his disciples, saying, 'Eat, all of you, of this.'" Jesus is the love that gives itself without stint—wholly—to teach us to devote, give, surrender, ourselves through love, to all that God wills; to all ministry, to every charge or office, to all souls indiscriminately, to every sacrifice.... It may be that we have given ourselves wholly, once and for all—but how often have we taken ourselves back, piece by piece! Let us hasten then to give ourselves back—sincerely and totally—so as to form but a single host with Jesus....

"This is my Body." Each of these words merits an explanation.

"This." The priest does not say, "This bread is my body," but employs the demonstrative pronoun, "this." This is because as soon as the formula is pronounced, that which was bread is bread no longer, but the Body of Christ. Christ is not the bread. (Impanation was the error of Berengarius, condemned by the Church.) What has taken place is a complete change; the replacement of all the substance of the bread by another substance—Christ. The "accidents," called also "species," and "appearances," (such as colour, form, and taste) continue to subsist by miracle.

"Is," and not "becomes," for the change is instantaneous.

"My." The priest says "my Body," and not "Christ's Body," because it is Christ who speaks through the lips of the priest.

"Body." That is, his whole Body; not his flesh alone, but also his blood; and the whole person of the living Christ—his soul, his human, and divine natures, God and Man, living, risen, and glorified. Thus Christ is present in his entirety; not dead, not his body alone, bloodless as it was after his death on the Cross; but the whole and living Christ.

The second Consecration will be a replica of the first. Jesus will be whole and entire under the species or appearance of wine.

"This is My Body"—ineffable words uttered by Christ, and that only he could utter. The priest repeats them; but in the name of Christ and in his power—and the great mystery takes place.... Jesus becomes present in the state of Victim; that he may unite us to himself, transform us into himself, and so offer fitting praise to the Holy Trinity. These words are meaningful: they perform what they say! They are more potent than those spoken at the creation of light and of the universe! For they bring about transubstantiation: this marvel of the supernatural order, which theology seeks to fathom.... A mystery as impenetrable as it is adorable!

In silence let us adore....

At this moment, the priest elevates the Host and holds it aloft for the adoration of the people. This is not the time to bow one's head, but to look at the Sacred Host, and make an act of faith in the Real Presence! In order to favour this act of faith, the Church grants an indulgence of seven years to all the faithful; who (either at the Elevation, or when the Sacred Host is solemnly exposed in the monstrance), recite with faith, piety, and love, this ejaculation: "My Lord and my God!" A plenary indulgence may be gained once a week, if this pious practice is followed daily; with the addition of Confession, Communion, and prayer for the intentions of the Sovereign Pontiff.

Before and after the two elevations, the priest, as if overcome by the presence of Christ, falls to his knees. This gesture of deepest veneration—the genuflexion—is made four times in succession at this sacred moment of the Mass; and will be renewed more than a dozen times before the ablutions.... Whereas, before the Consecration, the priest genuflected only once: namely, during the Creed.

One gesture of the server may have seemed strange to you; the one when, kneeling behind the celebrant, he lifts up the edge of the priest's chasuble. This gesture, often useless at the present time, is simply a survival from a former time when the chasuble had the form of a rather full cloak. The acolyte then lifted it up to facilitate the movements of the priest.

The Consecration of the Wine

189—What is said and done at the Consecration of the wine?

Immediately following the Elevation of the Host, the celebrant proceeds to *the Consecration of the wine.*

The priest lifts the pall covering the chalice, then rubs the thumb and index finger of each hand together over the chalice, lest any small particle should adhere to them. He then takes the chalice and places it before him. He next makes the sign of the cross over the chalice; then takes the chalice in both hands, and placing anew both forearms on the altar—pronounces slowly and secretly the words of Consecration over the wine.

He then genuflects; and again stands erect to present the chalice of the Saviour's Blood to the adoration of the faithful; just as he did after the consecration of Christ's Sacred Body.

Here again, we should look at the chalice; believe and adore.

Have you ever noticed, during the consecration of the bread and wine, how low the priest bends over the host and chalice? . . . So that his lips almost touch them? Almost as if he were trying to enter them? Love tends toward nearness, toward union, toward oneness. The soul ever dreams of some new and more intimate means of communication with its Friend. It gives, and renews the gift of self. . . . Sometimes it would—if it could—*live* in him. . . .

Have you ever had this dream of really close union with Jesus? . . . .

These are the words of the Consecration of the wine:

Simili modo, postquam coenatum est, accipiens et hunc praeclarum Calicem in sanctas ac venerabiles manus suas, item tibi gratias agens, benedixit, deditque discipulis suis, dicens:

Accipite et bibite ex eo omnes: HIC EST ENIM CALIX SANGUINIS MEI NOVI ET AETERNI TESTAMENTI (MYSTERIUM FIDEI) QUI PRO VOBIS ET PRO MULTIS EFFUNDETUR IN REMISSIONEM PECCATORUM.

Haec quotiescumque feceritis in meì memoriam facietis.

In like manner, after He had supped, taking this excellent Chalice into His holy and venerable hands, again giving thanks to you, He blessed it, and gave it to His disciples, saying:

Take, all of you, and drink of this,

FOR THIS IS THE CHALICE OF MY BLOOD OF THE NEW AND ETERNAL TESTAMENT (THE MYSTERY OF FAITH) WHICH FOR YOU AND FOR MANY SHALL BE SHED UNTO THE REMISSION OF SINS.

As often as you shall do these things, you shall do them in memory of Me.

190—Please comment on the words of the Consecration of the wine.

"*Simili modo*. . . . In like manner." Here again we have the same recalling of the circumstances of the Last Supper, the giving of thanks, the blessing and the gift; as for the Consecration of the bread. *Here, Jesus is going to give us his Precious Blood*: the Blood he shed on Calvary for our salvation and redemption from sin.

Bibite ex eo omnes—"Take, all of you, and drink of this." Once more we are all called to partake of this chalice, to profit from the abundant and superabundant redemption which Jesus merited for us. . . . Are we still deaf to his appeal? Sharing in the chalice of Jesus, means suffering with him. . . .

Hic est enim calix sanguinis mei, novi et aeterni testamenti, "For this is the chalice of My Blood of the new and eternal testament." This is no longer the chalice of the old testament—the chalice that contained only the figure or symbol of that which Jesus gives us now to drink. This is the chalice of the new and eternal testament—the testament of Infinite Love. This Blood of the new covenant is the Blood of Jesus, which merited for us redemption and everlasting life through our union with Christ, through our divine filiation, and the promise of our union with the Holy Trinity for all eternity.

Mysterium fidei—"the mystery of faith." We are here at the very heart of the Faith! This "mystery of faith" will be unveiled to us only in eternity. . . . *Then we shall understand the mystery of divine mercy and justice.*

It is halfway through the words of Jesus, that the celebrant injects this brief parenthetical phrase: the "mystery of faith." Its origin goes back to the eighth century. There was no sanctuary bell at this period. And in order that there be no risk of the Consecration's passing unnoticed, the congregation was notified in this way: as the priest consecrated, the deacon would say in a loud voice: "*Mysterium fidei!*" (The mystery of faith is now being accomplished.)

Qui pro vobis et pro multis effundetur in remissionem peccatorum—"Which for you and for many shall be shed unto the remission of sins." These words of Jesus at the Last Supper show the union between the Eucharist and the Cross—they reiterate the union of our Mass and the Cross. It was for us that Jesus shed his blood, and it is in the Mass that the fruits of the Sacrifice of the Cross are applied to us. Jesus said that his blood had been shed for "many" . . . Does this mean (as the Jansenists taught) that Jesus did not die for all? Not at all. Jesus wishes to say only that "many" avail themselves of this Redemption. Let us strive to increase their number; and for our own part, let us never render useless the sufferings which our Lord endured for us on Calvary.

Haec quotiescumque feceritis, in mei memoriam facietis. "As often as you shall do these things, you shall do them in memory of Me." Jesus, by telling his Apostles to do the same things that he had just done, ordained them priests and conferred on them the fullness of his priesthood. The whole Catholic priesthood is contained in these few words, and for all centuries to come. . . . Jesus, by telling his Apostles that he communicated his priesthood to them—that outpouring from his divine heart—charged them, every time that they should change the bread and wine of the Mass into his Body and Blood, to do it in his stead, in his name, in his memory, and while endeavouring to imitate his virtues. . . .

The words of the Consecration reveal the delicacy of Jesus' heart. He loved us; he wished to remain with us. He desired that his memory should remain present to men's minds. At the hour of the Holy Sacrifice, this memory was—in the plan of Jesus—to be so vivid, that as often as we should "eat this bread and drink this cup," we would "proclaim the death of the Lord; until he comes." (I. Cor. 11:26.) This memory ought to continue with us throughout the course of the day. Jesus' life is *our* life. Jesus himself is our ALL! In the Mass, we have something better than a relic of Jesus, something better than a document personally penned by him. We have *Jesus himself* in his state of Victim! Thus it was that he willed to remain with us until the end of the world.

It can be truthfully said that the Mass is contained in two minutes of time—the time that it takes the priest to say: "This is My Body." "This chalice is the chalice of My Blood.". . . And instantly, Jesus *is* there, with his true Body and Blood—consecrated separately and successively, in order to typify Christ's mystical death in this Sacrifice.

By these Masses, which are continuously celebrated on different portions of the globe, Jesus continues and perpetuates the solemn moment wherein with his last breath, he cried out, "It is consummated!" . . It is done. My task here below is finished. I have done my Father's will to the end!... Do likewise—in memory of me!"

Every Consecration makes Jesus present on earth, and within our reach.... It is as if a gulf of adoration, love, and light were permanently opened beneath our feet, before our eyes, inviting us to cast ourselves in, to lose ourselves in it, with all those souls we bear in our heart; in order to divinize us, to become "other Christs," and to bring about the great return to the Father's House.

191—Show how Jesus, at the moment of Consecration, gives us a beautiful lesson of obedience and humility.

1. *Lesson in obedience*

All your life, Jesus, you have been obedient, and (as St. Paul puts it) "even to death on a cross!" Even this was not enough for your big, generous heart. You wanted to obey even to the end of the world in your Eucharist. You wanted to obey not only your Heavenly Father, but also your creatures, your priests!

At the voice of a man, you descend on the altar; and you would seem to remain on the altar to obey men without the slightest show of resistance. You remain there without moving—you let yourself be placed wherever they will; whether exposed in the monstrance, or enclosed in the ciborium. You let yourself be borne wherever they will—through the streets, into houses—and you let yourself be given, in Holy Communion, to whoever wishes to receive you; whether saint or sinner....

Following Jesus' example, we ought to obey even inferiors out of love for God. Let us say in a spirit of submission:

O Jesus, may I say to you every day of my life: "All that you will, as you will, and only what you will! However hard and bitter for me your holy will may be, I want to conform myself to it the way you obeyed on the Cross—the way you obey on the altar. Even if it means death, or shedding tears of blood!"

2. *Lesson in humility*

After the Consecration, you are on the altar, O Jesus, Incarnate Word, God of all majesty.... But in what a state!

When on earth, you spoke. By your words you charmed men of good will. But on the altar you are mute—you have become the Great Silent One.

On Calvary, you lost all your beauty. Your Sacred Body was torn by scourges, nails pierced your hands and your feet; your holy Face, so benign, so majestic, was defiled and bruised by blows, by blood, by spittle; and a crown of thorns disfigured your kingly brow.... But sinful man still recognized the holiness of your humanity; and even in death, your enemies were forced to tremble and beat their breasts in sorrow as they cried out, "Truly, he was the Son of God!"... But on the altar, not only are you divested of every human aspect; but you are dumb, abased, and reduced to the appearance of a poor and humble wafer; which the tiniest breath of wind could waft away like a dead leaf.... Faith alone is able to recognize in you the Redeemer of the world and Upholder of the universe.

O Jesus, God of Love, grant me the grace to be humble; to do good without ostentation; to become a saint without knowing it; to strip myself of my self-love and pretentions; to associate with the poor and those in humble circumstances; to love you with the love that glowed in the heart of Mary, when she shared your life of poverty and silence in Bethlehem and Nazareth.

192—How are we to "live" the Consecration?

We live the Consecration by consecrating ourselves; that is, by effecting a kind of "transubstantiation" in our own lives.

Now transubstantiation takes place, so to speak, in two movements. (In reality, the Consecration is effected instantaneously—the way light dissipates darkness.)

1. At the very instant when the priest pronounces over the bread the words, "This is my Body," the outside only (the appearances, what is visible) remains unchanged; but the inside—the substance of the bread—is changed!

2. The second movement is still more marvellous. The words of Consecration uttered by the priest produce Christ himself. That is, they render him present under the "outside" of the host; changing the "inside" of this piece of bread into Jesus Christ— into his living Body, with his soul and divinity!

To live the Consecration of our Mass, then, we must effect in ourselves two movements:

1. We must die to self, empty ourselves.
2. We must fill ourselves with Jesus to overflowing.

Do not forget that we are "living hosts." . . . (*See* No. 115.) What the Consecration of the Mass does to the wheaten host, our mystical consecration should—in a certain manner—produce in us.

A change, a conversion, must take place in my life. . . . Taking part in the Mass without becoming better, is an anomaly. To do so, is *not* LIVING MY MASS.

It should be noted that the change which takes place in the host at the Consecration is no mere surface, exterior change; for only the appearances remain the same. The essence itself has changed.

A similar transformation should take place in us—a genuine conversion.

A veneer of Christianity will not do. We must become living members of the Crucified Saviour. We must be incorporated into him; live his life through sanctifying grace; reproduce his dispositions in ourselves; become, in a word, "other Christs."

Hence, "really to participate" in the Mass, and then return home unchanged, proud, hard, impatient, sensual, unforgiving, indifferent, is sheer hypocrisy and insincerity. . . .

As we said above, when the celebrant whispers over the bread, the words "This is My Body," everything disappears except the *appearances* of bread.

We, too, must "disappear"! Not all at once; but little by little, by degrees, with each Mass that we hear! We shall "disappear" by being humble, through forgetfulness of self, through self-denial, through death of self. In this way, we shall arrive at mystical death. This will be the first result of our Consecration. Then we shall be able to say with St. Paul: "It is no longer I that live."

This is the negative side of the Consecration.

The second effect, still more marvellous than the first, is to reproduce Jesus. We too must change ourselves into Jesus Christ; become his other "selves"—if not substantially, at least, spiritually, mystically.

We must so espouse Jesus' mentality, that only our "appearances" remain!

Have Your Own Way, Lord

I have not always understood these windings of the road
that you, O Lord, have made me take.
I searched for short-cuts;
but when I look back, I see
that you did choose for me
the **only** road!
Providential strokes, great joys, little cares,
trips, new friendships,
dark days followed by sunny days—
with all these has my life's path been strewn.
For all this the purpose was that I might come to you!

Map out then as you will, O God,
the path of my life! Let its detours
and curves be those of your own choosing.
Teach me to follow the way,
without trying to understand it—
with eyes closed, as if you held me by the hand;
living one moment at a time, trustfully;
doing in the present moment
the thing that you expect of me.
Thus will the unexpected, and vicissitudes of yesterday
all open out in your time
into the light resplendent—fidelity's reward!

Ric Photo

Luminous Grape-clusters

●

Admire these close-pressed
and luminous grape-clusters,
Swollen with a potentially
Luscious wine,
Bearing in hope
the Blood of a God,
Purveyors of the Holy Eucharist!
What a marvel is here!

Christians, these clustered grapes are we...
Each close-pressed against his brother,
Shoulder to shoulder,
Heart to heart,
Bearing, no longer in hope,
But in reality,
Through charity,
Christ himself!
The wonder of it!

Annette Wolff Photo

This must be so real, that whoever approaches us must feel himself becoming better at our contact, as if he were approaching Christ himself!

How go about transforming ourselves like this?

By always doing what our Lord would do if he were in our place; that is:

By thinking like Jesus.... So, away with bad thoughts, with rash judgments, lack of faith....

By loving like Jesus.... So, away with dangerous friendships....

By speaking like Jesus.... So, away with double meanings, with lying, criticisms, detraction, and slander....

By reading like Jesus.... So, away with bad books....

By praying like Jesus.... So, away with distractions, with selfish prayers....

By using our eyes to see what Jesus would see if he were in our place.... So, away with unchaste looks, and with bad movies....

By using our ears to hear what Jesus would hear.... So, no listening to off-colour jokes, to spicy stories or songs....

By using our hands the way Jesus would use his.... So, no stealing, no bad actions, no slipshod work....

By using our feet to go where Jesus would go.... avoiding night clubs, dance halls, the movies, and houses of ill fame....

In a word, we ought to consecrate our daily lives to Jesus; so that becoming the continuation, the prolongation, the extension of his life, they may be in a small way, like his, lives of sanctity, charity, apostleship, redemption, and glorification.

If we live this way, we can say with St. Paul, "Christ lives in me!" And we shall have realized the second effect of our mystical consecration.

We have said that after the Consecration, only the species, the appearances, of the wheaten host remain. Now Jesus employs these sacramental species or appearances for the living of his eucharistic life....

In proportion to the completeness of our mystical consecration, Jesus will likewise make use of us to live and act in the world.

He will make use of us to think, speak, love, serve, and suffer....

He will make use of us to combat and drive out Satan and sin.

He will make use of us to console, convert, and sanctify....

He will make use of us to make reparation, to atone, and to save....

In short, he will make use of us to "pass once more through the world, doing good!"

We shall thus fulfill, after a fashion, the divine rôle of the species, or the sacramental appearances, of the Consecrated Host. We shall ourselves be "species," living "appearances"—not sacramental, but spiritual, mystic—veiling Jesus, concealing his presence, and continuing his influence in the world. In this way, Christ will be seen in our lives, and we shall be one with him.

This, then, is the "consecration" we are called upon to make. Remember that we must transform ourselves, change ourselves, into Christ, giving him to use as he wills, all that we are and do!

It should be likewise understood that our consecration—never perfect, never finished—must be continuous; so that our life may be the constant consecration of our whole being.

This is another way for us to LIVE OUR MASS!

A GIRL'S PRAYER TO OUR FATHER

•

Dear Father who are in Heaven, I am your little girl—a poor little girl, timid but trustful, resting in your arms, like a little bird fallen in the snow from cold and nestled in hands that warm.

Dear Father, you know how my heart is all brimming over with high hopes and ambitions, and of love ready to give....

I do not want to be disquieted in the face of a future that may not bring me all it promises. Calmly and trustingly, with enthusiasm and joy, I await the morrow that you have lovingly prepared for me. You have given me youth and vitality enough to enable me to make it turn to your glory.

I am your little girl, trustfully resting in my Father's arms. Our Father who are in Heaven, I trust in you.

193—What distinction do you draw between the "Offering" and the "Consecration" of your life?

The consecration, ratifies, confirms, the sincerity of the offering. Offering is not everything—it is easy to offer!

The real sign, the real proof that you have given yourself, is when the gift goes on to sacrifice. It is when you sacrifice in deeds—and not just in words—your time and your life. This is the hard part! "It is not those who say 'Lord, Lord,' who enter into the Kingdom of Heaven, but those who do the will of my Father."

This is what the *Imitation of Christ,* Book II, Chapter XI, brings home to us:

"Jesus has many lovers of his heavenly kingdom, but few consent to share his Cross. Many there are who share his consolations, but few take pleasure in his sufferings. He finds many companions at his table, but few at his abstinence. All desire to rejoice with him, but few are willing to endure anything for his sake. Many follow Jesus to the breaking of bread, but few to the drinking of the chalice of his Passion. Many admire his miracles, but few follow the ignominy of the Cross. Many love Jesus as long as they meet with no adversity. Many praise him and bless him as long as they receive his consolations. But if Jesus hide himself, and leave them for a season, they murmur and are discouraged. But those who love Jesus for himself, and not for their own sakes, bless him no less amidst tribulation and anguish of heart, than in the greatest of consolation. And should he never give them any consolation, they would always praise and thank him."

194—What five prayers follow the Consecration and conclude the Canon?

Now that the words of Consecration have been uttered, the priest's lips cease to be the instrument of Jesus Christ and become once more the mouthpiece of the congregation.

In union with the people, the celebrant declares:

1. That he is offering the Victim of the Altar to God in his own name and in that of the Christian people. *(Unde et memores.)*
2. He beseeches God to accept this offering. *(Supra quae.)*
3. He prays that all those who partake of the Victim may be filled with every heavenly blessing. *(Supplices.)*

4. He begs that the Sacrifice may be applied to the souls in Purgatory and open Heaven to them. (The *Memento* of the Dead.)

5. He also pleads for the admission to Heaven of all those present. *(Nobis quoque peccatoribus.)*

These brief prayers are richly significant. We shall pause just a moment to extract a few thoughts from them to nourish our devotion.

UNDE ET MEMORES

195—What is the meaning of the prayer, *Unde et memores?*

The prayer follows:

Unde et memores, Domine, nos servi tui et plebs tua sancta, ejusdem Christi filii tui Domini nostri tam beatae Passionis, nec non et ab inferis Resurrectionis, sed et in caelos gloriosae Ascensionis: offerimus praeclarae Majestati tuae, de tuis donis ac datis, hostiam + puram, hostiam + sanctam, hostiam + immaculatam, Panem + sanctum vitae aeternae et Calicem + salutis perpetuae.	Wherefore, O Lord, we your servants, as also your holy people, calling to mind the blessed Passion of the same Christ, your Son, our Lord, his Resurrection from the grave and his glorious Ascension into Heaven, offer up to your most excellent Majesty, of your own gifts bestowed upon us, a Victim + who is pure, a Victim + who is holy, a Victim + who is stainless, the holy Bread + of life everlasting, and the Chalice + of eternal salvation.

This prayer is a formula of offering.

During the Offertory, the priest had presented the bread and wine, together with the offerings—the matter of the Sacrifice—to God, beseeching him to accept them. Now it is Christ himself, and us with him, that he offers to the Father. The same Jesus whom God gave us that he might bring us back to him. The same Jesus who is a pure, holy, and stainless Victim; procuring life everlasting to those who receive him.

196—What memories or what mysteries are recalled in this prayer, *Unde et memores?*

After instituting the Holy Eucharist and consecrating for the first time, Jesus had said, "Do this in remembrance of me."

Jesus' appeal has been heard. *"Unde et memores*—we remember," says the priest, immediately after the two Consecrations.

For the ritual formula evokes the memory of the principal mysteries of the Christian religion: the Passion, Resurrection, and Ascension of Christ.

These three mysteries had already been evoked in the prayer of the Offertory, "Receive, Holy Trinity. . . ." For together they form a whole, together they complete Christ's Sacrifice: Calvary marks the immolation of the Victim; the Resurrection is the solemn sign of God's acceptance of the Victim; the Ascension is the inauguration of Christ's eternal communion with the Father.

We have dwelt at some length on the Passion. Let us now say a word about the Resurrection and the Ascension. Let us determine what these great realities have to teach us:

1. *The Resurrection.* It was fitting that Christ's great Sacrifice —the Sacrifice dominating the religious history of mankind—should receive this supreme consecration.

After Christ had humbled himself, humiliated himself, even to the death of the Cross, the Father then desired to exalt him; that is, solemnly to ratify the proffered Sacrifice and manifest his acceptance of it, by resurrecting the Sacred Victim and taking him up into glory.

It was fitting that the oblation of Calvary, offered in an unrestrained burst of love and with an insatiable thirst to atone, should be consummated by a reciprocal proof of acceptance by the Heavenly Father, that should be no less complete.

Now, Christs' Resurrection is the guarantee of our own resurrection. But to rise again, a man must first die! Not only physically, but mystically, as well.

"Did not the Christ have to suffer these things before entering into his glory?"

If we would share in Christ's Resurrection and glory, we must likewise taste of his Passion. This is indispensable.

That is why, to the memory of Christ's Passion, is added the consoling memory of his Resurrection; which St. Paul interprets when he speaks of "the old man changed into the new man"—an expression signifying the substitution of the "self" of Christ for my own selfish and carnal self.

Admirable, indeed, is this resurrection of the soul—half, if not wholly, dead—to the life of grace: a resurrection which is the fruit of that rugged, painful, and ever unfinished task designated by the word, "asceticism." Asceticism is the practice of the spiritual purification of the whole being: the incessant effort to eliminate its unwholesome and morbid elements and lubricate the secret springs of the soul. It is that slow and laborious passage from the terrestrial and human to the celestial and divine, made through those thorny paths, strewn with trials and planted with crosses, which lead to mystical death and guide the soul to the summit of sacrifice.

A resurrection which is the price of perpetual acts of self-denial, of fresh beginnings, of revival, of brusque awakenings; alternating with boredom, disgust, discouragement, anguish, with numerous lapses, falls of surprise, tepidity, lassitude, paralysis of the springs of spiritual activity; and periods of enthusiasm as brief as they are vehement, spurts of fervour followed by sudden inertia, etc. etc! ..

2. *The Ascension.* The law for a victim is a life of oblation, directed toward God. With all its energy, the soul—Love's victim, the host of the divine will—lives outstretched in sacrifice to God.

For so long as its immolation endures, it aspires—with all its immolated being—for its return to the Father.

To this created life which reaches out and aspires, will correspond the aspiration of Uncreated Life, to receive and consume the proffered host.

So it was with Christ. So will it be with us....

Christ's Ascension, after his bloody oblation and immolation, proves, as Benedict XIV teaches, that "the Victim was received by God in the odour of sweetness and placed at his right hand."

The Ascension thus appears as the crowning of Christ's mysteries, wherein he descends into this world as the High Priest of the New Covenant, and ascends again to his Father as a glorified Victim. It is the return to the Father.

For each soul bent on perfection—as is the case with Tertiaries—the ascension has begun. The return is underway....

The ascension! How true this is of the ascension of our lives! A rugged, painful climb, continuing to the final summit, wherein is consummated the union with God the Father, through Christ Jesus, in the Sanctifying Spirit.

Christ walked this way before us. He is the Way. To his disciples, he teaches the secret of success: "If you have a mind to be perfect, go home and sell all that belongs to you: give it to the poor, and so the treasure you have shall be in Heaven; then come back and follow Me." [Knox.]

A clear, unequivocal statement, that; which, beginning with the Rich Young Man of the Gospel, has disconcerted and dismayed a great many. A statement, which, nonetheless, is the secret of a joyous ascension....

It is incumbent upon those generous souls whom the grace of vocation calls to the narrow way of the evangelical counsels, to rid themselves of all unnecessary baggage: of the weight of material goods, the anxious solicitude for which singularly retards the soul in its ascension toward spiritual and eternal goods: of the heavy burden of self, weighted down by the flesh, or by the tyranny imposed by evil habits, or by the demands of an undisciplined freedom.

Following Jesus, mounting toward the heights, means to leave everything: nets, boats, home, parents, brothers, sisters, friends—if not in fact, at any rate, spiritually. It means going on from progress to progress, until we reach that degree of perfection which God expects from us, and which corresponds with the graces of our state in life and with our God-given talents.

It presupposes the continuous and life-long gift of self.... Let it not be forgotten, that before Jesus ascended into Heaven, he began by being "lifted up" on the Cross on Calvary.... It is from the Cross that every Christian must begin his ascent toward his heavenly home.

The Mass is the invasion of a host by Christ. Let us make ourselves "hosts" alongside the priest's host; so as to be permeated within and all day long with Christ. He will come to transform, to "transubstantiate" all—lifting our smallest human acts to the divine.

197—Why does the celebrant make five signs of the cross at the conclusion of the prayer, *Unde et memores?*

In keeping with the rubrics of the missal, the priest makes three signs of the cross over the chalice and the Host together, then one sign of the cross over the chalice and Host separately.

These five signs of the cross after the Consecration, correspond to the five signs of the cross of the *Quam oblationem.* (See No. 185.) "After the Consecration," declares St. Thomas, "the priest no longer employs the sign of the cross to consecrate and bless, but solely to recall the virtue of the Cross and the manner whereby Christ's Passion was accomplished." (III. Q. 83, a.5 ad 4.)

SUPRA QUAE

198—What prayer comes next?

The *Supra quae,* as follows:

Supra quae propitio ac sereno vultu respicere digneris; et accepta habere, sicuti accepta habere dignatus es munera pueri tui justi Abel, et sacrificium patriarchae nostri Abrahae: et quod tibi obtulit summus sacerdos tuus Melchisedech, sanctum sacrificium, immaculatam hostiam.	Vouchsafe to look upon them with a gracious and serene countenance, and to accept them, even as you were pleased to accept the offerings of your just servant Abel, and the sacrifice of Abraham, our patriarch, and that which Melchisedech, your high priest, offered up to you; a holy sacrifice, and a spotless Victim.

199—What do we ask for in this prayer?

We ask God to "look upon" these offerings with a "gracious and serene countenance" and to "accept them."

But can we fear for a single instant that the object offered will *not* be acceptable to God, when we know that what we offer is the very Body and Blood of Christ?

Let us not forget too quickly, that alongside Christ's Sacrifice, we have placed the Church's sacrifice: that of all the members of the Mystical Body, and consequently, our own personal sacrifice—more or less worthily offered!

Let us not forget either that God is not only concerned with the presents that are offered him, but also with the purity of the donor. . . .

Now we ask the Father to look graciously upon and to accept, the Body and Blood of Christ; not as they are in themselves (which is, of course, infinitely acceptable), but as offered up by *our* sinful hands!

Do we not, then, have real cause to wonder if our offerings will be received?

At this moment, let us unite ourselves with the priest, and fervently implore God for this great grace: that he will deign to accept our offering.

200—Why does the priest make mention of the sacrifices of Abel, Abraham, and Melchisedech in the *Supra quae*?

If the sacrifices of Abel, Abraham, and Melchisedech (even though greatly inferior to the Sacrifice of the Mass) were acceptable to God, it was because of the excellent dispositions of these holy personages of the Old Testament.

These ancient sacrifices, moreover, prefigured the immolation of Calvary and the altar.

Abel offered up the first-born of his flock and was slain by his brother Cain. Jesus Christ, the First-born among his brethren, offered up himself, and was put to death by his brethren.

Abraham did not hesitate to sacrifice his son, Isaac. The Eternal Father sent his only Son to his death.

Melchisedech, a "priest forever," offered up bread and wine—the elements used in the Sacrifice of our altars.

The innocence of Christ is typified by Abel's sacrifice.

His obedience by Abraham's sacrifice.

His life-giving action by Melchisedech's offering.

Let us try to feel the way these olden friends of God did. And the infinite beauty of the Sacred Host will not be too disfigured by the manifest unworthiness of those who offer it, and themselves with it.

Supplices

201—What is the third prayer which follows the Consecration?

The *Supplices,* which follows:

Supplices te rogamus, omnipotens Deus, jube haec perferri per manus sancti angeli tui in sublime altare tuum in conspectu divinae majestatis tuae: ut quotquot ex hac altaris participatione, sacrosanctum Filii tui Cor + pus et San + guinem sumpserimus, omni benedictione, caelesti et gratia repleamur. Per eumdem Christum Dominum nostrum. Amen.	We humbly beseech you, Almighty God, let these offerings be carried by the hands of your holy angel to your altar on high, in the presence of your Divine Majesty; that as many of us as shall receive the most Sacred Body and Blood of your Son, by partaking thereof from this altar, may be filled with every heavenly blessing and grace, through the same Christ our Lord. Amen.

202—For what does the priest pray in the *Supplices,* and what are his accompanying gestures?

This prayer has a twofold objective:

1. *From earth to Heaven.* That our offerings may be carried by the hands of God's holy angel from our earthly altar to Heaven's sublime altar. This comprises the first half of the *Supplices.*

2. *From Heaven to earth.* So that from this "ascension," a "pentecost" of "heavenly blessings" may descend into our souls—soon to be nourished with the Body and Blood of Christ.

This second part particularly concerns those who by their reception of Holy Communion will partake of the Sacrifice. This prayer implores for them special blessings and graces.

The celebrant bows profoundly while reciting this prayer. His hands are joined and rest on the altar. This is the attitude of supplication and humility.

In the middle of the prayer, the priest kisses the altar. He thus attests his love for Christ, and his great desire to partake of the gifts of the altar—he is very close to Jesus!

He next makes two signs of the cross—one over the Sacred Host and the other over the Precious Blood. He thus indicates the gifts of which he and the devout faithful who are to receive Communion, will partake.

The priest then blesses himself with a large sign of the cross, as if he wished to be wholly covered with the graces acquired on Calvary and now distributed from Heaven's heights.

He ends his prayer by joining his hands, to mark the ardour of his desire.

203—Who is the "holy angel" mentioned in this prayer?

This once much mooted question, now seems settled. In the original formula, we find the very clear rendering: *Per manus angelorum tuorum*—"by the hands of Your holy angels."

The "holy angel," then, is neither the Holy Spirit nor the Incarnate Word (as some people have thought). It simply stands for the created angels—heavenly messengers who surround God's throne and who are about the altar during the celebration of the Holy Sacrifice. It is they who are charged with the mission of bearing our petitions to Heaven's sublime altar. (Cf. Apoc. 8:3.)

MEMENTO OF THE DEAD

204—What is the fourth prayer after the Consecration?

The Memento of the Dead:

Memento etiam, Domine, famulorum famularumque tuarum *N. et N.* qui nos praecesserunt cum signo fidei et dormiunt in somno pacis.	Be mindful also, O Lord, of your servants, *N.* and *N.* (here mention is made of those dead for whom one especially wishes to pray) who have gone before us with the sign of faith and who sleep the sleep of peace.
Ipsis, Domine, et omnibus in Christo quiescentibus, locum refrigerii, lucis et pacis, ut indulgeas, deprecamur. Per eumdem Christum Dominum nostrum. Amen.	To these, O Lord, and to all who rest in Christ, grant, we beseech you, a place of refreshment, light, and peace. Through the same Christ our Lord. Amen.

205—Please explain the "Memento of the Dead."

While reciting this prayer, the celebrant's gestures are the same as for the Memento of the Living. He joins his hands and bows his head as he prays: "Be mindful, also, Lord, of your servants, *N.* and *N.*. . . ." (Here he mentions in an inaudible tone those dead whom he especially wishes to commend to God.) Then, again extending his hands and holding them at shoulder level, he continues his prayer. So much for the accompanying gestures.

Formerly, the names of those to be given special mention during Mass were read off from the diptychs. This is why the Missal still makes mention of "*N.* and *N.*"

The word *also* refers back to the Memento of the Living.

Note that whereas the Memento of the Living precedes the Consecration, the Memento of the Dead follows it.

Why? Because the living are able to unite themselves with the priest and to offer the Sacred Victim with him and by his hands. The dead may only participate in the *fruits* of the Holy Sacrifice. Therefore, the Church implores divine aid for the living, at the moment in which they are about to fulfill the priestly function to which their Baptism entitles them. As for the dead, the Church prays that they too may have a share in the fruits of the Mass, during the time that the Divine Victim lies on the altar. It was, moreover, after his death that Jesus descended into Limbo. . . .

The dead whose names were read from the diptychs had to fulfill two conditions. They must:

1. Have been marked with the sign of the cross, in other words, they had to have received Baptism.
2. Have died in peace with the Church.

The beautiful expressions used by antiquity to designate death will likewise be noted in this prayer. The word *death* itself is never used; but rather, "those who have preceded us," who "sleep the sleep of peace," who "rest in Christ."

Heaven is designated as "a place of refreshment, light, and peace."

Besides those dead who are especially mentioned by the priest who celebrates, or by the faithful who offer the Mass, we likewise commend to God all those departed Christians who have not yet attained to the beatific vision. Here the Church appears as a true Mother. At every Mass she thinks of those abandoned souls who may have no one left on earth, and whom all have forgotten.

206—What ought we to do during the Memento of the Dead?

We ought to remember!

How easily we forget our dear departed!

How easily also we ourselves shall be forgotten at our death!

Bossuet has written a pithy statement: "Mortals take no less pains to bury all thought of the dead, than they do to bury the dead themselves."

Who still thinks to remember—at the Memento of the Dead—the most recently deceased Pope? . . .

If the Supreme Pontiffs, who were once mingled in the concerns of the whole world, are today forgotten, can we flatter ourselves that we ourselves shall not be forgotten too?

At our daily—or, at least, weekly Mass—we shall remember, then, our dear departed ones. . . particularly:

Our mother—our father—the authors of our physical being.

Our brothers: Bernard, Henry, Ralph. . . .

Our sisters: Louise, Jean, Elizabeth. . . .

Our brother and sister Tertiaries. . . .

Our benefactors. . . .

Our relatives: uncles, aunts, cousins, godparents. . . .

Our fellow-workers in the lay apostolate. . . .

Our associates in school, shop, or office. . . .

Those who are now by our fault in the flames of Purgatory, because we scandalized them and incited them to evil by risqué stories with double meanings. . . by our lack of modesty. . . by our lending them bad books, pornographic pictures and magazines. . . by immodest and daring caresses. . . by sinful dancing. . . by alcoholic beverages. . . by invitations to frequent dangerous places, with persons of evil reputation—taverns and clubs, corrupt films, dance halls, "wide-open" beaches, auto rides, etc.

Let us not forget our dead!

There may be souls dear to us in Purgatory, to whom we have sworn eternal friendship! What are they thinking now of our fine promises? Must the old proverb, "Out of sight, out of mind," always be true?

Alas! We have been only too quick to place them all charitably in Heaven!

"He was so good!" someone will say.

"He had such a beautiful death!" another will add.

This premature canonization soon exempts us from praying or doing penance for our dead. Yet, the sheer uncertainty of their fate, the thought of God's justice,—for nothing defiled may enter Heaven—ought to put us on our guard and stimulate our charity to help the Poor Souls; who unceasingly call out to us: "Have pity on us; at least, you, our friends!"

Let us, therefore, make it *a duty and a rule of conduct* to think of those who have gone before and who implore our prayers. Besides this is in our own interest. The souls thus liberated by us become our protectors in Heaven. Moreover, our Lord said: "With what measure you measure, it shall be measured to you." (Matt. 7:2.) If we have been thoughtful and generous in our prayers for the dead, we may confidently hope that God will cause us to reap the benefits of the prayers and Masses which our friends and relatives will send up to Heaven in our behalf, when death shall have ravished us from their affectionate embrace.

But if, forgetful and unfeeling, we have omitted to pray for the dead; even though we may have left a fortune to have Masses said for our souls at death, it is to be feared that God will give to us less freely—who will have merited so little—the riches of satisfaction accumulated by these Masses. Rather, he will make use of them to benefit other souls; less rich, perhaps, in banknotes, but more generous with their prayers and sacrifices.

Remembering our dead, then, means to pray for them; to make sacrifices for them; TO LIVE OUR MASS for them; to have Masses said for them; to gain indulgences for them.... There are a number of practices enriched with indulgences, applicable to the souls in Purgatory—the Way of the Cross, the Portiuncula and All Souls visits, with prayers for the Holy Father's intentions. Tertiaries may gain numerous plenary indulgences every month on feast days noted on their Third Order calendar. There are, in addition, the thirty Gregorian Masses, indulgenced prayers, the wearing of scapulars, and so on.

As will have been seen, working to relieve the souls in Purgatory is quite another thing from carrying flowers to the cemetery or laying them on the graves of the departed. "Consolation for the living," tersely commented St. Augustine, "but of no advantage to the dead."

Be mindful of our dead, and our dead will be mindful of us!

207—Does Purgatory last very long?

Certain indications would seem to favour the affirmative. St. Augustine prayed more than thirty years for his mother, who was a saint! And he asked others to continue these prayers. "O Lord God," he prays in Book IX of his *Confessions,* "inspire all those who in time to come will read these pages, to remember at the altar your servant, Monica, and her husband, Patricius. May they piously remember my father and mother!"

When dying at Ostia, St. Monica likewise expressed this desire: "Bury my body wherever you will, without troubling yourself about it. One thing only I beg of you, to remember me, wherever you may be, at God's altar."

The Church, moreover, permits the celebration of Masses for a deceased person for an indefinite period.

Strictly speaking, the exact duration of the sufferings of Purgatory is unknown. One thing is certain. The length of the stay in Purgatory depends on the gravity and number of one's unexpiated sins.

208—Do the souls in Purgatory suffer very much? Which is greater, the sufferings, or the consolations, of Purgatory?

These two theses might be formulated: "Beyond Heaven, nothing more consoling," and, "beyond Hell, nothing more terrible!"

Each of these two affirmations bears the signatures of many theologians and saints.

St. Catherine of Siena wrote a *Treatise on Purgatory.* This treatise has been praised by numerous theologians and approved by the Sacred Congregation of Rites and by Pope Clement X in the decree of canonization of the saint. (Father Faber offers us a résumé of this treatise in his book, *All for Jesus.*) This is what St. Catherine has to say:

"I do not think that apart from the felicity of Heaven, there can be a joy comparable to that experienced by the souls in Purgatory. An incessant communication from God renders their joy more vivid from day to day; and this communication becomes more and more intimate, to the extent that it consumes the obstacles still existing in the soul."

So much for the consolations.

Turn the page and you will read this:

"On the other hand, they endure pain so intense, that no tongue is able to describe it. Nor is any mind capable of comprehending the smallest spark of that consuming fire, unless God should show it to him by a special grace."

There is no contradiction between these two citations. It is correct to hold that *great joy and great suffering coexist in Purgatory.*

Suffering. The pain of loss, while not eternal, is terrible. (The term, "pain of loss," refers to the privation of the clear vision and possession of God.) "The more one longs for a thing, the more painful does deprivation of it become. And because after this life, the desire for God, the Supreme Good, is intense in the souls of the just (because this impetus toward him is not hampered by the weight of the body, and that the time for enjoyment of the Perfect Good would have come) had there been no obstacle; the soul suffers enormously from the delay." So says St. Thomas.

As for those in Hell—the damned—this "pain of loss" is more dreadful still, because it is unending. Their ceaseless need for God can *never* be fulfilled! . . . *And to think that there are persons living in the state of mortal sin who never give a thought as to HOW and WHERE they will spend eternity!*

As for the fire of Purgatory, it does not differ essentially from the fire of Hell—the only difference lies in its duration. In Hell the fire is eternal; in Purgatory, it is temporary.

Consolations. The first joy of the souls in Purgatory is that of not being able to sin any more. They are happy at having a means to purify themselves.

If, on your way to a party, a car were to splash mud from a puddle over you, would you like to go into the parlour, covered with mud from head to foot? . . . Even if you had been looking forward to this evening for a long time, you would not want to go in that way, without cleaning up! . . . It is the same way with the souls in Purgatory. They bless God for having created this place of purification, and they plunge into it themselves—all confused as they are at seeing themselves covered with the "mud" of sin!

There is no doubt but that these souls suffer. But their sufferings are endured with perfect submission, and they bless the pains which bring them nearer to the happiness of Heaven.

209—What lessons are taught us by the souls in Purgatory?

You know, of course, that the souls in Purgatory are suffering in the flames—without merit—to expiate for their unabsolved venial sins; and for the temporal punishment due to their sins—mortal or venial—absolved, but for which atonement has not been fully made.

Have you ever thought about the holy and exemplary lives these afflicted souls would lead, could they come back to earth and begin life anew? These souls understand now the value of time, the price of virtue, and the malice of sin—but it is too late! Their lot is fixed. Despite their sufferings, they can neither merit any more, nor augment their degree of glory.

Thank God, it is not too late—yet—for us! . . . Even though we may be very near to rendering our account to God. Why not live, then, the way we should like to be living at the hour of death? Why not take a leaf from the book of the souls in Purgatory? . . . The holy souls have so much to teach us! If we would but listen to them, how they would rectify our judgments; batter down our prejudices; check our unfounded enthusiasms for the world and its perilous pleasures. . . . And how they would stress the importance of a virtuous and sanctified life—the source of true happiness.

Among the many lessons taught us by the souls in Purgatory, let us consider two in particular. These are:

A. The importance of the moment that passes and does not return again.

B. The value we should place on little things.

A. *The importance of the moment that passes and does not return.*

We are sometimes tempted to waste time; whether because we count on having a long life, or because we place but small value on a life that a chance accident can take away from us prematurely. We are always prone to put off important things until tomorrow—a necessary

Confession—the breaking off of a sinful attachment—the practice of virtue.

Like the executioners, who crucified Christ, we "crucify" the present between the two thieves of Yesterday and Tomorrow.

We attach our memories and our regrets to a past which no longer belongs to us, and we hitch the wagon of our dreams and cares to a future that may never be ours. And these two thieves rob us of our only treasure that is ours to use—the present moment.

Our dead judge things more clearly! They see now how brief is the time for meriting, and how important it is to use it wisely. They know that minutes on earth stand for years in eternity. They know that a good work "remitted" is often a good work omitted, and that *"tomorrow" is often just another name for never.* They understand that God does not require of us a certain amount of good to be done "sometime"; but that he does desire the daily task; which is, in a sense, the "daily bread" he taught us to ask of our Father in Heaven. For is not work itself a grace? St. Francis of Assisi explicitly teaches this in his Rule of the First Order: "Those to whom God has given the grace to labour. . . ."

Our dead, then, teach us the value of time!

Would that we could understand its worth the way a young aviator, James d'Arnoux did, when he wrote in *Paroles d'un revenant,* this profound thought:

"The minutes of my life are all numbered. Soon my life will be over! Then I shall stand before my Redeemer and God. . . . What sheaf of souls have I to offer him? Oh, the value of time! O God, make me abhor every wasted moment. For in Heaven, my charity will know no increase—nor my glory—nor the glory that I shall be able to render to Jesus, and to my God."

To be practical, and profit from the lesson taught us by our dead, let us together look at a few situations wherein people waste time. . . and, as a logical consequence, DO *NOT* LIVE THEIR MASS. For example:

1. *People waste time by just doing nothing!*

Their minds are a vacuum—they do not know what to do with themselves, nor how to pass the time. Or if they do think of anything, it is of some idle day-dream, some impossible project. They waste hours in purposeless visits, in trifling small talk, in satisfying their curiosity, in non-important phone calls, in interminable pastimes.... How many days are squandered as they sit in front of that noisy little box they call their "radio" or "television set"!

Every rule has its exception. Hence, an ill person, for whom rest is imperative, fulfills his duty by *not* working. For such a person, *working* would be a waste of time; for he would be running counter to God's will.

2. *People waste time when they spend it in wrong-doing.*

This is the case with those who spend their lives criticizing, slandering their neighbour, reading dangerous books, frequenting dance halls and bad films, taverns and clubs, and places where the riff-raff meet—in a word, all the time spent in offending God.

3. *People waste time even doing good, outside the line of duty.*

This is the mistake made by those who forget that the duty of one's state of life comes ahead of everything else... of those who stay up when they should be in bed... of those who have no rule of life, and do everything at the wrong time—nothing at a fixed hour... of those who meddle in things that do not concern them....

4. *People even waste time doing good in the line of duty, and this in two ways:*

a. When they are in the state of mortal sin; for then all good actions are dead, that is, unprofitable for Heaven. All the good done in this state can only dispose God to grant the sinner the grace of conversion. Sometimes, certain sinners, aware of their incapacity to merit, abandon their religious practices altogether and plunge headlong into forbidden pleasures.... This is senseless and foolhardy. Even should God give them an opportunity for conversion before they die, would they be in the right dispositions, then, to correspond to his grace? And even if they should be able to go to Confession before they die, they forget that they must expiate in the flames of Purgatory all the temporal punishment due to their numerous sins! Besides, that is not the way a person acts who really loves God. Such a person does not remain a single day in God's disgrace.

b. When instead of acting for God, for his glory, and for the sanctification of souls, in a word, from a supernatural motive; the good works are motivated by vanity, self-esteem, natural sympathy, to satisfy some whim or fancy, to build up a reputation for sanctity, etc. Thus, a man who gives alms out of vainglory, wastes not only his time, but his money as well! He has already received his reward!

5. *Again, people waste time by doing poorly the thing that ought to be done.*

This is the case with certain souls who spoil the good they do by the ill grace with which they do it... by the disagreeable words that go with it... by their delay and carelessness in doing it.... If all the merit is not lost in this way, it is considerably diminished—and their Mass is *not* well lived!

6. *Finally, people waste time by making other people waste time.*

This happens when they fail to keep an appointment, or are late for one... when they carry on long, useless conversations or write long letters... when they make no attempt to perfect themselves in their profession or trade, or by their incompetence waste other peoples' time... when after accepting a responsibility or charge, they fail to carry out their obligations—thus causing endless annoyance to everyone....

That is how people waste time!

To go back to our first thought—"the importance of the moment that passes and does not return"—remember that if we live the present moment well, we may be certain that the past will be "repaired," the future prepared our eternity guaranteed.... and our Mass well lived.

Why return to the past? Why forsake the present moment to worry about an uncertain future?

Thought of a battle that lasts a lifetime may well be terrifying. But is it not easy to say to myself: "I will not offend God *now*... I accept this cross? In this present moment (the only one that belongs to me), I will serve the Master, love him and cause him to be loved. In this moment (the only one I have), I will abandon myself to God's will; I will do the thing that is hard; I will follow the dictates of duty and my conscience.... "

How brief a space in time is occupied by a minute! Yet, minutes are the warp and woof of the loom on which our days and lives are woven. The most bitter sufferings, the most painful duties of a lifetime, are borne, accepted, and fulfilled, second by second and minute by minute. And these brief moments extend into eternity, for God's glory and our everlasting happiness.

You may already have come across this thought: "I except to pass through this life but once. If, therefore, there is any good that I can do, or any kindness I can show to any living creature, let me do it now. Let me not defer nor neglect it, for I shall not pass this way again." [From the Sanskrit.]

How true and profound this thought! This minute just past has gone into eternity.... What use have I made of it? ...

B. *The importance we should attach to little things.*

Our dead teach us another truth akin to the first: attention to little things, to small duties....

We are tempted to attach great importance to that which shows, stands out, gets talked about....

We dream of doing *big* things, of performing heroic exploits; and when the big opportunity that would have permitted us to show our mettle, does not come, we capitulate daily before the humble, daily task.... We are capable (or so it seems to us) of tilting with giants; and we are appalled or grumble at a pinprick!

Our dead appreciate things better now in the light of eternity.... They see the details, proportions, and perspective of the picture.... They are able to grasp the reason why Jesus placed so high a value on the widow's mite in the Temple of Jerusalem.... Those now enjoying the beatific vision, realize that they have done nothing remarkable; and yet they have known the unspeakable joy of hearing the words: "Come, faithful servants, here is your glorious reward!"

And all about them (and perhaps more highly placed than they) they see saints who never did anything sensational on earth—saints who (like our own good mothers, and others as well) attracted so little attention, that the Church never even dreamed of canonizing them! They hear Thérèse of Lisieux telling them how when she died, her companions did not know how to fill the short biographical page that is sent, in accordance with custom, to the world's different Carmels when a nun departs for the Heavenly Father's home!

Yes, our dead teach us that true sanctity consists not in working miracles or in doing "big" things; but in doing one's daily duty the best one knows how, out of love for God and neighbour.

During the Memento of the Dead, let us ask our dear dead to help us understand this lesson. Our acts, however humble, are potent for eternity. Whether you work at sweeping floors, mending stockings, washing dishes, transporting garbage, or out in the fields, remember that Heaven is purchased with the small coin of the daily task—the duty of our state in life. This is the "thermometer" that God uses to measure the "degrees" of our eternal happiness and of our recompense....

All this calls for a kind of continuous heroism. Sometimes it would be easier to shed one's blood all at once, than to part with it drop by drop in an obscure and continuing martyrdom. Our war heroes—despite their heroic deaths—teach us the same lesson. Their greatness was no less when they endured weeks, months, and even years in the mud, than the day they bravely crossed the firing line and gave up their lives.

If we would see things the way our dead do, we must first convince ourselves of the importance of the present, and of faithfulness in small things.

Life comes to us every morning like the blank page of a book on which each moment leaves its imprint of what we have thought or done. And when night comes, this page is placed in God's archives. We must never forget that God gives us time—that unspeakable treasure—with which to build eternity. If your past life seems full of holes and ragged edges, do not give way to discouragement; but proceed at once to "mend your ways," by beginning today to LIVE YOUR MASS. Let us fill up these "holes" in our lives without loss of a single second.... The time for sowing is short—the harvest is eternal.

210—How can the Mass help the souls in Purgatory?

Perhaps you have already heard this beautiful story:

One day a wounded soldier lay dying, blood flowing from a frightful wound in his left shoulder. The blood was almost drained from his veins.... A fellow-soldier went up to the doctor (who despaired of saving his patient) and offered his blood to save the victim. The surgeon at once made the necessary incision, linking up the healthy man's arm with that of the wounded soldier. The strong man's blood passed into the weakened body; life took over; and the wounded lad's life was saved.

The Mass is a similar "operation." It is a "blood transfusion" of Christ's life into sick souls—the souls of the living on earth and the souls in Purgatory. A marvellous operation, "performed" by the priest when he brings down upon the altar the Sacrifice of Calvary.

It is easy to understand the importance and efficacy of the Mass for the relief of the souls in Purgatory.

Let us hasten their entrance into Heaven by having Mass said for their intention, and by taking part in it ourselves by really LIVING OUR MASS!

211—Is it better to have Masses celebrated for ourselves during life or after death?

It is certainly more advantageous and more prudent to have Masses celebrated for ourselves during life, and this is why:

1. While we are alive, we can collaborate in offering the Holy Sacrifice by our presence at Mass and by our offering. In Purgatory, our collaboration in the offering of the Holy Sacrifice will be limited to the remote contribution furnished by the payment of a Mass stipend before or after death, as indicated in our will.

2. While alive, our very collaboration is a source of merit. In Purgatory, we can no longer merit.

3. While alive, we satisfy unqualifiedly for the penalty due to our sins. In Purgatory, the Mass hands back the fruits of the Passion to God, who will distribute them to us—more or less abundantly, according to his good pleasure—no doubt taking into consideration the generosity or tepidity of our life on earth.

4. During our lifetime, when we contribute Mass stipends, we actually deprive ourselves and accomplish an often most meritorious act of self-denial. In Purgatory, we shall be depriving our heirs of a sum we had enjoyed the free use of to the very end. It is our heirs (not we) who will be "mortified"!

5. During life, we can be certain that the Masses we require are celebrated. In Purgatory, we may have to wait a long time before our heirs execute our last wishes—if they are ever carried out at all!

There is not the slightest doubt about it. It is all to our advantage to have Masses celebrated for ourselves during life, rather than to leave a fortune at death to have this done. If our purse does not permit of this, we can always come to Mass and take part in it. . . .

Moreover, if, during life, we have procured to the Holy Trinity —through the Christ of our Mass—the glory and adoration due him; if by means of these Masses, we contribute with him, through him, and in him, to offer infinite satisfaction to God; have we not reason to believe in the infinite condescendence of Him who does not forget the gift of a glass of water? These Masses during life are an insurance against Purgatory. . . . They obtain for us every morning, in exchange for the homage of satisfaction and praise God receives from them, an increase in our right to eternal beatitude and the remission of our debts. They, moreover, dispose us to receive—should we fall into the flames of Purgatory —speedy relief in the way of refreshment coming from the immolated Christ; who will remember to help in time of need, his collaborators of yesterday at the holy altar.

Hence the extreme importance of taking part in mind and heart as well as in body—in the Holy Sacrifice of the Mass—and of LIVING OUR MASS!

A YOUNG MOTHER'S PRAYER OF GRATITUDE

I thank you, Lord, for these children you have given me—
Flesh of our flesh, and blood of our blood.
I thank you for these darlings whose smile makes my heart beat faster,
And whose tiny hands caress my cheeks.
I thank you for this fair fruit of our love—
Of this love so beautiful since the day we plighted our troth,
And so beautiful all of our days.
I thank you for this love which every day grows greater.
Praise to you, O Lord, for having associated us in your work of creation!
We two sinners praise you together.
Be especially praised, dear God, by these little cherubs!
So fair are they and so pure, because they belong to you!

Nobis Quoque Peccatoribus

212—What is the last prayer of the Canon? What does the priest say and do?

The last prayer of the Canon is called the *Nobis quoque peccatoribus.*

Nobis quoque peccatoribus famulis tuis, de multitudine miserationum tuarum sperantibus, partem aliquam et societatem donare digneris cum tuis sanctis Apostolis et Martyribus, cum Joanne, Stephano, Matthia, Barnaba, Ignatio, Alexandro, Marcellino, Petro, Felicitate, Perpetua, Agatha, Lucia, Agnete, Caecilia, Anastasia et omnibus Sanctis tuis: intra quorum nos consortium, non aestimator meriti; sed veniae, quaesumus, largitor admitte. Per Christum Dominum nostrum.	To us sinners, also your servants, who put our trust in the multitude of your mercies, vouchsafe to grant some part and fellowship with your holy Apostles and Martyrs, with John, Stephen, Matthias, Barnabas, Ignatius, Alexander, Marcellinus, Peter, Felicitas, Perpetua, Agatha, Lucy, Agnes, Cecilia, Anastasia and with all your Saints. Into their company, we beseech you to admit us, not by weighing our merits, but by freely pardoning our offenses, through Christ our Lord.

As the priest says the three words: *Nobis quoque peccatoribus,* he raises his voice and humbly strikes his breast.

By this breaking of the great silence of the Canon, the celebrant seems to beseech the fullest attention from the faithful, and to invite them likewise to strike their breasts and acknowledge themselves sinners.

In former times, when the celebrant raised his voice, it was for a different reason which no longer exists; and to which we find an allusion in an ancient Roman Sacramentary of Bec Abbey, which reads as follows: "When the subdeacons, who, after the *Sanctus,* have remained inclined behind the altar, hear the intoning of the *Nobis quoque peccatoribus.* they shall lift up their heads and make ready the sacred vessels." The words, therefore, served as a signal.

213—What do we ask for in this prayer?

After praying in the Memento of the Dead for the eternal beatitude of the faithful departed, we likewise ask it for the living—for those who will one day be "the departed." In other words, for ourselves; who are at one and the same time "sinners" and "servants of God."

Note the humble tone of this prayer. It brings to mind the *Confiteor* and bears some slight resemblance to the Conclusion of the Preface. In it we acknowledge ourselves truly unworthy of being admitted to the happiness of Heaven in the Communion of saints. This is the reason why we ask for "some part"—for a little place—in the corner of Heaven!

Finally, the prayer brings out that this participation is to come, not because of our merits, but through the sheer mercy of God.

214—Do we not sometimes have reason—because of our sins—to doubt God's mercy?

Never, never, never! And again NEVER!

On the contrary, we have every reason to "put our trust in God's mercy" and to hope to be one day possessors of Heaven's bliss—even though we may have been the greatest of sinners! For God comes to the relief of our helplessness. To the sinner he extends infinite pardon, though he has only horror for sin. This is Love's mystery.

Doubtless, it will not do to allege God's mercy to authorize a life of sin: God is also *just!*

The thing important to remember, is that *we ought to have faith in God's mercy, regardless of the enormity of our sins!* If Judas had thrown his arms around the Saviour's neck, instead of putting his own neck in a noose, we should have had a "St. Judas" today. Judas' despair proved his undoing. Despair depicts God as inexorable and cruel. Despair deceives and blinds its victim and leads him astray. Despair is inspired by the Devil. After hatred of God, it is the greatest sin, because it slays the virtue which holds first place after charity—*hope.* It is a sin diametrically opposed to the divine mercy, because it directly attacks it. It would place bounds on God's mercy, which is boundless. It is the sin most odious to the Saviour. He came into the world to display his goodness before the eyes of sinners and to search for the lost sheep. He has never desired the death of the sinner; but, rather, his conversion.... After first pushing a soul into presumption by inducing it to commit every crime, the Devil suddenly shows it the enormity of its sins—plunging it into despair. Let us never fall into this snare of Satan.

Let us, rather, see the ways in which God's mercy "pursues" the sinner.

1. First, by remorse of conscience.

2. Next, by the loss of inner peace, moving the sinner to return to a life of grace and union with God.

3. By the timely warning which compels the erring soul to open its eyes. For instance: the death of an accomplice in sin, bodily illness as the consequences of sin, the loss of personal fortune, failure in one's undertakings, an accident, a chance meeting with a true friend, the artless remark of a child ("out of the mouths of babes"), a closed retreat, etc.

The sight of Divine Mercy pursuing the sinful soul—unwearied, undeterred by rebuffs—is both marvellous and touching.... Consider the traitor-apostle, Judas:

On Holy Thursday—the night in which Jesus was to institute the Holy Eucharist—Judas was in the Upper Room, seated at the same table as the Divine Master.... Jesus rose, and coming toward him (just as he did for the Eleven), knelt down to wash his feet—Mercy's first overture.

The Saviour wanted to let Judas know that He was fully cognizant of the whole evil plot.... So, amidst the pall of silence hanging over the hall, Jesus spoke: "Not all of you are clean!"

This is a direct attack!... But, obstinately, Juda's soul was closed to this new onslaught of Divine Mercy, eager to snatch him from damnation.... Judas feigned not to understand!

A third time, Jesus tried to move Judas before his final impenitence. Jesus had washed the feet of the Twelve; and again seated himself at table with them, explaining to them the profound meaning of his action. Then, abruptly, his conversation took another tack. "He who eats bread with me," remarked Jesus quietly, "has lifted up his heel against me. I tell you this now, before it comes to pass, that when it has come to pass, you may believe that I am he."

Judas could not help knowing that these words were meant for him. Although his crime had been plotted in secret, under cover of night, he perceived that Jesus knew all! The guilty apostle heard, understood, and remained— unmoved! Juda's sin had struck deep roots into his soul. The passion for gold (for another it will be the passion for fame, for the flesh, for culpable pleasures) had hardened his heart.

A fourth time, Jesus attempted to save Judas. The meal continued. This time, Jesus declared clearly, "One of you will betray me!"

Consternation was general among the disciples. Jesus profited from their great dismay to give Judas a veiled warning: "What you do, do quickly!"

The Master—ever considerate of the sinner—had carefully chosen his words. So carefully, that the other apostles thought they had to do with some purchase or other. But, Judas would go on to the end!

Where the offense abounded, grace abounded yet more!

A fifth time, Jesus attempted a rescue. Judas had received the price of his treachery—thirty pieces of silver. All that remained was to deliver up his Master. This was the signal: "The Man I shall kiss is he!"

The promise was kept. In the Garden of Gethsemani, Judas at the head of a cohort, went up to Jesus and kissed him!

"Friend!" replied Jesus.

What other heart but would have broken to hear itself so addressed by Jesus?... A searching look from the Master sufficed to restore Peter's soul after his triple denial. But Judas remained insensible and persisted in his crime to damnation. Despair incited him to suicide, to hanging! Why? Because of Judas' resistance to grace, because he said "NO!" to the divine overtures.... God created us without our help, but he will not save us without our help. He respects our liberty.

We may note in passing that Judas had been good. One day he had been generous and left all to follow Jesus. He lived with the Divine Master; listened to his exhortations; saw his miracles; experienced the discreet and penetrating attempts of Divine Mercy to save him when he was on the road to damnation—and after his betrayal, Jesus' friendship for him continued. "Friend!" ... But to no avail! This shows us the danger of an ill-contained passion. For Judas, it was money; for you, it could be something else.... Watch out! However beautiful our vocation, however close we are to Jesus by our state of life, let us beware of sinful attachments; let us never resist grace; let us break at once the chains that enslave us. Then let us plunge trustfully into the infinite sea of God's mercy!

Despite all Jesus' winning words, despite all the manifestations of his mercy, there are still sinners, and scrupulous persons, who cannot be reassured and who are in despair.... Poor souls! Why torture yourselves so? If God did not will your salvation, would he have let his only Son be crucified? Is your wickedness greater than God's goodness? If he is calling you, if as the Good Shepherd, he is seeking you, it is to forgive you.

God loves us more than do our father and mother, more than we could ever love ourselves. All confused as we are, he invites us to fling ourselves into his arms in utter trust, there to find the peace that he alone can give.

Let us believe in this merciful Love the way St. Thérèse of the Child Jesus did. After reading and rereading the Gospel, she wrote these admirable words:

"I trust in the heart of Jesus because I have read, reread, and meditated the Gospel story of the Prodigal Son received by his father with these words capable of touching the most hardened hearts: 'You were lost, and are found.' I have read in the Gospel of the adulterous woman and I heard the Sacred Heart say to her: 'I do not condemn you. Go and sin no more.' I have read the Gospel of the Passion, and my ears still ring with the pressing invitation of the Sacred Heart to Judas to save that which was lost: 'Friend, on what errand have you come?' "

How, after so many proofs of the Sacred Heart's infinite mercy, can one still doubt his forgiveness?

It is taken for granted, when, in our Mass, we recite the *Nobis quoque peccatoribus,* that we all hope—despite our numerous past sins —to share one day in the eternal happiness of the elect. But if we have lost sanctifying grace, let us hasten to recover it this very day. Tomorrow may be too late! Let us say with the Prodigal Son, "I will arise and go to my Father."

215—What saints are recalled in the *Nobis quoque peccatoribus?*

As in the *Communicantes,* we find here a definite number of martyrs, symmetrically and symbolically grouped.

We remarked in the *Communicantes,* that Mary, Mother of God, heads a list of 12 apostles and 12 martyrs.

In the *Nobis quoque peccatoribus,* we commemorate John the Baptist at the head of a list of 7 men and 7 women martyrs.

These fifteen confessors of the Faith seem to have been chosen to complete the list of the *Communicantes.* Let us say a word about each:

1. St. John the Baptist, the Precursor of Christ, occupies the first place (like the Blessed Virgin in the other list), because the Redeemer proclaimed him the greatest among the sons of men. (His feast is celebrated June 24.)

2. St. Stephen, first martyr of the New Law. It is fitting that the Jewish deacon, Stephen, should be the counterpart here of the Roman deacon Lawrence. (Dec. 26.)

3. St. Matthias was one of the seventy-two disciples. After the Saviour's Ascension, he was elected in the apostolic college to replace Judas. As the *Communicantes* already coupled the names of St. Peter and St. Paul (although the latter was not one of the Twelve), St. Matthias could not be named without exceeding the number twelve. This is how the name of this apostle was incorporated into the complementary list of the *Nobis quoque peccatoribus.* (Feb. 24.)

4. St. Barnabas was honoured by St. Paul with the title of "Apostle"; the Church does likewise. For the Holy Spirit had designated Barnabas and Paul to evangelize the pagans. (June 11.)

5. St. Ignatius, Bishop of Antioch and disciple of St. Peter, was thrown to the lions and died a martyr in Rome about A.D. 110. He is noted for his seven epistles, of which the most important and beautiful is the one written to the Christians of Rome. According to Renan himself, this epistle is one of the "gems" of primitive Christian literature. The following extract reveals the apprehension of the saint lest he escape martyrdom:

"I fear your charity. I fear lest the affection you feel for me be all too human. You might even prevent my death.... There can be no finer work for you than that which consists in letting me die.... Suffer me to be immolated while the altar is in readiness.... It is not fine words that make a Christian. It is greatness of soul. It is solid virtue. Should I ever—being in pain—let other sentiments escape from my lips, do not believe me!... Permit me to serve as food to lions and bears. I am God's wheat. I must needs be ground beneath their teeth, that I may become bread worthy of Jesus Christ."

Prayer to the Blessed Mother

●

Holy Mary, Mother of God,
Keep my heart childlike,
Pure and limpid as a spring.

Obtain for me simplicity of heart
A heart that dwells not on sadness;
Which freely gives itself, and
Is compassionately tender,
A heart faithful and generous,
Which forgets no benefit
And holds no rancour.

Make my heart humble and mild,
Loving without asking for return,
Content to be eclipsed in another heart,
Before your Divine Son.

A heart great and unconquerable,
Closed by no ingratitude,
Nor wearied by any indifference;
A heart wounded by love for Jesus,
With a wound only Heaven can heal!

Fr. LEONTIUS DE GRANDMAISON, S.J.

The Canticle of Divine Love

(Prayer of St. Francis of Assisi)

Chorus

O Christ, Thou hast ravished my heart!
My soul is rapt in Thine!
Thou hast transformed me into Thee.
I am consumed in Thy flame!

— 1 —

O Christ, Thou hast ravished my heart!
How place a curb on my love for Thee?
Thou hast transformed me into Thee—
So what can remain of my poor self?
Since Thou alone moveth in me,
And art my strength, and my being and life—
To Thee must the blame be imputed,
If I love Thee to excess—if I love Thee to folly!

— 2 —

For didst Thou defend Thyself
From the love that vanquished Thine omnipotence?
From Heaven, Thou didst descend to earth—
Despised and abject for our sakes from birth—
Without shelter, poor and suffering,
Thou didst repay with interest all our debts.
Living for us, dying for us,
Burning with boundless, immeasurable love!

— 3 —

Inebriated with this divine love,
Which, as a captive, urged Thee through the world,
Thou didst love us to the end.
Opening to all the fountain of Thy heart,
Thou didst cry out to all men: "Come and drink!
These waters will restore thy languid soul.
Thy burning thirst shall be assuaged
In the ever-flowing fountain of life!"

Giraudon Photo

6. St. Alexander, pope and martyr, was one of the seven sons of St. Felicitas. He it was who prescribed the highly expressive ritual of the tiny drop of water added to the wine of the chalice. (May 3.)

7. and 8. St. Peter and St. Marcellinus, the one an exorcist, the other a priest. Both were beheaded near a wild and solitary spot. (Feast, June 2.)

9-10. SS. Felicitas and Perpetua, two young mothers who were thrown to the beasts of the Carthaginian Circus because of their faith.

In the face of the entreaties of her father, who besought her to renounce her faith and so avoid martyrdom; Perpetua remained true to her God. "Daughter," pleaded her father, "have pity on my grey hairs! Have pity on your little child, who will be an orphan! Sacrifice to the health of the Emperor!"

"I will not sacrifice," replied Perpetua, "nor can I, for I am a Christian." (March 6.)

11. St. Agatha, the great martyr of Catania, died during the persecution of Decius, in A.D. 251. (Feb. 5.)

12. St. Lucy, born in Syracuse, underwent martyrdom under the reign of Diocletian, about A.D. 304. (Dec. 13.)

13. St. Agnes, a young maiden, defied the flames and the persecutor's sword. Despite her youth—eleven or twelve—she received the martyr's palm under Diocletian. (Feast, Jan. 21.)

14. St. Cecilia, virgin and Roman martyr, patroness of musicians, died during the third century. (Feast, Nov. 22.)

15. St. Anastasia, martyr, a native of Sirmium. She enjoyed great celebrity in Rome at the time of the Byzantine domination. Her feast is celebrated on December 25th.

Recalling such examples, can a soul whose vocation to sanctity calls for immolation, hesitate?

All of these saints, glorious martyrs, ought to stimulate us to show ourselves openly as Christians, despite the ridicule of our fellow-workers or of "the neighbours".... Let us, during the *Nobis quoque peccatoribus,* beg the Lord to impart to us some of their generous zeal; so that we may have the courage and "nerve" to conquer human respect and appear outwardly what we are in reality—true disciples of Christ, and of Christ crucified.

Conclusion of the Canon

216—What three prayers make up the conclusion *of the Canon?*

The prayers, *Per quem, Per ipsum,* and *Per omnia,* with the conclusion, "Amen."

Per quem haec omnia, Domine, semper bona creas, sanctifi + cas, vivi + ficas, bene + dicis, et praestas nobis.	By whom, O Lord, you always create, sanctify +, vivify +, bless +, and grant us all these good things.
Per Ip + sum, et cum Ip + so, et in Ip + so, est tibi Deo Patri + omnipotenti, in unitate Spiritus + Sancti, omnis honor et gloria.	Through + Him, and with + Him, and in + Him, is to you, God the Father + Almighty, in the unity of the + Holy Ghost, all honour and glory.
Per omnia saecula saeculorum. ℟. Amen.	World without end. Amen.

217—What is the meaning of the formula, *Per quem. . . ?* What are the celebrant's gestures, as he says this prayer?

The Canon is drawing to a close. In this brief prayer—a sort of résumé of those which preceded it—the priest brings out the fact that Christ is the Mediator between God and man in every offering.

The prayer may be paraphrased as follows:

Per quem. Through Christ, God created the wheat and grapes which represent Nature's gifts. In the Mass, he has sanctified them; changing them into the Bread and Wine of supernatural life. In the Eucharist, he has opened to us the source of his richest blessings; and now these are about to be offered to us in Holy Communion.

At the words "sanctify," "vivify," and "bless," the celebrant makes the sign of the cross three times over the chalice and Host.

We shall understand this brief prayer fully, only if we bear in mind that it is a vestige of the blessing formerly given over the unconsecrated offerings. As has been said, Christians in ancient times brought gifts in kind as offerings for the Holy Sacrifice. These offerings were, first of all, bread and wine; then oil, beeswax, wool, flour, grain, grapes, honey, and vegetables—in a word, the fruits of the earth. After removal of whatever was necessary or useful for the Holy Sacrifice, the remainder was left on the table of sacrifice. But, before being placed in the hands of the poor, it first received a blessing. This blessing took place at the close of the Canon. The *Per quem* is the brief and final form of the various blessings pronounced.

In olden times, milk, honey, and water were blessed on Pentecost Sunday.

On Ascension Thurday the new fruits, beans, etc., were blessed.

On August 6th, grapes were blessed.

In our time, the blessing of oil for the sick takes place on Holy Thursday at this place in the Mass: i.e. at the close of the Canon.

218—What is the meaning of the *Per ipsum?* What rubrics must be observed here?

Let us first consider the gestures of the celebrant. The priest uncovers the chalice and genuflects. Reverently, he takes the Host and holds it over the chalice, to indicate that Christ is contained entire and indivisible in both chalice and Host. Then, with the Sacred Host, he makes the sign of the cross thrice over the chalice.

At the same time, he proclaims that God is honoured:

"*Through* Him." Through Christ crucified, the One Mediator between God and man; who gives himself to make up for the incapacity of his creatures. "No one comes to the Father but through Me." (John 14:6.) He is the *Way.*

"*With* Him." All the members of the Mystical Body are united with their Head, that God may be fittingly glorified. We ought to follow Jesus "at all times and in all places." Without him, there can be no infallible, unchanging doctrine. Christ is the *Truth.*

"*In* Him." In a vital union of grace. We need to nourish our souls with the heavenly Bread Christ places at our disposal. He is the *Life.*

Through, with, and in, Christ! Is not this the complete program for achieving sanctity? For these words—"through, with, and in Him" —sum up the whole Mass, and the program of every Christian life; which ought to be one of integration, of union, with His life, and of eventual identification with Him.

Let us never lose sight of the fact that our divinisation, the result of our consecration, must be the work of Christ—the Way, the Truth, and the Life! (*See* Q. 7.)

The celebrant next makes the sign of the cross twice with the Sacred Host, as he pronounces the names of God the Father Almighty, and of the Holy Ghost. Nevertheless, these two signs of the cross are not made over the chalice; because the Father and the Holy Ghost are not hypostatically united to the Body and Blood of the Saviour. The act, however, indicates that it was Christ's death on the Cross which procured to the Blessed Trinity the honour due him.

Our own sufferings and crosses, united to the sufferings and Cross of Christ, will give to the Blessed Trinity the glory that we ourselves owe.

219—What can you tell about the minor elevation which now takes place?

After the *Per Ipsum, et cum Ipso, et in Ipso, est tibi Deo Patri omnipotenti, in unitate Spiritus Sancti,* and after the prescribed signs of the cross, the rubrics continue:

"Then, still holding the Host in his right hand over the chalice, which he holds in his left hand by the stem, the priest elevates it a little (just a few inches from the altar), together with the Host, saying the words, *omnis honor et gloria.* This is the minor elevation.

Up to the eleventh century, this was the sole elevation. Our present, or major, elevation (right after the Consecration) was introduced during the Middle Ages. Prior to the eleventh century, the minor elevation took place amidst a solemn pomp almost equal to that surrounding the Consecration today. At the sound of the *Sanctus,* all the clergy in the choir remained motionless and slightly bowed. In the nave, the people awaited in silence. When the celebrant had terminated the Canon, he placed the Sacred Host on the uncovered chalice and slightly elevated the sacred gifts. The clergy thereupon bowed lower, the church bell rang out, and the people looked upon and adored the Host and Precious Blood.

The whole Canon was considered at that time as a eucharistic prayer. That is why, at its conclusion, the people were shown the consecrated Species. At the same time, it was an invitation to the eucharistic Banquet. It is to be remarked also, that the priest was turned toward the people, making this elevation much more expressive—"Here is the Body and Blood of Christ!"

But in the eleventh century, a heretic named Berengarius, dared to deny the Real Presence, and went on from there to teach the theory of impanation. As a protest against this heresy, the Church wished to give a more manifest token of her faith, at the very moment when Christ descends on the altar. The Consecration was therefore accompanied by the separate and successive elevations of our Lord's Body under the species of bread, and of his Blood under the species of wine. The ringing of bells, the lighted candles, the fumes of incense, the profound inclination of the people—all these were in the nature of a protest against the heresy of Berengarius.

If, in our day, the minor elevation terminating the Canon is less noticeable; it is no less significant. It constitutes a sort of exaltation of the sacred Gifts, which accompany the honour and glory we ought to give to God. It is likewise an invitation for us to adore Jesus Christ present on the altar and generously to embrace our rôles as "victims of love," in union with the perfect Victim.

At this sublime moment, wherein the priest assembles all the "little victims" of Merciful Love and offers them up with the Body and Blood of Christ to the glory of the Blessed Trinity; let us—following the example set by St. Thérèse of the Child Jesus—repeat from our hearts this act of offering which she composed, and which she carried day and night over her heart, together with the Holy Gospels:

AN ACT OF OFFERING AS A VICTIM OF HOLOCAUST TO GOD'S MERCIFUL LOVE

In order that I may be a living act of perfect love, I offer myself as a whole burnt offering to your tender love; beseeching you to consume me continually; letting my soul overflow with the floods of infinite tenderness that are found in you; so that I may become a martyr of your love, O my God! Let this martyrdom make me ready to appear before you, and at last cause me to expire; let my soul cast itself without delay into the everlasting arms of your merciful love. With every beat of my heart, I desire, O my Dearly Beloved, to renew this offering an infinite number of times; until that day when the shadows shall vanish, and I shall be able to retell my love in an eternal face-to-face with you!

The priest has only to add (raising his voice): *"Per omnia saecula saeculorum"*—forever and ever. And all the little victim-souls have only to reply "Amen"! (So be it.)

You must have noted that the very text of the rubrics separates this conclusion—*Per omnia*—from the preceding doxology. In fact, in our days, the priest neither sings nor recites it until he has first placed the Host on the corporal; covered the chalice again with the pall, and genuflected.

Formerly, and until the twelfth century, this conclusion, *Per omnia,* belonged with—as is fitting—*omnis honor et gloria* (all honour and glory)—forever and ever.

To which the people replied, "Amen."

The people by their "amen" ratify all that the priest has done: that is, the entire eucharistic thanksgiving.

This "amen" which concludes the Canon, ought to be roundly said! For Jesus has renewed the gift of himself. This gift of self imposes a sacrifice. Giving, the gift of self, means to deprive, to deny, self. On the part of Christ, this immolation is very real. It ought to be accompanied by ours.

We ought to give ourselves, following Christ's example. And giving ourselves means renouncing ourselves, immolating ourselves; not in word, but in deed. . . .

This is how our Mass becomes a school of renunciation, of immolation, helping us in the gift of self.

There is an austere aspect to this sacrifice which ought to humble us, make the "old man" in us die, the better to give ourselves to God. Now, surrender to God constitutes our only, true, and final, happiness. Finding Him—instead of self—is our glory and the reason for our existence as creatures, as children of the Heavenly Father, as Christians and apostles. With Jesus, we become victims and mediators. And in order fully to give ourselves to God, we ought to immolate ourselves in the service of our brothers, to guide them toward the goal, and achieve with them the return to the Father's House. "Through Him, and with Him, and in Him, to God the Father, in the unity of the Holy Spirit, be all honour and glory. Amen!"

So concludes the Canon, Part II of the Mass of the Faithful. We can conceive of nothing more sublime.

And now is the time for Communion!

After its immolation, the soul becomes united to the Divine Victim to the point of making him its food!

IV. COMMUNION

The Soul is united

Preparation

- Pater
- Libera nos, quaesumus
- Haec commixtio
- Agnus Dei
- Pre-Communion Prayers
- Domine, non sum dignus
- Quid retribuam

Reception of the Divine Victim

- The Priest's Communion
- The People's Communion

Preparation for Communion

220—What name is given to the third part of the Mass of the faithful and what are its subdivisions?

The third portion of the Mass, extending from the Pater Noster to the end of the Mass, is called the *Communion.*

The Communion consists of two parts:

1. *The Communion proper*: The soul is united to Christ.
2. *Thanksgiving*: The soul gives thanks.

221—How is it that so many Catholics receive Communion so often, even daily, without becoming better?

This is an extremely important responsibility-packed question for such time-marking, tepid Christians!

A Freemason recently converted, told us that one of the things that kept him from believing in the Real Presence of our Lord in the Holy Eucharist was this very tepidity of Catholics after receiving Communion.

"If God is *really* there," he would say to himself, "these people ought to be saints!"

What would have been your reply to logic like that?

If instead of being a testimony, our lives nullify or contradict Christ's doctrine, how can we believe ourselves to be his faithful disciples?

Again, how is it that with so many priests and religious in contact with so many youths... so many Sisters in contact with so many girls... that this should produce the many so-called "good" Catholics, and so few real, burning, and zealous Catholics? ...

How is it that with so many churches and parishes, so many preachers and confessors, so many Confessions and Communions, so many works of piety and the apostolate, that all this makes for mere "good Catholics," who are neither fire nor water, flesh nor fowl, pepper nor salt? Again, how explain the fact that there are so few *Christians?*

Our Lord himself complains of this. Did he not say recently to a holy soul (Sister Benigna Consolata), *"I dwell in many hearts as a barren treasure. They possess Me because they are in the state of grace, but they do not turn Me to account.... Do you make up for this."*

Here each one should take stock of himself, and ask himself why he is not a saint and why he does not make others holy....

For too long, perhaps, we have been satisfied with being "alive," without thinking about becoming LIFE-GIVING....

Well, we can affirm without risk, that if we are not saints after our Communions, it is because we brought an insufficient preparation (or none at all) to our reception of Jesus in the Holy Eucharist. Or in a nutshell, it is BECAUSE WE ARE NOT LIVING OUR MASS.

We shall take up this point in our next question.

Is it necessary to mention here that *the state of grace* is ESSENTIAL for worthy reception? This is elementary, but! It happens only too often—especially in high schools, boarding, or private schools—that one or more pupils dare to commit the grave sacrilege of approaching the altar rail after the commission of mortal sin. The fear of being judged unfavorably, and human respect can make a person go that for! By all means, let us free ourselves from the fear of what others will say or think; and never, *never,* become guilty of such crimes, so painful to our Lord, who sees in this treason a renewal of the kiss of Judas.... Should anyone unfortunately find himself in this sad situation, let him lose no time in returning to God's grace; for no sin is too great for God to forgive.

Such was the case of a great saint, Blessed Angela of Foligno, a Franciscan Tertiary and mystic; whose mysticism may be compared to that of St. Teresa of Avila. This is how Blessed Angela herself describes her conversion:

"For the first time in my life, I contemplated all my serious sins." (It would appear that she had been untrue to her marriage vows.) "I became fully cognizant of their number and gravity, and my soul became terror-stricken. I trembled at thought of my damnation, and I shed copious tears. For the first time, I blushed for my sins. Such was my shame, that I quailed at thought of confessing them. I did not go to Confession—I dared not. I approached the Holy Table; and it was with my sins that I received Christ's Body. Day and night, therefore, my conscience rebuked me. I prayed to St. Francis of Assisi to find me the confessor I needed—someone who would understand me, to whom I could speak."

That very night St. Francis appeared to her: "My sister," he said, "if you had called on me sooner, I would have answered sooner. The thing is done."

In the morning, she found, in the Church of St. Felician, a son of St. Francis to whom she unburdened herself fully. It was the starting-point of a holy life.

The state of grace, therefore, is essential. This is easy to understand. One does not give food to a corpse. And the soul that has sinned seriously is dead. . . .

As we said above, however, for a soul to profit fully from the Holy Eucharist, the state of grace is not enough. There must be, in addition, *a serious and generous preparation, drawn from OUR MASS itself.*

222—Demonstrate that the Mass, from its beginning, affords the best preparation for Communion.

Better than all the prayers to be found in prayer books, and which many people say as a sort of "supplement" to the Mass during its celebration; the Mass itself—both by virtue of its prayers, and above all by reason of the inner sentiments it inspires in the hearts of those who wholeheartedly participate in it—affords the best possible preparation for the reception of the Holy Eucharist.

The person who would undertake to live his Mass in the way that we have endeavoured, up to now, to point out to him, would be in the best possible dispositions for participating in the eucharistic Banquet.

Let us call to mind first of all that the more a soul increases its capacity to receive, by means of charity, detachment, and the intensity of its godlike aspirations, the more room it makes in its heart for Love; and the more abundantly will it be filled with Christ's grace in Holy Communion.

Hence the extreme importance of preparing for our Communions.

Let us see how *living our Mass* gives us the right dispositions. (We give here only a broad outline of the preceding material):

1. We sincerely regret our sins and purify our whole life from the slightest attachment to mortal sin, and even from deliberate venial sin. *(Confiteor,* prayers at the foot of the altar, the *Kyrie.)*

2. We are enlightened by the Word of the Lord. (Epistle, Gospel, Sermon.)

3. We make a first Communion of Jesus, the Divine Word, at the Gospel, when our minds adhere to the truths revealed, by an act of faith.

4. Our union with God becomes closer. We accept our sacrifices, our pains, our daily task; and out of them we make a little host, white with purity, poor and detached, ready for the most absolute obedience to God; and we place it on the paten, alongside the large host. (Offering of the bread.)

5. We cast into the wine of the chalice the tiny drop of water of all our apostolate since our last Mass: so as to make our lives enter into the great Sacrifice and make them count for eternity. (Offering of the wine.)

6. The total offering of self calls for immolation. We become victims with the Victim of Calvary, hosts with the Host.... We offer ourselves to God: "Here is my body; here is my blood. Do with them what you will. Here is my soul, my energy, my strength, my possessions, all that I am and have. Take it.... Transmute the poor bread of my life into your divine life. Change my daily cross into a crucifix, so that it will no longer be I who live, but you, my Good Master, who live in me." (Consecration.)

7. We yearn for ever closer union, love calls for love. We offer up Christ to the glorious Trinity, and ourselves "with Him, through Him, and in Him," to the honour and glory of God. (Minor elevation.)

8. Love tends toward fusion, absorption. "I love Baby enough to eat him!" cried a fond mother. At the moment of Communion, Jesus enters so intimately into our heart and soul that our affections, desires, and thoughts may be said to be *his* affections, desires, and thoughts. Jesus has them first; then he communicates them to us IN PROPORTION TO OUR LOVE FOR HIM NOW. If our soul has but little love, Jesus is constrained to circumscribe himself within the narrow dimensions of that niggardly little heart and to limit his gifts. But to the communicant detached from creatures, dead to self, stripped of self-will, unreservedly ready for every sacrifice—to the pure soul which makes itself fully receptive to the influence of the Host and identifies itself with him—Jesus gives himself in exchange as only God can give. He sets up a circulation of divine life, a communication of spiritual goods, a unity of love, an intimacy, which defies description. The soul, penetrated by Jesus, is deified and becomes life-giving. (Communion.)

By its active participation in the various phases of the Holy Sacrifice, the soul is thus gradually prepared and wondrously enlarged for the abundant outpouring of the graces which flow from Communion. Again, generosity is required for LIVING OUR MASS and never taking ourselves back after offering and delivering ourselves to all Love's exigencies. . . .

223—Every time we go up to the altar rail, we speak of "receiving Communion." Is this expression adequate? Could this concept of "receiving" have anything to do with our failure to profit more from Communion?

It is true that Communion implies, and presupposes, the RECEPTION OF DIVINE LIFE—the reception of Jesus Christ himself. But Communion has another angle that we seldom envisage: the GIFT of our lives to God.

All love calls for love in return. God will give himself to us in the measure that we give ourselves to him. And we know how Jesus thirsts for us! Unceasingly, he calls, "Give Me your heart!"

You are going to communicate, with the intention of receiving supernatural life. . . . Have you ever thought of Jesus as receiving communion from *you?*

Every living creature which acquires a higher form of existence, must first give itself; must die; must let itself be devoured by a superior being. Plants swallowed by animals are transmuted into animal flesh; and the flesh of animals, eaten by man, becomes human flesh.

By a miracle of divine condescendance, the man who consents to die to the "old man"—to his habit of sinning—is divinized by Christ's life! The degree of this divinization varies with the completeness of his GIFT OF SELF to God.

Hence, no Communion is possible (or at any rate, fruitful), without consecration and immolation. Or, in other words, we live by what we give up!

Therefore, seeking Life without giving anything in return; drinking of the chalice of salvation without helping to replenish it; makes me a parasite on the Mystical Body and dooms me to a listless existence.

Thus communion presupposes sacrifice—daily suffering supported and generously accepted, the crucifixion of this egoistical "I," etc.

In a word, we give God time, and God gives us eternity!

We hand over our humanity, and God gives us his divinity.

We bring our nothingness, and he gives us his ALL.

The incredible thing about it is that we should show so little zeal for generosity in giving!

That man should be so loved by God is astounding, but not inadmissable, once one has an inkling of the immensity of the Heart of Jesus. But that man should not love back, is one of the most incomprehensible of mysteries!

Why is Jesus the Abandoned Lover?

"Why is LOVE not loved?" as St. Francis was wont to cry as he went up and down the streets of Assisi.

Why, when Jesus asks us for water, must we give him gall and vinegar to drink?

Why, as in Bethlehem, is there no room for Christ in our hearts?

Why? Very often it is because we love God only in words!

In our prayers, perhaps, we send up our protestations of love to Heaven; but we speedily forget that love is based on self-denial and sacrifice—even to the laying down of our lives. "Greater love than this no one has, that one lay down his life for his friend."

We accept the Gospel's teaching in theory; we may even teach it to others. But in practice, we do not believe it strongly enough to have the generosity to bring it into our daily lives.

Devout, pious, we love God—but in our own way! We lack courage to detach our minds and hearts from this trinket or trifle, from this or that person harmful to our sanctification, from this or that pet fault. " Dear Lord," we pray, "I give you everything but *that!*"

But "that" is the very thing God asks of us!

Again, to make progress in the spiritual life and to be effectual as an apostle, it is not enough for me to be in the state of grace, to frequent the sacraments, to receive Communion every day, to do spiritual reading, to practice a number of devotions. All these things are good, but they are not enough. *In addition, I must gradually and generously detach myself from creatures so as to be more closely united to God,* who ought to be ALL in my life, and King of my heart freed from the futilities of this world.

Here is an illustration of the harm that may be done to our souls by an inordinate attachment to a person or thing:

Supposing that to reach my friend's home at a certain hour, I have to cross a lake. So I jump into a boat. The boat is watertight, the oars are in good shape. With much effort and enthusiam, I start rowing. I row, I row—AND I row. *Nothing* happens. After fifteen minutes of this violent exercise, I haven't budged an inch!

Yet, the boat is good. (Soul in the state of grace.)

The oars are excellent. (Supernatural setup: virtues, gifts of the Holy Ghost, Sacraments, all other means of sanctification.)

And goodness knows I certainly did my part! I really rowed! What's wrong, then? Why, it's very simple. The boat is *moored* to the dock! There is an "attachment!"

How we shall suffer at the hour of death at having held up our sanctification because of an attachment we lacked courage to break! At being left "at the dock," despite our God-given graces and despite all our efforts!

While there is still time, let us sweep aside every obstacle cutting us off from, or distracting us from our life's goal—GOD!

Let us not be surprised at the exigencies of the Divine Master. Once a soul decides to sanctify itself, our Lord asks much of it. . . .

So let us not be niggardly in God's service. . . . Too many devout souls, who dream of breath-taking "flights" into divine love, easily forget (alas), that the price of spiritual progress and of an influential apostolate is combat, detachment, and suffering.

So today—tomorrow may be too late—let us root out pride, vanity, human respect, jealousy, envy, ambition, and grudges. . . . Let us root out the exaggerated love of ease and pleasure. . . the inordinate fondness for certain persons. . . or for forbidden pleasures. . . Let us root up avarice and the love of riches. . . . These will be so many idols destroyed in our heart!

When this heart shall be really empty of creatures, God will dwell in it and fill it to overflowing! Then we shall be able to communicate fruitfully.

It has been said with truth that words are moving, but that examples move to action. Here is an example of a generous life:

Pauline Reynolds was an English convert. At twenty-three, during a Day of Recollection, she came across these words written on the back of a holy card: "If you would be perfect, your heart must cling to nothing. Give Jesus *all* your love."

"I went over in memory," she writes, "the so many little things kept as precious treasures." (Big sacrifices, relatively speaking, are easy. But the *little* ones!) "I decided to sacrifice them all. I had prized letters kept from childhood. I was so fond of them, that I had never got rid of them. I bundled them up, not daring to look at them, and gave them to my confessor to burn (since for me, this would have been impossible). The heart-wrenching this cost me is inexpressible. . . . I looked over my room, and everything went—letters, locks of hair, photos, pressed flowers, were burned. This was an immense sacrifice for me. I don't think I ever did anything else so hard."

We see by her life, that God put just this "immense" sacrifice as the condition for his special graces.

"Since that hour," she adds, "I have never had the slightest attachment for any object whatsoever. For I had understood all the divine jealousy of Him who could not suffer even a letter or a flower to take up His place in my heart."

The day wherein we fully understand that Christian self-denial always brings enrichment in its train, the minute that we turn our gaze from the little we are leaving, to the EVERYTHING we gain; the chains that shackle us to earthly things will fall off of themselves. And it will be with joy that we shall forsake that which is passing, for Him who abides eternally.

224—Are not the trials God sends to us a providential means of purifying ourselves, of emptying our hearts of all idols, and of preparing them for Communion?

Without a doubt! Very often, we ourselves lack the courage for these necessary "amputations." So God, like a loving Father, comes to our aid....

For instance, He will send a financial reverse to a man too engrossed in business....

Loss of a child to a mother who idolizes her children too much....

Nervous fatigue to a book-worshipping intellectual....

Small-pox to one too concerned with her beauty....

He will permit the separation of two friends whose inordinate affection for each other has retarded the growth of charity in their hearts.... To love some people truly, we must give them up.

Like a good physician, God applies the right remedy. He always puts his finger on the sore spot—let us not be surprised, then, if it hurts!

Let us accept the divine surgery unresistingly, assured that the operation, far from being followed by "complications," will simplify our lives and make them bear fruit in abundance. "Every branch that bears fruit, He will clean, that it may bear more fruit." (John 15:2.)

A PRAYER FOR THOSE WHO CAUSE US TO SUFFER

Jesus, my Saviour, you whom I see on the Cross overwhelmed with suffering and covered with wounds, and who prayed for your enemies and persecutors, grant me the grace to do likewise. O generous Benefactor, you die for your executioners, and rejoice and offer for their salvation the divine blood which they make flow by nailing you to the Cross! Penetrated with a sincere desire to imitate you, I beseech you to look in your infinite mercy at all those who have caused me pain, and of whom I find cause for complaint—those who have saddened, humiliated, and wronged me. Dear Lord, do them good in this world and the next! Do not refuse them the grace of repentance, so that one day they may be given entrance into Heaven. Dear Lord, give me the courage and strength to avenge myself like the saints; by cheerfully rendering good for evil, every time I have the opportunity to do so. Father, forgive them, for they know not what they are doing. Amen.

225—We have seen that active participation in the various phases of the Mass, is the ideal preparation for Communion. With the approach of Communion, the Church intensifies her preparation by means of appropriate prayer and ritual. Of what does this proximate preparation consist?

In the liturgy of the Mass, this proximate preparation consists in:

1. The chanting or recitation of the Pater Noster, with its introduction *(Oremus)* and complement *(Libera).*
2. The ritual of the breaking of the Bread and of the commingling of the species, wit the *Agnus Dei.*
3. The kiss of peace and the three Precommunion prayers.

Let us consider each of these elements.

The Pater Noster

226—How does the Pater Noster begin? Please comment on the ritual and text.

After concluding the last prayers of the Canon, the celebrant rests both hands on the altar and prays aloud: *"Per omnia saecula saeculorum."*

"Amen," replies the congregation.

We have seen that these words belong to the Canon, which the priest says in a low voice. He now raises his voice, at the *Per omnia,* to permit the people (who have been silent all during the Canon) to take an active part in the drama unfolding before their eyes.

Next comes the introduction proper:

Oremus: Praeceptis salutaribus moniti et divina institutione formati, audemus dicere:	Let us pray. Instructed by your saving Commandments, and following your divine directions, we presume to say:

"Oremus," says the priest, joining his hands to attest his unworthiness at beginning a prayer couched in such bold terms—as if he must needs excuse himself. It was the Son of God himself who ordered us to use this prayer formula, and obedience to him concerns our salvation. "When you pray," therefore he taught, "say, Our Father."

Then, full of confidence, the celebrant extends his hands, keeping his eyes fixed on the Sacred Host, and begins the Pater Noster in the attitude of Moses praying on the Mount.

227—Is not the Pater Noster so sublime a prayer that we almost ought to apologize to God for daring to say it?

Coming straight from the Heart of Jesus, the Our Father is the prayer of prayers.

We say it several times a day: at Mass, outside Mass—on all occasions. Thus Tertiaries, to fulfill the obligations of their Office, must say twelve Our Fathers daily. What an opportunity, and what spiritual advantages they may reap from this! Unfortunately, if we know in theory that the Our Father is the greatest of prayers, in practice—through habit and the impact of other prayers—it has been somewhat lowered—in our minds only, for the Our Father has never lost its sublimity or value.

Christians of the early centuries had a less dimmed concept of the worth of the Our Father than we do. Their liturgy was a powerful aid in giving it their full appreciation.

To begin with, only the baptized could recite the Our Father. Outsiders were not permitted even to know of its existence.

The secret mysteries were gradually revealed to the catechumens during the rites initiatory to Baptism, and they did not know about everything until they took part in the eucharistic liturgy on the day of their reception into the Church.

Ancient rituals have preserved for us the explanation of the Our Father made to the catechumens; who, in many places, waited to become Christians before "daring" to say with their brethren—on the invitation of the pontiff or priest who baptized them—the Lord's Prayer, the prayer proper to the children of God, permitted to address their Heavenly Father ("Our Father who are in Heaven") by his name.

As we see, before being inserted into the Mass, the Our Father figured in the baptismal liturgy.

In this way, we understand better certain passages from the Fathers of the Church. St. John Chrysostom, commenting in a homily on the Lord's Prayer, remarked: "That this prayer is suitable only for the faithful (i.e. the baptized), is taught by the laws of the Church, and likewise by the very beginning of this prayer; for the yet uninitiated (baptized) cannot call God his "Father."

Theodoret of Cyrus, a writer of the same period (A.D. 458), likewise said: "We do not teach this prayer (the Our Father) to any of the non-initiated, but only to the faithful. No one not initiated would dare to say, 'Our Father, who are in Heaven,' etc., before having received the grace of the divine adoption."

Are we, who are baptized, aware of our dignity as were the first Christians, and do we appreciate at its just value the sublimeness of our vocation as children of God?

Christian tradition has always seen in the Our Father the model prayer and the compendium of our highest aspirations. It contains inexhaustible riches that ravish our intellects, as they gradually absorb the light of its true meaning.

May we learn to appreciate these divine words with as much profit as did the first Christians; and always use them to further our spiritual progress, as well as our participation in the Eucharistic Sacrifice, in accordance with the desire of the Church.

228—What are the divisions of the Pater Noster?

The Pater Noster, also called the Lord's Prayer, affords a magnificent compendium of the petitions we may address to God in the spiritual and temporal realms. It also gives us a graduated scale of values.

Its divisions:

1. A prologue or invocation; (2) three petitions for God; (3) four petitions for ourselves; (4) conclusion: Amen.

Prologue or Invocation

Pater noster, qui es in caelis!	Our Father, who are in Heaven!

Three petitions for God

a. Sanctificetur nomen tuum!	a. Hallowed be your name!
b. Adveniat regnum tuum!	b. Your kingdom come!
c. Fiat voluntas tua, sicut in caelo, et in terra!	c. Your will be done, on earth as it is in Heaven.

FOUR PETITIONS FOR OURSELVES

d. Panem nostrum quotidianum da nobis hodie.	d. Give us this day our daily bread.
e. Et dimitte nobis debita nostra, sicut et nos dimittimus debitoribus nostris.	e. And forgive us our trespasses, as we forgive those who trespass against us.
f. Et ne nos inducas in tentationem.	f. And lead us not into temptation.
g. ℟ Sed libera nos a malo.	g. ℟. But deliver us from evil.

CONCLUSION

Amen!	Amen!

229—Why do we say the Pater Noster at Mass?

No one will be astonished to learn that the Pater Noster was introduced into the liturgy of the Mass in the fourth century. And here is why:

1. Because the Our Father is the prayer proper to the Christian, the one defining his pre-eminent status as an adopted son of the Heavenly Father.

2. Because it is the "Lord's Prayer": the one Christ, when questioned by his disciples on how to pray, gave them as the model of perfect prayer. Hence, it is eminently fitting for us to say it during the Sacrifice.

3. Because it possesses a special purificatory value, by virtue of the words: "Forgive us our trespasses."

4. Because the fourth petition, that for daily bread, is applied, in a profound mystical sense, to Eucharistic Communion. "Give us this day our Daily Bread."

230—May the faithful at Mass say the Pater Noster aloud, along with the priest?

In the oriental Church, the Pater Noster is chanted aloud by the entire congregation—the faithful thus preparing themselves to approach the Eucharistic Banquet.

In the Latin Church, until recently, it was sung or recited by the priest alone.

According to the Instruction on Sacred Music and the Sacred Liturgy issued by the Sacred Congregation of Rites, Sept. 3rd, 1958, however, the faithful are now exhorted to sing the response: "Sed libera nos a malo" in a chanted Mass; and in a low Mass to recite the whole "Pater Noster" in union with the celebrant.

Our Father

231—Why do we say "Our," and not "my," Father?

We say *"Our,"* and not *"my* Father," because the Christian is not an isolated individual, but a member of a living organism; sometimes called the Church, and sometimes the Mystical Body.

Our Lord thereby teaches us to have done with our egoism. As members of a society, the Church, *our prayer ought to be social, universal, and catholic; without distinction of country, race, or tongue.*

God is not just "my" Father; he is *our* Father.

What is the difference?

This revelation of Christ revolutionizes human relationships. Knowing that we all have the same Father, I can no longer look on others in the same way. This stranger passing by, who without the Gospel—the "Good News"—would mean nothing to me, is my neighbour and brother. I pray with and for him. I ought to spend myself for his greatest good. Perhaps he is one of these "lost sheep" who must be brought back to the fold, one of these ears of wheat awaiting the harvesters. . . .

"Mr. X. treated me very shabbily; he was hateful. All bonds between us are broken. From now on, he is my enemy." Yes, this is how it would be without the Gospel, which teaches us the Our Father. But with the Gospel, I know that Mr. X is my brother and that I ought to forgive him. This is the law of charity, which alone can reign among members of the same family, the law incumbent on every Christian. Just try to picture a real Christian, a Tertiary, who would not forgive!

It follows that this fellow-worker, this servant, my boss, this spinster, this shut-in, this Negro, this German, this Englishman, this Jew, etc., are all my brothers and sisters; and we ought to love one another as such out of love for God, our common Father.

232—What does the concept of "Father" suggest in our relations with God?

Jesus' great revelation, the message of the hidden years, of his public ministry, of his Passion, can all be summed up in these few words: "God, who is Love, wants us to love him the way a child loves its Father, and he wants us to share in his divine life, in his eternal beatitude!

"Oh, how glorious, noble, and grand it is to have a Father in Heaven!" exclaims St. Francis of Assisi in his "Letter to all the Faithful."

Therein lies the great mystery of the divine thought. "If you knew the gift of God!" Think of it! We can call GOD our Father!

Unaided human reason is able to demonstrate the existence of a Supreme Being, a Sovereign Ruler, a First Cause of all things. But our reason, however powerful, has been unable to discover anything about the intimate life of the Supreme Being—the divine life is impenetrable without revelation.

So the Word of God became incarnate, inundating the world with his light. He came to teach us the "Good News" that God is our Father!

Who would not be thrilled and transported with gladness, joy, and gratitude! *God is our Father and we are his adopted children.* We have a share in Heaven's heritage!

It is Baptism that makes us enter God's big family and confers on us the title of adopted sons, a wonderful privilege and the basis of our spiritual life.

God adopts us then as his children, and this in a much more perfect manner than men are able to do by means of legal adoption. These can doubtless transmit their name and property to their adopted sons, but not their blood and their life. "Legal adoption," wrote Cardinal Mercier, "is a legal fiction. The adopted child is considered by his foster parents as their own child, and receives from them the heritage to which the fruit of their union would have been entitled. Society recognizes this fiction and sanctions its effects. Nevertheless, the object of the fiction is not, in reality, transformed. . . . The grace of the divine adoption is not fiction, but reality. St. John tells us that God grants the divine sonship to those who believe in the Divine Word. This sonship is not nominal, but effective: "Behold what manner of love the Father has bestowed upon us, that we should be called children of God; and such we are." (John 3:1.)

Adoption is the admission of an outsider into a family.

But to be adopted, one must be of the same race; to be adopted by men, one must belong to the human race.

Now we, who are not of the race of God; who are but poor creatures, farther from God by nature than animals are from man, how can we be adopted by God?

This is a marvel of divine wisdom, power, and goodness. God communicates to us a mysterious participation in his nature, which we call "grace." Grace raises us above our own nature, and we become, in a certain sense, "gods." We do not become equal to, but resemble, God.

This participation through grace in the divine life makes our souls, capable, as it were, of knowing God as God knows himself; of loving God as God loves himself; of enjoying God the way God is filled with his own beatitude—and thus we live the very life of God himself.

Such is the ineffable mystery of our divine adoption.

Our gratitude to such a good and generous Father ought to be simply boundless!

And it is because he loves us that he wants us to share as his children in his own happiness. "The gift surpassing all other gifts," says St. Leo, "is for God to call man his son and for man to call God, 'Father' " !

Each of us may truthfully say to himself, "It was by a special act of mercy, benevolence, and love that God created me, and called me by Baptism to the divine adoption; for in his infinite opulence, God has no need of creatures. By a special act of pure love, God chose me to be infinitely elevated above my natural condition, so as to enjoy his own beatitude forever; to realize one of his divine thoughts; to be a voice in the concert of the elect; and a brother of Jesus, eternally sharing in his heritage."

Let us not forget that it is through Christ that we go to the Father: "No one comes to the Father but through Me."

"This is what I came on earth to do," says the Divine Master to us. "I want all men to become my brothers. I desire my Father (who is also your Father) to grant to all of you the love that he has for me. I propose —if you do not oppose me by sin—to introduce you one day into the house of my Heavenly Father, and to make you sit down beside me as my true brothers. You belong to the adopted family of my Heavenly Father, and ought to help me win for him a multitude of sons. You will teach them not to be afraid of God any longer, but to approach him with confidence and trust. Begin now with me to love my Father as I love him, and let us say together, "Our Father who are in Heaven...."

That, in brief, is what Jesus, our Big Brother, revealed to us when he taught us the Our Father. It is easier to understand now what St. Teresa tells us of an unlettered nun who had attained to a high degree of sanctity and to perfect prayer simply by saying the Our Father. She recited it slowly, and was never able to finish, so enraptured was she by the first words!

And we? Do we "fall into ecstasy" when we say the Our Father? If not, could it not be because we recite it at top speed or in routine fashion? Instead of being "phonographs," let us be *prayerful hearts, burning with love!* Thus, we shall be more sure of being heard and answered.

233—What obligation do we contract toward God when we call him by the beautiful title of "Father"?

Knowing that God is our Father, are we not obligated to live like true sons of God?

Yes, we are. And since children of the same family look alike, we ought to model ourselves on Jesus, our Big Brother.

Alas! what a heartbreaking reality it is that these are souls wherein Christ's image has been marred by sin!

How many souls recite the Our Father with no fear of the odious lie they dare to proffer to God!

After the above, we can understand better why mortal sin—the grave, deliberate, and willful disobedience to God's law—is the most heinous of crimes.

It is the revolt of the creature against the Creator, of the child against its Father, of him who is nothing against Him who is All, of him who has received all against Him who has given all!

It is the brutal rejection of the divine friendship. God the Father is willing to admit man to terms of intimacy with him, and man prefers to God's gift of himself, the first gratification that comes along!

Mortal sin is the most incomprehensible of acts. Man, who desires happiness above everything else, refuses God's own happiness, so freely and mercifully offered!

May God keep us from falling into this misfortune; and help us to live in such a way that when we say the Our Father, we may never need to dread hearing Jesus say to us, "No, I do not own you as a child of God." Or hear Mary say to us, "No I do not find in you any of the humility, piety, obedience, purity, meekness, poverty, or holiness of my Divine Son!"

When we call God "Father," another obligation devolves upon us; which is to conduct ourselves toward God the way a child does toward his earthly parents—in other words, to practice spiritual childhood.

234—What is spiritual childhood?

Spiritual childhood is a state of soul for which we should all aim; and which consists in acquiring those spiritual dispositions which correspond to a child's natural dispositions.

This is the thought our Lord means to convey when he says to us, "Unless you become as little children, you will not enter the Kingdom of Heaven."

If we are to have some slight grasp of the meaning of spiritual childhood (unless we are already in the state of proficients), we need graces of illumination obtainable by prayer and detachment. . . .

Nevertheless, we are still able to get some idea, by comparing it with natural childhood. Fr. Grou in his *Manuel des âmes intérieures* (Manual for Contemplatives) draws an apt parallel, as you can see for yourselves:

"1. The child does not reason; does not reflect; possesses neither prudence nor foresight; and is without malice.

"1. It is the same way with spiritual childhood. The first thing that God does, when he places us in this state, is to suspend the operations of the intelligence. He arrests the constant flow of reasonings and reflexions, and replaces them by simple and direct operations; which issue, so to speak, from the soul. And he does this in such a fashion that the soul believes that it no longer thinks (although it continues to think, but in a manner more elevated, and more approximating the thought of God; since God has but one infinitely simple thought). The soul no longer reasons or reflects; and is not concerned with either past or future, but solely with the present. It forms no projects; but lets itself be guided from moment to moment—interiorly, by the Spirit of God; exteriorly, by his providence. Its actions and speech contain nothing of malice; because it does nothing, and says nothing, designedly or with premeditation.

"Stripped of its own prudence, the soul is clothed with that of God; who always causes it to speak and act opportunely, so long as it is faithful in not consulting its own reason.

"2. The child does not dissimulate. (As soon as he is capable of dissimulation, he is no longer a child.)

"2. Likewise, nothing approaches the candour of the spiritual child. He does not assume an "appropriate expression"; his recollection is not strained; all—words, actions, and demeanor—is natural in him.

"What he says, he means.

"What he offers, he wishes to give.

"What he promises, he wishes to fulfill.

"He does not attempt to appear other than what he is, nor to conceal his imperfections or sins. He does not have a special confessor for his serious faults.

"He tells the good and bad about himself with the same simplicity; he keeps nothing back from those to whom he ought to speak.

"3. The child manifests his love with simplicity. Everything in him expresses the sentiments of his heart. He is so much the more touching and persuasive, because his manner is unstudied.

"3. It is the same way with the spiritual child in his demonstrations of love for God, and in his charity toward his neighbour.

"He goes to God simply and unaffectedly. He lets his heart speak; without the use of fixed forms, or chosen words. He knows no other "prayer method" than that of being near God, looking at him, listening to him and possessing him; expressing all the sentiments inspired by grace —sometimes with words, and more often, without.

"He loves his neighbour sincerely and wholeheartedly; bearing him neither envy nor jealousy. He neither ridicules, criticizes, nor despises him; and never deceives him. He never flatters him (having lost the habit of those vain compliments which do not come from the heart). He takes from politeness only what the Gospel authorizes, rising above it by charity and cordiality.

"He loves no less when he reproves, than when he approves; when he condemns, than when he praises. He does good to others without affectation; under the eyes of God, without looking for gratitude.

"4. The child is docile and obedient. He feels that he was not made to do his own will.

"4. Likewise, the first thing that the spiritual child renounces is his own will; which he submits entirely to God's will; and to all that represents God to him. He does not wish to govern himself in anything; but abandons himself for his interior conduct, unreservedly to the Spirit of God, and to the director in whom his confidence has been placed. As for his exterior conduct, he willingly yields to all those in authority over him. In indifferent things, he prefers to accommodate himself to the will of others, rather than to bring others to follow his own will.

"5. The child has no self-knowledge, does not indulge in introspection; is incapable of self-study and of self-observation. He takes himself as he is, and goes straight ahead.

"5. The spiritual child, likewise, is not curious about turning his thoughts inward, nor to see what is passing within. He takes what God gives him, and is content to be at each moment what God wants him to be. He does not judge of the goodness of his meditations, Communions, or other practices, according to his passing moods; but leaves the judgment up to God.

"Provided that the innermost dispositions of his soul do not change, he rises above all the vicissitudes of the spiritual life. He knows that it has its winters, its tempests, and its clouds; that is, its dryness, its disgusts, its inner doldrums, and its temptations. He stoutheartedly goes through every trial and calmly awaits the return of fair weather.

"He is not anxious about his spiritual progress. He does not look back to see how much ground he has covered; but follows the path without thinking that he is walking, and advances so much the more because he does not look to see if he is advancing. Hence, he is neither disquieted nor discouraged. Should he chance to fall, he humbles himself, but at once picks himself up; and runs on with renewed ardour.

"6. The child is weak, and knows he is weak. This is what renders him so submissive, so distrustful of self, and so trustful toward those whom he knows have his welfare at heart.

"6. In the same way, the spiritual child knows that he is weakness itself—that of himself he is unable to stand, or to take so much as a single step without stumbling. Thus, distrustful of his own strength, he places all his trust in God. Far from him, then, is the thought of crediting himself with the good that he accomplishes or the victories he gains—he ascribes all the glory to God. He does not prefer himself to others, but is intimately convinced that, should God abandon him, he would fall into the greatest of sins; and that if others had the same graces as himself, they would have known better how to profit by them.

"For the same reason that he knows his frailty, he is not astonished at his falls. His self-love feels no affront; instead he calls God to his aid.

"He never undertakes anything on his own; but let God once speak, and he is willing to undertake anything and to expose himself to every danger—so certain is he of success, in spite of all the opposition of men and demons.

"7. Innocence, peace, and pure joy are the appanage of childhood. Children are happy without knowing it; they are carefree. The parents think of everything for them. Thus they are in a continual state of enjoyment.

"7. This is a very feeble picture of spiritual childhood. The happiness of spiritual childhood, like that of natural childhood, is unperceived and unplotted, but nonetheless real and enjoyed. God himself pours it into the soul. He thinks of everything; he provides for everything. This happiness endures in the midst of the greatest storms of the spiritual life. It is not that spiritual childhood makes us insensible; but it raises us, through our abandonment to God's will, to an imperturbable peace, far above all feeling.

"This may be judged of only by experience."

This is something worth meditating and living! St. Thérèse of the Child Jesus, with her "little way," and St. Francis of Assisi by his simple and obedient life, teach us nothing other than this. Let us learn from them and we shall achieve the same kind of sanctity!

235—Why are some souls so worried?

This is the way Dom Eugene Vandeur answers this question, in his book entitled, *Abandon à Dieu* (p. 180).

"I am worried! And what about?

"I am worried about myself; it is for myself I am frightened; it is for myself that I dread so many things.

"Worry and egotism! Are they not too often the same thing?

"Always this vision of 'me' in front of me; that is what wearies me; that is what wears me out.

"I must forget self. I must forget what I was, what I am, what I might be—and replace this memory by that of God; who is alone worthy to capture my thoughts or inebriate my heart.

"I worry about everything, because my Self is really *multiple.* It has multiplied itself into so many things, from which I never manage to detach myself.

"And each one of them causes me a particular worry, more or less acute according to the degree of the attachment binding me to it. I fear to lose the things I love, that I possess, that I have so painfully accumulated: honours, riches, position, food and raiment....

"My Self fears spoliation—and will have none of it. It spends its life trying to protect what it so jealously possesses.

"It spends its life thinking, scheming, attempting this, attempting that—a never-ending process.

"And peace is lost, that serenity of soul, which has, and can have, no other basis than the Immovable, i.e., God alone.

"But nothing is so disquieting as the future.

"The past, however painful, I have lived, suffered, and borne. It is over and done with. I have perhaps triumphed over it.

"The present, I live in, however hard. I know where I am; I know what my difficulties are; I am working to overcome them.

"But the future! The future! What will that be? What is going to happen to me tomorrow, the day after tomorrow, a year from now, ten years from now?

"Where shall I be? What shall I be doing? And what is to become of me and mine, and all those whom I love? (Oh, what a worry *that* is!) And my dwindling resources? And my growing children, noisy, venturesome, thrilled at life?

"And my poor health? And old age creeping up? And death that seems close, now?—All this disturbs me....

"The mystery of the future, which you would sometimes rather not face or think about, God has reserved for himself. He knows it. It is in his keeping.

"And this thought suddenly fills me with light, hope, calm, serenity.

"Dear God, my future is in your hands! Ah, if I were to decide at last to believe in this Providence that is you and whom I adore; why should you, God, if I believe in you, and hope in you, let me fall from that Hand which governs all that is, lives, and moves?

"Why should I hesitate a single instant to drive from my soul all worry about the future, all fear, and also all distrust?

"For is it not distrust of you to live this way all the time, in this state of soul so unchristian, so unworthy of you?

"'Do not fret, then, over tomorrow; leave tomorrow to fret over its own needs,' said Jesus. [Knox.]

"This is pure Gospel—if I want to believe the infallible Word of Truth.

"Father, it is done.... I entrust to you my future, whatever it may be—

"My joys. You will sanctify them in the humility of my heart.

"My sorrows. You will make of them an element of great saving penance.

"I surrender myself; I look no more; I do not want to worry any more.

"I am in your fatherly hands, O Supreme Providence; and I want to stay there always, with the help of your grace. Lord, never let me yield to temptation, to the trial of worry."

236—In our daily lives as Christians, do we have faith in Providence?

Acknowledging God as my Father means to have faith in Providence.

"Providence! Providence! Where does that come in? It's no good praying! My prayers are never answered!"

"What did I ever do to God, that I should be tried this way?"

And how many other blasphemous expressions we often hear from people irritated at their lot, understanding nothing of God's merciful guidance, leading them back more surely to the Father's House!

We always blame God, and we always forget to look within to see if we are not the authors of our misfortune.... Especially, are we ignorant of the important statement made by St. Paul that "for those who love God, all things work together unto good."

Getting down to brass tacks in our daily lives:

Sometimes it is a trial one finds too hard, a cross that appears too heavy; and we complain, "What have I ever done that this should happen to me?"

We are honest, we go to Mass, we do our duty. Therefore, we should deserve, if not a reward, peace, at least—and we get trials and worries instead! God takes a dearly loved child, an indispensable husband, a model wife; the house has burned down and we are left homeless, without money or clothing; a breadwinning son or daughter has unjustly lost his or her job!

"What have I done to God... ? Why did he will that?"

We never even ask ourselves if he might simply have permitted it! We do not look for anyone else to blame, anyone else to be guilty, but the Good Lord!

The questioning, the complaints, the lamentations, the murmuring, approximate indeliberate blasphemy!

Indeliberate! If lack of reflexion is an excuse, reflexion is a duty. Have we a right to blame God before looking around and before plumbing our own conscience?

We are free agents, and God always respects our liberty.

Do we really realize this?

A young man is instantly killed in a hunting accident in the mountains; where he went freely, despite the advice of friends and his parent's prohibition. He was free—but abused of his freedom. Why blame God?

A girl is dying of T.B. at twenty-one! She quit school to take a job, and have more money and liberty.... Instead of resting, she went out every evening, came home late, and several nights got no sleep at all. . . . Getting up late, she often left without breakfast. . . . In winter she forget about the change in weather; and to be fashionable, went out in nylon sheers and lightly clad. Four years of this, and she had ruined her health—she was dying in a sanatorium! Her tearful mother, blames Providence, but had *she* done her duty?

A small baby falls into a pond and drowns; another falls off a gallery onto the sidewalk and is killed. . . . Two little innocents? . . . Perhaps, two only sons! Well? Would you expect God to baby-sit, build fences, and repair porches; while Mother listens to the radio, and Dad reads the paper or goes out for a beer?

A young mother, after four or five years of marriage, weeps from morning to night because her husband gives her no money; but drinks up his salary. Furthermore, he comes home either dead drunk, or in a towering rage. He beats his wife and even his two little children suffering from rickets—the fruits of alcoholism. Where does God come into this? When this poor woman was keeping company, she was warned that her friend drank heavily. Friends, parents, and priests counselled an immediate break, but she would not hear of it. God *could* have prevented this disaster by hamstringing the boy's and girl's liberty. But both wanted their own way! Whose fault is it?

How many trials we could spare ourselves by shunning sin! Every fault brings its own punishment:

Before taking it out on Providence when things go wrong, let us first explore our conscience and ask ourselves if it is not we who are the cause of our sufferings and difficulties? Remember, our deeds follow us! Just think of the ravages caused by pride, greed, jealousy, impurity, and drunkenness!

As for the providential happenings which make up the warp and woof of our lives—joys, trials, success, failures, sickness, death, and all that happens without our always being able to understand why—this is the way we should act:

First, we ought to remind ourselves of the elementary and basic truths: God exists; God knows past, present, and future; God can do everything; God is All-Good; God loves us: God is our Father!

Whatever happens, let us bear in mind that GOD IS ALWAYS GOOD. If we could once persuade ourselves of this truth, and live it daily, we would never complain; and would be filled with inner peace!

Alas! The moment our puny minds are unable to explain the reason for the trial we undergo, or for God's delay in answering our prayers, we rebel and no longer believe in God's goodness and providence! Furthermore, we sometimes go on to revolt and despair!

We judge things from a too human point of view. Instead of trusting utterly in our Heavenly Father who loves us and desires only our good, we are unwilling to admit that we could be mistaken.

"In everyday life," writes Fr. Dohet, S.J., "you will find a sick man who wants health, a man faced with ruin, a father involved in an important temporal affair, some unhappy mortal calling for an end to a spiritual trial. All are firmly convinced that they are in the right. In their eyes, there is no doubt as to the reasonableness of their desires, and they defy you to show that there is the least danger involved. They declare and prove to you that they want only good. Not only are they sincere, but also (looking at it from a human standpoint), they are absolutely right! Is it not self-evident that health, money, or success would bring immediate happiness to these poor folk?"

But what good would immediate happiness be to us, if we were to lose eternal happiness?

"We behave like children," continues Fr. Dohet, "who might ask their father to lend them a dangerous object—a razor, matches, etc. Would such a man hesitate a single instant? Despite the insistence of his children, despite their conviction of no danger, despite all their promises to be careful, the father would say No. He would not let himself be swayed by their pleas, and everyone would say that he was perfectly right. Furthermore, he would consent to be misunderstood by his children whom he loves, to hear himself accused by them of being 'mean,' and even of making them unhappy. He would ask only for their trust.... The father would be good for the very reason by which his children would judge him heartless and unkind. Both sides believe they are right; but which side really *is* right?" (Cf. *L'Irréprochable Providence.* p. 24.)

Very often, this is our own life history! How we ought to thank God for not having answered our imprudent prayers and requests! And how sorry we should feel for murmuring against this Good Father; who in refusing, has only our interests at heart!

When St. Paul says that "for those who love God, all things work together unto good," he excepts nothing. Everything: sickness, health, poverty, privations, betrayal, bereavement, spiritual dryness, disgust, vexations, temptations, even our sins and our serious sins which may serve to make us more humble, more grateful to God, and more indulgent toward our neighbour. Therefore, everything works to the advantage of those who love God! There is no room for discouragement!

What Christian would still want to be delivered from his trials, if he were persuaded that these very trials were able to make him a great saint; and procure for him as well as for many others, a greater happiness for all eternity? Why not make an act of faith in God's all-powerful goodness toward us?

Let us, then, whether we be in the world or in the cloister, whether we experience joy or sorrow, poverty or plenty, success or failure, at all times and in all places, keep on believing in our Father's love for us; and keep on accepting with a smile, bad weather, life's inevitable contrarieties, and the unfortunate consequences of our actions; in the persuasion that all things will work together for our greatest good, because we love God!

This is the true attitude of a loving child, who, utterly trusting in its Father, willingly submits to his will; and, knowing him to be all-wise, accepts without recrimination and even without knowing the reason, all that he wills—even his slightest wish. . . .

Who are in Heaven

237—What does "who are in Heaven" add to the word, "Father?"

The phrase, "who are in Heaven," ought to remind us that on earth we are *pilgrims* and *strangers*. We have no lasting home here below. Our true country, our everlasting home, is above, in our Father's House. There it is that Jesus, our Elder Brother, has prepared us a place. When we settle down on this earth with every modern comfort, always desiring things to be "bigger and better," we, at least, lack wisdom and bear a strange resemblance to the Rich Fool of the Gospel who believed that his life would last as long as his fortune! After a big harvest, he had torn down his too small barns to build larger ones: he had stored up his crops.... And he had said to his soul, "Soul, you have many good things laid up for many years; take your ease, eat, drink, be merry."

"You fool!" said our Heavenly Father to him, "this night do they demand your soul...and the things that you have provided, whose will they be?"

"Lay up for yourselves treasure in Heaven," our Lord recommends to us, "where neither rust nor moth consumes."

What good would it do us, indeed, to gain the whole world, and lose Heaven forever?

If someone were to say to us (and this could very well happen), "This night do they demand your soul," would we not feel some regret —for instance, for having lived selfishly and so forgotten to work for Heaven?

From the spirit of "settling down," O Lord, deliver us!

Away, then, with the miserable preoccupations of a poor world whose fleeting joys may well dazzle frivolous souls; but which leave unassuaged that hunger for full and eternal satisfactions, whose torment all men have felt!

But where is Heaven?

It can be truthfully said that Heaven is where our Lord and the Blessed Virgin are, who ascended bodily to the dwelling-place of the elect. That is one way to localize Heaven.

St. Teresa of Avila, commenting on the Our Father, teaches that our soul is a "heaven," into which we must enter to find God:

"You know, of course," she writes, "that God is everywhere. Now, wherever the King may be, his court will be; hence, wherever God is, Heaven is. You can admit as an indubitable truth, that where the Divine Majesty is to be found, all glory will be found.

"St. Augustine tells us that after long seeking God in the objects about him, he found Him at last within himself. Meditate well these words, for understanding this truth is of the utmost utility to a soul who finds recollection difficult—to know that it is not necessary for it to ascend to Heaven in order to converse with its Divine Father and to find its delight in him; nor to raise its voice in order to be heard. He is so close to us that he hears the least movement of our lips, the most intimate word. We have no need of wings to go in search of him. Let us withdraw to a solitary place and look within ourselves—there is his dwelling. Let us speak to him with great humility, but also with love, like children to their father; exposing our needs before him with confidence, telling him our troubles, imploring his aid, expressly recognizing the fact that we are not worthy to be called his children."

It is because God is not far from us that our Lord bade us beware of long prayers and counselled us not to address long speeches to God; like the heathen who think that by saying a great deal, they will be heard. "You are not to be like them. Your Heavenly Father knows well what your needs are, before you ask him." (Matt. 6:8.)

"Those souls," continues St. Teresa, "who can thus shut themselves within the little heaven of their souls, wherein dwells He who made Heaven and earth; who accustom themselves not to look at anything without, and to pray in a spot where nothing can distract their exterior senses; ought to believe that they are walking in an excellent way and that they will soon slake their thirst at the fountain of life. . . ."

The thing to do, then, is to enter our own "little church" and to close the door tight after us to everything in the world.

A MORNING PRAYER

In the morning, like good children
Who never do a thing forbidden,
In dawn freshness dipped in dew
My waking soul cries out to You.
Let my early prayer arise
Like a morning sacrifice—
While I feel less shame of me,
While from sin I still am free,
In early morning liberty.
Father, cover me all day
(Like a cloak of satin gay)
With the dawn's fresh purity!
Now so soon as my prayer end,
I shall return to haunts of men.
Mid their clamour and their din
Keep my soul from stain of sin.
Make my thoughts lofty as this hill—
Rising high, and higher still!

LOUIS LEFEBVRE

You are probably wondering what "little church" we mean. A good Sister of Providence is going to describe it for us so well that you will recognize it at once:

YOUR LITTLE CHURCH

There is a little Church I know
Not very far away.
You'll be surprised to hear of it,
Yet see it every day.
You need not walk to reach the Church—
No riddle this, but true;
Nor wonder on what street it is.
That little Church is YOU!
Is not your noble brow the tower,
Your eyes the windows bright?
Your heart the sanctuary lamp
That casts its crimson light?
Is not your voice the organ sweet
That sounds the hymn of LOVE?
Your holy thoughts the altar pure
Whence God comes from above?
Is not your soul, your precious soul,
The tabernacle white?
And your poor body not the veil
That hides him from your sight?
Your tongue the table of the Lord,
Your lips the open door?
Your prayers the tinkling of the bell,
Your humble mien the floor?
Then place your hand upon your breast
A thousand times a day,
And in your own dear little Church
Oft loving visits pay!

See how one may taste of Heaven's bliss by anticipation.

238—What are the first three petitions of the Pater Noster and to whom are they addressed?

The first three petitions are three desires, three wishes, concerning God's honour and glory.

1. Hallowed be your name!
2. Your Kingdom come!
3. Your will be done on earth as it is in Heaven!

You may notice that the Pater Noster and the Gloria offer the same structure: a prologue, a first part pertaining more particularly to God's glory; and a second part relating chiefly to our own interests.

Hallowed be your name

239—For what do we pray in the first petition of the Pater Noster?

We ask that God's name may be hallowed.

When we speak someone's name, we evoke the person who bears it and is identified with it. This is readily seen by an analysis of our feelings when names like Jesus, Judas, Mary, Satan, St. Francis of Assisi, Voltaire, St. Thérèse of the Child Jesus, etc. are brought to mind.

If the name is taken for the person himself, is it so hard to hallow God's name, when it reminds us solely of excellent things?

God! This name evokes the concept of the one necessary Being; defined as Truth, Beauty, Goodness, Omnipotence, Liberty, Eternity, Beatitude, etc.

God the Father, who is the eternal and inexhaustible source of life, Creator, Providence, Abundance, Mercy, and universal Fatherhood.

God the Son, Word of the Father, substantial Truth made flesh to speak God's words to men, to reveal the providential plan of the Father's love for even guilty men; to furnish an adequate ransom to divine justice; to nourish our lives through his subsistence in the Gospel; in the Church through his priesthood; and in the Eucharist....

God the Holy Spirit, Love of Father and Son; Love, whose property is to shed light and warmth; Love, capable of transforming a darkened soul, faltering and sinful, but contrite and sincere, into a furnace of divine love....

What richness is evoked by this name, to which none other can be compared! Hallowing this divine name, means treating it with the reverence due to holy and consecrated persons or things.... It means separating it from every name into which enters an alloy of ordinary, vitiated, imperfect, elements.

On human lips, this Name should be pronounced only as a prayer, as an expression of faith, adoration, and piety.

The Jews of the Old Testament, much more accustomed to contemplating God in his justice than in his goodness and mercy, did not dare call God by his name. When they had to name him in their ritual prayers, they would substitute the name of one of his attributes: the Almighty, the Eternal, the Most High, the Just One, the Holy One, etc.

Jesus came to liberate us from the law of fear and to place us under the Law of Love. Henceforth, we may trustfully call God by his Name and venerate him as a Father.

Now, to LIVE OUR MASS, we shall endeavour to hallow God's Name; i.e., by uttering it with so much reverence, repentance, and love; that this reverence, repentance, and love, will to some extent atone for the contempt and hatred of those who insult and curse God, instead of venerating and honouring him.

Indeed, what could be more wicked and diabolic than these satanic words which are spewed forth as it were in a steady stream against God's providence and holiness; the unfathomable malice of perverse men, victims—consciously or not—of Satan—faithfully echoing his eternal cry of furious hate.

Blasphemies of the lips, pen, attitude, and action.

The coarse blasphemy of the unrefined and unthinking, or the calculated and reasoned blasphemy of the materialistic philosopher and scholar.

The bitter and sarcastic blasphemy of the sectary and revolutionary.

The blasphemy of a life made up of indifference and tepidity, scorning God's gifts.

The blasphemy of the perjurer, of the apostate, of the impious legislator.

The permanent blasphemy of a State, of a Government, flouting God's law, and encouraging laws favouring divorce, secular schools, Communism, Jehovah Witnesses, Freemasonry, etc.

Whenever we hear or read of some such infamous blasphemy, directly insulting Almighty God, let us send up to Heaven ejaculatory prayers; such as, "Blessed be the Name of the Lord," or "My God, I love you, I adore you! I implore your pardon for the poor unfortunates, for they know not what they do. . . ." These, or similar protestations of love, will make up for the blasphemers' cry of hate; and return fitting glory to God.

240—What did St. Cyprian say about this first petition of the Pater Noster?

The holy martyr-bishop gives us the following explanation:

"It is not that we desire that God should be sanctified by our prayers: what we ask is that his name should be sanctified in us. Besides, by whom could God—who is holiness itself—be sanctified? But since he says (Lev. 20:7) 'Be holy, for I am holy;' the thing we pray for—we who have been sanctified by Baptism—is that we may persevere in the state in which we have been placed by grace.

"And we offer this prayer daily, because we need to be sanctified daily; for we sin daily. Thus, we should wash away our sins in a continuous sanctification. Now the apostle reveals that it is sanctification that God vouchsafes to grant us. 'Neither fornicators,' says he, 'nor idolators, nor adulterers, nor the effeminate, nor sodomites, nor thieves, nor the covetous, nor drunkards, nor the evil-tongued, nor the greedy, will possess the kingdom of God. And such were some of you; but you have been washed, you have been sanctified, you have been justified in the name of our Lord Jesus Christ, and in the Spirit of our God.' (I Cor. 6:9-11.)

"He says that we have been sanctified in the name of our Lord Jesus Christ, and in the Spirit of our God. Let us pray, then, that this sanctification may abide in us; and as the Lord, our Judge, warns the sinner whom he has healed and quickened, not to fall again into his past sins, lest he receive a different treatment; so do we plead day and night that God will vouchsafe to preserve in us that sanctification and life, which we receive by God's grace."

Your Kingdom come

241—What is expressed in the second petition of the Pater Noster?

In this second petition, we beseech God that his Kingdom may come.

"Your Kingdom come" does not refer to unreasoning creatures; for these creatures, deprived of liberty, necessarily obey God's orders. They remain where they have been placed, and do not depart from the law that moves them. Stars always gravitate in the same orbit. Spiders have not varied the design of their webs, and bees always follow the same recipe for making honey.

What a lesson for us! We are supposed to be more reasonable than they—yet we have long disobeyed God's law and upset the established order!

This petition of the Pater Noster *envisages God's reign in every heart.*

We are begging God to reign over individuals, over families, over states—over the whole world!

God is a King of Love, and it is through love that he wills to reign.

For nineteen centuries we have repeated this prayer: "Your kingdom come!" Then how is it that the true God should be unknown to so many millions? How is it that he has so few friends who open their hearts wide to his burning love?

Let us first ask ourselves just how sincere we are ourselves, when we tell God to reign in our hearts through his love.

Are we not the first sometimes by our dislikes, our resentments, our suspicions, our jealousy, our detractions, our slanders, our attachments, and selfishness, to close our hearts to Love?

Just so long as we, who have certainly received more light and divine favour than many others, are lax in the service of the King of Kings, and rebellious to his Law of Love, there will always be numberless societies and individuals to prolong the cry of the rebellious angels: *"Non serviam!* I will not serve!"

Just so long as we are lacking in generosity and true love, there will always be multitudes to repeat the horrible blasphemy of the Jews confronting Christ in the praetorium of Pilate. "We will not have this Man rule over us! . . . His blood be upon us and upon our children!"

This is an age of social corruption. God has been banished from the home; the family is shaken by an avalanche of licentiousness and immorality; the "best people" have already been visibly contaminated, and stricken with the malady of an unbridled sensualism. The Christian woman who still considers herself pious, dresses, dances, and questions authority as if she had never been baptized; even daring to criticize the anathemas of the Pope and bishops against the pagan audacity of her manners and dress, and of her worldly amusements. . . .

Are you not struck at night by the sight—profiled in a maze of bright lights—of those theatres within which every crime is sanctioned? . . . Watch the human torrents that stream out from amusement and dance halls, from picture palaces and night clubs—and count their numbers if you can! . . . Count those who queue up for hours before the doors of branch stores of the Liquor Commission to purchase the poisoned beverage which assassinates joy and kills both body and soul! Alas! Numerous are the Christian men and women who make a practice of attending these scenes of moral laxness, and who applaud these antichristian spectacles which today's "good society" tolerates as necessary pastimes in modern-day living!

Innumerable are these wordly-minded Catholics, in open rebellion against God's law! In the name of "progress," of "civilization," and "fashion," they have sapped the foundations of the sanctuary of the home; they have profaned, and even sacrilegiously broken, the bond of Christian marriage! They have debased and frightfully "humanized" two things that God had ennobled and made almost divine—love and fruitfulness!

These unfortunate souls, adrift, rush headlong along the road to ruin, damning themselves for all eternity, because they will have none of God's dominion over them!

For such revolts, reparation is required. Our Bishops have recently asked us to lead lives of self-denial and mortification. What is more, they have told us to prepare for martyrdom! These are grave times. . . .

What can we do to fulfill the desire we express in the second petition of the Pater Noster—"Your Kingdom come"?

We can start by letting God be King of our lives, by placing ourselves wholly at his service.

First, we will let God rule over our bodies, by using their senses, and members only in conformity with the intentions of God, who created the body to be the servant of the soul, the temple of divinity, and the living ciborium of Christ, his Son.

We will let him rule over our minds, by living with intense faith and submitting our judgment to his laws and Providence.

We will let him rule over our hearts, by never putting an obstacle in the way of his love—for it is through love that he will reign over us. This will mean the sacrifice of all friendships not God-centered and God-directed. It will furthermore call for the generous surrender, at whatever cost, of all that our hearts may be attached to, that runs counter to his will.

We will let him rule over our wills, by our perfect obedience to his representatives. The third petition of the Pater Noster, "Your will be done," will tell us just what is meant by this reign of God over us.

Before taking up the study of this third petition, let us make reparation for offenses; especially those of Christians, and obtain peace for disoriented mankind, by reciting together with our family this act of reparation to Christ the King:

ACT OF CONSECRATION OF FAMILIES

O most Sacred Heart of Jesus, you revealed to Blessed Margaret Mary your desire to reign over Christian families. Behold, in order to please you, we stand before you this day, to proclaim your full sovereignty over our family. We desire henceforth to live your life; we desire that the virtues to which you have promised peace on earth, may flower in the bosom of our family. We desire to keep far from us the spirit of the world, which you have condemned.

You are King of our minds by the simplicity of our faith. You are King of our hearts by our love for you alone; with which our hearts are on fire, and whose flame we shall keep alive by frequently receiving the Holy Eucharist.

Be pleased, O Sacred Heart, to preside over our gathering together; to bless our spiritual and temporal affairs; to ward off all annoyance from us; to hallow our joys and comfort our sorrows. If any of us has ever been so unfortunate as to displease you, grant that he may remember, O Heart of Jesus, that you are full of goodness and mercy toward the repentant sinner. And when the hour of separation strikes, and death enters our family circle; whether we go or whether we stay, we shall bow humbly before your eternal decrees. This shall be our consolation, to remember that the day will come, when our entire family, once more united in Heaven, shall be able to sing of your glory and goodness forever.

Yes, Lord, establish here your dwelling, that we may live by your love, and in your company—we who proclaim you to be our King, for we desire no other than you.

Glory to the Heart of Jesus, our King and our Father!

YOUR WILL BE DONE

242—What desire do we express in the third petition of the Pater Noster?

We express the desire that God's will may be done on earth as it is in Heaven.

243—Are we sincere in formulating this third petiton of the Pater Noster?

How many prayers we recite paying no attention to the words our lips murmur from habit!

Of what worth are such prayers, so often belied by our conduct?

Péguy once wrote to a friend: "Just think! I have gone almost two years without saying the Our Father! And this is why. It is my opinion that a man ought to be sincere and really want what he prays for. Now in this prayer, there is one thing I could not accept, 'Father, your will be done'! Since I didn't want God's will, rather than offer useless prayers, I kept still."

Yes, Lord, how many useless prayers! How many beautiful formulas learned by heart and mechanically reeled off, often for hours on end (to the point of using up all our saliva!), but with the soul taking no part in them.

Let us try saying the Act of Charity with a pause after each word:

"O my God, I love you." (Do I?)
"Above all things." (Do I?)
"With all my heart." (Do I?)
"And I love my neighbour as myself!" (Do I?)

Picture a Christian kneeling in prayer. Listen to him!

"O God, I am a miserable sinner, I am jealous, I am selfish, I am nothing, I am no good. . . ."

Now just supposing that one of us kneeling beside him were to hear him, and then go up and say to him, "Brother! you're a miserable sinner! You're selfish! You're jealous!" (What a fine reception *we'd* get!)

What a pity! If a man does not live his Mass, his devotional life is not lived either.

A very frequent error consists in confusing the practice of an evangelical and Christian life with the practice of private devotions; and in measuring the extent of the one, by the multiplicity of the other. A person deems himself a good Catholic because he has accumulated a stack of long prayers, of rosaries upon rosaries, of novenas upon novenas; but without ever taking the trouble to discipline his "inner self," and make it tally with his mumbled prayers! Alas, there are many among us who could take to themselves this tirade of Christ to the Pharisees: "This people honours me with their lips, but their heart is far from me!"

Every time we say the Our Father, we pray to God that his name be hallowed; when perhaps because of us, his name is mocked. . . . Besides, are not these prayers, when said so thoughtlessly and insincerely, an irreverence toward the God to whom they are addressed?

We desire his Kingdom to "come," and we do little or nothing to extend his reign of love in and around us!

We continue, "Your will be done!" but do we sincerely have the intention of accepting God's will when we say these words?

We know that "God's will is for us to become saints"! Now Tertiaries saying their Office, and those saying the Rosary daily, have repeated twelve and fifteen times respectively this petition of the Our Father, "Your will be done"! And perhaps after many years of daily saying this sublime prayer, one still discovers in these people a secret pride, attachment to Self, selfishness, ill will toward their neighbour, rivalry in good works, sometimes tenacious and not inactive grudges, an extremely thin-skinned and touchy susceptibility that gets them "all wrought up" over trifles, with a loss of inner peace; a voluntary nursing of their ill humour, discouragement, revolt in trial, etc.

Again, when we pray, *are we sincere?*

244—What is involved in my asking to do God's will?

Asking to do God's will, implies asking for the grace or means of accomplishing, that will. We know that of ourselves we can do nothing, unless it be to sin. Let us possess a keen awareness, then, of our state of spiritual mendicity; and when we pray the Our Father, let us beg most fervently for the necessary aid to carry out God's will. The task of our sanctification is one that takes two to accomplish—God and ourselves.

Again, asking God that we may do his will, means asking God to let us know what he wants us to do; so that we may—with his help —do our very best.

St. Francis of Assisi had a life-long burning desire to carry out all God's will, both of counsel and precept, to the letter. "He desired to know," his first biographer, Celano, tells us: "what in his person would or could be most pleasing to the King of Glory. With all the zeal and devotion of his soul, he sought to know by what means, step, or desire, he could be perfectly united to God's will and plan. All his life, this was his whole philosophy and his chief ambition; and he asked of learned and unlearned, of perfect and imperfect alike, how he might enter into the way of truth and achieve a higher goal. For he had tasted the sweetness, the grace, and goodness of the God of Israel toward upright hearts who seek him in pure simplicity and in true purity."

Doing God's will is most important, for it is the only way to be sure of loving God and of becoming holy. This will be seen in the next question.

245—Show the importance of doing God's will "at all times and in all places."

To understand its importance and grandeur, it suffices to consider the extraordinary effect produced by Mary's *fiat* at the Annunciation! This sacerdotal word uttered by the Blessed Virgin, submissive to God's will—like the words of Consecration pronounced by the priest at Mass —made God descend on earth! "And the Word was made flesh, and dwelt among us." (John 1:14.)

Thus, in obedience to God's will, Jesus gives himself to us; he is incarnated anew in us in proportion to our conformity to his will, and we become for him as an "extra" human nature.

Doing God's will at all times and in all places, is the only way for me to tend toward perfection; to save my soul; and to achieve sanctity.

As we have said above, our sanctification is a task for two. God's action, plus our co-operation, is needed—the continual agreement of our will with the divine will.

The man who works with God profits from every instant; while he who turns away from him falls, or else wearies himself in misguided activity.

How many works appear complete, and for this sole motive are void! Not having been done with God (despite the effort they cost us); they will vanish in the light of eternity, like morning mists before the noonday sun.

If we would ascend to the summit of perfection—and we should all have this ambition—let us do God's will oftener and better each day. We shall rise to the extent that our submission, or better, our conformity to the divine will, becomes more universal in its object, more exact in its execution, more supernatural in its motives, more perfect as regards the disposition of our wills.

Read the life of Jesus, of Mary, of all the saints; and we shall soon realize that in this conformity, and not elsewhere, lies the secret of sanctity.

Do you want proof of your love for God? You may be sure that you love him, if you always do his will.

Loving means the merging of two wills into one. Love unified—this is the secret of the divine friendship. "If you love me," says Jesus, "keep my commandments."

This is essential. Many pose as saints, who are blinded by their stubbornness and enmeshed in the net of self-will!

"Everybody," said St. Francis de Sales, "envisions perfection in his own way. Some make it consist in the austerity of their clothing, others in that of their eating, or in alms-giving, or in frequenting the

Sacraments, or in meditating. And one and all deceive themselves, taking the means for the end, the accessories for the principal, and often, the shadow for the substance. As for myself, I know of no other perfection than to love God with all one's heart, and one's neighbour as one's self."

It is to be noted that the means pointed out by St. Francis are not to be tossed aside. Far from it. But it is an error to identify holiness with these means; which may be useful or necessary to some, but sometimes harmful to others.

Thus Mass and daily Communion are two excellent means of sanctification. But these two means would be harmful to the person who would make use of them to the detriment of the duties of his state in life. You can readily understand that a mother with young children to care for, or with a person ill in bed, will not sanctify herself by leaving the house to go to church to hear Mass or receive Holy Communion. Why? Because God's will is manifestly opposed to it. And just as soon as a person runs counter to God's will, charity either diminishes or disappears altogether; as the case may be. And without charity, there can be no sanctification!

St. Paul's beautiful eulogy on charity in the thirteenth chapter of First Corinthians belongs here:

"If I should speak with the tongues of men and of angels, but do not have charity," (St. Paul could just as well have said," If I do not do God's will,") "I have become as sounding brass or a tinkling cymbal.

"And if I have prophecy, and know all mysteries and all knowledge, and if I have all faith, so as to remove mountains; yet do not have charity, I am nothing.

"And if I distribute all my goods to feed the poor, and if I deliver my body to be burned, yet do not have charity, it profits me nothing. . . ."

246—What authors deal with the important question of the surrender of our will to God's?

Their number is legion. The following are the principal authors consulted:

St. Bonaventure: *His Works.*
Saint-Jure: *Connaissance de l'amour du Fils de Dieu, N.S.J.C.*
Rodriguez: *Christian Perfection.*

Lehodey: *Holy Abandonment.*
Gay: *Vie et vertus chrétiennes* (Christian life and virtue).
Caussade: *Abandonment.*
St. François de Sales: *Love of God.*
St. Alphonsus de Liguori: *Treatise of the Will of God.*
Graef: *Yes, Father.*
Lekeux: *Holiness is for Everyone.*

The various "lives" of the saints, in which examples and illustrations abound, etc.

247—How are we to recognize God's will?

There are two ways whereby God shows us what he wants us to do:

1. God's manifest will.
2. God's hidden will.

1. *By God's manifest will,"* we mean that God causes us to know clearly and in advance the truths which we ought to believe, the reward for which we should hope, the punishment we should fear, the Commandments we ought to observe, and the Counsels he desires us to follow.

God's manifest will, then, comprises, in résumé, the Commandments of God and the Church, the duties of our state in life, the inspirations of grace, and, for religious, obedience to the evangelical Counsels, as well as the Rule which they have promised to observe.

The great advantage the religious has over the simple layman, who is himself his only guide, is readily seen. For obedience detaches and purifies by the thousand and one renunciations it imposes; and even more, through the surrender of judgment and will. For self-will, according to St. Alphonsus, is "the ruin of virtue, the source of every evil, the sole door leading to sin and imperfection, a demon of the worst species, the tempter's favourite weapon against religious, the torturer of its slaves, and Hell anticipated." And St. Bonaventure tells us that "all the perfection of the religious consists in the abdication of his own will. This renunciation is of such value that it equals martyrdom. While the executioner's axe lops off the head of his victim; the sword of obedience immolates to God the will, which is the 'head' of the soul."

All this is called *God's manifest will,* because God clearly signifies and manifests what he wills and expects of us.

Therefore, we should submit ourselves to his will without a moment's hesitation.

If we have, in passing, let drop a hint as to the security and great advantages enjoyed by the religious under obedience; we hasten to add that the faithful may, if they will, benefit up to a certain point by some of these privileges. For the Third Order offers the advantages of religious life to people in the world: a postulancy, a novitiate, a profession, and a rule of life: all tending toward perfection.

Thus, even a person living in the world, may find it relatively simple to know God's manifest will and even to do it—provided he make use of the means!

Assuredly God wills:

1. That we keep his Commandments.
2. That we avoid serious sin; and so far as possible, even venial sin.
3. That we correct our faults.
4. That we faithfully perform the duties of our state in life.

The will of God is further manifested in the special rule of life mapped out by the individual for disposing of his free time. And whoever tends toward perfection can scarcely do without such a rule; which should receive the approval of an experienced director.

Finally, God's will is manifested by the voice of those in authority over us: the Church, the Government, parents, employers, and superiors. Whenever a doubt arises as to the morality of an order, the person should pray, think, and seek counsel.

2. *God's hidden will.* Again, God's will is revealed to us through circumstances; that is, by everything that happens to us: joy, trials, illness, success, failure, affliction, consolation, births, deaths, etc.

This manner employed by God to manifest his will and dispose of us in accordance with his good pleasure, is technically called, "God's hidden will."

In these providential happenings, we ought to see God's loving plan to purify and perfect us for our own good.

What God requires of us in all these circumstances is the submission born of patience; or better still, of love.

We shall see farther on, how we should behave in these various circumstances of life.

248—Please give a few examples illustrating the state of the soul that is submissive to the God's will.

A person who is really submissive to God's will, practices what is known as "holy indifference"; i.e. that person's ideas, desires, and tastes are not riveted to any object. He thinks, desires, and loves whatever God wants him to think, desire, and love; and he is ready to change whatever he is doing at the slightest indication of the divine will.

Holy indifference is not insensibility; and still less, apathy. On the contrary, *it presupposes great generosity and great faith.*

With this in mind, the comparisons which follow will be better understood:

The soul that is really submissive to God's will resembles a scale in perfect equilibrium, ever ready to incline to the divine will.

Again, it is like a formless liquid, which assumes the form of its container. Put it in ten different vases, and it will assume ten different shapes—and that, as soon as it is poured into the vase.

It likewise resembles a blank sheet of paper on which God may write what he will.

Or it may be compared to any rough material, such as marble, plaster, stone, and the like; and like them, it is equally disposed to receive whatever form the artist has in mind.

If the artist is to achieve his masterpiece, it is essential that the inert matter—the block of marble—should let itself be carved.... We are all "blocks of marble" in God's hands. What should be our behaviour in all this? Richard Graef, in his book, *Yes, Father,* supplies the answer:

"In each of us there is a hidden saint, as the likeness of Christ that a sculptor wishes to carve is hidden in the block of unfinished marble. The artist is the only one who sees this figure; and all that he needs is to remove with his mallet and chisel all that is useless, so that the figure may appear. It all sounds very simple, and yet only the artist is able to transform the block into a masterpiece.

"Just as the sculptor envisions his statue in the marble block, so does God see his image in us. He made us in his image—but sin ruined his masterpiece. Through Baptism or the Sacrament of Penance, that image has been restored; but its features need to be ever more sharply defined. For a masterpiece is to be created, the greatest and most beautiful conceivable; since it is to be conformed to the image of his Son." (Rom. 8:29.) Our good will alone will not suffice for this gigantic task; the Divine Artist must needs tackle it, and there is much for him to do. When he created the first man, he had only to fashion the slime of the earth. Here he must work with a much more resistant mass, for sin and passion have hardened man's heart. The mallet and chisel will be required; and we must have the courage to say with the poet, 'Smite, O Divine Sculptor! I am but a block of marble!'

"Smite, O Divine Sculptor! For all that is useless must be chiselled away. Self must go. Now God intervenes unceasingly in our lives; and to the degree that we consent to all that he sends or permits, the divine features stand out, and that which is human disappears. Who is capable of describing the love with which God gives himself over to this task? He sculptures each individual as if he were the only person in His 'studio' —as if, from all eternity, God had nothing else to do but to transform him into a masterpiece worthy of Himself!

"I am a block of marble." Because of that, I have no right to hinder the Artist in his work. 'Martha, Martha, how many cares and troubles you have! But only one thing is necessary.' [Knox.] Keep calm, talk less, don't get so excited. 'For not everyone who says to me, "Lord, Lord," shall enter the Kingdom of Heaven; but he who does the will of my Father in Heaven.' Why worry, and assume so many burdens, when God wants to make our task his own? All that we have to do is to let God act, while we consent and obey in all humility, and abandon ourselves to God's hidden will. God will do the rest. If we ourselves undertake this work, it will never turn out a masterpiece. Man spoiled it the first time, under pretext of becoming like God. We know what happened —the divine image was almost obliterated. But man was none the wiser for that. We never cease to impede divine action. The more freedom we give God to act, because, regardless of the cost, we keep still under his hand, the greater will be the resultant masterpiece; the more swiftly and more successfully will the work of the Divine Artist go on; and the more perfect will be its resemblance to the Prototype.

"Smite, O Divine Sculptor! God detaches us from everything—piece by piece, and instant by instant—if we let him cut. His chisel is so penetrating, that it extends 'even to the division of soul and spirit, of joints also and marrow.' (Heb. 4:12.) It is a continual death. Fortunately, we do not know at the beginning all the things from which we must be separated, or we should never have the courage to start. Often, we are tempted to feel sorry for ourselves, as if we were marching in our own funeral procession! Death appears sweeter to us than life. And yet, however painful this 'death' may seem, we know that it is the prelude to a life of peace and joy. The happiness merited, the beatitude attained, will make us forget all our distress. 'Your sorrow shall be changed into joy.' (John 16:20.) 'All discipline seems for the present to be a matter not for joy, but for grief; but afterward it yields the most peaceful fruit of justice to those who have been exercised by it.' (Heb. 12, 11.)

"Everything would turn out for the best, if only we would give God a free hand. Let us keep tabs on ourselves to see if we are always 'at attention' before God, and snap back into 'position.'

"Smite, O Divine Sculptor! I am your block of marble!"

249—What virtues are required to enable us to conform to God's will?

The practice of holy abandonment or conformity to the will of God, supposes a certain acquired habit of interior life; based on faith, humility, detachment, obedience, and love of God.

To attain this, we must start by doing away with negligence, dissipation, and attachments—with everything deliberately opposed to grace. For the road leading to conformity with God is hard and rugged, and that is why so few attain it. We become discouraged at the outset. But the first steps are the hardest. Once we have wholeheartedly entered upon this way, we find God, and have no further desire to look back. Thus when someone asked Tauler where he had found God, he replied, "Where I left Self behind; and where I found Self, it was there I lost God."

Humility and obedience are twin virtues, absolutely necessary in order to do God's will in everything; hence to accept patiently and supernaturally, contradictions, humiliations, and bodily and spiritual trials.

Without humility and obedience, the imperfect soul is totally unprepared to accept the divine will. "Whether the trial come from God or man," writes Lehodey, "unless the person feels that it is deserved or needed, he poses as one 'misunderstood'; adopts the air of a martyr, and either revolts or murmurs."

250—Are there degrees to this doing of God's will?

Certainly.

Msgr. Ambroise Leblanc, O.F.M., in his splendid volume, *La fécondité du sacrifice,* deals with this question most happily in the chapter entitled, "Les trois croix." (The Three Crosses.)

The author shows us three possible attitudes to take as regards suffering—those of the three crucified:

1. Suffering rejected—the Bad Thief.
2. Suffering accepted—the Good Thief.
3. Suffering desired—Jesus Christ.

(We refer the reader to this book, which should be read in its entirety.)

Basing his conclusions on the degree of generosity with which we accept God's will, Rodriguez recognizes three degrees:

"*First degree*: Instead of desiring and loving contradictions and afflictions, the person avoids them wherever possible. Nonetheless, he would rather endure them, than commit sin to avoid them. This is the lowest rung of the ladder, the first step to conformity—the simple performance of one's strict duty. For it is possible to be afflicted by an evil, to suffer and feel sorry for oneself in the grip of illness, to bewail the death of friends or relatives, and still be resigned to God's will.

"*Second degree.* Although the person neither desires nor prays for pain and suffering, nevertheless, when these do arrive, he willingly accepts and endures them; because he knows that these pains and sufferings are part of God's plan. Here there is a love of affliction out of love for God; and this it is which serves to distinguish this degree from the preceding. Once this point of resignation is attained, there is no trial so painful that one would not consent to accept it; not only with patience, but with a certain joy. In the first degree, the person suffers patiently; in the second, he smiles at suffering and eagerly accepts it as a guest from God.

"*Third degree.* In this degree—the most perfect—not only does the person gladly accept and suffer, out of love for God, all the pains God sends him; but, in an outburst of love, goes, so to speak, to meet them. He rejoices at their coming, because he knows that they come from God's hand and are the effect of his adorable will."

St. Paul had attained this third degree when he said, "We rejoice in tribulations!"

St. Bernard has an identical classification, based on the three theological virtues: "The beginner, moved by faith and fear, patiently endures Christ's Cross; the proficient, moved by hope, willingly bears it; he who is consummate in charity, or who is perfect, embraces it henceforth with ardour."

With the help of these "degrees," we can get some idea of our spiritual growth.

251—How should we behave in different situations of life: bad weather, financial loss, our surroundings, illness, and death?

After having seen, in general, what should be our attitude as regards God's will, let us cast a swift glance over the ordinary situations under which we live; so that, being better informed, we may the more easily conform ourselves joyously to the divine will.

1. *God's will and the weather*

Listen to Fr. St. Jure: "We ought to conform our will to that of God in those natural things, that are beyond our control: heat, cold, wind, hail, storms, thunder, lightning, pestilence, famine, in a word, all inclement weather, and the disorder of the elements. We ought to be pleased with whatever kind of weather God sends; and not endure it with impatience and anger, as people have the habit of doing when it is not to their liking. We must not say, 'What terrible weather!' or employ other terms which show how vexed and displeased we are. We ought to want the kind of weather we have, for God made it; and say with the three children in the fiery furnace of Babylon: 'Cold and heat, ice and snow, lightnings and clouds, bless the Lord; praise and glorify him forever!' These creatures do so unceasingly, through their obedience to God and their doing of his most holy will. In the same way, we ought to bless and glorify Him with them. Now to check these unjust feelings and unbridled words, we ought to think that if this weather inconveniences us, it is helpful to another; that if it hinders our plans, it furthers those of our neighbour; if it is not good for a part, it is useful for the whole. And should it be otherwise, is it not enough for us that it should always be good for God's glory; since it is according to his will and pleasure?"

Think this over on your next excursion, hike, or picnic!

2. *God's will and financial reverses*

"Because you were pleasing to God," said the angel to Tobias, "it was necessary for you to be tried by temptation." "Did not the Christ have to suffer these things before entering into his glory?" "The disciple is not above his Master."

These inspired texts supply the key to the mystery of our crosses and help us to bear them joyfully after Him who is the Way, the Truth, and the Life.

Someone asked St. Ignatius one day the shortest way to perfection and Heaven. The saint replied, "To suffer much adversity for love of Jesus Christ." One great adversity leads us to Heaven; several adversities guide us there more swiftly and further along the road.

One should never complain of poverty or financial losses; because the greatest service God can render a person is to detach him from that which is harmful to his sanctification, namely, riches.

According to St. Bonaventure, "the abundance of temporal goods is a sort of bird-lime which clings to the soul and keeps it from flying to God."

You know that riches incite us to seek comfort, to become tepid in God's service, to flee every mortification, to lead worldly and dissipated lives, to seek honour and glory, to rivet ourselves to earth, and so forget Heaven.

Therefore, "when inopportune events impoverish us, to a greater or lesser extent, such as storm, flood, drought, theft, lawsuits; that is the real time to practice poverty; serenely accepting our losses, and patiently and steadfastly adjusting ourselves to this impoverishment." And St. Francis de Sales continues: "Do not complain, then, of your poverty; for one complains only of what displeases. If poverty displeases you, you are not poor in spirit but rich in attachment to riches. Do not be distressed at not receiving all the help you require; for desiring to be poor without any inconvenience, is to desire the honour of poverty and the convenience of riches."

Blessed are the poor in spirit, for theirs is the kingdom of Heaven!

3. *God's will and our environment*

The world rings with lamentations. The number of those believing themselves victims of impossible situations, and who pose as martyrs, is legion. Everything would be better, they think, if they lived somewhere else.... Would they be happier transplanted in some earthly paradise? Not always—for they would find *themselves* there! Happiness is to be found within oneself.

The story of the man who wanted to change his cross should give them food for thought.

It seems that among the many people discontented with their crosses, one unhappy man used to complain to God for giving him the cross he had, instead of some other. One night he dreamed that he was in an immense workshop, strewn about with crosses representing every form of human suffering. He laid down his own cross at the door. Our Lord, the Divine Workman, was there, hewing out crosses of various weights and dimensions.

"And what brings you here?" asked the Lord.

"O Lord! This cross you gave me is very heavy! I know that we have to have a cross, if we are to follow you and go to Heaven. But the cross *I* bear is crushing me! Couldn't you please give me some *other* cross?"

"Here, heaped together, are all the crosses which, in my mercy, are designed to open to men the gates of Paradise. Since you find your cross too heavy, then choose another better suited to your strength."

The man was both content and fearful at the sight of this multitude of crosses which had been borne since the world began, and which are to be borne until the end of time. So he set to work inspecting, measuring, and "hefting" each one.... He tried one—but it was longer and heavier than he had thought. Then another, but it had sharp edges. Then a third one. But it was full of knot-holes, it was badly hewn, not well planed, and full of splinters. It seemed hard to choose!

There was the cross of remorse—the cross of jealousy—the cross of ingratitude—the cross of divided families—the cross of drink—the cross of poverty—the cross of humiliations—the cross of illness—the cross of lost vocations—the cross of calumny—the cross of betrayal—the cross of being forsaken... the cross of death....

The man tried every one of the crosses, and then laid each one aside, saying, "Not *that* one!" And he began to despair. "Dear Lord! *Must* I choose one?"

"No cross, no crown," replied Jesus.

The poor man retraced his steps then, and began a meticulous re-examination. Finally his glance lit upon a cross near the door that was smaller than the rest. He lifted it and sighed with joy. "At last! I have found a cross that suits me! True, it *is* a mite heavy, but I can easily manage it!"

"Take a good look at it," said the Divine Hewer of Crosses.

The man examined his cross more closely, and discovered that it was the self-same cross that he had laid down at the door when he came in—the cross that our Lord in his mercy had given him from all eternity, so that he might win Heaven!... The cross that he had found too heavy, thinking that others had less to suffer than he!

So the man hoisted the cross once more onto his shoulders and thenceforth carried it without a murmur.

Is not this our story too?

Have we not told our Lord that we are sometimes tried beyond our strength? That others are happy, while we——! How ungrateful we are to accuse the Good Lord of injustice! What presumption and imprudence to envy the lot of others!

Let us clearly understand, then, that it is by accepting the cross and living where God wants us to live, in the situation that pleases him, that we shall more readily attain to holiness in peace and joy.

Yes, let us bloom where we have been sown.

The crosses that come from our relatives are to be borne like the rest. We must learn to accept them!

In the midst of a group, a family, a community, a large share of our happiness or unhappiness depends on the way we get along with others.

Our Lord's recommendation: "Do to others, as you would have them do to you," and this other that completes it, "Do not do to others what you would not have them do to you," ought to be graven in our minds and hearts, that we may sow joy and love about us.

When we meet anyone, we ought to ask ourselves, "What can I do to help him and make him happy?"

Naturally, we sometimes run across cranky, unsociable people; who make life miserable for all around them; a splendid opportunity furnished by God himself for cultivating a bouquet of solid virtue: charity, patience, meekness, faith, hope, humility, kindness, self-denial—what heaped-up riches for eternity!

We find in the life of St. Thérèse of the Child Jesus, splendid examples of generous abandonment to God's will, in accepting community life, under circumstances particularly painful to nature!

Listen to her:

"For a long time, during meditation, I was near a Sister who was always rattling her rosary or some other object. Perhaps I was the only one who heard her. It would be impossible to say how much this sound annoyed me. So I tried to like this unpleasant little noise. Instead of attempting not to hear it (which would have been impossible), I listened with fixed attention, as if to a delightful concert; and my meditation (which was *not* the 'prayer of quietude') was spent in offering this 'concert' to Jesus."

And another time:

"I was in the laundry with a Sister who was washing handkerchiefs, and who splashed me continuously with dirty water. . . . I thought that I was very foolish to refuse the treasures which were being offered to me with such generosity, and I took care not to show the displeasure I felt. On the contrary, I made a great effort to receive a great deal of dirty water. So well did my efforts succeed, that at the end of half an hour, I had really acquired a taste for this new sort of 'aspersions'; and I promised myself to come back as often as possible to this favoured spot, where such great riches were distributed without cost."

This sounds like a passage from the *Fioretti,* giving us a description of "perfect joy"!

It is especially in the infirmary that Thérèse appears heroic. Toward the close of her life, she said, "If I had my life to live over, the office of Sister Infirmarian would be my choice. . . . I should want to pass under the windows of the sick Sisters, on purpose to give them a chance to call me and request some service."

Let us take a glimpse of her as she assisted cranky Sister St. Peter!

"I knew how hard (or rather, how impossible) it was to please this poor invalid. However, I did not want to miss such a good opportunity. So I humbly offered to help her. This meant following the good Sister while holding onto her belt. I did this as gently as possible; but if she chanced to stumble, she immediately thought I was holding her wrong, and that she was about to fall. 'Sister! You're going too fast! I'll hurt myself!' If I tried then to lead her more gently: 'Sister! Follow me! I don't feel your hand. If you let go of me, I'll fall! Oh, I knew you were too young to help me."

"Finally, with no further incident, we would arrive at the refectory. There, other difficulties would crop up. I had to install the poor invalid in her seat (skillfully, so as not to hurt her), then fold back her sleeves, always in a certain manner."

In spite of all the tyrannical crotchets of this sick Sister, this is what St. Thérèse said:

"When I led Sister St. Peter, it was with so much love, that it would have been impossible for me to do better if I had been leading our Lord himself!"

Another model in this sort of trial is St. Jane de Chantal.

"Widowed at the age of twenty-eight, she was ordered by her father-in-law to come with her four children to live with him. Jane at once foresaw the bitterness of the chalice she was about to quaff; for she knew the old baron's character, the disorders of his house, and those of his conduct which were greater still. This dour old man, before whom all else must bend, had let himself come under the sway of a servant; who commanded the castle as its mistress, dissipated her master's property, and made herself generally disliked. For more than seven years, the saint was to be treated as an outsider in the family circle. Her views were never consulted on anything, and she had no right to express an opinion. She was to be, so to speak, under the thumb of an insolent inferior; who did not even refrain from insults. It was her sorrow to see this servant's children put on the same footing as her own—or often, even given the preference. Jane was seized with indignation, and her blood boiled; especially in the beginning. But she stifled these cries of nature; and to such insolence opposed only mildness and cheerfulness. She even attained to this degree of heroism—that of caring for the servant's children like her own; and rendering them the most humble services with her own hands. And what was the secret of her victory? Solely occupied with her great task—the conversion of her father-in-law and the unworthy servant—her desire was to conquer both by the power of meekness. No effort or sacrifice was capable of deterring her. She profited from every available opportunity for doing them good, and no affront or violence was ever able to lessen her respect or discourage her patience.

"To this elevated motive, which sustained her for seven years in a life of such heroism; another, no less determining, was added. Jane was naturally a little haughty. In her blood, on her father's side, there was something of pride and imperiousness; that, at whatever price, she meant to put down. The opportunity of becoming humble that offered itself through humiliations, seemed ideal. And Jane succeeded in her efforts, beyond the power of words to express. It was in this harsh school —better than in the severest of novitiates—that God caused her to acquire that rare humility and perfect obedience, soon to make of her, under the guidance of St. Francis de Sales, the instrument which would accomplish great things." (Cf. Lehodey, *Holy Abandonment.)*

For they founded the Order of the Visitation, to which the Sacred Heart was pleased to reveal his secrets.

Similar occurrences are to be found in the lives of all the saints, We might have cited the adventures of the holy Curé of Ars with his viçar! Or the love of St. Francis of Assisi for rebellious lepers, or for the discontented prisoner in the Perugian prison, etc.

As a follow-up to these splendid examples, here is the advice Fr. Caussade gives to a soul having to contend with the same kind of individual:

1. "*Support patiently the involuntary revolt* that you will feel at this person's conduct, just as you would support an attack of fever or a headache. For your antipathy is an inner fever with its chills and hot flashes. How crucifying, humiliating, and painful all this is; and consequently, how meritorious and sanctifying!

2. "*Never speak of this person,* as others, perhaps, may do; but always speak well of him; for there is good in him. And who is there with no evil in him? Who in this world is perfect? Perhaps without willing or thinking it, you 'try' the other person, more than God tries you through him! 'God often polishes one diamond with another,' said Fenelon.

3. "*When you have committed a fault, pick yourself up at once,* humbling yourself; without voluntary exasperation either against the other person or yourself; without turmoil, sadness, or disquietude. Atoned for in this way, our faults become profitable and advantageous. It is by means of these little annoyances and daily failings, that God keeps us little and truly humble of heart.

4. "*In addition to this, do not trouble yourself about anything, beyond the degree that you are obligated by duty.* When you have done your duty, do not worry about anything else. Do not even think about it, except before God in prayer. Abandon everything to God's keeping. The one thing really important is for us to be wholly God's and to save our souls."

There you have it! As you see, it is all very simple!

From the very beginning of this book, we have not ceased to centre the Christian's whole life on the Mass; so as to help people to LIVE THEIR MASS. This method of envisaging the Mass permits of multiple developments as we study its prayers. Certain passages should be dewlt on more at length. Thus, this third petition of the Our Father, "your will be done" which is (as we explained in Q. 12) the essence of Christ's Sacrifice, causes us to LIVE OUR MASS INTENSELY. For the little extra time spent on it, each one will assuredly derive great profit, and the idea we are seeking to convey, will—we trust!—sink in more deeply.

252—How should the untalented, or those afflicted with physical deformity, behave as regards God's will?

One thing certain is that it is not talent nor beautiful bodies that further the sanctification of our souls. Sometimes, these natural advantages may even prove an obstacle.

A talented person or one fair as the dawn, unless very humble, has a greater tendency than another less favoured by nature, to become self-centered; and to take credit for the success or popularity he or she enjoys. From here to forgetfulness of God is only a step.

The logical conclusion is, that if we are talented, we ought to thank God; without neglecting to make use of our talents, not for our own advantage, but for God's glory alone. If, on the other hand, we are not talented, *again we ought to thank God,* in the conviction that our chances for sanctification are greater here than in the first instance.

This brings to mind the delightful dialogue between Blessed Brother Giles, Franciscan, and the Seraphic Doctor, St. Bonaventure:

"What!" exclaimed the holy lay brother, "an uneducated person can love God just as much as the most learned Doctor?"

"Yes, Brother. Even an ignorant old woman can love God just as much or more than a Doctor of theology."

And the holy brother, in a transport of joy, rushed into the garden and began to shout: "Come, simple and unlearned men! Come, poor and ignorant women, and love our Blessed Lord! You can love him just as much as—and more than—Brother Bonaventure and the most learned theologians!"

In the unequal distribution of talent and physical advantages, as in everything else, *we ought to submit to God's will;* and be convinced that we have received all that is necessary for fulfilling our rôle in the Mystical Body, as foreseen by Providence.

EVENING PRAYER

Father, I come at close of day.
If good I have done, my thanks record;
If evil, then may your charity, pray,
Pardon once more my unworthiness, Lord!
In this calm nocturn that, moonlit, gleams,
I think of the end of earthly dreams;
When my eyes shall behold the last day of my life.
Death is bound to come as nightfall is bound,
Like it irresistible, and like it, profound.
(Of all my nights, may it be the most fair!)
This night, for the hour of death to prepare
I offer my soul at this slumbering hour—
Father, receive it—God of all power.
May I feel it an instant from its prison tower
Hesitatingly rise, as if starting to fly;
So that falling asleep I may learn how to die.

LOUIS LEFEBVRE
(Extract from "La Prière d'un homme".)

Hand in Hand

●

Heedless of aggressive wave,
The young pair,
Lovingly,
Follow the shore.

From peril of wind and wave,
A strong rail—
For safety—
Shelters the two.

O Boy and Girl together!
Would taste love's ecstasy,
And not its pain?
Then, ere ever hand
clasp sister hand,
Place your own hand
In the hand of God!

Thus "through Him and for Him"
You will be vigilant;
Avoiding temerity,
And the long, sad hours of weeping,
Of a love that's been dethroned!

Niagara River
Ric Photo

The Great Rock

Portion of God's power,
The imposing "ship"
Profiles its figured prow—
Ready to cleave the blue waves.
Illusion! For, solidly anchored to the shore,
The immovable vessel refuses to budge.
It would defy the most cunning manoeuvres
Of the best of crews.

Only the Head Pilot
Could vanquish this Titan's inertia;
The opposition of its great hawsers—
And launch it into the deep.

The Head Pilot. . . or a man of faith;
For it is written
That faith removes mountains.
(But who so full of faith,
As to remove this sea-girded cliff?)

Because man now believes only in man,
He wastes centuries of days and nights
Seeking the secrets of motion,
And the forces of impulsion and propulsion;
Inventing all kinds of machines,
Which—too often—become engines of destruction—
And his pride grows.

Let us have faith!
Not for manoeuvering mountains,
But for living in all humility,
In dependency upon God—
Acknowledging his splendour
In the multiple visage of Nature.
His finger in each circumstance—
His voice in the depths of conscience.

The "Old Lady"
Forillon, Gaspésie
Ric Photo

St. Paul explains this clearly in writing to the Romans: "For just as in one body we have many members, yet all the members have not the same function; so we, the many, are one body in Christ; but severally members one of another. But we have gifts differing according to the grace that has been given us. . . . (Rom. 12:4 ff.) St. Paul develops the same idea when he addresses the Corinthians. He writes: "To one is given the gift to preach, to others, that of listening to preaching, to another, the gift of healing, the working of miracles, to another various kinds of tongues. . . . But all these things are the work of one and the same Spirit, who divides to everyone, according as he will." (I Cor. 12:10.)

In all this, there is no injustice on God's part.

"If we are less gifted than certain others, if we have some natural defect of body or mind—a less attractive appearance, a crippled limb, frail health, a poor memory, a slow mind, a less solid judgment, little aptitude for certain types of work—we should neither murmur nor complain because of the perfections we lack, nor be envious of those who possess them. A man would show but ill grace, to become huffy because the present given him out of pure generosity, was not so fine or rich as he should like it to be. Was God under any obligation to give us finer minds, or better bodies? Could he not have created us in a still less favourable situation, or left us uncreated? Have we merited what we have received from him? For it is sheer liberality on God's part, for which we are greatly in his debt. Who ever received a present, and complained about it afterward? Let us impose silence on our miserable pride which makes us ungrateful, and humbly thank God for the gifts he has deigned to give us." (Lehodey.)

"And who knows," inquires St. Alphonsus, "if, with more talent, with robust health, with a more pleasing exterior, we should not lose our souls? For how many have not their learning and talent, their beauty or strength, furnished the occasion for their eternal ruin; by inspiring them with sentiments of vanity and of contempt for others, or even inciting them to rush headlong into a thousand villainies? How many, on the contrary, because of their poverty, sicknesses, and deformities, have been sanctified and saved; who had they been rich, vigorous, or well-built, would have been damned? It is not necessary to have a beautiful face (the Holy Spirit declares beauty to be deceitful and vain!), or good health, or brains. One thing is needful, and that is to save one's soul."

Let us take heart. In Heaven there will be neither halt, nor lame, nor blind!

As for the earth, it was St. Paul who said: "But the foolish things of the world has God chosen to put to shame the 'wise,' and the weak things of the world has God chosen to put to shame the strong, and the base things of the world and the despised has God chosen, and the things that are not, to bring to naught the things that are; lest any flesh should pride itself before him." (I. Cor. 1:27-30.)

So, far from murmuring, those who have nothing should rejoice, for they are the very ones God has chosen to be the instruments of his glory! What an honour!

253—What should be our attitude toward God's will in sickness and other trials? What two extremes must be avoided?

Properly accepted, illness is one of the most precious periods in one's life.

"As for me," writes St. Alphonsus, "I call the time of illness the touchstone for the discerning of spirits; for it is at this time that the real virtue of a soul may be ascertained. If the ill person supports this trial without anxiety, without any desire of his own, if he is obedient to the doctors and to his superiors; if he remains calm, entirely resigned to God's will, it is a sign that he is well-stocked in virtue. What is to be thought of sick person who complains of the little care he receives from others, of his unbearable suffering, of the inefficacy of remedies, of the ignorance of the doctor; and who goes so far at times as to murmur against God himself, as if he were treating him too harshly?"

In sickness, two extremes are to be avoided:

1. Scorning to take care of oneself. Making fun of medicine and doctors. Taking needless risks, either through lack of prudence or through pride.

2. Taking an exaggerated care of one's health, complaining about the slightest ill, and seeking a sympathetic audience in bemoaning one's pitiful state.

This last pitfall is most common, and is a clear indication of egotism.

St. Teresa of Avila amiably chides those persons too preoccupied about their health, who, although capable of assisting at choir without being any the worse for it, do not go to choir one day "because they have a headache; the next day because they *had* a headache, and the next two or three days because they *may* have a headache." She adds: "It seems to me a great imperfection, to complain all the time about such trivial ailments. I do not speak of serious illnesses (for instance, a violent fever); though I desire that these should always be supported with patience and moderation. But I mean those slight indispositions one may have with-

SORROW AND I

I said to Sorrow, "Go!" and Sorrow then
Like stubborn cur rebuffed, returned again.
And still returned with ardor multiplied.
Pursued me night and day on every side.

"I hate, thee, pest, importune!" I shrieked,
"And loathe thee, for I fear thy shadow grim!"
She answered, "I adore thee, and enjoy
To stroke thee with my dark deceiving wing."

In utter misery I cried out then,
"Since Sorrow will not flee, than let her kill!
"Fall to, Barbarian!" Sorrow said "No."
(My soul, no stronger, fought against its fate.)

Then said I to my Sorrow, "Let's be friends!
"My heart is open. Come!" Serene she came.
Abandoned now my bitter dark revolt,
I took part, docile, in her sacred task.....

A charitable friend, with mildness now,
She calmed the terror she herself had caused;
Took care of me as would a sister dear;
And amply paid my loyalty to her.

I learned how gentle is her loving touch;
How kind and healing is her chaste embrace;
Which brings, instead of the desire for death,
The joy that comes from combat and from life!

out disturbing everyone else. As for serious illnesses, these speak for themselves and cannot be long hidden. Nothwithstanding, those persons who are really ill should say so; and let themselves be treated."

254—Is it permissable—without failing in submission to God's will—to complain when one is ill?

Sometimes the pain may be so intense, that the victim cannot help his groanings, and feelings of inner revulsion!

Jesus, the model of suffering souls and painful bodies, willed to know all our sufferings. Forcing back the joys of the beatific vision to the innermost recesses of his soul, he delivered up body and soul to the most fearful agony. He saw the mountain of our sins, he saw his Father ignored, he saw the souls which, despite his sufferings, would be lost, he saw the tortures and ingratitude awaiting him! Then, plunged into a sea of sadness, he abandoned himself to fear, loneliness, and revulsion. His soul was sad, even unto death; his body was covered with a bloody sweat. He thrice implored his Father's pity: "If it be possible, let this cup pass away from me"—immediately adding, "Yet not as I will, but as you will."

"Our Lord, in his Passion," says St. Francis de Sales, "teaches us three valuable lessons:

"1. It is no fault, nor even an imperfection, to experience feelings of suffering, fear, loneliness, repugnance, and disgust; provided that we do not cease to say with a resolute will: 'Not my will, but Yours, be done.' Our Lord is no less perfect or less great in the Garden of Gethsemani, than on Mt. Thabor or at his Father's right hand. To think otherwise would be blasphemy. Also, it is no small thing, when a soul, destitute of all sensible aid, amidst trials, suffering, and contradictions, remains so steadfastly faithful to God's will.

"2. It is no fault, nor even an imperfection, to complain to God with loving submission—the way a hurt child runs to its mother to 'show her where it hurts.'

"Complaints, and all the lamentations of Job and Jeremias, are allowed by love; on the condition that in one's inmost soul there is acquiescence to God's will." So speaks the gentle Bishop of Geneva. But he does blame us "if we never stop lamenting; if we cannot find enough people to complain to, telling them of our troubles in detail."

"3. It is no fault, nor even an imperfection in great trials, to ask God to take away the cup, if possible; and even to request it with a certain insistence—for our Lord did so. But if, after you have prayed to the Father to console you, it does not please him to do so; then strengthen your resolve to accomplish the work of your salvation on the cross, as if you were never more to descend from it. Behold your Master in the Garden of Olives. Having begged consolation from his Father and understanding that this was not his will, he thought no more about it. He did not insist upon it; he no longer sought it; but as if he had never asked for anything, valiantly carried out the work of our Redemption."

The thing to remember, then in great trials, is that moderate and submissive complaints are admissible. Excess only is blameworthy.

255—In connection with complaints in time of trial, can you tell the meaning of these two letters, "N.C."?

Father Edward Poppe, a Belgian, and fervent Franciscan Tertiary, dubbed the "Belgian Curé of Ars," gives us the key to the mystery, in his splendid book, *Entretiens sacerdotaux,* ("Chats with a priest.")

He refers to a resolution, taken by the youthful members of the Eucharistic Crusade at the end of a closed retreat. This resolution was abbreviated as T.S.W.C., meaning: To suffer without complaint. (Or, how to become a saint fast!)

Here is the quotation as reported by Fr. Martial Lekeux in *Sainteté et bonne volonté* (English translation, *Holiness is for Everyone)*:

"If we only knew how to welcome the crosses God arranges for us, if we were wise enough to give Him credit, to admit that everything coming from His hands is good, to say 'Yes' instead of groaning, we would have unlimited opportunity for sacrifice, and virtue would be all prearranged and prepared for us. Our progress in renouncement would be rapid indeed, and our progress in sanctity practically assured.

"Suffering is at your door every morning—either little or much. Each day brings with it its share of unpleasantries. Abnegation and love can be practiced many times a day. There are all kinds of opportunities to repeat: T.S.W.C., 'Yes.'

"You are supposed to go out, but it's raining. 'What awful weather! What a nuisance! What rotten luck! . . .' That's not the thing to say. It is not awful weather; it is God's weather. The rain is His decision. It's the best possible weather. It is not "rotten luck"; it's a grace. The conclusion: T.S.W.C.

"You return home in the evening, and put on slippers to rest your tired feet. At last, peace and quiet! The bell rings. Urgent business. You have to put your shoes back on. 'How annoying! There's never any peace around here!'—I wouldn't want to be the man who rang your bell!... Come, come, God sends him to you. Why? So that you may gain a lot of merit that night. He waits for your 'Yes': T.S.W.C.

"You are preparing for a trip. It's urgent, it's important. All of a sudden you shiver, sneeze, and notice you have a sore throat. Sure enough, the grippe. The trip is out and you look forward to eight or ten days of coughing. 'What luck! Why do these things always happen to me! Misery after misery after misery!...' Instead of kicking against the goad, isn't it better to think that God sends you this grippe for your good? Does He make mistakes? Have you ever stopped to think that each time you complain you insult Him? Be honest enough to admit He knows your needs better than you do, and simply say: T.S.W.C. You won't be any sicker for it.

"You've run into financial straits. Who hasn't these days? You become somber and morose. You worry. Obsessed by your debts, you curse the dog's life you are forced to lead. O man of little faith! Doesn't the Gospel say: 'therefore do not be anxious, saying, 'What shall we eat?' or, 'What shall we drink?' or, 'What are we to put on?' (for after all these things the Gentiles seek); for your Father knows that you need all these things. Seek first the kingdom of God....' (Matt. 6, 31-33). The road to Heaven is paved with difficulties. Why should you be surprised, why complain? C'est la guerre. Fifty years from now all will be forgotten. The awards will have been given out. Work, do your duty, and for the rest: T.S.W.C.

"You find out that someone has been running you down, calumniating, ridiculing you. You fume and swear and shout: 'What a foul thing to do! It's downright mean of him!' And plenty more in the same vein. What are you saying? Remember the eighth beatitude: 'Blessed are you when men reproach you, and persecute you, and speaking falsely, say all manner of evil against you for My sake. Rejoice and exult, because your reward is great in heaven' (Matt. 5, 11-12). Oh, if you knew how to profit from this wonderful thing offered you! One word would clinch it: 'Yes.' T.S.W.C.

"Examples could be multiplied. A mishap occurs: T.S.W.C. A toothache: T.S.W.C. A vexing word, a humiliation, a loss of money, a business venture gone wrong: T.S.W.C. Whatever it is, no distinction is made. The answer is always the same, because all these things come, ultimately, from God. After all, are you better off for balking and grumbling? Or are you just that much more unhappy? Swallow the pill, even if it is bitter. A "Yes" said willingly will sweeten it.

" 'That's all very easy to say, but in practice, when face to face with all these enemies, I cannot help feeling anger, sadness, revolt, and ill-humor.'

"Yes. But please understand. I am not asking you not to feel these emotions (that's impossible). All you are asked to do is not to consent to them. Don't let the dogs loose. Let them bark, if they must. The easiest thing to do, I think, is to do nothing. That's all that is asked of you."

It's a bargain, then! The better to LIVE OUR MASS, we shall make this generous resolution which contains in four letters: T.S.W.C. the half of holiness!

256—Can we, without failing in submission to God's will, ask to be delivered from our sicknesses and infirmities?

Doubtless it is permissable to pray for this. From time to time, God is pleased to reward, even with a miracle, prayers that are fervent and submissive.

Here again, it is to our interest always to add to our prayers, "Lord, your will and not mine be done."

We can so easily fool ourselves when we ask to be cured. "The Devil," writes Charruau, "does great harm to souls, by persuading them to pray always for God to take away their crosses. There are invalids who spend their lives asking for health; when after a certain time, it is clear that God does not will to grant their request. Instead of a cure, then, they should pray for the grace to support their infirmity. This grace is still more excellent." And let us add that it is a grace that is *never refused* to the one solliciting it in the *humility and sincerity of his heart.*

The following three stories will illustrate this point:

A certain sick man had a great devotion to St. Thomas of Canterbury. On going to the tomb of the holy archbishop to pray for health, his health was restored. Returning home, he said to himself, "What if sickness were more useful to my salvation than health?" Struck by this thought, he returned to the tomb of the saint, and implored him to pray to the Lord for whichever would be better for his salvation. After this prayer, he fell sick again, to his great consolation; for he was assured that God had permitted this illness for his happiness.

Again, Michael of Naples, who had lost the use of an arm and was unable to say Mass, besought our Lord to cure him. The cure was obtained! At once, Michael ran joyously to the sacristy to celebrate a Mass of thanksgiving. He was already vesting himself, when he recalled that he had prayed for his cure without the stipulation, "if it be for Your greater glory." Returning to the church, he again prayed to be cured, but this time, abandoning himself to God's will. He then felt his paralysis returning; and took it to mean that the sacrifice of his will, and even of his arm, was better for him, in God's plan, than offering up the Sacrifice of the Mass.

Surius likewise tells of a blind man, cured by the intercession of St. Vaast, who prayed that if the use of his sight would not be useful to his soul, it might be taken away. His prayer was answered, and he became blind as before.

"But my case is different!" someone will cry. "If I only had good health, what good I could do!... I would consecrate myself to God in religion.... I would become a priest.... I would be a breadwinner instead of a burden," etc.

Self-deception!

Remember the reply of St. Alphonsus de Liguori:

"Oh, the self-deception of those who say that they desire health; not to get rid of suffering, but to serve the Lord better, to observe the Community Rule, to go to church, to receive Holy Communion, to do penance, to study, work, and labour to save souls by hearing Confessions and preaching!...

"But I ask you, faithful soul, tell me, why do you wish to do these things? Is it not to please God? Then, why seek for another way, when you know with certainty that God's will for you is not in meditation, Communion, penance, study, preaching, and other works, but for you to support with patience this sickness and pain that he sends you? Unite your sufferings, then, to those of Jesus Christ.

" 'What is painful for me,' you reply, 'is, that being sick this way, I am useless, and even a burden to my community, or to my family.'

"But because of your resignation to God's will, you may hope that your superiors or your parents may be equally resigned to it; when they see that it is through God's will and not through any fault of yours, that you are thus a burden. Ah! these desires and complaints do not come from love of God, but from self-love seeking a pretext to depart from God's will. Do you wish to please God? Then, whenever you are sick in bed, simply say to God, '*Fiat voluntas tua!*—Your will be done!' And repeat it from the bottom of your heart a hundred times, a thousand times—always. By this word alone, we shall please God more than by all possible mortifications and devotions. There is no better means of serving God, than that of embracing his holy will with joy."

The venerable John of Avila wrote one day to a sick priest as follows: "Friend, do not set yourself to examining what you would do if you were well; but be content to be sick for as long as God pleases. If what you are looking for is God's will, then what does it matter to you whether you are sick or well?"

That is why St. Francis de Sales used to say that "a man served God just as well by suffering as by doing."

In other words, it is in reverting once again to the words of the Our Father: "*Your* will be done!" that we are sure *not* to make any imprudent requests.

This is the way the saints prayed. St. Alphonsus said: "I neither desire to get well nor stay sick. I want only what You want." And St. Bonaventure reports that when St. Francis was racked one day with extraordinary pain, one of his religious—an extremely simple man—said to him: "Father, pray God to treat you a little more gently, for it seems to me that his hand lies too heavy on you."

At these words, St. Francis uttered a cry, replying, "Brother, did I not know that it was from simplicity that you spoke to me as you did,

I would never want to see you again; because you dare to criticize God's judgments!" Then, feeble and extenuated as he was, he sprang out of bed; and kissing the ground, exclaimed: "Lord! I thank you for all the sufferings you send me. I beseech you to increase them still more, should this be your good pleasure. My desire is for you to afflict me and not spare me, because doing your will is the greatest consolation I can know in this life."

Let us often recite this beautiful prayer of St. Francis; and, conforming ourselves to its sentiments, we shall be able more easily to LIVE OUR MASS!

Here is another little story to add to what we have said previously on the will of God in time of trial:

Msgr. Foulquier, former bishop of Mendes, received a visit from a priest one day during his last long illness.

"You suffer, Your Grace," said the visitor, "but we are praying for you."

"Thank you," replied the aged prelate. "Yes, I've had quite a siege of it. But here is a little prayer— it's quite short—that I offer to the Heart of Jesus through his holy Mother. I want to teach it to you. It really is beautiful:

Dear Jesus, I have lost my sight. So be it!

Dear Jesus, I suffer from neuralgia. So be it!

Dear Jesus, I am deaf. So be it!

Dear Jesus, I can neither say Mass nor my breviary. So be it!

And in a merry tone of voice, he added, "Learn this prayer. You'll find it useful!"

Follow this kindly counsel. It is a good recipe. Believe me!

Let us say with Dom Vandeur:

"Humiliations, thwarted desires, broken plans, enthusiasms squelched, all this, O Lord, I accept. . . .

"Distress of my own will at seeing itself reduced to uselessness, to nothingness; all this, O God, I accept.

"Incomprehensible maladies of body and soul, which plague me without pause or letup. Malignity of men opposing my plans; unwilling to understand them, raising up opposition, resistance, obstacles of every kind, against them. To this I say, 'Yes.'

"Then, all Life's misunderstandings which separate men and bring sadness and discouragement. Yes, Lord, all this is good and useful to me, and I accept it.

"All this is your Will; or at least you allow it; and will or permission, I adore it. And why not?

"I am hidden in the earth with the little grain of wheat. I die daily in this sepulchre, which already bears the fragrance of a life to be reborn....

"And I really am reborn in God... I have become his flower, his fruit, his grain renewed, his host. I can be altar bread—bread glorifying my Father's Name.

"Trial has made me more alive than ever: more fruitful, more generous in the gift of myself to God and man."

257—Have you ever asked yourself why the Good Lord does not always deliver you from your trials, even after you have prayed about them for a long time?

The first thing to do in sickness or trial is to accept it, and to accept it as a visitation from God. It is USELESS to pray for health or a change, if we do not consent to God's will. It was to incline us, to make us obedient to his will, and give us an opportunity to prove our love for him, that the Master gave us the cross. "Willingly or unwillingly," says Msgr. de Ségur, "we must welcome the Divine Visitor. With deep faith, meekness, humility, and gratitude, we must accept the rude present his hand proffers."

Once you have said your fiat, "God will have thirty good reasons for curing you," writes Canon G. Panneton in *Vous qui souffrez.* ("You who suffer.") "He may cure you very soon.... On the other hand, God may have thirty good reasons for *not* curing you. If he does not cure you, look for the reason in the following list:

1. You do not have enough faith in God's power.
2. You do not pray (or), you do not pray well enough.
3. You do not receive the Sacraments with the right dispositions.
4. You lack confidence in the priest God sent you.

5. You do not love God above all things.
6. You do not love your neighbour as yourself for the love of God.
7. You are too attached to this world's goods.
8. You are too taken up with temporal affairs.
9. You are not concerned enough about your soul's salvation.
10. Sickness is calculated to sanctify you; good health would be your ruin.
11. Sickness will correct you of certain faults.
12. Sickness will straighten out your life.
13. Suffering will enable you to atone for your sins.
14. A victim is needed for the sins of your family.
15. Your sufferings will merit the conversion of a relative.
16. Your sufferings will keep God's wrath from falling on your country.
17. Your sufferings will help bring an end to a war or other calamity.
18. Your sufferings will assist missionaries to convert the heathen.
19. Your sufferings will help priests to save souls.
20. Your sufferings will sanctify consecrated souls.
21. You will obtain priestly and religious vocations.
22. You will open Heaven to the souls in Purgatory.
23. You will enrich the treasure of the Communion of saints.
24. You will fortify the Church the way the martyrs did.
25. You will extend Christ's reign over the nations.
26. You will make the works of Catholic Action prosper.
27. Jesus does you the honour of fastening you to the Cross with him.
28. Jesus is asking you to complete his Passion by your sufferings.
29. Jesus is asking you to help him save the world.
30. God wants to give you a more beautiful Heaven for all eternity!

Can you get around these reasons?

258—Can we be happy amid suffering and trial?

Why not? But on this condition: *We must have understood the usefulness and fruitfulness of suffering endured for the love of God and for the salvation of souls.*

St. Elizabeth of Hungary understood it that way. Disgracefully driven from her palace with her little brood and reduced to beggary, she had a *Te Deum* sung to thank God for having chosen her for the grace of poverty and suffering.

We suffer joyously when we really love God and when we know our sufferings are not in vain.

But of what use can suffering or trial be to us?

They are of great value! They often serve to atone for our own sins, or to obtain for others the grace of conversion. Or again, they bring us closer to Christ. You know that one must have suffered himself, if he is to understand those who suffer. Since our Lord is a crucified God, the more we suffer, the more we shall understand Christ's love for us; the more we shall love him and joyfully accept more suffering.

What comfort and inspiration have we not experienced at the contact of such souls! "One of the most beautiful spectacles to be admired on this earth," writes Fr. Anizan, "is that of a soul which goes its way, leaving a perfume from Calvary along its trail; purchasing with its own darkness light for its sisters, paying with its weakness the price of fruitful activities; obtaining through its own sufferings the happiness of others; paying with its own humiliations for the triumph of great causes; carrying out to the letter this law of contrasts, by means of which Jesus must needs pay for our lives through his own death."

If all afflicted souls but knew to what extent their lives of pain could prove fruitful for the salvation of multitudes, their sufferings would be immediately turned into joy.

In *La fécondité du sacrifice* (The fruitfulness of sacrifice), we read a passage which is well calculated to awaken our enthusiasm along these lines. It concerns a nun deeply afflicted by the sad state of the world. She expressed her anguish one day to our Lord:

" 'O Lord,' she asked, 'when will this devastating flood of immorality and impiety be stemmed?'

" 'Whenever you will,' replied Jesus.

" 'Whenever I will?'

" 'Yes, you,' continued Jesus. 'For if you were a saint, you would serve as a dike.'

" 'You would serve as a dike.' This is indeed a tempting possibility for a delicate and loving soul, but the condition imposed is formal: '*If* you were a saint!' Should this be frightening? No! For sanctity simply consists in the loving acceptance and total doing of God's will.

" 'Do you desire your life to be holy and God-filled?' wrote a pious Carmelite of Compiegne. 'Then accept everything that happens, every sacrifice, every trial, the way that you receive the Sacred Host every morning at Mass. Just as at this moment you forget the veil concealing the sacred Species, so as to direct your entire attention and your soul's adoration toward our Lord present in you to sanctify you; in the same way you must learn to bypass continually those secondary or intermediary causes, by means of which God desires to increase the degree of our union with him. Whether this created intervention goes by the name of interior suffering, inertia, dryness, temptation, spiritual affliction, sufferings relating to one's family, physical suffering, things hard to endure, difficult obedience, repugnant regulations, tiresome, tiny details of life, always say to yourself at once, 'It is a host!' Then receive eagerly and reverently this 'host of Providence.' And this without permitting your soul to struggle with the eternal 'WHY' of nature, blinded by suffering. Courageously, joyously, silently, and in the peace of genuine content, offer up your thanksgiving; so that you may receive the divine Gift in all its fullness.'

"The 'hosts of Providence' are not lacking. Holiness is thus within reach of all persons of good will. But, as 'Little' Thérèse remarked, 'Every soul is free to respond to our Lord's advances, to do little or much from love—in a word, to choose from among the sacrifices he asks.' Alas! How many souls hesitate and shrink at sacrifice! This is unfortunate. These souls who do just enough to keep from being damned, are saved and that's all. The influence they exert on their environment is virtually nil; their example has no compelling force; their prayers, more or less fervent, are scarcely pleasing to God. Hence, few of the elect will owe their salvation and eternal happiness to them. All in all, they will never be 'dikes.'"

Souls who refuse the cross are not happy. Jesus often leaves these inhospitable hearts; and takes this cross, wherein lie holiness and salvation, to others more generous, more worthy of him, and wiser.

Franciscan joy has become almost proverbial. In success and in trial, in sickness and in health, the Franciscan sings and smiles at life!

For many, this is a mystery! Fr. Gemelli, O.F.M., in his excellent book, *Il Francescanesimo,* "The Franciscan Message to the World" gives us an explanation of this joy and optimism in a chapter dealing with "Happiness", under the subtitle: "The Attitude of Franciscan Spirituality towards Suffering". (Pp. 324-327.)

"Franciscan optimism is by no means that of Doctor Pangloss. The Franciscan is under no illusion as regards the fundamental goodness of human nature. He places his trust simply in the promises and in the love of God. He loves life because it is a gift of God. He loves men because they are souls redeemed by the blood of Christ. Franciscan happiness does not depend on the evanescent beauty of material objects and on successive and fleeting instants of joy. It is neither simplicity, nor insensibility, but sagacity. St. Francis by means of one act of self-denial after another finally reached a point when he had nothing further either to gain or to lose. And in the same way a Franciscan eventually becomes immune from all those forms of sorrow which have their roots in the passions of men. For he energetically casts from him that sense of melancholy which is derived from self-importance, expels from his nature the fever of sensuality and the bitterness engendered by ill-fortune and thwarted designs. The absence in him of the acquisitive spirit protects him and enables him to stand foursquare against the winds of adversity. Nevertheless man on this earth can never entirely avoid suffering, even when he avoids those things which are the direct causes of suffering in other people. Suffering came to St. Francis himself in the form of ill-health and physical infirmities. The very Stigmata were a continual source of suffering to him, and he was deeply wounded too by lack of comprehension on the part of his own followers. And so, too, every Franciscan is well aware that both his body and his soul are vulnerable to pain, and when suffering comes he accepts it as a means of purification. The more good he is the more he is liable to suffer, from the very fact that goodness of heart makes the mind and nerves of a man

more highly sensitive. The tears shed by the Poor Clares over the bier of St. Francis, the way in which St. Bernardine of Siena mourned over the death of his travelling companion, and the fainting fit which overcame St. Leonard of Port Maurice when he learned of the death of his faithful servant, Diego, all show how delicacy of feeling in men of deep spirituality is so strong as to move them to tears. For the Franciscan is not afraid of suffering.

"From that September morning when St. Francis first uttered his tremendous prayer to Christ on the summit of the hill of 'La Verna': 'Permit me to experience in my body and soul the suffering of Thy passion: permit me to feel in my heart Thy love for mankind,' from that day every Franciscan has chosen as his special subject of meditation the cross. To awake and let one's eyes rest on the crucifix, to let the meaning sink deep down into one's soul; to convince oneself that a day well spent must be one in which one has nailed one's own will to that of God which is inflexible like a cross; to cast one's eyes once more on the crucifix in the evening and consider whether we have learned its lesson; to fall asleep with the crucifix resting on one's heart, in the hope that the sleep of death will begin in the presence of that one and only Friend who is not afraid to descend down with us into the tomb: this is the essence of Franciscan spirituality. Sorrow, whether physical or moral, does not debar either work, or song. And, like St. Francis after his experience at 'La Verna,' so too the Franciscan after a trial continues once more to pray, love, work, and sing. Nobody must know about the Stigmata, except those from whom it is absolutely impossible to hide them.

"Suffering is a gift of God and a mark of honour, which he bears with joy and pride because it is the sole thing of which it is ever possible to be proud. The more the Franciscan feels he is nailed to the cross, so that he has no longer any free movement, the happier he is. The more his heart bleeds the louder does he sing. The more the crown of thorns presses against his thoughts the more does he thank God for it, because he begins to feel that he may after all be worth something in His eyes, when he has ceased to have any value in the eyes of men.

"Old age is the natural Calvary of Life. Man retains his sensitive feelings only in order to experience suffering, his natural strength only in order that he may perform his duty. But the Franciscan never grows old, for every day there is born in him once more the desire of doing something more and something better for God, as he views this life merely as the antechamber of the next which will have no boundaries except love and light.

"For a Franciscan happiness becomes a duty. But it is an easy duty, for it is the logical result of his conception of Life. He eliminates all useless desires. He works unceasingly at whatever may be his natural bent in a quick, practical way which leaves no opportunity for day-dreaming and sentimentality. He strides forward always in the middle of the road and in the sunlight. He is satisfied with a very little, and yet enjoys everything. He lives from day to day in the freedom of poverty. He welcomes suffering as a friend, jealously, loving it as a mark of predestination. He has confidence in God and brings his own will into harmony with that of his Maker. All these things serve to create that state of mind which may be termed happiness. And yet this cannot be called Franciscan happiness unless it contains the essential elements of love and poverty, common sense and action; unless what is temporary be joined to what is eternal, and the whole universe be enclosed in one straight line, as simple and infinite as a circle, and the centre of which is God.

"Thus Dante in his youth described Franciscan love, and thus it is. For it is a type of love which, while it gives to those who yield to it the secret of happiness, tends at the same time to increase in all who come into contact with it a sense of the joy of living. And thus for seven centuries has it fulfilled its historical mission of giving a supernatural value to every manifestation of Life—from the inconspicuous incidents of daily life to sublime moments of suffering. It has presented Life as a gift of God of far higher value than mere pleasure or pain. Finally it has transfused into life the supreme treasure of Faith and harnessed to the service of Faith everything that is of value in life."

After this long and substantial quotation, let us pause an instant and ask ourselves if we really have the Franciscan spirit with regard to suffering? . . .

We shall have occasion further on to speak of perfect joy, as taught by St. Francis.

259—When someone has slandered us and ruined our reputation, are we still bound to submit to this as the will of God?

Why not? Certainly, this trial is one of the most painful to support in silence. Nevertheless, when we gaze on our crucifix, we can take heart. *He* did not open His mouth in the presence of false witnesses, and His silence led to Calvary! We should rejoice to bear some slight resemblance to such a Model!

Should it happen that—secretly or openly—evil tongues let fly their poisoned darts and damage our reputations, we should accept this patiently; conforming ourselves to God's will.

"Behind the men," writes Lehodey, "we must see God alone for whom—consciously or unconsciously—they serve as instruments. The Good Lord will require a reckoning of every word, and will render unto them according to their works. Meanwhile, he wishes to make use of mistaken zeal, thoughtlessness, and even malice, to try us. Our reputation belongs to him—he has the right to dispose of it as it pleases him. We believe that a good reputation is necessary to carry out our charge. He knows better than we, what is expedient for his glory, for the good of souls, and for our spiritual advancement. If he has resolved to test us on this score, he is the one to choose whatever instrument he pleases for this purpose. Despite the complaints and incriminations of nature, let us deliberately forget men and see God alone. And, kissing with filial submission the hand that strikes us with loving design, let us set about gathering all the fruits possible from this trial."

A ball hurled to the ground, bounces up all the higher. In the same way, a soul smeared by blackest slander, will—by its resignation to God's will—"bounce up" toward the sublime summits of divine love.

TO THE YOUNG... TO ALL...

Say nothing you would not want God to hear.
Do nothing you would not want God to see.
Write nothing you would not want God to read.
Do not read any book you would not want to be reading, should God suddenly say to you: "Show Me that book!"
Do not go anywhere you would not want God to find you.
Do not go with anybody with whom you would not want God to meet you.
Do not spend a minute in which you would not want to have God ask you: "What are you doing, child?"

—Msgr. Sylvain

TO A DISTRESSED SOUL

You suffer, soul? What makes you suffer?
"Everything!"
Who makes you suffer?
"Everybody!"

Yes, you are suffering this intimate and grievous martyrdom, this heart-stabbing martyrdom, this subtle martyrdom of noble, delicate, exceptional, souls, *disappointed at their failure to achieve their ideal....* for whom their star would seem designedly to hide behind a cloud. You suffer because you do not feel your wings are strong enough to soar above an atmosphere saturated with noxious miasmas....

You suffer at feeling yourself filled with unslaked desires—with wonderful, apostolic desires, almost as high above you as Heaven.

Dear soul standing at "wit's end corner," poor soul with refined sensibility from those last disappointing years, from intimate torture known to you alone: you are discouraged. You grumble at your lot: you are rebellious at this valley of tears which (you say) destroys your fairest dreams. A murmur rises to your trembling lips.... You would like to refuse your cross, quit fighting for good.

Poor soul, you are blinded by grief. All that you see is a grey and black horizon; for you forget, no doubt, that the heavy mists roll away and the skies become blue again. (But why *not* think of it?)

You think yourself misunderstood, perhaps. You feel yourself forsaken by friends on whom you have heaped benefits. If this be so, know that this trial is one that God sends only to great saints, to his *chosen,* his *special* friends.

You feel unloved—at least, less loved than you would like to be. You act with the best will in the world, and your actions are misinterpreted, your very intentions misjudged. And every new bruise brings new heartbreak.

A hand that you would have wished to see more loving gives repeated stabs, allegedly to lance an abscess; but the wound left is so deep and has so drained your energy, that *you know it will never be healed.*

O soul, what dismal, difficult, and crushing hours you are going through—to the point that you long now for liberating death. You are disgusted with everything, even with those things that formerly were the source of so much pleasure.

You feel disgruntled with everybody and everything. The merriment of others makes you gloomy and bitter. You would like to "crawl into your shell," or take off for the deep woods with your lost illusions and forget about your high aspirations.

There are days when you would like to cry aloud your distress, so that *everybody* might hear and share it. You would—what else, soul? Do you know, even? Oh, the pain of souls who suffer *because* they suffer!

You want, and you don't want. You lack vim and enthusiasm. You feel rejected of God himself, feel guilty, beaten, ashamed, undone, sick of yourself. Your wishes come flocking, your thoughts conflict like those in a poor fever-wracked brain. The inner hurt is deep and the torture so cruel, that for a few moments, at least, you wish you were someone else? . . .

The Devil holds up and exaggerates your mistakes; the list of your blunders and sins appears horrible. "Can I ever," you wonder, "pay a debt like that?"

Enough, soul! Be calm. Stop now, and listen to me. Let me pour balm into the great wound that is you. . . .

Every life is a Calvary. Your own cross seems the heaviest to you. But what do you know of the crosses of others—of those you rub elbows with every day? "But they smile! They are happy!" *Do you know this?* "Cheerfulness is the atmosphere of heroic souls; often it is also a defence against tears."

For your encouragement, think of the crosses you might have had and didn't: infirmity, sickness, betrayal, abandonment, etc. Think of those who suffer much more than you do. Especially, think of those who suffer and have not the Faith—or sanctifying grace—who suffer *alone!* Do not you, at least, have the Bearer of the first Cross to help you? Of the enormous, gigantic, immense Cross of guilty humanity?

Yes, soul, He is with you; He, the Friend who surpasses all others; the Only Friend who never deceives, who understands, who knows all, and who loves us with infinite love!

Jesus knows where our heart-strings lie, and touches them gently with his divine fingers. The Great Artist knows how to play on souls! But suffering "misunderstood and unaccepted" is not harmonious, and "hurts" his ears! It makes a man selfish, unsociable, nervous, and sometimes ill. Sorry sick are those whose sickness comes from a cross dragged along unwillingly, rather than loved!

Soul, let your heart-strings, like a docile instrument, send up to Heaven the sound so beautiful, pure, and meritorious of *serene resignation and conformity to the divine will.* Say the peaceful *fiat* of the great saints, the generous "Yes," that will streamline your progress and cause you to ascend to the heights, close to God!

Jesus makes you feel the thorns of his heart burning with love, only because he wants this heart to be *fastened* to his, so as to form but one heart—so great is his love for you! He would make you his own—he has an immense need of your sufferings! You love him, you want to please him, and win souls for him. (That soul whom you love and who may be lost, other souls.) Jesus pleads for them all your secret tears, seen by him alone. Give them to him lovingly and joyously. *He has great need of love!* So many others give him only hate! Do you be his faithful comforter! Dear soul, begin anew, and become the sweet Bethany where he will stop and rest.

Are you willing?

260—What should be our attitude as regards God's will in the face of death and bereavement?

"That one should shed tears over the loss of a relative or friend," said St. Alphonsus, "is a pardonable weakness; but to abandon oneself to all the vehemence of one's grief, shows a lack of virtue, a lack of love for God."

Certainly, the loss of a person dear to us is a heavy trial; but good always comes from the detachment it brings.

Some persons are so attached to their parents, that they lack the courage to leave them to follow God's call to become a religious or a missionary. One also comes across parents who so idolize their children that they will not permit them to give themselves to God. Selfishness can go to such lengths!... There are likewise "Philotheas" who become too attached to their director; so that spiritual direction for them is derouted....

And so, to save these endangered souls, God sometimes hits hard—death at times brings the necessary adjustment. It is hard, but salutary!

One day two artists were engaged in painting frescos on the walls of a cathedral. Both artists were working on a scaffold more than forty feet up. One of the two became so absorbed in his work, that he forgot where he was. He stepped back from the picture for a better view, and reached the very end of the plank. At this critical moment, the other painter suddenly turned, and stood frozen with horror at the sight of his companion's imminent peril.

Another instant, and the unfortunate painter would be dashed to death on the pavement below. Should the second man speak, the other was lost—and no less so, should he remain silent. Recovering at once his presence of mind, he seized a brush, plunged it in water, and flung it against the painting so that the latter was utterly spoiled.

At this, the man he was trying to save, rushed toward him with shouts of indignation and anger; but, struck by the woebegone face of his friend, he stopped short and asked him what had made him do so senseless a thing. Hardly had he learned from what frightful peril he had just escaped, than he burst into tears and clasped his companion in his arms—unable to express in words the vehemence of his gratitude.

Is not this the way God often deals with us? When we let ourselves become absorbed in visible, temporal things, forgetting those that are eternal, or when we become so attached to persons that we deviate from our duties toward God; the Lord in his mercy breaks in our hands the miserable trinkets that divert our affections from him. And, while we murmur and weep, he points out to us the abyss into which we risked falling through carelessness and spiritual torpor.

Some blessings enter the house by smashing the window-panes! Let us not look at the splinters that wound; but at the hand of our Heavenly Father, who blesses us and wills our good.

Not all deaths, of course, are therapeutic. Certain bereavements strike us in our most legitimate affections. If such were your own case, we do not believe that we can offer a better illustration of the dispositions one should have, than those shown by St. Bernard at the death of one of his dearly beloved brothers:

"I resisted the sentiments of my heart with all the strength of my faith; telling myself that death is the tribute paid to nature, the universal debt, the necessity of our condition, the order of the Almighty, the sentence of the Just Judge, the scourge of the All-Terrible—in short, the Lord's good pleasure. I might command my tears, but not my sorrow; and the more I repressed it, the more violent did it become. I admit that I was vanquished. You know how legitimate my grief is, how faithful a companion has left me; how vigilant, laborious, gentle, and pleasant he was. Who ever loved me as he did? Who was as necessary to me? When I was weak in body, he carried me; when I was pusillanimous, he encouraged me; when I was lazy and careless, he roused me; when I was forgetful and without foresight, he warned me. We were united less by ties of blood, than by spiritual kinship, by harmony of opinion and conformity of character. Our souls were one; the same blow struck both together; taking one half to Heaven, and leaving the other on earth. And Gerard was so fully mine—my brother by blood, my son by religious profession, my father by his pious solicitude; in mind another self; in affection, my very dear friend. He has left me; I feel the blow; I am stricken to the depths of my soul. I weep, but do not reproach the Hand that struck me. My words are full of sorrow, but not of murmuring. I acknowledge that one and the same sentence has punished the one and crowned the other—

each according to his merits. The Lord, mild and just, has shown mercy to Gerard, his servant; and has made me feel the weight of his justice. Lord, you gave me Gerard, you have taken him away. I weep because he is torn from me, but do not forget that it was from you I received him; and I thank you for having been able to enjoy him. You have claimed your deposit; you have taken back your own. My tears put an end to my speech; Lord, put a limit and an end to my tears."

Your will and not mine be done.

As a magnificent ending to all that we have said on the subject of surrendering our wills to God in life's different trials, let us often repeat the act of abandonment written by St. Francis de Sales:

"O God, the only thing I want in this world is you and your most holy will. I have the greatest desire to grow in your love and in every virtue; and to this end I desire to accomplish faithfully your known will. As for all those things which depend on you and not on me, I trustingly place myself in your hands, holding myself in readiness—in simple and filial expectation—to do whatever you may require of me.

"I desire nothing.

"I ask for nothing.

"I refuse nothing.

"I accept everything.

"I do not fear suffering, because you proportion it to my weakness. My one wish is to let you lead me as you will and lovingly to accept your good pleasure. Amen."

261—What are the fruits of our surrender to God's will?

The first fruit of the surrender of our will to God, *is a delightful intimacy with the Blessed Trinity.* "If anyone loves me," says Jesus to us, "he will keep my word, and my Father will love him, and we will come to him and make our abode with him!" Whoever does the will of my Father in Heaven, he is my brother, and sister, and mother!" (Matt. 12:50), i.e., he is closely united to him, even more closely than by all the ties of blood....

Hence, the divine familiarities with which the lives of the saints are filled. Let one read, for instance, the life of Sister Gertrude Mary.

On every page he will find the most touching tokens of God's goodness. God the Father calls her his "little earthly daughter" and speaks to her as tenderly as a mother to her child, while our Lord calls her his "little sister," his "daughter," and his "spouse."

The second fruit of surrender to God's will is *simplicity* and *freedom.*

Though the soul that always does God's will may have many duties to perform, it sees in all things only God and his adorable will. It will pass through sickness and health, dryness and consolation, temptation and repose, without being troubled and without criticizing; because it rises above these happenings to see only God, who directs all for his greater glory and the good of souls.

The soul that always does God's will thereby acquires great freedom.

Freedom from possessions and temporal evils, from prosperity and from adversity. Nothing of greed, ambition, or luxury holds it captive. Humiliations, sufferings, privations, and crosses of all kinds have ceased to dismay it. In all things it has recourse to God alone; assured of being in the divine friendship and on the road leading to Heaven.

It is free as regards man. Its great desire being to please God by an entire submission to his holy will, it lets itself be stopped neither by human respect nor by criticism and raillery—nothing can make it swerve from the path of duty.

In its relations with God, it freely wills all that he wills, and as he wills; and accepts everything with a smile.

Just as he who does God's will is free; so is he who does not wish to submit to it, a shackled slave!

For are sinners who follow their whims and fancies really free? The world and their passions tyrannize them; they are drawn into occasions of sin; they are dominated by human respect. They want to do good, and a thousand obstacles (voluntary attachments) turn them away from it. They hate evil, but lack strength to shun it. Even the devout (in their own way) who seek material consolation, are not free, because they are led by self-love.

A soul is free and disengaged to the extent that the passions are deadened, that self-love is vanquished, and God's will accepted.

The third fruit of submission to God's will is *peace and joy.*

Fr. Saint-Jure explains clearly this state of the soul that is submissive to the divine will:

"Souls following along this way enjoy an unalterable calm, and their lives are passed in a peace which only they can understand, and which is to be found nowhere else on earth. . . . For can one imagine a more blissful state than that wherein the soul is borne, reposes, and slumbers like a child in the loving and all-powerful arms of divine Providence?"

Do you wish a clear picture of the happiness enjoyed by this soul? Consider Noah during the flood. "He was at peace in the ark with lions, tigers, and bears, because God led him; whereas all the others, amidst the strangest confusion of body and soul, were pitilessly engulfed by the waves. Thus the soul that abandons itself to Providence, lets him steer the rudder of its ship, enjoys perfect peace in the midst of every trouble, and tranquilly sails life's sea; while undisciplined souls, fugitive slaves and rebellious to Providence, are in continuous agitation; and, having as pilot only their inconstant and blind will, after having long been the toy of wind and tempest, end up in a sorry shipwreck."

Abandonment to God's will also produces great joy, even amidst great suffering. "It is not rare," says Msgr. Gay, "for this to be sensible joy. At other times (and this the more often), it remains purely spiritual."

The crosses of saints are heavier than those of other men; nevertheless, they are more joyously borne, for the very good reason that the saints willingly accept them. We make our own crosses, when our wills clash with God's will. But when they are in conformity with his, the result is two parallel wills—two rails on which we roll swiftly and surely toward Heaven!

Listen to the holy Curé of Ars, an illustrious Franciscan Tertiary:

"It is the Cross that gave peace to the world; it is the Cross that we should bear in our hearts. All our troubles come from not loving it. Fear of crosses increases our crosses. A cross simply and lovingly borne, no longer brings suffering. Nothing makes us more like our Lord than does carrying his Cross. All suffering is sweet in union with him. I cannot understand a Christian who does not love his cross, or who flees from it! Do we not at the same time flee Him who willed to be nailed to it, and to die on it for us? Contradictions bring us to the foot of the Cross, and the Cross brings us to Heaven's gate. To get there, we must first be vilified, despised, crushed. Suffering? What of it? It is but for a moment. If we could spend a week in Heaven, we should understand the value of this moment of suffering—we should find no cross heavy enough, no trial bitter enough. The cross is a gift which God offers to his friends. We must pray to love our crosses, for in this way they become sweet. I experienced this for myself during four or five years. I had been slandered, contradicted, shoved about. Oh, it was almost more than I could bear! I began to beg for the love of crosses. Then I became happy. I said to myself, 'Really, crosses are the only source of true happiness!' We must never look to see where our crosses come from—they come from God. It is always God who furnishes this means of proving our love for him. Oh, when the day of judgment comes, how happy we shall be about our unhappiness; how proud of our humiliations; how rich in our sacrifices."

There would be no end to these examples from the lives of the saints. But among many others, there is an interesting episode from the life of St. Francis of Assisi that belongs here—the tale about perfect joy!

"One Day Francis was coming back from Perugia with Brother Leo. They had been on a preaching tour. Snow lay deep on the ground, and still more snow was falling as they struggled along, Leo leading the way. They had tied sacks around their feet. Their cowls were pulled down tight over their heads, and they kept their hands in their sleeves. The wind was blowing through their habits. But they fought their way ahead, praying and shivering.

"Suddenly Francis shouted: 'Little Lamb of God, even if all the Minor Brothers gave the finest examples of holiness and virtue, and healed cripples and could make the blind see, drive out devils, and even bring the dead back to life—remember and note that perfect joy does not lie therein!'

"Brother Leo did not answer, but kept on walking.

"A moment later Francis exclaimed again: 'Even if we knew all there is to know and could predict the future and read the secrets of men's consciences and hearts, note that neither is that perfect joy.'

"Again Brother Leo did not reply as he walked on. Out of respect for Francis, he did not want to disturb him in his meditation.

"A little farther on, Francis cried out: 'Even if a Minor Brother could speak the language of the angels, describe the course of the stars, know the qualities of plants and the strength of birds and men and fish and every creature on earth, note that neither in this is perfect joy.'

"Brother Leo leaned still more into the wind, which was blowing gusts of snow into his face. He was listening more and more intently, because he knew that something wonderful was coming.

"A moment later Francis again shouted: 'Little Lamb of God named after the lion, even if the Minor Brothers could preach so well that they succeeded in converting all the heathen to the religion of Christ, note that perfect joy does not lie in that.'

"Meditating thus, they walked another mile through the snow. But finally Brother Leo could no longer restrain his holy curiosity. And he asked what perfect joy really was.

"Then Francis cried out with great joy, like an organ pouring forth music from all its stops: "When we arrive at the Portiuncula in a little while, wet to the skin by the snow and freezing with cold, plastered with mud and tortured by a gnawing hunger, and then, when we knock at the door and the Brother Porter asks: 'Who are you?' and we answer: 'Two of your Brothers,' and he says: 'You are lying. You are two tramps who go around deceiving people and robbing the poor! Get out of here!', and he leaves us standing outside in the cold and the snow until late at night, and we humbly and meekly realise how well he knows us, and we knock again, and he angrily strikes us down and beats us with a club, and we endure it all willingly, without complaining and lamenting, out of love for Our Lord Jesus Christ—O Little Brother Lamb, note that that is perfect joy! For above all the gifts of the Holy Spirit which Christ gives to His friends is the grace of conquering oneself and of suffering pain, injustice, and mistreatment willingly, for love of Christ! We cannot take pride in any of the other gifts, because God grants them to us. Why should we glory in something that is not ours? But we can glory in the tribulations of the Cross, because we take it upon ourselves of our own free will, and it is ours. I want to glory in nothing but the Cross of Our Lord Jesus Christ!"

"Deeply moved, inspired, and inflamed by the beauty and power of Francis' soul, Brother Leo embraced him, weeping with joy." (From *"De Harp van Sint Franciscus,"—The Perfect Joy of St. Francis*, by Felix Timmermans.)

As a final illustration of this question, we quote the famous dialogue of the theologian and the beggar, narrated by Tauler.

A theologian (Tauler himself) prayed for eight years that he might meet a man who would show him the way of truth. One day, when he burned with this desire more ardently than ever, a voice from Heaven was heard saying, "Go and sit down on the church steps. There you will find the man who is to teach you the way of truth."

He went out then, and found a beggar with bare, sore, and muddy feet, clothed in rags not worth a thin dime. He greeted the beggar, saying, "God grant you a good day!"

"I do not recall ever having had a bad one," the beggar replied.

"May God make you happy!" rejoined the master in theology.

"But I have never been unhappy," retorted the poor man.

"God bless you," replied the theologian. "Only please speak more plainly, for I don't understand what you are saying."

"Gladly," replied the beggar. "You wished me a good day, and I replied that I do not recall ever having had a bad one. For when hungar harasses me, I praise God. If I suffer from cold, or if it is snowing, hailing, or raining—in fair or stormy weather—I praise God. When I am in need, subject to rebuffs and contempt, again I praise God—the result being that I never have a bad day. Next, you wished me a happy life, and I told you that I had never been unhappy. And that is true, because I live with God, and I am certain that whatever he does can only be very good. That is why, whatever I receive from God, or whatever he permits me to receive elsewhere—whether prosperity or adversity, sweetness or bitterness—I look on it as most fortunate and accept it with joy from his hand. I am, moreover, firmly resolved to attach myself to God's will alone; and I have so merged my will with his, that whatever he wills, I will also. Consequently, I have never been unhappy."

"But friend, what would you say if God willed to thrust you into the pit of Hell?"

"Thrust me into Hell, you say? If God willed to go to that extremity, well, I have two arms with which to clasp him firmly. With my left arm (which is true humility), I would grasp his most sacred humanity and cling to that. With my right arm (which is love), I would lay hold of his divinity, and grasp it tightly. So that if God willed to throw me into Hell, he would have to come with me—and I would much rather be in Hell *with* him, than in Heaven without him!"

By this the theologian understood that true resignation, joined to deep humility, is the shortest road to God.

"Where do you come from?" resumed Tauler.

"I come from God."

"Where did you find God?"

"I found him there where I left all creatures behind."

"Where does God dwell?"

"In pure hearts, with men of good will."

"Who are you, then?"

"A king."

"Where is your kingdom?"

"It is within my soul; because I have learned to govern my external and interior senses in such a way, that all the affections and powers of my soul are submissive to me. And this kingdom, you may be sure, is worth more than all earthly kingdoms."

"What brought you to this sublime perfection?"

"Silence, profound meditation, and union with God's will. In all that was not God, I was restless; and now that I have found my God, in him I find perfect repose and an inalterable peace."

Such was the conversation of Tauler with the beggar; who, by the total surrender of his will to that of God, was richer in his poverty than any king; and was happier amidst his sufferings, than are those who accord to themselves every satisfaction of the senses, and the pleasures which this world affords.

262—What does our Lord wish to convey by the words, "on earth as it is in Heaven," added to the third petition?

Merely doing God's will is not enough—God's will must be done with all possible perfection. It must be done on this earth as it is done in Heaven. And we know how the angels do God's will in Heaven.

They do it *promptly*—without loss of time, without delay, without remarks. They do not reason—they react. They do not deliberate—they act. That is why angels are depicted with wings, to signify their swift obedience. That is how we ought to do God's will: unhesitatingly, unwaveringly, without an instant's delay, without comment, and without asking why.

Again, the angels do God's will *lovingly* and *joyously*. It is not fear of God's judgments that induces them to act, since their state of glory is assured—it is solely the desire to please him. This desire ought to dominate us and be our only motive for doing God's will. We ought to do it solely to please him and be acceptable to him. Doing God's will from fear alone could not please him. He does not like to be served with too much fear. God loves the man who does his will with courage and joy, trusting him utterly.

The angels do God's will *perseveringly* and *faithfully*. They never grow weary; their zeal never slackens nor grows cold, but is ever wholehearted and prompt. That is the way we should do God's will, because only he who is generous and who "perseveres till the end," shall be saved. Let us strive to imitate the angels in their service of love.

Like those flowers aptly called sunflowers, which revolve on their stems, turning their faces toward the sun to bask in his kisses and light, let us follow the movement of the divine Sun. Let us always keep turned toward him, so that we may know and carry out his will. Let us never refuse him anything. Let us give our consent to every generous act, to every sacrifice; and prove to him that we love him better than those servants who merely obey their master's orders. Let us not be content with carrying out his orders; let us also acquiesce to his desires.

So shall we fully live the third petition of the Pater Noster: "Your will be done on earth as it is in Heaven!"

TO A FRIEND WHO SUFFERS

If heart and brain throb with intimate pain,
And your throat seems choking with sobs,
Pray and smile through the tears—
Pray and smile through the years!
If your questing mind to doubt be inclined,
This martyrdom must be endured;
Staunch in your faith and creed,
Accept this test you need!
If no ray of light illumine your night,
Murmur not. Complain not. O soul
To anguished fear a prey!
Be strong. Wait for the day!
Lest your body in vain be racked by pain,
Do offer it up as a host.
Expiate—with Christ's grace—
For the sins of our race!
Suffering, truly, of all friends is best;
Its worth to mankind is most sure—
For it detaches, sanctifies, and makes pure!
Accept it gayly, and you will descry
God's will beneath flower and thorn.
To grow one must suffer—to live one must die!

MILICENT

Give us This Day Our Daily Bread

MY BROTHERS

I thought of all other famished ones who do not eat, of so many famished ones, of innumerable famished ones.

Of all those poor souls who seek, who hunger, who are athirst. . .

Of all those, my God, who do not know you, who are afar off from you. . .

Of all those without consolation; who do not want that anyone should console them, who are disgusted with consolations.

And of all those who no longer hunger, because nothing can ever nourish them any more.

They will walk in the distress and in the hunger of each day.

Who will nourish them?—for they no longer desire anything.

And yet have I given them food. . . but what of that?

What are these efforts, these sacrifices for them? I cannot give all things to all men.

And yet, I would that I had a thousand arms, a thousand hearts for them.

For all that I do is so little.

PÉGUY

Ric Photo

Waves in Motion

Lord, give to us the perseverance of the waves,
That dash themselves untiringly against the shore.
Make each recession, like the waves' recessions,
Form the starting-point of an advance.

Give us the freedom of the sea's horizon—
The peace of its immensity—
That eddies of the surface
Are unable to disturb.

Give unto our souls the purity,
The lucidness, the limpidity,
The freshness of its depths—
And the calm after the tempest.

Niagara River

Ric Photo

263—What are the last four petitions of the Pater Noster, and who benefits from them?

The first three petitions have pointed out the goal: God, the glory of his Name, his Kingdom, doing his holy will.

The last four petitions show us how to reach the goal: our daily bread, forgiveness of trespasses, victory over temptation, and deliverance from evil.

At this point, the Lord's Prayer takes a new tack. After being concerned with the Father's interests, it now turns to our own.

These are the last four petitions:

1. Give us this day our daily bread.
2. Forgive us our trespasses as we forgive those who trespass against us.
3. Lead us not into temptation.
4. But deliver us from evil.

Give us this day our daily bread

264—What is the fourth petition of the Pater Noster, and please explain it.

The fourth petition asks God for our bread. "Give us this day our daily bread."

265—Why does our Lord tell us to say: "Give us?"

The word *give* reminds us of our condition as creatures owing everything to the Creator. When we beg for our daily bread, we admit our extreme indigence. Our true attitude toward God is that of a beggar who excepts everything from charity. "Without me," says Jesus, "you can do nothing."

The verb is in the imperative. Our Lord wants us to be hungry folk clamouring for food. This is to be the confession of our bodily and spiritual hunger.

Do we, when we say the Our Father, really have this devouring hunger for spiritual things?

We say to God, "Give us," because we know that we deserve nothing.

We do not say (like the servant to his master or the employe to his employer), "Pay us," for God owes us nothing. It is we who owe him all that we have and are.

Nor do we say, "Advance us"; for if the past left us with only debts, it is to be feared that the future will still find us insolvent.

We do not say to God, "Lend us," for what could we give him back?

But we say to him, "Give us! Give, without expecting its return."

In this petition we make a great act of humility and faith. We confess our destitution; and at the same time, filled with humility, prove our trust in Him whom we address.

266—Why do we say, "Give us our bread," and not, "Give me my bread?"

We say, "Give us," and not "Give me," because every petition in the Pater Noster is first made for the general benefit of the Christian community. Our Lord so willed it; because he wanted to teach us that the best way to make our prayers efficacious for ourselves is never to forget others. God is charity and loves only charity. If we let selfishness creep into our prayers, we spoil their purity. We deprive them of the splendour and charm which would make them acceptable to God. But when we think of others more than ourselves, we touch God's heart; who then thinks of us and showers us with his blessings, to reward us for forgetting self out of love for our neighbour.

By having us say "our," and not "my," bread, our Lord likewise wishes to stir up in us that feeling of brotherhood which should unite all men.

We could paraphrase this petition as follows:

Lord, give bread to the rich; but give it as well to the poor, without its costing him too many humiliations and entreaties.

Give it to the worker. May work never be lacking for his arms; nor his arms be lacking for the work!

Give it to the feeble old man, to the widow, to the orphan.

Give more bread where the need is greater, where there are more mouths to feed.

Give more strength to him who must endure greater fatigue, more courage to him who has greater perils to face.

Give to all your children (our brothers) the necessities of life. Let there not be found one among them having only rags to cover him, poor and insufficient food to sustain him, and an unwholesome, airless, sunless hovel to house him.

The bread for which we plead, O Lord, is lawful bread, earned by the sweat of our brow; not the bread of injustice or theft.

There is no jealousy in our hearts; we cast on our brethren no envious glance. We do not ask you to despoil them to make us rich. We ask your help to live by the work of our hands to provide for our lawful needs.

When our Lord tells us to say "our" bread, he wants to remind us again that this bread is not given to us for our exclusive use; but to share with others as we are able and as they have need. He wants to tell us that almsgiving is not only a counsel but a precept for all those able to give. At the Last Day neglect of this duty will be enough to condemn us without mercy. "I was hungry, I was thirsty, I was in rags—and you did not help Me. Go into everlasting fire!"

The obligation of the rich to assist the poor by the distribution of their superfluity to them, is so great that the Fathers and Doctors of the Church hold those who did not do so to be thieves.

"It is theft and rapine," says St. John Chrysostom openly, "not to share one's goods with the poor. Our riches, from whatever source, belong to the Master we serve. God gives them to us in abundance; not to be dissipated on pleasures, on gluttony, on sumptuous garments, and luxury, but to be distributed to the poor. And just as a treasurer who receives the king's revenues, and would neglect to distribute them according to orders but would employ them for his own pleasure, deserves to be punished and to lose his charge; so a rich man should deem himself the treasurer and steward of God's goods, who commands him to distribute them to the poor. That is why if he takes for himself more than his own needs require, let him know that he will be severely punished. For what he possesses does not belong to him, but to his fellow-servants in need."

The rich of this earth are God's stewards, the supervisors of his providence. God created the rich to assist the poor; and he made the poor to prove and sanctify the rich, by giving them an opportunity to be charitable. The poor have no right to take anything away from the rich, but it is a duty for the rich to give to the poor.

It is not enough, then, to feel sorry for the unfortunate, to be aware of the distress of those without their daily bread, to ask it of God in a general manner. Those who have received more than the necessities of life have a duty to perform—to give to the poor from their abundance. "I command you," says the Lord, "open your hand to the poor and needy in your land."

St. James, in his Epistle, has some very strong passages on the duty of almsgiving, a subject we touch only lightly on here:

"Of what use is it, my brethren, if a man claims to have faith, and has no deeds to show for it? Here is a brother, here is a sister, going naked, left without the means to secure their daily food; if one of you says to them, 'Go in peace, warm yourselves and take your fill,' without providing for their bodily needs, of what use is it? Thus faith, if it has no deeds to show for itself, has lost its own principle of life." [Knox.]

We might ask ourselves here just exactly what kind of faith we have!

A little farther on, St. James describes the torments of those rich who will be buried in Hell, because of their hard heartedness in the face of human misery:

"Come now, you rich! Weep and howl over the miseries which will come upon you. Your riches have rotted, and your garments have become moth-eaten. Your gold and silver are rusted; and their rust will be a witness against you, and will devour your flesh as fire does.

"You have laid up treasure in the last days! Behold, the wages of the labourers who reaped your fields, which have been kept back by you unjustly, cry out; and their cry has entered into the ears of the Lord of Hosts. You have feasted upon earth, and you have nourished your hearts on dissipation in the day of slaughter. You have condemned and put to death the just, and he did not resist you. . . ." (James 2:14 and 5:1.)

Saying "Give us our bread," places the poor man at the rich man's door; and the rich man at God's door. Rich though he may be, the person the most blessed with this world's goods, ought to "beg" from God," and give to those having less, in God's name.

Men will talk no more of Communism and of bloody revolutions, in that day when the rich shall be truly rich and the poor truly poor.

In that day the rich will treat the poor as unfortunate brothers and generously assist them.

The poor will cleave to the rich as to their second providence.

They will be saved together, each by the other: the poor by their resignation, humility, and gratitude; the rich by their moderation, generosity, and the charity which they will receive from the poor in return for their alms.

267—To what "bread" does the Pater Noster refer?

In this fourth petition of the Pater Noster, we pray for two kinds of bread: (1) bread for the body, and (2) bread for the soul.

268—In what does the bread for the body that we ask for here, consist?

By bread for the body, or material bread, must be understood not only:

The bread that appeases our hunger.

But also:

The water that quenches our thirst.
The air we breathe.
The clothing—Modesty's handmaid—that covers us.
The roof that shelters us. . . .

In a word, that which is strictly necessary for the life of the body. If we ask for more, we no longer pray the way Jesus taught us.

"We do not say to God," writes St. Gregory of Nyssa, " 'Grant us riches, the pleasures of opulence, purple raiment, gold and precious stones, numerous contingents of men and beasts as slaves to our luxury, the talents of an orator, or the recompense that men award to merit.' All these things but deflect the soul from its primary need. No, we pray for bread."

By having us pray for bread, our Lord teaches us to be content with the necessities of life, with that which is indispensable to our subsistence; and to desire nothing superfluous. "But having food and sufficient clothing, with these let us be content!" exclaims St. Paul. Jesus preaches to us here detachment from all earthly things.

Only too rare, unfortunately, are those willing to be content with the necessities—those who make this request sincerely. Too many have the fever of gain, of growing richer every day, of amassing wealth, of accumulating riches—for their heirs! The more they have (it seems), the more they want. "Greed and ambition," says Fenelon, "are more discontented at what they do not have, than satisfied with what they have." Always discontented and worried, these men are ceaselessly occupied in creating new needs for themselves and in wondering how to go about satisfying them. How dare they, then, say to God, "Give us this day our daily bread," i.e., the necessities of life, when they are not content with them, and their desires and ambitions always go beyond them?

Doubtless, the desire to improve one's situation and enjoy more comfortable circumstances, is not forbidden; provided it does not get out of bounds. The thing that really clashes with our request, is the inordinate greed, the culpable cupidity, of so many. Often they misuse God's gift. It was not for hoarding or for extravagant spending, that they received more than they needed; but it was to come to the assistance of those lacking the necessities, while contenting themselves with the amount required by their state or condition.

This is the material daily bread for which our Lord desires each of us to pray.

269—How do we thank God for the material bread he gives us every day?

Too often, alas, we respond to God's daily benefits by daily offenses!

Every day the Good Lord prepares our food; either by sending rain to make the seeds sprout, or cold to destroy destructive insects, or else by bringing the sun's rays nearer the earth to ripen our crops. There is no day in which God is not occupied with us; no instant wherein his solicitude for us slackens. His goodness is daily and unceasing, just as our falls and backslidings are daily.

This is the way a priest one day in a sermon deplored man's ingratitude towards God: "When you think of Him least of all," he said, "while you are busy displeasing Him, He is mindful of you and works for you, and destines for you the moil and toil of creation. Consider the nobility and gentleness of this truly royal and divine Heart. At the very moment that you are most forgetful of Him, or even offending Him, He causes the dew from heaven to fall on your hills; He causes the fruits on your trees and the vegetables in your gardens to grow. He creates the delights of your table, and says to you—not in words, but in deeds—'The displeasure you cause Me is extreme. You commit sin, which causes Me infinite displeasure. But for all revenge, behold these perfumed flowers, these delicious fruits, I give you. "Taste, and see that the Lord is good." ' And is He not indeed good to shower down upon you so many delights, in return for the vexations you offer Him every day?"

Yes, how good God is to provide for our temporal needs!

How many times He has given us our daily bread, without our having thought to ask Him for it! Let us say to Him constantly, "Dear God, thank you for all the good things you have daily heaped upon me. I thank you especially for the daily bread you send me to sustain life.

Thank you for the bread you gave me yesterday, and for the bread you will send me tomorrow. 'Thanks be unto you for all your benefits' !"

To keep from ever forgetting to thank God, *let us adopt the holy and devout practice of saying grace before and after meals.* (Tertiaries who do this, are simply obeying their Rule.)

Since everything we have comes from God, is it not fair to thank him for the food he gives us, and of which we would be deprived without him?

Let the rich, whose tables are laden with all sorts of dishes, while the poor have nothing, thank God for his goodness in giving them not only the necessities, but that which is useful and agreeable as well.

Let the poor not forget that though they eat the bitter bread of tears; it still comes from God; who, if they are willing to surrender themselves to his will and to serve him, will give them another Bread—the true Bread, the Living Bread come down from Heaven, the Bread that will make them forget their poverty; for it brings with it all heavenly sweetness and consolation.

270—In what does the bread for the soul that we pray for in the Pater Noster consist?

In this fourth petition of the Pater Noster, we pray our Heavenly Father not only for bread for the body, but also and especially for the still more important bread for the soul! For material bread is for this fleeting moment; whereas bread for the soul is for all eternity.

But what is this spiritual food we beseech God to give us, when we say, "Give us our daily bread?"

By bread for the soul or spiritual bread, is meant:

1. The Word of God.
2. Spiritual reading.
3. Prayer.
4. Divine grace.
5. The Sacraments (especially the Holy Eucharist).

THE WORD OF GOD

Jesus himself formally spoke of this, when he said to the Tempter: "Not by bread alone shall man live, but by every word of God." He added that his words are "spirit and life."

Spirit is the powerful inspiration that sweeps man up into the current of light and love, opened by His Gospel to the mental and emotional activity of the man of good will who meditates on His words.

Life is the vital energy that determines and moves the will in conformity with those true concepts of which the Divine Word is the fruitful seed.

We have already mentioned the Word of God in Question 99 (in treating of the Sermon), to which we refer the reader.

SPIRITUAL READING

We shall find this "spirit and life" in spiritual reading; whose proper object is to foster prayer, by penetrating the soul sweetly and deeply with the divine precepts appropriate to its varied states of distress, calm, disquiet, trust, peace, or turmoil.

This reading is called "spiritual," because it treats of spiritual things and of the soul's relations with God.

The first spiritual book which every soul eager for perfection ought to read is the Bible, and in particular, the Gospels. (See questions 82-93.)

In addition to the various treatises dealing with the interior life and Christian perfection, there are the *Imitation of Christ,* the *Spiritual Combat,* the *Introduction to a Devout Life,* St. Bonaventure's *Three Ways of the Spiritual Life,* the lives of the saints, and all writing apt to elevate the soul.

Thoughtful, devout, and recollected spiritual reading, makes the good seed enter into the "furrows" of the soul opened by grace, to be fructified by prayer, and made to germinate by the daily examination of conscience.

If so many Christians remain unproductive and mediocre, if so many have lost the Faith, it is because they were satisfied with the elementary religious notions learned at school at the time of their First

Communion, without ever thinking afterwards to consolidate these rudiments of religious knowledge by recourse to books and spiritual writers.

Let us make this resolution today. Let no day pass—however busy and crowded—without opening one of these books in which theory and practice combined, assist our sincere effort to make new progress along the path in which Jesus has placed us that we may be transformed into him. Let us read, faithfully, if only for 15 minutes a day!

Spiritual reading, like the spoken Word, is a "seed" that grows in us according to our inner dispositions. It is a means of Communion with Christ, who is hidden beneath the words.

Meditation or mental prayer

Prayer is a heart to heart talk with God!

Blessed is he who, not content with the study of doctrine, applies his mind, heart, will, and all his strength, to assimilating the divine thought and love in the sanctifying colloquy of prayer. Who can tell what marvellous transformations a fervent heart to heart talk with Jesus under the gaze of and with the help of Mary, has wrought in a soul daily practicing the devout and soul-nourishing practice of meditation!

Certain authors delight in complicating this intimate communion of the soul with God! St. Teresa of Avila shrewdly hits the nail on the head when she says, "the best method of meditation is not to have one"!

"Yes, Father," said Fr. Poulain, S.J. to Fr. Letourneau, pastor of Saint-Sulpice, "we Sulpicians and Jesuits may as well face it! For years we have held souls back, by restricting them to a too complicated method of mental prayer. We have insisted on three preludes, three considerations, three examinations, three colloquies, three resolutions, and three conclusions. We have wearied many souls with this technique. We ought to allow freer play to the affections." *L'Oraison simplifiée* (Simplified Meditation), by Matthias Croonenborgh, O.F.M., p. 12.

Contrarily to discursive meditation, prayer gives priority to the heart and will over the intelligence—hence its effortlessness. The most perfect prayer is that wherein one reflects the least. If one *must* think, meditate, and reflect, let it be before or after—at the hour of spiritual reading or no matter when—but not during one's prayer period! "You talk too much and exert yourself too much," said our Lord one day to a soul. "That is why you are unable to hear me, for I speak in silence, solitude, and recollection."

Would you like to pray? There is nothing simpler. After having driven from your mind and senses all worldly cares, place yourself in God's presence by an act of faith. (Is it not with him that you wish to speak?) Next, consider briefly the mystery which is to serve as the object your prayer. This requires neither an ingenious mind nor long reflection. In fact, the intellect has very little to do. Whoever knows all the truths of the Creed, has enough knowledge to love—and therefore, to pray. Then let your heart be moved by the affections awakened by this contemplation of the subject chosen. Speak to God with your heart and tell him that you love him. Speak to him of yourself, of your affairs, of his interests. But above all, let him speak to you; and listen to what he says to you. From these loving thoughts, from these silences rich in divine communications, the closing "resolutions" come of themselves. For can we really talk sincerely to God, without feeling the need to prove our love for him?

Who does not see that this method of procedure is psychological, simple, and at the same time profitable? Is not this the way one proceeds among friends? For a visit with a friend, do you arm yourself with "subjects of conversation in three points"? Do you adopt stiff, stereotyped attitudes? Do you discuss some abstruse, lofty theory? Hardly! You warmly clasp your friend's hand and you begin to talk. Of what? Of anything and everything; especially about your friendship, if it is alive and deep. Then if your friend and you just sit there after that, you smile at each other—each of you finding it a real pleasure, a real joy, just to be together. It's as simple as that.

Why should people act so much differently with God, our Best Friend; who understands us so well, and who loves us with infinite love?

At the start of the spiritual life, beginners may sometimes require a certain method. To these we say: Make use of a method for just as long as you find it useful. Some day soon, however, you will need to lay it aside as soon as it becomes no longer helpful. This you will do with a certain sense of relief, much as a man who for some time has had to help himself along with crutches. He is only to glad to lay these aside, once he no longer needs them.

In this search for God and in dealing with him, let the fervent Christian adopt as soon as possible, the informality of the child. In this way, he will more readily be apt to pray "at all times and in all places," a little like St. Francis of Assisi. "Whether he was seated or walking," St. Bonaventure tells us, "inside the monastery or out, working or resting, St. Francis seemed to have devoted his body and heart, his work and his time, to prayer. He was always attentive to the voice of the Holy Spirit and never let his visit pass without profiting by it. Whenever he presented himself, St. Francis abandoned himself to him and enjoyed his sweetness for as long as God permitted. If he were on the road, he would stop; letting his companions go on ahead, while he savored the divine grace in his inmost soul."

When we say the fourth petition of the Pater Noster, let us not forget to ask God for the grace of prayer—the spiritual bread of our souls.

Divine grace

In order that the Word of God, spiritual reading, and prayer might produce their sanctifying effects in our soul, another "bread" is needed, namely, grace, which is at one and the same time:

1. A force aiding us to resist the Devil and triumph over temptation.

2. Light as to what we should do or avoid.

3. A flame to warm our hearts and attach them to the Divine Master.

4. The source of all our good thoughts, good resolutions, and meritorious good works for Heaven.

5. The life of our soul, in such a way, that in being deprived of grace, it becomes dead before God.

We must obey the inspirations of grace with docility and promptitude, then, and not render it vain; but co-operate and communicate with it to the best of our ability. For a single one of these graces may become the means of winning the happiness of Heaven forever!

Lord, how is it, that there are Catholics who neglect, over long periods of time, to recover lost grace? How can they deprive themselves a single day of this spiritual Bread? . . .

The Sacraments

This grace comes to us through the sacraments. The sacraments were instituted to:

1. Communicate Christ's merits to us.
2. Restore supernatural life to us, if we have lost it.
3. Increase this supernatural life, if we possess it already.

Among the sacraments which we may receive frequently, there is one which is endured, rather than loved—the Sacrament of Penance! Yet, is there a more consoling sacrament, or one more readily accessible? If, instead of dwelling on the misery and sin we bring to the confessional, we were to think more of the graces we bring back from it; our Confessions would no longer be a painful duty, but a devotion loved for its richness. This is so true, that after Confession, we ought to make our act of thanksgiving, just as we do when we receive Holy Communion.

Especially the Holy Eucharist

The fourth petition of the Pater Noster especially envisions the Bread of the Eucharist.

Jesus desired not only to nourish souls with his divine Word, with his thoughts, with his love and grace, but he furthermore wished to nourish them with his substance!

The property of love is to give. But love has degrees, an upward ascent. . . .

He who gives little, loves little.
He who gives much, loves much.
He who gives all, loves with his whole heart!

Now when Jesus gave us the Bread of the Eucharist, he loved us with his whole heart, for he gave himself to us totally: his Body, his Blood, his soul, his adorable Person, his divinity, his whole life!

"Greater love than this no one has, that one lay down his life for his friends"!

271—Why does our Lord give himself to us under the form of bread?

Simply so that we might eat Him!

Passing strange, is it not, that we do not let a day pass without eating the material bread which nourishes our bodies; but that we should so easily, for weeks at a time, deprive ourselves of the Eucharistic Bread, without which we cannot long preserve the life of grace within us! "Unless you eat the flesh of the Son of Man. . .you shall not have life in you," our Lord says.

We sometimes complain about the violence of our temptations, and of our powerlessness to resist them. . . .

Strength to resist is within reach of all—Holy Communion! But it must be received!

272—Are those souls in the state of grace right, who approach the Communion rail with fear and trembling?

It is not our intent to speak at length here on the subject; which will be dealt with in the part of the Mass treating of Communion.

Let us say merely that Jansenism has warped many minds by making the Good Lord into a redoubtable Being whom we should beware of approaching too closely! . . .

But let us not be more demanding than the Church herself; who permits her children to receive Holy Communion as often as they desire —daily, if possible—provided they are in the state of grace and have the right intention.

Everybody knows what is meant by the state of grace. A soul is in the state of grace when it possesses divine Life; and consequently, when no grave sin has driven this Life from the soul.

As to the purity of intention required by the Church for worthy Communion, this is what the decretal on frequent Communion says to us:

"Ardently desired by our Lord and by the Catholic Church, frequent and daily Communion should be accessible to all the faithful, of whatever class or condition; so that no one, if he be in the state of grace and approach the Lord's Table with an upright and pious intention, may be turned away. . . . The right intention consists in the communicant's not being guided by custom, vanity, or human motives; but in being desirous of conforming himself to God's good pleasure, of being more closely united to him through charity, and of opposing this Divine Remedy to his infirmities and faults."

If we have these dispositions, let us hesitate no longer. Our fear and lack of trust in God's mercy would deeply wound the Heart of Jesus. If we are weak and if we feel all the weight of our misery, then we need Communion more than do others! Let us never forget that the Holy Eucharist is both food and medicine.

IS IT REALLY TRUE?

Time: 8 A.M. Place: Hospital X——during Mass. The hospital chaplain was speaking. In the first row of patients sat a kindly-appearing old man with a great bushy beard. The left sleeve of his shirt was folded back and the ends fastened with a safety pin.

Two months before, they had sawed off Old Mark's arm, a few inches below the shoulder.

Father chaplain spoke from the altar rail:

"Friends, Holy Communion is the food and medicine of the soul.

"*Food. Medicine.* Remember this, and you will have understood everything. I shall draw no conclusions, and utter no fine phrases.

"1. Because I don't have the time, and neither do you.

"2. Because you have brains, and I would rather have you preach your own sermon (which will be much more profitable to you).

"3. Because our Lord made no long speeches on the subject; but repeated the same word, the same thought, a dozen times under different forms, then let the Jews and the apostles think it over.

"Now I am going to do the same thing. You all know what medicine is—and when people take it.

"You all know what food is—and when and why you eat.

"Well, Communion is a food—the food of the soul— just as it is a remedy against disease. Food and medicine. Medicine and food. And this is true. Not "almost" true, but completely true.

"Our Lord took the trouble to tell us: *'My flesh is real food.'* Real, do you understand? Not metaphorically or comparatively speaking, but, Real! And unless you eat it, you will not have life in you. That is, you will die, the way people starve to death who do not eat; the way people die of a sickness for want of care.

"Pope St. Pius X, in his two decretals, and more recently, Pius XII, have repeated this and explained it for those who failed to understand. I do not wish to add anything myself, for you are capable of understanding this yourselves. Then you will see what you have to do. You are not children any more.

"I repeat, then. Why did our Lord leave us Holy Communion, the Eucharist, on the night before he died?

"So that they might be food and medicine for our soul. Medicine and food. Amen!"

Old Mark, up to the end of Mass, had a thoughtful air. Head lowered, he was mumbling something. But what he said, no one understood.

The chaplain knew Old Mark only as a good, albeit slow-thinking farmer. A good fellow, but uncommunicative.

A man who never missed Sunday Mass or evening Benediction. Why, one day, he almost lost his temper because a medical check-up made him miss "his" Benediction!

The next morning after Mass. In the Ward, Old Mark had drunk his coffee, and seated on his bed, awaited the doctor's visit, a forbidden cigarette cupped in the palm of his hand. He had the same thoughtful air as the day before.

"Good morning, Mark!"

It was the chaplain making his rounds.

Old Mark tossed his cigarette in the aisle, hopped out of bed and gave a military salute.

"Good morning, Father!"

"Everything O.K.? You look worried! No bad news, I trust!"

"Father, yesterday morning, you said. . . . "

"Yes, Mark?"

"You said 'food and medicine. Medicine and food.' Is that true?"

"Certainly."

"You mean completely true, Father?"

"Completely true, Mark!"

Old Mark's forehead was furrowed with thought. The stump in the empty sleeve jerked about.

"Yes?"

"Well, I thought about it yesterday, and all last night, and again this morning. I've been repeating your 'pass words' over and over to myself. Food, medicine. Medicine, food.

"It's just as you said, Father! We aren't children! It's time to be thinking seriously now. . .about Heaven!"

"That's right, Mark."

"Yes. Well, anyway! If it's true that Communion is food. . .food for. . . . "

"Yes, Mark?"

"Well then! It's not enough to receive the way I do, just on Easter! Even with Christmas and special feasts thrown in! We don't eat just once a year! Food is for every day, medicine for when you're sick. So a man ought to go to Communion *every* Sunday! Or even. . . . "

"Or even, Mark?"

"Or even———. Well, maybe this will sound dumb! But if Communion IS just like food, why a man ought to go to Communion *every* day!

"That's right."

"Right?"

"Right as rain. The Pope says nothing different. Nor our Lord! You say the Our Father every day?"

"Morning and night. Before coffee and after the soup!"

"Then, at least twice a day, you say, 'Give us this day our daily bread.' "

"That's right."

"Now this 'daily bread' that our Lord wants you to pray for and want, is first of all, bread for the soul, or Communion. So———. Think it over, Mark!"

Twice a week after that, at 6 A.M., the chaplain brought "Old Mark" Holy Communion.

And although the ward boasted a few "freethinkers," nobody lifted an eyebrow. They simply commented, "It's Old Mark's idea."

And about that "idea," Old Mark had not said his final word. He simply announced to the chaplain, "When I get back home, you'll see!"

And when that day came, Mark's whole family started going daily to the Communion rail!

273—Why do we say "this day" in the fourth petition of the Pater Noster?

It is today's bread only for which Jesus has us pray: "Give us this day our daily bread."

According to the Gospel, do we have a right to beg for tomorrow's bread?

"For today, today's troubles are enough." Why should we worry about tomorrow?

The Good Lord wishes to remind us thereby that every day may be our last. Our lives are in God's hand. God, who gives us life in the morning, may well have decided to take it away from us this night....

The Hebrews in the desert gathered manna every morning; and if some of them thought to gather more than enough for one day, the manna spoiled and became worthless.

The "this day" that Christ inserted in the Pater Noster, and the miracle of the manna, have still another meaning. Our Lord wishes to teach us that we ought to pray every day; and often renew this sublime prayer—from the start of the day—so that God may bless our labour, and make it fruitful for us; and likewise make us a little less unworthy of the eucharistic Bread which we should long for daily.

Our Lord, then, gave us the Our Father to be said, not now and again during life, but as often as possible. He asked us to pray always. How are we to acquire this habit without regularly saying the prayer he himself deigned to teach us?

274—Why do we say "daily"? Isn't that simply a repetition of "today"?

"Today" is not the same as "daily."

The word *daily* is a temporal adverb. It refers to the time in which what we pray for is to be given us. This time is "today", the present day.

"Daily bread" pertains to the amount of food to pray for. It is fixed in proportion to the necessities of the present moment.

By having us ask for just the quantity of bread we need every day, our Lord wants to teach us not to worry about the future (as so many often do); but to reply in complete trust on Providence, which will never abandon us. God has provided for our needs in the past, and he will do so every day of our lives.

Jesus puts us on our guard against mistrust, with these beautiful words: "If any one of yourselves is asked by your son for bread, will he give him a stone?... Why then, if you, evil as you are, know well enough how to give your children what is good for them; is not your Father in Heaven much more ready to give wholesome gifts to those who ask him?" (Matt. 7:9) [Knox.]

"Do not fret, then, asking, 'What are we to eat?' or 'What are we to drink?' or 'How shall we find clothing?'...You have a Father in Heaven who knows that you need them all.... Do not fret, then, over tomorrow. Leave tomorrow to fret over its own needs." (Matt. 6:31-34.) [Knox.]

"See how the wild lilies grow. They do not toil or spin; and yet I tell you that even Solomon in all his glory was not arrayed like one of these.... If your Heavenly Father feeds the birds of the air; if he so clothes the grasses of the field; which today live and will feed the oven tomorrow, will he not be much more ready to clothe you, men of little faith?" (Cf. Matt. 6:25-28.)

Does this mean that we are supposed to fold our arms and do nothing?

No. *This petition of the Pater Noster does not dispense us from working, each in his own sphere and state in life.* Every man must eat his bread by the sweat of his brow; either by tilling the fields, by manual labour, or working in an office, or as students "sweating" over their lessons! Prayer does not dispense us from this work imposed on man, and without which nothing bears fruit. For our Lord desires to have something of ourselves enter into the fruit of our labours: either bodily sweat or the efforts of mind and heart—and often both. But just as the farmer's toil is not enough to fructify the soil without the dew from heaven, so is the Lord's blessing needed for true success in our affairs. Those who try to get along without it, either do not succeed in their undertakings; or if they do succeed, these temporal and transitory successes often become a source of real misfortune for them.

When our Lord exhorts us to trust in God, he does not mean to forbid every care and thought for the future. There are cares and even preoccupations which are lawful, natural, and quite in the order of things.

God does not condemn prudence and foresight; but exhorts us to sow in youth, so as to reap in maturity. He sends the sluggard to the provident and hard-working ant, which prepares in time for its future needs. And when Jesus gives us as an example the birds which neither toil, nor sow, nor gather into barns; he does not say that they do not fly in search of what they need, following natural instinct. It would be tempting God to want to lean wholly on his providence, waiting for him to give us what we need every day without working.

It is one thing to think of the future—worrying about it is another.

Providing for the future and its needs is a sensible and praiseworthy prudence, which God does not condemn. On the other hand, he does condemn the lack of foresight of those who spend money recklessly and extravagantly—foolishly throwing away in a day enough to live on for a week—particularly parents, who ought to look out for their children.

The thing that God reproves is this torment and worry, this continuous anxiety, which causes a person to hold on to his possessions too greedily; or to be too solicitous in acquiring others. This excessive solicitude is a fault; for it comes from a lack of confidence in God; because it shows that the person counts only on himself and his own industry, and not on God; and because it prevents him from concerning himself about his soul and his religious duties—all absorbed as he is by the idea of getting rich and increasing his property.

God did not will for us to ask once and for all for the necessities of life. If we had been satisfied too soon, we might have forgotten our divine Benefactor in the long run. So many in this world are ungrateful to Providence! . . .It is to spare us from this fault of ingratitude, to keep us close to him in filial intimacy, so that every day we may give him a fresh proof of our trust in him; that he asks us to remind him every day that we are in need of his liberality, by praying: "Give us this day our daily bread."

So every day we shall pray the Our Father, and prudently and trustfully ask for the bread necessary to life.

Prudently, by seeking only the bread needful for our subsistence —the strictly necessary—without desiring more.

Trustfully, abandoning ourselves to our Heavenly Father's generosity. Abandoning! What a beautiful expression—surrendering self, giving up self, forsaking every care; letting oneself be taken, governed, succoured, helped, and saved!

What a feeling of peace this gives to the soul!

Our Father, give us this day our daily bread!

Forgive us our trespasses as we forgive

275—What is the object of the fifth petition of the Our Father?

We ask God to forgive us our sins, as we forgive those who have offended us.

276—Because of our frequent offenses against God, can we always believe that our sins are forgiven, when we confess them with contrition and a firm purpose of amendment?

There is nothing that so wounds the heart of Jesus, as do the doubts of certain souls as to his mercy toward sinners.

Jesus made this loving complaint one day to St. Teresa: "Few souls understand my mercy. Feeling themselves peccable and frail, they cannot believe in my tender love for them, despite their weakness. This lack of faith in my love wounds me deeply."

"You could not believe what joy it gives me to fulfill my mission as Saviour!" he said another time to Sister Benigna Consolata, confidant and secretary of his merciful Heart. "When a soul repents of its sins, and deplores them with all its heart, do you think that I am too hard-hearted to receive it? If that is what you think, then you do not know my Heart!

"My most loving Heart so thirsts for the salvation of souls, that when they come to it, I cannot contain my joy. I RUN TO MEET THEM.

"As fire feeds on fuel, and its flames shoot up in proportion; so does my mercy feed on the misery it consumes. And the more it finds, the more it increases!

"People do not realize how they offend God by doubting his goodness! The sins may be enormous and their number great. But if the sinner returns to me, I am always ready to forgive all, and to forget all. . . .

"Yes, my love is fed by the misery it consumes, and the soul that brings me the most of these—provided it be with a contrite and humble heart—is the soul that pleases me most; for it furnishes me the opportunity of more fully exercising my office of Saviour. But the thing I want above all to say to you, Benigna (and that I condense in a few words), is this: LET A SOUL NOT BE AFRAID OF GOD, FOR GOD IS ALWAYS SWIFT TO GRANT MERCY. And the greatest happiness that the heart of your Jesus can have, is to bring to its Father the greatest possible number of sinners."

And (added our Lord) "my heart is not only compassionate, but it rejoices more, where there is more to be atoned for—provided there is no malice. . . . Even the gravest and most shameful sins, become stepping stones to perfection for the repentant soul!"

After such evidence, can we still doubt? How do otherwise than throw ourselves trustingly and confidently into this SEA OF LOVE AND MERCY?

Yet it is a fact that many sincere souls desirous of perfection, become paralyzed at one time or another at the memory of the sins of their past life. The Devil delights in thus checking fervent souls, by making them doubt God's infinite mercy. The soul thus ensnared is sometimes tempted to ask itself, "Dare I hope that God has fully forgiven me for my many serious infidelities against him?"

"Or supposing he has, can he love me—can I love him with a tender, devoted, and childlike love, like someone who has never offended him?"

"Can I ever hope to be really close to God?"

"Shouldn't I conduct myself before God like a criminal who has been pardoned, but still bears the brand of his ignominy on his brow? . . ."

These are the thoughts which often sadden a soul sincerely returned to God. Happily, these ideas are false. God's infinite mercy works miracles here, which are never met with (nor can they be) in man's dealings. Thanks to this mercy, we may completely expunge the guilty past and become once more God's beloved children; finding again in superabundance our lost treasure of sanctity.

Let us never forget that in an instant God can make the wilderness flourish!

277—With the Gospel as your inspiration, please quote words or facts revealing our Lord's infinite mercy.

Here we touch upon a subject as deep and vast as the Heart of Jesus himself! We shall content ourselves, however, with touching on it, leaving to each the joy of further research.

There is no better way for understanding our Lord's infinite mercy, than opening your New Testament, for that means opening the very heart of Jesus!

Listen to Him. It is perhaps the hundredth or thousandth time that He calls us to Him with all our sins and troubles:

"Come to Me, all you who suffer, who are troubled, alarmed, tempted, deceived, accused, betrayed, slandered, misunderstood, rejected, despised, threatened, harried, forsaken, crushed, discouraged, despairing.... You who walk in darkness...you who are in bitterness of soul... whose heart bleeds...whose life is broken.... You who weep—whatever may be your grief, its intensity, duration, or cause—come, all of you! I am waiting to console, to mitigate, and to heal!"

Victor Hugo redeemed many ignominious pages when he wrote:

"You who weep, come to this God, for he weeps!
You who suffer, come to him, for he heals!
You who tremble, come to him, for he smiles;
You who are passing, come to him, for he abides!"

Yes! Everyone may truthfully say, " There is Someone who thinks of me in my distress! Someone who is interested in my troubles! Someone who wants me near Him, when everybody and everything forsake me!

The "Someone" is Jesus; the Comforter of the afflicted, the sinner's Friend!

For as long as we live on this earth, the God of the Gospel is not a Judge, but a furnace of infinite love; who in an instant, forgives, regenerates, and sanctifies.

The greatest sinner can become a saint!

Let him but consent to believe in the merciful love of Jesus, who is ever present and about him, calling him, awaiting him. "Behold, I stand at the door of hearts," he cries, "and I knock!"

Let the sinner, then, at last surrender.... Let him break clean with sin.... Let him renounce the error of his ways and consent to be loved! The Blessed Saviour waits for nothing else....

Let him but love—and behold him at once, a Son of God and heir of Heaven!

But let us glance through the Gospels again. The few passages taken here and there for your consideration, will strengthen your faith in the merciful love of Jesus—the only Friend who never deceives! Let each of these precious words be graven in your hearts:

"Have faith in God!...I have compassion on the crowd!...Come to Me, all you who labour and are burdened, and I will give you rest!... Learn from Me, for I am meek and humble of heart!...These things I have spoken to you, that in Me you may have peace!..."

And with tears in his eyes, Jesus adds: "Ah, if you, too, could understand, above all in this day that is granted you, the ways that can bring you peace!...What is impossible to men, is not to God...How often would I have...but you were not willing!...Peace to men of good will!...If you can believe, all things are possible to him who believes!... I am the Light of the world. He who follows Me does not walk in the darkness!...I am the Way, the Truth, the Life, and the Resurrection! He who believes in Me, though he be dead, shall live!...Without Me, you can do nothing!...Ask, and I will do!...I am with you all days, even to the consummation of the world!...All power in Heaven and on earth has been given to Me!.. Let not your heart be troubled!...You believe in God, believe also in Me, your Saviour!.."

The Blessed Virgin says to us, as she did to the servants at the wedding feast of Cana: "Do whatever He tells you!...Listen to Him.."

Oh, if only we listened to our Lord, instead of resisting him because of his moral demands on us, our thirst for the infinite would be surely satisfied! Alas! "He came unto his own, and his own received him not!" How many playboys, pleasure-seekers, and egoists, still imitate today the wicked rich man of the Gospel, by their rejoicings and banquets alongside so many poor Lazaruses—homeless, hungry, unemployed—who beg for the crumbs that fall from their surcharged tables!...And in vain!...If St. John the Baptist were to come back, he would say to us again, "There is One standing in your midst of whom you know nothing!" And our Lord could add: "Have I been so long a time with you, and you have not known Me?...I am the Good Shepherd...I search for the lost sheep until I find it...."

Perhaps you are this "sheep" loved by Jesus!

"It is not the will of your Father in Heaven that a single one of you should perish. Him who comes to Me, I will not cast out.... I was not sent except to the lost sheep.... A bruised reed I will not break, nor quench a smoking wick.... The Spirit of the Lord is upon Me, because He has anointed Me to bring good news to the poor. He has sent Me to heal the broken-hearted, to proclaim release to the captives, and sight to the blind; to set at liberty the oppressed."

Listen to the Saviour praying for his executioners on Good Friday: "Father, forgive them, for they do not know what they are doing!"

Let us likewise imitate the Good Thief with his prayer come from a heart filled with repentance and trust: "Remember me when you come into your kingdom!" The response of the Sacred Heart is prompt to this poor, repentant sinner: "This day you shall be with Me in Paradise!"

All these words taken from the Gospel ought to be for us an assurance and a comfort! To our misery they bring an alleviating and liberating solution, giving wings to the spirit!...They help us to understand Jesus' goodness toward sinners! They explain why he showed himself so merciful to Mary Magdalene, so condescending to the Samaritan woman, so indulgent toward the adulteress!

Our past sins are not an obstacle to our love for God. Instead of dragging them behind us like so much dead wood, let us cast them into the furnace of God's love. They will be consumed in a twinkling and will preserve in our minds the consoling twofold aspect of our misery and of Christ's infinite goodness!

St. Thérèse of the Child Jesus had grasped well the immensity of Jesus' merciful love for sinners, when she wrote to one of her spiritual brothers:

"You may well sing of God's mercy, for it shines in you in all its splendour. You love St. Augustine and St. Magdalene, those souls to whom many sins were forgiven because they loved much. I, too, love them. I love their repentance, and even more their loving audacity! When I see Magdalene advancing toward Simon's many guests and watering with her tears the feet of her adored Master, which she touches for the first time, I sense that her heart has grasped the depths of love and mercy in Jesus' Heart; and that not only is he disposed to forgive her, but to shower upon her the blessings of his divine friendship and raise her to the loftiest summits of contemplation. Oh, my brother, since it has been given to me, too, to understand the love of Jesus' Heart, all fear has been driven from my heart. The memory of my sins humbles me and causes me never to lean on my own strength (which is only weakness); but even more, this memory speaks to me of love and mercy. For when one casts one's sins with childlike trust into the devouring furnace of love, how can they be otherwise than utterly consumed?"

St. Denis the Areopagite reports that a bishop named Carpus, having with much difficulty converted an idolator, only to learn that another idolator had, in an instant, made him renounce his faith; prayed earnestly to God all night to take vengeance on such an insult to his divine majesty by punishing the guilty persons. In the very thick of his prayer, Carpus suddenly saw the earth open, and the idolator and the apostate appear before him standing on the brink of Hell, with demons trying to push them in.... Raising his eyes to Heaven, he saw our Lord, who came up to him and said, "Carpus, you pray for me to take vengeance. You do not know me! Do you know what you are asking me for, and what sinners have cost me? Why do you want me to lose them? I love them so much, that I would be willing to die a second time for every one of them, if that were necessary." Then, approaching Carpus and showing his bared shoulders, our Lord said to him, "Carpus, if you want vengeance, strike me, rather than these poor sinners!"

After that, how can we still live in fear and doubt of God's mercy?

Everyone has heard of Margaret of Cortona, the Magdalene of the Franciscan Order! This poor unwed mother, who lived in the second half of the thirteenth century, is the perfect type of the repentant sinner, rehabilitated by grace. Admitted to the Third Order after her youthful errors, she thenceforth wished no other lot than the Saviour's Cross, tears of repentance, and the austere joys of severe mortification. Transformed by divine love, she rapidly scaled the summit of perfection.

We especially wish to call our readers' attention to the kindness shown by the Divine Master to his humble servant, in the first years of her conversion.

Kneeling before a crucifix in the Church of St. Francis in Cortona, Margaret gave free vent to her tears. "Dear God," she exclaimed. "Do you, who suffered so much for me, forgive?"

"I, the Son of the eternal Father and your Saviour, crucified for you," replied Jesus, "absolve you from all the sins you have committed to this day."

Margaret is transported, her soul thrills with indescribable joy. "O Lord," she cried, "Eternal and Omnipotent Priest! Be blessed forever! And you, choirs of angels, lend me your voices! Let us sing together the infinite goodness of the Saviour toward this least deserving of sinners!"

And this signal favour was only a prelude to the still more precious graces reserved for her, by the God who takes pleasure in showering souls with his benefits, according to the good pleasure of his holy will.

Praying in her little cell, Margaret considered her past errors and—despite them—the blessings of Providence. In an astonishment in which deep gratitude was mingled, she realized that patience, mercy and the proof of boundless charity were the Saviour's only "revenge" against a wretched, sinful creature.

"O God, how can you look upon me, who am but dust and ashes, darkness and mire?"

Suddenly the voice she had already heard several times replied: "I plumbed earth's depths, and chose you; because I take pleasure in exalting the humble, in justifying repentant sinners, and in making precious what is vile."

"But, why, Lord Jesus, grant so many favours to so despicable a creature?"

"Because I have destined you to become a net to catch sinners. I want you to be a light for those seated in the darkness of vice. I desire that the example of your conversion may speak hope to those who have offended me. Finally, I want those living in future times to be convinced that I am always ready to open the arms of my mercy to the prodigal who sincerely returns to me."

A beautiful and serious theme for meditation for those of us who have (alas!) sinned only too often!

278—Have we any right to allege God's mercy for continuing to sin?

God is infinitely merciful. We saw this in the preceding question. We could have demonstrated this even more, by commenting on the classical Gospel passages treating of mercy; as the parable of the Prodigal Son, the stories of the adulteress, the Samaritan woman, Mary Magdalene, etc. We leave it up to each reader to contact the Gospels directly and revel in their charm.

Here, without taking back anything that we said above, we would warn the presumptuous not to abuse God's mercy.

As we know, presumption consists in expecting God to forgive, while one plunges headlong into sin.

These temerarious souls feel no regret for their sins. Assured (they say) of God's indulgence and pardon, they despise his law and voluntarily expose themselves to evil.

If God is infinitely merciful, he is also infinitely just. There is no conflict among the divine attributes. "Every praise of God's mercy is a blasphemy," said Tertullian, "when it is opposed to his justice."

Indeed, whoever imprudently prolongs a life of sin, under the pretext that God will (as in the past) continue to pardon; proffers a horrible blasphemy and places himself on the road to perdition. For this sinner—by his abuse of God's goodness—willfully closes the door to grace; and by the very fact, paralyzes the action of mercy.

"Do not delay your conversion," says the Wise Man, "and do not put it off from day to day; for the Lord's wrath will suddenly break forth, and in the day of vengeance you shall perish." (Eccl. 6:6.)

Remember, then, that the Good Lord is infinitely merciful to the contrite and repentant sinner. But that his justice is inflexible toward the sinner who willfully persists in wrong-doing, giving himself license to do evil because God is good.

279—What conditions does our Lord impose for the forgiveness of sin?

Our Lord indicates the conditions for forgiveness in the fifth petition of the Pater Noster: "Forgive us our trespasses, as we forgive those who trespass against us"!

What a "trap" is this, set by divine love! God will forgive us in the proportion that we forgive those who have offended us!

"With what clarity," writes St. Teresa of Aliva, "do the words used by Jesus Christ in this petition of the Our Father, reveal God's esteem for this love we should have for one another! For our good Jesus *could* have offered other motives to his Father to induce him to forgive us. Thus, he *could* have said to him: "Forgive us, Lord, because we pray to you frequently. Forgive us because we strictly observe the prescribed fasts, or because we have forsaken all for you. Forgive us because we have a great love for you and are ready to sacrifice our lives for you." But he says nothing of all this, nor anything like it, contenting himself with saying: 'Forgive us because we forgive.' And perhaps this is why: seeing how attached we are to this world's miserable 'honour' (the main source of all resentful feelings), and that nothing is harder for us than to forgive whatever touches it; the Divine Master believed that he could offer his Father nothing more pleasing from us than this 'honour,' and so he has sacrificed it to him in our name."

How many times has Jesus repeated this great precept of the forgiveness of injuries! Of the necessity of doing good to one's enemies!

"Blessed," says he, "are the merciful, for they shall obtain mercy!... Forgive, and you will be forgiven!... If you do not forgive men their offenses, neither will your Heavenly Father forgive your offenses!... If someone strikes you on the right cheek, turn to him the other also!" Whoever does not forgive, even if he is baptized, does not deserve the name of Christian. He is a pagan, a Jew, or whatever you will; but he is not a child of the Gospel, and the words of the Our Father are not fitting on his lips!

"You know what has been said to the ancients, 'You shall love your neighbour'; to which the doctors of the Law added, 'and hate your enemy.' But I say to you, love your enemies, do good to those who hate you, and pray for those who persecute and calumniate you, so that you may be children of your Father in Heaven; who makes his sun rise on the good and the evil. For if you love those who love you, what reward shall you have? Do not even the Publicans do that? And if you salute your brethren only, what are you doing more than others? Do not even the Gentiles do that?

"If you are offering your gift at the altar," continues the Divine Master, "and there remember that your brother has anything against you, leave your gift before the altar, and go first to be reconciled to your brother, and then come and offer your gift."

"I proclaim aloud," says St. John Chrysostom, "and confidently uphold it. Let him who has an enemy not dare to approach the Lord's table. Let him first go and be reconciled. It is not I who say this, but the Lord."

Not content with having imposed this obligation of forgiveness, our Lord places the words in our mouths; so that if we fail to forgive, he will say to us, as he said to the wicked servant, "By your own mouth I judge you.... You asked for forgiveness, on the condition that you forgive."

280—Why should we forgive?

We should forgive because (as we have just seen) God commands it.

We should forgive, because God has been infinitely merciful to us!

We should forgive for our own sakes—this is the condition imposed for our own forgiveness.

At the end of our life, Jesus will appear before us to judge us. His words will be: "Did you forgive?... Did you refuse to forgive? If you forgave, I forgive you. If you did not forgive, I do not forgive you. My mercy depends entirely on your mercy toward your neighbour."

We hold, as it were, the forgiveness of our sins in our own hands!

We recall the parable of the wicked servant to whom the king had just remitted the enormous debt of ten thousand talents. (Say

$10,000.) This unworthy servant came across a friend of his who owed him a hundred denarii (or $50). Seizing him by the throat and almost strangling him, he cried, "Pay what you owe me!" The poor wretch went down on his knees and begged for a little more time, but in vain. He was cast into prison! We know the rest. Learning what had happened, the king had the servant called to him. "Wicked servant! I forgave you all that debt, because you entreated me! Should you not have had mercy on your fellow servant, even as I had mercy on you?" And his master, being angry, handed him over to the torturers until he should pay all that was due to him. "So also my Heavenly Father will do to you, if you do not forgive your brothers from your hearts." (Matt. 18:21.)

Let us, then, avail ourselves of this sure way to be forgiven—by ourselves forgiving others.

This is likewise a way to taste true happiness on earth.

When we have forgiven someone, our hearts—relieved of the feeling of oppression that weighed them down before—feel lighter. A great joy descends in us—we are happy.

But if we do not forgive, then goodbye to inner peace.... Take a look within your soul. It is the sea unleashed with all its wrath and tumult! Do the winds of adversity beat upon your enemy's head? We are filled with joy. But it is an evil joy, which lessens us in our own eyes and serves to increase our own unhappiness.... This enemy—the very sight of him turns us pale. We shudder at the sound of his voice. When it would be so easy to make friends with him and find again the joy of living—and of dying!... If we would only be willing to take the first step toward reconciliation!

Finally, forgiving our neighbour is a condition for setting out on the road to sanctity.

The first effort we must make to place ourselves in the state of sanctity, consists in separating ourselves from our selfish, susceptible, "I"; who sometimes engenders resentment, rancour, or even revenge. Now, forgiving means giving up bitter feelings and even bitter memories, and all thoughts of revenge.

So how can we believe ourselves headed for holiness, if we close our heart's door to charity, for lack of a sincere and generous word of pardon?

281—Whom should we forgive?

Our Lord said, "Forgive men their offenses."

The law of forgiveness admits of no exception.

1. *Let us forgive those who have offended us.*

Who has never had to suffer anything in his life from his neighbour? How many times have we not felt our heart pound with indignation at some crying injustice, at some cutting insult—ready to erupt like a volcano? If, seething within, we were to listen then to ourselves, we should say to the one who has cruelly offended us; "Go away! I hate you! I'll get even with you, if it's the last thing I do!"

But there is something better to do than this, something lovelier, bigger, more Christian. It is to shake hands with this person and say to him kindly, "I forgive you."

2. *Let us forgive those whom we dislike.*

Around us, near us, are people who have never done us any harm; who may wish us well or who even help us; but whom we do not like. We naturally dislike them and find them displeasing, either because of some physical defect or some character trait. We should prefer not to accept any favours from these persons, so greatly do they get on our nerves. It may be that, giving free rein to our ill humour, we take a malicious pleasure in ridiculing or slandering them. (Envy, jealousy, or pride, are often the cause here.) Here again, let us not be dominated by our impressions, but at least let us forgive those who have *not* offended us! To do so, let us follow the advice of St. Francis de Sales: "If a man had a hundred faces, I would always look at the handsomest one!" Or let us have the delicacy of Joubert, who wrote: "If my friend had only one eye, I would always look at him in profile"!

3. *Let us forgive those whom we have offended.*

Tacitus, a Roman historian who lived up to his name, since he could say so many profound things in few words, wrote this: "It is natural for the human heart to bear ill-will toward those whom we have injured." Unfortunately, this is human nature! After nineteen centuries of Christianity, the aphorism of the ancient writer has lost none of its truth. Have we behaved badly toward someone? *We*, it seems, must "get even," and the more innocent the other, the less do we forgive him!

There is a great deal of pride in this. Unwilling to acknowledge we are at fault, we try to make ourselves believe we are right, by maintaining an unjust attitude.

If we have committed the fault of holding resentment against our neighbour because of our own conduct, let us at least not commit a new one by our persistence. Let us be infinitely indulgent toward those whom we ourselves have offended, and hasten to make amends.

282—Before replying to the question, "How ought we to forgive?" please name and explain the qualities of divine mercy.

The qualities of divine mercy can be brought down to four:

1. Universal
2. Unwearying
3. Accessible
4. Generous or magnanimous

Let us say a word as to each of these qualitites.

1. *Universal*

Jesus excluded no one from his love. He died for all. Hence, his forgiveness extends to all sinners, without exception:

Even to Peter, who denied him three times in succession.

Even to the Jews—favoured with his blessings—who crucified him.

Even to Jerusalem, the deicide city!

Even to Judas, the traitor, if only he had chosen to profit by it!

After selling his Master, Judas, listening to the Devil, told himself, like Cain: "My crime is too great for God to forgive." This unfortunate apostle, who had a heart as circumscribed, hard, and sordid as his gold, did not even suspect the immensity of God's mercy! However, our Lord was ready to forgive him, if only he had shown the slightest sign of repentance. (See Q. 214.)

Whatever our sins, let us never for a single instant doubt God's mercy. To do so, would be to add still another to our sins and wound still more the merciful heart of Jesus.

2. *Unwearying*

Our Lord is always ready to pardon the repentant sinner.

Of this, there are astounding words in the Gospel. Jesus said, "As for your brother, if he is in fault, tax him with it; and if he is sorry for it, forgive him. Nay, if he does you wrong seven times in the day, and seven times in the day comes back to you and says, I am sorry, you shall forgive him." [Knox.]

Have we ever tried to carry out these orders of our Lord? ... Let us try it this very day! We shall be blessed indeed, if we succeed in forgiving the same person three times in succession on the same day!

The thing our Lord teaches to others, is the thing he does for us every day. His whole life was one long and merciful pardon! He has even set up "courts" (confessionals) on every corner, so to speak; so that he can more easily forgive those who offend him!

Do you know of any earthly king who would do that so as to pardon his subjects for their crimes of high treason?

3. *Easy*

The most remarkable thing about God's forgiveness is its extreme facility. God forgives the way he created—with a word! "Let there be light! And there was light!" "I absolve you!" And at once a sinful soul is restored to grace!

"Our Lord forgives a contrite sinner faster than a mother would snatch her child from flames!" said the holy Curé of Ars.

Doubtless, when God forgives sin, he does not dispense the sinner from the expiation due to sin's penalty. But this penalty, this expiation, is considerably mitigated by Calvary's Sacrifice.

An anecdote from the life of Msgr. de Ségur will help us understand this.

One day a workman who had profaned a Consecrated Host, came and threw himself at the feet of this Tertiary priest. During the Confession, the priest remained calm. After hearing this very grave admission, he said to the sobbing man: "For your penance, you will say three Hail Mary's."

"That's *all?"* asked the dumbfounded young man.

"Yes," replied the priest. "I will take care of the rest."

And to make reparation for the abominable sacrilege, Msgr. de Ségur slept for a long period of time on the bare floor, stayed awake entire nights, fasted, and had hundreds of Masses said.

This admirable passage from the life of a saint, helps us to understand why Jesus does not impose long and painful acts of reparation on those sinners he absolves. He himself paid mankind's debt on Calvary... and in the Mass, Jesus comes down on the altar in this attitude of reparation for our sins. Here we see once more, the incomparable expiatory value of the Holy Sacrifice of the Mass...and how, by our attendance, it is possible to atone for those who do not atone for themselves.

4. *Magnanimous*

When Jesus forgives, it is forever!

After the Resurrection, Jesus did not reproach the apostles for their cowardice and flight, nor St. Peter for his denial. No, he appeared to all in great joy and treated them as friends. To the Good Thief, he said, "This day will you be with me in Paradise!" For our Lord, to forgive is to forget!

Sometimes, when those wronged are urged toward reconciliation, some will reply starchily, "I will forgive, but I can never forget." In other words, they do not forgive at all. For deep in their hearts, these persons harbour a secret bitterness, a grudge, which at the first opportunity will break forth and produce another quarrel! This is to be expected.

There is no such pettiness in the heart of Jesus. When he forgives our sins, he throws them behind his back, and they are as though they had never been.

283—How ought we to forgive?

Our forgiveness, like that of our Lord, ought to be:

1. Universal: without exception.
2. Unwearying: prompt and without counting the number of times.
3. Effortless: with kindness and indulgence.
4. Magnanimous: forgetting all, once we have forgiven.

Besides giving us an example, our Lord has told us how we ought to forgive, and the steps to take.

The first step is to love our enemies.

It is not enough to forgive with our lips—our hearts must be in it too. And we must not put off our forgiving; for the longer we wait, the harder it is to "make up." Let us take the first step.

Here we need to understand what kind of love is meant. Let us take care not to make this love of enemies consist in a natural attraction, in a liking for them. When our Lord commanded us to love our enemies, he asked nothing like this of us. This is readily explained by the words, "Do good to those who hate you, and pray for those who persecute and calumniate you." Therefore, this is a supernatural love, a love based on our love for God.

The Sister of Charity who cares for lepers and cancer patients, feels no natural attraction for these repulsive diseases. Her acts of charity are so much the more meritorious. In the same way, should your feelings of resentment persist, do the acts required by our Lord and let your mind be at rest.

The second step is to render good for evil to our enemies.

"If your enemy is hungry," says St. Paul, "give him food. If he is thirsty, give him drink. If he is naked, clothe him. If he is in need, fly to his relief." This is the way a Christian "takes vengeance" by kind deeds.

Opportunities for doing good are not lacking, if you look for them. A Christian merchant was once an object of envy and hate on the part of a neighbour, his business rival. So what did he do? Every time that a customer came to his store in search of some article he did not find, he would send him to his enemy's store. Finally, the latter was vanquished. His hate melted and he came and apologized for his past enmity. Thus repeated acts of kindness are as fire which melts the ice of the most hardened hearts. Try it and see!

It is not always possible to render material service to an enemy; but it is possible and even easy to speak a good word for him, to emphasize his good points, etc. This is worth doing, and when your kind words reach an enemy's ear, he is touched by them, and is sometimes more pleased than by a service that might be rendered.

Finally, the final step is prayer.

Prayer for our enemies is most advantageous for us. It calms our irritation, unburdens our heart, and leaves us with a deep feeling of inward sweetness. It draws souls together and prepares for the joy of reconciliation.

While Saul was having Stephen stoned, the latter prayed for his tormentors, "Lord, do not count this sin against them." His prayer was heard. God stopped Saul on the Damascus Road, threw him to the ground, and from a tyrant made him his apostle! Saul become Paul will himself complete this "divine vengeance" by chastising his body and purifying his soul, by working every day to overcome this besetting sin —this tyranny of his passions which had carried him to such extremes of violence.

Such are the miracles which may be wrought by prayer for one's enemies. Or rather from one's opponents, for a Christian has no enemies.

284—Wouldn't thinking sometimes about the many times God has forgiven us, be enough to help us be quick to forgive our neighbour?

Now if you were to go over your whole life from year to year and from week to week, and think about the places where you have lived, the dealings you have had with others, the jobs you have held—surely you would be amazed at the countless sins God has forgiven you!

Just think of the sins committed during childhood. . .adolescence. . .youth. . .adulthood!

Of the sins committed against God. . .against our neighbour. . . against ourselves!

Now if God has been so merciful to us, how can we be so hard and demanding toward others? What right have we to act this way? Did we, who are so hard on our neighbour, die to save him? Let us show a little more meekness and leniency toward him! . . .

"But," perhaps you will say, "how can we love the Church's sworn enemies, who spend their days labouring to tear the very idea of God out of the hearts of their brethren?"

Not only we can, but we ought. As we have said above, God's forgiveness admits of no exception. He wishes ours to be likewise. This is a supernatural love.

Oh, it is so natural to hate and detest those who have done evil to us! To fight back with evil for evil, eye for eye, tooth for tooth—and even a little bit more! ! ! It is so easy to think we are in the right in striking back unmercifully and by fair means or foul, at these benighted souls; without once asking ourselves if they, too, like us, do not have a soul to save—a soul loved by Jesus and for which he died....

We forget that the Christian's best weapon is always charity! How easily we confound the sinner with the sin, treating both with the same rigour! Too numerous still are those who prefer strong-arm methods in the apostolate! In our Lord's day, the apostles wanted to have fire destroy the sinful village. In our own day, many persons think the best way to teach certain people how to live is to kill them!

Before protesting our own innocence, let us ask ourselves what charity we cherish in our hearts toward Jews—Germans—for so and so...we don't take to....

If instead of disliking these persons, what if we were to lay siege to their hearts, and through a true (because supernatural) love, try to win them for Christ? ! What do you say?

And to come back to our starting thought, let us ask ourselves where we would be today, if God had struck us down right after the first serious sin that we have perhaps committed in the course of our life?

LET IT PASS

Let it pass—that word that wounded you, and you will have peace in increased measure. Do not let that opportunity to say a kind word go by without seizing it. By thus bringing pleasure to another, you will have done yourself good as well.

Let it pass without a murmur—that dark cloud in your sky—and you will have grown in patience and in serenity. Do not let a joy or sorrow go by without first offering them up to God. In this way you will have increased joy's sweetness, softened the bitterness of sorrow, and augmented the merit of both.

Let it pass without notice—that lack of courtesy—and without loss of dignity, you will have developed your humility. Do not let an act of courtesy go by without showing your appreciation. You will thus show that you were worthy of the kindness shown, demonstrated your good breeding; and encouraged the other to renewed acts of courtesy...

Let it pass unavenged—the cruel word that is cutting to you alone. Do not let go unavenged an insult against God or religion, or a word that causes scandal to the soul of a child, or a calumny. For your silence, which began by cowardice, would become complicity and finally furnish an encouragement to evil.

—Fr. Bellouard, O.P.

285—To help us to forgive our neighbour promptly, wouldn't it be enough to recognize our share of responsibility for our mutual dislike and ill-will?

Indeed, yes! How many quarrels, grudges, and surly moods, would soon disappear in certain homes, if only we would stop a moment to adjudge with a more impartial mind and more merciful heart the reason for the wall of separation between our neighbour and us.

There are persons living in the same house, sometimes belonging to the same family (and hence intended by God to live together in the bond of charity), who have not been on speaking terms for years! And these people still go to church and dare to deem themselves disciples of Christ! As if, without love, we could be Christ's disciples! Our Lord said, "By this sign shall men know that you are my disciples, if you love one another" . . . Such persons ruin their own lives and poison the existence of others!

And the cause? This is often to be found in a *profound selfishness, in a pride that makes no allowance for human weakness, in an extreme susceptibility, headstrongness, and blindness as to one's own conduct— or simply a misunderstanding!*

With a little humility and good will, it would be so easy to understand one another and to make allowances.

If we are to form an accurate judgment of some wrong imputed to our neighbour of which we claim to be victims, and better appreciate those clashes attributed to the malice of others, would it not be better to place ourselves on the scales too?

Besides, when we complain of an offense, do we take into consideration our own touchiness, emotionalism, or susceptibility? So many people exaggerate, or interpret innocent words or actions in the wrong light. A word dropped in conversation, or thoughtlessly written—with no harm intended—is taken wrong by a suspicious mind. Thus a mountain is made out of a molehill, a big thing out of nothing! A gay wisecrack becomes a catastrophe to a sensitive soul; who takes note of and stores up everything said or done, tying it up with previous observations and painting a canvas which his imagination loads with sombre colours at will! These folks go out of their way to torture themselves—and to torture other folks!

The pessimists, of course, are always dead sure that they have good reasons for distrusting those around them who "deceive" and "hoodwink" them. . . . Now, if this is the case, are they really sure that it was intentional? And supposing that it was, have they not provoked it? . . .

If we are so sure that our neighbour has not treated us right, why not sincerely ask ourselves if we have always acted toward him the way we should!

Again, misunderstandings arise from our inability to understand others. Thus, man is ignorant of feminine psychology, and vice versa! How many troubles each could avoid, if each *did* understand the other! Woman is especially hard to fathom! St. Teresa of Avila is supposed to have said that the Devil himself is not clever enough to comprehend a woman's soul, so numerous are the enigmas it presents! (All the same, it is too bad that Old Satan found Mother Eve so easy to beguile!)

Be that as it may, it would not be a bad idea to read a few books on practical psychology, if we would live in peace with the world in general.

286—How should we act when a quarrel or misunderstanding does arise between us and our neighbour?

This! (After we have prayed and cooled off a bit.)

1. Give our neighbour the benefit of the doubt. If we cannot excuse the deed, we can always excuse the intention. So let it be our aim to see that the wrong done us by our neighbour comes less from willful perversity and hostility, than from the sum total of different influences which have obscured his judgment and conscience. For mercy always seeks to lessen the responsibility of the "other fellow."

2. Let us—in the light of humility—sincerely recognize our own faults, mistaken conduct, and even our ill will toward others. (Without mentioning the countless times we have—all unconsciously perhaps—rubbed the other person's fur the wrong way!) It is so easy for us to see the speck in our brother's eye, and so hard for us to see the beam in our own!

3. Keep in mind God's infinite mercy toward us; and remind ourselves that if we have received more, we ought to give more to God, by way of kindness and indulgence toward our neighbour.

4. Let us be prompt to "make up" with the person concerned. We should never let a grudge or a quarrel continue, even for a day. "Let not the sun go down upon your wrath," we read in the Bible. As soon as we are aware that our neighbour has suffered from our words or actions, we ought to seize the first opportunity that offers, to straighten things out—to undo as soon as may be, the bad effect. For this, we may make use of the current polite formulas of "Forgive me," "excuse me," "I'm dreadfully sorry," "I'm so sorry I forgot" (or) "that I was rude," "that I was unkind," "that I was impatient," "that I hurt you."

St. Teresa of Avila points out that in this petition of the Pater Noster, the verb is in the present and not in the future. Our Lord does not have us say, "Forgive us our trespasses as we we are *going* to forgive those who have trespassed against us," but "as we *forgive.*" Jesus gives us to understand here that it is something already done! ! ! "Our Lord," says the saint, thereby teaches us that whoever sincerely prays to God, "Your will be done," ought to have already forgiven his neighbour completely; or, at least, be sincerely and firmly resolved to do so."

5. Let our constant attitude toward those who refuse all reconciliation be one of good will. We should never give up hope. By his outgoing love, St. Francis of Assisi won over the most thankless, rebellious, and hardened hearts. Remember his apostolate to the lepers! (See *Mon Cercle d'Etude,* May, 1946.)

Let us likewise think of St. Francis de Sales, who said to a person who had insulted him: "Even if you were to tear out one of my eyes, I would look at you as lovingly with the other, as at the best friend I have in this world!"

Let us mull over, too, this beautiful saying of the holy layman, Thomas More, high chancellor of the Court of London: "We must write our wrongs on the sand, and carve our blessings on marble!" "Carving our blessings on marble," means keeping their memory green in eternally grateful hearts. "Writing our wrongs on the sand," means effacing them forever from memory, the way our foot wipes out the characters we have just traced in the dust of the road.

And to wind up, let us say to God: "Our Father, who are in Heaven, many are our offenses against you. We beg your forgiveness for them; may they be for us as if they had never been. Cast these transgressions afar off—let them no longer be present in the thought of your justice. We thank you for having made this grace for which we beseech you, to depend on us. You have assured us of your forgiveness, if we forgive our brother. It is from the heart, with the last vestige gone of enmity or hate, that we remit the debt he contracted toward us by offending against us. We shall do good to him whenever we have the means or opportunity to do so.

Forgive us our trespasses as we forgive those who trespass against us. Amen!

A PRIEST

"What joy for a Catholic to think that he has had a part in the formation of a priest; and is thus as it were in part responsible for the merits accumulated by the priestly ministry of this "other Christ." When the bells of his parish church peal out their harmonious prayer to the Consecrated Host, by virtue of the divine power of the priest, what a joy to think that he has co-operated in this mystery of love."

—Msgr. Roger Marien

* * *

A vocation is not the result of chance. People do not gather lilies from thorns; nor are saints discovered in suspicious places. Likewise, vocations do not usually spring up in families devoid of a Christian mentality. A priest or a religious is the reward of a family pleasing to God, the crown of two lives united in self-forgetfulness, of duty perfectly performed, of sacrifice joyously accepted.

Vocation! The greatest factor in success—here, as in every other field—still lies in the power of folded hands. For a vocation is before everything else a call of God and a free gift of his condescension. Who can claim to have merited such a gift? Humble and fervent prayer alone can justify asking God to look upon a family and choose from it a soul of his predilection.

Lead us not into temptation

287—What is the sixth petition of the Pater Noster?

The sixth petition is "Lead us not into temptation."

288—What is meant here by the word, "temptation?"

The word, "temptation," as employed in the Pater Noster, comes from a Greek word, meaning not only, as in English, "a suggestion to do evil," but all sorts of trials, persecutions, and sufferings.

289—How many kinds of temptation are there?

According to the preceding question, temptations may be divided into two groups: good and bad. Or what would be still better:

1. Temptations to good.
2. Temptations to evil.

"To tempt" means to test, to incite someone to speak, to make himself known, so as to see what he is capable of doing. Thus a person may be incited to good or evil.

In the first case, the temptation is good and comes from God.

In the second case, the temptation is, at the very least, dangerous, and comes from the Devil or his agents. As we shall see later on, even Satan's temptations or evil suggestions may serve to sanctify us, because of our resistance. It is for this reason that God does not will them, but permits them. It is of the second class of temptations—incitement to evil—of which St. James speaks when he tells us that God never tempts us: "Let no man say when he is tempted, that he is tempted of God; for God is no tempter to evil." (James 1:13.)

To think that God incites us to evil, would be a frightful blasphemy. God is infinitely perfect, for is he not Perfection itself? Now, as Perfection, God can neither will, counsel, nor love sin, nor incite anyone in any way to commit it. How could God have us pray, "Lead us not into temptation," if he were the one who sent the temptation? Doubtless, God permits dangerous temptations, but he permits them only as we are able to bear them, and he has in view our spiritual advancement by the victory he hopes for us. But we cannot think or say that God is the author of temptations to evil, for that would be saying that God wills evil.

When we pray, "Lead us not into temptation," we are praying God to remove from us every danger, and to give us the means to resist temptation, to overcome it and to triumph over it. For our weakness is so great, that without Heaven's aid, victory could easily elude us. So little lies, sometimes, between feeling and consenting!

290—Is the "temptation to good" included in the sixth petition of the Pater Noster?

Yes, because good trials may sometimes—because of our lack of faith—discourage us and cause us to fall.

When God wishes to raise a soul to perfection, he subjects it to trial. He requires of it acts of the difficult virtues—sometimes most difficult—but never above its strength.

We all know the heroic sacrifice that God asked of Abraham, when he ordered him to take his beloved son, Isaac, and offer him up as a burnt offering! Abraham obeyed, but an angel stayed the arm of the holy patriarch. This was an extremely difficult trial; which Abraham came through with flying colours, and greater in the eyes of God, who richly rewarded him.

When trials or temptations assume frightening proportions for our human nature, they are usually the reward of a holy life, or the starting point of a higher perfection.

Such is the case of the holy man Job and of Tobias.

When the trial of the latter had ended, the archangel Raphael gave him this explanation, which sheds light on God's dealings with us. The archangel reminded Tobias of all his good works, fastings, and prayers: "When you, Tobias, were praying, and with tears, when you were burying the dead," (this had been at the risk of his life) "leaving your dinner untasted, so as to hide them all day in your house and at night give them funeral, I, all the while, was offering your prayer to the Lord. Then, because you had won his favour, needs must that trials should come and test your worth." (Tob. 12: 12-13.) [Knox.]

Note this last line; "Because you had won his favour, needs must that trials should come." Once we have understood this, we shall not be astonished at being subjected to difficult and painful temptations.

When we are visited by trial, we should neither murmur nor become discouraged; but follow St. James' advice instead: "Esteem it a joy, brethren, when you fall into various trials, knowing that the trying of your faith begets patience. And let patience have its perfect work, that you may be perfect and entire, lacking nothing."

Souls tending toward perfection do not ask to be delivered from the trial type of temptation. St. Teresa of Avila, explaining the sixth petition of the Pater Noster, says to us: "One thing I am sure of, and that is that the perfect do not ask God to be delivered from suffering, temptation, persecution, or combats. Far from fearing them, they desire them, they ask for them, they love them; like soldiers, who greatly prefer battles which give promise of advancement, to peace and idleness which reduce them to peacetime pay with no hope of advancement."

However, if it is a question of great trials like those of Job or Tobias, the part of wisdom would be neither to desire them nor pray for them. For there is always the danger of yielding to presumption and vainglory.

The sixth petition of the Pater Noster is readily applicable to the "good" temptations, as we have explained them. For we may lack courage, cowardly shrink from them, or give way to murmuring—all of which, in a sense, is to yield to temptation. As we have discussed these trials at some length in commenting on the third petition of the Pater Noster, we shall not dwell on them here.

HOLINESS

Holiness is simply a full and perpetual "Yes" that is said by the creature to the Creator. A living "Yes" in which one voluntarily puts his whole being. A fervent, active, practical "Yes". A "Yes" that separates and raises above all that is low, in order to devote, consecrate, and deliver one as a "thing," a victim, and a word to that which is high— or rather, to the Most High, Christ, Son of God and true God; of whom the Church sings in imitation of the angels, "You alone are holy! You alone are the Lord. You alone, O Jesus Christ, are most high."

—Msgr. GAY

291—Is temptation to evil a sin?

Of itself, such temptation is indifferent, or at the most, dangerous. Even though it may be engineered by the Devil for our damnation, we can make use of it for our sanctification. It is evil only in its author—the Devil—or in its object: an invitation to evil. For us, everything depends on the use we make of it.

Fire, of itself, is a dangerous element. But we use it to heat the stove and cook our food. What could be better? If we use fire to burn down our neighbour's house, fire becomes evil because of the evil use we make of it.

292—Where do temptations to evil come from?

They come from three sources:

1. The Devil and his wiles.
2. The world with its seductions and maxims.
3. Ourselves with our concupiscence or inclination to evil.

1. *The Devil*

Temptation to evil comes first of all from the Devil, this fallen angel for whom God had to create Hell. The Devil is filled with hatred toward Him who so justly condemned him, and with jealousy toward us—seeking our ruin by every means in his power.

He it was who tempted and ruined our first parents, and he would like to ruin all their descendants called to take his place in Heaven. To this end, he employs all his wiles, mind, and malignity. "The Devil," says St. Peter, "goes about roaring like a lion to find his prey." (1 Peter 5:8.) [Knox.]

2. *The world*

The second enemy that tempts us is the world; that is, the sum total of visible creatures which solicit us to love them for themselves, independently of God, because of the pale reflection of the divine beauty they present to our gaze; and which charm us to the point of making us believe that we shall find in them the happiness for which we were created and which God alone can give.

Again, the world is the sum total of human beings who, by their bad example, their advice, and their ridicule, seek to turn us away from God and virtue. In particular, it is the tyrannical demands of fashion, of worldly pleasures, of dangerous amusements and spectacles, etc.

The world is a powerful tempter; and that is why so many wishing to attain Christian perfection, have left it and shut themselves up in cloisters, in deserts, and in solitudes—placing between themselves and the world an insurmountable barrier. These have understood the Divine Master's curse on the world: "Woe to the world because of scandals!" (Matt. 18:7.)

Those true Christians who have not shut themselves up in monasteries, but have remained in the world, have adopted means for living in the world as not of the world. They have not lent their ears to its perverse speech. They have not attached their hearts to the deceptive lures it dangles before their eyes. They have fled the giddy whirl of worldly pleasure, of corrupting spectacles. They have understood that if we would enjoy all the world's pleasures, we lose our souls; but if we forsake all false pleasure to attach ourselvevs to virtue, we find true joy: a quiet conscience, the esteem of good people, a taste for spiritual things, and the assurance of Heaven's happiness.

These true Christians have found in the Third Order the protection enjoyed by religious in their monasteries for vanquishing this second source of temptation—the world with its lures.

3. *Ourselves*

The enemy most to be feared, the closest to us and most dread, is our own flesh: this flesh prone to sin which easily leads us into vice, this flesh which wars against God's Spirit, and which opposes in us the penchants of nature as over against the impressions of grace. This enemy is so much the more deadly because we carry it always with us, because it is none other than ourselves.

There is not one of our senses or faculties which does not tempt and expose us to temptation. The passions ferment to a greater or less extent in every heart and mind: pride lifts us up, avarice sets a snare for us, envy torments, impurity would defile body and soul, anger irritates us, gluttony degrades us, laziness and idleness teach us every vice. . . .

This trial of the flesh is extremely painful for those who would be good. The flesh is an enemy we cannot get rid of, no matter what we do. We can subdue it; we can dominate it; but it is there; alive and demanding, murmuring when we do not gratify it, giving itself over to every excess when we slacken the reins.

Listen to St. Paul, the great apostle, whose soul was caught up to the third Heaven, where it had the honour of being admitted to share in the divine secrets: "There was given me a thorn for the flesh. . .to buffet me. . . . For I do not do the good that I wish. . . . When I wish to do good, I discover this law, namely, that evil is at hand for me. For I am delighted with the law of God according to the inner man, but I see another law in my members, warring against the law of my mind and making me prisoner to the law of sin. . . . Unhappy man that I am! Who will deliver me from the body of this death?" (Rom. 12:7, 7:19:ff.

All of us—more or less—have these temptations to combat. To us, as to St. Paul, our Lord says, "My grace is sufficient for you."

293—What are the two kinds of dangerous temptations?

1. There are dangerous temptations which appear dangerous—those directly opposed to the virtues.

2. There are dangerous temptations which do not appear dangerous. These are more insidious, because dissembled in the guise of virtue.

1. *Temptations directly dangerous*

There is no need to insist on this kind. They are readily recognized as dangerous. One need only name the seven capital sins to recognize nearly all of them.

We shall see further on how to cope with them.

2. *Temptations indirectly dangerous*

Here we ought to list our delusions!

294—What do you mean by temptations "indirectly dangerous?" Please give examples.

Temptations indirectly dangerous are those that present themselves to us under the appearance of something good that may be realized or of some spiritual advantage that may be procured. They are a snare of the Devil, who well knows the little quirks of us humans! "They will kill you," says our Lord, "and think that they are offering worship to God!" To such a sorry pass can blindness sometimes lead!

Before being committed, sin has one look: the Devil offers it to us from the aspect of pleasure and interest.... Recall the temptation of our first parents in the Garden of Eden. The Devil offered a luscious fruit with excellent promises for the eater: "You will be like God."

After commission, sin's look changes, for the Devil wishes to discourage the guilty soul and keep it from Confession. This is the aspect of responsibility, of the gravity and enormity of the sin committed, that he injects into minds already racked by remorse. "My crime is too great to be forgiven!" cried Cain after he had slain his brother Abel. The Devil had passed that way.

Before sinning, the sinner is proud and says, "What fun!" Now, he blushes and cries out, "How miserable I feel!"

Before, his only reply to warnings was, "Oh, it's nothing!" Now his response to proffered pardon is, "Leave me alone! It's too late! I'm done for!"

Duty makes stern demands; pleasure allures. Caught between the two, the soul often wavers; and without too much self-analysis, invents for itself reasons and pretexts for excusing conduct good only in appearance.

People are right when they say, "The Devil oft makes the worse appear the better reason!"

Let us take a glimpse, then, at the way the Devil acts with those souls already in the way of perfection. Let us remind ourselves first that the Devil is the father of lies. Trickery, guile, deceit, and falsehood—these are his methods!

Here we see him at the door of a soul docile to grace, but who has not yet extirpated the root of pride within. Listen to him:

"You are no longer a child!" You have a right to know what is in this book! Forewarned is forearmed.... You know enough to distinguish truth from error!... And doesn't your apostolate require you to be better informed on these things?"

To another he will say: "This film. . .this friendship. . .this date. . . this evening out of town. . .this dance. . .are not so dangerous as they try to make out. Only a fool sees evil in everything. Besides, there is always time to pull yourself together, to turn over a new leaf, and (should you need to) go to Confession!"

To this accumulation of lies, trickery is added. For the Devil acts with consummate art. He chooses his hour for the open attack after the softening up process. Serpent that he is, he unfolds his coils one by one.

He takes great care not to frighten. It is only little by little that he deadens the violence of the first scruples and creates habits of laxity.

Certain temptations are more subtle and may trouble the well-intentioned. For instance, the Devil will try to keep souls away from Holy Communion, through the fear of making unworthy Communions or under the pretext that Holy Communion is of no benefit to them. This temptation is peculiar to those souls who wish to judge for themselves of the benefit they reap from their Communions—a thing they should never do.

Another temptation and delusion is that of thinking that one can "do more good" by abandoning prayer and meditation, so as to be able to devote more time to one's apostolate. This temptation comes when the soul is going through a trial of dryness. Not finding in meditation any good thoughts or sensible affections, but being on the contrary besieged by distractions and even by bad thoughts, they have the impression that they are accomplishing nothing. Hence, the temptation to hurl oneself into the feverish activity of one's apostolate! This is sheer delusion. For meditation spells the death of self-love and begins to bring about this result only when it is dry, tasteless, and without consolation. Giving it up at this stage, means doing considerable damage to the progress already made and running the risk of falling into a purely natural activity.

Another delusion is a sugary, sentimental piety, made up of long prayers and novenas to numerous saints. This is a piety tinctured with superstition, having its roots neither in self-denial nor a true spirit of faith.... A piety incapable of buckling down to the austere acceptance of the small, daily task, but which dreams of immolations and holocausts!

It is a delusion and a temptation to propose for ourselves any other good than that which God requires of us. For instance, neglecting the duty of one's state in life, to do some task more to one's liking or to exercise a more showy apostolate! How frequent is this temptation! Under pretext of charity, zeal, or edification of one's neighbour, how duty is distorted! The worst of it is that this neglect of our own responsibilities lays heavy burdens on those who must carry on, in addition to their own work, the tasks that we—under a mistaken pretext of zeal—failed to do! Remember always that our apostolate begins at home, at school, at the office, wherever God has placed us. And before launching out into supernumerary works, let us start by carrying out the duties of our state in life. In this way, we shall not expose ourselves to this aberration—so much the more subtle because its alleged motive is fraternal charity!

Another form of delusion and temptation is that of practicing charity to the detriment of justice, by giving alms with other people's money! When we owe a person money, we ought to pay him back first; and then, and then only, give alms.

Delusions are of frequent occurrence. If we started listing them, we should never finish.

How insincere we are! How many excuses (the fair sex excels here) we make to salve our consciences, and leave untouched the comfortable *status quo*.

With a great deal of psychology and humour, Fr. Faber depicts in his *Spiritual Conferences,* the delusions of those worldly-minded individuals, who nevertheless consider themselves fervent Christians! "A permanent scandal for the world," (he writes) "is this strange admixture of worldliness and devotion, so common among those persons making a profession of piety, that the world (without taking the trouble to reflect) admits of no exception.

"For people think to combine prayer and elegant fashions, almsgiving and extravagance, the sacraments and love of the table, humility and snobbishness, spiritual conferences and worship of the great, balls and communions, benedictions and the theatre, works of charity and intrigues, the interior life and costly furniture; the whole being blended, combined, and entangled in such confusion as to furnish the subject matter for a year's conversation altogether!"

"Worldliness," he says a bit further on, "consists in an infinity of things which a man might permit himself taken separately, but which lead to an end for which no permission could be given; either because taken altogether they are bad, or because they acquire too great a hold on our affections. Things which in themselves are not bad, become blameworthy when they stand between God and us; and odious a thousandfold when they assume God's place in our hearts. We do not see the true malice in each of these elements of worldliness, taken alone; because ignorant of ourselves as we are, we can neither distinguish nor estimate the unfortunate effects which render such and such an amusement dangerous, or, taken in strong doses, fatal for us."

It has been said that self-love is the art of modestly covering up one's faults! Of how many delusions is not this immoderate love of self the cause!

1. The delusion of pride—which becomes "legitimate self-respect!"

2. Tricks our vanity plays—under the pretext of "a more fruitful apostolate"!

3. Susceptibility—taken for "sensitiveness"!

4. Stubborness—become "strength of character"!

5. Rudeness—dubbed "frankness"!

6. Softness—surnamed "meekness"!

7. Avarice—metamorphosed into "economy"!

8. Gluttony—confounded with a concern for "conserving one's strength"!

And to wind up the list, delusions anent one's health!

If we should avoid overwork, we must not fall into the opposite extreme of giving exaggerated care to "brother ass"! (St. Francis of Assisi, little accustomed to pampering himself, called his body by the picturesque name of "brother ass.")

Alongside those who neglect their health, are others who take too good care of it. Under the pretext of working better later on, they have quit working altogether! They listen to their heartbeats, look at their tongue, take their pulse, watch their weight, and never risk going out in damp or rainy weather. They gulp down incalculable quantities of pills and potions, follow a strict diet and—are always ailing! Their favourite prescription reads: "Eat heartily, and never work between meals!"

More delusions! How many saints with delicate health still got through a disconcerting amount of work! The *Imitation* tells us that "a holy life is to be preferred to a long life."

Everybody has his pet delusions—especially, perhaps, young people! That is why in cases of uncertainty or doubt, a spiritual director is particularly necessary.

Further on, we shall see how to overcome temptation.

295—Should being tempted surprise us?

Not at all. And why not? *Because God has permitted the temptation for his glory.*

The reason for temptation is not sin. Temptation comes before sin. Before their rebellion, the angels underwent trial or temptation. Adam and Eve were tempted before their fall. Even if Adam and Eve had never sinned, we should all have had to go through temptation.

We have said that the reason for temptation is the glory of God. This is part of the divine plan. God *could* have given us Heaven without asking anything in return, but this would have been less glorious for him. For there is more glory in being chosen, or (if you wish) in being loved with a preferential love.

Many say to us, "But why does God make creatures so attractive to us, if we are supposed to become detached from them and prefer him?"

This is why! You need to feel this attraction for created objects; so that they may, in a certain fashion, "vie" with God. And so that we may have the merit of making a free choice and of saying to God, "I am very fond of creatures. I thrill to everything that you have created. But I prefer You to all of them!"

This is the way Catherine de Montalembert talked when she was twenty-two. Entering one day the study of her father, the famous Count of Montalembert, her face illumined by a sort of supernatural light, she said: "Father, I love everything! I love to have a good time. I love wit, the world, dancing, my family, my studies, my friends, my age, my life, and my country; but I love God more and I want to give myself to him wholly in religious life!" (Cf. *Quand Dieu invite* ("when God calls") by Msgr. Marie-Antoine Roy, O.F.M., p. 35.)

This choice between God and creatures is not achieved without a struggle. "A bird in the hand is worth two in the bush," says the proverb. We sometimes find that Heaven's promised happiness seems afar off, while creatures are within reach! That is why this choice presupposes a great spirit of faith, much self-denial, and the help of God's grace.

Remember that feeling attracted to creatures is not evil, and is not sinful. The more we feel attracted, the more we should rejoice; for we can sacrifice more to God, and, by that very fact, give him greater glory!

"No gain without pain!"

If before the fall of the first man, temptation was on the divine program; still more is it after that fall, and for this reason:

With the advent of sin, the Devil became bold. He is jealous of man, destined to take his place in Heaven and be happy forever.

We find two texts in the Bible which tell us much of the Devil's rage toward mankind. "The Devil's envy brought death into the world." *(Book of Wisdom.)* "He was a murderer from the beginning." (John 8:44.)

In order to understand this attitude of the Devil, the circumstances of his fall must be recalled. Lucifer was a very perfect, intelligent, and handsome angel. (Ezek. 27 and 28.) To test him, God supposedly revealed to him the Incarnation of the Second Person of the Blessed Trinity, the Word. Jealous at seeing a Man preferred to him, a Man predestined to the hypostatic union, and whom he—perfect angel and pure spirit—was to serve, he rebelled. "*Non serviam!* I will not serve! I will not obey!" he shrieked.

> "What, fallen from Heaven, Lucifer, that once did herald the dawn? Prostrate on the earth, that once did bring nations on their knees? I will scale the heavens (such was your thought); I will set my throne higher than God's stars, take my seat at his own trysting place, at the meeting of the northern hills; I will soar above the level of the clouds, the rival of the Most High. Yours instead, to be dragged down into the world beneath, into the heart of the abysss." (Isa. 14: 12-16.) [Knox.]

To avenge themselves of their fall, the fallen angels attempted through envy to thwart the Incarnation. They unleashed their fury against man and tried every conceivable means to make him fall; so that God would destroy mankind or at least refuse to become incarnate in a sinner. But the Devil reckoned without God's infinite mercy, and without the Blessed Virgin, born without stain of sin, who was to crush the head of the malignant serpent!

Nevertheless, this explains why we should not be surprised at temptation. Since sin's advent, moreover, our resistance to evil has been weakened. But we may be sure that the temptation will never prove stronger than God's grace always at our disposal.

Another consideration. *It is no shame to be tempted.* Many persons find it difficult to speak of these assaults, as if they were the only ones at grips with the world, the flesh, and the Devil! As if being tempted were equivalent to sinning! Our Lord was thrice tempted by the Devil. The greatest saints have been severely tempted. Listen to St. Augustine: "My former passions thronged around me. They grasped me by my robe of flesh and tried to drag me into evil!" And what of the victorious battles of St. Francis of Assisi over his rebellious flesh? (See *Corps mystique et modestie chrétienne.)*

Not only should temptation not surprise us, it should also reassure us. Thieves never bother beggars! Soldiers in wartime have never attacked a city which laid down its arms and surrendered. So if we are much troubled by attacks of the Devil, it means that we have not yet been conquered. It also means that from a spiritual standpoint, we are rich! And this is just what makes the Devil jealous! He would like to draw us away from the love of Christ—his constant Foe!

St. Ephrem, the Syrian, once had a vision. At the gates of a city where vice was rife, he saw a demon drowsing on the walls, who turned over in his sleep now and then. But in the desert he saw a veritable swarm of demons around a holy hermit—all in the greatest activity. For the Devil does not tempt those who belong to him already, but those who are escaping or struggling against him! That is why St. John Chrysostom said that where we find a great number of temptations, it may generally be concluded that a great number of virtues are present.

Therefore, let us keep cool in these storm-tossed moments and trust in Him who strengthens us.

296—What are the advantages of temptation?

Temptation is of great advantage to us:

1. It arouses us from our lukewarmness, the way the touch of the spur rouses a horse. . . .

2. It purifies us from our imperfections, the way the heaving billows cast off debris and rubbish. . . .

3. It increases our energies; the way a tree shaken by storms plunges its roots deeper into the soil—and sheds its dead branches. . . .

4. It furnishes us with an opportunity of proving to God that we really love him; and it augments this love, just as fire burns brighter when fanned by the wind. . . .

5. It helps us to atone, even on this earth, for the penalties due to our sins, by means of the sacrifices it imposes. . . .

6. It makes us practice several virtues at once; for every resistance to evil is an act of volition, faith, hope, and love. . . .

7. And above all, temptation is a source of humility for us!

For nothing is more calculated to show us our nothingness and vileness, than the different forms of temptation and the sudden and violent onslaughts of Satan. Were it not for temptation, we might sometimes imagine ourselves to be filled with virtue and freed from the original taint. Temptation warns us that we are always frail and inclined to evil; and, therefore, inclined to fall without God's support. St. Paul confesses that he was tormented by most humiliating temptations, and for what cause? "Lest the greatness of the revelations should puff me up." He calls these temptations the "buffetings" of Satan. He prays to be delivered from them, and God refuses! "No," he says to Paul, "my grace is sufficient for you." Virtue is perfected in infirmity; that is, in our awareness of our weakness.

"Temptation does not make us bad," says the *Imitation.* "It merely shows us as we are." How dare we be proud and critical of the conduct of others, when within ourselves we find so much weakness, so much lack of consideration toward God and our neighbour?

Temptation (if we know how to use it as a Christian) likewise does us the great service of detaching us from earth and uniting us more closely to God. This life is a place of pilgrimage and exile—Heaven is our home. God does not want us to take the place of our exile for our homeland. We should be in danger of this, if on earth we encountered only the sweet joys of virtue, and the exaltation and intoxication of spiritual consolation! So the Lord sends us a mixture of joy and suffering. He permits this life to be subject to temptation and trouble so as to make us long for Him who is the journey's end and Love's true centre.

Thus temptation is very useful, and the Devil really does a service when he tempts us! Now we understand better why God permits temptation.

The teacher gives his pupils tests, so that he can give them good marks. God permits temptation to place us in a difficult situation so as to afford us the opportunity of proving our loyalty to him and of acquiring a right to a heavenly reward. In his mercy then, he has only our good in view. Thus one may say that temptations are a sign of divine favour. It is up to us to use them well, as we shall see further on.

297—What difference do you see between "feeling" and "consenting?"

"Despise those evil imaginings that you falsely take for culpable thoughts," once wrote Msgr. de Ségur to a tortured soul. "The sin of bad thoughts does not consist in having the thought of evil in one's mind; but in VOLUNTARILY picturing evil actions to oneself as if doing them and taking pleasure in the doing. All these little sparks that the Devil flashes before our eyes, are but will-o'-the-wisps, not worth bothering about."

How many refined and pious souls are troubled about temptations of the flesh! They are sometimes assailed by long and severe temptations, conducive of disquieting sensations, and they fear for the state of their conscience! These worries often come from ignorance, in which we must never remain.

Here are a few rules. Every temptation leading to sin or to merit, consists of three parts or stages:

1. The evil *suggestion* or proposition—a thought or imagining induced by the world, the flesh, or the Devil. For instance, the thought of vengeance, or of committing some wrongful act.

2. The *delectation* or pleasure which the person takes in the thing proposed. Instinctively, before any appeal to reason, the thing suggested pleases or displeases. This object may even provoke (independently of the will) a sensation of pleasure. For example, that revenge would be sweet, or the doing of something wrong.

But "feeling is not consent." No sin so far. Everything depends on consent.

3. *Consent or refusal*

Consent can take two forms:

1. I consent to the suggestion. For instance, I acquiesce in the desire of vengeance. "Yes, I *will* get even with him!" There is sin here, whether I take vengeance or not.

2. I consent to the delectation. For example, I refuse to carry out the evil desire, but I voluntarily hang on to it and savour it. I like and dwell on the feeling this gives me. Here again there is sin.

So then, only consent is sin. Refusal to consent is an act of merit.

Here in outline is the process or progressive march of temptation:

Indifferent act

1. The evil suggestion.	Otherwise said, "to be tempted."
2. Sensation and delectation.	Otherwise said, the feeling of pleasure.

Moral act

	Otherwise said:
3. Consent	Consenting (sin)
or	or
Refusal.	Not consenting (act of merit).

It is thus only at the last stage that our responsibility arises; because this is where the will intervenes, which alone imparts moral value to our actions.

We could be troubled for days at a time by impure thoughts or by doubts concerning the Faith, and subject—in these times of fierce struggle—to sensations of pleasure.... We still have no cause for alarm. Up to now the will has not entered into the picture, so there is neither merit nor sin.

But now we must take a stand. This is the third stage in which we freely choose: God or sin!

If our will, enlightened by our intelligence as to the malice of this temptation, gives its consent, we have sinned.

But if our will refuses its consent, far from having offended God, we have accomplished an act of merit for which we shall be rewarded in Heaven, even if—quite independently of our will—we have experienced a sensation of pleasure.

Many persons say to us, "I fear lest I consented!"

To this, St. Francis de Sales replies: "So long as the temptation is displeasing to you, there is nothing to fear. For why is it displeasing to you, if not because you do not will it? For consent presupposes an agreement so complete, an acceptance of the will so total, as to leave no room for doubt." Doubt is then in your favour, especially if you have a tender conscience.

The holy Bishop of Geneva says elsewhere: "Our hearts are like mirrors. The glass shows us the thing opposite it, but this object is not in the mirror. So it is with our hearts, which are mirrors on which the Devil can depict the most infamous objects; but our will alone can open the door and admit these horrors. So let the Devil grimace as he will and form the most fearful pictures before your eyes. All this does not make you guilty of sin."

A FRANCISCAN'S PRAYER

Lord Jesus, who are our Way, our Joy and our Life, we pray you to teach us along the roads where you are our companion:

The spirit of Poverty, which liberates from vain things.

The spirit of Humility and Simplicity which delivers from slavery to self.

The sense and generous understanding of the Cross which stands at all our crossroads—our hope of salvation and of resurrection.

Especially cause us to live (your grace fructifying our efforts) in intimate fellowship with you; and in outgoing fellowship with our brothers.

Lord, keep our hearts open to the vast horizons; and to every inspiration which comes to us from the "Mighty Deep." Keep our hearts open to all your graces; so that on Joy's highway, we may merit to bring to you all those with whom we come in contact.

We ask it through—

Our Lady of the Way, your Mother and ours.

St. Francis of Assisi, our Little Poor Man, whom we have chosen for our Chief; and whom Pope Pius XI proclaimed Patron of Catholic Action. Amen.

298—Are we not sometimes tempted beyond our strength?

Never! The temptation of Job makes plain that the Devil's power is no greater than God permits; and that when God leaves us exposed to violent temptations, he gives us sufficient grace to resist them. The more violent the temptation, the more potent the grace; the greater the peril, the more forcefully does God come to our aid. No one can excuse himself, then, by saying that the temptation was too strong.

Let us be convinced that in time of temptation, God is near. "Dear Lord," prayed a saint with streaming eyes, "where were You during my trial?" And she heard him reply, "Deep within your heart! I did not forget you a single instant. I collected your sighs, prayers, and tears. I saw all your combats and sufferings. I counted your efforts, your victories, and your merits. I was always there to watch over you, inspire you, and uphold you, and to dry your tears as a mother does for her suffering child. Be of good cheer. What you have sown in tears, you shall reap in joy."

Consoling words, these, which we cannot meditate too often.

Just as the potter does not leave his jars too long in the oven, lest they be shattered; even so does God watch over his children, never submitting them to a trial which would be beyond their strength.

Let us remember always that whenever we feel the weight of the Cross, Jesus is not far away; because Jesus is always on the Cross! And if we are with Jesus, who can be against us?

299—How can we manage always to resist evil temptations?

Before listing some positive means for overcoming temptation, we would point out that it is elementary first of all to shun the occasions of sin!

Everyone knows himself, and past experience should doubtless be conducive to prudence.... It is useless to throw straw on the fire and then pray God for it not to burn. If you voluntarily place yourself in a proximate occasion of sin, doing nothing to get out of it, do not be surprised if you are strongly tempted, or if you fall....

There is no playing with temptation. Giving in an inch means weakening yourself, but not the temptation. Far from it! The first concession is the source of many falls. "Give me a hair," said the Devil to St. Francis, "and I will weave a cable from it."

"It is easier," wrote Eymieu, "to chase the first thought, than to suppress all that follows. It is easier not to plant the acorn, than it is to uproot the oak."

So first of all, comes avoidance of the occasions of sin.

Now here are ten means we would suggest for vanquishing the wiles of the world, the flesh, and the Devil:

1. *An intense interior life*

A comparison, such as we find in the Gospels, will help us to grasp the thought that to make sure of vanquishing temptation, an intense interior life is imperative:

If you look at the leaves on the trees, especially when the sap is flowing freely through their veins, you will notice that they are strongly attached to the branch. You will never find them in springtime scattered over the ground. But in the autumn, the sap gradually withdraws, the leaves fall from the tree at the least breath of air, and die. This is the picture of tempted souls. Just so long as the life of grace abounds in souls because of their union with Christ—the Tree of Life—no amount of shaking, however violent, is able to separate them from him. But let the divine life become rare, or almost cease to circulate—that is the time to watch out! At the slightest temptation they fall; and risk being separated, perhaps forever, from Jesus Christ, the Tree of Life!

Blessed Jordan of Saxony wrote along these lines: "The heart without Christ is like chaff from which the grain has been removed, driven by the wind. Empty, the heart is tossed hither and yon by temptation. But the chaff still containing the grain, is fixed by the latter's weight. In the same way, the heart strengthened by the indwelling Christ, even when agitated by temptation, is not dragged hither and yon, nor carried away by it."

2. *Keeping busy*

Idleness is the mother of every vice. "Always be doing something," said St. Francis of Assisi, "so that the Devil will find you busy." While St. Francis de Sales had this to say, "If the Devil finds you busy, he has nothing to do. If he finds you doing nothing, than *he* gets busy!"

It has been said that flies do not like to light on a hot plate... and thieves are not fond of going into a house where they hear someone working. In the same way, the Devil shuns busy folks.

3. *Joy and singing!*

Habitual melancholy predisposes to temptation. A sad saint is a sorry saint! So let us be cheerful, and always in good humour. When we are tired of working, sing—and the Devil will dance with rage!

4. *Self-mastery*

The habit of self-control is of great assistance in gaining the victory over temptation. For instance, the mortification of those senses that are the "windows of the soul." Whoever is unable to watch over his eyes is unable to watch over his heart," says St. Augustine. "The look produces the thought which may provoke the desire, the consent, the habit, the necessity, and death." This helps us to understand the reflexion of a man who became blind: "I have lost my two biggest enemies!" The holy king David yielded to a serious temptation because of a curious, followed by a covetous, look.

If we had not read that book—if we had not seen that movie—if we had not danced that dance—if we had not listened to that story—if we had not eavesdropped—read someone else's letters—if we had not repeated that piece of gossip—etc., is it not true that we should have avoided many sins?

5. *Watchfulness*

The Divine Master himself counsels vigilance: "Watch therefore, for you do not know the day or the hour" .... "Keep the lamp of faith lit" .... "Watch and pray, that you may not enter into temptation" ....

Vigilance makes us shun the temptation without delay, as soon as it appears. Let us nip it in the bud. Otherwise, if we let it grow, we may not succeed.

Temptation is like a spark capable of burning a whole forest, but that can easily be stamped out now. What imprudence, if instead, we were to permit it to flare out of control!

St. Augustine compares the Devil to a chained dog which can bite only those who approach him. He can bark, or frighten people; but he can bite only those who want to be bitten. It is up to us to watch.

Hymn to Labour

(In the mode of St. Francis of Assisi)

As my brothers, the birds, as my brother the sun, and my sister, the moon;
Be blessed, Brother Labour, who presided unwearied at the creation of the world.
Be blessed, Brother Labour, who did make so pleasant the first hours of the universe.
Be blessed, Brother Labour, who after the Fall, led us through the punishment that atones, to the glory of rehabilitation.
Be blessed, Brother Labour, who make us co-operate with God himself, in all forms of our activity.
Be blessed, Brother Labour, in the instinctive activity of those animals that are under heaven; in the play of the fins of the fish of the sea, in the system of aerial oars of the birds of the air, in the mysterious contexture of nests and the ingenious construction of bee-hives, in the muscular effort of four-footed beasts.
Be blessed, Brother Labour, in my own labours—those of my arms, those of my brain, those of my heart.
For the dignity of your origin;
For the necessity of your trials;
For the efficacity of your expiations;
For your marvellous power of rehabilitation;
For this collaboration you permit me with God the Creator, in everything I invent that brings progress to the world;
For the collaboration you permit me with God the Redeemer, in all my sacrifices for the redemption of others, and for my own redemption.
Do not forsake me, but rather go with me to the final eve of my last day upon earth; and so guide all my footsteps to Eternity's threshold, where I may unfold still further in the inexhaustible activity of God.
Brother Labour, be blessed—both now and evermore.

EDOUARD MONTIER

Ric Photo

In Father's Arms

It is so good to be in Father's arms!—
So pleasant and so safe!
With arms 'round Dad, the little fellow's face
Bespeaks his heart's content

For this trusting little fellow,
The strong arms mean support,
Security and strength, comfort; joy and gentleness;
And who would dare gainsay a certitude like that?

Father and son. What magic in these words,
Made of union absolute and of complete devotion,
On Father's part. And for his son—
Complete and utter trust.

Father who are in Heaven, Father infinitely good,
Infinitely faithful, and better far
Than all earth's fatherhood;
Why should I hesitate to seek a refuge sure
In your own outstretched arms?
Give—that my faith may never fail—
But childhood's eager heart!

Ric Photo

6. *Mortification*

"This kind of devil," says our Lord, "can only be cast out by prayer and fasting."

We know that the saints imposed severe mortifications on themselves, to vanquish the assaults of the Devil. They scourged themselves, fasted, and mastered their rebellious flesh. And we?

7. *Humility*

If we would avoid yielding to impurity, let us be humble. Humility has ever been the source of purity. It is because we are unwilling to be humble and obedient that God permits certain falls. . . . The Devil does not stand a chance with a humble soul.

A good way to put the Tempter to flight is to let our confessor know all about our temptations. "As soon as anyone reveals his bad thoughts to his confessor," says Philip de Neri, "the temptation is half vanquished already." The Devil always urges silence—speaking to God's representative upsets his plans!

8. *Prayer*

Here is one of the most important means of overcoming evil. "Without me," says our Lord, "you can do nothing." Prayer is the elevation of our whole being toward God. Now the Devil is like a serpent crawling on the ground—he cannot touch anyone uplifted toward Heaven. Live in the thought of God's presence. "Think of your final end, and you will never sin," we read in the Scriptures.

Let us have recourse to prayer like the apostles on Lake Geneserath in the tempest, for then there will be "a great calm" in our souls.

When tempted, let us trustingly repeat the names of Jesus and Mary. Praying the Hail Mary is effective. "At the name of Mary," says Thomas à Kempis, "the demons fall down affrighted like a man who has just heard a thunderbolt hit hard by." And St. Bonaventure writes: "Wax melts near the fire, and demons lose their power when we piously invoke the name of Mary."

9. *Sacramentals*

Specifically, these are holy water and the sign of the cross.

The Devil flees from the Cross like a dog from a stick. St. Teresa of Avila writes: "Evil spirits fly from the crucifix, but soon return to the attack. They flee farther from holy water and do not come back so soon." The potency exercised by holy water comes from the prayers of the Church.

10. *Holy Communion*

The Holy Eucharist fortifies us against temptation; for here we receive not only grace, but the Author of grace, Jesus himself, the Victor over Satan. (We shall have more to say about this later on.)

Be trustful. If we are faithful in being where we ought to be, doing the thing we ought to be doing—humbly, from a supernatural motive—we may be assured of victory now, while we await an eternal reward. . . .

To conclude this explanation of the sixth petition of the Pater Noster, let us listen to St. Jerome as he tells us how he achieved the mastery over temptation in the wilderness of Chalcis, by means of fasting, penance, and prayer.

"How often when I was in the desert, in this vast solitude, which, parched by the sun's rays, affords but a fearsome dwelling-place for monks, did I imagine myself to be still in the midst of Roman delights! I was a sight to behold under the shapeless sackcloth which covered my limbs, with my unkempt exterior, which gave to my skin the aspect of a member of the Ethiopian race. Every day brought fresh tears and groans. When (despite my efforts to the contrary) sleep finally overpowered me, my loose-slung joints were crushed by the bare ground. I say nothing of food or drinks; for even the ill had only cold water to drink, and a hot meal appeared as laxity. As for me, who through fear of Hell, had condemned myself to such a prison, and whose only society consisted of wild beasts and scorpions, I often found myself mingled in thought in the dances of the Roman maidens. Fasting had given pallor to my features, but my heart burned with desire in a body grown cold; for my flesh had preceded the total death of my person—only the flames of guilty passion continued to burn within. Thus, devoid of all aid, I cast myself at Jesus' feet, watering them with my tears and wiping them with the hairs of my head; and by whole weeks of fasting altogether, I sought to subjugate my rebellious flesh. I did not blush at my misery. Rather I wept at no longer being what I once was. I remember that often

I continued to lament, even when day had succeeded night. I did not cease to smite my breast, until at the word of the Lord, tranquility was restored to me. My very cell, considered as accomplice of my evil thoughts, became a horror to me. Irritated, and cruel to myself, I buried myself alone in the wilderness. Clefts in valleys, mountain crags, and cliffs became my places of prayer and served as prisons for my miserable flesh. But the Lord is my witness, that after much weeping and contemplation of Heaven, it sometimes happened that I believed myself to be admitted amidst angelic hosts. Satisfied and joyous then, I would sing, "We run after You in the odour of Your ointments!" (Cavarella, *St. Jerome et son oeuvre,* t. 1, p. 40, letter XXII, 1922.)

Here we see the fierce temptations which saints have had to undergo even in the wilderness, far from the world! Let us especially bear in mind the energy and generosity they put into repelling their temptations, then go and do likewise!

But deliver us from evil

300—What do we pray for in the seventh petition of the Pater Noster?

We pray to be delivered from evil.

From what kind of evil?

From every evil that could hinder or ruin the work of our sanctification, of our divinisation, of our identification with Christ, the final end of the mass of our life. Or specifically:

1. From tribulation.
2. From sin.
3. From Hell.

1. *From tribulation*

Among the physical evils capable of afflicting us, are those beyond our power to foresee or avoid, such as those catastrophes and disasters which suddenly spread devastation and ruin in town and country. These include earthquakes, cyclones, tidal waves, floods, avalanches, microbes, carriers of pestilence, contagious diseases, crop-destroying insects, etc. The Church, in the Litany of the Saints, has us pray: "From plague, famine, and war, O Lord, deliver us."

These woes in the physical order known as calamities, are not necessarily harmful to the work of one's sanctification. "To him who loves God, all things work together for good," even physical evil, affording as it does the opportunity to pay one's debt of sin and to co-operate in the redemption of souls.

Nevertheless, with the Church, we pray the Lord to deliver us from these misfortunes so difficult to accept supernaturally for the majority, with its wavering faith. This prayer, however, should always be contingent on God's will. Like our Lord in Gethsemani, we ought to say, "Not my will, but Yours be done."

There is another kind of physical evils of which we are the authors. It depends only on us to abolish them.

These evils are the result of a violation of the laws of nature through the abuse of liberty: disease, degeneration, premature aging, infirmities, arising from the disorder introduced into vital organs by excess in the use of those things placed at our disposal, and by disobedience of the laws of nature imposed by the wisdom of nature's Author. Alcoholism and vice deeply brand the flesh. This does not mean that all sick persons are sinners. Far from it! The Gospel episode will be recalled in this connection, where Jesus met a man blind from birth. His disciples asked Him, "Master, who has sinned, this man or his parents, that he should be born blind?" Jesus replied, "Neither has this man sinned, nor his parents, but the works of God were to be made manifest in him." And this young man's infirmity gave our Lord the opportunity to perform a miracle.

As for those evils of which we are the author, the practice of virtue and of mortification will suffice to deliver us from them.

2. *Sin*

The seventh petition of the Pater Noster is especially aimed at the evil which attacks the vitality and health of the soul and its progress toward God, and delays or prevents its return to the Father's House.

Above everything else, we pray to be delivered from sin. Of all evils that can happen to us in this world, the greatest is sin. How many understand this? Alas, we feel much sorrier for a man suffering from cancer or financially ruined, than we feel sorrow when we have committed a sin! And yet, the smallest venial sin ought to grieve us more than all the woes in the temporal order that could ever fall to our lot.

We ought to feel sorrier for having given way to petty outbursts of temper, to secret jealousy, and to trifling intemperance, than we would to be robbed of everything we own!

We ought to experience greater sorrow at our petty detractions, at the seekings of self-love, at the lack of application and attention in our religious exercises of which we have been guilty, than we would to be stricken with leprosy, tuberculosis, blindness, deafness, loss of a limb or any other possible affliction to which we might fall victim!

To say nothing of serious sin!

With the help of the world's maxims and the prejudices received from a "liberal" education, one is easily persuaded that sin is rather forgetfulness than offence; or that God is not sensitive to this offence—his all-greatness placing him infinitely above our affronts. These are two errors to which it is necessary to oppose two truths:

1. Sin is the most injurious outrage made to God.
2. Sin is the most sensitive outrage made to God.

Sin is the most injurious outrage made to God

We all know that the greatness of an injury is measured by the greatness of the person injured. The slap in the face that I give to a king is much more serious than the slap that I give to a tramp. If the gravity of the affront grows with the dignity of the person offended, when it comes to God it must be infinite; for God's greatness and majesty are infinite. But since we do not comprehend this infinite greatness and majesty of God, we are incapable likewise of estimating all the malice of sin.

Still, we have an inkling of how good our Heavenly Father is! God is love—*Deus caritas est*—says St. John. Now sin makes of God a Love unknown, or rather, unrecognized.

Sin means despising God! "Listen, heavens, says the Lord, and earth, receive my words. I had children whom I loved with immeasurable tenderness. With what care did I nourish them! To what sublime rank did I lift them up and exalt them, making them to share in my divine nature! I have heaped gifts upon them, overwhelming them with them! And what have they done for me?... Do you know what they have done? They have despised me." (Cf. Isa. 1:2.)

GOD despised! Think of it! And he has always been good to us....

Before we came into existence, God loved us. His love for us dates from all eternity. He it is who created us; and ever since we entered the world, he has preserved our lives. Every step that we take on the road of life, we owe to him. Let him but suddenly cease his sustaining action, and we are blotted out from the number of the living. His goodness follow us everywhere; his love envelops us and protects us. For us, he became a little Child. For us, he preached the Gospel and founded his Church. For us, he shed the last drop of his blood. For us, he has gone so far as to let himself be eaten—by the institution of his Sacrament of love, the Holy Eucharist! For us, he has prepared a place in his Heaven!

What gratitude and love should be ours toward Him who has shown us only goodness and mercy! How we should show forth our tender and loving gratitude for the immense benefits we have received from Him, never wearying of blessing and admiring Him, and of tasting the ineffable sweetness of His love, making it the constant object of our contemplation.

And yet, when a God so good asks a bit of our hearts in exchange for all that he has done for us, we often dare to refuse! When he asks us to yield our wills to his by keeping his laws, we despise his precepts that we may satisfy all our caprices. In short, we despise God himself.

Treating our good God as a despicable thing, seems simply incredible! Yet, that is what we do every time that—torn between our conscience and our unbridled passions—we have wounded the former that we might follow the latter.

The friendship, the possession of God, such was the treasure that was ours to keep—or to lose.... Must we say it, Dear Lord? We have compared and calculated Your worth, and the worth of a moment's pleasure.... To the honour of serving You, we have preferred sin, the death of our soul—and sometimes the death of other souls as well! This choice of ours is so much the more humiliating for You, Dear God, in that if anyone else but You—if the world, if our health—had demanded of us the sacrifice You asked, we should have made it without hesitating or weighing the pros and cons. We sinned, because sinning, we offended only You, lost only You! You said to us, "Son, give me your heart by keeping my law. This heart belongs to Me; I want to make it happy. If you yield to temptation, where do you go? Can he who would incite you to rebel against your God and Father, wish you well? Think of the abyss of dreadful woe toward which he drags you. . . ."

Alas, all Your efforts have been in vain! The Devil has carried the day. We have preferred degradation and Hell with Satan, to glory and Heaven with You! To such a point can our contempt go!

The saints, though, understood sin's ugliness, in proportion to their comprehension of God's love for us.

By means of a wholly diabolic clairvoyance, based on hatred of God, the wicked have understood the outrage that sin is to God.

The heretical emperor of Constantinople, being one day violently irritated at St. John Chrysostom, who had reproached him for his iniquities; remarked in the presence of his courtiers, "How I would like to avenge myself on this bishop!" There upon, four or five among them gave their opinion. One advised, "Send him into exile, so far away that you will never see him again." "Confiscate his goods," said another. "No," said a third courtier. "Put him in irons and cast him into prison." "The fourth counseled, "Are you not the master here? Have him killed! Get rid of him!" To this, the fifth courtier, who was more knowing than the others, retorted, "No, Sire! That is not the way to avenge yourself of him and punish him! If you send him into exile, the whole earth becomes his country. If you confiscate his goods, it is from the poor that you take them, and not from him. If you cast him into your dungeons, he will kiss his irons and esteem himself happy. If you condemn him to death, you open Heaven to him. The only way to avenge yourself, Prince, is by causing him to commit a sin; for this is the only thing in the world he fears. He dreads neither exile nor the loss of his property; neither fetters, torture, nor flame. The only thing in the world he fears is sin."

Indeed, on another occasion, as great threats were being made to the holy bishop on the part of the empress to whom he had refused something he was unable to grant, the bishop replied aptly, "Go tell the empress that John fears only one thing in this world—sin."

Such should be our sentiments, if we are to judge things in the light of faith.

Sin is the most sensitive outrage made to God

Who is unmoved by the complaints made by our Lord to the ungrateful Jews? "Many good works have I shown you. . .for which of these works do you stone Me?"

There is no sinner to whom God could not address the same language. How can we think that God is indifferent to sin, when he sacrificed his only Son to atone for it at the cost of his life?

"Why do you despise and contemn me?" asks our Lord. "What have I done to you? What is your complaint? Is it because I have given you intelligence, a heart, will, reason, and freedom that you use my gifts to insult me? Is it because of my benefits that you insult me? Is it because I created you, that you sacrifice me to the creature? Is it because I rescued you from the chains of a cruel enemy, that you treat me like an enemy? Are you punishing me for having loved you too much?"

What is our reply to these reproaches—we who are all sinners?

From now on, let us strive to understand a little better the malice of sin. Thus, at the close of the Our Father, it will be with a burning desire to be heard that we shall pray, "Deliver us from evil!"

3. *From Hell*

If sin is a tremendous evil, then dying in sin, in God's disgrace, is the greatest evil that could possibly happen to us! For this means Hell for all eternity! We do well to beseech Heaven to be spared from such a calamity!

Incidentally, is it in good taste to speak of sin and Hell to souls with marked aptitudes for ascetisim and mysticism?

These rather gloomy subjects are, in certain circles, both disillusioning and boring. "Here we go again!" they sigh. "We're in for a lecture and some more proofs of the obvious principle that we mustn't be bad! A lot of 'thou shalt nots'—the negative approach!"

To know whether meditating on sin and Hell is opportune or not, let us consult the Gospel.

Jesus, who taught us the Our Father, sets forth two petitions out of seven, to supplicate his Father not to let us yield to temptation and to deliver us from evil.

Again Jesus appears to us (St. Luke 12) as teaching, not the multitude, but his disciples: "But I say to you, my friends. Do not be afraid of those who kill the body, and after that have nothing more that they can do. But I will show you whom you shall be afraid of; be afraid of him who, after he has killed, has power to cast into Hell."

In the Gospels, Jesus constantly puts his disciples on their guard against sin: "The spirit indeed is willing, but the flesh is weak. . . ." "You are the salt of the earth, but if the salt loses its strength, what shall it be salted with?" To the Twelve: "One of you will betray me!" And to Peter: "Before a cock crows, you will deny me thrice!" Let us also recall Jesus' last talk, in which the Divine Master beseeches his Father to keep those whom he had given him from evil, etc.

We also read in the Holy Scriptures that there is a way to keep from offending God, and that this way is: "Think of the four Last Ends, and you will never sin"! Now Hell is (together with death, judgment, and Heaven) one of the Four Last Ends.

Enlightened by these considerations, what would you say of the "method" of the preacher of a ladies' retreat, who would say: "As for sin, I will not insult you ladies by believing you capable of committing it! Let us pass on to another subject!"

Is it true that anyone can assert without batting an eyelash, that the woman of today (or anyone else, may it be said) does not—at parties, dances, beach-parties, or from dress, reading, refreshments, movies, and dating—run the least risk of sinning? Speaking to her of sin is "rude," and a priest ought to know enough about "etiquette" not to bring up so boring and useless a subject! The most elementary tact prescribes that he should shut his eyes to certain inevitable peccadillos. ("Let us pass on to another subject"!) For the all-important thing is to vaunt the virtues in which these ladies abound! Be careful not to disturb them once they are settled down in their selfish, tepid, worldly lives!

Now who is right? Our Lord or these others?

Listen to the voices of holy personages. St. Paul, deeming himself the last of all: "For I am the least of the apostles; and am not worthy to be called an apostle, because I persecuted the Church of God." (I Cor.

15:9.) "For I formerly was a blasphemer, a persecutor, and a bitter adversary.... Jesus Christ came into the world to save sinners, of whom I am the chief. But for this reason I obtained mercy, that in me first, Christ might show forth all patience." (I Tim. 1:13.)

After the miraculous draught of fishes, St. Peter groaned, "Depart from me; for I am a sinful man, O Lord!" (Luke 5:8.) After his threefold denial, he wept bitterly. (Matt. 26:75.)

During Jesus' apparitions to St. Margaret Mary, he often reproached her—as he did St. Paul—for her past sins, "lest the greatness of the revelations" should puff her up!

The saintly Curé of Ars wished that his superiors would retire him to some remote corner, where he might weep over his poor sinful life!

And does not the Church cause us to repeat daily in the Hail Mary, "Pray for us sinners"? This is an inexhaustible subject. We leave it then to each one to go into it more deeply.

A. WHAT IS HELL?

We know that Hell is a place of torment. Every conceivable pain and evil is to be met with there.

There bodies and souls are tormented.

As for the bodily pain, we will say only that it is universal, violent, and perpetual.

Let us reflect for a few moments on the sufferings of the souls of the damned; which are even more fearsome; and no less eternal. (We have taken the following considerations on Hell from the *Meditations* of Fr. Chaignon, Vol. 1, p. 272.):

Torment of the imagination: This faculty torments the damned soul incessantly, by means of the most distressing representations. It vividly depicts to it what it was on earth, what it might have been in Heaven, what it must be forever.... It *had* procured for itself satisfactions and forbidden pleasures—*now* there is only torment.... In its troubles, it *could* promise itself a brighter future; it sometimes heard a word of compassion, encountered the face of a friend.... *Now* it sees nothing anywhere but hate and fury. Hated by demons, hated by men, and by its own self, it can only curse itself, gnash its teeth, and call for the death that does not come. Which will *never* come!

O eternity! O ever-present thought of eternity! The damned soul buries itself in this abyss; it heaps up millions of centuries upon millions of centuries, and seeks an end to that which has no end! Oh, if it be dreadful to suffer forever, is it not almost as dreadful to *know* that one will suffer forever?

Torment of the mind: This faculty clearly shows the damned soul all the folly of its conduct, all the injustice, all the shame, all the abomination of its sins. It shows it the greatness of God, his ineffable perfections, and above all, his infinite goodness.... "Wretch! You have outraged your Benefactor!... Perjurer! You have violated all your oaths!... Murderer! You have slain souls, and are responsible for Christ's death on the Cross!" No, Hell is not too long to punish so many crimes: "O Lord, you are just and upright in your judgments."

Torment of the will: This is the greatest torment! Scarcely is the soul separated from its body, when it rushes toward God, its Final End. A thirst devours it, a hunger consumes it. Panting, it hurls itself toward God, its Necessary End, for whom it was created. "God! God! I must have God!" Such is the cry of its whole being. And God excites still more the flame of its desire, by his beauty that he permits to be glimpsed or suspected. He draws it with the omnipotence of his infinite charm. But while it makes incredible efforts to unite itself to God, God repels it; God thwarts it by eternally repeating. "Depart from Me! Depart from Me! God is not for you! During your earthly life, you would have none of Me! I know you not! Depart from Me!" ... This is known as the torment of the damned.

This soul, seeing the uselessness of its efforts, enters into a transport of rage. Gladly would it strip God of all his perfections, which render him so amiable, so attractive; or else tear out from itself its inmost being—this compelling inclination to love God. Doomed to failure, the soul blasphemes God and overwhelms itself with reproaches and curses. O appalling fate! Forever to will with the most burning passion, the thing that can never be! Not to will that which must be forever! "Hell is like Heaven," says St. John Chrysostom, "in that 'eye has not seen nor ear heard, nor has it entered into the heart of man,' the torments God has prepared for those who forsake him with no desire to return—and the happiness for those who love him."

B. Who goes to hell?

One mortal sin is enough to condemn a man to Hell.

Who can say, "I have never committed one," or especially, "I never will commit one"? We all have on our lips the kiss of Judas—we are all capable, in a moment of weakness, of giving it and betraying the Divine Master!

A surprising thing is that it is the saints who are most afraid of falling! St. Paul, caught up to the third Heaven at the very time when he was engaged in exhausting toil for the glory of God and the salvation of souls, feared lest he find his reprobation in the very midst of his apostolic labours. "I chastise my body," he wrote, "and bring it into subjection; lest perhaps after preaching to others, I myself should be rejected." (I. Cor. 9:27.)

We have seen St. Jerome burying himself in the deep solitude of the desert, giving himself over to mortification and prayer. Would you like to know why he delivered himself to this penance? He tells you himself: "I condemned myself to this prison because of my fear of Hell."

St. Philip Neri often used to pray: "Lord, watch out for your Philip, for he may play you a mean trick!"

St. Teresa of Avila saw in a vision the place destined for her in Hell, if she did not correct herself of the worldly-mindedness that motivated her whole life. This vision made so decisive and lasting an impression on her that she became a great saint.

Let us exercise prudence, shunning sin and all that leads to it; eschewing sensuality, drunkenness, pride, stubbornness, etc. Let us throw ourselves at the feet of the priest, the minister of reconciliation—in the arms and on the merciful heart of Jesus. Let our conduct prove the sincerity of our repentance, as we say to Jesus: "Lord, if we must burn, let it be with the fire of your love! We beseech you to deliver us from evil—from the evils of tribulation, sin, and Hell. Amen!"

Amen

301—What is expressed by the "Amen" at the end of the Pater Noster?

This "amen" sums up the whole prayer. The whole Pater Noster is epitomized in this one little word, "amen," implied after each petition. Yes, Dear God and our Father, we earnestly beg again for all that has just been prayed for.

Hallowed be your Name. With all our heart we desire it. May it be known, adored, loved, or in a word, glorified. For your name is you!

May it be hallowed by every creature come from your hands, even by the tiniest, even by those closely bound to matter. (And fair already will the hymn be!)

Let it be hallowed by angels; because living in your friendship at the court of Heaven, these pure spirits are better able to know and praise you. (And fairer still will be the hymn.)

May it be hallowed by men; because man, centre of two worlds—the world of the spirit by his soul and the world of matter by his body—is the born poet of creation. May all men sincerely reverence this name above every name—with reverence in word and in deed. (And wonderful will be the hymn. Amen!)

Your kingdom come! May it come through constant increase in the number of faithful, through the more and more intense development of Christian life—this life of which the Apostle formulated the law: "Grace with me, and I with grace."

But what we see on earth is the reign of human passions, the reign of pride, pleasure, and self. May it come, O Lord, the kingdom of your grace, precursor of your divine glory. O Jesus, rule our hearts, minds, and wills! Reign over all men, over all the earth. Amen!

Your will be done on earth as it is in Heaven! Yes, may all men do your holy and adorable will! For conformity, submission, to your will, is the epitome of Christian perfection. To obey when you command, when you forbid, or better still, when you but counsel. Or better still, when you but desire. Never to will anything save what you will, and as you will—this is everything.

However crosses and trials may come to us—whether from your hand, that loves even as it smites; whether from the hand of man or through the inexorable trend of events, matters little. For it is always by your order or else with your permission. Cause us to accept them bravely and patiently, as is fitting for Christians obedient wholeheartedly and in advance to your holy will. Amen!

Give us this day our daily bread. We have first prayed for your glory, O Lord. We pray you now to look after our needs, both temporal and spiritual.

Give us the bread needful for our subsistence, bread for our bodies; bread for our minds, which is truth: bread for our hearts, or charity; bread for the soul, which is the Holy Eucharist—the greatest gift, the "Bread of the strong," the Bread required for our arduous march toward eternity. Amen!

Forgive us our trespasses as we forgive those who trespass against us. Forgive us our transgressions, which are numerous, which are grave, and which have placed us in your debt. Grant us forgiveness of our sins —are not you the infinitely good God? Grant us this freely, in the most abundant measure; as we in turn (You are our witness, O God) forgive all those who have offended us. Amen!

And lead us not into temptation, that you send to try your just ones, nor into that temptation raised up by the Devil to induce men to sin. For we are not only guilty, but weak.

"For your adversary the Devil, as a roaring lion, goes about seeking someone to devour," says St. Peter.... Peter was speaking from first-hand knowledge when he wrote that in his Epistle!

The flesh, with its unwholesome concupiscence and appetites, may rightly be termed, "the demon within."

The world is a great slayer of souls....

If you forsake us, we must fall.... Stretch forth your hand, O Lord. Save us from the combat, or render us victorious. Amen!

But deliver us from evil. Deliver us from all evil.... Deliver us from those greatest evils, sin—and Hell.

Deliver us from that evil of the mind which is error, doubt, a worldly or materialistic mentality; from "optical illusions": spiritual myopia, or presbyopia, rash judgment, insincerity, self-sufficiency, stubbornness—in a word, from pride in all its forms. Give us humility and faith. . .

Deliver us from that evil of the heart which manifests itself as selfishness, jealousy, envy, the search for emotions and thrills, for sensible consolation, and sensual enjoyment. Give us purity and a more supernatural love.

Deliver us from that evil of the will made up of instability, inconstancy, irresolution, and disobedience. Grant us obedience and perseverance. Amen.

The Our Father, that incomparable prayer learned from Jesus, corresponds to all our needs. With what fervour and what reverence should we pray it; especially at Mass, when He who taught it to us reposes before our eyes! "It is as short in words, as long in sense," says Tertullian. We shall never exhaust its meaning!

One day a priest said in a sermon: "Try to pray the Our Father by making a brief pause after each of the words in this divine prayer. Give yourself time to weigh and understand every word. You will be surprised at the result."

The "result" will be that produced by a kind word on a suffering, forsaken, bruised heart, hungry for affection.

Calmly, softly, and lovingly, you will say to God, "Father!" And softly and lovingly you will hear, "My child!"

You will say to God softly and lovingly, "Hallowed be your name. . .Your Kingdom come. . .Your will be done on earth as it is in Heaven. . .and softly, lovingly, you will hear, "Thank you, child."

Softly, lovingly, you will say, "Father, give us this day our daily bread." And softly, lovingly, you will hear, "Yes, my child, you shall not want."

You will say to God softly, "Forgive us our trespasses." And lovingly, you will hear, "As you forgive, shall I forgive. Abide in my peace."

Finally, you will say to God softly and lovingly, "Father, lead us not into temptation. . .but deliver us from evil." And God will say to you kindly, "I watch over you. Be good, and you shall have a foretaste even on earth of Heaven's happiness, until you enjoy the bliss of Heaven through all eternity!"

302—Are you familiar with the commentary on the Our Father composed by St. Francis of Assisi?

St. Francis, God's troubadour, composed a paraphrase of the Our Father that he prayed night and morning, before and after the canonical hours, and before the Office of the Blessed Virgin.

Upon his conversion, that is, as soon as he had abandoned a worldly life to live according to the Gospel, Francis did not stop singing; but now he sang to praise God and to invite men to praise and serve the Lord.

"The question has been raised," writes Fr. Leo Veuthey, O.F.M. C., "as to whether the spirit of St. Francis was christocentric; i.e., directed toward Christ as toward its centre, or directed toward the Father. Both opinions have their defenders. For us, both are true; provided they are not mutually exclusive and are placed in their proper order. It is certain that Francis made Christ the centre and foundation of his whole life. But it is no less certain that he did not stop with Christ; but with him and in him, went on to the Father. At the beginning of Francis' religious life, although he had wholly given himself to Christ, he clearly manifested a great love for God the Father. Francis' earthly father was demanding restitution of his goods, that Francis had desired to distribute to the poor. The latter, in an impulsive movement of love for holy poverty, divested himself of his garments, and shouted: "Listen and hear this, all of you! Up till now, I have called Peter Bernardone my father! But as I purpose to serve God, I give him back this money for which I have been put to so much inconvenience; and the clothing I have received from him! So that henceforth I can say with more reason, 'Our Father who are in Heaven,' and no longer call Peter Bernardone my father! Until this day, I have called upon my earthly father. Henceforth, I can say in fullest confidence, 'Our Father who are in Heaven, with whom I have placed all my treasure!' " *(Life of St. Francis* by St. Bonaventure, Vol. 2. 4.)

"Is not this an utter outgoing of love toward the Father, from whom comes every perfect gift; and to whom all things should return in love? This is the theme of the Franciscan paraphrase of the 'Our Father.' "

The following is the authentic text of St. Francis of Assisi:

"*Our Father* most holy, our Creator, Redeemer, Saviour, and Comforter.

"*Who are in Heaven*: in the saints and angels, illumining them that they may know you, because you, O Lord, are Light; inflaming them with love because you, O Lord, are love; living within them and filling them with bliss because you, O Lord, are the highest Good; the eternal Good from whom all goodness proceeds, and without whom no good could exist.

"*Hallowed be your name,* that we may know you more clearly, so as to comprehend the breadth of your benefits, the length of your promises, the height of your Majesty, and the depth of your judgments.

Your Kingdom come, that you may reign within by your grace; so that you may make us enter into your Kingdom, where men see you face to face, in perfect love, blessed union, and eternal joy." (St. Francis touches upon here, without suspecting it, the problem of heavenly beatitude, at that time a highly controversial subject among theologians.)

"*Your will be done on earth as it is in Heaven.* May we love you with our whole heart, by ever thinking of you: With our whole soul, through constant desire of you. In our minds, by directing all our intentions toward you, and seeking your honour in all things with all our strength—expending all our faculties and senses of body and soul in the service of your love alone. Let us love our neighbour as ourselves, doing our best to draw all the world to your love; rejoicing in the good of others as of our own, sympathizing with them in affliction, and giving offense to none.

Our daily bread. Give us today your dear Son, Jesus Christ, our Lord, to bring to mind, and cause us to comprehend and venerate, his love and all that he has said, done, and suffered for us.

Forgive us our trespasses, by means of your ineffable mercy, through the Passion of your beloved Son, Jesus Christ, our Lord, and the intercession of the Blessed Virgin Mary and of all your elect.

As we forgive those who trespass against us. And whatever we do not fully remit, cause us, O Lord, to forgive, fully, to truly love our enemies for your sake, devoutly praying for them, rendering evil to no man, and striving to serve them all in you.

And lead us not into temptation, either hidden or manifest, sudden or persistent.

But deliver us from evil—past, present, and future! *Amen!*

Libera nos

303—What does the celebrant do after the Pater Noster, and what prayer does he say?

After the Pater Noster, the celebrant takes the paten—placed at the right under the corporal—(or held by the subdeacon, enveloped in the humeral veil, during a Solemn Mass). He holds it in a vertical position as he says the prayer. "Deliver us."

The paten is a symbol of peace. At the words, "Vouchsafe us your peace," he kisses the paten as if to draw peace from its source; and makes over himself a large sign of the cross.

He next places the Sacred Host on the paten. From this moment, the paten becomes not only the sign of peace, but its throne.

The prayer, *Libera nos*—"Deliver us—which the priest says immediately after the Pater Noster, is a continuation or development of the last petition, "Deliver us from evil." Here is the prayer:

Libera nos, quaesumus, Domine, ab omnibus malis, praeteritis, praesentibus et futuris: et intercedente beata et gloriosa semper Virgine Dei Genitrice Maria, cum beatis Apostolis tuis Petro et Paulo, atque Andrea, et omnibus sanctis, da propitius pacem in diebus nostris: ut ope misericordiae tuae adjuti, et a peccato simus semper liberi, et ab omni perturbatione securi. Per eumdem Dominum nostrum Jesum Christum Filium tuum. Qui tecum vivit et regnat in unitate Spiritus Sancti Deus.

Per omnia saecula saeculorum.
℟. Amen.

Deliver us, we beseech you, O Lord, from all evils past, present, and future; and by the intercession of the blessed and glorious Mary, ever Virgin, Mother of God, and of your holy apostles Peter and Paul, of Andrew and of all the saints, graciously grant peace in our days; that through the help of your bountiful mercy, we may be always free from sin, and secure from all disturbance. Through the same Jesus Christ, your Son, our Lord, who lives and reigns with you in the unity of the Holy Ghost, God.

World without end.
℟. Amen.

304—What is expressed by this prayer?

In this prayer, we renew our petition to be delivered from all evil, past, present, and future.

This prayer deals, then, with evil having its roots in the past: the effects of Original Sin—a wound never closed, and that down the generations continues to enlarge—the effects of Original Sin, mortal or venial i.e., of bad habits contracted and which manifest themselves from time to time.

It likewise deals with the evil that thrives in the present: vitiated native tendencies to which the world and the Devil strive to give a wrong impulse and direction.... daily faults, sins of tepidity and of spiritual mediocrity.

It also includes evil dreaded in the future; for the root of evil in us is never extirpated, the ashes of slumbering passions never extinguished.... There is the "demon of noontide," and the "demon of evening"—the crises of maturity and old age follow those of adolescence and youth. A surprise is always possible. That is why our Lord warns us to watch and pray without ceasing.

This prayer of deliverance recalls not only the seventh petition of the Pater Noster, but likewise our Lord's sublime discourse on the eve of his death.

It was the evening of the Last Supper during the hour of thanksgiving which followed the institution of the Holy Eucharist. Jesus, moved to compassion over his disciples, whom he did not wish to leave orphans; and desirous of commending them anew in a special manner to his Father, prayed over them the prayer reported to us by St. John, the apostle of love. This chapter has been called by common consent, "Christ's priestly prayer." One may also see in it the memento of the bloody Mass that Jesus was on the point of celebrating:

"Father, the hour has come! Glorify your Son, that your Son may glorify you, even as you have given him power over all flesh; in order that to all you have given him, he may give everlasting life. Now this is everlasting life, that they may know you, the only true God; and him whom you have sent, Jesus Christ. I have glorified you on earth; I have accomplished the work that you gave me to do. And now, Father, glorify me with yourself; with the glory that I had with you before the world existed."

(The first intention formulated in this memento is the glorification of Christ's sacred Humanity. The second intention is, as we shall see, the sanctification of the apostles and disciples.)

"I have manifested your name to the men whom you gave me out of the world. They were yours, and you gave them to me; and they have kept your word. Now they have learnt that whatever you have given me is from you; because the words that you gave me, I have given to them. And they have received them, and have known of a truth that I came forth from you; and they have believed that you sent me.

"I pray for them; not for the world do I pray, but for those whom you have given me, because they are yours (and all things that are mine are yours) and yours are mine; and I am glorified in them. And I am no longer in the world; but these are in the world, and I am coming to you. Holy Father, keep in your name those whom you have given me, that they may be one, even as we are. While I was with them, I kept them in your name. Those whom you have given me I guarded; and not one of them perished except the son of perdition, in order that the Scripture might be fulfilled. But now I am coming to you; and these things I speak in the world, in order that they may have my joy made full in themselves. I have given them your word; and the world has hated them because they are not of the world; even as I am not of the world. I do not pray for you to take them out of the world, but for you to keep them from evil.... Sanctify them in the truth. Your word is truth. Even as you have sent me into the world, so I also have sent them into the world. And for them I sanctify myself, that they also may be sanctified in truth.

"Yet not for these only do I pray, but for those who through their word are to believe in me, that all may be one, even as you, Father, in me, and I in you; that they also may be one in us, that the world may believe that you have sent me. And the glory that you have given me, I have given to them, that they may be one, even as we are one: I in them, and you in me; that they may be perfected in unity, and that the world may know that you have sent me, and that you have loved them even as you have loved me.

"Father, I will that where I am, they also whom you have given me, may be with me; in order that they may behold my glory which you have given me, because you have loved me before the creation of the world. Just Father, the world has not known you; but I have known you, and these have known that you have sent me. And I have made known to them your name, and will make it known; in order that the love with which you have loved me may be in them, and I in them." (John 17: 1-26.)

This rather long quotation belongs in this part of the Mass. This prayer, or rather, this effusion of love, by which our Lord terminated in a sense his evangelical mission in this world, is the same whereby we also terminate the prayer that we address to the Father in the Pater Noster. "Keep them from evil," he prayed, speaking of us. And he has us pray, "Deliver us from evil." It is the same prayer, the same petition, the same desire, that we express in the *Libera nos.*

It is the wish of the father and mother embracing their son who is taking leave of them for a long journey. "May God be with you, Son! May he guide you and protect you wherever you go, and bring you back safe and sound. May he keep you from all harm."

The same love in the heart of Jesus made him desire the same thing for us, and he wants us to pray for it with him to his Father.

So what should be our attitude toward evil? First, we shall shun it—he who exposes himself to danger perishes. Next, we shall place ourselves in the way of God's grace, enlarging our souls to receive the heavenly gifts. For just as our desire to be free is efficacious and sincere only if it is accompanied by an effort which tends to realize it, God delivers us from evil only to the degree that we lend ourselves to this often painful operation. And, since in this kind of medicine there is no anaesthetic or drug to stop or alleviate the pain or the bitterness of the remedy; we must take the scalpel of renunciation in our own hands to cut the bonds that hold us captive to evil, and we ourselves must cut out or burn out the infected or gangrenous parts. There is a spiritual penicillin called grace—but grace without our co-operation can do nothing.

In the second part of the *Libera nos,* we pray for "peace in our time."

The perils to which the Church is exposed both within and without are the worst evils threatening her.

This prayer for peace comes reinforced by the invocation to the saints named: Mary, the apostles Peter and Paul, Andrew, and all the saints.

The word "peace" represents a concept which the Church continues to develop in the prayers which follow, and which finds its complete expression and its conclusion in the kiss of peace. It is under this term that the Church conceals the thing dearest and closest to her heart. This peace is to be given to us in substantial form by the Lamb of God.

THE BREAKING OF THE HOST

305—With what words and gestures does the celebrant accomplish the breaking of the Host?

At the end of the *Libera nos,* while saying the words, *Per eumdem Dominum nostrum,* the priest slides the paten under the Host, then uncovers the chalice and genuflects to adore the Precious Blood. He then breaks the Sacred Host over the chalice, so that any particles may be mingled with the Precious Blood. He first divides the Sacred Host lengthwise into two equal parts, placing the right-hand portion on the paten. From the lower part of the other half, he now detaches a triangular fragment which he retains in his right hand; meanwhile placing the larger portion beside the other on the paten, while saying the words, *in unitate.* In his right hand, placed over the chalice, he holds the triangular small portion which he has just broken off, as he says (this time aloud) the concluding words of the *Libera nos.*

Per omnia saecula saeculorum. ℟. Amen.	World without end. ℟. (The people:) Amen.

With the particle retained in his fingers, the celebrant then makes the sign of the cross over the chalice, as he says:

Pax + Domini sit + semper vobis + cum. ℟. Et cum spiritu tuo.	May the peace + of the Lord + be always + with you. ℟. And with your spirit.

In the early Church, the breaking of the Sacred Host took place after the giving of the peace, of which the *Pax Domini sit semper vobiscum* of the priest was the signal. All the Christians present then gave each other a holy kiss as a token of peace.

Finally, the celebrant drops this particle of the Sacred Host into the chalice, as he says in a low voice, "*Haec commixtio.*"

306—What Gospel event is recalled to us by this breaking of the Sacred Host?

This ritual ceremony takes us back to the Last Supper, when our Lord broke the bread before giving it to his apostles.

It was by the breaking of bread that the disciples of Emmaüs recognized Jesus. Here, as in the Upper Room, the Divine Master had blessed the bread before distributing it. It seems evident that this was a true Consecration, and the first renewal of the Last Supper. (Luke 24:30.) Let us likewise recall the two miracles of the multiplication of the loaves.

The "breaking of Bread" was the primitive name for the Mass. **The first Christians** met together for the "breaking of Bread," that is, for the eucharistic meal. "To break bread" or "to eat" were synonymous. The bread was not cut. The loaves, in the shape of flat cakes, were broken by hand and distributed by the head of the house.

The Church remained faithful to this ritual. During the first centuries of Christianity, it was, moreover, the necessary prelude to the distribution of the Eucharist. For it was necessary that the loaves brought by the faithful at the Offertory, and consecrated by the celebrant, should be separated into several pieces. When all those present communicated, the result was a long and imposing ceremony. In Rome, for example, the acolytes bore the consecrated loaves in linen sacks, to the bishops and priests taking part in the papal Mass. At a sign from the pontiff, all broke the loaves at the same time.

307—Why does the celebrant divide the Host into three parts?

This tripartite division recalls the practice in the early Church. The celebrant communicated himself with the first portion; the deacons broke the second portion and distributed it to the congregation or bore it to the sick. The third portion (which the celebrant now places in the chalice for the commingling), was either placed in reserve to be mingled with the Precious Blood in the morrow's Mass; or else sent by the bishop to the priests celebrating in other churches, there to be deposited in the chalice, in token of the unity and continuity of the Sacrifice celebrated in different places and at different hours; and likewise to affirm the communion existing among celebrants.

These ceremonies have disappeared, but how blessed their memory! The billions of Hosts which ever since the Last Supper have been sown in souls, form but the one and same Jesus Christ. All those which today, from one end of the world to the other, are raised aloft above our misery, renew the one redeeming Sacrifice and cause us to enter more deeply into the Unity.

308—Please explain the symbol of the breaking of the Host.

The breaking of the Host is the expressive symbol of the Saviour's violent death, of the rending asunder of body and soul. It is made over the chalice, to remind us that the Blood therein contained flowed from the wounds and torn body of Christ.

COMMINGLING OR MINGLING OF THE SACRED SPECIES

309—What is symbolized by the commingling or mingling of the particle of the Host with the Precious Blood?

Up to this point, the division of the species of bread and wine figured the Saviour's death. Now, the reunion of these species becomes the image of his Resurrection. The Body and Blood of Christ are manifestly reunited. It is like a new consecration, resurrection, or pledge of eternal life for those about to receive.

310—What prayer is said by the celebrant during the commingling or mingling of the species?

Dropping the eucharistic Particle into the Precious Blood in the chalice, the priest prays in a low voice:

Haec commixtio, et consecratio Corporis et Sanguinis Domini nostri Jesu Christi, fiat accipientibus nobis in vitam aeternam. Amen.	May this commingling and consecrating of the Body and Blood of our Lord Jesus Christ avail us, who receive it, unto life everlasting. Amen.

This prayer, which accompanies the rite of the mingling of the divine Body and Blood, implores the fruits of everlasting life for those about to receive.

Everlasting life is the life of the Resurrection. Our Head has risen. We, his members—if we remain united—shall likewise be resurrected. The Eucharist is a union. And already on this earth, we ought —as Christians regenerated by Baptism, dead with Christ, and resurrected with him through grace—to inaugurate this life of light, sanctity, and purity. This life of grace which Holy Communion will develop, is a foretaste of the life of Heaven. Or better still, it *is* this life everlasting: but in germ, veiled, not having yet attained its full development. The rose in bud! Heaven will bring the complete unfolding of this earth's sanctifying grace. Faith will be transformed into vision, hope into possession, and charity become in glory, beatific love. But it will be the same life of adopted sons united to the Perfect Son, Jesus Christ, the Incarnate Word!

Let us be more than ever assured that Holy Communion which we are about to receive, is destined to procure for us everlasting life.

Let us do our best to prepare to receive the Lamb of God!

Agnus Dei

Let us say first, that from the beginning of the Church until the eighth century, the part of the Mass called the "Communion," consisted of two actions, rather than of special prayers: the breaking of the bread and the Communion of both celebrant and people, both preceded by the kiss of peace given one another by the congregation. The oldest prayer preparatory for Communion was the Pater Noster. The other prayers— the Agnus Dei, the three Oratios, the *Domine non sum dignus,* and the Confiteor—were added in the course of centuries by the piety of bishops and faithful; the better to express their faith in the Sacred Victim of whom they are about to partake, their mutual charity of which it is the efficacious symbol and type, their humility, and their holy desires.

Let us study the Agnus Dei.

311—What is the source of the first words of the *Agnus Dei*?

After covering the chalice again with the pall, the priest genuflects.

He then joins his hands, and profoundly inclined, strikes his breast three times as he says:

Agnus Dei, qui tollis peccata mundi: miserere nobis.	Lamb of God, who takes away the sins of the world, have mercy on us.
Agnus Dei, qui tollis peccata mundi: miserere nobis.	Lamb of God, who takes away the sins of the world, have mercy on us.
Agnus Dei, qui tollis peccata mundi: dona nobis pacem.	Lamb of God, who takes away the sins of the world, grant us peace.

This triple formula is borrowed from St. John the Baptist, who thus designated the Saviour: "Behold the Lamb of God, who takes away the sins of the world!" (John 1:29.)

312—Please explain the meaning of the *Agnus Dei*.

Up to this point, we have addressed ourselves to God the Father. The Victim of the Altar has appeared in a certain sense to be out of the picture. But after the commingling or mingling of the Lord's Body and Blood—symbol of the Resurrection—the Church addresses herself directly to our Lord himself, the Lamb of God.

We give to Jesus a name made up of tenderness, meekness, and trust—but a name also recalling his Sacrifice, and his position of victim for sinners, and so for us....

Filled with repentance and contrition, we should strike our breast with the celebrant and implore the Lord's mercy on all those evils of which our sins are, to a great extent, the cause. Have mercy, O Lord—

On those families without employment and without bread, crowded into one or two rooms, reduced to leading a life of heroism and martyrdom—overwhelmed by discouragement, and also by hate!...

The old folks without hearth or home, with no one to care for them or show them a little affection....

The joyless young, homeless, despairing of ever having a home of their own; and for whom vice lies in wait in interminable steady dating. . . .

The children for whom hunger and abandonment have become so soon familiar, but who seldom taste the sweetness of a kiss or caress. . . .

The little babies with no fathers or mothers. . .and whose only cradle is some straw or a heap of rags on the ground, and whose tender flesh causes them to suffer that much more cruelly from hunger and cold. . . .

The sick, forsaken of all, and eaten up by boredom. . . .

Those rich who never think of filling the hands of the poor. For these, enkindle the torch of charity in their hearts. . . .

Those without peace of soul. . .those not at peace with You. . . nor with others. . .nor with themselves. . . .

Us, who have so often offended You. . . . Grant us peace. . . .

As we see, the Agnus Dei, thrice repeated, is related to the Kyrie, of which it is the echo. (See Q. 69.)

Priest and people repeat this prayer thrice, because there are three kinds of sins: of frailty, of crass ignorance, and of malice.

The third time, instead of "have mercy on us," we pray, "Grant us peace."

You will have remarked that in Masses for the Dead, the celebrant replaces the two invocations, "Have mercy on us," by "Grant them rest"; and that to the third invocation, he adds the word *eternal*. Since his prayer is for the dead, he does not strike his breast.

We pray then for peace. "Grant us peace," we pray in the third Agnus Dei. "Grant them eternal rest," we pray for our dead.

The Agnus Dei directly prepares for the kiss of peace, and indirectly for Communion. The Sacrament of love about to be given to us is so great and demands such purity, that priest and people feel the need of imploring the mercy of this Divine Lamb for the forgiving of sins committed and for peace of soul.

Lamb of God, O God of meekness and love whom we are soon to receive. . . . O immolated Deity, you who take away the sins of the world, and have assumed the enormous weight of our sins—the shortcomings and failures of yesterday—have mercy on us! Dispose our hearts to worthy reception of you. Look upon our weakness. Come into our hearts not as a judge, but as a charitable physician. Give us peace! O Good Master, come into our hearts (whether really or spiritually) to give us the peace, the calm, the tranquility suitable for all, in keeping with the needs and duties of our state in life. Make our souls to be no longer "dens of thieves," but houses of prayer wherein you love to dwell with us, as in a sanctuary wholly consecrated to your interests. Amen.

313—What is expressed in the first Communion prayer?

Bowing humbly, hands joined, and resting on the edge of the altar, and his eyes fixed on the Host, the priest prays in a low voice for the precious gift of peace. He asks it for himself and for the whole Church:

A PRAYER FOR PEACE

Domine Jesu Christe, qui dixisti Apostolis tuis: Pacem relinquo vobis: pacem meam do vobis: ne respicias peccata mea, sed fidem Ecclesiae tuae; eamque secundum voluntatem tuam pacificare et coadunare digneris: qui vivis et regnas Deus per omnia saecula saeculorum. Amen.

O Lord Jesus Christ, who said to your Apostles: Peace I leave you, My peace I give you, look not upon my sins, but upon the faith of your Church; and vouchsafe to grant her peace and unity according to your will, who live and reign God, world without end. Amen.

As we can see for ourselves, the entire preparation for Holy Communion is organized under the sign of peace.

Already, in the *Libera nos,* which continues the Pater Noster, the contrast stands out between peace and sin. A few moments later, the celebrant expresses his desire for peace for the faithful, by making three signs of the cross with the sacred particle—the *Pax Domini.* The priest concludes the Agnus Dei with this invocation: "Grant us peace." And now, immediately before the Pax, comes a new insistence upon peace!

This repeated sollicitation of peace apprises us with certitude as to the importance of this gift! Standing out in such sharp relief, peace appears to us as the indispensable condition for carrying out the final act of the Mass—Holy Communion!

But then, arrived at this point in the Mass of our life, how could there still be any room for disturbance, fear, or disunion?...

Now for the explanation of this beautiful prayer:

"O Lord Jesus Christ." Here we are addressing Christ himself, really present on the altar, under the species of bread and wine. The first thing to be noted is that it is only at the moment of Communion that the prayers are addressed to Christ (from the Agnus Dei to the Communion verse exclusively). It is the only departure from the general tenor of the prayers of the Mass, all addressed to God the Father through Christ. This is readily explained by the need of speaking to Jesus at the moment we receive him.

Another observation is that these prayers are relatively recent, and are of private origin. During the ceremony of the Pax, the priest adopted the custom of private recitation of prayers preparatory to Communion. These were also introduced into the private devotion of the faithful; and finally, inserted in the missal. (These prayers, in the first person singular as they are, bear the stamp of their origin.)

"Who said to your apostles: Peace I leave you, my peace I give you." The peace that Jesus gives us is not the false, perilous, death-dealing peace of the world; which leaves the soul ignorant of itself, forgetful of its destiny, sunk in sin, and sliding to the brink of that abyss within whose depths Death may at any moment hurl it beyond recall. But the peace Jesus gives to his disciples—and that means all of us—is that which establishes a soul in filial abandon in the arms of the Heavenly Father; by whom it knows itself to be loved, and whom it loves.

It is a peace which engenders a serene trust in Him who can do all things and who watches over us. It is a peace which maintains union with God in spite of temptations, doubts, anguish, interior aridity, and the grave and incessant cares which the duty of our state and the zeal for our apostolate create. This is the peace brought to us by Jesus, our only true Friend, soon to give himself to our souls.

Here again, we ought to imitate Christ, our Divine Model, and before uniting ourselves to him in Communion, turn toward our neighbour in a mutual gift of peace. This fraternal charity is a gift, a heritage from Christ. Let us hold fast to it; and if, unfortunately, we have broken this bond of peace, let us endeavour to restore it as speedily as possible.

We next consider the object of this prayer. It is twofold—the forgiveness of our sins and peace and union with the Church.

"Look not upon my sins." Do not look upon my transgressions. The reference here is to all venial sins, but more especially to sins contrary to the second precept of charity—love of neighbour. Remember what we have said above on this subject; namely, that we shall be forgiven in proportion as we forgive others from our hearts.

"But upon the faith of your Church." But look upon the faith of your Church. Think of the holiness of her component membership.... You who would have pardoned Sodom and Gomorrah, if in them there had been found ten just men; permit me, O good Jesus, to beseech you for the members of your Church, the thing I implore for myself and for those Christians, my brothers, here present, and all others—this peace, this spirit of love and reconciliation.

"And vouchsafe to grant her peace and unity, according to your will." Vouchsafe to grant peace and unity to this Church, i.e., to all members of the Mystical Body. (To "grant peace," means to cause peace to reign among them so that they become one heart and one soul.)

Is there a better preparation for Communion?

"O Jesus, that I may approach you with more confidence, draw me closer to my neighbour. Grant me peace with all men. Grant me charity, particularly toward those with whom I go up to the communion rail today. For is it not there, partaking of the same Bread, that we become members of your Body and Blood—members of one another, and one body with you? Could it be, O my Master, that filled with willful aversion or dislike for a single soul I would dare to profane and break the Sacrament of union? Would I dare to sit down at the banquet table of the God of love without the wedding garment of charity? No, for you would cast me forth—far from your loving Heart, so good to every one of us." (Dom Vandeur.)

"When you are tempted because of someone," wrote St. Thérèse of the Child Jesus, "even to the point of anger, the way to recover your peace is to pray for that person; begging God to reward him for the suffering he caused you." The way not to fall is to soften one's heart—or if need be, to subdue it!

The Lighthouse

Without the moving light
At the door of Night,
Lost ships would crash on the reef.

Without the "Man in White" in the Vatican—
Christianity's guardian—
The Church—storm-tossed—
Would ever be off course.

Without the priest in our midst—
Preacher of the Gospel—
Our souls—apart from Christ—
Would be forever lost.

Without that inner eye
That men call conscience,
Our heedless hearts
Would stumble into sin.
My soul—on guard!

Lighthouse at Cape des Rosiers, Gaspé.

Ric Photo

From Shore to Shore

"Luminous pathway,
who art thou, then?"
"Hope that appears
to mortal men."

"Who art, thou, Night,
obscure and bare?"
"Man's ignorance,
and man's despair."

"O Hope, what dost thou
'neath the skies?"
"I guide God's sons
to Paradise."

"Ignorance, wouldst thou
walk in light?"
"Gladly I walk, for now
I see. . . .
The light of truth
illumines me."

Lislet, at St. Fabien sur mer

Ric Photo

314—What is the origin of the Pax or kiss of peace?

During a solemn Mass (a Mass celebrated with a deacon and subdeacon), there takes place the very significant ceremony of the Pax.

After the first of the three Communion prayers, which follow the prayer for peace, the celebrant kisses the altar and gives the kiss of peace to the deacon. Without inclining his head, he places both hands on the arms of the deacon and offers him his left cheek, while saying: "*Pax tecum*—Peace be with you." During the prayer for peace, the deacon knelt. He now kisses the altar with the celebrant; bows, receives the Pax from him, and responds to his wish with the words, "*Et cum spiritu tuo*—and with your spirit."

Next, both join their hands and bow to each other. The deacon gives the Pax to the subdeacon, who transmits it to the members of the choir, and last of all to the acolyte.

Formerly, in the early Church, the ordinary greeting of the faithful to one another, as well as in liturgical functions, was this exchange of the kiss of peace in token of charity and union.

Four times St. Paul writes: "Greet one another with a holy kiss." (I. Cor. 16:20; II Cor. 13:12; I Thess, 5:26; Rom. 16:16.) Likewise, St. Peter: "Greet one another with a holy kiss." (I. Peter 5:14.)

The Pax was first given before the Offertory, later on after the *Pax Domini,* and finally came to occupy its present position.

Formerly, the ritual kiss was given with the mouth. In the thirteenth century, it was replaced by the accolade. It was at this time that, under Franciscan influence, the "instrument of peace" was employed. This was a framed square or oblong plaque with a handle, and with our Lord's picture engraved on it. The priest or the people placed the kiss on this sort of reliquary.

Why was this "instrument of peace" used for the faithful, when it was already employed in the ceremonial of bishops? Because the Pax (as we have said) was transmitted by the suddeacon or the acolyte to the people; from men to men, and from women to women. It was even the main reason for the separation of men and women in church. Now in the thirteenth century, in many churches, this arrangement no longer existed. It is easy to see what abuses might arise. . . .

315—What is the meaning of the Pax?

The Pax is the symbol of charity and union. This is so much the more close because it is realized in Christ. It is expressive of the bond uniting the faithful to one another and to Christ.

It is a sacramental, conferring actual grace and purifying the soul. It is likewise an excellent preparation for Communion, which infuses charity and fortifies the peace existing among communicants.

This kiss comes from the altar; that is, from Christ himself, of whom the altar is a symbol. Thus, it is Jesus who gives his kiss to those participating in his Sacrifice. This bond of brotherly love is bound first by the priest's "peace pact with Christ," which he concludes by kissing the altar. In the Middle Ages, to indicate clearly that this peace was borrowed from Christ himself, the priest first kissed the Sacred Host or else the chalice, next giving the Pax to the deacon. Thus, the transmitted peace derives directly from the Eucharistic Sacrifice: from the altar to the priest; from the priest to the deacon; from the deacon to the subdeacon; from the subdeacon to the choir; thence to the acolyte and from him to the people.

Out of horror for the treason of Judas, the Pax is suppressed on the final days of Holy Week. (Croegaert.)

In former times—and this omission is to be regretted—when the faithful mutually gave one another the accolade of peace, certain formulas were employed. Thus, in Paris, this form was used: "Peace to you, Brother (Sister), and to God's holy Church!" Sometimes, this was added: "that you may be fit to approach the most sacred mysteries."

If the faithful no longer give one another the kiss of peace, the brotherly love of which it is the sign, should nonetheless dwell in their hearts. For, without love, it is impossible for us to make a good Communion. Did not our Lord warn us that "any man who is angry with his brother must answer for it before the court of justice" ? . . . "If you are bringing your gift, then, before the altar, and remember there that your brother has some ground of complaint against you, leave your gift lying there before the altar, and go home. Be reconciled with your brother first, and then come back to offer your gift." (Matt. 5:22-25.) [Knox.]

From this text we ought to conclude that without charity—love of neighbour—no act of religion can please God. So even if we go to

Mass every morning and receive Holy Communion, we shall not be pleasing to God, if we hold a grudge in our heart against our neighbour.

Did you ever think of this?

If then, we have brought pain to our neighbour—have said or done evil against him, have damaged his reputation—let us go at once and apologize, promising reparation. Then, and then only, can we sincerely tell God that we love him and approach the Blessed Eucharist with fruit.

And if it is against us that this evil has been committed, let us be ready to forgive. And more is required. Not only should we lay aside all resentment, every uncharitable memory, and inwardly wish for peace and reconciliation with our neighbour (who partakes, as we do, of the Body and Blood of Jesus Christ); but we furthermore should play the rôle of peacemakers.

So it is not enough to avoid quarreling. Ours is the positive duty of discreetly working to bring back peace and concord between two adversaries, two antagonists—perhaps in our own family, neighbourhood, or parish.

It must be admitted that this is not always easy, but that is no reason for not trying. "With God's grace and a little tact, the thing can be done. Let us endeavour to play the rôle of "shock-absorbers." Let us pour oil on the troubled waters! Let us become angels of peace!

A PRAYER FOR PEACE

(A prayer attributed, because of its spirit, to St. Francis of Assisi.)

LORD, make me an instrument of your peace. Where there is hatred, let me sow love; where there is injury, pardon; where there is doubt, faith; where there is despair, hope; where there is darknss, light; and where there is sadness, joy.

O DIVINE MASTER, grant that I may not so much seek to be consoled as to console; to be understood as to understand; to be loved as to love; for it is in giving that we receive; it is in pardoning that we are pardoned; and it is in dying that we are born to eternal life.

316—What do we read in the *Ordre de la Penitence* anent the peacemaker rôle of Tertiaries?

We read that before playing the rôle of peacemaker to others, "the Tertiary is to establish peace and maintain it first of all within. Let Tertiaries be really meek and peaceful. Let them despise or ignore their real or fancied hurt feelings and lack of consideration shown them. Let them have only good and kind words on their lips, replying neither to injuries nor insults! This calls for self-conquest." (See *L'Ordre de la pénitence,* p. 32.)

Farther on, we come across some means for peacemaking: amiability, meekness, pleasantness, patience, and tact.... "Sometimes, to act immediately would not be prudent; but by setting their minds to it, Tertiaries will profit by the least opportunity, the merest incident, which might work into their plans for concord." (Pp. 33-34.)

317—How are we to practice our rôle of peacemaker in a practical manner?

Here are a few suggestions:

1. Meditate at length on the Gospel so as to become a "living Gospel."

2. Intensify your inner life.

3. Once self-mastery has been acquired, watch out for critical situations. Foresee that you are going to meet such and such a disagreeable person, who will shoot some barbed shaft in your direction; but tell yourself in advance that you will pay no attention to it.

4. Keep still, and do not smile when a person fails in charity in your presence.... Try to change the subject.... Say something good about those who are attacked.... If you are the one in charge, impose silence on the detractors. It is better to ruffle an evil tongue, than to let a reputation be torn to shreds.... A good way to embarrass detractors, is to excuse the accused by ascribing a good intention to him!

5. Accept an unpleasant task without murmuring.

6. Listen indulgently to those who like to brag. (Sign of a weak mind...strongly mixed with conceit.)

7. Be content to go your own way in life, without envying those who surpass you.

8. Do not demand of others a perfection which you yourself do not have.

9. Do not jump to the conclusion that the one who wounded you, did so on purpose. Avoid creating imaginary troubles for yourself, and throwing the blame on others.

10. Forgive others, for the very reason that you yourself have much to be forgiven....

All of us ought to scale the mount of perfection. But mountains are not scaled without paying the price of repeated and persevering effort. Let us not flinch from the task, but do our part. The Good Lord will surely do his!

318—Can you mention any episodes in the life of St. Francis where his "technique" of peacemaking especially stands out?

The following is an example quite characteristic of the procedure of St. Francis of Assisi for bringing peace to souls hardened by habitual vice.

Three notorious brigands, pressed by hunger, and affecting a humble and piteous air, had knocked at the door of the convent of Mont-Casale to beg for alms in God's name. The Father Guardian, who recognized them, roughly repulsed them, reproaching them for their nefarious means of livelihood.

Filled with rage, the robbers withdrew, not without breathing forth a flood of blasphemy and the most dreadful imprecations against the religious.

Now at this very moment, St. Francis arrived at the convent. As the Guardian, still excited, hastened to tell him what had happened praising himself for having treated according to their deserts, these wretches who had had the audacity hypocritically to try to snatch from the friars the bread they had so painfully begged. Good Father Francis, looking very sad, reproached the Guardian for having gone far afield from the spirit of the Divine Master, telling him he had behaved very ill. Such sinners (said he) are more easily converted by mild and compassionate reproof, than by bitter and violent rebuke. Scornful rebuffs, far from softening their hearts, only end up by hardening them still more.

Had not St. Francis written in Chapter 7 of the First Rule the following words: "Let the friars, wherever they may be, in hermitages or in other places, beware of appropriating any of them or of defending them against anyone whatever. And let whoever comes to them—friend or foe, thief or brigand—be kindly received"? Small wonder, that in place of congratulations, the Guardian drew down upon himself a stern reproof!

"Truly, brother," he continued, "you do not know of what manner of spirit you are! Your conduct is unworthy of a religious! In the name of holy obedience, I command you, as punishment for your fault, to go and find the robbers. They are your brothers; they are suffering from hunger. Cast yourself at their feet; and after you have asked their pardon, offer them the best bread and choicest wine in the house; inviting them kindly and courteously to eat the little you have brought them. And when they have finished their meal, beseech them from me to give up their evil ways and to give their word that they will not harm anyone any more. If they promise this, you are to bring them food the next day. The third time that they see you serving them, God will deign to open their eyes and bring them back on the right road."

The Guardian, quite abashed, promptly carried out the orders of his charitable Father. Meanwhile, St. Francis began to pray and beseech God to touch the souls of these robbers and bring them to do penance.

Wonderous to relate, the three notorious brigands, conquered by so much charity, and not knowing which to admire most—the humble obedience of the religious prostrate at their feet or the meekness of the one who sent them their food and invited them to repentance—reformed. They decided to go to the Saint, who received them with open arms, and, like a father, pressed them to his heart. From that day on, their lives were transformed. Instead of cutthroats, they became true servants of the Lord. They became reconciled with God and spent the rest of their lives expiating their crimes by rigorous penance.

That was one of the methods used by St. Francis to win over rebellious hearts to peace. As you see, he did not hesitate to use human means to achieve his ends—he won the brigands through their stomachs. But even here, St. Francis had a way with him! And besides, St. Francis prayed!

Here is another example of how St. Francis, by his great meekness, succeeded in bringing peace to a troubled soul, given over to despair and rage.

One of the most cherished works of the Friars Minor was that of service to lepers. As a general thing, these poor unfortunates, on whom the good friars—at the risk of their lives—lavished all kinds of care and consolation, as to suffering members of Christ; responded to their unwearied devotion by the most touching tokens of gratitude. How many souls in whom vice festered in bodies eaten away by hideous sores, were instantly purified and healed by the action of grace! From these hospitals a chorus of thanksgiving and praise went up to Heaven.

Nevertheless, by a monstrous exception, there happened to be in a hospital one of those unfortunates, who, naturally of a gloomy temperament, had allowed himself to become so embittered by his malady, that he repaid the tender care of the friars by coarse insults, sometimes even by blows; never ceasing to pour out horrible blasphemies against God and Christ.

St. Francis was told of this. At once, yielding to the impulse of his heart, he hurried to the leper firmly resolved at all costs to shower his brother with affectionate care.

Entering the sick man's room, he cast himself at his feet in greeting, saying to him in kind tones, "Friend, may God grant you peace! I come from him to serve you as my brother!"

"So? And what can *you* do for me more than your companions?" shrieked the leper in a frenzy of despair. "God has abandoned me! I have been rotting in this place for months, devoured by this horrible disease! There is no hope for me! I can't live this way, consumed by all the fires of Hell!"

At this language, which bespoke the deep discouragement of the unfortunate, pain-distracted man, the saint raised his eyes to Heaven and withdrew to pray. A few minutes later, he returned to the leper; and greeting him as before, addressed these words to him in a most affectionate tone of voice: "Brother! Friend! Command me to do whatever pleases you. I will obey you in all things."

The suppliant attitude of the man of God, and his look of sympathy, touched the infuriated man, who burst into tears. Francis anticipated his desires. Gently, he drew aside the rags covering the man; and carefully bathed all his members, devoured by leprosy, in a bath prepared with medicinal herbs. At the mere touch of his blessed hands, the fiery wounds with which the poor leper was covered, disappeared forever. At the same time, the invincible and marvellous meekness of the saint, restored the sick man to health and brought his soul back to God—snatching him from the depths of despair.

That was the way St. Francis subdued the most rebellious souls by this indefatigable gentleness.

We could add here the marvellous incident of the "conversion" of the dreadful wolf of Gubbio! But since the story is well known to everyone, we prefer to relate some lesser known examples.

Conquered by Love!

On his way to Perugia, St. Francis met a beggar whose features were distorted by violent rage; and said to him, "Brother, why are you so angry?" The man was cursing like a trooper against his liege lord, whom he accused of having stolen all his goods. Francis, seeing him persist in this deathly hate, had great compassion on his soul, and said to him gently, "Brother, for the love of God, forgive your master, so that you may save your soul. It you don't, you will lose, besides what he took away from you, your poor soul, which is worth much more."

"No!" retorted the man. "I cannot possibly forgive him, unless he gives me back what he stole!"

Then Francis said with angelic sweetness, "Here! I give you this cloak. It is all that I have, and I beg you to forgive your lord for the love of God." And taking off his cloak, he gave it to him. The beggar received it with a softened countenance, suddenly burst into tears, and, vanquished by love, forgave!

* * *

Born at a time when civil and religious society were torn by class conflict, St. Francis deserves his title of "the Angel of Concord." St. Francis brought peace in 1209 to the citizens of Assisi, and, later on, to the bishop and podesta (mayor) of the city. So in 1224, he could add this consoling stanza—breathing the Franciscan spirit—to his Canticle of the Sun:

"Be praised, my Lord, through those who
pardon give for love of you,
And bear infirmity and tribulation:
Blessed are they who suffer it in peace,
For of you, Most High, they shall be crowned."

As a final quotation, here is an unusual testimony. In the archives of the church of Spoleto, an original, contemporary document has been preserved of the impression made by the personality and words of St. Francis. Here it is in its touching simplicity:

"I, Thomas, a citizen of Spoleto and archdeacon of the cathedral church of the same city, while studying in Bologna in the year 1220, saw —on the day of the Assumption of the Mother of God—St. Francis preaching in the square, before the 'Little Palace'; where almost the entire city was assembled. His sermon heads were 'Angels, men, and demons.' He spoke of these intelligent beings so well and with so much precision, that many men of letters who heard him admired such a discourse coming from the lips of a simple man. He did not follow the ordinary manner of preachers; but like a popular orator, spoke only of the wiping out of enmities, and of the necessity of making treaties of peace and union. His habit was of cheap material and ragged, his appearance, frail, his face pale and lean. But God gave such efficacity to his words, that a great number of noblemen, whose cruel and ravenous fury had caused much bloodshed, became friends again. The affection and veneration felt for the saint were so universal and extensive, that men and women crowded up to him, deeming themselves happy if they could but touch the hem of his robe."

One may observe, in these lines penned by a contemporary of St. Francis, the great influence the saint had over them!

Why should we not do as much in our environment?

319—Do we say the prayer for peace in a Mass for the Dead?

No, nor is the Pax given. This is because the prayer for peace applies especially to the Church Militant. The Pax is likewise exclusively addressed to the faithful on earth. Now in a Mass of Requiem, Christ's grace descends first of all on the faithful departed.

320—For what do we pray in the second pre-Communion prayer?

The celebrant formerly received Communion right after the prayer for peace and the Pax. Later on, a number of priests wanted to make a final prayer for better dispositions just before eating the Bread of Life. At first, the Church let every priest follow his devotion; but as these prayers multiplied, she intervened nine hundred years ago, to choose two of them and leave out all the rest. It is these two prayers officially adopted as an immediate preparation for Communion, that we are about to explain.

In the first prayer, the priest begs for an increased spiritual life, and the removal of whatever might impair it:

PRAY FOR GRACE

Domine Jesu Christi, Filii Dei vivi, qui ex voluntate Patris, cooperante Spiritu Sancto, per mortem tuam mundum vivificasti; libera me per hoc sacrosanctum Corpus et Sanguinem tuum ab omnibus iniquitatibus meis et universis malis: et fac me tuis semper inhaerere mandatis, et a te numquam separari permittas: Qui cum eodem Deo Patre, et Spiritu Sancto, vivis et regnas Deus, in saecula saeculorum. Amen.

Lord, Jesus Christ, Son of the Living God, who according to the will of the Father, and through the co-operation of the Holy Ghost, have by your death given life to the world; deliver me by this, your most sacred Body and Blood, from all my iniquities, and from every evil. Make me always adhere to your Commandments and never suffer me to be separated from you; who, with the same God the Father and the Holy Ghost, live and reign, God, world without end. Amen.

This prayer recalls in a few words all the economy of the divine plan of the Incarnation and Redemption which the Mass perpetuates, and the precise rôle of the Blessed Trinity in the work of Redemption. (See Q.5.)

"*Lord Jesus Christ.*" Christ is directly addressed, as in the preceding prayer.

"Son of the Living God." To the initial invocation is added the essential quality of Christ: "Son of the Living God." This formula recalls to us the Gospel scene wherein Jesus is proclaimed by St. Peter as the "Son of the Living God." This act of faith of the Prince of the Apostles invites us to make a similar act. For this, let us impose silence on flesh and blood and hear only the Heavenly Father who testifies: "This is my Beloved Son in whom I am well pleased." Yes, before the Host on the corporal, let us tell Jesus of our faith in his presence under the appearances of bread, burning with love to communicate to us this divine love which gives true peace.

"Who, according to the will of the Father, and through the co-operation of the Holy Ghost, have by your death given life to the world." It was the will of our Heavenly Father to save us by sending his only Son into the world: "For God so loved the world, that he gave his only begotten Son; that those who believe in him may not perish, but have life everlasting." (John 3:16.)

God the Father, after satisfying the requirements of his justice with regard to our guilty first parents, lets mercy take over again, and promises a Saviour.

God the Son offers himself: "Father, you did not want sacrifices mingled with iniquity. Here I am as a Victim."

God the Holy Ghost created in Mary the matter of the human body of the Word of God. The Holy Ghost's co-operation continues during the Saviour's entire earthly existence.

"Have by your death given life to the world." Why did Jesus die? To give us life! And what a life! Not the life that becomes vile and corrupt by a degradation of the senses and by ill-contained passions; nor that culpable life which precipitates a soul into hell-fire forever, as was the case with the evil Rich Man. But a divine life, a life purified and transformed by the Sacraments, a life which leads the Christian toward likeness with Christ.

Jesus makes use of the death inflicted on him to open Heaven to his executioners. And we murmur at suffering! And what will we not do to avoid it!

Our Lord once said to Bl. Angela of Foligno: "What the Father gave to his Son, the Son often gives to his own. That is why many receive tribulation, not with patience, but with joy, as a token of friendship."

Suffering makes the soul cleave to God, turns it to him, and binds it to him. Sometimes it makes Christ increase in us, like a shower that makes the land fertile. If we knew its value, we not only would not shun it, but would go out to meet it—searching for it as for a treasure.

"Deliver me by this, your most Sacred Body and Blood, from all my iniquities." By virtue of this Body and Blood of Christ, which I shall presently receive, deliver me from all my past sins, whether venial or mortal. Those that I myself have committed, and those of others for which I have been more or less responsible.

"And from every evil." This formula recalls the Our Father. Yes, Lord, remove from my life the insincerity, the distractions, the feverish agitation in place of the serene action; the preoccupation with being esteemed by others, the seeking of my own comfort and ease, my love of the limelight. . . . "Deliver me," writes Fr. Desplanques, "from this tendency to push myself, to show off, instead of showing You to souls."

But before undertaking to liberate the souls of others, we ought —and this is essential—to have already begun to liberate our own soul. The more courage and will-power we put into the work of our own personal sanctification, the more right we shall have to hope to win others, one by one. Every soul is worth a world, and deserves our whole life's devotion—so much the more, because every soul cost the Blood of Jesus Christ.

"Make me always adhere to Your Commandments." The divine friendship is conditioned by the observance of Christ's precepts. "You are my friends," he has said, "if you do the things I command you." (John 15:14.)

Let us beware of falling into the delusion, which would make us gauge our love for God by our burning protestations of love, or by the prayers fed by seraphic ejaculations taken from books of devotion; while our lives may be a network of disobedience to God's Commandments! True love is proved less by words than by deeds. . . .

"And never suffer me to be separated from You." The greatest evil that could possibly happen to us, is separation from Christ. And yet a single mortal sin plunges us into this misfortune! Now it is not possible for a just person to persevere for a long time—especially, to the end— in God's friendship, in the state of grace, without special actual grace.

The Holy Eucharist obtains this grace for us. Moreover, if we would live the Consecration of our Mass to the end, we must die to self, to enable Christ to live in us. For the harder we work at separating ourselves from self, and at substituting the self of Christ, the greater becomes our assurance, the surer our perseverance in Christ's friendship, and the more indissoluble does this friendship become.

Yes, Jesus always with me, and I always with him. His life mine, and my life his!

How far-reaching is this petition! How much of insistence we should put into it! Many may be the obstacles and difficulties—we know this only too well—but by Christ's power, nothing will be able to separate us from him. "Who then will be able to separate us from the love of Christ?" No one!

The doxology which follows is a protestation of faith and trust in the Blessed Trinity; and an adoration of Christ, whose life and Kingship is forever, world without end.

I WANT WHAT YOU WANT

•

Dear Jesus, every time I say, "The Lord be praised," or "God's will be done," I intend thereby to accept whatever your providence may have planned for me, in time and in eternity.

I desire no other state in life, no other place to live, no other food, or clothing, or state of health than it may please you to give me.

I want no other work, no other talents, no other lot in life than you have destined for me.

If your will for me is failure, broken plans, lost lawsuits, and the loss of all I possess, this is my will, too.

If your will is for me to be despised, hated, forsaken, defamed, and ill-treated, even by those I love most, this is my will, too.

If your will is for me to be stripped of everything, banished from my native land, shut up in prison, and living in continuous suffering and anguish, this is my will, too.

If your will is for me to be always sick, covered with sores, crippled, stretched on a bed of pain, and forsaken by all, this is my will, too.

321—What is expressed by the third pre-Communion prayer?

This prayer, as we shall see later, inspires the one about to receive his God with the horror of an unworthy Communion, and also with the requisite humility for approaching God. It implores the salutary fruits to be brought to us by the Friend of our souls:

A PRAYER FOR HEALING

Perceptio Corporis tui, Domine Jesu Christe, quod ego indignus sumere praesumo, non mihi proveniat in judicium et condemnationem; sed pro tua pietate prosit mihi ad tutamentum mentis et corporis, et ad medelam percipiendam: Qui vivis et regnas cum Deo Patre in unitate Spiritus Sancti Deus, per omnia saecula saeculorum. Amen.	Let not the receiving of your Body, O Lord, Jesus Christ, which I, all unworthy, presume to receive, turn to my judgment and condemnation; but through your loving kindness may it be for me a safeguard and a remedy for soul and body, who with God the Father, in the unity of the Holy Ghost, live and reign, God, world without end. Amen.

Still more humble than the preceding, this prayer is most expressive. As if the prayer for deliverance from evil and of perfect fidelity, still appeared too general and too ambitious in scope, this restricts itself to imploring Jesus' mercy that the Communion may not turn to the condemnation of a too tepid or unworthy soul; but may produce its salutary effects, and be, at least, a remedy, if soul and body are weak and ailing.

"O Lord, Jesus Christ." This prayer, like the preceding, is addressed to Christ present on the altar.

"Let not the receiving of Your Body." As no mention is made of the Blood, this formula has a purely private character and pertains equally to faithful and celebrant.

"Which I, all unworthy, presume to receive." Alas! We can never forget that we are unworthy to approach the Holy Table of the thrice holy God! For the question is not one of approaching Jesus only; but of uniting ourselves even to assimilation, to compenetration, through Holy Communion, to Him who is Holiness itself! To the extent, moreover, that we live our Mass, we shall know ourselves better and have special light

with regard to God. All of which makes us more aware of our unworthiness.

But thank God, we can count, and ought to count, on divine mercy! Jansenist doctrine erred on just this point, in that it forever separated God's justice from his infinite mercy; and despite the sincerest repentance a sinner could show, Jansenism halted him on the threshold of Communion, inspiring him with terror at the thought of uniting himself to Him who had said: "Come to Me, all you who labour and are burdened under the weight of your misery. Come to Me, and I will give you rest!"

"Turn to my judgment and condemnation." "Holy Communion can bring you to judgment and condemnation," St. Paul wrote to the Corinthians. When? When a person receives it unworthily. Now only one thing can make us really unworthy to receive; and that is mortal sin of which we are cognizant, and for which we neglect to ask forgiveness in Confession.

"But through Your loving kindness." Before going on to enumerate the positive effects, we appeal here to Christ's loving kindness, to his divine mercy, praying:

"May it be for me a safeguard and a remedy for soul and body." The Eucharist is a salutary protection for soul and body.

For the soul: At the end of a life truly Christian, as the all-important day of final union with God approaches, our minds, hearts, and wills seek a sure refuge in the Heart of Him who calls Himself Love! The Eucharist comes in answer to our soul's aspirations and to fortify it in the combats it must sustain in the world.

For the body. Holy Communion is even good for the body! By the reception of the Eucharistic Bread, our bodies become living ciboria —vessels of divine life. The Holy Eucharist, moreover, extinguishes in us the devouring fire of the passions and deposits within us a germ of eternal life.

"A remedy." The sacred Council of Trent made this effect of the Holy Eucharist stand out admirably: "It is the remedy, the antidote, which preserves us in the future from mortal sin, and which consumes in our souls everyday venial faults." (Sess. 13. C. 2.)

We cannot insist too strongly on the salutary effects of Holy Communion. They are almost completely unrecognized. Modern piety, for the most part, aims only at tasting the sweetness brought over and above to the soul by the eucharistic food. We live too much for thrills and are too avid of sensible consolations. When God takes away these little spiritual dainties from a soul still too attached to the sensible, it happens that many persons believe their Communions to be less good or even without fruit, because they no longer *feel* anything! This is another delusion.

St. Ambrose, in his admirable commentary on Luke's Gospel, indicates those maladies of the soul which the Eucharist as remedy is designed to combat. The saint comments here on the incident of the healing of St. Peter's mother-in-law, confined to her home by a violent fever. Here is St. Ambrose's text: "Now our 'fever' is cupidity, avarice, voluptuousness, luxury, vanity, ambition, and anger; i.e., the seven capital sins. It is the compendium of every vice, the source of every sin. These are the ills from which our souls suffer, and which often place our supernatural life in peril."

"Who live and reign with God the Father, in the unity of the Holy Ghost." You who work miracles of sanctification by the action of Your Holy Spirit; You who—coming in us—are about to give us this Divine Spirit, who is the principle of the spiritual life of our souls—O you who reign on earth, and world without end. Amen.

These three prayers admirably unite solid dogma and religious fervour. Let us pray them then, with the priest, giving them precedence over all other prayers.

RECEPTION OF THE DIVINE VICTIM

From the Pater Noster to the end of the third prayer on which we have just commented, we have considered that portion of the Mass which we call the *"preparation for Communion."*

With the *Panem caelestem* and the *Domine, non sum dignus,* we come to the Communion proper.

The Communion is the last act of the Mass drama, of which the Consecration is the climax. It is the consummation on earth of our union with God; it is the means of bringing about our return to the Father's House.

Offered and consecrated with Christ, the soul is ready for Communion.

Ready? Up to a certain point, with divine aid.

That is why we should, like the celebrant, repeat our triple protestation of humility: "Lord, I am not worthy. . . ."

Panem Caelestem

322—By what words does the priest express his desire for Communion?

Overflowing with confidence, the priest genuflects in adoration, saying as he takes in his hand the two parts of the Host:

Panem caelestem accipiam et nomen Domini invocabo.	I will take the Bread of Heaven and will call upon the name of the Lord.

The solemn moment approaches. All—priest and faithful alike—ought to dilate to the maximum the receptive capacity of their hearts; in order to receive in their fullness the torrents of grace which Holy Communion imparts.

323—From what are the words of the *Domine, non sum dignus,* taken?

These are the words of the centurion of Capharnum, who asked Jesus to heal his servant. This pagan drew from his faith-filled heart, this admirable formula: "Lord, I am not worthy that you should come under my roof; but say the word only, and my servant will be healed." This profession of faith in the mouth of this foreigner so touched Jesus' heart, that he expressed his great admiration and granted the favour asked. Now, the servant was paralyzed; and, as we know, bodily paralysis is an image of the state of sin. In order to adapt this beautiful formula to the communicant, it was sufficient to replace the word *puer meus* (my servant) by *anima mea* (my soul).

While reciting this prayer, the priest inclines, reverently holding in his left hand the two halves of the Sacred Host and the paten, and with his right hand strikes his breast three times, as he prays in a modulated voice, "Domine, non sum dignus. . . ."

Domine, non sum dignus, ut intres sub tectum meum; sed tantum dic verbo, et sanabitur anima mea.	Lord, I am not worthy that you should come under my roof; but say the word and my soul will be healed.
Domine, non sum dignus, ut intres sub tectum meum; sed tantum dic verbo, et sanabitur anima mea.	Lord, I am not worthy that you should come under my roof; but say the word and my soul will be healed.
Domine, non sum dignus, ut intres sub tectum meum; sed tantum dic verbo, et sanabitur anima mea.	Lord, I am not worthy that you should come under my roof; but say the word and my soul will be healed.

Let us—before Christ present on the altar—renew the accusation of the sins of our life, especially, the most humiliating. Pitilessly acknowledge our real weaknesses, spiritual misery, and our many repeated falls into the same sins. . . . And with deep conviction of our spiritual indigence, let us repeat—not alone with our lips, but inwardly humiliating ourselves more deeply than we bow our heads—"Lord, I am not worthy that you should come under my roof, should enter my heart. . . . I have no right to a single one of your graces. . . . I have so abused your goodness. . .but if you will, you can heal me."

And it is true! He *can* do anything! Out of a sinner, he can make a saint—like the Good Thief who got to Heaven ahead of the Blessed Mother!

Oh, if we would only trust Him! If only we, too, were willing!

> "If the Mass did not exist, the world would long since have been crushed under the weight of its crimes."
>
> —ST. LEONARD OF PORT-MAURICE, O.F.M.

The Priest's Communion

324—What are the words and gestures of the celebrant at his own Communion?

After the *Domine, non sum dignus,* the priest takes the two halves of the Sacred Host in his right hand and with them makes the sign of the cross, while saying.

Corpus Domini nostri Jesu Christi custodiat animam meam in vitam aeternam. Amen.	May the Body of our Lord Jesus Christ keep my soul unto life everlasting. Amen.

Sacrifice is inseparable from Communion—the signs of the cross with the Host and Chalice recall this to the priest at the moment when he is to receive the Body and Blood of Christ.

Taking his stand on Christ's promise, "He who eats My Flesh and drinks My Blood has life everlasting, and I will raise him up on the last day," the priest, in the *Corpus Domini,* prays that the Divine Food may imprint his soul with the seal of a blessed immortality.

Then, bowing deeply, the celebrant reverently receives the Eucharistic Body of the Sacred Victim; who sheds divine life on him in abundance, and carries him along in his sacrificial ascension toward his Heavenly Father. This is the great return, through and with Christ, to the Father's House.

The priest now lays the paten down, joins his hands, and remains a few moments in recollection and in meditation on the divine mysteries.... A delightful pause, this, reminiscent of the repose of St. John on the Heart of Jesus at the Last Supper. But this halt is of short duration; for the Mass is an action, and the celebrant must bring it to a conclusion.

Next, he uncovers the Chalice, genuflects before the Precious Blood, as he did before the Sacred Host, and asks himself this question (with words borrowed from the 125th Psalm)!

Quid retribuam Domino pro omnibus quae retribuit mihi?	What shall I render unto the Lord for all the things he has rendered unto me?

The priest now attentively examines the corporal to see if any particle of the Sacred Bread still remains, and uses the paten to collect these with the greatest of care. (The Greeks gave the name of "pearls" to these particles of the Sacred Host. And indeed, nothing on earth is more precious; since so long as they are perceptible to our senses, they remind us of the Real Presence of our Lord Jesus Christ.)

We Catholics as well, following the example set by the priest at the altar, ought to gather up most preciously our "pearls," these tiniest fragments of the Consecrated Host; which are for us none other than the opportunity of making "little sacrifices." (For is not Christ concealed in these particles just as much as he is in the large Hosts?) This is possibly the only means we have of proving our gratitude to our Lord! Follow in this the example of Little Thérèse of Lisieux, and say with her: "O my Beloved, I do not want to refuse You *anything* today!"

The priest, placing the paten over the chalice, uses his thumb and index finger to cause the "pearls" to fall into the cup; and holding the chalice in his right hand, and the paten with his left, answers his recent question with these words:

Calicem salutaris accipiam et nomen Domini invocabo. Laudans invocabo Dominum, et ab inimicis meis salvus ero.	I will take the chalice of salvation and call upon the name of the Lord, and I shall praise him, and I shall be saved from my enemies.

The celebrant desires to show his gratitude to God for the ineffable Gift which he has just received, by consuming the Sacred Host—the Gift in which all other gifts are comprised.

"What shall I render unto the Lord for all the things he has rendered unto me?" he asks. What can he offer, if not the chalice of salvation? Christ himself shall be the magnificent homage of his gratitude—the only praise worthy of the Father in Heaven.

Thus at the word, *calicem,* he takes the chalice, and finishing the prayer, makes with it the sign of the cross, just as he did with the Sacred Host; this time saying:

Sanguis Domini nostri Jesu Christi custodiat animam meam in vitam aeternam. Amen.	May the Blood of our Lord Jesus Christ keep my soul unto life everlasting. Amen.

Finally, raising the paten under his chin with his left hand, he reverently partakes of the Precious Blood of the Saviour, and of the fragments of the Sacred Host which had been previously deposited in the chalice.

The mystery of eucharistic love is consummated—the Sacrifice is complete. The priest has obeyed Christ's injunction to all his priests: "Drink, all of you, of this."

Our Lord's heart is open like the corolla of a lily, to pour into the heart of his minister, a delicious honey—his own divine life!

But let us never forget that Communion does not bring with it spiritual delights alone. The Chalice has its significance which must never be lost sight of, for it is the symbol of the suffering of our Lord's Sacred Heart.

Partaking of the Lord's chalice means sharing in his Passion! It means affirming our desire to continue through suffering the task of the whole world's Redemption.

Think of it! We ought to be living hosts!

At the Consecration, the Spirit of Love had already united all the congregation to the great Victim of the altar. Holy Communion draws still closer these bonds of friendship between each communicant and Christ.

Love calls for love—the hour has sounded for the Communion of the faithful!

325—Is not the Communion of the faithful coming immediately after that of the celebrant (as the whole liturgy of the Mass calls for), a thing to be hoped for?

Undoubtedly. For the Mass from its commencement, provides an admirable preparation for Communion.

At the Offertory the faithful offered themselves to God; at the Consecration they agreed to become co-victims with Christ. The spiritual transformations thus effected by the Holy Spirit in their souls have predisposed them for mutual union with Christ.

Communion before, after, or outside of Mass, is an act performed out of season. Necessity alone can justify it.

In this connection, we take pleasure in citing a particularly luminous page from the writings of Canon Croegaert. Canon Croegaert demonstrates (in a style perhaps slightly too technical for the uninitiated) that *Communion is not a private devotion, but an integral part of the Mass Sacrifice.*

"A great many authors," (he writes) "consider Holy Communion to be an independent rite, a sort of 'pious practice.'

"They seem not so much as to dream that this sacred rite constitutes an integral part of the eucharistic Sacrifice, instituted along the lines of a predetermined plan laid down by the Great High Priest at the Last Supper. Holy Communion constitutes the last act in the sacred drama of the Mass.

"Is it not unmistakably clear for whoever reads the Gospel accounts of the Last Supper or the text of the Missal dealing with the Institution of the Eucharist, that 'He took bread, and blessed and broke and gave it to His disciples'?

"And does not the same order govern the ritual of the Eucharistic Sacrifice?

"The last act of a secular drama does not constitute a separate element to be staged independently of the rest of the play, nor ahead of the other acts, to which it is organically linked as their complement.

"Undoubtedly, it is the Body and Blood of Christ that we receive in Holy Communion, but it is essential to define these sacred elements. It is the Body and Blood of Christ as offered up by us to the Father. It is the Lamb of God, the Sacred Victim of our own sacrifice, in the oblatory state.

"For this reason, the Communion, situated and integrated as it is within the very framework of the sacrificial or oblatory institution established by Christ, should signify and constitute a most intimate participation in the Sacrifice; a co-oblation, both active and passive, with the Divine Victim; a penetration into the victim state of Christ offered, and an assumption into his oblatory reascension toward God.

"All the liturgy of the Communion, from the Breaking of Bread (the Pater Noster) to the Postcommunion, is subordinate to the consecration; because it constitutes the complete participation of priest and people in the oblation of the one Sacrifice of Jesus Christ, rendered present in an unbloody, or eucharistic manner, by virtue of the Consecration.

"The general line of the oblation is ascensional. It ascends toward the Father. A full participation in this sacrificial oblation, Communion is primarily oriented toward the Father.

"Wrenched from the sacrificial framework of which it formed an organic part, and where it is clearly directed toward the Father, Communion was treated as a 'pious practice,' and applied exclusively to the individual; and—by virtue of this exclusiveness—stripped of its sacrificial significance.

"Scan the countless books of devotion. The first, foremost, and only question is invariably this: 'What is its value?' (In the spiritual sense!) Or, 'What blessing will I receive?' Or again, 'What are the fruits of Communion?'

"The question is doubtless important, and a noble preoccupation (which the Church herself makes use of in the innumerable variety of her postcommunions), but one which—because of its unconscious exclusiveness and its unilateral objective—has for many persons, completely divested the Communion of its significance as a sacrifice.

"As has been said above (see Q. 186), devoid of the act of oblation essential for a sacrifice, the Consecration becomes nothing more than a rite of transubstantiation, a rite productive of Communions, one not directed primarily toward God, but toward US for the purpose of realizing our utilitarian ends; for replenishing our ciboria and monstrances, and assuring us of the Blessed Sacrament reserved—Food of our souls and object (at last!) of our eucharistic worship.

"Hence, so many faithful communicating—without the slightest motive—after Mass, before Mass, without any Mass at all!

"It was not until the thirteenth century, however, that distribution (in the case of an affluence of worshippers) of Holy Communion apart from the Mass began.

"Communion at Mass, with the priest, and with a Host consecrated during the Mass—such is the perfect Communion."

326—What do we read about this in the encyclical, *Mediator Dei et hominum*?

After encouraging Communion of the faithful in its proper place, the Holy Father admits of exceptions. His text follows:

"It is eminently fitting, (and is, moreover, established in the liturgy), that the people should approach the Holy Table after the priest's Communion; and, as We have written above, those persons are to be commended, who, assisting at the Mass, receive Hosts consecrated in it; in order that the prayer may be realized: 'That as many of you as shall receive the most sacred Body and Blood of Your son, by partaking thereof from this altar, may be filled with every heavenly blessing and grace.'

"Nevertheless, it is not unusual that motives should arise for the distribution of Holy Communion either before or after the Sacrifice itself; or again—although the Host is distributed immediately after the priest's Communion—of making this distribution with Hosts previously consecrated. Even under these conditions (as We have already observed above), the people partake normally of the Eucharistic Sacrifice, and it is not infrequent that they can thus more readily approach the Holy Table. If then, in her maternal indulgence, the Church endeavours to anticipate the spiritual needs of her children, these, in turn, should not lightly disdain what is counselled by sacred liturgy; and, unless hindered by a reasonable motive, they should carry out whatever brings out more clearly at the altar the living unity of the Mystical Body."

327—What is the ceremony for the Communion of the faithful?

As the celebrant receives the Precious Blood, the faithful go up to the altar rail and pray the Confiteor with the server, either aloud or inaudibly, according to custom. The Confiteor so prayed is an act of humility and repentance; and, at the same time, a sacramental with the peculiar virtue of obtaining for us the forgiveness of venial sins.

After the Confiteor, the celebrant genuflects before the uncovered ciborium. Then, hands joined, he turns toward the people, and begs God's pardon for the sins of those about to receive, saying, the *Misereatur*: "May Almighty God have mercy on you, forgive you your sins, and bring you to life everlasting."

To which all reply: "Amen! So be it!"

He then adds, "*Indulgentiam*.... May the Almighty and merciful Lord grant you pardon, absolution, and remission of your sins!" While saying these words, he makes the sign of the cross with his right hand over those who are going to receive Communion. The reply is the same: "Amen!"

Again genuflecting, he takes the ciborium in his left hand, and in his right (between the thumb and index finger), a Host. Turning toward the congregation, he slightly raises the Host so as to show it, saying: *"Ecce Agnus Dei....* Behold the Lamb of God! Behold Him who takes away the sins of the world!"

Words which sum up all that we have said above: "Behold the Lamb—the sole Victim worthy of God! Behold Him who immolated Himself for His Father's glory! Behold Him who takes away the sins of the world, and has atoned for them with His Blood!" The celebrant shows Him to the people and seems to say: "Are you willing to share in the dispositions, in the spirit, of this holy Victim?" (Here, each one should answer for himself.)

Three times the priest repeats for the people, the *Domine, non sum dignus*: "Lord, I am not worthy that you should come under my roof; but say the word and my soul will be healed." Let us inwardly repeat this public profession of our unworthiness, and of our confidence in the effcts of Holy Communion.

And now the celebrant approaches the communicants, beginning with those kneeling on the Epistle side. To each, he presents the Sacred Host; and as this is the Victim of Calvary, he makes with it the sign of the cross over the ciborium, saying:

Corpus Domini nostri Jesu Christi custodiat animam tuam in vitam aeternam. Amen.	May the Body of our Lord Jesus Christ keep your soul unto life everlasting. Amen.

And Jesus is in your tongue! He descends in your heart!

A moment ardently desired by Him!... An inestimable moment for you!... For it marks the fulfillment of the desires expressed in the Pater Noster!

Jesus coming into our hearts, effects as it were a new incarnation. He brings to us his spirit, his loving dispositions, his divine life.... Henceforth, he will live in us. He will employ us to adore his Father, to be for him a holy and pleasing sacrifice, insofar as we do not resist....

God's name will be hallowed through Him in us.

God's Kingdom will be realized in our lives, for Jesus is in our hearts as a King. We should let him direct our affections and desires. In this way, we shall more easily do God's will....

We are now in possession of the Bread for which we prayed! Like a devouring flame, the divine love which this Bread brings, burns and consumes our venial faults and keeps us from falling again into mortal sin.

The soul, thus regenerated, feels itself fortified against temptation. By this very fact, evil, that is, sin, is driven from our soul's dwelling, and within there is a great calm.... Thus again the prayers for peace are answered, which we pray after the Our Father. For the Lamb of God gives us inner peace, calming our passions and turning our affections toward God.

"Si scires donum Dei!" If all the faithful but knew the gift of God, no one would deprive himself of Communion—even once!

328—Can you tell briefly how the faithful received Communion in the early Church?

In the early Church, celebration of Mass comprised two processions of the faithful toward the altar.

The first, at the Offertory, when they offered bread and wine.

The second, at the Communion, when they received their consecrated offerings.

In Christian antiquity, the faithful communicated standing. It was not until the Middle Ages, along about the thirteenth century, that the custom of kneeling for Communion was introduced.

Everyone communicated under both kinds.

The deacon convoked the people to Communion by crying in a clarion voice, *"Sancta Sanctis!"* "Holy things for the holy!"

The faithful received the Eucharistic Bread on the outstretched right palm, the left hand being crossed under it. For this reason, the faithful washed their hands at the fountain situated at the portico, or front of the church, before entering the basilica. For reception of the Holy Eucharist the communicants covered the hand with a white linen cloth called the *dominicale,* or "Lord's cloth."

In his celebrated *Catecheses,* St. Cyril of Jerusalem (+386) describes the reception of Communion:

"Then (after the Pater Noster) the priest says, 'Holy things for the holy!' For holy is the eucharistic Bread which is offered, after it has received the visit of the Holy Spirit from on high. Holy are you likewise, when you have become worthy of the Holy Spirit. So what is holy is proper for those who are holy. Then you say, 'One holy One, and one Lord, Jesus Christ.' For in truth, there is only One who is holy by nature. We are holy, too, not by nature, but by participation, by mortification and prayer. You now hear the chanting of the Psalm which, by a divine melody, invites you to partake of the holy Mystery, saying, 'Taste and see how the Lord is good.' This is to be referred not to the physical mouth, but to faith, which resolves all doubts.

"Therefore, when you approach, do not do so with your hands out flat or fingers extended; but make of your left hand a sort of throne for your right hand, since it is the one to receive the King. Then cup your hand and receive Christ's Body, as you say, 'Amen.'

"After you have piously sanctified your eyes by gazing upon the venerable Body, consume it; taking care not to lose any of it. For if you do, be sure that you lose in a fashion one of your own members. Tell me. If someone gave you some gold dust, would you not receive it with the greatest precaution; and would you not take care to see that none of it was lost or damaged? Should you not be so much the more careful not to lose the tiniest crumb of what is more precious than diamonds and gold?

"Then, after partaking of the Body of Christ, approach the chalice of his Blood. Do not stretch out your hand; but, on the contrary, bow and respond 'Amen,' in an attitude of adoration and reverence. Sanctify yourself by your reception of the Body and Blood of Christ. Next, be attentive to the prayer, and thank God who has made you worthy of so great a mystery."

The reception of the Holy Eucharist on the hand was not without peril. The particles *could* be lost, and profanation of the Sacred Bread by the unworthy was not impossible. On the other hand, the form of the Eucharistic Bread gradually became reduced in size, and the use of small hosts became more and more widespread. Also, by the ninth century, the faithful almost everywhere received Holy Communion, not on the hand, but on the tongue.

For the reception of the Precious Blood, communicants drank directly from the chalice. Later on, a slender gold or silver tube was used. You can imagine the inconvenience of this! This usage disappeared completely by the thirteenth century.

Nowadays, by a decree of the Sacred Congregation of Sacraments, dated March 26, 1929, communicants should—in addition to the Communion cloth—make use of a small gold or silver metal tray, called a paten, to collect any particles that might chance to fall during distribution.

All of these modifications made during the course of centuries, do not change in any way the value of the fixed dogmas of the Christian religion, nor the efficacy of Mass or Communion.

Christ being whole and entire under the species of both bread and wine, the faithful receive the whole Christ when they receive him under the species of bread. If the Church no longer gives Communion to the faithful under the species of wine, it is solely because of the inconvenience entailed; and also as a protest against those heretics who wrongly asserted that in order to receive the whole Christ, it was necessary to communicate under both kinds.

329—Of what is a person who misses one Communion by his own fault deprived?

The loss is irreparable! The person who *could* receive Holy Communion, but does not trouble himself to do so, deprives himself of:

1. The personal visit of Jesus Christ!
2. An increase in sanctifying grace!
3. The power of the sacramental grace of the Eucharist!
4. A valuable remedy against temptation!
5. The remission of venial sin!
6. The total or partial remission of the temporal penalty due to his sins!
7. An increase of his happiness in Heaven!
8. The gaining of plenary indulgences on certain days !
9. A fruitful ministry among souls!

Have you thoughtfully reflected on ALL THESE LOSSES?

How is it that so many are indifferent to Jesus, or feel so little desire for him?

Love proves itself by the gift of self. The more perfect the love, the more abundantly and fully is it given. Jesus loved us and gave himself up for us. How can we do otherwise than give love for love, to a God who has loved us so much?

St. Thérèse of the Child Jesus might well write: "It is not to remain in the golden ciborium that Jesus descends daily from Heaven but to find another Heaven—the Heaven of our souls, in which he takes delight."

As a matter of fact, we ought to communicate every time that we are present at the Holy Sacrifice of the Mass. For if we attend a banquet without partaking of it, do we not do dishonour to the feast, as well as to the one who invited us? Besides, those who rarely receive Holy Communion, make but little progress in holiness.

This was the experience of an engineer, who tells us in engineer's terminolgy, of the lowering of his spiritual power, when deprived for several days of the Bread of the Eucharist. He states:

"While on a business trip last month, I had to miss Communion for several days. Now, right away, I noticed a distinct lowering of my 'moral voltage.' It was like a break in a dynamo—the 'light' didn't come on! I was practically helpless when faced by temptation. I thank God for having permitted this experience. It made me understand these words of St. Pius X: 'Daily Communion is the preliminary condition for leading a Christian life.' This had always appeared to me like sheer exaggeration. I know now, from my own experience, that it is a formula of moral dynamics, as exact as is the classic formula of the mechanical equivalent of heat. It is like a theorem in geometry—a mechanics of life. For me, no system of geometry or mechanics is better established."

And for us? . . .

330—To appreciate better the worth of a Communion, show how enriching were the contacts of Jesus with the Jews during his public life.

If a simple rapid visit of Jesus through the cities and villages of Palestine produced so many cures, both spiritual and physical, what will not his sojourn in our hearts through Holy Communion accomplish?

Think of his passage through Cana, where he worked his first miracle, changing water into wine.

Recall the Samaritan woman, a model for apostles of Catholic Action. She comes to the Master to draw from the Source of living waters, and immediately rushes to the conquest of her fellow citizens. "I have found the Christ!" she cries. "Everybody come and listen to Him!"

Her interview with Jesus was of short duration—shorter, perhaps, than a Mass! But how fruitful this conversation with the Saviour for this fallen woman, whose heart had been in the keeping of five husbands!

We, as well, if we go (perhaps discouraged) to church with the empty amphora of our hearts, will find that Jesus (who thirsts to give us to drink) will not fail to give us living water springing up into life everlasting. . . .

And consider Zacchaeus, short of stature, but long in generosity! He wanted to see Jesus; and our Lord, who saw him up in a tree, anticipated his desire by telling him that he wanted to visit him. The Master's visit brought forgiveness and salvation to this sinner. "Today salvation has come to this house." For Jesus inspired this sinner with so complete a detachment of this world's goods, and with so remarkable a spirit of charity and justice, that he became a saint on the spot!

Recall the story of the sick woman who touched but the hem of Jesus' garment, and was instantly healed. How could our contact with the flesh, heart, and divinity of Christ in Holy Communion do otherwise than transform us?

One day when our Lord entered St. Peter's house, he instantly cured the malignant fever of the mother-in-law of the chief of the apostles. "And she arose, and began to wait on them."

Why did Jesus Christ raise Lazarus from the dead? As a reward for the hospitality which he had so often received at Bethany. As for us! What should *we* not obtain, if only the doors of our heart were open to Him daily?

One look of Jesus at the Apostle Peter, who had just denied his Master, was enough to change his heart and convert him!

At our Lord's touch, the deaf hear, the blind see, the lame walk, the dead are raised up, sinners are converted, and generous souls become more fervent. . . . Some ask for life, the rest for healing; and none goes away unsatisfied.

What Jesus did during his mortal life, he continues to do in his eucharistic life. . . . How explain that so many Christians are not interested? It's a mystery!

"Would you like to know," writes Abbé Mark, "what you lose every time you leave a Host in the ciborium? Imagine what might have happened if Mary Magdalene had not gone to the house of Simon the Pharisee when inwardly invited by the Master to do so? She might have died in her sins! She knew the peace and glory of holiness, the day that she took refuge at the feet of her God. Let us never forget that every day Christ descends in our cities. He comes with full hands that he would fain open, and everyone may come to him. Our churches are open, and are more inviting than was the Pharisee's house. Who is keeping you—yes, who is keeping you—from crossing the threshold, from coming with *your* "alabaster vase" (your heart) to pour out your perfume, your cares, and your tears over the feet of the Waiting One? Who will say to you, "Many things are forgiven you, because you gave Me a proof of your love, by receiving Me into your house"?

This house of your heart—how eagerly Jesus desires to enter it! "I have longed and longed to share this paschal meal with you before My Passion," is what He says to every one of us! He would restore, adorn, and embellish our soul's dwelling—and too often we close the door! As in Bethlehem, there is no room for Him in the inn, where He insistently knocks.

This is deplorable, and yet this is the way we treat Incarnate Love! *For some people, daily Communion is a "mortification" for Lent! (Going to church to receive our Best Friend, a penance?)*

Again, with what torrents of grace does not Jesus wish to fill us by his coming to us in person! Not a few feet away, but in our inmost being. Not in passing, but to dwell within! How great the happiness of those who receive Jesus with hearts enlarged by humility, trust, and love!

Certainly, many Catholics seem unaware of the immense treasure of divine love that pervades the soul in Holy Communion. Let us make use of a comparison to help us understand this. If, for a wonder, we were to attempt to shut up in this tiny glass vase, the mighty globe of fire called the sun, what would happen? ... It is not hard to guess! At the sun's approach, the little vase would be shattered. When we communicate, only a miracle enables the fragile "vase" of our hearts to receive and contain without becoming shattered, Jesus, the Sun of justice and of holiness, the Omnipotent Source of light and love!

Indeed, if we but understood the worth of a single Communion. we would approach the altar rail on our knees!

331—In order to appreciate still more the real value of Holy Communion, list the miracles performed by Jesus to come to us in the Host.

To give himself as food for our souls, Jesus upsets the laws of nature, and works numerous miracles, of which the principal are:

1. The bread and wine, whose appearances we see, actually no longer exist. Christ's Body and Blood have taken their place.

(By "species" or " appearances" of bread and wine, must be understood that which appears to our senses, as the colour, form, and taste of bread and wine. The sacred species are called "appearances," because they are like the subsisting shadow of a vanished body. All our senses say, "This is bread." "This is wine." However, neither one nor the other substance or nature now exists. By virtue of the words uttered by the priest at the Consecration, it has been changed into the Body and Blood of Jesus Christ.)

2. When the eucharistic species corrupt, the Real Presence ceases.

3. Christ is present at the same time in Heaven and in the Host, wherein his soul accompanies his Body.

4. Just as our soul is present in every part of our body, so Christ is contained entire in every part of the Host. He is to be found as completely in the smallest particle as in the large Hosts. For Christ is present in the Holy Eucharist under the mode of substance. Now a substance is just as entirely contained in a small quantity, as it is in a large. Thus, the substance of water is to be found just as well in a tiny drop as in the entire ocean.

5. Christ is contained at the same time and entire, not only in one Host, but in the millions and billions of Hosts consecrated by priests daily in the whole world.

When you break a mirror, observe what happens. (Besides your feeling of displeasure!) First, before the mirror was broken, it reflected your image. Now that the glass is in splinters, your image (fortunately for you!) is not broken, but multiplied. And in every fragment, it is just as complete as it was in the whole mirror.

Alongside the miracles of might, should be noted the miracles of love!

Jesus has "spoiled" us. That is likely the reason why we are not surprised at being surrounded by so many benefits!

Our Lord *could* have given the sublime power of consecrating his Body and Blood to a few rare privileged souls, who would have exercised it once a year at a given spot on the globe. And that would have been wonderful enough. But this would not have satisfied his love. Just as he gives to every priest the divine power to forgive sins in his name, so does he desire that every priest should bring him down upon the altar to become our Food. And what is more, he has foreseen all the outrages that he was to receive in the Holy Eucharist. He knew that many persons would misuse and desecrate the Sacred Host. Despite this, seeing the small number who *would* profit, he did not flinch.

Jesus is silent in his Sacrament of love, bearing all things. Because he loves us, he has become our Food! He remains subject to our call, day and night, like a prisoner. He lets himself be touched, taken up, carried, and sometimes given to souls in the state of mortal sin. . .so as to unite himself and divinise those living in the state of grace. (Even though in the past, they have many times betrayed him.) He consents to every humiliation. . . . He goes still further. He stoops even to begging for the hearts of his creatures; who pass with indifference before his tabernacles, where his heart watches—awaiting us, as if he had only us to love!

But do not forget that the Eucharist, while the most touching of marvels, is likewise the most pressing of obligations. Love calls for love!

"Alas!" writes Father Baeteman, "who then has no cause to smite his breast? Alongside all the miracles wrought by Jesus in profusion as if they were child's play, in order to come to us, there is another miracle which men have reserved for him; and which equals or surpasses his own! It is the "miracle" of hatred, scorn, indifference, and coldness, which Christ encounters every day; and which ought to detach him from, and disgust him with us forever!

"Oh, what would become of us, if some day, tired of so much ingratitude, disgusted with so much hatred, the God of the Eucharist were to say to us: 'So you will have no more of Me? Then give Me back My chalices and My ciboria! The pagans are waiting for Me. I am awaited in the heart of the desert, there where new converts walk fifty miles to embrace those altars that you no longer visit—and which are to be found at your very door! If I willed to punish you, I would have no need to wield My thunder—it would be enough to leave you alone with your empty tabernacles! Then you would see what would happen to your faithless countries, when My Host should no longer be there, like a lightning arrester, to make intercession for you!'"

It is quite true. We never miss the water till the well runs dry!

O God, give us the power to become eucharistically minded, living by you and bearing you through the world as a luminous and radiant flame. Make us comprehend your love for us, and respond to it in a manner less unworthy of you!

332—Please demonstrate the necessity of Holy Communion in the life of every Christian.

Here, each is free to draw on his own experience. The subject is inexhaustible and vast. We have already touched on it in Question 329. Let us add this:

A soul is like a furnace. It needs attention. "Wood" must often be thrown on the "fire." It must be kept close to the great Source of life and love. Very often have our moral forces wavered, when we failed to renew them in the Heart of Jesus.

Without Jesus, we might perhaps comprehend where our duty lies, but it is certain that we should never accomplish it. "Without Me, you can do nothing!"

Jesus has shown us what we ought to do. He has set us the example of every virtue. He has taught us to suffer, to offer up, to consecrate ourselves; in short, to LIVE OUR MASS. But it is not enough to know *what* to do; we must be capable of doing it as well!

Picture to yourself a giant raising aloft a two-hundred pound weight in front of a ten-year-old boy. Our athlete says, "Well, son, *this* is the way to do it! See? Now, it's *your* turn!"

Naturally, such a feat of strength is impossible for a youngster. He simply hasn't the strength. If the strong man wants the boy to imitate him, he ought to give him his strength. The things that are impossible to men, are possible to God.

This is what Jesus does in Holy Communion. He gives us his divine strength, enabling us to follow his example.

In the history of the Canadian martyrs, a fact is related which illustrates this thought:

"Fr. John Brebeuf, founder of the mission to the Hurons, was taken prisoner in March, 1649. The savages began by tearing out the nails from his fingers and toes. He was next bound to a stake; and a 'collar' of hatchets heated to white heat was placed around his neck. Then he was given a 'belt' made of bits of birch bark, smeared with tar and pitch; and after half flaying him, they set fire to the belt; while, in a mockery of Baptism, they poured boiling water on his head.

"Amidst these atrocious sufferings, the martyr continued to pray —his prayers serving only to double the rage of his tormentors. They split the corners of his mouth to his ears, cut off his lips, and forced a firebrand down his throat.

"Then an Iroquois, knife in hand, jumped on the dying man; and opening his chest, tore out his heart. 'This Black Robe,' he shouted, 'is a strong man! Let us drink his blood, so we, too, may become as brave!'

"And each in turn, sucked blood from that heroic heart, to acquire his strength and courage."

Our Lord, both God and Man, nourishes us with his own Blood and gives us his supernatural power; which enables us to follow his example and practice his teachings.

In the *Life of Grace,* Fr. Norbert-M., O.F.M., relates a significant story in this connection. "One day after a great battle," he writes, "a doctor said to a seriously wounded soldier, 'You need fresh, pure blood, boy, to get you feeling fit again.'

"Another man in the outfit held out his arm, saying, 'Doc, you need blood. Here, help yourself!'

"In a twinkling, the transfusion took place and the soldier soon recovered his strength. Later on, the man said to his benefactor with profound gratitude, 'We aren't just pals any more, but brothers, for your blood is flowing in my veins.'" And he embraced him.

You who read these lines, may have a soul seriously wounded by sin. But there is a true Friend, who, stooping down to you, says, "My boy, your soul needs fresh, pure Blood." And this Friend is Jesus, who offers you his Precious Blood as your soul's life and nourishment. Often —frequently—let this Blood of your God flow over your soul in Holy Communion. Then you will live *in* God, *of* God and *for* God. Remember these words of St. Cyprian, "It is to be feared that he who abstains from Communion, separating himself from the Lord's Body, withdraws at the same time from eternal salvation. For He Himself warns us and declares: 'Unless you eat the flesh of the Son of Man, and drink his Blood, you shall not have life in you.' "

Again, it should be noted that elite souls who have done their allotted task well, were all frequent communicants.

The changed life of Eva Lavallière, the famous actress of the French stage, who became a Tertiary, began only on that day when she decided to become a frequent communicant. God aided her to carry out her good resolutions. Without him, her desire for goodness would have been a flash in the pan.

Fr. Foucauld's greatness dated from the day when he began to receive Christ daily. . . .

One reads in the life of the famous Italian apostle and Tertiary, Pio Perazzo, that the Holy Eucharist was the motive force of his activity. Without paying any heed to feelings of illness or other temporary obstacles, every morning found him at the communion rail. "I could not do anything," he used to say, "until I had received Communion!" And indeed, a day without Communion is something like a day in which the sun does not shine.

When Pio Perazzo was travelling, if it was going to be impossible for him to reach his destination before noon, he would interrupt his trip so as to be able to receive the Bread of Angels. Early in the morning he would rise and go to the nearest church, speaking to no one in the house or on the street. His preparation for Holy Communion had begun the evening before. The next morning he would assist at a first Mass as an immediate preparation for the great Act, while a second Mass served for his thanksgiving. Those who saw him at that time, say that he conversed with our Lord with so visible an expression of reverence and love, that they were moved to tears. After spending at least an hour and a half in church, he would return home; the members of his household not daring as yet to address him, since they saw him still absorbed in prayer. He was transfigured and as if in ecstasy. (See also "Pier-Giorgio Frassati," Q 338.)

But were we to continue, we should need to draw up a list here of all the saints, and of all those who have accomplished something lasting in this life!

Let us merely add that *the Holy Eucharist is likewise indispensable to our apostolate.* It is impossible to give Christ to souls, if our own hearts are not filled to overflowing with him! And to possess Christ in this way, our souls need to be fed, if possible, by daily Communion.

Our rôle as Christians is to radiate Christ. Even if we cannot speak in public, Communion makes of us living monstrances.

Now a monstrance, however rich in gold and precious stones, is but a piece of the goldsmith's art and useless, so long as its centre does not contain the Host. So it is with the lay apostle. Whatever his degree of culture, his oratorical gifts, his talents, or his possessions, if Jesus is not in his heart as a living reality, he will speak, preach, stir crowds, and organize good works in vain. He will accomplish little or nothing. For "without Him," (we repeat) "it is impossible to do anything that counts in God's eyes."

And yet, how many young men and young women—and older persons as well—we launch into the lay apostolate without first having prepared them by means of an intense eucharistic life! Or who are perforce kept away from the holy table by frequent and prolonged night meetings, on the pretext of the conquest of souls and of apostolic life! Thus, instead of Jesus, they give *themselves* to the world! The results should not surprise us.

333—Has the Church always favoured frequent Communion?

Yes, always! How could it be otherwise, when we stop to think that frequent Communion is the surest means to sanctity?

Together, let us look at the record of frequent Communion in the history of the Church.

In the very beginning, the disciples of Jesus after Pentecost "continued steadfastly. . .in the breaking of bread and in the prayers." (Acts 2:42.) Now we know that the expression, "the breaking of bread," signifies Communion.

A little later on, in Rome, the faithful communicated every time they heard Mass. They did not imagine that it could be otherwise—that one could sit down to a meal without eating.

Furthermore, during the period of persecution, the Church permitted her children, even lay persons, men and women, to take home consecrated Hosts; so that they might communicate at home, when unable to do so in church.

Those waiting in their prisons to be led into the arena to be devoured by beasts, were not forgotten. Devoted and courageous Christians fearlessly exposed themselves to deadly peril to bring them the Holy Eucharist. In this way Tarcisius, a little lad of ten (as everyone knows) endured martyrdom on his way to bring his God to the victims of persecution.

There were times when fervour diminishing together with faith, or piety being but ill understood, frequent Communion ceased to be the practice among Christians. But the doctrine of the Church did not change. Doctors and saints rose up vigorously against these errors. One should reread the numerous texts expressive of their indignation. Here are a few:

St. Augustine said, "Live in such a way that you may receive Communion daily."

St. Jerome from his Bethlehem solitude, gave the same advice: "The Eucharist is a daily Sacrifice. It is the daily food of the faithful."

St. Thomas Aquinas admitted his preference for those Christians who, impelled by their love for and their trust in our Lord, receive him frequently; rather than for those who from a reverent, but ill-founded fear of making a bad Communion, stay away from the Holy Table.

St. Catherine of Siena in the fourteenth century, was determined to receive Communion every morning. No one could have stopped her; not even her spiritual director, to whom she would say, "Father! I'm *hungry!*"

We have mentioned what an ardent apostle of the Eucharist St. Francis of Assisi was. (One has only to reread Q. 40.)

The desire of the Church is particularly made known through the decrees of Councils and the writings of the Popes. Now everywhere and always in these documents, the Church shows herself favourable to frequent, and even daily, Communion.

The Catechism of the Council of Trent gives this order to shepherds of souls: "It is a duty incumbent upon priests to exhort the faithful to frequent and even daily Communion. They will remind them that the soul, as well as the body, requires to be fed daily."

Pope Innocent XI in the seventeenth century, published this decree: "The bishops will see to it carefully that Communion, even daily Communion, is to be refused to none; and they will seek to foster so salutary a devotion in their dioceses."

In our own twentieth century (in the year 1905 to be precise) what impetus was given by St. Pius X—called with reason the "Pope of the Eucharist"—to the practice of daily Communion! No one has a right now to argue the point. The question has been settled. "Frequent and daily Communion, being ardently desired by our Lord and by the Catholic Church, ought to be accessible to all the faithful, of whatever class or condition."

Here, as in everything else, the Church is but the mouthpiece of Christ, her Divine Founder. Now Jesus did not expressly state in the Gospel, "You are to receive Communion frequently." Nevertheless, his will is no less evident. It stands out from what we have just said: namely, that the practice of the early Church was certainly the logical consequence of the Saviour's expressed intention.

But the matter becomes unmistakeably clear to whoever reads the celebrated announcement of the Eucharist: "I am the Bread of Life. Your fathers ate the manna in the desert, and have died. This is the bread that comes down from Heaven, so that if anyone eat of it, he will not die. I am the living bread that has come down from Heaven. If anyone eat of this bread, he shall live forever; and the bread that I will give is my flesh for the life of the world. . . . Amen, Amen, I say to you, unless you eat the flesh of the Son of Man, and drink his blood, you shall not have life in you. He who eats my flesh and drinks my blood has life everlasting, and I will raise him up on the last day. For my flesh is food indeed, and my blood is drink indeed. He who eats my flesh and drinks my blood, abides in me and I in him. . . . He who eats of this bread shall live forever." (John 6.)

Thus the Eucharist is like the manna that daily fell from Heaven to feed the Hebrews in the wilderness. For the Christian—likewise walking toward the Promised Land— it is his daily food.

The Eucharist is the bread of the soul that would live by Christ. The *bread!* Jesus utters the word eight times in these few lines. . . . What is bread? The "staff of life," synonymous with life. "Eating bread" means "living." "Bread-winning is earning one's living.

The Eucharist is food. A man cannot have life within him here below; nor hope for life everlasting in Heaven above, who does not eat it. Could Christ possibly make clearer the analogy he draws between the life of the body and that of the soul? To live naturally, one must eat. To live spiritually, one must also eat. When? Every day.

Would your body be satisfied, if you ate just now and then? The same thing holds true for your soul.

Finally, in the Our Father, Christ clearly indicates his will, when he has us pray our Heavenly Father for "daily bread"; which is pre-eminently the Holy Eucharist. (See Q. 267.)

Every morning the table is set in our churches. Jesus waits for us —sometimes in vain—to give himself as food for our souls. . . .

"If you only knew," said our Lord one day to his faithful servant, Sr. Benigna Consolata, "how greatly I desire to come to you in Holy Communion! When you receive me later than usual, my longing for you increases. . . ."

May we—starting tomorrow—no longer disappoint Him, but be faithful to so life-giving a rendezvous!

THE TWO HOSTS

When with my whole faith I come to Thy side,
For the proffered riches of love I see,
Lord, may it be with my arms opened wide,
Saying, "Lord take me. Take even me!"

Lo, I saw two hosts on the paten lie.
One was for me—and the other was I!

Alongside my nothingness there did rest
Almighty God stooping to my distress!

Let me be lost wholly in Thee, my Love—
No longer "I" living in me, but Thee!

To my heart descend from Heaven above,
With Thy heart replace it, and love in me!

Crucify me with Thee to earth. My goal
With Thee in glory and love to rise,

Make me a victim and saver of souls;
Offer me to the Father in sacrifice.

M. D'ERLYS

334—List and refute the poor excuses some people make for their infrequent Communions.

Even today, there are those who have a distaste for frequent Communion, that is almost invincible. . . . For some, it is the dread of increased responsibility; while for others, it is that of having to make an effort, and the fear of sacrifice. The first group is still tinctured with Jansenism. The second is paralyzed from human respect and the spirit of the world!

And yet, frequent Communion corresponds to a *pressing need* of our age; for the present perils threatening faith and morals have never been so pronounced and universal. Good Catholics have to cope with this formidable sensualism which employs a thousand means for leading them to perdition: unwholesome literature, immoral movies, shameless dress, alcoholism. . . . Young people brought up to indulge their every whim, have a horror of sacrifice. They plunge headlong into the frantic love of pleasure and display a scandalous scorn of the sacred laws of marriage; unless they have been accustomed from childhood to live their Christianity to the hilt and to base their lives on frequent Communion—guardian of purity and source of all self-sacrifice.

Frequent Communion, requiring as it does, the state of grace, is the best remedy for all our ills. Let us together refute then the most common objections.

1. I'm not good enough.
2. My sins keep me from Communion.
3. I'm troubled by temptations.
4. I lack fervour. I don't "feel" any devotion.
5. I'm not making any progress. I'm afraid of receiving through routine.
6. I haven't time.
7. I don't want to attract attention.
8. Daily communicants are no better than others.

I'm not good enough

First: "I'm not good enough!"

People who say that are perfectly right! It is dead certain that they are *not* "good enough" to receive our Lord. (No one *is!*) If only those who were "good enough" were allowed to receive, we should be obliged—without more ado—to empty all our ciboria and fence off the Communion rail! Why the Church herself reminds us of our unworthiness before every Communion: "*Domine, non sum dignus*—Lord, I am not worthy for you to come to me."

Were the apostles "good enough" on Holy Thursday? There was Judas, the traitor. Peter, who was going to deny his Master. Thomas, who in a few days would refuse to believe without seeing, thereby giving proof of a very shaky faith. And the rest who would abandon—on the very eve of his arrest—the One who had been so good to them! There they were with their human weaknesses, and without courage in the face of sacrifice. Even John, the "disciple whom Jesus loved." ! He was not to do as Peter did, or Thomas and the rest; but he did fall asleep in the Garden of Olives, while his Master sweat blood and water in his fearful agony; drawing down upon himself the same reproach as the other two: "Could you not then watch one hour with Me?"

So. . .*were* the apostles "good enough"? Jesus knew their unworthiness; but still he gave them his Mystery of love, saying to them, "Take and eat. . . . All of you drink of this!" Note that our Lord did not say, "Adore," or "Pray"; but he said simply and clearly, "All of you take and eat of this!" For he became a Host that he might become our food.

And how about the first Christians? Were they—fresh come out of paganism and idolatry—"good enough"? Did their Baptism make them shed all their faults on the spot? And yet the Church did them signal favours. She distributed the Host to them every time they attended the Holy Sacrifice; and in order not to deprive them of Communion, permitted them in serious circumstances to take it home with them.

"If our Lord had had our worthiness in view," said the holy Curé of Ars, "he would never have established his beautiful Sacrament of love; for no one in the world is worthy of it, whether saint, or angel or archangel, or the Blessed Virgin! But he considered our needs—and we all have need of it. . . ."

Let us—at the risk of astonishing some people—go further. *It is our very unworthiness, which, far from keeping us from the holy table, ought to make us rush to it!* We shall understand this, if we stop looking on the Eucharist as a reward or as some sort of "dessert." This is the wrong slant altogether. The Eucharist is a necessary remedy for our spiritual infirmities, an indispensable food for the life of our souls. (See P. 496)

Listen to Jesus himself in his parable of the Great Supper (Luke 14), which the Church connects with the Eucharistic Banquet.

When everything is ready at the appointed hour, the host sends for his guests. These all excuse themselves (just like today): "I have bought a farm and I must go out and see it." Or, "I have bought five yoke of oxen, and I am on my way to try them." Or, "I have just got married, so I cannot come."

That is the usual thing: pleasure, money, and luxury.

One person does not communicate, because he does not want to put himself out; or because he is engrossed by his business or temporal concerns. Or more often, alas, because, a victim of impurity, he is a slave to mortal sin. . . .

But the thing we want to bring out in this parable, is the conduct of the man who is organizing the Great Supper. He doesn't want to go to all this trouble and expense for nothing. "Bring in," says he, "the poor, the crippled, the blind, and the lame." That is, all who are hungry or who would like to be healed. That is the Master's way. He abandons those who disdain or hate him to their sorry lot. "I tell you none of those who were invited shall taste of my supper." But he does call, he does urge, the others: the people of good will who do not deem themselves worthy; the "poor, the crippled," who would never have dared hope for such good fortune. Jesus invites them to satisfy their hunger and receive help for their ills. To the poor, he will give a treasure that no man can take from them; to the sick, health; to the blind, light; to the lame, a springy step.

No, we are not worthy. But who among us is not in some sense spiritually impoverished, crippled, blind, or lame?

"Never say that you are sinners," insisted the holy Curé of Ars. "that your misery is too great, and that that is why you do not approach the Sacrament of Love. I would as soon hear you say that you are too ill, and that is why you do not want to call the doctor."

Let us lay aside this poor pretext. "After all," wrote St. Pius X, "it is not a question here of safeguarding the honour and reverence due to our Lord, nor of making the Holy Eucharist a sort of prize and recompense accorded to the virtue of communicants. There exists no ecclesiastical precept demanding more perfect dispositions for daily, than for weekly, or monthly Communion. Moreover, daily Communion produces more abundant fruits than does weekly or monthly Communion."

Remember, we don't eat whenever we "deserve" to eat. We eat when we are hungry! We don't take medicine when we are well, but when we are ill.

Finally, the *Imitation* places these reassuring words on Christ's lips: "I will supply for whatever you lack. Come and receive me."

MY SINS KEEP ME AWAY FROM COMMUNION.

A distinction should be drawn here between past and future sins.

1. Past sins are obliterated, because you have confessed them with a contrite heart. (If not, then by all means do so!)

Speaking of mercy, we have shown how generous God is when it comes to forgiving. (*See* Q. 275.) As a final clincher, here are some more texts from the Bible:

"O My people, I have cast your sins behind My back; I have cast them into the depths of the sea."

"I am a God of mercy. My wrath does not endure forever; I will not take vengeance on you according to your sins." (Luckily for us, or else Heaven would again be closed!)

"As far as the heavens are above the earth, so great is My mercy toward you."

"As far as the east is from the west, so far have I removed your transgressions from Me."

"As a father pities his children, even so will I have pity on you, because I know from what clay I have created you; I know that you are dust. You pass like the wind, like the flower that withers; but My mercy is everlasting."

If God deigns to forget our transgressions, why should we persist in building a wall of separation between him and us?

We should trust, despite repeated falls. A saint is not someone who never falls, but someone who always picks himself up again. The greater our misery, the more God is honoured by our trust in him. The holy king David, who had committed most serious sins, exclaimed, "Lord, you will pardon my iniquity, for it is very great!" And the Curé of Ars: "The Lord bears with us in spite of our sins. He has mercy on us in spite of ourselves!" Throw yourself into God's arms," wrote St. Augustine. "It will not be to let you fall, that he will open them!"

Finally, for those who still hesitate, remember what our Lord said once to a person who, because of his sins, did not dare approach him. "Child, I forgive and forget, not count, the sins of those who love me!"

We could go on citing such testimonies at length.

2. As for future sins, the refutation is easy. There is no doubt but that we shall sin again, but Communion remains the most efficacious remedy for sin. Receive often, and we shall fall less often!

Remember that the Holy Eucharist is not a reward for virtue, for who would venture because of his purity and holiness to receive God in his heart? No, Communion is a viaticum, a food, a medicine, a support for the weak and sick.

Let us hesitate no longer. If you have a soul purified by repentance and love, then receive Communion. Thus from one Communion to the next, we shall become a little less unworthy to receive Jesus in our hearts.

I AM TROUBLED BY TEMPTATION.

Since we have already answered this question in Question 297, we add here merely this piece of advice: "To you who are overwhelmed by temptation, receive Communion; and receive it because you *are* tempted!"

What does the labourer do who must work hard? He eats good, solid food. Well, to wage a winning battle over temptation, eat the "Bread of the strong" and you will be victorious! The Holy Eucharist is the best means of weakening temptation's power. It would be illogical to deprive yourself of it when you need it the worst!

Some will say that they are more tempted on the days they communicate! This is a good sign. The closer we get to God, the more we are attacked by the Devil! Temptation has made great saints; and it will sanctify us, too, by making us humble and giving us a chance to win big victories, which will be richly rewarded in Heaven.

Let us remind ourselves that temptation of itself is not a sin.

I LACK FERVOUR. I DON'T FEEL ANYTHING.

Many wrongly gauge the degree of their love for God by their feelings. This is to confound devotion with feelings of devotion. The latter are by no means necessary, and we can have true devotion without "feeling" devout.

God customarily gives this delectable sweetness, this strong emotion which delights the soul, to beginners in the spiritual life.

But little by little, God "hides" himself to permit the soul to purify itself; and to seek him, rather than his consolations. The result is dryness, or aridity. And for how long? For as long as God wills. Great saints have spent years in this state, and it was just this that sanctified them.

"Far from fearing Communion in these states of desolation and dryness," wrote Bossuet to Sr. Cornuau, "this is the time to desire and practice it still more. For only *He who is* can move our nothingness and draw us out of it."

I'M NOT MAKING ANY PROGRESS. . . . I'M AFRAID OF RECEIVING THROUGH ROUTINE.

On what grounds do you base your assertion? "The child who grows and develops attains to adulthood before he is aware of it," wrote Msgr. Millot. "We can grow and develop spiritually, without *feeling* growth."

Even supposing that despite your Communions, you are not making any progress, would it be a sensible thing to stop? On the contrary, you would need to receive more often and with increased fervour. For Communion received with good dispositions cannot help fostering spiritual development and augmenting the life of grace! "Being given the state of grace and a good intention," specifies the Decretal on Frequent Communion, "it is impossible for those who communicate daily not to correct themselves of venial faults, and gradually, of their affection for these faults," and as a result, become better.

As for routine, this must not be confused with habit; which by dint of doing, makes a thing easy to do. In order to avoid routine, we should carefully prepare our Communion; receiving as if for our first (or last!) Communion! And with no omitted Communions!

I HAVEN'T TIME

Really!

You find time to nourish your body three and perhaps more, times a day. You find time for vanity. (How many hours are wasted before a mirror!) You find time for idle talk—not always in accord with charity. You find time to bow to fashion's decrees. You find time for social evenings which wear you out, because they last till dawn! You find time for pleasure, for your temporal interests, for your every whim. But when it comes to taking a short half hour a day to attend Mass and receive the "Bread of the strong" to insure your soul's salvation and the success of your apostolate, you "haven't time"! ! ! Sad, isn't it?

You find time for your temporal affairs, but not for those of eternity? What does it profit a man to gain the whole world, if he loses his soul?

You think that you lose time by receiving Communion? Don't fool yourself! The more you are "swamped" with work and responsibility, the more you ought to receive Communion; the better to fulfill the duties of your state in life.

Someone reproached Thomas More, England's great chancellor, one day, for communicating too often, with all he had to do. This was his reply (which might be your own, if you only attached enough importance to the really worthwhile). "You give me the very reasons I have for receiving Communion daily. I have great distractions; Communion brings recollection. Occasions for offending God present themselves to me every day; every day I strengthen myself against them by Communion. I need wisdom and light for unravelling knotty problems. That is why I go every day to consult Jesus Christ in Holy Communion."

Would you, by any chance, be busier than the great King of France, St. Louis, patron of Tertiaries? Here is what one of his biographers tells us: "Although burdened and weighed down by affairs of state, he heard two Masses every day, said Vespers and Compline with his chaplain, visited hospitals every Friday, went to Confession, and often listened to sermons, and frequently attended spiritual conferences; and with all this, he never lost sight of the public weal and of foreign affairs, which he administered diligently."

Can you still seriously insist that you "haven't time" for Communion?

I don't want to attract attention

Is it a disgrace to receive Holy Communion?

Unfortunately, in certain circles, human respect makes great inroads! A remark, a criticism, a smile, a trifle, can paralyze the weak in faith!

Kindly be a little more reasonable. Do not compromise your eternal welfare, for fear of what people may say!

"Rejoice," says our Lord, "when the world despises you, and says all manner of evil against you falsely."

"Concern yourself little with what the world thinks," writes St. Francis de Sales. "Despise both its esteem and its scorn, and let it say what it will of good or ill."

Tell those who taunt you about your frequent Communions, that you will meet them at the Last Judgment!

Daily communicants are no better than others

Everywhere we meet with Catholics who forget all day long that they are living tabernacles of the Divine Master received that morning. Just as we also run across people who do not profit from the food they eat. But is that any reason for other folks refusing to eat?

None of these pretexts are serious. Loving, devout souls whose motto is GOD FIRST SERVED, are not to be stopped by similar subterfuges.

335—What should a scrupulous person do about Communion?

It is not our intention to write a treatise on scruples. Nonetheless, the scrupulous are sufficiently numerous and distressed for us to devote a few lines to them, while speaking of Communion.

Let us say right now that scruples are not a form of insanity!

Scruples do not constitute an act of the intellect or reason. (In exceptional cases, scruples may be caused by ignorance as to the morality of certain human acts. In this case, as soon as the scrupulous person is exactly informed, he recovers peace of soul.)

Definition. Scruples consist of panic in the faculty of perception, of emotion characterized by fear, a sort of anxiety phobia, occasioned by an obsession of doubt; by the impossibility of achieving certitude, especially with regard to Confession and Communion. Many scrupulous persons wrongly believe themselves to be damned. This is the way they express their anxieties:

"I think," (says the scrupulous person to himself) "that I may have committed such or such a sin. It seems to me that this sin must have been serious. So just to be on the safe side, I'll accuse myself of it once more in Confession. I think I *may* have consented to that bad thought! I am not sure that I remembered to accuse myself of this other sin in my former Confessions. I'm not sure that my confessor understood me, or that I expressed myself clearly. It seems to me as though I gave my consent to that wrong feeling that haunted me all day." (Etc. etc!) "To have peace, I will make another general Confession."

Such, briefly is the state of mind of a scrupulous person.

For the most part (as we said above) the doubts of the scrupulous are not intellectual ones, or else they would disappear as soon as the answer had been given by a competent person. The fact is that the unfounded fear of having committed mortal sin persists. Doubt continues to torture him, producing an anxiety phobia which racks his mind and paralyzes his reason in the field of moral judgment, in which he is no longer master.

The sufferings of the scrupulous individual are heightened by the knowledge that he is intelligent, and yet incapable of dominating his distress, or of concealing it from others.

"Not only does the scrupulous person suffer from his scruples," writes Fr. Arnaud d'Agnel, "but he experiences because of them a feeling of shame. In his own eyes, this is an infirmity, a disgrace, which he does his best to hide. A queer thing is the energy put forth by a person so weak, so in the throes of his obsession, to conceal under a smiling mask the anxiety by which he is devoured. What a torment, indeed, to be conscious of thinking—it would be better to write 'of feeling'—in an unreasonable manner; while he inwardly feels himself to be a sensible man."

Scruples being most often the effect of an extreme sensibility, are more frequently encountered in women than in men. But for both, a cure is possible.

We all know, from reading the *History of a Soul,* that St. Thérèse of the Child Jesus was tortured for two whole years by scruples. Indeed, her definite deliverance from them favoured the sanctity of her life. She writes: It was during my second Communion retreat that I saw myself assailed by the terrible disease of scruples. To understand this martyrdom, one must have passed through it oneself. To describe what I suffered for nearly two years, would be impossible! My most simple thoughts and actions were turned into subjects for distress and anguish. I had no rest until I had entrusted everything to Mary. . . . As soon as I laid down my burden, I would taste a few minute's peace. But this peace vanished with lightning speed, and my martyrdom began all over again!"

Despite the acuteness of her distress, St. Thérèse found peace after two years. The scrupulous person, then, can be cured. But how?

First of all, he must want to be cured.

Next, since this acute sensibility often comes from overwork, the scrupulous individual should learn to rest and to live in great peace—a peace peopled with agreeable distractions: drawing, painting, the stimulus of outdoor life, together with the contemplation of beautiful scenery and of Nature's marvels, in the mode of St. Francis. . . .

The morbid state of the scrupulous individual may also be the effect of faulty gland functioning, or of some other ill of a physical nature, requiring the doctor's care.

As for the moral treatment, (and it is of this especially that we wish to treat), the best remedy for a case of scruples is Communion! Yes, frequent Communion without Confession! The Communion that avoids stirring up the conscience beforehand.

"Communion! *That* is the remedy!" writes Dr. A. F. G. "The patient knows this well. He feels it. He has an immense desire to receive his God, but how he does exaggerate the conditions! Always there is this lack of proof! This perplexity as to the value of his Confession, as to his 'firm purpose of amendment,' his contrition! Did he do his sacramental penance right! Didn't he sin again after his Confession (which most often dates from last night, sometimes from a few hours ago)? Has he broken his fast? And (if he receives during Sunday Mass) wasn't he voluntarily distracted during the Holy Sacrifice, thus obliging him to hear another Mass?

"Notice that there is no certitude, no proof! Always the anguish of doubt is accompanied by nervous distress and symptoms. So much is at stake! What if he were to make a sacrilegious Communion? . . . The painful excess of false logic checks the patient and deprives him of the benefits of Communion.

"If the will has been sufficiently strong, and the Communion accepted, a glimmer of calmness brings a moment of respite to the poor soul; which will, thanks to the ordinary preoccupations of existence—studies, professional activity, household cares, the rearing of children—be prolonged."

A scrupulous person who accepts Communion is already half cured. The main thing is to get him to agree to this. The intervention of the director of conscience is indispensable here. The latter should act with gentle firmness, and demand prompt obedience from his penitent.

Scrupulous souls may become great saints, on the condition that they are willing to obey and to trust themselves entirely to their director.

Another method is that of recalling this maxim in theology: "No doubtful obligation is binding." So, confronted with a doubtful obligation, the scrupulous person is free.

"A scrupulous person ought to despise all his doubts," writes Fr. Dubois. "That is, he ought to regard and treat as being perfectly null and void all doubtful laws, obligations, or prohibitions, or all doubtful fears of having sinned. He furthermore should deem and despise as doubtful all laws, obligations, prohibitions, or fears of sinning which are not absolutely certain; i.e. as clear as the fact that two and two make four."

Let us suppose that a scrupulous soul does decide to go to Communion, and that at the altar rail he is besieged by doubts and fears of having committed sin. What should he do? Well, he knows that it is a very serious offense to take a false oath. So let him ask himself if he could place his hand on the Gospels and swear that he has committed such and such a sin that troubles his mind. If he cannot take this oath, then let him communicate in all security.

So, short of positive proof, a scrupulous person should not reason with himself when assailed by doubts and fears, particularly in matters having to do with purity. The debate should be closed at once by this affirmation: "I did not consent, and I am going to receive Communion."

Fr. Eymieu in *Self-Government* gives this rule of gold: "When it comes to an obligation binding in conscience, under pain of mortal or venial sin, or imperfection, only FACTS count—a calm, complete, and dazzling CERTITUDE. If all available evidence points to an imperfection, there is no sin. If it has bearing only on sin without stating whether the sin is mortal, then the sin is not mortal, but only venial."

It is in the light of these principles and in obedience to his spiritual director, that the scrupulous person should chart his course.

Scrupulous souls, go to Communion, and go frequently (without, however, going to Confession each time.) You will find peace and joy and healing at last.

THE PRIEST

•

He is another Christ—respect him;
He is God's Representative—trust him;
He is your benefactor—be thankful to him.

AT THE ALTAR
He offers your prayer to God—do not forget him.
He prays for you and yours in Purgatory—ask God's mercy for him.

IN THE CONFESSIONAL
He is the physician of your soul—show him its wounds;
He directs you toward God—follow his admonitions;
He is judging—abide by his decision.

IN HIS DAILY LIFE
He is human—do not hastily condemn him;
He is human—a word of kindness will cheer him;
If you must tell his faults—tell them to God,
That He may give him light and strength to correct them;
He has a great responsibility—ask God to guide him in life,
And to be merciful in death.

DREAM OF THE CHRIST

Dear God, when you thought of the priesthood,
How did you think of me?
In the cavalcade of a Peter
Unworthy am I to be!
Dear God, when you thought of the sunrise
In the chaliced heart of the East,
Saw you the Host in my fingers
And a table set for a Feast?
Dear God, when you thought of the sunset,
Enthroned in the Golden West,
Did you not vision the monstrance
With yourself as the Little White Guest?
Dear God, when you arched the rainbow—
A promise of hope from above—
Did you not think of Confession,
And a priest to lavish your love?
Dear God, when you thought of the sunbeam,
Did you not dream of your grace—
Sharing your life with the faithful,
Giving your love to the race?
And God, when you thought of the crescent
Enframing a queenly throne,
Did you not think of your Mother—
The Mother you gave as my own?
While you were dreaming of beauty—
A lily, a star, or a fir—
While you were dreaming the lovely,
Were you not dreaming of her?
Dear God, when you thought of the harvest
Ripe for the gatherers' hands,
Saw you the legions immortal
Directed to you by these hands?
When you beheld the moonlight
Sheening majestic the stream,
Thought you, dear God, of a priesthood
That only a God could dream?
Dear God, as a priest I pledge you
The best that mine heart can give.
The battle-cry of my service:
"Live, Jesus, my God! Live! Live!"

—Father Nugent, C. SS. R.

(Note: Fr. Nugent's poem carries the imprimatur of Cardinal Stritch of Chicago.)

336—What should be my physical dispositions for reception?

Whatever deserves doing at all, deserves doing well. If there is any act which calls for serious preparation, it is certainly the reception of Christ in the Holy Eucharist.

For worthy and fruitful Communion, two dispositions are necessary: those of the soul, and those of the body; because Communion is the food of the soul through the body. Both should be fit to receive our Lord.

From the physical standpoint, two things are required:

1. The eucharistic fast.
2. A modest and reverent exterior.

A. THE EUCHARISTIC FAST

The eucharistic fast was formerly much more strict.

New conditions created by modern life, have inspired the Church to modify this fast, so as to enable a larger number to partake of the eucharistic banquet.

By requiring this slight mortification, the Church wishes to invite us to make an effort, a "sacrifice," and to teach us that spiritual food ought to come before material food. Is not Jesus our first necessity? We ought to seek him ahead of everything else.

The purpose of this reminder of the penitential aspect of the eucharistic fast is to bring home again to the communicant the full significance of the Mystery of our altars—"celebrated in memory of Christ's Passion."

You will find below the *Motu Proprio* of His Holiness, Pope Pius XII, published March 19, 1957, setting forth the new privileges of the eucharistic fast.

MOTU PROPRIO

An extension of the privileges of the eucharistic fast.

To enable the faithful to receive Holy Communion frequently, and more readily satisfy the precept to hear Mass on Sundays and feast days, We promulgated in the beginning of the year 1953, the Apostolic Constitution, *Christus Dominus,* modifying the law of the eucharistic fast. We have granted to Ordinaries the faculty of permitting the celebration of Mass and reception of Holy Communion in the evening, under certain conditions.

We have reduced, then, to three hours for solid food and one hour for nonalcoholic beverages, the time of fasting to be observed before celebration of Mass and the reception of Holy Communion in the evening.

Moved by the abundant fruits flowing from these privileges, the Ordinaries have expressed their deep gratitude to Us; and several among them have besought us for the greater good of the faithful to authorize them to permit Mass to be celebrated daily in the afternoon or evening.

The Bishops have also petitioned Us to establish an identical period of fasting for the celebration of Mass and reception of Holy Communion before noon.

In view of the considerable changes affecting the working world, as well as society in general, We have deemed it Our duty to accede to these repeated requests of the Bishops; and We have established the following dispositions:

1. The Ordinaries, with the exception of those vicar generals *sine mandato speciali,* may permit daily celebration of Mass in the afternoon if the spiritual welfare of a large number of faithful requires it.

2. The period of eucharistic fasting to be observed by priests before Mass and by the faithful before Holy Communion, is reduced to three hours for solid food and alcoholic beverages, and to one hour for nonalcoholic beverages. Water does not break the fast.

3. The same rules likewise apply to priests who celebrate the Mass and to those who receive Holy Communion at midnight or in the first hours of the day.

4. The sick, including those not bedfast, may take nonalcoholic beverages and medicine, whether solid or liquid, up to the celebration of Mass or the reception of Holy Communion.

But we strongly urge priests and faithful who are able to do so, to observe the ancient and venerable discipline of the eucharistic fast.

In gratitude for these privileges, they will endeavour to lead more perfect Christian lives, and especially to practice the works of charity and penance.

Nothwithstanding all prescriptions to the contrary, even those worthy of special mention.

Who?	What?	When?
Everyone	Water	At all times
Everyone	Solid food Alcoholic beverages	3 hours before Communion
	Non alcoholic beverages	1 hour before Communion
The sick (even those not bed-ridden)	Non alcoholic beverages Medicine — liquid or solid	At all times

Given at Rome, near St. Peter's, on the feast of St. Joseph, Patron of the Universal Church, March 19, 1957, in the nineteenth year of Our pontificate.

Pius XII

2. A MODEST AND REVERENT DEMEANOUR

Do you always think of your body as a temple, a "little church," a "sanctuary"; becoming, with reception of the Holy Eucharist, a real tabernacle?

Before giving the Eucharistic Bread to his disciples, our Lord first washed their feet. . . .

Cleanliness is a mark of elementary etiquette when assisting at a banquet. For assisting at the Eucharistic Banquet, it is eminently fitting that our hands and faces should be clean and our hair neat—avoiding, however, that exaggerated concern for one's appearance which smacks of worldliness. "Bodily cleanliness is often a sign of purity of soul," observed St. Francis de Sales. Those who wear lipstick, should—at least, for Communion—use it lightly and unobtrusively.

Decency and *modesty* in dress are still more imperative. (The fair sex should check themselves on this, especially during the summer months.)... Humble attire is nothing to be ashamed of. Jesus, who was born in a stable, delights to be with the poor, his favourite friends.

The deportment should likewise be reverent. "Races" to the Communion rail, and looking around, should be avoided. Let uur step be dignified, our recollected air showing our awareness of the grandeur of our act.

337—What should be prepared in a home to which the priest brings Viaticum or Communion?

This question (which takes us away somewhat from the Mass) will be briefly treated. We shall simply make a list. Needed then, are:

1. A table covered with a white cloth.
2. A crucifix and stand.
3. Two candlesticks with blessed candles.
4. A glass of ordinary water in which the priest may purify his fingers. After the ceremony, this water should be poured in the fire, or in the ground. (For example, in a flower pot containing earth.)
5. A glass of holy water with a blessed palm or holy water sprinkler.
6. A white cloth for the sick person's reception of Communion.

And nothing more! Flowers and pictures do not belong on this table.

When the sick person is to receive, in addition to Viaticum, Extreme Unction, there must be added:

7. A small dish containing six or seven balls or wads of cotton batting, for the priest's use in wiping off each of the parts of the body (representing the five senses) which have been anointed with holy chrism.
8. Another small dish containing a crumb of bread for the priest to use in wiping his fingers. (For this, a rather thick slice of bread should be cut, from which the crust has been removed.)

Here again, the wadding and crumb of bread should be thrown into the fire after use.

Needless to say, the sick person and his room should be scrupulously clean.

338—What should be our dispositions of soul for worthy Communion?

We have already replied to this question, when discussing the Pater Noster, in the introductory portion of the third part of the Mass of the Faithful—the Communion. (Q. 222.)

We have said that the best preparation for Communion is the Mass itself. Whoever LIVES HIS MASS is ready for Communion. We added that reception of Communion requires the state of grace and a right intention. (Q. 272.) Let us clarify these dispositions for reception before adding the others:

1. *The state of grace is required*

Holy Communion or the Eucharist is a Sacrament of the living. It can produce its effects only in souls that are alive, not in those that are dead. "But let a man prove himself," says St. Paul, "and so let him eat of that bread and drink of that cup; for he who eats and drinks unworthily. . .eats and drinks judgment to himself." (I, Cor. 11: 28.)

The Eucharist is God, the All-Holiest. It is a profanation to receive him in a soul foul with mortal sin. "What fellowship has light with darkness?" cries St. Paul again. This is forcing God to dwell in a place in which his enemy, the Devil, holds sway; a place wherein sin, the thing God most abhors, resides. It means committing an odious sacrilege, a profanation much greater than that of Balthasar, who attacked the sacred vessels of the temple. For unworthy communicants attack God himself!

The Eucharist is a banquet. Each guest present must have on the wedding garment of sanctifying grace. (Reread the Gospel parable of the wedding feast. Matt. 22:1 ff.)

We remind the reader that a person in mortal sin cannot go to Communion after making an act of contrition. Confession is of obligation.

2. *The intention must be right*

As for the right intention, it suffices to recall that the communicant should receive the Holy Eucharist, not through custom or vanity, to make a good impression on others, or for any other human motive; but to please God, to unite oneself more closely to him, to be strengthened against the forces of evil, or for some other supernatural motive.

Here are some other dispositions of our souls for worthy Communion.

3. *The heart must be detached*

The Holy Eucharist is the Sacrament of Union with Jesus, who is love. If then, we discover some voluntary attachment in our hearts to our own way of thinking or to self, or to deliberate venial sin (particularly, if we observe an addiction to those habitual sins which cause divisions: jealousy, grudges, detraction, calumny, rivalry, etc.), we may rest assured that just so long as we are satisfied with this state of affairs, the fruits of the Sacrament in our souls will be limited.

But if we make a resolution to correct ourselves of our bad habits; if we make serious efforts to get rid of them, if we approach our Lord in order to obtain the necessary strength to do so; we may rest assured that Jesus will be favourably disposed toward us, will bless our efforts, and fill us with his grace.

Remember that our dispositions do not cause the grace of the Sacrament—they merely give it free course, by removal of obstacles. We ought to open our hearts as wide as possible to the bestowal of the divine Gift. An excellent disposition, then, is to refuse nothing to Jesus. "A soul habitually disposed to remove from its life whatever might offend the eyes of the Divine Guest, and to hold itself in readiness to accomplish the divine will, is admirably 'adapted' to the sacramental action." (Dom Marmion in *Christ, the Life of the Soul.)*

4. *A great spirit of faith*

We must often renew by acts of faith our belief in Christ's presence in the Eucharist.

God's creative word brought all this universe that we see out of nothing. This same word has lost none of its power with regard to the miracle of love, which changes bread and wine into the Body and Blood of Christ.

What happened when God said, "Let there be light!"?

There was light.

What happened when Jesus said to the raging sea, "Peace, be still!"?

There was a great calm.

What happened when Jesus said to the blind, the lame, and the halt, "Be healed!"?

They were instantly healed.

What happened when Jesus said to Lazarus, "Lazarus, come forth!"?

Lazarus came forth and lived.

Well, then! When Christ pronounced the words of Consecration over the bread and wine, saying, "This is my Body. This is my Blood," what happened?

What happened was that Christ was present in body and soul, under the species or appearances of bread and wine.

And when the priest, who has received from Christ the divine power to consecrate, repeats these same words in the Mass, the same miracle of love takes place; and Jesus becomes present in our midst, ready to give himself to us.

So true is this, that even Luther, the apostate monk, one of the founders of Protestantism, would have liked to deny the reality of Christ's presence in the Eucharist; but however hard he tried, he could never succeed. "*This is My Body!* These four words crush me!" he once exclaimed in an access of frankness and fury. "It is too clear *not* to be true!"

Lord, I believe, but increase my faith!

It is told of St. Louis, King of France, that he was deep in recollection and meditation in a retired corner of the Sainte Chapelle, when someone came to tell him that the priest had been obliged to interrupt the Mass, because our Lord had appeared in the Host in the form of a child! And as the man pressed him to come and see the miracle:

"I am not going," replied the king. "I believe that Jesus is in the Host, and that is enough for me." On his deathbed, it was he again who said these beautiful words, "I could not believe more strongly in His divine presence, if I saw Him the way the apostles did during His earthly existence."

Blessed is he who has not seen, and yet has believed!

One Sunday as Pope St. Gregory, celebrating Mass in the basilica of St. Peter, distributed Communion to the congregation, a Roman lady came up with the others; and when the Pope uttered the customary words, "May the Body of our Lord Jesus Christ keep your soul unto life everlasting," the woman, with an incredulous air, began to laugh. Pope Gregory took the Bread of the Eucharist away from her and gave it to the deacon to take back to the altar and keep, until the Communion of the faithful should be finished. After which, the Pontiff, addressing the woman, inquired, "Tell me, I pray, of what were you thinking, when, just as you were about to receive Communion, you started to laugh?"

"The piece of bread that you offered me," she replied, "was the very same piece that I brought to the Offertory. I couldn't help smiling, when you gave the name of 'Body of Jesus Christ,' to a loaf that I had made with my own hands."

Turning, then, toward the people, the saintly Pontiff asked them to unite their prayers to those of the priests to adjure the Lord to dispel this woman's incredulity. He then returned to the altar.

As he did so, the Bread deposited on it became transformed. The entire congregation, beginning with the woman, beheld with indescribable emotion, the bleeding Body of Christ appear, instead of the appearances of bread, which up until then, had hidden it from view.

When the unbelieving woman had yielded to the evidence, and recognized the presence of our Lord's Body in the Eucharist; the Pope again picked up the Host, which now had as before the appearance of bread. A small portion, however, remained bloodstained; as one may see it today in the Bavarian village of Andechs, where the portion of the miraculous Host which was not given in Communion to the converted skeptic, is still preserved.

5. *Profound humility and sincere contrition*

"One ought to be God," said St. Alphonsus, "to receive a God!"

"If you had the purity of the angels," we read in the *Imitation,* "and the holiness of St. John the Baptist, you would not be worthy to receive the august Eucharist."

You may have been a great sinner. In that case, it would be audacity to wish to serve as the Lord's abode, without first humbling yourself.

Let us, then, renew before our Blessed Saviour the accusation of the most serious sins of our lives, especially, the most humiliating. Pitilessly acknowledge our profound weakness, moral misery, and our many and repeated falls into the same faults. And with deep humility, let us say from the heart, the Act of Contrition. Above all, let us promise Jesus never to offend him again.

6. *An ardent desire to receive Him*

Desire enlarges the capacities of the soul, sharpens its powers, and prepares for reception of the Desired One. The more the soul calls God, the more fully does he come.

If we thought more about who gives Himself to us, how our burning desire for Holy Communion would inflame our hearts with love! Who will impart to us a longing for the altar, a zeal for frequent Communion? When shall we be able to say sincerely with St. Ignatius of Antioch, "The fire which consumes me cannot abide any earthly nourishment! . . . No corruptible food, no worldly delights or savours are able to satisfy me. The thing I desire and want is the Bread of God, the Bread of Heaven, the Bread of Life, which is the Flesh of Jesus Christ. The thing I desire and want is the beverage of God, the Blood of Christ, which is indefectible charity and eternal life."

St. Francis de Sales counsels: "Begin the night before (at least) to prepare yourself for Holy Communion by loving ejaculations. Should you awaken during the night, fill your mouth with fragrant words, that your soul may be perfumed for its reception of the Bridegroom. In the morning, arise with great joy and go with confidence to receive this heavenly Food, which nourishes unto life everlasting."

Once more we remind the reader (for many persons misunderstand this point), that while burning desires may sometimes be sensibly felt, they do not consist chiefly in impassioned outbursts; but are, above all else, repeated and generous acts of Christian virtue.

Starting today, in preparation for your next Communion, make an effort, then, to vanquish temptation, to triumph over selfishness, curiosity, ill humour, and idle talk. Make a resolution to spread happiness about you, to radiate goodness, to perform promptly, exactly, and perfectly the duties of your state in life. Then (just as the person who has

Unity in Diversity

Mounting up like a prayer
Toward the light,
Six immense boughs joined together
In a parent trunk.

Whether rich or poor,
Learned or ignorant,
White, black, or red,
We have all issued
From one divine Source.

As the sap through the boughs,
Let us have flowing through us
Unifying charity;
That together we may build—
Harmonious and fair—
The City Eternal!

Ric Photo

The Cross on the Shore

So tall is the cross that stands facing the sea,
That it links Ascension to Calvary.
The sailors behold it from near and afar—
The crucified God whose disciples they are.

In uncertain voyage, in lengthy sojourn,
They pin to its arms their hope of return;
As Christ's face uplifted toward Heaven so fair,
Maintains still its vigil of waiting and prayer.

The sailors set out now for far distant shores,
Heedless of breakers and tempest that roars;
Beneath the calm gaze and the most sacred sign
Of the Master of waves and God-Man benign.

In all of our crossroads the Cross towers above—
Perennial sign of undying love.
It offers two rules to souls that would soar—
They are "closeness to God," and "loving men more".

Lourdes

"La Rosa" Photo

worked hard, has a better appetite), you will hunger for God; and to-morrow, as one truly famished, you will approach the Communion rail to restore your spiritual forces, to the end that you may better serve him.

Finally, did not our Lord manifest the urgency of his will to give himself to us, when he said to his disciples: "I have greatly desired to eat this Passover with you before I suffer"? If Beauty had so great a desire to unite itself to the ugliness of a soul that has sinned; Riches to poverty; Wisdom to ignorance; Power to weakness; Purity to imperfection; Supreme Beatitude to deepest distress; in fine, God to man; without any possibility that this union can add anything to God's perfections; with what eagerness should not man long for union with God—a union that will deliver him from all his faults and fill him with every good thing!

A PRAYER FOR THE CONVERSION OF A LOVED ONE

•

O God, you who expressly command us to love our neighbour and deign to promise such magnificent rewards to those who, for love of you, charitably do good to their brethren; it is in the name of Mary, immaculate Virgin and refuge of sinners; it is in the name of Jesus, this Divine Lamb immolated on the Cross for the sins of the world; it is in the name of your infinite mercy, that I come to beseech you to forgive a sinning soul, to bring back a lost sheep to the fold. Ah, if this unfortunate soul but understood its sad state! If it but realized what it loses by separating itself from you, by setting its heart's desire on this land of exile, by living as if it had no heavenly home! If it only knew—this poor soul—the fate reserved for it in eternity after a lifetime of suffering, without true consolation and without hope!... O God, deign by your divine light and by the power of your grace to open its eyes; impress its mind with the dangers of its position; and, finally, take away from it the love for those things that perish. Vouchsafe, O Lord, to inspire this new prodigal son with a burning and efficacious desire to return to you, his tender Father. Receive him in your arms; restore his right to your love and grace; and to you, O Lord, be the glory. Amen.

7. *Great charity*

In reality, everything boils down to divine charity—love which receives and gives. (Q. 223.)

Is it not enough simply to recall the motive of Christ's institution of the Holy Eucharist—the Sacrament of love—to be so intimately united with us that he and I are one? "He who eats my flesh and drinks My blood abides in Me, and I in him" . . . "As I live because of the Father, so he who eats me, he also shall live because of Me."

Jesus gives himself to us to the degree that we surrender ourselves to him without reserve.

Do not forget that we cannot love God, without at the same time loving our neighbour. "If anyone says, 'I love God,' says St. John, "and hates his brother, he is a liar."

For this reason, Bossuet writes: "One of the sins least tolerated by the Eucharist is that of dissension and hate of one's brother; for the property of the Eucharist is to unite us into one body, according to the words of St. Paul. Whoever, therefore, receives this Bread of Life, which, being distributed to many, is always and invariably the same, tolerating no division in its substance; ought to be one with all the members, even as he ought to be one with Jesus Christ."

How indeed, is one to receive Love in a heart filled with hate? Or, in a nutshell, the value of our Communions depends on our preparation.

"Put all the good works in the world over against one good Communion: it will be as a grain of sand compared to a mountain," said the holy Curé of Ars. "Oh, my people," he added, "how beautiful in eternity will be a soul who has frequently and worthily received its God! Our Lord's Body will shine through our bodies, his adorable Blood through our blood, and our souls will be united to our Lord's soul through all eternity."

Yes, let us endeavour daily to prepare ourselves better for this divine feast, and it may be that some day we shall have the joy of hearing the Sacred Heart say to us as he did to St. Margaret Mary: "It gives me such happiness to come into your heart, that if I had not already instituted the Holy Eucharist, I should have done so expressly for you!"

A MODEL: PIER-GIORGIO FRASSATI

Here is a passage taken from the life of a young Italian Tertiary of our times, who centered his life on the Eucharist:

At the age of sixteen, at the suggestion of his professor, Fr. Lombardi, Pier-Giorgio Frassati adopted the practice of daily Communion; to which he remained faithful all his life.

"But why," someone will say, "bother to mention a practice so common today?" Let's take a closer look. Sixteen is the age at which many students give up their childhood practice of daily Communion. For Frassati, going to college marked, not a backward step, but spiritual progress. Thus, faithfulness to daily Communion, far from being childish fervour or mechanical routine, was for him the result of conviction and of gradual spiritual maturity.

Hence, nothing—changes of residence, his occupations, holidays in the country, his love for the mountains—made him swerve from the line of conduct he had mapped out for himself. During examination time, he contented himself with a fervent Communion.

Already, through this strict fidelity, may be discerned a need for God and a steadfast will, which disregards sacrifice.

Only too easily, frequent Communion puts an end to fervent Communion. A sacred action repeated, quickly loses its nimbus of glory and tends to become commonplace. A man who communicates every morning may speedily forget that he receives God's Body. His preparation is often carelessly made, and his thanksgiving abbreviated and without fervour.

None of these things were true of Pier-Giorgio. Every morning saw him enter the yard, swarming with students, of the Jesuit college. For so vivacious a temperament, the temptation to stop for a moment's chat with his fellow students must have been strong. But Pier-Giorgio contented himself with a friendly greeting. Then, without saying a word, he headed for the chapel to prepare—in perfect recollection—for Communion. During the space of a whole year, no one ever saw him stop to chat.

To the fast of words was added that of food. In September 1923, he accompanied a youth group to the Eucharistic Congress held at Genoa. During the night voyage, his companions unabashedly munched almond cookies and other dainties until morning. At Genoa, they experienced both admiration and shame at seeing Pier-Giorgio—still fasting—go up to the altar rail.

Small wonder then that these generously prepared for Communions should cause heads to turn toward young Frassati at Communion time! In the youth's parish Church of Crocetta, a commemorative plaque hung near his usual place, recalls his assiduity and fervour at the Holy Table. Every morning saw the university student kneeling in this spot in deep recollection. Often he would rise and go to the sacristy to ask the priest if he would hear his Confession. He would then approach the Communion rail with such earnestness, modesty, and devotion, that one of his fellow students exclaimed, "You don't have to tell *me* anything about Pier-Giorgio in church! I've *seen* him!"

We have already mentioned another young Italian Tertiary, Pio Perazzo, whose eucharistic devotion bears much resemblance to that of young Frassati's, by reason of its fervour of conviction. (Q. 332.)

A SECRET OF SANCTITY

•

I am going to reveal to you a secret of sanctity and happiness. If every day during five minutes, you will keep your imagination quiet, shut your eyes to all the things of sense, and close your ears to all the sounds of earth, so as to be able to withdraw into the sanctuary of your baptised soul, which is the temple of the Holy Spirit, speaking there to that Holy Spirit, saying:

O Holy Spirit, soul of my soul, I adore you. Enlighten, guide, strengthen and console me. Tell me what I ought to do and command me to do it. I promise to be submissive in everything that you permit to happen to me, only show me what is your will.

If you will do this, your life will pass happily and serenely. Consolation will abound even in the midst of troubles. Grace will be given in proportion to the trial as well as strength to bear it, bringing you to the Gates of Paradise full of merit.

This submission to the Holy Spirit is the Secret of Sanctity.

—Cardinal Mercier.

339—What are the fruits or effects of Holy Communion?

A. THE HOLY EUCHARIST IS THE SACRAMENT OF UNION

1. *It unites us to God in charity.*

"Just as two pieces of wax that are melted together," wrote St. Cyril of Alexandria, "become one, the communicant is so intimately united to Christ, that Christ is in him and he in Christ."

Of course, in Communion, it is not the Body and Blood of Christ that are changed into our substance, for a superior substance is not changed into an inferior. But a change does take place. In a certain sense, we are transformed into Him. St. Augustine once heard a voice from Heaven saying, "It is not I whom you shall change into yourself, as you change your food into your flesh; but it is you who shall be changed into Me." *(Conf.* 7:10.)

Note that Communion does not unite us to our Lord in such a way as to form but one person (for in such a case, man would become God); but with this reservation, it is impossible to imagine a closer union between two beings.

2. *It unites us with one another.*

It is impossible to unite ourselves to the Head of the Mystical Body without becoming united to the other members. Communion means entering into the movement of charity which comes from God and returns to God, by uniting all things in Christ Jesus.

Ah, if all communicants were but willing to fathom the significance of their Communions, even to the loving of one another as Christ has loved them! Unwearyingly, without becoming discouraged, in spite of everything—"to the end"!

A lover of the Eucharist radiates his goodness, faith, and love in his environment, family, office, shop, factory, or on the street. Such a one starts by giving the example of what he would obtain from others. How powerful is the force of example! Next, such a person seeks to imbue those with whom he rubs elbows, with his Christian ideals. This is not done single-handed. It is the force drawn from his morning Communion, which gives him the courage to accept the many refusals and to sustain the underhand attacks and bitter taunts.

The morning's Communion has transfigured his soul and rekindled the sacred fire of self-sacrifice. He now wishes to transform his environment and scatter light and joy about him. He does not wish to lose a single opportunity for doing so; and, if need be, he will even create opportunities for making Love who is not loved, beloved, and for uniting divided hearts. (How many there are around us who live and die without ideals, all shut up, as they are, in self!)

This is the effect of Communion in a generous heart.

B. The holy Eucharist brings an increase in sanctifying grace

More than the other Sacraments, the Holy Eucharist increases sanctifying grace within us, because it gives us the very Author of grace!

Communion means imbibing draughts of sanctifying grace, no longer from some small stream, but from the Source!

Communion means eating and drinking Christ!

Communion means eating and drinking Life!

By the very fact that it increases sanctifying grace in our souls, the Holy Eucharist increases our eternal glory; for to the degree of our grace on earth will correspond our degree of glory in Heaven.

C. The holy Eucharist remits venial sin and the temporal penalty due to our sins: and preserves us from mortal sin

Who would not be happy at the hour of death, to pass directly from earth to Heaven without going through Purgatory? The expiatory power of a single Communion is such that it would suffice to pay all our debts to the last farthing, and the debts of many other sinners as well, provided our dispositions were sufficiently holy! Hence the great care we should take to prepare our Communions.

The Council of Trent defines the efficacy of Communion when it declares that it is "a remedy whereby we are delivered from daily faults and preserved from mortal sin."

We have just pointed out another fruit of the Holy Eucharist; namely, our preservation from serious sin. The Scriptures call Communion the "Bread that comes down from Heaven; so that if anyone eat of it, he will not die." (John 6:50.)

D. The holy Eucharist weakens the power of concupiscence

"The increase of charity," says St. Augustine, "produces a decrease in covetousness." The soul, impregnated with the grace and charity of Christ, dies to self and forearms itself against the pull exerted by its fallen nature.

"A woman. . .who for eighteen years was bent over and utterly unable to look upwards," was cured, the Gospels tell us, by Jesus' touch.

Perhaps you have been "bent over" in misery for a similar period by sin. Take heart! Communion will "straighten you up" again, deliver you.

E. The holy Eucharist is a source of joy

Holy Communion brings to souls a foretaste of Heaven! It is a source of spiritual consolation, for it is the Sacrament of love. Our hearts find in it assuagement for their desires and solace in distress.

St. Teresa received so many consolations from Holy Communion that her heart almost burst with joy and love. Often when discouraged by temptation and distress, she recovered her inner peace and spiritual joy in Communion.

Listen to what was said in the last century by Bl. Theophane Venard, the martyr missionary of Tonkin. From the iron cage in which he was a prisoner, he wrote, "Communion in church is a great joy; but Communion in an iron cage, the day before one is to be beheaded, realizing that the Sacred Host goes through bars to reach the depths of one's soul—this is ecstasy, the height of ecstasy."

Frederick Ozanam, the great promoter of the "St. Vincent de Paul Conferences," went so far as to invoke the joys of Communion as an argument in proof of the divinity of the Christian religion. He said: "If the whole earth were to repudiate Christ, there is a power of conviction in the inexpressible sweetness of Communion and in the tears it causes to flow, that would make me embrace the Cross all over again and defy the whole world's incredulity."

Here is another testimony, cited by Msgr. Millot in "Eucharistic Retreat":

"You may perhaps know of Father Hermann, the Jewish convert. Much sought after in the world, he was outstanding for his brilliant mind and his talents. And yet, filled with sadness and weary of disappointments, he dragged through life, finding nothing in material pleasures capable of satisfying his intelligence or his empty heart. One day, sad, and still disillusioned with everything, he entered a church; stopped a moment, and all became light! The veil covering his eyes was rent and Jesus manifested himself to him, touching his heart at the same time that he enlightened his mind. Rapt in ecstasy, he now believes in Christ; hopes in the One whom his fathers blasphemed; loves—and loves ardently—the One they repudiated and cruelly put to death. A few moments later, the Jew rose up a Christian!

"Thenceforth, he lives only for Christ, yearns only for that Heavenly Bread, whose sweetness he divines. He thirsts for the Eucharist; for he knows that it alone will give him the Object of his love and adoration; alone is able to unite itself to him and merge his life in that of the divine Object, without which he can no longer live. And still, as an 'unbeliever,' for forty days the Bread of Life to which his burning lips unceasingly aspire and for which his soul is famished, is refused to him!

"The pain of this long trial is evinced in the later cry of the young religious: 'In the world, men speak of love. Of *love!* Ah, what are your enthusiasms and joys, your transports, compared to these inexpressible delectations, these unutterable ravishments, which cause every fibre of your heart to quiver; when one believes in Jesus Christ and would fain be admitted to the mystic Banquet, where he himself is Food?' "

Sad and unhappy amidst this world's joys and pleasures, Fr. Hermann found happiness in the God of the Eucharist. Listen again to him as he expresses the felicity with which his soul overflows:

"O Jesus, my Love, how I long to kindle in the hearts of my former friends, the zeal with which I am inflamed! How I long to show them the happiness You give me! No! I make bold to say, that if faith did not teach me that the delight of contemplating You in Heaven is greater still; I should never believe it possible for a greater joy to exist, than that I know at loving You in the Eucharist and receiving You in my poor heart, made so rich by You! What delicious peace!... What beatitude!... What holy joy!... Miserable riches, sorry pleasures, humiliating honours, are those I hotly pursued with my former friends! Now that my eyes have seen, my hands touched, and my heart felt the heart-beats of a God, how I pity you in your blind pursuit of those pleasures powerless to satisfy your hearts!

"Come, then, to this heavenly Banquet which Eternal Wisdom has prepared. Come, leaving behind your chimeras and your baubles; and with a heart new and pure, quench your thirst at the limpid fountain of his love."

Such are the sentiments of a soul which has fallen in love with its God!

Let us, however, define the nature of this joy. It is, before aught else, spiritual; that is, existing in the mind and not in the feelings; in the intelligence and not in the imagination; in the will and not in the heart of flesh.

Nevertheless, it may be felt; but this is not essential. Hence, it follows that we may receive from Communion the joy it brings, without feeling it. This joy is no less real, sweet, and peace-producing.

MATT TALBOT AT MASS

Matt Talbot, Irish workman and inveterate drinker, was a disgrace to his aged parents.

One day, on a Saturday in the year 1894—sixty-six years ago—doubtless enlightened by God's grace, he decided to reform. But how was he to resist the instances and gibes of his comrades? In a flash, Matt saw the solution—his promise would be made to God himself. Without an instant's delay, he ran to nearby Holy Cross College; asked for a priest; went to Confession; and made a vow of total abstinence.

The next morning, Sunday, at five o'clock, Matt crossed the threshold of St. Francis Xavier Church; heard Mass and received Holy Communion. Renewed and strengthened in spirit, he returned home. Every morning found him at five o'clock Mass. So convinced was he that the Mass is the greatest source of grace and divine power, that he could not get along without it. One day the five a.m. Mass at St. Francis Xavier Church was discontinued. It was impossible for Matt to wait for the six o'clock Mass, for he must be at work in a few minutes. Unhesitatingly, he gave up the trade of mason which he loved and in which he excelled, and hired himself out as a simple workman to a lumber merchant at a place where the work did not start until 8 o'clock.

At sixty-nine, Matt was still a simple workman; but every day found him at 6 o'clock Mass. And it was on his way to Church that on Sunday, June 7, 1925, he collapsed on the sidewalk. People rushed up to him; he was dying. He started for Church and arrived—in Heaven!

Matt Talbot was a Franciscan Tertiary.

(Adapted from the life of MATT TALBOT, OUVRIER, by Martial Lekeux.)

340—Carrying out the symbolism of bread and wine, can you draw a parallel with the Holy Eucharist, the better to bring out the effects of this latter?

In the following lines, we shall see why our Lord chose bread and wine as the matter of the Sacrament of the Holy Eucharist:

Material bread	*The Bread of the Eucharist*
1. Maintains physical life without giving it.	1. Maintains spiritual life without giving it.
2. Imparts physical strength, and protects us from bodily ills.	2. Imparts spiritual force and protects us from temptations and falls.
3. Assuages bodily hunger to the point that we are satisfied, desire nothing more.	3. Assuages the soul's hunger and thirst, satisfying and filling it —creatures no longer mean anything to it.
4. Brings peace and repose to the body; which desires nothing more.	4. Brings peace and repose to the soul; which desires nothing more.

Wine	*The Holy Eucharist*
1. Produces gaiety.	1. Produces spiritual joy.
2. Intoxicates.	2. Intoxicates with joy.
3. Makes delirious, impels one to senseless acts.	3. Drives men not mad, but makes them wise with that divine wisdom called the "folly of the Cross," causing them to do things which appear senseless to worldlings.
4. Makes men forget their earthly preoccupations—the things of earth—and not think about anything at all.	4. Spiritual intoxication makes men forget earthly things, and think only of heavenly things.
5. Renders communicative.	5. When we have God within, there is a pressing need to make him known to others.

We also know that a person who neither eats nor drinks is sick and cannot live very long. The same holds true in the spiritual realm for the person who forgets to nourish his soul!

Let us bow before the mystery of the Eucharist; and with burning desire, thrilling at the thought of Jesus soon coming, and with emotions of profound gratitude, often repeat before Communion the following beautiful prayer:

TO JESUS IN THE BLESSED SACRAMENT

Soul of Christ, sanctify me.
Body of Christ, save me.
Blood of Christ, inebriate me.
Water from the side of Christ, cleanse me.
Passion of Christ, strengthen me.
O good Jesus, hear me!
Within Your sacred wounds hide me;
Never suffer me to be separated from You.
From the malice of my enemies defend me.
At the hour of my death call me,
And bid me come to You.
That with all Your saints I may praise You
Forever and ever. Amen!

The supplication, "Anima Christi," recommended by St. Ignatius, appeared at the start of the fourteenth century. In 1330, Pope John XXII attached indulgences to the prayer, of which he possibly is the author. (Ind. 300 days. Ind. 7 years after Communion. Plenary once a month. Pius IX, 1854.)

341—Can we receive Christ apart from the Eucharist?

Yes, for in addition to sacramental Communion, there is spiritual and mystic Communion.

The Host which the priest has offered and consecrated has become Christ.

The priest receives the Host in the same way that one receives food—placing it in the sanctuary of his soul. This is sacramental Communion; namely, the most intimate and divine union of the priest with Christ.

We have already amply shown the grandeur and necessity of sacramental Communion for every Christian. Here we need say only that the best form of Communion is actual reception of the sacramental Christ. But to LIVE YOUR MASS during the day, you ought often to receive Jesus spiritually. Besides, to do this is an excellent means of preparing your soul for sacramental Communion.

342—In what does "spiritual Communion" consist?

Spiritual Communion consists in a desire to receive the Holy Eucharist, and in the sentiments of fervour whereby the soul endeavours to make itself worthy of doing so. This Communion is recommended by the Council of Trent, which urges the faithful to receive at least spiritually during Mass.

Spiritual Communion has been esteemed by all the saints, who sought in this way to unite themselves to our Lord.

One may make a spiritual Communion at any time, day or night, particularly when we pay a visit to the Blessed Sacrament.

Spiritual Communion draws down precious graces to souls. "This is what the Lord himself has given us to understand," said St. Alphonsus of Liguouri, "to his faithful servant, Sr. Paula Maresca, foundress of the convent of St. Catherine of Siena at Naples. He showed her two precious vases, one of gold and the other of silver, saying that the gold vase was for His sacramental Communions and the silver one for His spiritual Communions." Cardinal de Lugo goes so far as to say that "the soul because of the vehemence of its desires, may sometimes receive greater graces from spiritual, than from sacramental, Communion," Thus the sick, and those not near a church, may console themselves by trying to make up for the physical or moral impossibility of communicating, by an ardent desire to be united with Jesus in his Sacrament of love.

343—How does one make a spiritual Communion?

This is how in a nutshell:

We place ourselves in the presence of God.

We purify ourselves from our sins by a good Act of Contrition.

We stir up our faith in Christ present in the Holy Eucharist.

We are eager to receive Him in our hearts.

We make acts of adoration, love, thanksgiving, petition, and so on.

344—In addition to sacramental and spiritual Communion, what other ways are there of uniting ourselves to Christ?

We may often "receive" Jesus during the day. For, in a sense, is not every act uniting us to our Lord a true Communion?

The thing to do, then, is to seek out the places where Jesus is to be found; to discover the places of his hidden presence, and to receive him lovingly.

The sad thing is that we brush unseeingingly against His garments every moment! We lack the spirit of faith. We have eyes and see not, ears and hear not!

The person who sees in a poor man only a poor man, in a sick man only a sick man, in a sinner only a sinner; does not see deeply enough to treat the poor man, the sick man, and the sinner as they should; and that is, as a means of Communion with Christ.

The Christian apostolate begins the moment that we are able to discern, behind the appearances of human beings, their immortal reality; and in this reality, Christ. If we separate God from the universe, it becomes meaningless, and lacking in all that is worthwhile. If we separate Christ from men, we leave them to their isolation and strip them of their high significance.

When St. Paul wrote that the Church is the Body of Christ, that Christians are the members and Christ the Head, and that Head and members together form the total Christ; he was writing what Jesus had already said: "As long as you did it to one of these least, you did it to Me." And again, He said in the same sense, "When you visit the sick, the prisoners, you visit Me. When you feed the hungry, you feed Me."

Christ loved all those for whom he died. He loves them; they belong to him; they are part of him. His love for them, the interest he bears them, the indissoluble vital union he has established between himself and them, gives them an astounding value, which makes us receive Christ at every charitable contact with them.

So all these poor mortals are transfigured, illumined with a new light. Thenceforth, our estimate of them is different. The pains we take for them, are taken for Christ.

The sun gives light, beauty, and life to creation! What the sun is for things, Christ is for men, Through Him, with Him, and in Him is revealed their high dignity and the importance of the immortal drama that is staged in their fleeting existence. Doubtless, their pettiness remains, their ugliness, their faults; and everything which to eyes of flesh renders them disappointing, discouraging, and sometimes, even repulsive. Hence, whoever fails to see Christ in them, sees only themselves in all their misery—and runs a great risk of no longer finding in them that subject of compelling interest which came to them from Christ himself!

The almost incredible charity of the saints for the most wretched, was indefatigably fed by the burning conviction that Christ is all to all men; that in all men he calls us and waits to give himself to us; and that, suffering in some and hungering in others, it is he in them whom we love. It is for him in them that we exhaust our kindness, and it is he in them whom we receive.

The apostle for whom this lofty truth is not a certainty, will soon fall a prey to discouragement. At the contact of men malodorous with evil, he would instinctively withdraw.... For to be attracted by the fragrance of roses, one need only pass near them; but a compassionate halt beside withered weeds, calls for assurance that the Master of the field loves them and desires them for Heaven's barns.

We have said above that we can receive Jesus wherever he may be found; and we have shown that Jesus is particularly hidden in the poor, the sick, and the sinner. Naturally, his presence in the sinner is less than in the righteous; but Jesus is still to be found in a certain fashion in the sinner, by reason of the love he bears him (for did He not die for him?), and by his eagerness to save him.

But Jesus dwells in many other places where he may be received. Canon Astruc helps us in our search by saying:

Jesus is to be found in the Gospel.
Jesus is to be found in souls in the state of grace.
Jesus is to be found in the "little ones"—the humble.
Jesus is to be found in our superiors.
Jesus is to be found in everything we do.

1. *Jesus is to be found in the Gospel*

Jesus is in the Gospel, which is a sort of "incarnation" of Christ, "hidden under words." When you meditate on God's Word (and here I am merely quoting Msgr. Landriot, who sums up the doctrine of the Holy Father on spiritual Communion of Christ), when you comprehend the spiritual meaning, and get down to the pith and marrow of it, a real "eucharistic mystery" takes place in your soul. The Divine Word enters, nourishes your intelligence, warms your heart, renews your life, and transforms you into Him—you receive in Communion Jesus hidden in the Gospel.

2. *Jesus is to be found in souls in the state of grace*

He himself has declared formally and publicly that He abides with them. "If anyone loves Me, he will keep My word, and My Father will love him, and We will come to him and make Our abode with him." (John 14:23.) Christ declared the same thing on a number of other occasions. So whenever you are united either by thought, affection, or charity to souls in possession of the life of grace, you receive Jesus living in them.

3. *Jesus is to be found in the "little ones"*

Jesus is found in little children, the humble, the poor, the suffering. Again, He Himself has said: "Amen, I say to you, as long as you did it for one of these, the least of My brethren, you did it for Me." So when you are engaged in the intellectual, moral, or religious formation of little children; when you render service to and assist those in need; when you visit the sick and care for them; when you play the rôle of a "ministering angel" and of Simon the Cyrenian to those with a cross to bear and a Calvary to climb; when you give a little joy and happiness to the poor and outcast, you receive Jesus in Communion.

4. *Jesus is to be found in your superiors*

Do you recall the delicately supernatural words of the young Carmelite, Sr. Elizabeth of the Trinity? One of the Sisters who was visiting her in her humble cell during her illness, said to her upon leaving, "I am on my way to see our Mother Superior."

"Oh!" exclaimed Sr. Elizabeth. "You are going to see Mother! Profit well by your visit, for it is a sacramental!"

So whenever your are with your superiors (for instance, your father, mother, or spiritual director), and you listen closely to their commands and counsels; when you obey them and follow their directions to the best of your ability, you receive Christ present in them.

5. *Jesus is to be found in everything you do*

"Every action, every sacrifice, every tiny detail of your daily life," wrote Fr. Faber, "forms so many 'sacraments'; so many 'real presences'; for God is in them." (The word "sacrament" is used here in a broad sense; i.e., as the sensible sign of our union with God, a union that enriches in accordance with our interior dispositions.) Thus, when following the counsel of St. Paul, "Have this mind in you which was also in Christ Jesus," you endeavour to think, will, love, and feel like our Lord himself, do you know what you do? You "receive" his mind, will, heart, and soul.

When, in fulfillment of the Master's precept, "For I have given you an example; that as I have done to you, so you also should do," (John 13:15) you apply yourself to reproducing his way of life—the way he dealt with persons, events, and objects, what is it that you do? You partake of his inner life.

When you suffer in body, soul, and heart; when, bearing your cross, you painfully scale the Calvary of your life; when, stretched upon your cross, you atone and make reparation, merit for yourself and for others; are you aware of what you do? When Fr. Faber said, "The greatest sacrament is suffering," he implied that you are sharing in the Saviour's Passion.

When you visit the poor and the sick and do good to those that suffer; when you assist in the sanctification of souls by teaching Catechism and engaging in other works of zeal; when you give those about you an example of Christian virtue; when you say a word in season, a word that does good, that consoles, encourages, edifies, and makes souls better, do you realize what it is that you do? You "communicate" in Christ's apostolate.

When you pause for a moment of recollection, when you pray, when you meditate, you partake of Christ's prayer.

As you see, whenever you unite yourself to Jesus, whether sacramentally or spiritually, participating in his interior or exterior life, you receive him as the priest does. But you must carry out this resemblance to the end. The priest saying Mass is not selfish—he shares his Host with his brethren. Go and do likewise! You receive Jesus, but do not keep Jesus within you for yourself alone—let Him pass into other souls. Be, for members of your family and your friends, for all those living with you, a "living eucharist," a living "table of the Lord." Make them sit down to the banquet of your soul and heart. Share your thoughts, affections, words, and good works with them, distributing charitably and generously to each, Jesus within. Following the dictum of St. Francis de Sales, "always have Jesus Christ in your brain and heart, in your eyes, in your tongue, in your ears." And then serve him, give him, send him to all who come, to all who approach you. "You are My living sacrament," said Jesus to a mystic of our day. "I give Myself to you, and through you to souls." He says this to YOU as well!

Let us then make of our lives a continuous Communion, so that we may LIVE OUR MASS and its third act—Communion with Christ.

A PRAYER FOR THOSE WHO ARE SICK

•

Our Father who are in Heaven, hear the prayer of all your sick.

Lord, I suffer. Here are my sufferings. Accept them—you who refuse nothing to your children. You know that I suffer, you who suffered more than all others. ACCEPT MY SUFFERINGS. I give them to you—I give them to you!

United to yours, BECOME YOURS, they can serve to atone for my sins and the sins of those whom I love, or who have done good to me (or evil to me), so as to bring me closer to you.

Make them into happiness both for them and for me, on earth as in Heaven.

Lord, I suffer! I offer, give, you my sufferings. Have mercy on me—you who love me more than I am capable of loving you. Help me.

Dear Father, make my prayers and sufferings fill up what is lacking of the sufferings of Jesus; so that as a member of his Mystical Body, I may be worthy of him, my Head; and live of his life and divinity in abundance.

Glory to you, Father, you who take care of me.

Glory to you, the Son, integrated in me.

Glory to you, Holy Spirit, dwelling in me. Amen.

V. THANKSGIVING

The soul gives thanks

- The orations of the two ablutions
- The Communion antiphon
- Postcommunion

Let us never forget that the Mass is a social, and not an individual, action. Therefore, *the participation of the faithful should not end with reception of Holy Communion.* Their personal thanksgiving will not come until after the Mass. The Church has her official thanksgiving, in which one must take part if he would think like the Church.

The liturgical thanksgiving is very brief. And in the primitive Church, the liturgical service ended even more rapidly than today. The schola or chorale stopped chanting the Communion Psalm when distribution of Holy Communion was finished. In the name of the entire congregation, the Pope then recited a brief concluding prayer before the altar. The deacon dismissed the people with the well-known formula of the *Ite missa est;* and after the response, *Deo gratias,* the cortege of sacred ministers returned to the sacristy. Along the way, the people bowed as the Pontiff passed, blessing them with the words, *"Benedicat vos Dominus!"* "The Lord bless you!"

Our present ceremony (fixed between the ninth and fourteenth centuries) is somewhat more developed. And, first of all, the celebrant proceeds to the ablutions.

345—What do we mean by "ablutions"?

The ablutions are the purification of the chalice, lips, and fingers of the celebrant, and of the ciborium when it is emptied. This name is also given to the water and wine which serve for these purifications.

For it sometimes happens that a few drops of the Precious Blood adhere to the sides of the chalice after the priest's Communion. So the priest has a little wine poured into the chalice, in order to facilitate reception. Previously, he has carefully collected with the paten, the particles of the Sacred Host which may have fallen on the corporal, as well as those that fell on the Communion paten during distribution of the Bread of the Eucharist. These particles are emptied into the chalice and consumed with the Precious Blood. In the same way, out of reverence for the Holy Eucharist, the priest purifies the lips and hands that have touched the sacred species.

346—What does the celebrant pray as he purifies the chalice?

As the server pours wine into the chalice, the priest prays this ancient prayer going back to the sixth century, when it served as a Post-communion.

Quod ore sumpsimus, Domine, pura mente capiamus: et de munere temporali fiat nobis remedium sempiternum.	Grant, O Lord, that what we have taken into our mouth, we may receive with a pure mind; as a temporal gift, may it become unto us an eternal remedy.

This first thanksgiving prayer asks of God that the divine Food we have just received may transform our soul and be a remedy for it, keeping us unto eternal life. The sacramental species are quickly gone; but may the divine Gift that they conceal remain with us, heal our weakness and make us worthy of Heaven's happiness!

Receiving the Body of Christ is not enough. We must also live by his spiritual life, thoughts, affections, and holiness; so that the temporal gift may become for us an eternal remedy, making the living waters of charity spring up in our hearts for the life that is, and is to come.

347—Of what does the second ablution consist, and what prayer is said by the priest?

After consuming the wine, the priest goes to the Epistle side to purify his fingers which have touched the Sacred Host. He places the thumb and index fingers of each hand over the chalice and the subdeacon or server pours a little water over his fingers.

Once more, the celebrant beseeches the Lord to make him profit abundantly from his Communion. This prayer dates from the seventh century.

Corpus tuum, Domine, quod sumpsi, et Sanguis, quem potavi, adhaereat visceribus meis: et praesta; ut in me non remaneat scelerum macula, quem pura et sancta refecerunt sacramenta: Qui vivis et regnas in saecula saeculorum. Amen.

May your Body, O Lord, which I have received, and your Blood which I have drunk, cleave to my heart. Grant that no stain of sin remain in me, whom pure and holy Sacraments have refreshed. Who live and reign world without end. Amen.

In this second prayer, we pray with the priest that the Body and Blood of our Lord may cleave to us and purify us of every stain. That same charity which the Saviour came on earth to bring, consumes the stains of the soul. It is through Holy Communion especially that he continues to enkindle and maintain it.

O Jesus, my mouth has eaten your Body and drunk your divine Blood; but what will it avail me to have eaten your Body and drunk your Blood, if I do not receive you with a pure heart, with a heart filled with the fear of losing you, of separating myself from you? Alas! St. Peter, when he received you for the first time, did not tremble with the fear of losing you! He was so sure of himself, that he promised you he would die with you before he would forsake you. And yet, the very night of his first Communion, he denied you three times, and affirmed with an oath that he did not know you!

And I, your disciple, am I stronger than he? Alas, my passions, my past falls, the perils of this world, the horror felt by my flesh for all that mortifies, its frenzied inclination for all that flatters, my pride which revolts at humiliations, and which has already made me commit so many imprudences, my laziness which is disgusted at duty done with precision and promptness—all that I am, O Jesus, would make me tremble, if you were not infinite goodness and mercy!

Penetrate my inmost being—not just its surface, but its innermost fibres. And make it so that where your infinite Purity passes, no trace of the ancient stains may remain—no dust of the flesh, nor my foolish self-sufficiency.... Yes, penetrate me from head to foot, for I am yours.

You who are in my heart—abide with me. Ah, well I know that when you come into a soul, you are never the first to forsake it; and that you are ever with it, unless this soul forsakes you.

Good Master, grant me the grace to hate every voluntary sin, however small. . .and should you see that I shall some day depart from you by sin, make me die now while I am in your grace.

Body and Blood of Christ, cling to me; attach me to you forever. . . . This stain of sin, the terrible inclination toward sin, in short, this appalling habit which sin imprints in soul and body of the one who let himself be drawn into it; O God of the Eucharist, destroy it by extinguishing ever more in me who have just received you, the fire of concupiscence. Give me ever-increased strength in well-doing and in the fulfillment of my apostolate.

348—What do the celebrant and server do after the ablutions?

As he dries the chalice and covers it with the purificator, pall, veil, and burse, in which he has been careful to place the corporal that he has just folded, the celebrant continues to converse with Jesus present in his heart.

The server carries the missal from the Epistle side and places it as for the Introït; and kneels at the Gospel side, as for the beginning of Mass.

The priest is now going to read in the missal the Communion antiphon, return to the middle of the altar, kiss it, turn toward the people, say *"Dominus vobiscum,"* return to the book, and read the prayer (or prayers) called Postcommunions, after which he closes the missal.

Why this shifting about of the missal?

Because the Epistle side, which is also the side where the bishop or priest sits, is the natural place for the missal; and the one where it would always be left, were it not for this mysterious reason which determined the reading of the Gospel on the north side—the region of cold and darkness, symbolizing the abode of the Devil—whose coming darkens minds and congeals hearts. It is facing the north, then, that the priest reads the Gospel; the very Word of God, which illumines the mind and warms the heart. There is also the question of convenience. In olden times, the altar had to be cleared for the offerings to be brought, and for the ensuing ceremonies.

The Communion Antiphon

349—What is the origin of the Communion antiphon?

When all the faithful received under both kinds, distribution of Holy Communion was a long drawn-out ceremony. To hold the people's attention, it therefore became necessary to chant a Psalm. After the distribution, the chorister intoned the Gloria Patri; then the antiphon was repeated.

After discontinuation of the long Communion service, the chant was shortened. Soon there remained only an antiphon, considered as a thanksgiving chant, and placed after the Communion. It is this brief antiphon, referring almost always to the day's feast, that the priest prays on the Epistle side immediately following the ablutions.

After reading the Communion antiphon, the priest returns to the middle of the altar and kisses it; then, turning, he addresses the customary salutation to the congregation, *"Dominus vobiscum."* This time the salutation has a different meaning, giving it a joyous ring.

"Dominus vobiscum! The Lord *is* with you!"

It is more than a wish; it is a reality. Through Communion, God has come into our hearts. It is then with a heart burning with love that the priest says these words. He possesses within himself the All-holy God, whose only desire is to shed more abundant graces on the faithful who have devoutly assisted at the Holy Sacrifice.

"Et cum spiritu tuo! He is with your spirit!" the people reply with equal gladness.

Then the priest goes toward the Epistle side to pray the Postcommunion, which properly constitutes the thanksgiving of priest and people.

350—What is the Postcommunion?

As the word indicates, "Postcommunion" means "after Communion." We give this name to the one or several prayers which the priest prays after the Communion antiphon.

The number of these prayers varies with the importance of the feast. Important feasts have only one Postcommunion (just as they have but one Collect and one Secret) because of the excellence and importance of the mystery celebrated, which claims our exclusive attention; while for Masses of semi-double or simple rite, as on penitential days, there are always several *oratios.*

As we have already said, the number of Postcommunions always equals that of the Collects and Secrets. But their theme is not the same.

The *Collect* refers exclusively to the feast of the day and characterizes it.

The *Secret* particularly pertains to the oblation of the Sacrifice.

The *Postcommunion* has thanksgiving as its principal object. It thanks God for the gift of the Holy Eucharist and beseeches him to make the divine gift fruitful in the souls that have just received it.

We do not wish to pass over in silence a prayer which is added to the Postcommunion only on the ferials of Lent; i.e., on those days in Lent in which no feast of a saint is observed. This oratio is called the *oratio super populum*—"the prayer over the people." After saying, *"Oremus,"* the priest adds these words, *"Humiliate capita vestra Deo,"* "humble your heads before God." And he pronounces this additional prayer, written in the spirit of the penitential season.

351—Why is the Church's official thanksgiving (virtually limited to the Postcommunion prayers) so short?

At first glance, the shortness of the Church's official thanksgiving is surprising, so much the more by its contrast with these wordy formulas of thanksgiving and these prolix protestations of gratitude to which books of devotion and prayer books have accustomed us.

And what is more, in the Postcommunion, gratitude to God is often expressed in an unheard of manner—by begging for favours!

And yet all liturgists unanimously recognize in the Postcommunion the official thanksgiving of the Church.

The key to the mystery is this:

The Church leaves it up to every communicant to express his personal feelings of gratitude after Mass to the God of the Eucharist.

"But why" (you will say) is the thanksgiving presented in the form of a request?"

There is teaching here that enlightens us at one and the same time as to the riches of the Heart of Jesus and the frailty of the heart of man. Begging favours of the Master of all good is an excellent act of religion, for it means honouring his infinite might and inexhaustible liberality. It means adoring One who has no need of our presents, but who is pleased to make known to us his goodness by his gifts. Man, for his part, confesses the greatness of his poverty and his infinite weakness by imploring God's gifts.

As we have just pointed out, the private thanksgiving of the people should be made only *after* Mass. (As we shall discuss here.)

Alas! How few understand this! Many prefer by far to become absorbed in their personal and silent thanksgiving; as if the conclusion of the Eucharistic Sacrifice held no interest for them, did not concern them! As if these official prayers afforded an unwelcome interruption to their conversation with our Lord!... What a mistaken idea!... What a distorsion of facts!...

Participation of the faithful in the Holy Sacrifice should not cease with reception of Holy Communion.

We repeat that your individual thanksgiving does not come until *after Mass*...or (better) consists less in word than in action. The best thanksgiving to our Heavenly Father for the precious gift of his Divine Son, received in Holy Communion, will be your day, your week, with its toil, duties, struggles, and suffering.... It will consist in the practice of brotherly love.

But meanwhile, do not forget that the Church has her official thanksgiving, in which one must take part when one really has a "liturgical mentality;" or, in other words, possesses the mentality of the Church.

Then, up to the end of Mass, we ought to be engaged in this common and social Action. Besides we have but to glance at the Postcommunion to see what food it can furnish for our personal thanksgiving; which we can prolong to our liking *after* Mass.

During these final prayers, prayed in the plural, we shall give a final thought to all the congregation which offered up the Sacrifice with us, and to all the Church's faithful. We shall also give a thought to those unable to receive, and more particularly to those, who, by a heedlessness without a name, deprived themselves of Holy Communion by their own fault. For each one we shall beg immense graces of fervour or of conversion, according to the case.

VI. CONCLUDING RITES

Of the Holy Sacrifice

- Dominus vobiscum
- Ite missa est (Dismissal)
- Placeat
- Benediction
- The Last Gospel
- Personal thanksgiving

352—How is the Mass concluded?

After the Postcommunion, the celebrant returns to the middle of the altar; kisses it; turns toward the people, again saying *"Dominus vobiscum"*; and in this position adds. *"Ite, missa est."* In solemn Masses, it is the deacon who, turning toward the people at the same time as the celebrant, chants the *"Ite, missa est."* The server or the chanters respond, *"Deo gratias."*

The Mass formerly terminated with the *Ite, missa est.*

In the Middle Ages, along about the eleventh century to be exact, the *Placeat* and the priest's blessing were added.

The most recent element is the Last Gospel. It appeared isolated in the thirteenth century; and up to the time of Pope Pius V in the sixteenth century, was also frequently recited as the priest returned to the sacristy.

ITE, MISSA EST

353—What meaning should be given to the Ite, missa est?

These three words may be translated, "Go, you are dismissed"!

Missa (for *missio*) signifies *dismissal* or *sending away,* not "Mass."

By means of this formula, the celebrant simply says to the crowd, "You may go now. The assembly is dismissed."

L'ami du clergé ("The Priest's Friend") published (in April 1948) an interesting commentary on the *Ite, missa est,* which we quote here, almost in its entirety:

"The eucharistic Sacrifice is not a private prayer, which each begins at will and ends when it pleases him. It is the eucharistic assembly, the meeting of the whole family, of the entire Christian community; under the 'chairmanship' of the celebrant. It is 'opened' by him; at his signal, it is 'adjourned.'

"Hence the employment of the profane formula at the conclusion of our Mass: 'Go, you are dismissed!' In olden times, this 'signal' was given by the archdeacon, on the order of the bishop-celebrant after the Postcommunion terminating the eucharistic Sacrifice. Today, after this same prayer, the priest turns toward you; gives you a final greeting and officially dismisses the assembly. This he does in a joyful tone of voice, in thanksgiving for the abundant graces received from the Holy Sacrifice. Thus it is with a heart vibrant with joy—from this same motive—that you send back your own brief but buoyant, '*Deo gratias*—Thank you, God!'

"You understand now what incorrectness, and incivility toward God, the 'chairman' and the whole liturgical assembly, is committed by the parishioner who deserts the church before the official 'dismissal.'

1. *Meaning of the expression*

"Ite, missa est." Singular fortune of this tiny word! Originally, merely the culminating point of the liturgical ceremony, it was soon to designate the ceremony itself. The faithful of Rome no longer said 'the breaking of bread' or 'the Lord's Supper' to indicate the eucharistic assembly; but *Mass—missa.*

"Together let us seek for the full meaning of this solemn dismissal.

"Needless to say, the Church's formula has nothing in common with the 'Thank goodness, *that's* over for another week!' of the mediocre Catholic, docile for once to his pastor's voice; and who ever since the ablutions has been striving to collect gloves, bag, and umbrella, so as to be able to offer a 'running commentary' to the priest's invitation.

"But let us also quickly add that the liturgical formula of dismissal is a far cry from the prayers to be found in modern books of devotion; in which one expresses (with sighs) his desire to 'remain forever at the foot of the altar'! The Church speaks a different, more virile language! '*Ite, missa est!* Go!' (Nevertheless, we must take into consideration all that the Holy Father has had to say anent the importance of the private thanksgiving of the faithful after Mass. *(See* Q. 364.)

This numerous, splendid congregation of all God's sons and daughters, which has just realized a bare few minutes ago, its perfect unity in communion; I, your Mother, Christ's Holy Church, dismiss without fear! Go! Let each one of you return now to his labour and occupations!'

"Or would it be the intent of the Church to say to us, 'You have performed your religious exercises and devotions toward God! Now you can shut up shop and go home! You're free again! Free to go back to your regular pursuits!'?

"Certainly not! The Church could never admit of a closed, water-tight compartment between a man's religious practices and his everyday life. She would never agree that one could don his religion with his topcoat every Sunday morning and put both back in the clothes closet Monday until the next Sunday.

"For she knows that our whole lives come from God and belong to God. Among man's diverse activities, she recognizes that certain ones (spiritual activities) are privileged. But she nonetheless maintains that all possess a divine worth in the eyes of Almighty God. 'It is through your Son, Jesus Christ, that you bless, sanctify, and vivify all these things,' thereby alluding to our offerings as represented by our lives and work. And that is the precise reason why, at the dawn of a new week—or of a new day—we have come to Christ.

"I, who have taken part in the Mass, ought to leave the church more of a Christian. For in truth I have become 'another Christ.' The Christian is 'another Christ,' said my brothers, those first Christians. And this is true! I am then invested with the mission *(missa—missio)* of being joyfully in the world this coming week, 'another Christ.'

2. *This dismissal is likewise an assignment.*

" 'You may go,' says Christ to me. 'I send you away, and I remain with you; and what is still better, *in* you. Make of your day, of your week, a continued Mass in union with those constantly offered up by the Holy Father, bishops, and priests on the earth's surface. Return to your duties as mother, employer, clerk, employe, workman, student—but transformed by me—and continue my Mass in the kitchen, at the office, in the factory, at the shop, at school.... Generously you will offer in union with me to God the Father—in the course of each one of your days—even your most commonplace actions. Your weariness and afflictions have already been presented in advance at the Offertory of your Sunday (or daily) Mass. In this you have done well. The important thing now is to carry out this anticipated offering, this burst of generosity enkindled at the altar; throughout the day and all week long in union with my continuous offering on all the altars in the world.

" 'You have received my Body and Blood in your daily or Sunday Mass. You did well to receive; but communicate likewise, now, throughout this new day or this new week with all that I will.'

"You complain of not having enough time for your thanksgiving after Mass? Do not worry! Your best thanksgiving, the 'thank You' that pleases me most, is the one expressed not in words (which are often deceptive), but by actions that are true, performed in fulfillment of duty every day in a Christian way.'

"*Ite, missa est.* It is likewise the assignment of all the children of God to the divine harvest fields of the Elder Brother. 'Go,' Christ says to you. 'My Mass will never be finished as long as there still remains a famished body, a bruised soul, a wounded heart, a face that does not respond—just so long as God is not all and in all.

"Go, then, like the priest after his Communion...Distribute around you, in your parish, this God whom you have received. *Ite, missa est.* Go! Nothing is finished; everything begins. After the liturgical action, comes the hour of apostleship, of Catholic Action.

"*Ite, missa est.* But after all, is not the liturgical word merely the echo of the words of the Gospel to every Christian: 'You are the light of the world, the salt of the earth, humanity's leaven'? Lamps are not lit to be put under bushels; salt is not meant to remain in the salt cellar. The Catholic who waits for the *Ite, missa est,* is the yeast placed in the dough.

"St. Luke tells us that the apostles after the last blessing of Christ —leaving them for good to return to Heaven—returned to Jerusalem; not with their eyes filled with tears, but with their hearts filled with joy. 'This is queer,' you will say. Not at all! They freely give themselves over to joy; because fortified as well by the assurance of Christ's continual presence in them, and by the promise of his Spirit, they will now be able to bear witness and conquer the world for the mystery of the Cross; uniting their prayers, their labours, and their sacrifices to the Sacrifice of Christ.

"It is likewise with a joy-filled heart and for the same motives that the Catholic should return to his home. Without daily or at least, Sunday Mass, his life would be uncommenced and incomplete. It would be sterile. But thanks to the Sacrifice of the Altar, HIS LIFE IS A MASS. Begun in time, it will terminate in eternity. At life's close, his last word will be, 'It is finished. My Mass has been said. *Ite, missa est.*'

And soon, in Heaven, he will be able eternally to reply, 'Thank you, God! *Deo gratias.* Amen!' "

So when the priest says, "*Ite, missa est,*" it is as if the Church said to us, "Now that you have received the grace of the Holy Sacrifice, this grace ought to suffice for you to show yourselves to be Christians in work, suffering, patience, and love.... Go, and live accordingly!"

354—Does not the *Ite, missa est* remind you of something said by our Lord on the Cross, just before his death?

Indeed it does! Our Lord—the First Priest—knew the *Ite, missa est* of his Mass when he uttered—for the first time on earth—these words of triumph: "All is consummated! The redemption of the guilty world is complete!... My Father is glorified! "...

His work is finished. But what about ours?

When Jesus cried, "All is consummated," he thereby declared that he had perfectly accomplished his work—had so well performed it that there was nothing more to be added.

And we? Can we say as much of our daily task, of our whole lives, of our "lived" Mass?

"Too many among us", says Bishop Sheen, "COME TO THE END of our lives, without COMPLETING our lives. A life of sin comes to an end; but a life of sin is never finished, is never complete.... The world is full of half finished Gothic cathedrals, of half finished lives and of half crucified souls. Some people bear the Cross as far as Calvary and abandon it there; others let themselves be crucified, but climb down from the Cross before it is set up; still others let themselves be 'lifted up' on the Cross, but in response to the world's challenge, 'Come down from the Cross,' they do come down after an hour...or two hours...or two hours and fifty-nine minutes! The only true Christians are those who persevere to the end. Our Lord held fast to the very end. . . ."

The priest remains at the altar until the Sacrifice is over.

Do you?

Do you continue to the close of your prayers? . . . Do you frequently ask yourself if you have said your "Amen," your *fiat?*

Do you always persevere? Certainly, a good start is an act of generosity drawing down Heaven's blessings. But starting is not enough. One must also finish!

"Well begun is half done," says the proverb. Fine, but work that is "half done," is not well done!

"The first step is the hardest," goes another old saw. This is not altogether true. If the second step (under the momentum of the first) is easy; then the last step is correspondingly hard! To take it, one must fight fatigue, monotony, obstacles, discouragement, neglect, treachery, and goodness knows what else besides!

At the end of every action is a minute which will either cover it with glory, or with ignominy.

Oh, that last step! . . . That last line! . . . That last moment of life!

All the saints who are in Heaven today are there because they were able to say, "I fought, I worked, I willed, I kept on to the very end!"

This is the thing asked of you when you are invited to tend toward perfection—and to LIVE YOUR MASS to the end!

355—Does the celebrant always say the *Ite missa est?*

Not always. He says it only on those feast days on which he has either recited or sung the *Gloria.*

The other days, after greeting the people with the *Dominus vobiscum,* the celebrant again faces the altar and says (or chants in Masses of requiem) *"Requiescant in pace."* "May they rest in peace"; to which the server replies, "Amen." In other Masses wherein the Gloria is omitted, (see Q. 71), the priest says *"Benedicamus Domino"* (Bless the Lord); to which the response is *"Deo gratias"* (Thanks be to God.)

The Bloodroot

Like a snow-white hand—
Emerging from green velvet—
With a questionable superfluity of fingers,
Does not its name
In its own way
Recall the duty of apostleship?

There are in the world
Hands so liberal,
That one would think
They had extra fingers for giving!
So prompt is their charity,
So ready their gift for doing
The task of those unable to toil;
And for bringing swift assistance
To a neighbour in need.

Like the sweet-scented bloodroot,
May we be "open-handed";
And may its octoform petals
Preach to our five fingers
Of self-effacement and devotion.

Ric Photo

The Chasm

From the green-spired towers
To the last granite step,
The immense mountain castle
Seems but to exist
For the dazzling white torrent
Contained in its depths.

We seek for God on the surface of our lives—
God prefers the secret, solitary dwelling place.

To discover His battlements,
Accept each detachment;
Imposing sharp silence on clamour of earth,
Consenting to enter within our own souls.
Let us delve and sound out the depths,
Insinuating ourselves in the passage
His unrecognized Presence illumines.

In this supreme solitude,
With your light resplendent,
Where the soul knows beatitude—
Call me, O God!

Sunwapta Canyon
Canadian Rockies
Ric Photo

Placeat

356—What is the significance of the prayer "*Placeat,*" said by the priest after the *Ite, missa est?*

At the two extremities of the Mass, we remark two little anomalies which you may have found surprising. First we have the Introït signifying "overture" or "entrance," and which opens nothing and causes no one to enter! For the celebrant (who has already entered) commenced Mass by reciting prayers at the foot of the altar!

So it is with the *Ite, missa est,* which ends nothing and dismisses nobody!

But let us not forget that we are in the twentieth century. The prayers preceding the Introït (like those that follow the *Ite, missa est),* are late additions introduced by the piety of priest and people. They were not definitely prescribed until 1570, with the publication of the new Missal by St. Pius V.

Let us take a closer look at them.

After the *Ite, missa est,* the priest has turned again toward the crucifix. He now holds his hands joined and resting on the altar. His head is bowed, as he says in a low voice this admirable prayer to the Holy Trinity; which begins with the word, *Placeat*:

Placeat tibi, sancta Trinitas, obsequium servitutis meae, et praesta: ut sacrificium, quod oculis tuae Majestatis indignus obtuli, tibi sit acceptabile, mihique, et omnibus, pro quibus illud obtuli, sit, te miserante, propitiabile. Per Christum Dominum nostrum. Amen.

May the lowly homage of my service be pleasing to you, O most Holy Trinity, and grant that the sacrifice which I, all unworthy, have offered up in the sight of your Majesty may be acceptable to you, and because of your loving kindness, may avail to atone to you for myself, and for all those for whom I have offered it up. Through Christ our Lord. Amen.

This time, the celebrant speaks in his own name, and not as the peoples' delegate. The reason for this is simple. From the ninth century on, this prayer was recited privately by the priest after Mass; just as the Psalm, *Judica me,* was said by the celebrant from the sacristy to the altar.

To begin with, let us recall that God does not always communicate to us during celebration of the Mass, all the fruits of the Sacrifice that are destined for us. Sometimes, we do not receive these graces until a considerable time afterward. That is why in the *Placeat,* which sums up in a sense all those sentiments of adoration, supplication, humility, and trust which made the priest's heart vibrate during Mass, he begs the Holy Trinity anew for the realization of all these things through Jesus Christ our Lord.

Thus, the celebrant, by his sincere recitation of the *Placeat,* makes reparation for the distractions which may have slipped in during the celebration of Holy Mass.

Instead of preparing to rush out of the church as if it were on fire, don't you think that it would be better for you to examine your conscience for a minute and then ask yourself how well you participated in the Mass just ending? . . . You might find your need to say the *Placeat* greater even than that of the priest himself!

Yes, at this moment, let us enlarge our hearts, imploring the Blessed Trinity to pour within them the graces flowing from the Mass we have just offered up.

AN OFFERING AT LIFE'S SUNSET

•

O Good Jesus, I offer myself to you, to support through you, with you, and in you, old age with its infirmities, loneliness, powerlessness, discouragements, distress, and sufferings. I unite this offering to your immolation on the Cross and on our altars.

I accept this work of the destruction of my body; since I "die daily" (St. Paul) a little, to pay homage to the Supreme Creator and Master of Life.

O Jesus, I would die with you, that I may live again with you in eternity.

I believe in the resurrection of the body. At the end of the world, I trust to share in your triumph in my glorified body. To this end, I want to sanctify myself ever more and more; so that I may merit to enjoy Heaven's happiness with the Angels and Saints, and sing the praises of the Blessed Trinity forever and ever. Amen.

"One day during Mass, St. Mechtilde saw our Lord take his heart between his hands and raise it aloft. This heart was transparent and filled with a delicious balm. The hearts of all those present likewise floated in space along with that of the Saviour. Some were filled with the balm flowing from the Heart of Jesus, and shone with great brilliance. Others, on the contrary, remained empty and dull and fell back heavily on the ground. The first hearts were of those present who were attentive to the Holy Sacrifice; the second, of those persons whose minds remained filled with earthly thoughts." *(Revelations,* Book I, chap. 19.)

Let us always take care to place ourselves in the first category; so as to leave behind us a luminous trail and always to shed abroad the fragrance of Christ.

The final blessing

357—What does the celebrant do after praying the *Placeat?*

He gives the blessing.

The accompanying gestures, in detail, are as follows:

The priest kisses the altar. (This kiss is never omitted, even in Masses for the Dead), raises his eyes toward Heaven, and also his hands; extending and rejoining them. He bows to the crucifix, at the same time saying in an audible voice:

"Benedicat vos omnipotens Deus." (May Almighty God bless you.)

Then, hands joined, and eyes lowered, he turns toward the people; and with right hand extended and fingers joined, and placing his left hand on his breast, he says:

"Pater + et Filius et Spiritus Sanctus." (Father + Son and Holy Ghost.)

"Amen!" replies the acolyte in the name of the congregation.

Let us follow carefully each one of the priest's gestures; for they are most instructive.

While saying, "May the Lord bless you," he raises his eyes and hands toward Heaven. It is from there that all blessings come.

He rejoins his hands, to show that God has given him the solicited favours.

He salutes the crucifix in homage and in recognition that though all blessings come from Heaven, they were procured for us by Calvary's Sacrifice.

He turns toward the congregation, over which he is about to act in the Name of God, as his minister and representative.

He makes the sign of the cross over the people in the name of the Triune God: God the Father to whom the Sacrifice has been offered; God the Son, who was the Victim; and God the Holy Spirit, who during Mass inspired them with sentiments of faith, piety, fervour, and charity.

358—Does not the priest's blessing at the end of Mass remind you of another blessing which Jesus gave before leaving the world?

Yes, this blessing reminds us of a particularly touching scene in Jesus' life. After eating for the last time with his apostles and giving them his final counsels, Jesus conducted them to the Mount of Olives. There he raised his eyes and hands toward Heaven for a final blessing; and before their eyes, ascended up into Heaven.

Speechless with surprise, the disciples stood as if thunderstruck; when two angels appeared and reminded them of the mission imposed upon them by the Master—their dispersion for the conquest of the world. . . .

Something similar is to be seen in the life of St. Francis of Assisi.

Before sending out his disciples, Francis had assembled them before the little chapel of Saint-Mary-of-the-Angels, also called the "Portioncula" because of its small size; and there where they had been accustomed to pray, he made them a meaty exhortation. As was his manner, he spoke to them with a peculiarly penetrating sweetness, of the Kingdom of God they were to bring to men; teaching them that they themselves must first of all despise the world, renounce the desire for riches, and dominate their bodies:

"Go, my dear sons," he said, "and preach the Gospel of peace and of conversion! Be patient in trial; humbly reply to all those who ask you anything; bless those who treat you unjustly or calumniate you; for great will your reward be in Heaven! And do not let the thought that you are unlearned men, disquiet you; for you will not speak of yourselves, but the Spirit of your Father in Heaven will speak through you!

Be assured that you will find many good and peaceful believers who will joyfully receive you and your words! But it is true that you will come across others, and in greater number, who being God's enemies, will resist you and speak against you. Be prepared then to support all things with humility!"

Having said this, Francis had embraced his friars one after the other, "as a mother embraces her children"; blessed them, and given them these words of Holy Writ as viaticum: "Cast all your anxiety upon Him, because He cares for you!"

And so the friars, two by two, went piously through the world to bring back the lost sheep—often transformed into ravenous wolves—into the Gospel fold. Joy inundated their souls.

In this instant of the Holy Sacrifice, we witness an analogous fact.

All during the Mass, the Lord was among us. He now asks us to quit his eucharistic Presence in the tabernacle to find him anew in the duty of our state in life, in our work of apostleship and Catholic Action. In a word, he "sends us forth" in the world. We have received much; we must now give much. We shall have much to combat this day (or this week), as the Lord knows full well. To fortify us, he gives us a final blessing.

359—Does the priest give the blessing at every Mass?

No. At a Mass for the Dead, the priest does not bless the congregation.

Why not?

This is to show that all the fruits of the Sacrifice are to be applied to the Departed.

SPIRITUAL COMMUNION

Come to me, O most lovable and most desirable Jesus, and enkindle in my soul a thirst so burning and a hunger so extreme for your holy love, that it may be a continual martyrdom for me not to love you enough; and so that nothing in this world can so afflict me as to love you too little.

—St. John Eudes.

The Last Gospel

360—What Gospel is read at the end of Mass?

Most frequently, the priest reads the beginning of St. John's Gospel.

There are a few exceptions:

Private Masses on Palm Sunday, in which the Gospel of the Blessing of the Palms is used.

The third Mass of Christmas in which the Gospel of the Ephiphany is read.

Needless to repeat, you should not leave the church before the reading of the Last Gospel!

If you would return home joy-filled, take care to profit by the eucharistic Sacrifice up to its final point!

361—Please comment on the Last Gospel.

Before the thirteenth century, we find no trace in the liturgy of the Mass of this reading of the Prologue of St. John's Gospel.

Since that time, many priests recited it from devotion while returning to the sacristy or when removing their priestly vestments.

In the fifteenth and sixteenth centuries, popular piety practically forced priests to recite it at the altar—a usage which became universal. Be it noted in passing that our ancestors were more devout than we!.. It must also be said—for your consolation!—that the faithful of the Middle Ages accorded the value of a sacramental to this Prologue of St. John. That is why the priest on leaving the altar, often recited this Gospel at the insistance of the people—to ward off evil. Even today, it is read to obtain good weather.

Nowadays St. John's Prologue is part of the Mass liturgy, forming as it were the summary and résumé of all that has gone before.

The text follows:

℣. Dominus vobiscum.	℣. The Lord be with you.
℟. Et cum spiritu tuo.	℟. And with your spirit.
Initium sancti Evangelii secundum Joannem. (I. 1-14.)	The beginning of the Holy Gospel according to St. John. (I. 1-14.)
℟. Gloria tibi, Domine.	℟. Glory be to you, O Lord.

I. CHRIST BEFORE THE WORLD WAS

In principio erat Verbum, et Verbum erat apud Deum, et Deus erat Verbum. Hoc erat in principio apud Deum. Omnia per ipsum facta sunt: et sine ipso factum est nihil, quod factum est; in ipso vita erat, et vita erat lux hominum: et lux in tenebris lucet, et tenebrae eam non comprehenderunt.	In the beginning was the Word. And the Word was with God; And the Word was God. He was in the beginning with God. All things were made through him, And without him was made nothing that has been made. In him was life, And the life was the light of men. And the light shines in the darkness; And the darkness grasped it not.

II. THE PRECURSOR

Fuit homo missus a Deo, cui nomen erat Joannes. Hic venit in testimonium, ut testimonium perhiberet de Lumine, ut omnes crederent per illum. Non erat ille Lux, sed ut testimonium perhiberet de Lumine.	There was a man sent from God. His name was John. This man came as a witness, To bear witness concerning the Light, That all might believe through him. He was not himself the Light, But was to bear witness to the Light.

III. ENTRANCE INTO THE WORLD

Erat Lux vera, quae illuminat omnem hominem venientem in hunc mundum. In mundo erat, et mundus per ipsum factus est, et	It was the true Light That enlightens every man who comes into the world. He was in the world,

mundus eum non cognovit. In propria venit, et sui eum non receperunt. Quotquot autem receperunt eum, dedit eis potestatem filios Dei fieri, his, qui credunt in nomine ejus: qui non ex sanguinibus, neque ex voluntate carnis, neque ex voluntate viri, sed ex Deo nati sunt.

And the world was made through him,
And the world knew him not.
He came unto his own,
And his own received him not.
But to as many as received him
He gave the power of becoming sons of God;
To those who believe in his Name:
Who were born not of blood,
Nor of the will of the flesh,
Nor of the will of man,
But of God.

IV. BIRTH OF THE GOD-MAN

Et Verbum caro factum est et habitavit in nobis: et vidimus gloriam ejus, gloriam quasi Unigeniti a Patre, plenum gratiae et veritatis.

℟. Deo Gratias.

And the Word was made flesh,
And dwelt among us.
And we saw his glory—
Glory as of the only-begotten of the Father—
Full of grace and truth.

℟. Thanks be to God.

362—Please comment on the Last Gospel.

We shall make but a summary study of this Gospel Prologue of St. John. (A suitable commentary would require several volumes!) Never has a man said so many profound things in more simple terms. The Fourth Gospel is the loftiest summit of the incomparable and vertiginous group of "mountain peaks," which together make up the inspired volume!

Let us ask the Holy Spirit to illumine us, so that we may be able to penetrate still further into the knowledge of Christ and of the truths which he revealed to us on coming into the world.

Without further ado, let us come to the commentary:

I. In the first part, John speaks of the Word, the Second Person of the Blessed Trinity, before his entrance into this world:
   a. The Word himself, before time, and apart from time.
   b. The Word in relation to the Father.
   c. The Word in relation to creation.
   d. The Word in relation to man.

II. The second part shows us the Precursor who announces the entrance of the Word into the world:
   a. Parallel between the Word and the Precursor, John the Baptist.
   b. The mission of the Precursor.

III. The Mission of the Word in the world—to enlighten.
   a. The world rejects the light.
   b. Divine sonship conferred on those who accept it.

IV. God the Word made man—climax of the Prologue:
   a. The Word becomes flesh.
   b. The witness of St. John the Evangelist.

Let us take up again now the text of the Last Gospel with a few explanations. The quotations are from Geslin, exegete and commentator of the Scriptures.

I. The word

a. *In himself*

"In the beginning was the Word."

"In the beginning," that is, before anything else existed, the Word was—therefore the Word is not comprised in time. Therefore, he is eternal like God, whose Thought he is.

"Was." The imperfect tense, 'was,' is the most apt for signifying eternity.

"The Word." This is a scholar's term for the Second Person of the Trinity. Everybody knows what a thought is. It is the mental image of the object about which we are thinking. The Greeks and Romans gave the name of *word* to thought. In point of fact, a word *is* a thought exteriorly expressed; and thought is the interior word. Now the Greek term for "word" is *logos,* and the Latin, *verbum;* whereas English utilizes an Anglo-Saxon derivative, *word.* We know, moreover, that God has a thought, and that his thought transcends our thoughts; just as God's being transcends our being. In other words, God's thought is the most perfect thought; just as the being of God is the most perfect Being. Hence the expressions of "Logos" or "Word" employed by writers of the first centuries to indicate the "Thought" of God; just as one uses the term "Being" to designate God."

Before continuing these explanations of the Prologue, let us introduce here a passage from the Book of Proverbs, in which Wisdom (another name given to the Word), already had related in the language of imagery, his eternal origins and divine filiation. The speaker is Wisdom (or if you prefer) the Word:

"Yahweh (God) possessed me in the beginning of his ways,
Before anything was made.
From eternity I was formed,
From the beginning, before the world was.
There was no abyss when I was conceived,
Nor fountains filled with water.
Before the mountains were confirmed,
And before the hills, I was brought forth.
When no rivers or land existed
Nor the elements of the globe.
When he laid out the heavens, I was there;
When he drew a circle at the surface of the pit.
When he confirmed the clouds above,
And tamed the fountains of water,
And imposed limits on the sea,
Lest it overflow its bounds.
When he laid the foundations of the earth,
I was beside him as a workman,
Unceasingly playing before him,
Playing on the globe of his earth—
Making the sons of men my delight.

(Prov. 8:22-31.) [Vulgate.]

In addition to the eternal origin of the Word, this passage reveals that like God the Father, he was engaged in the creation and organization of the world; as St. John is to say farther on: "All things were made through Him," (the Word) and without Him was made nothing that has been made."

Let us continue our commentary:

b. *In His relations with the Father*

"And the Word was with God." It is certain that a thought presupposes someone who thinks; a word, someone who speaks. A thought does not hang suspended in the air; words are not to be found in clouds. Therefore, the Word belongs to God.

Now God is eternal. Therefore, his Thought, his Word, must be eternal like God in whom it dwells.

Every thought has an object which it reflects. What then is the object of the divine thought? Toward whom or what is it directed? What does it reflect?

"The thought of God is God! . . . God thinks of himself; and it is in thinking of himself that he produces his Thought, his Word; and the Word looks at God, faces God, and says 'God' to God; as a mirror says 'Peter' to Peter. Therefore the Word of God who proceeds from God without leaving God, goes to God without entering God. Jesus will express this truth later on by saying (John 14:11): 'I am in the Father, and the Father in me.'

" 'And the Word was God.' The Word, marvellously enough, is a *Person,* like the Person from whom he emanates. He is not only eternal, is not only in God, but *is* God. He is not only divine (a term indicative of substance alone); but is God (a term indicative of personality). Nevertheless, the divine substance remains simple: the Word—another Person—is not another substance *(i.e.* another God). We all remember the answer in our penny catechism: 'In God, there are three Divine Persons, truly distinct and equal in all things: the Father, the Son, and the Holy Ghost.' And this other answer: 'The three Divine Persons are only one God.'

c. *In His relations with creation*

"All things were made through Him, and without Him was made nothing that has been made." All that exists outside of God has been created by him through the intermediary of his Word, his Thought.

Everything without exception, has been created by the Word, nothing that exists has come into existence without him. The Word never had a beginning. Therefore, the Word has always been.

Hence, Thought is anterior to matter. The First *was* when the second *became;* and it is the First that caused the second to become; namely, which caused it to pass from nothingness into existence. The necessary conclusion then is that the Thought of God, his creative Word, is like him, eternal. (With no apologies to Communists, materialists, and all the "godless," who foolishly reject God's existence and affirm the eternity of matter.)

d. *In His relations with mankind*

"In Him was life, and the life was the light of men." The preceding paragraphs had reference to the relations of the Word with creation in general and in the natural order. Here, St. John envisages the relations of the Word with mankind in the spiritual order.

"Life" and "light" designate "the life of grace" and "the light of revelation."

The Word brings life and light. It is in the Word that divine life, all life, is to be found. He is the first Foundation; the source of eternal life, of the divine life in us. This life is for all men a source of light. The word is to souls what the sun is to animate creation.

Envisaging this text from another angle, Gosselin expresses it:

"Just as the workman's thought is put into his work, the architect's into his building, the painter's into his painting, the sculptor's into his statue, the musician's into the cantata he is composing, and the writer's into the book he is writing, so God puts his thought—his Word—into his work, the universe. Hence the Word of God is in creation.

"Now what do men look for in a masterpiece? The creator's thought. And this thought, when they have found it, enlightens, illumines, and delights them. Life of the work, as it is, the creator's thought becomes a light for the spectators. Likewise, God's thought, become the life of the world, constitutes the light of men. . . .

"Take a book. What is it? An accumulation of paper, made out of rags—a lifeless thing. But let someone just put his thought, his word, into it! The volume that I despised and would have tossed aside as a lifeless thing, I now keep because it has come alive. And how did it come alive? By the thought that the author injected into it. . . .

I read and reread this book. I consult it. Why? Because I find enlightment. The author's thought has become the life of the book, and the life of the book my light. . . .

"Whoever then studies nature and seeks out its laws, receives the Word of Light, the Word of Wisdom; and so attains to God. Therefore, the Word is the ultimate Object of man's investigations—its Science and Truth. If man, once he knows the truth, transforms his knowledge into blessing, praise, thanksgiving, and song, he has fulfilled his destiny and achieved his goal. . . ."

"And the light shines in the darkness, and the darkness grasped it not." As we pointed out in question 5, God's wonderful plan for creation was thwarted. Here is the way Geslin briefly explains this:

"Adam had received from God sanctifying grace to be transmitted to us by generation. This grace was accompanied by other favours. For our faculties, by gifts which rendered our intelligence sharp and penetrating; our wills active and generous; our bodies, endued with the gift of immortality. But Adam sinned, and sinning, lost divine life and its accompanying favours. Out of his fault came a darkened intelligence, a weakened will, a body passible and mortal. All his children were born in the same fallen state. The light of the Word which God had caused to scintillate on the mirror of the universe, continued to emit its rays; but they fell on blinded eyes. . . . The book of creation had become a riddle. Man for whom it was destined, read the letters, without perceiving their lesson. The meeting between God and man, which was to have taken place through the medium of creation, failed to materialize. In a word, the light indeed shone; but man, become darkness (as St. John and St. Paul put it), grasped it not."

Men by their sins could withdraw from the Divine Light, from the influence of grace; but whatever they might do, and however numerous the errors they taught, they could never prevent the Light from shining. Ever, until the end of time, good will coexist with evil; the good grain with the tares; and the light so shine in the darkness that none shall be able to reproach God for their failure to distinguish truth from error. . . . God's grace does not fail men. It is men who fail grace! Every sin clouds the soul—just as every absolution bathes it with light. . . .

II. The precursor:

a. *Parallel between the Word and John the Baptist, the Precursor*

"There was a man, one sent from God, whose name was John." We find here a striking parallel between the Word and John the Baptist, precursor of the Messiah.

Above, St. John had written, "In the beginning was the Word. The word *was,* as we have said, expresses eternity.

Here, St. John writes: "There was a man." Hence, someone who at a given moment, arrived in the world and began to exist.

Above, St. John had said, "The Word was God" . . . and continues to be God while assuming a human nature.

Here, St. John presents us the Precursor, not as a god or an angel; but as a man.

Above, St. John tells us that the Word is God, and with God.

Here, the apostle presents John the Baptist as the one sent from God. . ."and his name is John." It is John the Baptist who is referred to, and not St. John the Evangelist who wrote these admirable unsigned pages. Ingenious research was required to discover that St. John, "the son of Zebedee," was the author of the Fourth Gospel. . . .

b. *The mission of the Precursor—St. John the Baptist.*

"This man came as a witness, to bear witness concerning the light, that all might believe through him." The rôle of John the Baptist is that of an ambassador come to testify. Testify to what? Concerning the Light; who is none other than the Word, the Second Person of the Blessed Trinity.

Why this witness of John the Baptist? That all might have faith. "He was not himself the Light; but was to bear witness to the Light." Although John the Baptist enjoyed a great reputation as a saint, to the point that people took him for a prophet like Elias, Jeremiah, or even for the Messiah; the Evangelist protests that John the Baptist was not himself the Light, but the dawn; not the Messiah, but the herald of the great King; a voice crying in the desert to bear witness to the Light now manifest. . . .

St. John here echoes Isaias, with the same striking solemnity. The Church, in the offices of Christmas and Ephiphany, has us read the prophet's sublime vision, wherein the same simple and magnificent terms announce the Incarnation of the Word:

"The people who walked in darkness have seen a great Light. Upon those who dwelt in the region of the shadow of death, the Light has arisen!" Arise and shine, Jerusalem!

III. The mission of the Word in the world—to illumine

"It (the Word) was the true Light that enlightens every man who comes into the world." A great event has occurred: the Light, that is, God's Thought, his Word, his Life, has come into the world to enlighten men. And yet the unexpected happened:

a. *The world rejected the Light*

"He was in the world, and the world was made through Him; and the world knew Him not." Unfortunately, the world failed to recognize its Creator.

"The Word of God who desired to be read by men in his work, the universe; wherein he was so deeply graven, so finely written, so clearly expressed, did not succeed. Why not? Because of the iniquity of one man, Adam; who in blinding himself, blinded all his descendants. And that is why St. John, after saying that the Light was in the world and had made the world, adds with accents of profound sadness that "the world knew Him not"—had not received, had not understood Him. The Light, it is true, is always shining; creation continues to speak—today as in the first days of the world—like a book which does not cease to express the author's thought, though the eyes of the reader turn away from it or no longer see. Nonetheless, let us say that man's eyes are not completely blind. He sees, though painfully; he grasps thought, though feebly. And the Vatican Council declares anyone a heretic, who claims that man is incapable of discovering through reason the existence and principal attributes of God in creation. Purity of soul is of great assistance for seeing God in creation. For did not Jesus say, "Blessed are the pure in heart, for they shall see God"? . . .

He was the Light "that shines in the darkness, and the darkness grasped it not"; namely, all those whom their passions have truly plunged into darkness:

Proud souls failed to understand Christ's humility. . .

Superficial souls failed to understand his examples. . . .

Self-interested, selfish souls failed to understand his denial of self. . . .

Presumptuous, haughty souls (as were the Pharisees and doctors of the Law) completely failed to understand Jesus; who remained for them a riddle and a mystery.

In the account of the Passion, the sad tale is told of the outrages inflicted on Jesus, when the soldiers, in a refinement of cruelty, veiled his face.

When the Christian commits sin, he inflicts anew this humiliating outrage to Christ. He "veils" (as much as lies in his power) the face of his Saviour. For when a soul is in the state of grace, the eyes of God rest upon it with complacency. But if the soul loses sanctifying grace because of sin, God turns his eyes and face away from it. This, alas, was the punishment of those Jews unfaithful to their trust—so blinded that they are still waiting for the Messiah.

God turned away from them; and in turn, put a veil over their eyes. We put this veil over the "eyes" of our soul, every time that we offend God; and just so long as we continue to offend him, we remain in a state of darkness which prevents us from seeing God and from comprehending the truths of religion.

Our Lord said to Blessed Angela of Foligno one day: "It was likewise for your eyes with which you have so often admired vain and dangerous objects, that I accepted this humiliation during my Passion. It was in expiation of your offenses that I shed bitter tears; that I had my eyes veiled; and that they were bathed in the blood that flowed from my head."

All that our Lord suffered for his faithful servant, Blessed Angela, he has suffered—and with much greater reason—for us poor sinners.

For who can count the number of sins—perhaps even mortal sins —of which our eyes have been the guilty instruments, and which have prevented us from "seeing" God (i.e. from comprehending his will and teaching)?

And how many times also, have we not wanted to fool ourselves into thinking that God did not see! . . .

The Good Lord might have left humanity in its original fallen state. With sanctifying grace lost, we were excluded from Heaven. . .But

God in his infinite mercy, showed clemency toward us and sent his Son to us with a message: the Good News!

The first to be invited were the Jewish people, who rejected the invitation! "I know that you are the children of Abraham; but you seek to kill me," said Jesus to the Jews; giving as the reason, "because my Word takes no hold among you." (John 8:37.)

Then, as we shall see, Jesus turned toward the whole world.

"He came unto His own, and His own received Him not." This is the principal thought, the theme developed throughout the Fourth Gospel.

This phrase, of great consequence, merits our consideration.

"For two milleniums, God had cultivated a little people; which he had, as it were, brought out of complete obscurity, loving and cherishing it. Become a hardy shrub, the people of Israel had put forth leaves and flowers which bespoke fruits in abundance. At the set time, the Word descended among this people in the chosen tribe of Juda; in the privileged family of David. And in this family, he willed to be the presumptive heir of the royal crown. Thus St. John is able to say with justice that the Word came unto his own.... Then, heart-distressed, he adds, "and his own received him not." "His own," that is, his own people, "received him not"; for the Jews cast their King, the Word of God, out of the Jerusalem capitol and there crucified him." An abominable crime, that; and unfortunately, one still renewed in our day....

What can be sadder than this expression taken from St. John's Gospel : "He came unto His own, and His own received Him not" ? We read it every day at the end of Mass and wind up—by dint of repetition —by not paying any attention to it. A very little reflection, however, is enough to bring out all its bitterness.

"He came unto His own." Here is the father of a family, tired and old—whom his children no longer want around. He gave them everything; spending himself for them without stint. He let them live in the house his ancestors built, and till the fields he had bought and made fruitful by his toil. Now that he is worn out and no longer able to work, his children show him the door. Let him go where he will to die. He is no longer needed!

"He came unto His own." Here is the elder brother; who, after a long absence from his country, returns home and raps at the door of his younger brother. He looks forward to an affectionate welcome; for he arrives from distant lands—his arms loaded with gifts. He has presents for everybody, great and small; even for those he has never seen and knows only by name. The door opens a crack, and then closes again; for he has become the stranger who cannot be trusted; the enemy for whom one has only hatred, jealousy, and scorn. The happiness of entering the house is not to be his. His own receive him not.

"He came unto His own." It is the childhood chum, the constant companion, the confident of his friend's joys and sorrows. In the old days, the friends shared work and play. Then came separation. Today, he returns, his heart filled with old memories, and a song in his soul of faithful friendship and of bygone days. But no one wants to remember him now; and when he gives his name, his old friends pretend—after much searching of a voluntarily faulty memory—not to recall him at all. He could insist, of course; but what good would that do? When hearts are closed, it is better to go back, without having been "received."

We could insert the story of perfect joy, here, as described by St. Francis. But since this savoury episode has already been related on page 474 we simply refer our reader to that page.

"He came unto His own." God, our Creator and Heavenly Father has come. At each instant, he knocks at the door of our hearts. He reveals to us the mildness of his springtide, the magnificence of the world, which he made so fair, and the heavens which sing of his glory. He makes his sun to shine above, to ripen our crops and make us glad. He makes his beneficial rain to fall on our fields at the very hour we need it. But we do not recognize him in the work of his hands; we close our eyes to the Light and live like unreasoning brutes, incapable of lifting our eyes toward Heaven and of expressing our gratitude.

He visits us in time of sorrow and trial. He makes suffering to be the privileged harbinger of his coming. He strives to make us understand the vanity of this passing world; to detach us little by little from this world's goods, in order to orient us toward eternal realities. We understand still less the significance of this warning. We murmur at the Cross. We refuse to listen to the call of sickness and death; which is none other than the call of God. Sometimes, we even dare to blaspheme this incomparable token of divine affection, calling us to the honour of suffering and of dying for love!

He visits us in the secret of our hearts, when he inspires us with generous thoughts, sends us the desire for perfection, of devotion, or of pardon. But we speedily drive far from mind and heart these inner summonses to a better life. "Of what use will it be to me?" we think. "Are we not placed on earth to make money, to have a good time, to profit by the passing moment and our fleeting youth? And, like the good seed that fell among thorns, our aspirations toward the ideal are choked by earthly cares and remain fruitless. The voice of the world is louder than the voice of God; which speaks in silence and in solitude....

He visited us when he sent his only Son on earth, confiding to him the mission to enlighten us and to teach us to know and love him. Many times already, before taking this final step, He had communicated his Word to the prophets; but one after the other, the prophets had all been despised, outraged, beaten, and put to death. Then God said to himself, "Perhaps they will reverence my Son."

We know what they did to that only Son, to that beloved Son. He was betrayed, mocked, scourged, and condemned. He was led to his death, and expired upon a Cross like the last among malefactors.

He visits us again when he permits Calvary's Sacrifice to be renewed on the altar by his priests. But it is in vain that the Redeemer's blood continues to flow. By their sins, men unceasingly crucify afresh the Son of God!

He visits us in Holy Communion; where he is (more or less) well received.... He visits us in the Sacrament of Penance; which we receive without too much contrition or too "firm" a purpose of amendment.... He visits us by the preaching of God's Word; which we so readily let fall on the ground—preferring more mundane speech.... This is deplorable.

God came unto his own, and his own received him not! Let us not say that these words do not apply to us and have not been written for us! Even we, who like to look upon ourselves as being "better," and who very often, feel only a pharisaic disdain for our brothers, the publicans and sinners, the poor and needy...have not always consented to receive God's visit. We have, of course, received and welcomed the Divine Master's coming.... But how often, how much more often, have we not shown him the door or received him with a grumble? . . . For your convincing, simply consider the way you accepted your last trial! . . . Or the man who just now rang your doorbell! And yet, as we have said. the visit was from God!

We know this well enough, though we are not always willing to admit it! God has never ceased to call us, only rarely have we responded with fitting generosity. This is because God called us to self-denial He invited us to walk in the royal road of the Cross. Sometimes, he merely asks us to smile instead of pout; to forgive instead of hate; to pray instead of blaspheme. . . . He wanted to make us saints. All this seemed too hard for us; so much so, that when the time came for following Christ *all* the way, we pusillanimously drew back. . . .

Jesus, the Son of God, Love unappreciated, came unto his own. In the days of his new life, how many did he find to love him with their whole heart and be steadfastly true to him? Today, how many does he find who respond to his love with equal love, in terms of complete self-surrender? We admire the great number of those who recognize him, but think of the multitudes who disavow him! . . .

Truly, God is not loved. If St. Francis were to come back in our twentieth century, he would have still more reason for going along the streets weeping and crying out to everyone, "LOVE IS NOT LOVED!" Alas, the world continues not to recognize Christ. His own receive him not!

Since we desire to be numbered among those who do know and love Him, let us correct whatever is defective in our conduct and pray hard that we may measure up to our Christian vocation.

b. *Divine sonship conferred on those who accept Christ*

"But as many as received Him, He gave the power of becoming sons of God." "One man's loss is another man's gain," we sometimes say. The light rejected by the Jews has been accepted by the Gentiles or pagans.

Since sin's advent, humanity has been divided into two camps—those who accept Christ, the Light of the world, and those who reject him. We must not be surprised at the battles we shall have to sustain against the sons of darkness. This opposition is often recalled in the Scriptures. "The stone which the builders rejected," wrote David (Ps.

117) "has become the cornerstone," the cornerstone on which the Gentiles consented to be placed in order to constitute the universal Church.

Christ's reward for those willing to acknowledge and accept him is magnificent. "He gave the power of becoming sons of God."

Note that God excludes no one. "As many as received Him," says St. John. Hence, it depends only on us.

A son of God! What grandeur! And to which none could hope to aspire without God's infinite goodness, who grants this privilege to all who are baptized and believe.

A son of God. This means having a soul freely washed from the taint of original sin and mercifully purified from every mortal sin that we may have committed afterward.

A son of God. This means having a soul sanctified (by a holiness that is, of course, perfectible) by means of the divine life infused into it by the Holy Spirit.

A son of God. This means having a soul adopted by God himself as his child and honoured by his fatherly affection.

A son of God. This means having a soul wherein God dwells as in a ciborium; in order to love it, embellish it, and enrich it with spiritual goods.

A son of God. This means having a soul integrated into Christ: "grafted" on him, and to which he transmits in fullest possible measure, his own life of sonship.

A son of God. This means having a soul divinised, not only in itself, but also in its faculties and potentialities, in such a way that it is made capable of performing divine and supernatural acts, meritorious for Heaven.

A son of God. This means having a soul marked by anticipation with the seal of the elect and destined to everlasting glory. . . .

If this title of 'son of God' is so glorious, let us ever be grateful to God for having so readily conferred it on us. And let us never do anything that could make us lose it!

To the Christian engaged in the combat against the solicitations of evil, St. Augustine recalls that there is no more powerful stimulant than the memory of one's adoptive sonship, with regard to his Heavenly Father; or, if you prefer, than his title of "son of God." "When the flesh solicits you to shameful pleasure, reply, 'I am a son of God, called to too high a destiny to become the slave of base passions!' When the world tempts, tell it, 'I am a son of God. Heavenly riches are laid up for me. It is unworthy of me to attach myself to mud!' When the Devil attempts to attack you, and promises you honours, say to him, 'I am a son of God, born for an everlasting kingdom. Get behind me, Satan!' " Never depart from those lofty thoughts becoming to sons of God!

Wordy protests that we do not intend to deny our title of sons of God, when we run after gross pleasures; when we yield to unworthy actions reproved by the Divine Master; when we burn the bridges between him and us; mean that we seriously fool ourselves. For this is treason! Doubtless, God does not require of his child to be perfect to start with. But he does expect him at least not to be ungrateful or rebellious and to constantly tend toward perfection....

One condition, however, is a "must" for becoming a "son of God." St. John points this out when he says that God gave this power "to those who believe in His name."

Hence, the indispensable condition for becoming a son of God is faith, and faith in the Word—in the Son of God, incarnated to glorify his Father and to save us.

In order to preclude all misunderstanding, St. John adds that the divine sonship is not earthly in origin, but proceeds from God's creative power. This is the thought expressed by St. John when he writes: "He gave the power of becoming sons of God; He who was born not of blood (adultery), nor of the will of the flesh (concupiscence), nor of the will of man (free and reasonable act), but of God.

IV. God the Word Becomes Man

1. *"And the Word was made flesh."*

We genuflect while saying these words. "Here, we are at the climax of the Prologue," writes Renié. "Nothing expresses better than this simple phrase, the unfathomable mystery of the Incarnation—the Word, uniting to himself human nature, becomes flesh. What an antithesis in terms—God and flesh! This last word was not chosen at random; but marvellously expresses the reality of Christ's humanity and the immensity of the Divine Mercy, whose love went to such lengths of abasement. The 'flesh' signifies the infirmity of our human nature."

"Before this time," declares Geslin, "the Word was separated from the world. As pure Spirit, he was distinct from matter. Now he has entered into, has plunged into, matter. He has robed, clothed himself, with it. How? He has become as it were 'material' by virtue of his alliance with a human body, even to personal union. Indissolubly, matter is attached to the Word and the Word to matter. To whatever heights he is to ascend on Ascension Day, matter will rise with him, participating in his triumph and glory. And it is not merely to one atom among billions that he is united. He consents that all matter should follow him in His Ascension. He will make of all men who believe in Him, His cloak, or better, His Mystical Body; and we shall draw behind us in our ascension the lower creation, our servant."

Let us pause a moment at this unique fact in history. God made man! God, who stoops so low, that we may rise so high! For if I were to assume the nature of a rat or an earthworm while remaining a man, I should be a thousand times less humiliated than the Word was in becoming a mortal and passible man.

"And the Word was made flesh." These words make us think of the humiliations of Bethlehem's Crib, where Jesus took so lowly a place that no man could take it from him! Have you ever studied the meaning of these five little words which we read regularly at the end of Mass? "The Word was made flesh"?

"The Word." The eternal Word of life!

"The Word." He who is the Light of the world, the Light that shines without ceasing and which penetrates every soul open to receive it!

"The Word." He to whom Eternity belongs, the Almighty, Infinite Wisdom, is made flesh!

O my soul, adore and measure if you can, the prodigious abasement of the Word of God and the extent of his love!

A God is made, and will remain, flesh; without ceasing to be God. Jesus Christ our Lord is "Love incarnate." He who exists from all eternity closely united to the Father through the Holy Spirit; He in whom the Father is well pleased, comes to us, becomes one of us!

He is going to take upon Himself all our misery; and as soon as He enters this world, He offers Himself up to His Father in place of the holocausts with which He was not pleased. Reparation begins, and the torrent of perfect adoration now ascends toward the Divine Majesty on behalf of all creation.

O Jesus, Incarnate Word, shall not my heart fly toward You, as Yours toward me? Unite me to You by faith and love and truly be my life's All. Unite my will to Yours, and may Your law likewise be in my heart.

O Word, eternal Truth, silence within me all other voices; that I may learn to hear You and act ever in accordance with Your teachings.

And you, Mother of Jesus, the first to offer Him to the Father, uniting your oblation to His; help me to deny myself. Help me to respond to Love by love; to be most faithful in receiving the Word of God; never to impede his action within; that I may gaze at Him forever in His glory and become inebriated with His splendour. Amen!

"And He pitched His tent among us." So reads the Greek, with much more of depth than the "dwelt among us" of the vulgate. "Just as in Old Testament times," writes Pius Parsch, "God pitched his tent among his people, notably on the desert trail, Christ is among us. He built no fixed dwelling in our midst; it was only a tent—as are all our tabernacles—for He did not wish to remain on earth." So He "camped" among us, crossing Life's wilderness with us, to lead us out of the Egypt of sin from whence He took us, to the Promised Land of Heaven into which He desires to introduce us—there to dwell with Him forever!

"And the proof of this?" we ask the evangelist.

2. *St. John's testimony*

"And we have seen, grasped, contemplated, and admired His glory," St. John tells us, "the glory that an only Son, full of grace and truth, is capable of receiving from His Father."

The Beloved Disciple is a sure witness, a man who has seen Christ, his miracles, transfiguration, and Resurrection with his own eyes, and has been enraptured by his public teachings and private confidences. "This glorious and resplendent majesty," declares the apostle, "was that which was fitting that the Father should communicate to his Only Son."

Such, briefly commented, are the sublime thoughts contained in St. John's Prologue that we read every day at the close of the Holy Sacrifice. St. John touches upon the most profound mysteries of our holy religion: Divinity, Trinity, Eternity, Creation, Incarnation, Revelation, Redemption, Life, Light, Truth, Grace, divine sonship, everlasting happiness! All in a few words!

Should we be surprised at the effort required to penetrate the meaning of this Gospel, the crown and epitome of the Mass? Let us often come back to this admirable passage, begging the Holy Spirit to grant us the Light which will illumine our minds at the same time that it warms our hearts; so that in every Mass we may be able to glimpse the glory contemplated by St. John—the glory of the Son of God, full of grace and truth.

363—What prayers does the celebrant say, kneeling at the foot of the altar, before leaving the church?

Pope Leo XIII ordered the recitation of prayers to the Blessed Virgin and to St. Michael after a Low Mass:

Three Hail Marys.
The "Hail, Holy Queen."
A prayer imploring Mary's intercession.
A prayer to St. Michael.

Pope St. Pius X. permitted following these prayers with a threefold invocation to the Sacred Heart. (Note that these prayers are not said after a High Mass, and are omitted at Low Masses accompanied by a certain solemnity; as, for instance, liturgical chant, a sermon, a marriage, etc.)

These prayers were ordered by Leo XIII on the occasion of the furious assault launched against the Church by freemasonry. Their aim is to obtain the end of the satanic persecution against God and his Church. As these battles waged by Satan and his minions by whatever name—Communists, Jehovah Witnesses, Freemasons, etc—are constantly renewed, these prayers are always timely. Let us unite with the celebrant and devoutly say these prayers for these intentions.

THE CHRISTIAN WIFE'S PRAYER

•

O Lord, bless, and preserve the man whom you gave me for my husband. Grant him a long and holy life, free from domestic troubles. Make me a blessing and a helpmeet for him; sharing his joys, comforting him when he is sad, a faithful companion, an assistant in this world's vicissitudes. Make me always pleasing in his eyes, and ever dear to him.

Dear Lord, unite his heart to mine in a deep and holy love. Unite my heart to his, in a love that is filled with sweetness and a mutual desire to please. Preserve me from discontentment. Make me always sweet-tempered and reasonable. Render me "humble" and "obedient"; useful to my husband, discreet, sensible, and prudent.

Cause us to live together in peace and harmony, even as your divine Word commands us to do! May we together share our love in your service forever. Amen!

—Cardinal Vaughan

THE PRIVATE THANKSGIVING OF THE PEOPLE

How little do we know how to thank!

"One of the miseries of the human heart," writes Abbé Mark in "*Le Christ dans nos cités* ("Christ in our cities"), is its gift for forgetfulness.

"Someone has rendered us a benefit.... At the time, our hearts are touched and go out to the person.... Then our enthusiasm cools.

"It is the same way with regard to Christ after our Communion.

"After we leave the church wherein the great mystery of Love has been accomplished in our souls, we are tempted to let ourselves be too soon caught up again by life and to 'forget' the One who gave himself to us and lives in us....

"We do not know how to prolong our thanksgiving by linking the Saviour to our lives, occupations, cares, joys, and sorrows....

"We are ignorant of the art of utilizing his beloved presence—this Light, this Force, this superior Life, which he represents and desires to impart to us.

"This is really a great misfortune.

"Once, crowds surged toward him, thirsting to see, hear, and touch him. They followed him in the desert. They sought to hold onto him....

"The Holy Women followed his footsteps....

"The disciples of Emmaus cried, 'Lord, abide with us!'

"Magdalene at Easter dawn, wandered aimlessly around the empty tomb....

"And we bear the world's Saviour in our hearts and fail to profit by it! We leave him alone—all alone.

"The day that follows Communion ought to be a continuous thanksgiving. How?

"First, let our purpose be to preserve a modicum of recollection in the fever of action. When we close the church door behind us, let us keep the door of our own inner sanctuary open. . .Let us—from time to time—come for a swift visit with the silent, but so mighty Guest who has given himself to us. Is it not a fault on our part to turn our backs on Him—to pay no heed to his visit? He has come from so far to prove His love and to place Himself at our disposal!

"So, after we have returned home, let us keep in contact with Him. Let us not permit the incense still floating beneath the vaults of the temple to become dissipated.... Let us entrust to our guardian angel and to our Lady the task of prolonging our adoration.... We are still in Heaven; let us not fall down to earth again too soon....

"Let us have an intuitive awareness that the Mass continues in us (and it does continue). Christ gives himself on the altar stone of our soul.... With the angels, he celebrates the divine liturgy.... He prays for us...for those whose names we have whispered to him.... He commences to offer our first acts of the day—did not St. Paul say: 'Whether you eat or drink, do all for the glory of God'?

"Life, our simple, quite material life, is not commonplace.... It is something envisaged by God—having its beauty and merit—on the condition that we live it with Jesus. And living it with Jesus is easy, when we have just received Him.

"The more the day advances, the more we must uplift it, make it divine, render it fruitful, by never losing sight of our Guide.... Unceasingly, we must return to Him.... In a swift mental flash, let us think of our soul as being truly a 'Jacob's well,' wherein Christ longs to give us living water; as the boat wherein he reposes and longs to calm our troubled mind, as a 'Bethany' where He comes for refreshing, as a Mount Thabor where we may glimpse the beauty of His transfigured face, as a Garden of Gethsemani where we may easily keep Him company, as a road to Calvary, where—like vigilant Veronica—we ought to have the courage to wipe away the spittle left on His face by sinners.

"What may not be accomplished by an earnest and loving soul!...

"And you visited by trial? Do not tremble.... Dominate your fears. Press closer to the Divine Heart and let the storm blow over.... You will be happy at your conquest.

"Has a shadow passed over your soul—a sin of surprise? Place yourself in the Saviour's wounds. A drop of blood will fall, purifying your soul. Even so, are our spiritual cures effected.

"Do you come across souls in distress? Do not be satisfied with merely showing your sympathy. Bring them in prayer before the One capable of restoring them. It is so easy to do! And so rarely done! How many Catholics pray for their fellow-Catholics, for their friends?

"Is your soul weary and broken, powerless in the face of grief? Cease your sterile laments, and rather, take one step toward the Divine Comforter. Rest your burning forehead on his Heart.... The gesture is daring—it is not forbidden. The Prodigal Son did no other thing, and the Father clasped him in his arms.

"Do you seek a way to remain worthy of Him who visited you this morning? Every hour, recollect yourself for a second or two. Think of some beautiful thought that struck you, of a counsel given, of a beautiful memorized prayer.

"I know souls who repeat certain prayers from the Mass...of others who go over one by one the Stations of the Cross, under the very eyes of the Crucified Saviour...of others who place themselves anew before the mysteries of the Rosary that they may glean their fruits...of still others who place the sufferings of all mankind in the priest's chalice —alongside Christ's Blood....

"What an inspiration all this can be to the soul! This is the way to dwell on the mountain peak and to bring down upon earth the torrents of God's power.

"I could continue, but to what avail? You have grasped the method—it is yours to apply. You can tell everything to Him, who while on earth, treated us with unparalleled goodness. What must have been Christ's greatness of soul to receive and uplift Magdalene...to have mercy on the Apostle Peter...to give immediate entrance to Heaven to the dishonoured but repentant Thief, and to utter these amazing words: 'I have come to call not the just, but sinners!'

"Now it is this good and mighty Being whom the Host brings every morning to the shores of our soul. He enters our 'ship'...bears us company...helps us...strengthens us...consoles us on Life's voyage.

"Finally, let us realize that a few moments adoration on a kneeler are not enough. We must bring Christ into everything we do, into the very centre of our lives. "A real thanksgiving does not last ten minutes; it lasts all day."

364—What judicious counsels does His Holiness, Pope Pius XII, give us in the encyclical, *Mediator Dei et hominum*, concerning thanksgiving after Communion?

Signaling the importance of our thanksgiving, for the purpose of thanking God and for making our Communions fruitful, the Holy Father reminds the communicant of his duties toward the sacramental Christ:

"When the sacred Action, regulated by these special liturgical laws, is finished, the person who has received the Bread of Heaven is not dispensed from giving thanks. It is, moreover, eminently fitting, that after he has received the Holy Eucharist and the public ceremony is over, he should recollect himself, and intimately united to the Divine Master, converse with Him—so far as his circumstances permit—sweetly and to his soul's benefit. Those persons deviate from the path of truth, who, holding more to words than to thought, affirm and teach that once the Sacrifice is finished, no reason exists for prolonging it by this type of thanksgiving; not only because the altar is in itself a thanksgiving; but also that this is a matter of personal and private devotion, which concerns the individual and not the good of the community.

"On the contrary, the very nature of the Sacrament requires that the Catholic receiving it should draw from it abundant fruits of sanctity. Assuredly, the public meeting of the congregation has been dismissed; but it is needful that each individual, united to Christ, should sing the hymn of praise ceaselessly in his soul, 'giving thanks always for all things in the name of our Lord Jesus Christ.' (Eph. 5: 20.) The liturgy of the eucharistic Sacrifice exhorts us thereto in these terms: 'Grant us always and in all places to give thanks unto You. . .and never cease to praise You.' *(Roman Missal.)* So, if there is not a single moment in which one should not give thanks to God, and if we must never stop praising him, who dare blame or accuse the Church for counselling her priests and people to converse at least a short time with the Divine Redeemer after Holy Communion; and for having introduced appropriate prayers, enriched with indulgences, into liturgical books; by means of which prayers, her sacred ministers may suitably prepare themselves before exercising their liturgical functions and nourishing their souls with the Eucharist; and having terminated Holy Mass, may express their gratitude to God? Far from stifling the inmost sentiments of the individual Catholic, the sacred liturgy rather animates and stimulates them, that they may bear a resemblance to Christ and be oriented by him toward God the Father. It is for this reason that it teaches and invites all those whose souls have been nourished at the Holy Table to render due thanks to God. For the Divine Redeemer loves to hear our prayers, converse with us familiarly, and offer us a refuge in his burning Heart.

"Such individual acts, moreover, are essential to our more abundant enjoyment of the treasures from on High, with which the Eucharist abounds; and in order that we may, according to our capacities, shed them abroad on others, so that our Lord may attain in every soul the fullness of his power.

"Why then, Venerable Brethren, should we not praise those, who, following reception of the Eucharistic food (even after the congregation has been officially dismissed), tarry in intimate familiarity with the Divine Redeemer; not only to hold most sweet converse with him, but likewise to thank him and pay him due homage; and especially to beseech his aid; for separating from the soul whatever might lessen the efficacity of the Sacrament, and for realizing their full share of whatever is capable of furthering the omnipotent action of Jesus Christ? We exhort them to do this in a special manner, by carrying out their resolutions, by the practice of Christian virtue, by adapting to their own needs the gifts received from his royal bounty. Surely the author of the golden book of the *Imitation of Christ,* speaks as one inspired and in accordance with liturgical precept, when he gives this counsel: 'Remain in the secret place and enjoy your God, for you possess Him whom the whole world cannot take from you.' (Book 4:12.)

"Let all of us, then, closely united to Christ, endeavour to plunge ourselves in a manner into his most holy love; and attach ourselves to him that we may participate in those acts whereby he himself adores the august Trinity in a homage extremely pleasing to him; whereby he renders supreme praise and thanksgiving to Almighty God, which with common accord reverberate in Heaven and on earth; in accordance with the word, 'All the works of the Lord, bless the Lord,' by means of which, united together, we implore God's help at this most opportune moment for asking and obtaining aid in Christ's name; and whereby we especially offer and immolate ourselves as victims; saying, 'May we become for You an everlasting gift.'

"The Divine Redeemer incessantly repeats his urgent invitation, 'Abide in me.' Now by the Sacrament of the Eucharist, Christ does abide in us and we in him; and just as Christ abiding in us lives and acts; so must we, abiding in Christ, live and act through him."

In response to the Holy Father's desires, we shall propose to you in the following questions, some considerations or suggestions as to modes of giving thanks.

THE ECHO IN THE WOOD

•

Filled with loneliness and woe,
In the dark, mysterious wood,
I cried (my courage ebbing low)
"How sad my lot is here below!"
Echo only answered: "OH!"

I, in most touching accents sighed,
"Death for me would be a blessing!"
Echo only answered: "SING!"

"Echo of the Wood!" I cried,
"My cross fills me with dark mistrust!"
This time Echo answered: "TRUST!"

"My heart is filled with thoughts of hate!"
'T'were blasphemy to say, 'I love!'
Echo calmly answered: "LOVE!"

Epilogue:
Echo of the Wood, I know
That your advice has changed my fate!
I sing, I trust, I love, and so
My heart goes singing here below!

THEODORE BOTREL

365—Do people know how to make their thanksgiving after Communion?

Apparently not!

In the last century, Father Faber sadly noted that the short quarter hour consecrated to our thanksgiving is the hardest quarter hour of the day!

Had he lived in our century, he would hardly modify his judgment!

Is it really so hard to say "Thank You"? *Is God the only Person toward whom we feel free to be ungrateful and rude?*

The Scriptures tell us that after the angel Raphael took his departure, Tobias and his son remained for three hours, foreheads in the dust, thanking God for sending such a visitor to help them!

As for us! What is our conduct, not toward an angel, but toward Almighty God, who deigns to visit us and enrich our souls?

Alas! Sometimes (not to say frequently) we act in a heedless manner.... We lack the generosity to impose on ourselves the strict minimum of recollection; that we may enter within ourselves and keep our Lord company.... Our Communions have become routine.... Our Lord is within us as in a tomb.... He passes through our souls like a stranger in an empty house. When he enters, we leave; and furthermore, we seem in a hurry to go! Our Guest is with us, but we are not with him! We should consider uncouth anyone who would leave a king who had come to visit him all alone in a room. And what is an earthly monarch alongside Heaven's King?

Besides, our Lord does not come as an ordinary visitor, simply to see us. He comes to make us rich!

"If a man were to plunge his hand into liquid gold," wrote St. John Chrysostom, "he would draw it out all golden. The Holy Eucharist does even better for your soul. It makes it all divine; it clothes it with Jesus Christ himself!" Once more, then, how can one be so showered with blessings without warmly expressing his gratitude?

Much selfishness and heedlessness is involved in this, also much ignorance. That is why we shall attempt to give a very simple method of thanksgiving.

366—Do you know what St. Philip Neri did to cure people who received Communion without giving thanks?

Noting that one of his parishioners always left the church right after Communion, and knowing that no compelling duty required such haste, St. Philip Neri hit on the idea one fine morning of having the man escorted to the street by two altar boys bearing lighted candles, just as is done for the Blessed Sacrament! Imagine the man's surprise at this procedure! Taking the hint, he turned back and made a quarter hour thanksgiving in church.

"But," you will ask, "what if our duties make it absolutely impossible for us to stay? Would it be better, then, not to receive?"

Not at all. Go ahead and receive; but go silently to your work, so as to make the thanksgiving you missed in church, on the way.

It was the same St. Philip Neri who said with regard to this: "Leaving the church right after Communion because of duty, or to practice some act of charity toward one's neighbour, is leaving Jesus Christ for Jesus Christ; i.e., giving up the spiritual sweetness of his conversation, to go where duty calls or to win souls for him."

The important thing is our *"Thank you."*

367—What do you think of the habit some people have of burying their noses in a prayer book right after Communion?

Let us say right off the bat that those few moments that follow reception, in which Jesus is substantially present in our soul, are of great importance for our sanctification.

"There is no time more precious in your whole life," wrote St. Magdalen of Pazzi, "nor more favourable for conversing with God and inflaming your soul with his love. Let us not trouble ourselves, then, at this time with masters of books, for we have Jesus Christ himself to teach us how to love. . . .

"What are we to think," contributes Msgr. Landriot, "of these printed prayers with which some souls surfeit themselves after Holy Communion? They may be useful, if they sustain fervour; but if they are multiplied, they drown the soul, under pretext of watering it. They may simply degenerate into a play of the imagination. We would, for our part, compare these prayers, these cut-and-dried formulas, with artificial flowers—pretty to look at, but without life or fragrance. The Lord would prefer the tiniest *living* flower plucked in your heart's garden—

a word you *feel,* a simple word springing up alive and richly from the soil of your heart."

It *does* seem inconceivable that in return for the immense benefits and countless graces of Communion, we should be so cold that we need to borrow somebody else's sentiments to thank God!

Experience shows, though, and as Pope Pius XII reminds us (cf. Q. 364), these beautiful after Communion prayers are of use, especially on days of dryness. We would be wrong to reject them. However, in such a case, let us always start (at least, for a few moments) by making acts of profound adoration and gratitude toward our Lord, present in us. Next, if we wish, let us read very slowly a few of these prayers, without feeling in duty bound to read them all. The important thing is to reproduce within ourselves the sentiments expressed by the words we are saying.

Moreover, as the Holy Father remarks, many of these prayers are indulgenced (such as the prayer "O Good and Sweetest Jesus," to which a plenary indulgence is attached). It would be ungracious to omit them. Let us stick to the golden mean and we shall not go wrong.

368—What method would you suggest for making a good thanksgiving after Communion?

The word "method," is perhaps ill chosen; since the thoughts and sentiments which should be ours during our thanksgiving, cannot be regulated by slide rule and have no other law than the inspiration of the Holy Spirit. Nothwithstanding, there are certain important acts that we should like to indicate to assist those experiencing any difficulty. We repeat here the things we said about meditation. In the beginning of the spiritual life, you may perhaps feel the need of a method. In that case, make use of one for as long as you find it helpful; but when the day comes that you find it becomes a hindrance, lay it aside and follow the Holy Spirit's inspiration.

Here is how we can make our thanksgiving:

1. Keep silent and adore.
2. Listen to Jesus.
3. Speak to Jesus.
4. Ask of Jesus.
5. Give to Jesus.
6. Radiate the Host.

1. *Keep silent and adore*

Let there be silence in your soul!

This is no small affair! "Putting the brakes on one's tongue is not enough for maintaining interior silence. We have said that we are temples of Divinity, God's "little churches." We ought to close "doors" and "windows," i.e., lower our eyes, become deaf to the world's din, mortify our imaginations, and let no worldly thoughts or too captivating images of any creature enter in. Jesus dwells in our "little church"; he ought to dwell there alone—let us make a sanctuary of love and recollection for him.

"I do not ask great things of you," our Lord told Sr. Benigna Consolata, "but simply a word kept back, a glance suppressed, a pleasing thought cut short—in a word, whatever mortifies and constrains. These little things, united to My infinite merits, acquire great value. If you only knew how souls please Me who thus immolate themselves in silence!"

As you see, we are not talking about daydreaming, or idleness, or distractions, but silence. Or, in other words, of a delightful and mute contemplation, of a heart to heart converse with our King, with our Beloved. It is all to our advantage, then, to forget ourselves and to think only of Jesus. He will take care of us. He is active within us. We have merely to *let* him act; to let him divinise us; and look at him lovingly, with one of those looks inexpressible in human speech, into which all that is best in our soul passes. Two hearts, as it were, beat in our breast —the Saviour's heart and our own. And these two hearts—if we do not put some obstacle in the way, will beat in unison—one *for* the other, and One *in* the other. He will love us, and we shall love Him; He will look at us, and we at Him. In Him we shall find life: a life of intimate union.

Our lives of consecration or of apostleship invite us to friendship with the Saviour. He made the first overtures—we have only to surrender ourselves to Him. Our thanksgiving cannot be the same as that of the ordinary Catholic. Our responsibility for souls, our commission as apostles, obligates us more. Hence, our thanksgivings should have a warmth, a special intensity, and likewise a value of mediation.

Our hearts have a right to, a need for, love. Jesus is the only Friend toward whom our marks of affection and tenderness are never misplaced. On Him should be expended our faculty for loving—especially reserved for Him. For it is in Him and for Him that we should love all other creatures.

In order to taste to the full these precious moments of intimacy with our Lord and profit by his brief visit, during which he is able to transform us—snatching us from mediocrity—awakening within us our slumbering "better self"—answering all our prayers—pouring into our souls the torrents of his inmost life, we ought to be recollected and silent.

2. *Listen to Jesus*

Jesus speaks in the silence. He always has something to say to us, some confidence to impart to us. If we do not hear him, it may be because we do not know how to be silent, being too eager to say certain prayers; or, again, being too interested *not* to hear, lest our Divine Friend ask of us some thing we do not wish to promise, or some sacrifice we do not wish to make! Sometimes, too, we avoid his eyes; sometimes, too, we close our ears to his divine appeal.... Such shall be our conduct no longer. Let us rather say, "Speak, Lord, for your servant hears."

Let us open the "ears" of our heart, and Jesus will say to us as he did in the Gospel:

"If you knew the gift of God, and who it is who says to you, 'Give Me to drink,' you perhaps would have asked of Him; and He would have given you living water...springing up into life everlasting."

"Come, follow Me...."

"What would you have Me do for you?..."

"Why are you weeping?..."

"If you have faith like a mustard seed!.."

"Do you love Me more than these?..."

"If you want to be perfect, abandon all things and come, follow Me...."

"Give Me your heart...."

"Take courage, I am the Good Shepherd...."

"I looked for someone to comfort Me, but I found none.... Can I count on you?..."

"Could you not, then, watch one quarter hour with Me?..."

"If you, too, could understand, above all in this day given you, the ways that can bring you peace!... I was willing...but you were not willing...."

"I forgave you your debt because you entreated Me. Why have you not been merciful to your neighbour? Why do you hold these grudges in your heart?

And so on. What wonderful things our Lord would say to us, if we knew how to listen!

3. *Speak to Jesus*

We, in turn, converse with our Lord. We speak to him simply and sincerely, as to a friend.

We start by thanking Him for coming to us. We talk to Him of our love for Him. . .our wishes. . .our worries. . .our sins. . .our temptations. . .our plans. . .our joys. . .our troubles. . .our apostolate. . .our parents. . our friends. . .our enemies. . .sinners to be converted. . .all the Church's needs, etc.

Farther on, you will find a model thanksgiving, wherein you will note still more things that we can say to God in these precious moments after Communion.

4. *Ask of Jesus*

We possess God in our hearts and have nothing to ask him? Nothing? "Ask and you shall receive. Hitherto, you have not asked for anything," said Jesus to his apostles.

We ought to avoid drawing down the same reproach upon our heads! How many favours we have to ask for! Here again, read the Gospel and see how our Lord loves to answer the prayers of those who pray to him in faith and love.

Here we see Jairus who has just lost his little twelve-year old daughter. "Do not be afraid," Jesus told him. Only have faith and she shall be saved." And the little girl arose!

Again, we see the widow of Naim, whose son had just died. This poor widow was following the bier. She does not run and fall at Jesus' feet. Wrapped in grief and blinded by tears, she does not even see Him! But Jesus sees *her*—is moved by this silent woe. He cannot bear to see this poor mother suffer any longer. "Do not weep," He said to her, and restored the young man alive to his mother!

Here we see the centurion whose servant was at the point of death and who asks Jesus to save him. "I will come," said Jesus, "and cure him."

These are all the miracles of Jesus we need mention here to demonstrate the power of prayer. The Lord is ever ready to listen. Night and day, he urges us to pray. And we shall never leave him without having been comforted and solaced.

During our thanksgiving, then, we shall beg Jesus for spiritual and temporal graces or favours for ourselves and others:

Graces of detachment from creatures, and of union with God.

Graces of illumination and strength for performing the duties of our state in life.

Graces of fervour and of sanctity.

Graces of patience and of obedience to God's will.

Graces for overcoming temptation and bad habits.

Graces for exercising a fruitful apostolate.

We would never finish listing the many favours we can beg of Jesus. Let each one ask according to his needs, always avoiding selfishness in his prayers. As in the Mass, let us pray for one another and we shall be more readily heard.

5. *Give to Jesus*

Some people are always asking for things, but never think of giving!

Jesus gave us everything we have, and then gave himself wholly to us!

What are we offering Him in return?

Perhaps a generous resolution too long deferred?

A renunciation? A detachment too long unbroken yet?

A reparation too long refused? . . .

A bad habit too long cherished?

A susceptibility we ought to root out? Etc.

If we would have our Communions always good and fervent, let us also precede and follow them with sacrifice. Sometimes we feel ourselves so overwhelmed by our own infirmities and misery and the immenseness of the graces received, that our hearts cannot be otherwise than generous to prove their love. Sacrifice is then the response of human love to the love of a God who died for us!

Let us not be satisfied with fine words and promises. Our sincerity is proved by deeds!

Let us say, as we make an act of oblation of our whole being to God, this beautiful prayer written by Abbé Edward Poppe, an eminent Belgian Tertiary:

"My Jesus, I give You my hands to do Your work and to distribute Your blessings.

"I give You my feet, to follow in Your footsteps.

"I give You my eyes for You to direct their vision, and make them glow with mildness.

"I give You my mind, that it may think like You.

"I give You my tongue, that it may speak Your words of wisdom, Your words of love and pardon.

"I give You my soul, that You may teach it to pray.

"Especially do I give You my heart, that You may fill it with love for Your Heavenly Father and for all men, my brothers.

"Let my personality be effaced, and Yours develop in me; so that it may no longer be 'I' who live, work, and pray, but You, O Jesus.

"Jesus living in Mary, live in us, Your servants.

"I want to disappear in You, so that You may appear in me and in my stead. . .so that You may continue in me, untrammeled, Your priestly life of praise to the glory of the Father, Your life diffused in the Church.

"Life of Jesus, vivify me.

"Look of Jesus, transfigure my eyes.

"Gospel of Jesus, speak through my lips.

"Light of Jesus, fill my heart and beam from it.

"Love of Jesus, burn within my soul and in my words.

"Meekness and humility of Jesus, permeate my whole life!

"Spirit of Jesus, be my spirit! Amen!"

6. *Radiate the Host*

The man who has received Communion cannot be, should not be, like the man who did not receive! When a lily has been in a room, the room is filled with its fragrance. When incense is burned in the sanctuary, the odour lingers. Thus when the Host has sojourned in our souls, we ought to emit the good odour of Jesus Christ. Like living monstrances, we should show forth Christ, so that people seeing us after each of our Communions may say: "Look! The Blessed Sacrament is passing by!"

If it is the nature of a sacrament to produce what it signifies, then the Eucharist is better designed for that purpose than are the other Sacraments. For it does not merely show us a picture of the loving Christ, suggesting that we should love him, like one of those likenesses of the Sacred Heart inspired to artists by St. Margaret Mary. It is not limited like the other Sacraments to imparting the remote influence of Christ reigning at his Father's right hand. Present in body and soul in our inmost being, Christ warms and inflames our hearts, like a flame giving rise to another flame. "It is fire that I have come to spread over the earth, and what better wish could I have than that it should be kindled?" (Luke 12:49.) [Knox.] Today He desires that this flame of love should continue to spread. To this end, he particularly applies himself in Communion; which completes in each of us individually the work for which he came into the world. Let our contact with this incandescent Source of love set us on fire! After Communion, we ought to be "gulf streams"—these warm currents that raise the temperature and influence all the regions through which they pass. Our touch must melt icy egotism and worldly prejudices! Aversions, rancour, and the clash of conflicting interests which plague our century, must melt and vanish before our flaming words! Then will the door of hearts of humble and proud alike open in a mute evocation of love—according entrance to our Gospel message of goodness, meekness, and love.

Sowers of peace and joy, we shall carry on Christ's mission and that of his servant, Francis of Assisi, Patron of Catholic Action; who recommends to every heart universal brotherhood in the love of our Blessed Lord!

We read in the life of St. Ives (Tertiary and patron of lawyers), that he habitually carried on his person a pyx containing the Holy Eucharist; that he might distribute it to the sick.

After our Communion, we, too, are "Christ-bearers." Now since zeal is the "direct object" of a fervent Communion; we, too, shall bear God to all those souls we meet with on our way, especially those dying of inanition because of non-reception. By means of our transformed lives, our good examples, our edifying words, we shall stimulate others to the practice of virtue. We shall radiate the Host of our Communion, and so prolong—during that day or that week—the thanksgiving of OUR *LIVED* MASS!

369—What is the meaning of the word ARDOR?

ARDOR is used here simply as a memory word to help us remember the principal acts to make during our thanksgiving. Q.E.D. ! :

A—Adore.
R—Return thanks (thanksgiving).
D—Demand (supplication).
O—Offering.
R—Resolution.

A Model for Thanksgiving

O Jesus, I adore You here present within me. With loving boldness, like the Beloved Disciple on the night of the Last Supper, I repose on Your Heart. I myself am a "tabernacle," wherein You repose, surrounded by adoring angels! Jesus, You have said, "He who eats My flesh and drinks My blood, abides in Me, and I in him." I bear Heaven within my heart! My God, how good You are!

I thank You, now, Jesus, for creating and redeeming me, and for having forgiven me so many times!... Especially do I thank You for having given Yourself to me so often in Holy Communion...for the graces You shower down upon me daily, and the calls to goodness which are so many visits from Your divine Heart to my soul....

I implore pardon for my unfaithfulness, for my resistance to grace, my frequent transgressions, my refusals to serve You, my lack of courage in following you to the end!...

Dear God, I kneel here before You...poor...little...destitute... a beggar.... I can do nothing...but You can do all things.... I have nothing.... but You possess all things.... I am weak...but You are strong...I am poor...but You are rich.... I am a sinner...but You are holy.... I am ignorant...but You are learned....

You are my God and my All.... You are my Master.... I belong to You.... Search me and know my heart.... Cut...burn.... Take from my heart whatever in it is not like Yours....

Lord, have You something to say to me?... Speak, for Your servant is listening!...

What do You think of me?

Of my heart? . . . Of my affections? . . . Of my thoughts? . . . Of my intentions? . . . Of my whole life? . . .

Am I a real Christian? . . . A real Tertiary? . . . A real militant of Catholic Action? . . . A really consecrated soul? . . .

What do You want me to do?

To please You, what things must I avoid and give up? Straighten out and purify? . . . Keep and defend? . . . Strengthen and improve? . . .

Tell me, Lord! . . . You know all things. . . . You know how weak I am. . . .

You know my thoughts, my temptations, my worries, my wishes, my needs, and the needs of all those dear to me, and of all those who are to die today. . . .

I leave everything to You, Lord. I trust in You and I know that I shall not be deceived. I am ready for anything. Here I am!

Do you want my time? I give it to You.

Do you want my strength? It is at Your service.

Do you want my life? I sacrifice it to You.

Give me a heart that is steadfast and strong, generous and dauntless, grateful and compassionate. . . .

Jesus, I kneel at Your feet like a most insignificant beggar, but (I know!) a beloved beggar. I plead not for myself alone, but for all mankind.

I recommend to You this person. . .this friend. . .this enemy.

I recommend to You this sick person. . .this sinner. . .this straying soul. . . .

I pray for those who suffer. . .for those who lament. . .for those who weep. . . .

I pray for those who do not pray. . .for those who do not know and love You. . .who insult You. . .for the millions of unbelievers and heretics. . . .

I pray for the Church, the Pope, the Bishops, and priests, for the missionaries and lay apostles who work for the salvation of souls. . . .

I pray for all consecrated souls. . . .

I pray for my confessor and for all those who have done good to me. . . .

I pray for all those who have desired to do me evil or harm me —and I forgive them....

Finally, I pray for myself. I undergo temptation...trouble, sorrow...discouragement...failure... bad habits...falls.... Help me and love me just the same!

O Jesus, above all I ask that I may love You more. O Good Master, Friend divinely good, full of tender mercy, forgive my sins and purify my soul. Make me less unworthy of You; and then, my Jesus, let us truly love each other.

Dwell within me so intimately that I may illumine all about me...that I may shed joy—much joy—and peace, in the souls of those whom You place on my pathway today.

O Jesus, you have proved Your love by dying for me and by giving Yourself to me! I want to prove my love for you by living for You! Yes, Jesus, I love You; and I thank you for all Your goodness. Show me how to prove my gratitude with deeds, for it was not just in words that You loved me!

Today I will love You particularly in this. (Here each mentions his sacrifice or good resolution.)

You are so good! Dear God, make me understand the blessings of the apostleship, the grandeur of my mission, the rôle You desire me to fill in the Third Order, in Catholic Action, in those other groups of which I am a member.

Tomorrow I will come to You again.

"LORD JESUS, YOU WHO HAVE GIVEN SOME AS APOSTLES"

"Help me to remember..."

When confronted by pleasure, modes, a desire to "be in the swim," imposing obstacles, etc., I am often tempted to forget (please help me to remember)—especially when I am alone, with no official title—that I ought always to be a "presence," so that my every action, and my smallest desires, may everywhere be a "light"! Help me to remember....

"That I have charge of souls...."

I am responsible. Here and there, souls wait for me! God has graces for them that are to come only through me. We are on a team—the team is life!

"Make we worthy to be..."

Lord Jesus, despite my frailty and my slips, of really living this work of incarnation, of sowing life in souls, in my environment. By your Incarnation in me, let me never cease to be...

"To youth..."

To those to whom you have united me in this generation, my brothers and sisters in You, those who struggle, who suffer, those...

"Forgetful of You..."

Of You, who think of them, who call them, who offer them Your Strength and Your Love, and for whom You make me...

"A missionary of Your light..."

Just as You were sent by the Father to preach the Good News. I would be to all...

"An apostle of charity, peace, and joy..."

These fruits of the Spirit, first-fruits of Heaven's happiness, authentic effulgence of true sanctity.

Lord Jesus, for this divine mission, in the name of all Your apostles and in my name, I thank You, I offer up my thanks.

THE PRESENCE OF GOD AND PRAYERFULNESS

Accustom yourself gradually to let your mental prayer spread over all your daily external occupations. Speak, act, work QUIETLY as though you were praying. Do everything without excitement, simply, in the spirit of grace. As soon as you perceive natural activity gliding in, recall yourself quietly in the presence of God. Hearken to what is prompted by the leading of grace, and say and do nothing but what the Spirit of God teaches. You will find yourself infinitely more quiet, your words will be fewer and more effectual, and your labours will bear more fruit.

You should try, without any painful effort, to dwell upon God as often as a longing for recollection comes upon you, and not regret that you cannot cultivate it more. It will not do to wait for disengaged seasons, when you can close your door and be alone. The moment in which we crave after recollection is the moment in which to practice it. Turn your heart then and there to God, simply, familiarly, trustfully. The most interrupted seasons may thus be used; not merely when you are out driving, but when you are dressing, even when you are eating and others are talking. Useless and tiresome details in conversation will afford you similar opportunities. Instead of wearying you, they will give you time for recollection. Thus, all things turn to good for those who love God.

—ARCHBISHOP ALBAN GOODIER

PRAYER TO CHRIST CRUCIFIED

(To be said before a crucifix)

O good and sweetest Jesus, / before Your face I humbly kneel, / and with the greatest fervour of spirit, /I pray and beseech You / to fix deep in my heart / lively sentiments of faith, / hope, and charity, / a true sorrow for my sins, / and a firm purpose of amendment, / the while I consider / Your five most precious wounds, / having before my eyes / the words of David, the Prophet, / concerning You, my Jesus: / "They have pierced my hands and my feet. / They have numbered all my bones."

10 years every time. A plenary indulgence after Communion under the conditions of Confession and Communion and prayers for the Holy Father's intentions. (Our Father, Hail Mary and Glory Be.)

A PRAYER FOR PRIESTS

Keep them, I pray Thee, dearest Lord,
Keep them, for they are Thine,
Thy priests whose lives burn out before
Thy consecrated shrine.
Keep them,—Thou knowest, dearest Lord
The world, the flesh are strong.
And Satan spreads a thousand snares
To lead them into wrong.
Keep them, for they are in the world
Though from the world apart;
When earthly pleasures tempt, allure,
Shelter them in Thy heart.
Keep them, and comfort them in hours
Of loneliness and pain
When all their life of sacrifice
For souls seems but in vain.
Keep them, and oh remember, Lord,
They have no one but Thee;
Yet they have only human hearts
And human frailty.
Keep them as spotless as the Host
That daily they caress—
Their every thought, and word and deed,
Deign, dearest Lord, to bless.

(Author unknown)

THE PRAYER OF ST. BONAVENTURE

Seraphic Doctor of the thirteenth century

O most sweet Lord Jesus Christ, pierce the very marrow of my soul with the delicious and health-giving dart of Your love, with a true, tranquil, apostolic, and most holy charity; so that from sheer love and desire of You, I may faint and melt away, longing for You and fainting in Your courts, desiring to be dissolved and be with You. Vouchsafe that my soul may ever hunger for You, O Bread of Angels, food of holy souls, our daily bread, full of strength and sweetness, bread in which those who eat of it, find every sweet delight! O You, whom the one desire of Angels is to contemplate forever, may my soul hunger for You, and feed on You; and may it be filled with the sweetness which comes from having tasted of You! For You may my soul forever thirst, O font of life, source of wisdom and all understanding, river of eternal light, torrent of delight, riches of God's house. May I have no other ambition than to possess You; may I seek You and find You; may I ever follow You and ever reach You; may I think only of You, speak only of You, and do all things for the honour and glory of Your holy name. May I be humble and discreet, loving and joyous, willing and eager, persevering to the end. And You, O Jesus, be ever my only hope, all my trust, my wealth, my delight, my love, my joy, my tranquility and my repose. Be my peace and my sweetness, my pleasing perfume, a goodly taste, my food, my Comforter, my refuge, my help, my wisdom, my inheritance, my wealth and my possession! In You alone, O Jesus, in You fast-fixed, may I, in heart and soul, deep-set be rooted, nor thence be moved forevermore. Amen.

LOVE OF CHRIST CRUCIFIED

All the nails in the world could not have held Christ to the Cross, were it not for the mighty bond of his love for us. Before Christ crucified, we must needs fall on our knees and cry with St. John, "I know Him who is Love and believe in Him." Love breathes everywhere from the Cross. The wounds of Christ crucified are as so many mouths crying out to me: "Behold, My child, and know whether or not I love you! For I have loved you as one mad, have loved you even to the 'folly of the Cross' ! "

Ah, but did I but know how to look upon even once, as I should, Christ crucified! Then I would understand; then I would believe; would surrender self! How can I help loving a God who has loved me so much?

If I love so little, it is because I have not looked upon Him as I ought, especially at those beautiful, divine eyes, which from the summit of the Cross—dimmed with tears and blood—sought me down the distance of the centuries and looked upon me with an expression of suppliant tenderness. "Child, are you not willing to believe in My love, and to give Me your love, all your love, without reserve? Have I not done enough for you? Have I not paid dearly for you?"

And this is what He says to me whenever I look at Him.

I must love You, my Jesus! Make me love You!

And this is how, with God's grace and a little good will, ALL OF YOUR MASS CAN BE LIVED 24 hours a day and 365 days a year!

May this study of the Mass have helped you to understand and love our Lord better!

May you have understood as well that the Mass—centre of our lives—is the chief means of glorifying the Blessed Trinity; and of effecting, through Christ, our return to the Father's House.

May our whole life be a continuous participation in the Mass—an offertory, a consecration, and a communion with Christ and with his Mystical Body. For then we shall become saints, and even great saints—and never will we consent by our own fault to miss a single Mass!

ARGUMENT

People do not argue with the wind—they simply close the window.
People do not argue with a fire—they simply throw water on the flames.
People do not argue with poison—they simply do not drink it.
Likewise:
One does not argue with Satan—one simply sends him away.
One does not argue with vicious friends—one simply avoids them.
One does not argue with a bad book—one simply throws it away.
One does not argue with one's duty—one simply performs it.
One does not argue with the Gospel—one simply practices it.
One does not argue with God—one simply serves and adores him.

A SPOKEN CHORALE ON THE MASS

•

THE MASS PRELUDE

First tableau: Lord, we have need of truth; illumine us.

Christ, the Choirmaster: I am the Way, the Truth, and the Life. / Come unto Me and you shall have light and life.

First Chorus: Lord, / we confess our sins / that we may come to You. (Confiteor.)

Second chorus: Lord, we are reconciled with our neighbour, so that we may be permeated by the light. *(The kissing of the altar.)*

Third Chorus: Lord / unto You we lift up our hearts / that we may possess life. *(Incensing of the altar.)*

Christ, the Choirmaster: Now you must desire Me, / call Me, / and receive Me.

First Chorus: Lord, / we desire You. *(Introït.)*

Second Chorus: Lord, / we call You. *(The Kyrie.)*

Third Chorus: Lord, we would receive You, / You, the glory of the Father. *(Gloria.)*

Christ, the Choirmaster: To desire Me and hear My voice, / one must be drawn by My Father.

The three Choruses: We humbly desire this grace. *(Collect.)*

Christ, the Choirmaster: To respond to My voice, / you must consent to be illumined by My doctrine.

The three Choruses: Our desire and will is to be illumined by your doctrine. *(Epistle.)*

Christ, the Choirmaster: Hearing My voice and responding to My call is not enough. / You must follow in My train, in My steps. . . .

The three Choruses: We would follow in Your train and in Your steps, O Lord. *(Gradual.)*

N.B. Although treating of the Mass, this spoken chorale should not be said during celebration of the Holy Sacrifice. It may be used instead during a catechism instruction or a forum on the Mass.

Christ, the Choirmaster: Do you know what will spur you on in My train, in your combats?

The three Choruses: Joy, that proceeds from Your grace, / O Lord. *(Alleluia.)*

Christ, the Choirmaster: And from whence do you derive this joy in My service?

First Chorus: From self-denial!

Second Chorus: From love of neighbour!

Third Chorus: From love of God!

The three Choruses: From the Gospel, O Lord. *(Gospel.)*

Christ, the Choirmaster: And do you believe the Gospel with all the fervour of your soul?

The three Choruses: We believe, / O Lord. *(Creed.)*

Christ, the Choirmaster: Because life, / before being a conquest and a witness, / is a gift, / what is to be your attitude toward the Heavenly Father?

The three Choruses: We shall offer You to the Father and ourselves with You, / since every perfect gift comes to us through You / from the Father of light. *(Offertory.)*

THE OFFERTORY

Second tableau: Lord, we have need of peace. Reconcile us with Your Father and among ourselves.

Christ, the Choirmaster: Behold the solemn hour of My Oblation to the Father. / Unite yourselves with Me.

First Chorus: Almighty Father, / we offer You Christ, our Peace, / and ourselves with Him. *(Suscipe.)*

Second Chorus: Almighty Father, look less upon our sins than upon the sweet Victim, / Jesus, come down to us in humility and love. *(In spiritu humilitatis.)*

Third Chorus: Purify, O Lord, our minds and hearts, / so that we may become in every way, / victims pleasing to You. *(Lavabo.)*

The three Choruses: Holy Trinity, / make our hearts to be in accord with Christ, / our Master. *(Suscipe, Sancta Trinitas.)*

Christ, the Choirmaster: Unite yourselves in mind and heart with My priest, for he is one with Me.

The three Choruses: We beseech You, O Lord, / to accept the Sacrifice from his hands, / to the praise and glory of Your name, / for our spiritual benefit, / and that of the whole Church. *(Suscipiat Dominus.)*

Christ, the Choirmaster: Your life should be a silent prayer, / and prayer the atmosphere of your whole existence.

The three Choruses: May the silent supplications / of the priest / bring this to pass. *(Secret.)*

Christ, the Choirmaster: Your life should be a song of praise, / a prelude to that of Heaven.

The three Choruses: We associate the whole Creation in our Offering, / O Lord, / the better to thank You here below and on high. *(Preface.)*

Christ, the Choirmaster: Be grateful to the Trinity for having associated you with his happiness.

The three Choruses: May all Heaven unite with us / to sing the sanctity of the Father, Son, and Holy Ghost. *(Sanctus.)*

THE CONSECRATION

Christ, the Choirmaster: Do you consent to be consecrated as Host with Me, your Head? / With My earthly representatives /—the Pope, bishops, and priests?

The three Choruses: We do consent, O Lord. *(Te igitur.)*

First Chorus: Remember, O Lord, Your servants and handmaidens.

Second Chorus : Especially all those present at Your Sacrifice.

Third Chorus: Or who are unable / to unite their offerings to Yours / for the glory of the Heavenly Father and the redemption of their souls. *(Memento.)*

Christ, the Choirmaster: Do you consent to carry out the crucifying obligations / that your consecration as baptized, comfirmed, and offering Christians at Mass / imperatively imposes on you?

The three Choruses: We do consent, O Lord, / fully to carry out our obligations as baptized, confirmed, and offering Christians at Mass. *(Communicantes.)*

Christ, the Choirmaster: Unite yourselves to Me, / so that your whole life / may pass into what will soon become My Body and My Blood.

The three Choruses: We unite ourselves, O Lord, / to Your Oblation, / so that ours may become what You wish, *(Quam oblationem)*, that is, full and pleasing to God. *(Hanc igitur.)*

Christ, the Choirmaster: Be recollected. / The consecration of the Offering / is about to be consummated.

First Chorus: Christ, the Master, / is about to offer himself as a holocaust / for our ransom. *(Qui pridie.)*

Second Chorus: It is no longer bread, / but the Body of Christ. *(Hoc est enim Corpus meum.)*

Third Chorus: It is no longer wine, / but the Blood of Christ. *(Hic est enim Calix Sanguinis mei.)*

Christ, the Choirmaster: Remember what I have done for you.

The three Choruses: Make the remembrance of this oblation and this sacrifice / O Lord, / pervade this day and our whole life. *(Unde et memores.)*

Christ, the Choirmaster: I consent to consecrate this Memorial in your lives, / if you will do for your neighbour / what I have done for you.

The three Choruses: May the virtue of Your Precious Body and Your Precious Blood / effect this in us and through us, / *(Supra quae)* we beseech You, O Lord. *(Supplices.)*

First Chorus: Be mindful, O Lord, / of our Dead. *(Memento.)*

Second Chorus: Vouchsafe that we all may attain to our Heavenly Home. *(Nobis quoque peccatoribus.)*

Third Chorus: To enjoy the vision and possession of God, / through all eternity. *(Per ipsum, Per omnia.)*

Christ, the Choirmaster: To act through Me, with Me, and in Me, on earth, while awaiting Heaven, / what have I told you to do?

The three Choruses: To pray, but above all to live, the Our Father. *(Pater Noster.)*

Christ, the Choirmaster: On what conditions may you be reconciled with the Father?

First Chorus: By hallowing His blessed Name. *(Sanctificetur Nomen tuum.)*

Second Chorus: By working for the extension of His Kingdom. *(Adveniat Regnum tuum.)*

Third Chorus: By doing His divine Will. *(Fiat voluntas tua.)*

Christ, the Choirmaster: On what conditions may you be reconciled among yourselves?

First Chorus: By approaching the Holy Table / to receive You. *(Panem nostrum.)*

Second Chorus: By sincerely—with Your graces—/ forgiving our neighbour. *(Et dimitte.)*

Third Chorus: By victory over temptation. *(Et ne nos inducas.)*

The three Choruses: By being delivered from all evil / with Your grace, O Lord. *(Sed libera nos a malo.)*

Christ, the Choirmaster: What I have done for you, / do also to others.

First Chorus: The Mass brings to mind / what God has done for every one of us.

Second Chorus: Communion gives us the strength to do for our neighbour / what Christ has done for every one of us.

Third Chorus: Let us prepare ourselves, then, with this intention, / to receive the Bread of the Strong / and the Wine that makes Virgins.

COMMUNION

Third tableau: Lord, we have need of love. Reign over us!

Christ, the Choirmaster: To prepare yourselves to receive Me, / you must acknowledge your wretchedness, / forgive your neighbour for the wrong he has done, / and trust in My mercy.

Frist Chorus: We acknowledge our wretchedness, O Lord. / Have mercy on us. *(Libera nos.)*

Second Chorus: We sincerely forgive our neighbour. / Grant us Your peace. *(Pax Domini. Pax tecum.)*

Third Chorus: Lamb of God, who take away the sins of the world, / reign over us by Your great love. *(Agnus Dei.)*

Christ, the Choirmaster: Since you are ready to receive Me, you must beseech Me, and likewise the Father and the Holy Ghost, / that this Communion may have its desired effect.

First Chorus: For this, we have recourse to the Divine Goodness. (First Communion prayer: *Domine Jesu Christe.)*

Second Chorus: May the Divine Sacrament deliver us from eternal woe, / and preserve us in charity and love. (Second Communion prayer: *Domine Jesu Christe.)*

Third Chorus: May this Communion / be for us an assurance of everlasting life, and not of reprobation. *(Perceptio Corporis.)*

The Three Choruses: We are not worthy, / but You are almighty and merciful. *(Domine, non sum dignus.)*

Christ, the Choirmaster: In return for so great a benefit, / everyone who has offered himself to Me through the priest / must be clothed with the sentiments of the priest.

First Chorus: Gratitude is essential. *(Quid retribuam Domino.)*

Second Chorus: And purity of heart, / mind, and body. *(Quod ore sumpsimus.)*

Third Chorus: And godlike and brotherly love / in Christ and through Christ. *(Corpus tuum.)*

Christ, the Choirmaster: Your Communion should fill you with joy, / humility, / and with utter trust in the Father.

First Chorus: Lord, preserve us in that true joy / of which You alone are the Master. *(Communion antiphon.)*

Second Chorus: Jesus, meek and humble of heart, / make our hearts resemble Yours. *(Postcommunion.)*

Third Chorus: Preserve us in truth, peace, and love, / so that the Mass may become our life / in all assurance and fullness. *(Ite, missa est.)*

Christ, the Choirmaster: For this, My priestly prayer / must not be just words, / but permeate your whole life.

First Chorus: May the Holy Trinity / help us to this end. *(Placeat tibi, Sancta Trinitas.)*

Second Chorus: May the priest's blessing / impart to us the power that comes from the Cross. *(Benedicat vos.)*

Third Chorus: May Christ's Holy Gospel / bring us the truth, peace, and love we so need, / and may Christ reign over us. Amen. *(Last Gospel.)*

—Fr. Dominic Bonin, O.F.M.

* * *

THE LITURGICAL YEAR

●

A PROGRAM OF SPIRITUAL LIFE TAKEN FROM THE LITURGY

These few notes on the liturgy are a supplement to our study of the Mass.

L 1—What does Pope Pius XII teach us about the liturgical seasons in his encyclical, *Mediator Dei et hominum*"?

After saying that *"Jesus Christ is the centre of the liturgy,"* the Holy Father adds: "Sacred liturgy proposes to have all believers participate in the mysteries of Jesus Christ, those of his humiliation and hidden years, and those of his redemption and triumph."

Speaking of the *liturgical seasons,* His Holiness continues: "Thanks to those arrangements and dispositions of the liturgy, which permit it to propose the life of Jesus Christ at determined periods for our mediation, the Church places the examples we are to imitate before our eyes, indicating the treasures of sanctity we may appropriate to ourselves. For whatever is sung with the lips, must be believed with the mind; and whatever the mind believes must enter into our private and public lives."

The Holy Father next gives us briefly the characteristic note of each liturgical season:

ADVENT: "During the holy time of Advent, the Church arouses in us the consciousness of the sins we have committed. She exhorts us to curb our desires and voluntarily to mortify our bodies, in order to compose ourselves by devout meditation; and to give ourselves over to ardent longings to return to God; who alone, by his grace, is able to deliver us from our sins and from their evil consequences."

CHRISTMAS: "With the return of our Redeemer's birth, it seems to bring us back to the cave of Bethlehem, there to learn the absolute necessity of being born again and of radically reforming ourselves; which can only be possible when we unite ourselves intimately and vitally with the Word of God made man, and become partakers of his divine nature to which we have been elevated."

EPIPHANY: "By the solemnities of the Epiphany, she recalls the vocation of the Gentiles to the Christian faith, intending thereby for us to give thanks daily to God for this great blessing; for us to seek with great faith the true and living God; to apply ourselves to acquiring a deep and devout knowledge of spiritual realities; and to take delight in meditation and silence, so that we may more easily contemplate and receive heavenly gifts."

SEPTUAGESIMA: "At Septuagesima and during Lent, our Mother the Church indefatigably insists that each of us should consider his miseries and apply himself to a real reform; and especially that he should detest his sins and blot them out with prayer and penance. For it is by persevering prayer and regret for our sins, that we obtain that divine aid without which all our efforts are vain and fruitless."

PASSIONTIDE: "In that holy time when the liturgy places the cruel suffering of Jesus Christ before our eyes, the Church invites us to Calvary, there to follow in the steps of our Divine Redeemer; so that we may willingly carry the Cross with him and awaken in our minds his sentiments of expiation and propitiation, and all die together with him."

EASTER: "With the paschal solemnities which commemorate Christ's triumph, our souls are penetrated with a deep inner joy. It is therefore fitting to remember that united to the Redeemer, we must also rise from a cold and dead life to a more fervent and holy one, fully and generously giving ourselves to God and forgetting this miserable world to aspire to Heaven alone. 'If you have risen with Christ, seek the things that are above. . .mind the things that are above.' "

PENTECOST: "Finally, comes the time of Pentecost. The Church then exhorts us by her teaching and works to be docile to the action of the Holy Spirit, who enflames our souls with the fire of divine charity;

so that progressing daily with greater eagerness in virtue, we may become holy like Christ our Lord and his Father in Heaven."

The encyclical concludes this passage as follows:

"The liturgical year must be envisioned as a hymn of praise, which the family of Christians causes to ascend to the Heavenly Father through Christ, its perpetual Conciliator. It also demands of us a diligent and sustained effort, so that every day we may better know and love our Redeemer. It likewise requires our application and tireless effort to imitate His mysteries and to walk willingly in His sorrowful way, so as finally to share in His glory and eternal beatitude."

A little farther on, the Holy Father notes that "through the course of the liturgical year, not only the mysteries of Jesus Christ are celebrated, but also the feasts of the saints in Heaven. By means of these feasts, the Church continues to pursue—albeit in an inferior and subordinate order—the same end; namely, to propose models of sanctity to the faithful, thus moving them to put on the virtues of the Divine Redeemer."

In the first rank must be placed the *Blessed Virgin.*

Such are the broad lines of the encyclical, *Mediator Dei,* on the subject of the cycle of the mysteries of the liturgical year. In accordance with the desire of the Supreme Pontiff, we shall come back to these leading ideas, in quest of all the riches they contain, with a view to Christian LIVING of them.

L 2—What part does the liturgy play in our lives?

We have two "men" inside us—the "old" man and the "new" man (Rom. 6:6); the "carnal" and the "spiritual" (Rom. 7:14); the "child of wrath" and the "son of God." (Eph. 2:3; Rom. 8:15.) We have two "lives," two "minds," two ways of thinking and acting, the one, *natural* and *earthly;* the other, *spiritual* and *Christian.*

Now the Christian's one business on earth is to become a *little more spiritual every day.* Every moment of our lives we have to *choose* between God's voice and the voice of the flesh or the Devil. The Christian life, the Christian mentality, must be impressed on our worldly minds, baptizing them, disinfecting them, and perfuming them with the "good odour" of Christ; so that we may come to think, will, and act like our Lord himself, our Perfect Model. "Have this mind in you which was also in Christ Jesus," St. Paul tells us. (Phil. 2:5.)

As a means of realizing this ideal, the liturgy offers itself to us and presents to us in simple language—because it is addressed as much to the senses as to the intellect—Jesus and his doctrine of life, his Blessed Mother, and his friends the saints, his perfect imitators. The liturgy is thus as it were the Church's yearly "catechism" for *adults*. It is the form of spiritual life offered for life to the faithful. The duty, then, devolves upon educators to prepare children to understand the liturgy, and to accustom them to spiritual living in accordance with its *seasons, prayers,* and *gestures.* Otherwise, there is bound to be a gap between one's catechism training and one's Christian life.

A PRAYER FOR THE ABSENT

•

O Lord, in whose presence is delight, and so have willed to be ever present in our midst;

You who have said, "My delight is to be with the children of men,"

And who added, "Behold, I am with you all days, even to the consummation of the world," you are not ignorant of the fact that one of the infirmities and miseries of our earthly existence is the absence of those whom we love.

O God, cause the inevitable pain which comes from the absence of our friends, to be useful for our salvation and serve to atone for our past sins.

Make those absent to be protected by your presence, illumined by your light, and sanctified by your grace.

Let them never be absent from your heart, or from our hearts.

But may they ever abide in communion of spirit, sentiment, and hope with you, O God, who are true Life.

And with us who implore the grace to love them with a holy love like yours. Amen.

L 3—What do we mean by "liturgical year"?

The liturgical year is the *living film of Jesus*: a film that "unwinds" in the course of the Church year, from the first Sunday of Advent till the last Sunday after Pentecost.

Daily, and especially on Sunday, the Church recalls a part of the story of Christ and his Kingdom. The Church takes twelve months—a whole year—to go over the whole story. This is known as the liturgical year. It does not begin on the first of January, *but toward the close of November.* It is not divided into months, but into several *periods* of varying length, called the *liturgical seasons.* The liturgical seasons together make up the liturgical year. The *manual* for this adult "catechism class" is the missal.

During the liturgical year, the Church is not content with recalling the story of God's Kingdom—this is not necessarily a class in history. When the Church relates the events in the lives of Christ and the saints, her chief aim is to make us LIVE like Christ and the saints. Every liturgical season has its special Christian way of thinking, feeling, and acting. Thus Advent is a time of waiting, of spiritual longing; Lent, of penitence; Easter, of joy, etc.

L 4—Please give a complete division of the liturgical year.

The liturgical year is divided into two cycles: two non-consecutive, but inter-related frameworks.

A. *The temporal cycle,* or proper of the time, celebrates the mysteries of the life of Christ.

B. *The cycle of the saints,* or proper of the saints, celebrates the life of Christ in the souls of his faithful ones—the saints.

The temporal cycle is subdivided into *two periods*:

1. *The Christmas cycle,* or the Incarnation.
2. *The Easter cycle,* or the Redemption.

1. *The Christmas cycle comprises three periods*:

   a. *Advent*: preparation for Christ's coming.
   b. *The Feast of Christmas*: the birth of Christ.
   c. *The time after Epiphany*: Christ's hidden life.

2. *The Easter cycle likewise comprises*:

a. *A period of preparation*: Septuagesima, Lent, and Passiontide.

b. *The solemnities themselves*: Easter and Pentecost.

c. *The time after Pentecost*: The application by the Church of the fruits of the Redemption.

ADVENT

L 5—What is recalled by the Advent season?

Advent is the first part of the liturgical year. It lasts about a month and comprises four Sundays before Christmas.

Advent recalls the centuries of waiting for the Messiah after the fall of the first man. Hence, it is the beginning of all world history, from Adam (first to be redeemed) to Christ (Redeemer of all men).

The centre of this first cycle is *Christmas*, which is prepared for by *Advent* and continued by the *Epiphany*.

L 6—What should be our soul's attitude during Advent?

During *Advent,* we should instill a *great desire* in our heart to receive Jesus; that is, to bear an inner resemblance to him. We ought, then, to prepare our souls for the second (spiritual) coming of Jesus in our hearts by means of sanctifying grace, either repossessed or augmented. We shall furnish proof of this great desire by much prayer in union with Isais (the most complete of the messianic prophets), with St. John the Baptist (the precursor of the Messiah), and above all, with the Divine Saviour's Mother, the Blessed Virgin.

We shall increase this great desire by wishing for millions of Confessions and fervent Communions for our Lord on Christmas, for genuine conversions, and for graces of sanctification for multitudes of generous souls. In so doing, we shall imitate the zeal of the Jews in olden times, who waited four thousand years for the Messiah's coming!

We shall choose our ejaculatory prayers from among the words and chants of the liturgy: *"Lord, come to me!"—"Come in the soul of...*

and. . . !"—"Come on earth everywhere!"—"Lord, prepare my heart to receive You; come and tarry not!"

We shall love to sing the songs and hymns of Advent: *Rorate caeli* ("Let the heavens distill dew"), *Come, O Divine Messiah, Alma Redemptoris Mater,* and the great "O" antiphons, followed by the *Magnificat,* etc.

Our Communions will be better prepared. We shall ask the Blessed Virgin for her spirit of recollection, of union with Jesus living in her, for her desire to give him to everyone she met, etc.

We shall impose some penances on ourselves, especially on the Wednesdays, Fridays, and Saturdays of Advent, and on the vigils of the Immaculate Conception and of Christmas. Formerly, in the sixth century, a fast of forty days was imposed on all the faithful in preparation for the feast of Christmas. Today, this luxury is reserved for monks! Thus, Franciscans prepare for the feast of Christmas by a fast beginning on the feast of All Souls, the first of November!

Today the fasts of the Ash Wednesday, the Good Friday, and the vigil of the Immaculate Conception and the second day before Christmas are the only ones of obligation. And even so, people will find ways to dispense themselves from them! . . . Poor health!

L 7—How does the Church, in her rubrics, show forth the spirit of Advent?

In order to point out that the time of Advent is a time of *purification* (and not of joy), of *expectation* (and not of possession), she has the priest who celebrates Mass do so in violet-coloured vestments. *Violet,* the colour of Lent and Advent, is a *sign of penance.*

The *Gloria* (the hymn indicated to salute Christ's coming at Christmas) is not said in the Mass. The *Ite, missa est* and the *alleluias* are omitted.

Marriages with solemn nuptial Masses and the nuptial blessing are not permitted, etc.

L 8—What is the theme for the Sundays of Advent?

The dominant theme here is expectation, the desire for Jesus' coming.

First Sunday of Advent: This desire arises first of all from the depths of misery of man shackled by sin. It is a poignant cry for help: "None of them that wait on You shall be confounded." (Introït.)

Second Sunday: The light approaches; hope changes into the certitude of deliverance: We shall have our Liberator!

Third Sunday: Irresistibly, this certitude releases the sober but sincere joy of Gaudete Sunday. "Rejoice!" intones the choir leader at the Introït. Violet is changed to rose.

Fourth Sunday: At last the awaited Liberator is named—He will be called Jesus! The Son of a Virgin who already dwells in our midst.... He will come and not tarry.

Last week: During the seven days immediately preceding the feast of the Nativity, the great "O" antiphons of the Magnificat announce Christ's coming for "tomorrow": *O Wisdom, O Adonai, O Root of Jesse, O Emmanuel, etc.*

Advent is a time of *profound silence* and of *intense prayer*. As Christmas nears, we ought to become more composed, more recollected. *"You will become heroic,"* a soul was told, *"only on that day when you become completely recollected within."*

Wherever we go, let us cultivate inner silence, become more calm. Let us watch over our senses, especially our eyes and tongue! Let us be less eager for news of the world than for the *Good News*....

THE VALUE OF A COMMUNION

Ah, Christians, if even once you have understood the value of a Communion, never at the cost of the thing you most prize, will you be willing to let a single day pass without sitting down to the eucharistic Feast. "So great is my desire for Holy Communion," wrote St. Margaret Mary, "that if I had to walk barefoot over a path of fire, I think that the pain would be nothing, compared to deprivation."

Listen to this model of devotion to the Sacred Heart. We ought to engrave these words in our hearts and regulate our conduct by them. Remember that devotion to the Sacred Heart is devotion to the FLOUTED love of our Lord. Hence, the soul truly devoted to the Heart of Jesus, seeks to increase the love of God in her by the most efficacious means. She strives to console the Sacred Heart by the most effective means; namely, Holy Communion... And she should never rest until she has made a resolve to communicate every morning.

The Child — God's Image

●

Some one had said—
"Your little girl is like a doll!
With her charming ways, chubby face,
Little hand uplifted,
And fingers wide apart!"

"Perhaps," concedes the invisible mother,
Who from the room corner smiles at her darling,
Whom careless remark has just classed as a toy!

Let us say, rather, Friend,
That this dainty miss is like a small Jesus,
With her transparent, snow-white soul,
Innocent laughter and candid, clear eyes
Reflecting, untarnished, the image of God!
Let us surround childhood with reverence.

"Whoever causes one of these little ones who believe in Me to sin, it were better for him if a great millstone were hung about his neck, and he were thrown into the sea.

(Mark. 9:41).

Ric Photo

The Spinner

Teach me, O Blessed Virgin,
To work the same way that one prays,
With calm and serene recollection,
In silent expectancy.

Just as this humble woman,
Who silently there in the sun,
Spins out the calm thread of her life-span
To the musical whir of her wheel.
(Fit tool for a labour-filled life,
And symbol of fortitude!)

Ric Photo

THE SAVIOUR'S ESCORT

L 9—What are the principal feasts celebrated in December?

The principal feast of the cycle of the saints for the month of December is unquestionably the Feast of the *Immaculate Conception.* (Dec. 8.) This feast shines with a particular lustre, for it was our Lady's *fiat* that gave us the Incarnation! On this great feast day, let us briefly recall the life of the Blessed Virgin—she who alone can lead us to her Divine Son.

In a tiny village of Galilee, called Nazareth, lived a maiden named Mary, of the royal family of David. Her Father was called Joachim and her mother, Ann.

This maiden, at first sight, appeared like many others. She was neither rich nor powerful. And yet, it was she whom God had chosen before the creation of the world to be the Mother of the Messiah. So the Creator made Mary's soul more beautiful than other souls—the fairest he had ever made!

Could we have had a glimpse into Mary's soul, we should very likely have been struck first of all by the fact that this young maiden had never wanted to do anything wrong: to be vain, proud, lazy, self-sufficient, mean, jealous, envious, impure, or greedy. On the contrary, she found it perfectly simple and natural to obey, work, do someone a service, and pray. She was fond of solitude and recollection, so as to converse more easily with God and to read the inspired Scriptures.

If Mary was free from concupiscence; i.e from the desire to do wrong, it was because God, when he created her, gave her his friendship (as he once did to Adam in the Garden of Eden, Mary—the sole exception—was preserved from Original Sin because she was to become the Mother of Christ, and because of Christ's merits. That is why we call her *Mary Immaculate,* that is, the all-pure One, born without the stain of Original Sin.

Not only was Mary's soul free from sin, but she was, in addition, *full of grace* because her soul was filled with God! Unceasingly, Mary kept herself in God's presence, humble, modest, and docile to the teachings of the Holy Spirit. As soon as she had reached the age of reason (which for Mary came early), she presented herself to God to do his will.

Mary must have remarked that others around her—with the exception of her parents, who were saints—committed many sins; and because she had an immense love for God, this must have caused her much suffering. When she was able to read or hear the sacred volumes explained, she understood sin's origin; she learned of the transgressions of her people, and also of the promises that had been made to them. And then she began to long for the Messiah's coming—not a glorious Messiah, an earthly king—but a suffering Messiah, a messenger of peace and charity. She prayed with her whole heart to hasten the coming of this long-awaited Saviour.... And, we already know that Mary's prayer was so perfect, that God was soon to answer it....

So Mary has become a young maiden. In accordance with Jewish custom, a marriage was arranged. Now it was not princes who sought in marriage the future Queen of Heaven. Mary was betrothed to a young workman, a carpenter by trade, called Joseph, and also of the royal family of David. Mary obeyed her parents and consented to become engaged to Joseph. But deep in her heart, she knew that her body and heart belonged wholly to God, and that she herself wanted to be entirely in the service of God's Kingdom. How was this desire, this inner certitude, to be reconciled with married life? Soon, and very probably because of this problem of Mary's, the angel Gabriel came to her to reveal God's plan.

As for Joseph, he was a just man, who must have surmised something of the beauty of Mary's soul. He was happy to have her as his future bride, though ignorant as yet of her "vocation," and of the treasure of purity he was to protect.

Shortly after their betrothal, and six months after the visit of the angel Gabriel to Zachary, the father of St. John the Baptist, the same angel Gabriel was sent to Mary.... Here we ought to re-read the Gospel of St. Luke (Luke 1:25-38), where the story of the Annunciation is told, and the interesting dialogue between the angel and the Blessed Virgin.... *"Hail, Mary, full of grace! The Lord is with you! Blessed are you among women!*

Note the words of the angel. They are the fulfillment of the prophecy of *Nathan* (II Sam. 7:12), the source of the popular expectation of the Messiah.

The angel added: *"It is the Holy Spirit alone who will give you this Child."* It is for this reason that he shall be the Son of God, for *nothing is impossible to God.* Here is a proof. Your cousin Elizabeth, who is aged and barren, will soon give birth to a child.

The Blessed Virgin did not understand everything that was hidden beneath the angel's words. She did understand that her Son was to be the Messiah, the Son of God in a unique way, and that it was God's desire that she should become the Mother of the Messiah. For her, this was enough. She trusted and obeyed.

Mary knew that her son was to be the Messiah, and hence, Israel's Saviour. In accepting the great honour of becoming the Mother of God, she accepted at the same time bitter pain of being the Mother of the Crucified Saviour. She thus consented first and foremost to be God's collaborator in the work of Redemption. Her maternity was first of all in the spiritual order.

(For more details, see William: *Life of Mary.)*

At this time, the greatest event in the history of the world since the fall of our first parents, took place. Eve had disobeyed and caused Adam to disobey, and this disobedience had caused humanity's fall. Mary obeyed, and this obedience merited for us the coming of Christ the Saviour who was to uplift fallen humanity.

Thrice daily, the *Angelus* bell reminds Christians of the coming of the Angel and of Mary's generous response.

The Visitation

Let us again read St. Luke's Gospel. (Luke 1: 39-56.)

Mary must convince her holy parents (for there is no reason for believing them to be dead) that she is to be the Mother of the Messiah. For this, she has a sign to offer, the one of which the angel spoke—the approaching motherhood of her aged and barren cousin Elizabeth. To convince her parents, and also to announce the Messiah's coming to Elizabeth (who is already halfway in the secret), Mary hastens to visit her cousin. She hastens to bring Jesus to others, to make him known. Elizabeth, already alerted by the Holy Spirit, and feeling John the Baptist leap in her womb, believes that Mary is truly the Mother of the Messiah. She believes in the Messiah and felicitates Mary for having believed.

Instead of becoming proud, Mary begins to praise and thank God in his name and in that of his people. She sings the *Magnificat.*

The Marriage of the Blessed Virgin

Mary remained three months with Elizabeth, returning then to Nazareth. She was still as yet only betrothed to Joseph. The latter was then apprised—doubtless by Mary's parents—that she was to become the Mother of the Messiah. At first, Joseph was disconcerted, not knowing what to do. A just and judicious man, he considered quietly breaking off with his fiancee. Then it was, that an angel came to advise him in sleep that his betrothed was to have a Child who would be given her by God, that God was the Father, and that Joseph should take Mary as his wife in order to protect her and the Child. Then Joseph, too, believed. One day, then, Mary was conducted with great pomp to St. Joseph's home. It was the marriage of these two holy personages.

We can imagine how much the pair, who knew their mutual vocation, loved each other with a deep and reverent love.

Awaiting Jesus' birth

While Mary was waiting for her Child, she prepared his tiny layette.... Perhaps Joseph made the cradle?

More than aught else, Mary thinks of what her Son will be! She renews her resolutions to be always his humble servant and to assist him in his "vocation" as God directs. She adores God's mysterious plans and thanks him for having fulfilled his promises. Trustfully she waits and prays. Such should be *our* interior dispositions.

Around this resplendent "Morning Star," are grouped the great heroes of the Christian Faith:

Dec. 2. *St. Bibiana,* virgin and martyr.

Dec. 3. *St. Francis Xavier,* the intrepid spostle of India and Japan.

Dec. 4. *St. Peter Chrysolog,* bishop and doctor, called Chrysolog, "speech of gold," because of his great eloquence. On the same day, feast of St. Barbara, virgin and martyr, invoked against sudden death.

Dec. 6. *St. Nicholas,* Bishop of Myra and defender of the faith in Asia, the protector of childhood.

Dec. 7. *St. Ambrose,* Bishop of Milan and Doctor of the Church.

Dec. 10. *Translation of the Holy House of Loretto.* This feast recalls the miraculous translation by angels of the house of the Holy Family at Nazareth to the little city of Loretto in Italy, where pilgrims may still visit it.

Dec. 11. *St. Damasus,* pope and confessor.

Dec. 12. *Our Lady of Guadalupe,* Patroness of the Americas.

Dec. 13. *St. Lucy,* virgin and thirteen-year old martyr, mentioned in the Canon of the Mass.

Dec. 16. *St. Eusebius,* bishop and martyr.

Dec. 21. *St. Thomas,* one of the twelve Apostles. It is to him that we are indebted for this cry of faith, "My Lord and my God!" which we repeat at the Elevation of the Host.

Dec. 26. *St. Stephen,* deacon, first martyr to shed his blood for faith in Jesus Christ.

Dec. 27. *St. John,* one of the twelve disciples, who was Jesus' favourite. He is called the "Apostle of Love."

Dec. 28. *The Holy Innocents.*

Dec. 29. *Thomas à Becket,* Bishop of Canterbury, martyred in his cathedral.

Dec. 31. *St. Sylvester,* pope and confessor.

In the Franciscan family, for the month of December, we honour several of these humble ones, who, like the shepherds, merited favours from the Infant Christ.

Dec. 1. *BB. Anthony Bonfadini,* priest; *Bentivola* and *Gerard,* Franciscan Brothers.

Dec. 5. *Bl. Nicholas of Tavila,* priest, martyred at Jerusalem by the Turks.

Dec. 11. *Bl. Peter of Siena,* a humble Tertiary, a manufacturer of combs in the fourteenth century, the model of silent souls. He had understood how rare it is to be able to converse with men about spiritual matters; and that the greater part of conversations lie in the realm of business, vanity, and trivialities, when they do not spill over on one's neighbour in the guise of detraction and slander. Peter admitted that it took him fourteen years to succeed in speaking only when obliged to do so by charity or necessity.

Dec. 11. *Bl. Hugolin Magalotti,* hermit Tertiary.

Dec. 13. *The Finding of the Body of St. Francis,* commemorates the joy of finding again, the body of the Saint of Assisi, several centuries after its disappearance.

Dec. 14. *Bl. Conrad of Offida,* zealous, Franciscan missionary of the early days; also *Bl. Bartholomew,* Tertiary priest, and *Bl. Nicholas Factor,* Franciscan priest.

Dec. 15. *Our Lady,* Queen of the Seraphic Order.

Christmas

L 10—What does the Church commemorate on Christmas?

Christmas commemorates the birth of Christ!

The liturgy of this day celebrates Christ's triple birth by three Masses:

1. *His temporal birth* as the Son of Mary (first Mass).
2. *His eternal birth* as the Son of God (second Mass.)
3. *His spiritual birth* in our souls (third Mass).

Christmas commemorates the world census ordered by Caesar Augustus, the painful voyage of Mary and Joseph in obedience to the emperor's edict, the improvised refuge of Mary and Joseph in a cave which served as a stable; the poverty, cold, and abandonment, the miraculous birth of the Child, the first motherly care given the Child (Luke 2:7), the shepherd's visit, the heavenly concert—"Peace to men of good will"—the prompt and enthusiastic visit of these guardians of the sheep, etc.

L 11—What should be our interior dispositions at Christmas time?

Christmas is a feast of inner *peace* and *joy.* Our sentiments, then, will be those of the men of good will who surrounded the crib. We shall have the trust and simplicity of the shepherds, who gave an immediate response to the angelic summons and ran joyously to pay homage to the tiny Babe they acknowledged as their God.... We shall be like St. Joseph, full of faith and reverent before Jesus and his Blessed Mother. Together with our Lady, who cared for the Infant Christ, we shall say, *"I am Yours, in Your service. I will help you in Your task.*

I will save the world with You. And with her, we shall meditate and keep in our hearts all the lesson's of Christ's life.

It will be especially from the Infant Christ that we shall borrow our sentiments. His *extreme humility;* he abased himself in a certain fashion at the Crib by becoming man without ceasing to be God, by taking the lowest place, by his willingness to have the shepherds as his first adorers. Like him, we, too, shall accept the sting of *poverty,* the lack of ease and comfort—contenting ourselves with the strictly necessary. In short, we shall resemble our Divine Saviour, who appeared to us as *a little child, lovable, mild, and smiling,* by practicing *spiritual childhood.*

Jesus chose the Blessed Virgin as his first cradle because she was *pure!* He thereby indicates how pure our hearts should be for his visit in Holy Communion.

L 12—How does the Church express the spirit of Christmas, and how can we prolong the season's liturgy in our home life?

In order to point out that Christmas is a *time of joy,* the Church employs *white* or *gold brocade* for the priest's vestments and for the ornaments of the altar. Flowers, song, and music are all expressive of joy. The *Gloria* is sung in the Mass—the song of the angels on Christmas night. Every church has a reproduction in miniature of the stable of Bethlehem, etc.

As we know, St. Francis of Assisi was one of the first to popularize the mystery of Jesus' birth by reproducing, in the forest of Greccio, the *living tableau* of the Incarnation. An example to be imitated....

The life of the liturgy should not be confined to the inside of the church, but should influence our whole life. *Every home* ought to show that it is Christmas! Mother and Big Sister ought to think out ways of trimming the house and making it look like Christmas. Every home should have its Christmas crèche, before which the family will meet in the evening for prayer.... An excellent means of creating a Christian atmosphere is that of making Jesus the centre of attention for the whole family!... Sickrooms, hospital wards, schoolrooms, etc., are ideal for introducing this manifestation of the life of the liturgy.

Dad or Mother might tell the little ones (and through them, the bigger ones who will end up listening too!) the *beautiful and true stories of Christmas*—of the Annunciation of the Archangel Gabriel to our Lady—of the Visitation—of Caesar's edict—of the departure of Mary and Joseph from Nazareth to Bethlehem (indicating the journey on a map), the crowded inns—the appearance of the angels to the shepherds —the visit to the manger—the Presentation of Jesus in the Temple—the Wise Men and the Star—their long journey and its unforseen events —their adoration—their gifts—Herod's jealousy—the massacre of the Holy Innocents—the Flight into Egypt (with map indications)—the return to Nazareth after Herod's death, etc.

In the same way, on Christmas night the children could be told the story of St. Stephen's martyrdom, in preparation for the morrow's feast. On the eve of the 26th, the life of St. John may be told, on the 28th, the martyrdom of the Holy Innocents, etc.

Our *beautiful folk songs and Christmas carols* should not be forgotten in our family gatherings. Christmas is likewise a time for exchanging gifts in memory of the great Divine Gift, the Incarnation.

Our first gift should be offered to Jesus. *This gift will be our good will* (the effective desire to correct ourselves of such or such a fault, to acquire certain virtues, to avoid even venial sin, to celebrate the Christmas holidays like Christians, leaving liquor out of them), followed up by our alms at the Crib, to poor children, and impoverished families, our Christmas gifts to relatives and friends, etc., to strengthen friendly ties on this feast of brotherly love.

L 13—What feast do we observe on January first, and what traditions should we keep on New Year's Day?

On January first we observe the feast of our Lord's *Circumcision.*

Christ having clothed himself with our human nature, though without sin, nevertheless willed to submit himself to the Law of Moses promulgated for sinners. Now this Old Testament law ordered that all little Jewish boys must be circumcised eight days after birth. This was a purificatory rite, an image of Baptism in the future.

On this occasion, just as today for Baptism, the Jews gave a *name* to the newborn baby. For the Jews, the name expresses the peculiar rôle, the chief characteristic, of the person. That of the Son of Mary was dictated by God himself and revealed by the angel of the Annunciation. The Child was to be called *Jesus,* signifying Saviour. The *Name of Jesus* is so great and rich in meaning, that the Church desires to celebrate it with a special feast. *The Feast of the Holy Name* is set for *the Sunday after the Circumcision.* In the fifteenth century, *St. Bernardine of Siena* championed devotion to the Holy Name.

Coming back to New Year's, let us say that it is customary for us to exchange New Year's greetings. This is a custom worth keeping, provided these wishes are sincere and Christian, and not a mere formality.... How many times has not this exchange of greetings served as the occasion for pardon and reconciliation!... Let us profit, then, by this custom, by ridding our hearts of all ill will and grudges. For the love of Christ who has forgiven us so many times, let us send at least a greeting card with a few words *in our own handwriting* to those who have offended us most deeply. Let us make the first move.

An old tradition is the New Year's Day *blessing* given by the father to his children. The mother could easily accustom her little ones to ask their father for this blessing themselves. In this way, when they grow up, they will carry on this beautiful tradition, which honours human parenthood and draws down rare blessings on the family.

Here is a form of blessing that can be used by fathers of our fine Canadian families:

May God bless you, children,
Even as I bless you.
In the name of the Father, and of the Son
and of the Holy Ghost. Amen.

Finally, we again ask parents to make every sacrifice, so that young people can receive their friends in their homes. In some families, this is strictly forbidden by parents, who lead children by the very fact into the temptation of going outside to look for sometimes undesirable entertainment. If young people go wrong because their friends are not welcome at home, who must answer for it before God?...

Our Christian festivities will be for us occasions of joy or sorrow, according to the use we make of them. Be unselfish and you will be happy!

EPIPHANY

L 14—What does the Feast of the Epiphany commemorate?

The Epiphany, celebrated on January 6, is the greatest liturgical solemnity in the Christian cycle. This feast recalls the *manifestation of Christ* not only—as on Christmas—to his chosen people, the people of Israel; but to the *whole world,* including pagans, represented by the Magi.

Epiphany means *manifestation.* So it is to us that Christ is manifested on this day. We ought to acknowledge his divinity and offer him our gifts.

Who were the Magi?

It is difficult to be dogmatic about them. Popular tradition envisions them as three *kings,* named *Melchior, Balthasar,* and *Gaspar.* Others look upon them as *scholars, astrologers,* whose business it was to scan the heavens. Be that as it may, these Magi knew certain prophecies dealing with the Messiah, such as that of Balaam: "*Behold, a star shall come out of Jacob, a sceptre shall arise out of Israel.* Besides this, they were enlightened by the Holy Spirit, so as to be able to declare: "We have seen His star in the East, and have come to worship Him."

Everybody knows of the great journey made by these pagan Magi, of the disappearance of the star at Jerusalem, of the information requested from Herod, of the latter's uneasiness and jealousy, and finally of the arrival in Bethlehem, where the Magi found the Child Jesus who stretched out his arms to them with a smile.

It is interesting to note that the Holy Family are no longer living in the stable, but in a house in Bethlehem become vacant after the departure of the crowds come for the census. Furthermore, the Magi's visit was doubtless some time after Jesus' birth; since Herod's intent was to slay all children up to two years of age. That Mary should have desired to remain near Jerusalem, where many persons had already acknowledged her Son as the Messiah, instead of returning to Nazareth where incredulity would be total, is understandable. No one is a prophet in his own country.

So after the poor and the Jews (shepherds), Christ drew the rich and pagans to him. We ought to thank our Lord today for saving the whole world.

The Flight into Egypt reminds us that Jesus, still a tiny Babe, already suffered from the wickedness of those he came to save. The closer we live to Christ, the more we shall suffer with him and the greater will be our share in his glorification.

L 15—The time after Epiphany relates Christ's hidden life. Can you tell the story?

The time after Epiphany commemorates *the thirty years of the hidden life of Jesus at Nazareth.* The Gospel tells us very little. However, the little information we do find, and the study of Jewish habits and traditions, suffice to give us an idea of the life led by the Holy Family at Nazareth.

1. *What we see*

Joseph is the head of the family, the one in authority. He is a worker in wood; a cabinetmaker and carpenter, for the people of his home town. The more frequently, no doubt, he works in the courtyard under the shade of a fig tree.... Morning and night he recites in the name of all the profession of faith that he will teach Jesus as soon as the Boy is big enough. On the Sabbath Day, Joseph does not work; but goes to the synagogue, for this is the *Lord's* day.

Every day Mary grinds the flour for their "daily bread" and takes the dough to the village oven to be baked. She goes to the fountain for water. She spins and weaves the flax and wool for the making and mending of tunics. She does the cooking and gathers the fagots for the fire. She washes the clothes, etc.

Jesus, like any small child, stays close to Mary's side. He looks at her, asks her questions, follows her everywhere. As Jesus grows, Mary asks him to help her. Jesus runs errands, plays with his little neighbours, speaks much of God, and loves to pray with Mary....

2. *What we do not see*

In Mary and Joseph. Their feeling of deep reverence toward this mysterious Child, destined to sit on the throne of David. They are in his service. They admire—and meditate.

In Jesus. A great respect for Mary and Joseph, who represent for him the authority of his Father. Deep gratitude, and likewise divine satisfaction with those whom he has chosen to carry out his Father's will.

3. *Jesus at the age of twelve*

Jesus "advanced in age and wisdom before God and men." Up to Jesus' twelfth year, he had not manifested himself as the Messiah. He is simply a pious and obedient child. What great faith Mary and Joseph must have had to recognize the Messiah in this Child! But when Jesus is twelve, an incident reveals that Jesus knew within who he was and why he came, and that he was already working for our salvation.

Now twelve is the age at which a Jewish boy becomes a man, after which he must go in yearly pilgrimage to the Jerusalem Temple. So Jesus goes up to the Temple with his parents and the other inhabitants of Nazareth for the Passover Festival.... What an impression it must have made on Jesus at this age of increased awareness of life, to enter once more into *his Father's Temple* and be present at the offering up of the sacrifice he had come to perfect! Jesus thought of how *he himself* was to be the *Victim* of the Sacrifice of the New Law. Small wonder that he tarried in the Temple and desired to question the Doctors of his people. For his parents find him "listening to" the Doctors in Israel and "asking them questions," as good pupils were wont to do. The Doctors are delighted with his questions and answers. As for Mary and Joseph, they are amazed. They are astonished to see Jesus who has left them thus, and appears unconcerned about them. Mary's motherly instincts prompt her to speak: *"Son! Why did you do so to us?"*

Jesus himself seems astonished. *"Did you not know that I must be about*—that I am on earth *especially* to be about—*My Father's business? It is quite normal for Me to remain in the Temple—and not always to remain with you."*

Jesus wants to make Mary understand that his vocation obliges him to "detach" himself from his earthly family. Mary does not fully understand yet, but she keeps all these things in her heart. Besides, Jesus' hour has not yet come—he becomes again the "ordinary child."

Here, each one may make his personal application. Youths who have heard the call of vocation ought to have the *courage* to leave home to follow Christ. Parents ought to have the generosity to give their children to God without hesitation.

4. *Christ the Worker*

It would appear that Joseph died shortly afterward, for the Gospel makes no further mention of him. No doubt, he died in the arms of

Jesus and Mary. This is why Joseph is the patron of a holy death. Jesus then succeeded Joseph for a decade as the village carpenter. The workmen are proud to have Jesus at their head. Jesus' hands are those of a labourer. His is an obscure life, duty-filled, filled too with neighbourliness.

As Man, Jesus continues to acquire experience of the creation, of man and of God. He observes nature, admires the lilies of the field, is present at seed-time and harvest, at the wheat-growing season. Perhaps he has a plot of earth. He is familiar with good plants and with weeds; he dwells amidst vines, olive trees, and fig trees. He knows the mysterious wind that blows over Palestine and is familiar with weather signs. Perhaps, too, Jesus owned sheep: he knows their habits and the way they act toward their shepherd. He thinks of how he is the Good Shepherd of men.... He knows that the property of salt is to preserve food.... He knows that a lighted lamp is made to give light and not to be covered up.

Jesus studies the people around him. He learns to know men, their good will and their weaknesses.... How easily they commit sin, and often with little malice.

He has seen that pride is the sin that shuts the soul off from grace...that pride is a terrible danger...that kindness and love win unhappy and repentant souls. Incidentally, let us ask ourselves if, because of our stubborn pride, we may not possess one of those souls impervious to grace?... If so, let us hasten to put our house in order by a humble and sincere Confession.

Jesus hears the Bible read and explained in the synagogue. He reads it himself; and understands the mystery of this Jewish history better than do the greatest of the doctors, for to him everything is prophecy and type. He sees himself in *Isaac* bearing the wood of his sacrifice, in *Samuel,* in *David,* in *Jeremias,* in the text of *Isaias* (surnamed "the fifth evangelist," so clearly has he written of the Messiah).

Through nature, men, and the Jewish people, Jesus learns to praise his Father who is so good, who watches over the lilies of the field and the birds of the air—how much more closely, then, over men, for whose salvation he has come to give up his life.

Thus it is that in the obscurity of a humble and toil-filled life, Jesus is not wasting his time. Already his life is of great value for our salvation, because he loves and obeys his Father. In addition he acquires experience for his public life, for which he conscientiously prepares himself. In peace, prayer, and labour, he awaits the moment of his Heavenly Father's signal to start preaching—and he waits for it thirty years!

5. *Lessons from the hidden years*:

Thus out of a life lasting thirty-three years, He who is Eternal Wisdom, willed to pass thirty of them in *silence* and *obscurity,* in *obedience* and *toil!* Herein lies mystery, and a teaching that many devout souls have been unable to grasp in its fullness.

For is it not mysterious and disconcerting to human reason? Had we been aware of Christ's mission, would we not have said to him—as some of his relatives did later—*"Manifest yourself to the world, for no one does a thing in secret if he wants to be publicly known"?*

This mystery of the hidden life contains many a lesson. The first is that nothing great is done in God's eyes that is not done with Christ's grace for his glory. And that we are pleasing to God in proportion to our resemblance to his Son, Jesus.

Christ's status as Son of God gives infinite value to his slightest acts. Our Lord was no less adorable or pleasing to his Father when he wielded the chisel or plane, than when he died on the Cross to save mankind. We—God's adopted sons—see all our activity become divine in its roots by means of sanctifying grace, and we are thus made worthy like Christ, in our small way, of his Father's pleasure.

As you know, the rarest of talents, the most sublime thoughts, the most generous and most dazzling deeds are without merit for eternity, *unless vivified by grace.* The world may admire and applaud, but they are not received and do not count for eternity. *What does it profit a man to conquer the whole world by force of arms, by the charm of eloquence, or by the authority of knowledge, if, not having grace, he is shut out of Heaven?*

On the other hand, see this poor workman painfully earning a living, this humble servant unknown to the world, this destitute individual disdained by all—their commonplace lives attract and hold no one's attention. But their souls are animated by Christ's grace, and so are a delight to the angels and a continual object of love to the Father. For these souls bear within them, through grace, the distinguishing traits of Christ.

Remember that our exterior activity, our apostolate, will be fruitful spiritually only to the extent that it is bound up with this interior and divine life of grace. "We shall be able to exert an influence on others only to the degree that we ourselves are temples of divinity, within which the supernatural source of our interior life burns more brightly."

"Let it be clearly understood that we shall do more for the Church, for the salvation of souls, and for the glory of our Heavenly Father, by seeking rather to be united to God by a life made up wholly of faith and love, having him as its sole object; than by an engrossing and feverish activity which leaves us with neither the time nor the leisure for finding God in solitude, recollection, prayer, and self-detachment. Now nothing so favours this intense union of the soul with God as does the hidden life."

Lord, teach us the virtue of being "dead and buried" to self!

THE HOST OF PROVIDENCE

Would you have your life be holy and God-filled? ... Then receive every happening, every sacrifice, every trial, the way you receive the Sacred Host every morning at Mass. Just as at that moment you forget the veil concealing the sacred Species in order to devote all your attention and your soul's adoration to our Lord present within for your sanctification, likewise learn to always bypass the secondary causes through which God desires to advance by a degree your union with HIM. Whether this created intervention be called interior suffering, lassitude, dryness, temptation, distress of soul, family worries, physical suffering, things hard to bear, a difficult obedience, an observance repugnant to you, or little wearisome details of life—always say to yourself—and promptly—"It is a HOST."

Receive eagerly and reverently this "host of Providence." Shut it up in your soul, within the ciborium of your heart, and adore it; as you "communicate" the thought your Heavenly Father had in offering it to your generosity and love. And without permitting yourself to struggle with the endless "WHY?" of nature blinded by suffering, make with courage, in silence, and in the peace of a living faith, your Thanksgiving; that you may receive the divine gift in all its fullness. And since it is in weak stomachs, digesting food with difficulty that the sacred Species remain the longest, just so often as this sentiment of suffering returns to besiege your sensitive and delicate heart, do not be troubled; but think that the "real presence" of this host still remains; and renew your acts of adoration and thanksgiving.

L 16—What is the theme of the Sundays after Epiphany?

You will notice that there are *six* Sundays after Epiphany. Not all these Sundays are used, however, when Easter comes early. In this case, the twenty-four Sundays after Pentecost are increased up to twenty-eight, the Sundays added being simply the two, three, or four Sundays after Epiphany which could not be observed before Easter.

Without further preliminaries, here is the theme of the Sundays after Epiphany:

First Sunday (within the octave): Here the Church is anxious to lay especial stress on Christ's infancy. This is the Feast of the *Holy Family.* The Gospel relates the story of Jesus' coming to the Temple at the age of twelve. Joseph and Mary lose him, and find him after a three day's search!... *Should you have had the misfortune to lose Jesus, do not rest until you have found him again!*... The theme of this first Sunday after Epiphany (overshadowed by the Feast of the Holy Family) is *"the will of God above everything else."* Let us pray today for the rechristianization of families. Let us pray that husbands and wives, parents and children, may love one another like Jesus, Mary, and Joseph.

The Octave of Christian Unity (from the Feast of St. Peter in Rome, the 18th of January, to the Feast of St. Paul's Conversion, January 25th): It is most unfortunate that all believers in Christ are not Roman Catholics—that there should be lack of unity among Christians. *(Catholic, Protestant, Orthodox.)*

Christ's will is for all his disciples to be one: *"That they may be one, even as we are one."* Let us pray hard this week for a return to unity, and that there may be but one fold and one Shepherd.

O Jesus, do away with divisions among Christians! Grant to all more charity and light, so that we may form but one family together with You!

The hymn of Christian unity: *Ubi caritas et amor.*

Second Sunday after Epiphany: Following her outbursts of joy at the Saviour's Advent, and in conjunction with Christ's manifestations to the angels, shepherds, and Magi, the Church now considers Christ manifesting himself through his miracles and sermons—the beginning of Christ's public life. Together with faith, hope increases in the hearts of the faithful. (The colour of the priest's vestment is *green,* the colour of hope.)

Here we are present at Christ's first miracle—the changing of the water into wine. This is the first sign of divinity that Jesus gives to his first disciples. This sign is, as it were, *within arm's reach.*

Act of faith: *Lord, we believe in You.*

Third Sunday: A sign at a distance. Jesus cures the centurion's son without even going to see him. God acts everywhere—just as well at a distance as he does close to us. *The conditions*: Going to Jesus with great humility and also with great faith in him.

"Lord, I am not worthy that You should come under my roof, but only say the word and my soul will he healed."

Fourth Sunday: Constant trust, even in the time of storm, of violent temptation, of persecution. Jesus seems to sleep, in order to try our faith; but he watches over us. As in this Sunday's Gospel, he has but to stretch forth his hands over us for the "great storm" to cease and for a "great calm" to come.

Lord Jesus, we trust in You; but increase our faith. Having You, we fear nothing!

Fifth Sunday: Judge not! The Gospel of the good seed and the weeds confronts us with the perplexing problem of the existence of evil-doers. How can the infinitely good and wise God tolerate them? We do not know. God knows and that is enough. *Trust!*

Just let us suppose that the Lord had replied "Yes," to the apparent zeal which causes us to ask with the servant of the parable, "Will You have us go and gather up the weeds—liquidate the undesirables?" Who would be the first to be weeded out? We know the answer to *that* one in a flash! Does this mean that we would be acting before God in justice? Is it not much more likely that with our judgment darknened by ignorance and our hearts hardened by selfishness, we should—nine times out of ten—pull up the wheat instead of the weeds? So much so, that we might even end up by asking ourselves seriously if the first sinners to be speedily liquidated ought not to be *us!* No, let us leave the judging up to God. As for ourselves, let us strive by our example and charity in action, to convert the lost.

Jesus, teach us to love one another.

Sixth Sunday: The Kingdom of God is in our midst, or within us. It appeared in the person of Christ, who came among men. He was given to us very small, like a seed, like the grain of mustard in today's Gospel. He wants to increase.

1. In *us,* through the task of our personal sanctification.
2. Among *men,* by our apostolate. (The leaven that leavens the whole batch!)

What are you doing to make God's Kingdom grow—in and around you?

O Jesus, merely listening to You is not enough! We must do all that You tell us to do. Give us the strength to carry out Your teachings.

L 17—What are the principal feasts celebrated in January?

A. CALENDAR OF THE UNIVERSAL CHURCH

Jan. 5. *St. Telesphorus,* pope and martyr.

Jan. 11. *St. Hyginus,* pope and martyr.

Jan. 14. *St. Hilary,* Bishop of Poitiers and Doctor of the Church.

Jan. 15. *St. Paul,* hermit, who died a centenarian after a life of asceticism in the desert.

Jan. 17. *St. Anthony,* abbot, hermit, the farmer's saint.

Jan. 18. *St. Peter's Chair in Rome,* nominal anniversary of the taking possession of the episcopal see in Rome.

Jan. 20. *SS. Fabian and Sebastian,* both martyred at Rome.

Jan. 21. *St. Agnes,* young Roman virgin martyr of thirteen, who was beheaded.

Jan. 23. *SS. Vincent and Anastasius,* martyrs. The *Espousals of the Blessed Virgin and St. Joseph.*

Jan. 24. *Conversion of St. Timothy,* disciple of St. Paul.

Jan. 25. *Conversion of St. Paul,* struck down by grace.

Jan. 26. *St. Polycarp,* disciple of St. John.

Jan. 27. *St. John Chrysostom,* Doctor of the Church, the "golden-voiced" preacher.

Jan. 30. *St. Martina,* virgin martyr.

B. *FRANCISCAN CALENDAR*

Jan. 14. *BB. Odoric, Roger, and Giles,* Franciscans.

Jan. 16. *St. Berard and his companions,* first Franciscan martyrs (while St. Francis was still alive). When St. Francis learned of their glorious death, he exclaimed, "At last, I have five real Friars Minor!"

Jan. 19. *BB. Thomas of Cori, Charles, and Bernard,* Franciscan Brothers.

Jan. 29. *St. Francis de Sales,* cordbearer, patron of journalists and writers, Doctor of the Church.

Jan. 30. *St. Hyacinth of Mariscotti,* virgin of the Third Order regular.

Jan. 31. *St. John Bosco,* Tertiary priest, founder of the Salesians, protector of youth.

L 18—What is the origin of the Feast of the Purification? What is the meaning of the ceremonies?

The Purification of the Blessed Virgin Mary (Feb. 2), sometimes called "Candlemas Day." The principal feast of February, and the one giving this month its distinctive character, is the Feast of the Purification, on which the Church celebrates the Presentation of Jesus in the Temple and the Purification of Mary. This solemnity marks the transition between Christmastide and Eastertide. Jesus is still a child, but already he is presented to his Father by Mary for the Sacrifice which is to be consummated thirty-three years later on Calvary.

HISTORIC ORIGIN OF THIS FEAST, THE FEAST OF THE DIVINE LIGHT

In the beginning of the Christian era, a nocturnal torchlight procession was organized in the pagan quarters of Rome, known as the *Lupercalia,* a licentious festivity.

The Church, therefore, wished to replace this pagan festival by another, Christian, festival of light. Thus it is in a spirit of expiation that the priest wears violet vestments during the procession. In Rome, the pope used to walk barefoot during the procession.

The Church has profited by this ceremony to bless the candles for her liturgical use, and for the use of the faithful in their homes. (It is commendable to light blessed candles during a thunderstorm, in time of peril, of great necessity, during temptation, etc.) Two candles must also be lit for the distribution of Holy Communion to the sick, for Viaticum, and Extreme Unction.

This *feast of light* corresponds to the fortieth day following Christ's birth. It is the day of his *presentation in the Temple* as the first-born, in keeping with the Mosaic Law. Now it is on this day that the aged Simeon, speaking by inspiration of the Holy Spirit, proclaimed Christ as *a Light of revelation to the still pagan peoples.* This is why we have a "feast of light" or Candlemas Day.

The significance of the ceremony

1. The candles symbolize Christ. (In the composition of every candle, (a) the *wax* is produced by worker bees, and not by the *queen bee* (the only fertile bee in the hive, all the other bees being, in a sense, "virgins"). The Body of Christ came from the Virgin Mary. (b) The *wick* concealed in the wax represents Christ's soul, (c) the *flame,* his divinity.

2. Light is the symbol of God and truth; whereas darkness is the emblem of the Devil and his works: sin.

We have seen in commenting on the Last Gospel that Christ is the Light of the world.

3. The holding of a lighted candle in our hand recalls our vocation as *"children of light,"* or of God. Hence, our obligation to shun darkness—i.e. sin—and to give light in a positive manner by constituting ourselves messengers of the *Good News.*

The Church makes us think of this, by placing a lighted candle in our hand at the important events in our lives: at our Baptism, (Receive. . .), at our First Communion, at a religious profession, at an ordination, and finally, at our last hour. (During the prayers for the dying, someone holds a crucifix.)

The Church has us hold a candle twice during today's Mass, for the two times that Christ the Light appears in our midst—at the Gospel and the Consecration. For we are all light-bearers, going before Christ the Light. (We should carry lighted candles in this way at every Mass, but the acolytes have replaced us for this.) The Church wishes to remind us of our duty as Christians to *bear witness to the truth, to be lights of the world*, to walk in Christ's light, and always to act in such a way as to bring souls to Christ by our good example.

The procession reminds us of Life's true meaning. Going out of the Church and entering it again in a solemn manner, following the crucifix and bearing lighted tapers, teaches us that we ought to go through life with Christ, our footsteps turned toward Heaven.

Our sentiments during this ceremony

1. Sentiments of reparation for our negligence and that of Catholics in general in the missionary apostolate. (Christ's light has not yet shown over all the earth. We still have 1,000,000,000 pagans, 200,000,000 Protestants, 160,000,000 schismatics, 16,000,000 Jews, and several million ignorant or indifferent Catholics. So during this ceremony, let us think of the Gospel which must be brought to every soul; and pray for missionaries, without forgetting to be more generous to missions.)

2. Sentiments of faith and hope. We are Christians. It is easy for us—with divine grace—to believe and to live in the hope of Heaven. Let this belief appear in our lives. Let us be true "Christ-bearers." Let there always be "oil in our lamps"—taking our cue from the parable of the wise virgins.

As we said above, this feast is at the same time *a day of OFFERING.* Officially, (i.e., as a first-born son), our Lord offered himself to his Father through the hands of Mary. *This was the first Offertory of the Sacrifice of the Cross.*

It is also *the feast of HUMILITY.* Mary goes to the Temple for purification, just as if her motherhood were like that of other mothers. (The ceremony of churching.)

It is likewise *the feast of a MEETING.* Simeon, at joy's summit, sings his life's evening prayer. (Let us here recall the beauty of Sunday Compline.)

L 19—What other important feasts are on the February Calendar?

A. *CALENDAR OF THE UNIVERSAL CHURCH*

Feb. 1. *St. Ignatius of Antioch,* celebrated for his joyous pursuit of martyrdom.

Feb. 3. *St. Blaise,* bishop and martyr. The Church recognizes his prerogative of curing all throat ailments, and has established a special blessing with two candles for this purpose.

Feb. 5. *St. Agatha,* virgin, and martyr of purity, mentioned in the Canon of the Mass.

Feb. 8. *St. John of Matha,* founder of the Trinitarians.

Feb. 9. *St. Cyril of Alexandria,* the valiant defender of the glories of Mary.

Feb. 10. *St. Scholastica,* foundress of the Benedictine nuns and sister of St. Benedict.

Feb. 11. *Our Lady of Lourdes,* the feast which recalls the most beautiful title to glory of the Blessed Virgin—her Immaculate Conception.

Feb. 14. *St. Valentine,* bishop and martyr.

Feb. 23. *St. Peter Damian,* who contributed toward making the custom of consecrating Saturday to the Blessed Virgin, universal.

Feb. 24. *St. Matthias,* the Apostle who replaced Judas.

B. *FRANCISCAN CALENDAR*

Feb. 4. *St. Joseph of Leonissa,* Capuchin missionary.

Feb. 5. *St. Peter Baptist,* martyred in Japan, together with twenty-three Franciscan and Tertiary companions.

Feb. 7. *BB. Richer, Giles, and Anthony,* Franciscans.

Feb. 13. *Bl. John of Triora,* Franciscan martyr.

Feb. 14. *St. Jane of Valois,* foundress of the Sisters of the Annunciation.

Feb. 15. *Translation of St. Anthony.*

Feb. 16. *BB. Philippa, Eustochim, and Viridane,* Poor Clares and Tertiary.

Feb. 17. *BB. Luke, Andrew, and Peter of Traja,* Franciscans.

Feb. 19. *St. Conrad of Piacenza.* Tertiary hermit.

Feb. 22. *St. Margaret of Cortona,* Tertiary and penitent, called the "Magdalene of the Franciscan Order."

Feb. 25. *Bl. Sebastian,* Franciscan.

Feb. 28. *Bl. Antoinette of Florence,* Poor Clare; *Louise of Albertoni and Angela of Foligno,* Tertiaries. The latter, in an "all out" gesture, gave away her castle and all its contents as an expiatory sacrifice for her past briefly sinful life.

II. THE PASCHAL CYCLE
PREPARATION

L 20—How do we prepare for the Feast of Easter?

The remote preparation for Easter—the peak of the second cycle of the liturgical year—takes place in Septuagesima, Lent, and Passiontide.

Septuagesima begins nine weeks before Easter including three Sundays (or weeks that are reckoned as three ten-day periods).

Lent lasts for forty days, exclusive of Sundays. (For in the mind of the Church, one does not do penance on Sunday.)

Passiontide lasts for eleven days, namely, from Passion Sunday to Wednesday in Holy Week.

SEPTUAGESIMA

L 21—What thought stands out from Septuagesima and its three Sundays?

After exalting the mystery of the Incarnation in the Christmas cycle, we bring out here the mystery of the Redemption, having the Resurrection as its culmination. Everything in this second cycle is orientated toward the exaltation of Christ—Easter and the Ascension. During the three Sundays of this liturgical period (Septuagesima, Sexagesima, Quinquagesima), a wonderful ascending scale recalls the various phases of our Redemption:

1. Our vocation to salvation.
2. Our instruction for the attaining of this.
3. Our illumination by faith, resulting from this instruction.

To each of these three divine operations man should correspond by:

1. Combatting evil. (Adam.)
2. Working for good. (Noah.)
3. Loving God. (Abraham.)

Each of these three stages in our spiritual preparation are symbolized by an Old Testament character, successively evoked on these three Sunday mornings: Adam, Noah, and Abraham.

Septuagesima Sunday. Our vocation to salvation is recalled in today's Gospel by the parable of the workers sent by Christ into his vineyard. This vocation, this calling, is the work of God; who has called us to his eternal glory. (I. Pet. 5:10.)

The work corresponding to this, St. Paul teaches us in the Epistle, is the combat against evil in order to receive an "imperishable crown" of glory. The concrete exampe is *Adam*: the creature called to glory by virtue of his creation, but constrained—as the result of his sin—to attain it only through struggle.

Sexagesima Sunday. Our *instruction*—necessary for determining the road to take—is the work of the Divine Sower of today's Gospel. "The seed is the Word of God." (Luke 8:11.) It is *His* work.

Man's corresponding work is the *work for good* that St. Paul proposes to us in this Epistle—this titanic work which he himself undertook in order to become a sower of truth; the work that we, too, ought to undertake, so that God's Word may be fruitful in our souls. Of this, the patriarch *Noah* is the living symbol. *Noah,* the workman who built the Ark, is the figure of the Church, wherein safely reposes the only deposit of Christian life and truth capable of confronting the "deluge" of centuries and of men.

Quinquagesima Sunday. Our *illumination*—the gift of seeing all things as they should be seen, that is in God—is received by us through the action of Christ, like the blind man of the Gospel whose sight Christ restored. Lest Christ's words become *obscure* to us, let us pray with this poor man plunged in darkness, *"Lord, that I may see! May I look at things in a Christian way—with the eye of faith!"*

To this illumination by faith—the work of God—man's work should correspond. How? By what part of our being should we cling to this gift of God which is faith? With our minds to be sure, but also with our hearts. *Corde creditur.* (Rom. 10:10.) St. Paul likewise deals at length with *love,* with charity, in today's Epistle. *"Without charity,"* he says, *"I am nothing." "It is selfishness that creates unbelievers,"* remarked Joergensen, commenting on the thought of St. Catherine of Siena. When selfishness is vanquished (by love), faith comes of itself—the "blind man" becomes a believer.

Abraham is the biblical character in whom this state of the believer's soul is embodied in a striking manner. Abraham's great spirit of faith leads him to the most heroic proof of his love for God—his consent to sacrifice his only son, a symbol of Christ's Sacrifice. "Greater love than this no one has, that one lay down his life for his friends."

L 22—How does the Church manifest the spirit of Septuagesima in her liturgy?

The directives of the Church for this period are as follows:

1. For the Mass: Omission of the *Gloria.* The *Tract* replaces the *Alleluia* after the *Gradual.* The *Benedicamus Domino* is substituted for the *Ite missa est. Violet ornaments* (for penance) are required.

2. For the breviary: Omission of the *Te Deum.* The *Laus tibi Christe* replaces the *Alleluia.*

We are not yet in Lent, but in a time preparatory to this period of penance. It is fitting—in order to live in harmony with the Church—to soft-pedal noisy celebrations, and lead a more intense interior life, centred on Christ, our Model.

L 23—What are the principal feasts on the calendar for March?

A. *CALENDAR OF THE UNIVERSAL CHURCH*

March 4. *St. Casimir,* confessor, and *St. Lucius,* pope and martyr.

March 6. *SS. Perpetua and Felicity,* two martyr mothers, mentioned in the Canon.

March 7. *St. Thomas Aquinas,* Dominican, called the "angelic Doctor," because of his learning and purity. He is also the patron of all Catholic schools.

March 8. *St. John of God,* founder of the Hospitaliers, patron of the sick and of those caring for them.

March 10. *The Forty Holy Martyrs.*

March 12. *St. Gregory the Great,* pope and doctor. He established Gregorian chant.

March 17. *St. Patrick,* Bishop and Apostle of Ireland; patron of the Irish.

March 18. *St. Cyril of Jerusalem,* bishop and Doctor of the Church.

March 19. *St. Joseph,* virginal spouse of the Blessed Mother and foster father of the Child Jesus; Patron of the Universal Church and of a happy death; the model of workers and of interior souls. Let us trust him implicitly, study his virtues, and what is more important, imitate them.

March 21. *St. Benedict,* abbot, founder of the Benedictines and head of the monks of the West.

March 24. *St. Gabriel Archangel,* chosen by God to announce the mystery of the Incarnation to Mary.

March 25. *The Annunciation of the Blessed Virgin Mary.* It was on this day that, as a result of Mary's *fiat,* the mystery of the Incarnation was accomplished in her womb, a miracle that gave Mary her fairest title of "Mother of God." Like our Lady, we will say "Yes," to every divine inspiration with which our lives are filled; and Christ will increase in our souls!

March 27. *St. John Damascene,* Doctor of the Church and defender of the veneration of images.

B. *FRANCISCAN CALENDAR*

First Friday in March. *Mystery of the way of the Cross.* The Way of the Cross is a devotion coming straight from the heart of St. Francis. Let us profit, then, by this particularly Franciscan feast, to renew in us the sentiments of compunction and of compassion for Christ's sufferings, in imitation of the stigmatized Saint of LaVerna.

March 5. *St. John Joseph of the Cross.* Franciscan and contemplative.

March 6. *St. Collette of Corbia,* virgin and reformer of the Order of Poor Clares.

March 9. *St. Catherine of Bologna,* virgin and Poor Clare. *St. Frances of Rome,* Tertiary, widow, and the model of housewives.

March 11. *BB. John Baptist of Fabriano, Agnello and Christopher,* Franciscans.

March 14. *Translation of St. Bonaventure.*

March 18. *St. Salvador of Orta,* Franciscan lay Brother.

March 20. *BB. John of Parma and Mark,* Franciscans, and *Bl. Hippolyte Galantini,* Tertiary.

March 22. *St. Benvenuti,* Bishop of Osmiso.

March 26. *Bl. Didacus Joseph,* Capuchin priest.
March 28. *St. John of Capistrano,* great Franciscan preacher.
March 30. *St. Peter Regalado,* Franciscan.

LENT

L 24—How should we envision Lent?

Lent is particularly the time of *spiritual combat.*

Advent is the time for awareness of one's weakness and of God's call—for humble and trusting desire.

Christmas corresponds to the simple, naïve, and admiring joy of the beginnings of the spiritual life.

Soon comes testing, the time of mortification, of combat, of self-denial. This combat does not cease to be "joyous," since it comes from love and is impregnated with hope. The term, "gloomy Lent," is a misnomer; and Jesus tells us not to be sad when we fast. Lent is a time of austerity, of mortification, which is penance, sin's penalty; as is the case for every struggle, for every combat. But penance can be a joy if we think of the good we acquire by it, rather than of the "evil" it imposes on us. For Lent's purpose is to leave sin out of our lives, and take God into them instead!

We must cast off the "old man," then; or in other words, act like children of God. Let us learn to bear our daily crosses, for ourselves and for sinners; so that we may become like Christ, *who was made sin for us.*

This is the goal of all our sacrifices and of the practices the Church requires of us. Almsgiving ought to detach us from exterior goods and their lure. Fasting and abstinence ought to make us stronger than our passions.

So it is in this spirit of "liberation, joy and resurrection," that all our daily crosses should be more generously accepted. During Lent, the sins and imperfections that we encounter in and around us, will be burned off—painfully but joyously—in the flames of intense charity and love. This joyous struggle against sin ought to increase in intensity as Holy Week approaches.

The Lenten liturgy becomes intelligible, if we recall how in former times, this period was employed to prepare public sinners for the reconciliation with the Church on Holy Thursday and the catechumens for their Baptism on Holy Saturday. Now *we* are these sinners that are to be "reconciled" by the penance of Lent; and there are many more sinners—public or otherwise—in my parish, in my city, to be brought back to the Church. We are likewise these souls to be "renewed" by the grace of Easter. Our resurrection—but let us not anticipate!

The Lenten liturgy likewise recalls the labours, combats and sufferings that Christ had to face before being glorified. For Christ's manifestation at Christmas and Epiphany had raised up enemies for him. Jesus met up with sin and sinners. For this reason, his task could only be accomplished through suffering and death.

We, too, in our journey toward Heaven, will encounter sin within and around us. To live as true children of God and to go to Heaven, we ought to struggle unceasingly against our faults and sinful habits (pride, sloth, jealousy, impurity, selfishness, etc.). We will also seek to win souls.

THE LAW OF ABSTINENCE

The law of complete abstinence forbids the use of meat and meat juices as food, as well as the fat, marrow, or blood of land animals. Eggs and dairy products (milk, cream, butter, and cheese), as well as margarine, and condiments and seasonings (even though prepared in fat) are allowed.

Every Catholic over seven years of age is bound to observe the law of abstinence.

THE LAW OF FASTING

On days of fast only one full meal is allowed. Two other meatless meals, sufficient to maintain strength, may be taken according to one's needs. The amount consumed at these two meals, however, should be notably less than that ordinarily eaten. (The complete meal may be eaten either at noon or in the evening.) Eating between meals is not permitted; but liquids, including milk and fruit juices are allowed. By this modification of her laws, the Church has made observance of the precept for fasting possible to a greater number of Catholics.

Every Catholic between the ages of twenty-one and fifty-nine years is bound to observe the law of fasting, unless dispensed.

NEW REGULATIONS ON FAST AND ABSTINENCE

(January 20th, 1960)

1. The days of abstinence are:

   Every Friday of the year.

2. The Days of fast and abstinence are:

   Ash Wednesday

   Good Friday

   The Vigil of the Feast of the Immaculate Conception (December 7th unless this happens to be on a Sunday.

   The second day before Christmas (December 23rd) unless this happens to be on a Sunday.

HOLY DAYS OF OBLIGATION

Besides every Sunday in the year, there are six holy days of obligation on which all the faithful having attained their seventh year are obligated to, 1, abstain from all unnecessary servile work, and, 2, attend Holy Mass. These days are:

1. The Circumcision of our Lord, Jan. 1st.
2. The Epiphany, the 6th. of January.*
3. The Ascension of our Lord, (the Thursday after the fifth Sunday after Easter).
4. All Saints, Nov. 1st.
5. The Immaculate Conception, Dec. 8.
6. Christmas, Dec. 25th.

(* In the United States, the Feast of the Assumption (Aug. 15) is a holy day of obligation, whereas the Epiphany is not.) [T.N.]

N.B. In Canada, by virtue of a decree emanating from Rome, and in force since November 1st, 1956, servile work, with the permission of the diocesan bishop, is permitted on the four following feasts of obligation: Epiphany, Ascension, All Saints, and Immaculate Conception. Mass, however, is of obligation on these days.

These new regulations abrogate from this day forward all prior legislation concerning fast and abstinence so that the Lenten Fast is reduced to fasting on Ash Wednesday and Good Friday, that the partial abstinence of the Ember Days no longer exists and that in general all other days except those mentioned above do not come under the Church law on fasting.

L 25—How does the Church's liturgy manifest the spirit of the Lenten season?

The Church points out Lent to us as a time of combat and mortification by:

A special daily Mass, celebrated with violet vestments, without the *Gloria* and the *Ite, missa est.*

A supplementary Postcommunion prayer "over the people."

The use of the folded chasuble (a sign of penance).

Prohibition of the solemn nuptial blessing.

Daily fasting (except Sunday). Of obligation.

Imposition of the ashes—a token of penance and humility.

Vespers before dinner to recall the former fast which was unbroken until Vespers.

Alms-giving (the Lenten pardon).

More frequent: Our prayers, Masses, Communions.

Recommended devotion: the Way of the Cross.

Everyone should adopt his own personal Lenten mortifications, according to his needs! For instance, trying to "ration" our selfish, pleasure-loving minds, by LIVING IN THE STATE OF GRACE. This is elementary. We might draw up a "Lenten schedule" for ourselves in keeping with our habits, as: no beer or alcoholic beverages, no (or, at least, fewer) cigarettes, no soft drinks, no candy or sweets, fewer dates! No dancing, less TV or radio, an all-time ban on immoral magazines or newspapers (burning the bad ones). A banishing from memory of songs and stories with double meaning, being kinder, more helpful to others, less envious, more indulgent, patching up old quarrels, practicing great modesty of the eyes and clothing, more charity in our dealings with our neighbour, a ban on useless visits and criticism, etc.

Bird Sanctuary

Thousands of white-winged seagulls
Over the St. Lawrence River—
Brushing its waves with their wing-tips,
Seeking subsistence and slaking their thirst.
They mount up in rapid flight,
Only to glide down again softly,
Like delicate air-borne petals
Under the wind's caress.

Like the wandering seagulls, our thoughts
Fly off in many directions.
Those not lost in space,
May take refuge in a human soul;
While still other thoughts
May find winter shelter in a book.

* * *

Heaven grant that our thoughts by their flight
May enrich, not impoverish, others!

Percé
Ric Photo

The Waterfall

If every drop of water
that falls on the forehead of the baptized
were gathered together...
If all the graces poured into souls
were formed into rivers
and hurled from the top of a cliff,
And if, by some miracle, we were able
to see this sight,
Unspeakable ecstasy would send us to our knees!

We never think of it, and yet...
What are visible torrents;
churnings of water, impetuous liquid masses,
tumbling down the world's mountains,
overflowing flood waters,
compared to this imperceptible spiritual dew,
without weight and without measure,
that inundates souls?

Lord, I give thanks to you for the fair
spectacle of creation.
I offer you infinitely more praise for the miracles
of your divine munificence
taking place within!

Saint Fereol
Ric Photo

Included likewise should be assiduity in attending our parish retreat and in praying for the success of these retreats, bringing the disinclined to the retreat, and so on.

L 26—What ceremony marks the beginning of Lent?

The imposition of ashes marks the beginning of Lent. "Remember, O Man, that you are dust!"

Now we were never meant to eat dust! So let us be logical. Picking ourselves up out of the dust where sin has laid us low, let us break away ourselves, from our narrow, petty egotism, and become what we really are—*sons of God and heirs of Heaven!* The fight is on!

In the fullest meaning of the word, Christian penance means a "change of mind." From pagan, our minds must become Christian. In other words, we must be *converted*—a work primarily of the will, assisted by grace.

As soon as the will does an "about face" and detaches itself from the world, it begins to see things more clearly. It ceases to be darkened by the mists arising from the swamplands of self. The eye of the mind becomes limpid, and in its midst (as St. Catherine of Siena once said), is the "pupil of faith."

The most profound liturgical content of the Lenten period is the struggle between light and darkness, which furnishes the subject-matter for the next question.

L 27—Please demonstrate, in the themes for the Sundays of Lent, this struggle of Darkness and Light, and the triumph of Light over Darkness.

First Sunday of Lent: This struggle between light and darkness, characteristic of the Lenten season, has (explains Parsch) two phases—the *defensive* and the *offensive.*

The *defensive* appears especially in the Gospel for this first Sunday, wherein we see Christ at grips with the spirit of darkness. Jesus is tempted in the desert by Satan.

Second Sunday. A first triumph of the spirit of light. Jesus transfigured shines resplendent on Mount Thabor.

"If we were to spend a quarter of an hour in Heaven," said the holy Curé of Ars, "there is no suffering that we would not endure on earth!" Thabor ought to encourage us to ascend to Calvary.

Let us not forget during the first week of Lent, the *Ember Days,* days of more intense penance and of greater zeal.

The great duel of Light vs. Darkness, characteristic of the Lenten period, has passed its first phase—Christ and his Church on the defensive against the Devil.

By a generous spirit of penance, the soul is trained to resist evil. It has defended itself against the spirit of darkness.

Third Sunday of Lent. Now, the *offensive!* Christ, victorious in resistance, is still more so in the attack. He is the *stronger man,* mentioned in the Gospel of the day, who triumphs over the "*strong man*"—the unclean spirit. Thus the soul is liberated. "You were once darkness," says St. Paul (Epistle), "but now you are light in the Lord. Walk, then, as children of light (for the fruit of the light is in all goodness and justice and truth)."

Fourth Sunday of Lent. "Laetare!" Rejoice! The first fruit of the victory over this deceptive darkness, wherein our fallen nature gladly gropes, is interior joy. *"Write that this is perfect joy to conquer self and to suffer all things willingly for the love of Christ."* (St. Francis.) That is why the Church, no longer in violet, but in *rose* vestments, exults today. *Rejoice!* The "old sinner" that we all are, more or less, is going to be "buried" in the death of the Cross and be "resurrected" to the life of grace. Then he will be fed with divine food—the Easter Communion!

L 28—Please name the principal feasts listed on the calendar for April.

A. *CALENDAR OF THE UNIVERSAL CHURCH*

Apr. 4. *St. Isidore*, bishop and doctor of the Church.

Apr. 5. *St. Vincent Ferrer,* Dominican wonder-worker.

Apr. 11. *St. Leo the Great,* Pope and Doctor. He withstood Eutyches and Nestorius.

Apr. 13. *St. Hermenegild,* martyr.

Apr. 14. *St. Justin,* martyr. He established the first school of Christian philosophy.

Apr. 17. *St. Anicetus,* Pope and martyr.

Apr. 21. *St. Anselm,* bishop and doctor.

Apr. 22. *SS. Soter and Caius,* popes and martyrs.

Apr. 23. *St. George,* soldier martyr, invoked for the cure of skin diseases.

Apr. 25. *St. Mark,* disciple of St. Peter, one of the four Evangelists. On this day the Church chants the Litany of the Saints in procession to implore God's blessing on the fruits of the earth.

Apr. 26. *SS. Cletus and Marcellinus,* two martyred popes. In some places, *the Feast of Our Lady of Good Counsel* is celebrated.

Apr. 28. *St. Louis-Marie Grignon of Montfort,* the apostle of true devotion to Mary.

Apr. 30. *St. Catherine of Siena,* virgin and stigmatic; the next to youngest in a family of 24 children.

B. *FRANCISCAN CALENDAR*:

Apr. 2. *Bl. Leopold of Gaiches,* Franciscan.

Apr. 3. *BB. Gandolph and John of Penna,* Franciscan priests, and *William of Sicily,* hermit of the Third Order.

Apr. 4. *St. Benedict the Moor,* Franciscan Brother; a Negro.

Apr. 6. *Bl. Mary Crescence,* virgin of the Third Order regular.

Apr. 8. *Bl. Julian of St. Augustine,* Franciscan Brother.

Apr. 16. *Profession of St. Francis* with his first companions. The feast on which all members of the Franciscan family renew their engagements or vows.

On the same day, *St. Benedict Labre,* mendicant cordbearer, and *St. Mary Bernard Soubirous,* virgin, cordbearer, both patrons of the Archconfraternity of the Cord of St. Francis.

Apr. 18. *Bl. Andrew Bibernon,* Franciscan Brother.

Apr. 19. *BB. Mark of Bologna* and *Angelo of Clavasio,* Franciscans. *Bl. Conrad of Ascoli,* cardinal-elect.

Apr. 21. *St. Conrad of Parzham,* Franciscan.

Apr. 22. *Bl. Francis of Fabriano,* Franciscan.

Apr. 23. *Bl. Giles of Assisi,* Franciscan.

Apr. 24. *St. Fidelis of Sigmaringien,* martyr priest. Capuchin.

Apr. 28. *Bl. Luchesio* (the 28th,) first Franciscan Tertiary, also *St. Paul of the Cross,* Tertiary and founder of the Passionists.

Apr. 30. *St. Joseph Benedict Cottolengo,* Tertiary priest.

PASSIONTIDE

L 29—Of what does Passiontide remind us?

The last two weeks of Lent are called *Passiontide.* With Passion Sunday, we enter into the final Lenten phase—that terminating in the bloody drama of Calvary. The Church, who during the preceding four weeks, wept over the sins of her children; now mourns the death of her Heavenly Spouse. Except at the close of the Psalms in the breviary, she prohibits the recitation of the Gloria. Her lessons for Matins are taken from the Lamentations of Jeremias, who wept over Jerusalem—a type of the Church of Christ.

In the expectation of the final denouement of Good Friday, the cult paid to the saints (whose statues are veiled) is relegated to second place. Even the glory of the Master is eclipsed; for since yesterday—at Vespers of the Saturday preceding Passion Sunday—the Cross itself is concealed from the eyes of the faithful; in order to express the humiliation of the Redeemer, constrained to conceal himself to avoid being stoned to death before his appointed hour.

The Church consecrates the final fortnight of Lent to the sufferings and death of Christ. She desires her children to prepare their souls, through compassion for the Saviour's sufferings, to receive the abundant fruits of the immolation of the Divine Lamb. Christ's Passion ought to be our dominant thought during this period. For this we have gradually paved the way by daily readings from the New Testament; which show us the incessantly increasing hatred of the Scribes, Pharisees, and Chief Priests toward the Messiah. (Especially the Gospel for Tuesday of the fourth week of Lent.)

The second object of the Church's preoccupation at this time, is the instruction of the catechumens who are to receive Baptism on Easter eve. Their initiation into the mysteries of their salvation draws to a close, and in a few days the symbol of faith is to be given them.

"The reconciliation of public penitents," writes Dom Guéranger, "whom the Church will again welcome to her bosom, on the Thursday of the Lord's Supper. . .likewise draws on apace. In sackcloth and ashes, they carry out their task of expiation. The consoling readings that we have heard will continue, bringing ever greater refreshment to their souls. The approach of the sacrifice of the Lamb augments their hope, for they know that the blood of this Lamb is of infinite worth and takes away every sin."

The Church asks of us, then, in this Passiontide, not idle tears; but contrition for our sins ond heartfelt compassion.

L 30—How does the Church express the spirit of Passiontide in her liturgy?

The Church *veils* the statues and crucifixes in purple. (Why not repeat this liturgical gesture in homes, schools, and offices by veiling crucifixes and crosses? Children, and likewise adults, will better understand the nearness of the great mysteries of the Redemption; and will be reminded a hundred times a day of the duty of suffering and dying with Christ, in order to "rise" with him, when at Easter, crosses and crucifixes are unveiled!)

As in Masses for the Dead, the Psalm, *Judica me* and the *Gloria Patri* at the *Introït* and at the *Lavabo* are omitted.

The chanting of the Passion.

The Gospels at Mass for these eleven days relate the hatred for Christ of the "great" among the Jews.

In the breviary, there is the reading of the prophecies of the suffering Christ, taken from David, Isaias, Jeremias, Jonah, and Daniel.

L 31—In what spirit should we spend Passiontide?

In a spirit of *submission to God's will,* by accepting to suffer and die with Christ!

That we may better acquire the dispositions which should be ours at this season of the liturgical year, we shall meditate for a few moments on a commentary on the Passion by Jesus himself, taken from the *Revelations to Sr. Josefa Menendez.*

The passage in question relates the episode of Simon of Cyrene who was requisitioned; that is, who consented to carry Jesus' Cross because he hoped for something in return:

" 'So it is with many souls who follow Me,' said Jesus. 'Doubtless, they agree to help Me carry the Cross; but continue to be concerned with consolation and repose. . . . They consent to come after Me, and to this end have embraced the life of perfection; but without giving up their own interest, which remains for them as the first line of conduct. Hence they waver, and let My Cross fall when its weight becomes too heavy.

" 'They seek to suffer as little as possible; doling out their abnegation, avoiding this humiliation, this fatigue, that work; and, regretfully remembering all they have given up, they try to give themselves, at least, some enjoyment. In a word, there are souls so moved by self-interest, and so selfish, that having begun to follow Me more for their own sakes than for Mine, they accept only what they cannot avoid or what is of strict obligation.... These souls help Me bear only a small portion of My Cross; and in this way are barely able to acquire the merits indispensable for their salvation. But in eternity, they will see how far behind they lagged on the way.

" 'In contrast to these, there are souls (and they are numerous) who, pressed by the desire for salvation, but still more by love of Him who suffered for them, decide to follow Me on the road to Calvary. They embrace the life of perfection and give themselves over to My service, not just to carry part, but *all* of the Cross. Their sole aim is to assuage My sufferings and to console Me. They offer themselves for whatever My will requires of them, and seek only My good pleasure. They think neither of the reward nor of the merit they may acquire, nor of the suffering and fatigue that may result. Their one desire is to prove their love and to console My Heart.

" 'Let My Cross present itself to them under the form of sickness, or conceal itself under an occupation that runs counter to their tastes or aptitudes—let it assume the appearance of some chance slight, or of a certain opposition on the part of their associates—they recognize and accept it with all the submission of which their wills are capable.

" 'Sometimes, impelled by a great love for My Heart and a true zeal for souls, they do the thing they believe best in a certain circumstance; but all sorts of troubles and humiliations result. Then these souls, inspired by love alone, discover My Cross under this failure. They adore it, embrace it, and offer up for My glory all the resultant humiliation.

" 'Ah, such souls indeed bear all the weight of My Cross, with no other interest, and with no other recompense, than love! They it is who assuage My Heart and glorify it.

" 'And you may be sure, that if your self-denial and sacrifice are slow to bear fruit, or seem, indeed to be sterile, they are nonetheless neither futile nor vain. The day will come when the harvest will be great.

" 'The soul that truly loves, does not dole out what it does, nor weigh what it suffers—it stints neither labour nor pains. It does not work for a reward, but does all for God's greater glory.

" 'And because of its sincerity of purpose, regardless of results, it seeks neither to excuse itself nor to protest its good intentions. And because it acts from love, its pains and efforts tend ever to God's glory. Hence, it is never worried or flustered.... Still less, does it look upon itself as contradicted, nor even humiliated or persecuted. For the sole motive of its acts was love—and Love its only goal!

" 'Such souls are selfless and seek only My glory. They have taken up My Cross and bear all its weight on their shoulders.' "

Such are the dispositions that should be ours, if we are to live closely united to Christ during Passiontide.

It is likewise well to point out that the desire for God's glory does not exclude our own happiness. The positive language of the mystics merely serves to show the totality of their gift to God and his interests. For working for God's glory, means working at the same time for our own salvation.

L 32—Please explain the general theme for each of the principal days of the last fortnight of Lent.

With Passiontide, the immediate preparation for the great mystery of our Redemption begins. The Church mourns her suffering and dying Spouse....

Passion Sunday: Christ's enemies give the signal to attack. "They took up stones to cast at him." (Gospel of the Day.) Yes, They want to stone him to death!

Friday of this week. Consecrated to the Compassion of the Blessed Virgin. The Passion of Christ seen through the Heart of Mary. The Blessed Virgin brought forth the Son of God in joy. Now she is present to co-operate in our birth as children of God—born of the death of her Divine Son. Today, let us invoke Mary under her title of *Our Lady of Dolors.*

Palm Sunday: Today marks the first act in the great drama. Here is no mere commemoration, but a new "performance"; in which we are not just spectators, but *genuine actors.* Once, Christ suffered all alone; now he desires to suffer in us. Or what, after all, amounts to almost the same thing. For ever since that day when we were identified with him by Baptism, everything that he has belongs to us; and everything that we have—hence also suffering—belongs to him. Of this, the blessed palms are the insignia. For the palm is the emblem of martyrdom. *Martyr* indicates *witness.* We ought to be witnesses of Christ in our daily lives. Of this, the blessed palm hung up in our homes should serve as a reminder. The reading of the Passion—the remembrance of Christ's gift to his Father—also gives us a pattern for making our gift to God through Christ.

1. *The Procession*: The Church reproduces the triumphal cortege of Christ's entry into Jerusalem. Christ is truly the King announced by the prophets. It is to signify this royalty that he has accepted and willed this triumph and the people's shouts of joy. "Hosanna to the Son of David! Blessed is He who comes in the name of the Lord!" The faithful should take part in this procession.

Christ is soon to take possession of his kingship. His victory is close at hand.

Palms and olive branches are blessed (symbols of victory, meekness, and joy. We shall carefully preserve these blessed palms. In our homes and near our sick and dead, they will be tokens of victory over sin and death. They are a sacramental.

During the procession we shall think of how we, too, have taken up arms against sin; and of how, like Jesus, we shall some day "come forth" as conquerors.

2. *The Mass.* But Jesus' victory (like ours) must be made through the Cross. His triumph on Palm Sunday is only a sign, a promise, accepted by our Lord in fulfillment of prophecy. But Jesus himself cuts short the celebration. On his arrival at the Temple, he conceals himself from the crowd. Thus the Mass confronts us with the Cross.

And Holy Week commences.

We contemplate Christ "obedient to death on a Cross," (Epistle). In the Gospel, we read the Passion according to St. Matthew. (On Tuesday, St. Mark's account is read; on Wednesday, the narration of St. Luke; and on Good Friday, that of St. John.)

We, too, encouraged by the assurance of triumph, and of Christ's grace; will fight with still more zeal this week against sin in us and in others.

Catholics used to make an effort to pass Holy Week as much as possible in silence and recollection—in a recollection penetrated with regret and compassion. They attended the services, which did not appear to them too long—adapting their day to the prescriptions of the liturgy. They took time off from their occupations and pleasures; so as to spend at least a few hours daily with the Divine Victim, whose death and Resurrection is the price of their salvation.

They were likewise more generous with their penances. Why can we not do, what those before us did?

One may have reasons of age, position, or health for being dispensed from that corporal fast which consists in going without food; but no one can have any excuse for not keeping the spiritual "fast," which calls for complete conversion.

Now should someone have forgotten to keep one (or both) of these fasts from the beginning of Lent, he would do well to give proof of his generosity during Holy Week, so as to make up for lost time. Here is what one should have done since the start of Lent, and that should be carried out without delay:

First, a fast of the mind. A withdrawal of one's mentality from worldly thoughts, so as to occupy it only with thoughts of the great eternal truths. A "fasting" from earthly plans and schemes, to busy oneself with Heaven's plans and the insuring of a happy death. . . . By helping others to save their souls; by breaking off with every dangerous or culpable attachment, etc.

Next comes the *fast of the senses.* Making my eyes and ears "fast" by little checks imposed on their curiosity. For how many sins are committed with our eyes and ears, in conversation, reading, and movies, by the passion to see and hear everything! So then, a "fast" for this indiscreet and dangerous curiosity, and another one for my tongue. How many sins are committed by a "yen" for telling everything one knows, and by quizzing people so as to be sure to know everything! A fast for my imagination and its dreams of vengeance or an "easy life," And, finally, a doing without unnecessary "treats," of too worldly finery and dress. . . .

And now, a fast with regard to one's neighbour—a "fast" on quarrels and antagonisms among family and friends. . .of detraction and digs, a silence imposed on natural antipathies. A little more reserve and a little less effusion in my affections. A keeping God and myself company.... A "fast" on murmurs and complaints about importunate neighbours or untoward events.... The practice of charity in all its forms.... These are habits to acquire and to practice all one's life.

On *Holy Thursday, Good Friday* and *Holy Saturday* the *Office of Tenebrae* (Matins and Lauds) formerly chanted at night, is now said in the morning.

For this Office, a *triangular candelabrum* on which are fixed fifteen candles is placed in the midst of the choir. Each candle is extinguished one at a time, at the end of each Psalm; with the exception of the last and highest, which represents Christ. This candle is concealed behind the altar, thus expressing Christ's death. A muffled blow is then given with it, to imitate the earthquake which took place at Christ's death.

Holy Thursday. It is the eve of Christ's death. Jesus, therefore, makes his will; bequeathing us HIMSELF! Himself complete in his Sacrament of love, the *Holy Eucharist.* Hence the Last Supper is at the centre of today's liturgy. In addition, Christ bequeaths us the *priesthood*—an outflow from his loving heart.

It is especially in the Mass that this thought of the Eucharist and the Priesthood predominate—bringing joy to Christians. The vestments are white, the Gloria is sung, the bells are rung; thenceforth to be silent until the Easter Vigil.

Let us meditate this day on the Holy Eucharist; the sign of Christ's love for us, a sign equally of charity among Christians. Let us thank our Lord for all our Communions since our First Communion; imploring his pardon for all those Communions omitted through our own fault; and for those lacking in fervour or genuine love. Let us likewise pray for priests, imploring holiness for them. Let us also thank God for all the spiritual advantages of which—thanks to the ministry of priests—we have been the object.

In cathedrals, the Bishop consecrates the holy oils during the Mass of Holy Thursday: the *oil of the sick* for Extreme Unction; the *holy chrism* for Baptism, Confirmation, the consecration of bishops, and the dedication of churches, for the consecration of altars and chalices, and the blessing of bells; the *oil of catechumens* for Baptism, the blessing of baptismal fonts, the coronation of kings, and the ordination of priests.

This Mass consecrating the Holy Oils is celebrated in the morning, after Terce, and in the cathedral only. But the Mass commemorating the Last Supper of our Lord must be celebrated in each church in the evening, between 5 and 8 p.m.

The ceremony of the washing of the feet takes place immediately following the Gospel in this Mass. Today only one priest in each church may say Mass.

Before the altar of repose. We must not be content on the evening of Holy Thursday and on Good Friday with merely visiting one or several altars, to look at the flowers and lights. We must pray before the repository: meditating on the events of this great day, on the presence of Jesus among us, and on the way in which he asks of us now to take up our crosses and follow him.

Let us profit by this opportunity of passing a few hours with Jesus, in proof of our love for him, and to make reparation for the outrages and profanations of which he is the Victim in his Sacrament of Love.

Good Friday: "Where there is a testament, the death of the testator must intervene. In the same way, in order for the gift of Christ in the Eucharist to be valid, it was necessary for Christ to die. It is therefore on the Cross that Life, passing through death, gives himself to us. Christ died, bringing us salvation and restoring us to life! We will communicate supernatural life to others in the measure in which we are dead to self. *"Unless the grain of wheat fall into the ground and die, it remains alone. . . ."*

The reading of the Passion according to St. John offers the Church's only subject for meditation today.

Between 3 and 6 p.m., the liturgical ceremony takes place, followed by adoration of the Cross and Communion.

Let us live all day in union of thought and heart with Jesus on the Cross, like Mary; and so make a better offering to the Father of our work, difficulties, and daily sufferings.

On this day, let us love to make the *fourteen stations of the Way of the Cross,* and stir ourselves up to contrition for our sins.

Let us meditate on the *seven words of Christ on the Cross. . . .*

Let us venerate the Cross. . .remembering that the Mass brings down on the altar daily Calvary's Sacrifice. . . . Let us promise our Lord to participate more frequently and more actively in his Sacrifice.... Let us thank him for having sacrificed his life for our salvation.... Let us, like Jesus, be obedient unto death....

Holy Saturday. A time of great silence! The Heavenly Spouse reposes in his tomb, and his Bride (the Church) gives herself over to sorrowful recollection in a waiting time filled with trust. It is a day of great mourning, in which the Church lingers near the Saviour's tomb, meditating on his passion and death, and abstaining from the Mass Sacrifice. The altar is stripped until—after the solemn vigil or night passed in expectation of the Resurrection—free course is given to the joys of Easter, to be poured out in abundance over the following days.

A day of mourning, Holy Saturday is likewise a day of complete fast.

Yet, already the liturgy of the paschal vigil anticipates the great solemnity of Easter. The light that was put out on the summit of Calvary, is reborn in the flame of the paschal candle—a glowing symbol of the resurrected Christ.

In this Easter vigil, the Church no longer has her eyes fixed on the Cross. Her soul is no longer filled with sorrow; but with the certainty of the approaching Resurrection, and with wonder at the way employed by God to save us—with the Redemption, more admirable than the Creation.

She blesses the *new fire* and the *paschal candle;* symbol of Christ, the Light of souls.

She sings of this blessed night, more fair than that which brought delivery to the Egyptians. (Chant of the *Exultet.)*

She reads or chants the prophecies summing up Jewish history, and explaining the mysteries of the Redemption.

She blesses the baptismal fonts wherein souls—by Christ's grace —are reborn to the life of a child of God. (Catechumens were formerly baptized on this day, after the blessing of the baptismal fonts, then immediately confirmed.)

Then, from the baptismal font—chanting the litanies—we proceed to the altar. It is the commencement of the Mass of Easter. At this Mass, the *alleluias, the Gloria,* and the *pealing of bells* suddenly burst forth. The neophytes (or newly baptized) are clothed in white robes and receive Christ in Holy Communion. If we are pure, or purified by the Sacrament of Penance, we too may communicate.

Love has conquered hate!

Light has triumphed over darkness!

EASTERTIDE

L 33—What does Eastertide express?

Renewal and joy!

It is Spring. Already the first buds have appeared. Nature has come to life again. By Pentecost, the sap will be rising, and flowers bursting into bloom.

Nature and our physical selves rejoice in springtime, and so do our souls and the whole Church of God! For this is Eastertide, the time in which the Church meditates on Christ's Resurrection. Christ our Head has conquered sin and death. Jesus is now transformed, glorious, and about to ascend to Heaven. And we likewise are assured of being one day resurrected with him, provided that we start at once to work at transforming and renewing our souls.

The Paschal Season lasts from Easter Sunday to the Saturday after Pentecost, and is really a single continuous feast. It is the most important part of the Church year, because of the mysteries it recalls to us.

On *Christmas,* the Sun rose; whereas at *Easter,* it is *high noon.*

L 34—How does the Church express the spirit of Easter in her liturgy?

The colours of the Mass vestments are *white* or *gold brocade.*

Flowers, the organ and hymns of triumph with "alleluias" everywhere, are all expressive of joy and gladness.

The *Vidi aquam* (instead of the *Asperges)* recalls the imposing ceremonies of Baptism.

The *Regina Caeli* (prayed instead of the *Angelus),* is said standing—the victor's attitude.

And finally, the *paschal candle* which will be lighted in the sanctuary until Ascension Thursday, symbolizes Christ's presence in our midst.

L 35—What shall we do during Eastertide?

We shall start (while awaiting our complete transformation by the glorious resurrection of our bodies) to prepare ourselves for this by the interior transformation of our souls.

We shall live in a state of thanksgiving and joy.

We shall—while working on earth—*live* for Our Father in Heaven.

It is this grace of transformation for which we shall pray.

During Lent, if we did some tiring job, we would say to ourselves, *"I accept this fatigue in expiation for my sins. . .I offer it up to God in proof of my love,* of *my repentance, etc."*

But during this Eastertide, confronted by the same difficult task, we shall say instead, *"This little difficulty is nothing compared with my joy at knowing that Jesus rose again and that I am going to rise with him. This little difficulty is helping to prepare for my own resurrection. . . ."* Alleluia! Life is beautiful!

EASTER

L 36—What is recalled by the Feast of Easter?

Easter is the greatest feast of the year!

Easter is an *outburst of joy.* Of joy for Christ. Of joy born of hope for our own future resurrection.

Easter is the feast of liberation. The Jews of old had their Passover festival, recalling the night of their deliverance from the Egyptians; the night on which the angel of the Lord who slew the first-born of the Egyptians, had spared their own houses marked with the blood of the lamb.

But the *real* Passover, the *real* "festival of deliverance," of which the first was but a figure, is the death and Resurrection of Christ; wherein the true Lamb, by his Blood, saves the whole world from the only *real* death. So, for the Church, the Easter Feast is the centre of her liturgical life. *All the time before Easter is a preparation for Easter*— Advent, Christmas, Epiphany, Lent, and Holy Week. *All the time that comes after Easter merely recalls the consequences of the Redemption:* Pentecost and all the history of the *Church.* Every Sunday is a "little Easter"; recalling not the end of the work of Creation (as did the Jewish Sabbath), but the "end" of the work of Redemption—the *Resurrection!*

Easter is a movable feast. It is celebrated on the Sunday falling after the full moon which follows the *21st of March* (the vernal equinox). Easter, therefore, falls between the *22nd of March and the 25th of April.* It is the date of Easter that determines the dates of Lent, Ascension, Pentecost, etc.

In order to comprehend the joy of Easter, we must recall that Easter was once the feast of the newly baptized.... The joy of the Church was in having new children. Today the Church's joy is found in having children, who, having "fought the good fight" during Lent, have merited a more beautiful Christian life. It is likewise the joy of seeing many sinners approach the Sacraments and return to Christ.

L 37—What lesson should we derive from Easter?

Lent gave us an opportunity to die to self. *Easter is to be our resurrection.* Like Christ, we must "come forth" from the "sepulchre" of our sins—breaking off definitely the bonds of our bad habits. For just as the risen Christ dies no more, so we ought to preserve the life divine within us. (Augmenting it, if it already is ours.)

It is essential that Christ should be able to say of us: "He is no longer in his former state of tepidity and disgust for spiritual things. He no longer lives in that forgetfulness of God, that wandering imagination, that mental dissipation and thoughtlessness, in which virtually all his days were spent. He is no longer a slave to vanity and pride, selfishness and jealousy, indolence and anger, impurity and drunkenness.... He is no longer dominated by those importunate anxieties and feelings of depression which formerly troubled his soul.... He is no longer seen to succumb to those imperfections and vicious tendencies which slowed down his spiritual progress and arrested in him the divine workings of grace. He is truly risen with Christ; and it is Christ who lives in him, speaks through him, loves and prays with him.... *He rejoices; he has become a disseminator of joy.* Alleluia!

L 38—What is expressed by the five Sundays after Easter?

The Passover festival of the Jews lasted a week. The Christian Easter likewise lasts a week. In olden times, the whole week was a religious holiday. Those baptized on Easter—the newly-born to grace—wore the white robes of their Baptism all week in token of their joy.

Clothed in white, the neophytes attended Mass daily, received Communion and listened to the instructions on the Resurrection and Holy Eucharist. For this reason, the Eucharist occupies an important place in this week's liturgy. It is the time to thank God for the grace of Baptism and the great gift of the Eucharist.

First Sunday after Easter or Low Sunday. Its Latin name of *Dominica in albis,* comes from the fact that on this day the newly baptized laid aside their white robes.

On this day, the Church gives faithful counsels to the newly baptized and to us. "This is the victory that overcomes the world, our faith." Let us not be unbelieving like Thomas (Gospel), but believing. *Blessed are those who have not seen, and yet have believed!*

Second Sunday after Easter: This is the Sunday of the *Good Shepherd.* During the entire paschal season, ours is a joyous meditation on the work of deliverance accomplished by Jesus for us. Today we are filled with admiration for the Good Shepherd who laid down his life for his sheep.

Third Sunday: A new outburst of joy *(Jubilate)!* We think more particularly of how we are on pilgrimage from earth to Heaven. It is a wonderful journey! However, the Epistle warns us to "behave yourselves." Grant us, O Lord, ever to remain in the right path which leads to Heaven." Jesus already announces his approaching Ascension. We shall see him again.

Fourth Sunday: Our joy continues, for despite persistent temptations, our arrival in Heaven is certain. In trials, our Easter joy—the thought of Heaven—ought to be stronger. Keep smiling! "Grant, that... amid the changing things of this world, our hearts may be fixed where true joys are to be found." (Collect) Jesus' departure is the condition for the coming of the Holy Spirit. "If I do not go, the Advocate (the Holy Spirit) will not come to you; but if I go, I will send him to you."

Fifth Sunday: The cry of joy continues. Here, inaugurating the Rogations, it is transformed into a joyful petition. "Ask and you shall receive, that your joy may be full." (Gospel)

"Grant...that we may ever think on such things as are right, and by Your guidance ever do what is correct." (Collect)

L 39—What are the principal feasts on the calendar for May?

A. *CALENDAR OF THE UNIVERSAL CHURCH*

May 1. *St. Joseph, the worker.*

May 2. *St. Athanasius,* bishop, confessor, and doctor, who combatted the Arian heresy.

May 3. *Discovery of the Holy Cross,* by St. Helen, mother of Constantine.

May 4. *St. Monica,* widow, who for more than twenty years, wept and prayed for the conversion of her son, who became St. Augustine.

May 5. *St. Pius V.,* Dominican. One of the glorious popes of the sixteenth century.

May 6. *St. John before the Latin Gate.* This feast recalls the martyrdom of the Apostle St. John.

May 7. *St. Stanislaus,* bishop, murdered while saying Mass.

May 8. *Apparition of St. Michael the Archangel,* and *St. Acacius,* invoked for headache.

May 9. *St. Gregory Nazianzen,* bishop and doctor.

May 10. *St. Antonius,* Bishop of Florence, Dominican.

May 11. *SS. Philip and James,* Apostles of our Lord.

May 12. *SS Nereus and Achileus,* officers, first century martyrs.

May 14. *St. Boniface,* martyr.

May 15. *St. John Baptist de la Salle,* founder of the Brothers of Christian Schools.

May 16. *St. Ubald,* bishop.

May 18. *St. Venantius,* a martyr at fifteen.

May 19. *St. Peter Celestine,* pope and founder of the Celestines (a branch of the Benedictine Order).

May 25. *SS. Gregory VII and Urban I,* two martyr popes.

May 28. *St. Augustine of Canterbury,* archbishop and apostle of Britain.

May 29. *St. Mary Magdalen de Pazzi,* Carmelite and virgin. Her motto: "To suffer, and not to die."

May 31. *Mary, Queen of the world* (also, in many places, Our Lady of the Sacred Heart).

B. *FRANCISCAN CALENDAR*

May 12. *St. Ignatius of Laconi,* Capuchin Brother.

May 14. *BB. Benedict, Julius, and James,* Franciscans.

May 17. *St. Paschal Baylon.* Franciscan Brother, named the patron of Eucharistic Congresses and processions by Pope Leo XIII. Let us strive to reproduce within ourselves the eucharistic virtues of this humble and holy Franciscan Brother, that he may obtain for us from God the grace of true devotion to the Eucharist.

May 18. *St. Felix of Cantalice,* Capuchin Brother.

May 19. *St. Theophilus of Corte,* Franciscan priest.

May 20. *St. Bernardine of Siena,* Franciscan priest, promoter of devotion to the Holy Name.

May 21. *BB. Ladislaus,* Franciscan, and Crispin, Capuchin Brother, and Bl. Waldo, Tertiary.

May 22. *BB. John Forest, Godfrey Jones, and Joachim of St. Ann,* Franciscan Martyrs.

May 23. *BB. Bartholomew, Benvenito, and Gerald of Villamagna,* Franciscans.

May 24. *BB. John of Prades, John of Cettina, and Peter Duenas.* Franciscan martyrs.

May 25. *Feast of the Dedication of the Patriarchal Basilica of Assisi and Translation of St. Francis.*

May 26. *St. Anne Mary of Jesus,* virgin and Tertiary, called the "Lily of Quito." Patroness of Ecuador.

May 29. *BB. Stephen and Raymond,* priests. Franciscan martyrs.

May 30. *St. Ferdinand III,* Tertiary and King of Castille; also St. Joan of Arc, virgin and Tertiary, secondary Patroness of France.

ROGATION DAYS

L 40—What are Rogation Days?

Rogation Days (from the Latin *rogare, "to ask, beg,")* are three days of special supplication before Ascension Thursday.

In the fifth century, following a series of public calamities which afflicted the diocese of Vienna, *St. Mamert* inaugurated a triduum of solemn penitential processions before this glorious feast. In 816, Pope Leo III adopted the custom in Rome and soon it spread to the entire Church.

Until now, we have prayed for spiritual benefits. During these three days we shall likewise pray for material benefits: to be delivered from disease, war, and famine; and, in particular, to obtain a good harvest.

"Lord, give us strength to support all our misfortunes with fortitude." *(Postcommunion.)*

During these three days, we shall recite the Litany of the Saints and orations and the *Miserere.* We shall chant the *Parce, Domine.*

ASCENSION THURSDAY

L 41—What is recalled by the Feast of the Ascension?

The Feast of Easter continues to unfold. Today Christ ascends into Heaven. He is exalted and enters into his reward. He goes to take possession of his throne. This is the feast of his official triumph, his whole life's crowning victory.

The Evangelists give us an account of this memorable event. The apostles, who had come to Jerusalem as Pentecost approached, were in the Cenacle when Jesus appeared to them and ate his last meal with them. He then led them out of the city by way of Bethany, on the Mount of Olives, which is the highest of the mountains surrounding the capitol. Jesus then blessed his apostles and ascended into Heaven. It was noon. A cloud concealed him from their sight; and two angels told them that Christ, who had ascended again into Heaven, would return again at the end of the world.

Ascension Day, then, marks the departure of Jesus for Heaven on the fortieth day after his Resurrection.

The Church rejoices—however hard the separation—because of her love for the Beloved. Today Jesus enters into his glory and has gone to prepare ours. Having shared in his sufferings on earth, we shall share in his glory and in his elevation to Heaven.

We ought to dwell today especially on Heaven, in the thought that our Lord's Ascension is an assurance of the happiness that awaits us above, where he has gone to prepare a place for us. As there are "many mansions" in Our Father's House, we shall be rewarded in proportion to our generosity. . . .

"Grant, we implore You, O Almighty God. . .according to our belief in the Ascension into Heaven of Your only-begotten Son, our

Redeemer, that our minds also may dwell in heavenly places." (Collect and Postcommunion.)

This departure is well expressed by the liturgy. After the reading or chanting of the Gospel, the paschal candle is extinguished until next year. Since Easter, its light has reminded us of Christ's presence among his disciples. Now begins the interior reign of the Holy Spirit .

In these days separating us from Pentecost, we ought to prepare ourselves for the coming of the Holy Spirit—like the apostles and our Lady in the Cenacle—by an ardent novena of prayer. (The daily recitation of the *Veni Creator* or of the *Veni, Sancte Spiritus),* and by daily Mass and Communion.

Let us live in recollection, silence, and solitude, so that we may be ready to receive the gifts of the Holy Spirit. He it is who is to teach us all things. He it is—the Spirit of Love—who will renew the face of the earth and transform our souls and our lives.

Sunday within the Octave of the Ascension. Thought for the day: What must I do to go to Jesus? I must do everything for the love of God and my neighbour, under the Holy Spirit's inspiration. I must also be a witness for Christ.

What does this mean? *Witnessing means bringing Christ's invisible love into my daily life.* An example of witnessing; Henri Ghéon became a convert because he "saw God in a man," and that man was Peter Dupouey.

A PRAYER FOR PRIESTS

O God, pour forth in its fullness the spirit of sacrifice upon your priests! For their duty and glory is to be victims; to be consumed for souls: to live without human joys; and frequently to suffer from injustice, persecution, and mistrust. May they think of the words they repeat each day at the altar, "This is My Body. This is My Blood..." May they remember these words and apply them to themselves: "It is no longer I that live, but Christ and Christ crucified. I am like the bread and wine, a consecrated substance that has ceased to be itself!"

O God, I burn with desire for the sanctification of your priests! I desire that the lips that have uttered words of such sublimity at the altar, may never stoop to trivial speech. May everything about your priests bear the imprint of their noble functions. May all men see in the priest a soul that is simple and grand like the Host—superior to all men, yet accessible to all.

Cause your priests to come away from today's Mass athirst for the Mass of the morrow; and, filled themselves with the Gift which they bestow on others, may they receive the grace to do so lavishly.

PENTECOST

L 42—What does Pentecost teach us?

The paschal feast ends at Pentecost, which is *"red Easter"*, the colour of blood, fire, and charity. It is the feast of Springtime—of life bursting forth everywhere.

For the Jews, this was the feast of the First-Fruits, in which the first loaves made with the wheat from the new harvest were offered to God. This feast likewise recalled the promulgation of the Law of God by Moses on Mount Sinai. It was the "Feast of the Law."

For the Church, Pentecost is the feast of the first fruits of the Resurrection—of the first converts. It is the birthday of the Church. It is also the feast of the New Law; not the Law of fear, but the Law of love, brought by the Holy Spirit. With Pentecost, the reign of the Spirit of Jesus is inaugurated. The Redemption passes from the Head to the members.

It was indeed life that we received on Easter; but a life for ourselves—not yet manifested. New life—*is not the Easter egg its symbol?* And the fearful apostles behind the bolted door of the Upper Room!

Under the inspiration of God's Spirit, this life comes forth. A veritable divine tempest beats down upon this embryo Church composed of the Eleven cloistered in the Cenacle. A flash of light—*tongues of fire*—and the fire that Jesus came to bring on the earth is kindled. The doors shake like an egg-shell under the pressure of new life. And those who a few brief moments before trembled like little children, set out to take the dreadful world by storm. At Peter's first sermon, we witness three thousand conversions in a single day! Three thousand new "Christs" conceived by the Holy Spirit! The next day five thousand! From pusillanimous, fearful, timid men, the apostles, filled with the Holy Spirit, become heroes, going on to martyrdom!

Every Christian is called on to reproduce Christ in his life. This is his chief task. Let us not forget that Christ is conceived only by the Holy Spirit. This is the grace of Pentecost, the one for which we shall pray today above all other graces.

Yes, let the Spirit enter with his *seven gifts,* and make us understand, will, and live a Christianity that is dynamic and apostolically fruitful. It is for all these intentions that we shall communicate, after a good Confession and a fervent vigil.

In olden days, on this vigil (of a solemnity equal to that of Easter), those persons were baptized who had been unable to receive Baptism on Holy Saturday. That is why six prophecies are read, followed by the blessing of baptismal water. Fast and partial abstinence are obligatory today.

Throughout the octave, the Church prolongs her prayers for the newly baptized and for all of us; and during the three *Ember Days,* especially on Ember Saturday, she prays that priests ordained on these days may receive the Holy Spirit's gifts. Let us unite our prayers to this great intention of the whole Church—the sanctification of God's ministers.

Each day of the Octave of Pentecost is consecrated to the meditation of and acquiring of a gift of the Holy Spirit. "During this week," counsels Dom Vandeur, "Read, drink, penetrate, and inwardly digest the liturgy of your missal. This for the intelligence. Exercise your heart in the love of God, with the help of the indwelling Holy Spirit. This for the heart. Decide to undertake something great, good, holy, or (if need be) heroic, for God. This for action."

This is the week of important resolutions inspired by the Holy Spirit—have you made yours yet?

L 43—How is the time after Pentecost divided?

Just as for Christmas or Easter, Pentecost comprises a preparation and a continuation:

1. The preparation. The ASCENSION, or ten days of prayer and waiting.

2. The celebration. PENTECOST and its octave.

3. The continuation. THE TIME AFTER PENTECOST. (From Trinity Sunday to the close of the liturgical year—twenty-five or twenty-eight Sundays, depending on whether Easter is late or early.

L 44—How does the Church express the time of Pentecost by her liturgy?

1. *For Ascension Thursday*

a. The disappearance of the paschal candle, extinguished after the Gospel.

b. *By white* vestments, like those of the two angels. mentioned in the Gospel. White recalls the joy of angels and of souls (those detained in Limbo and now introduced into Heaven with Christ), and signifies the purity required to receive the Spirit of Holiness.

c. By the proper of the Mass.

2. *For Pentecost*

a. *Red* vestments to signify the Spirit of Love and the tongues of fire.

b. The proper of the office, the blessing of baptismal fonts, the hymn *Veni Creator,* and sequence, *Veni, Sancte Spiritus.*

3. *For the time after Pentecost*

a. *Green* vestments to signify hope (of Heaven) and the abundance of the fruits of the Spirit in souls. The *Angelus* replaces the *Regina caeli.*

b. The Corpus Christi and Sacred Heart processions.

c. Various feasts in honour of our Lord, of our Lady, of angels and saints, All Saints, All Souls.

Every Sunday after Pentecost and every feast brings with it a special grace which the Church prays God to grant to us. It is up to us, then, to co-operate by taking an active part and by putting the lessons learned into practice.

L 45—What are the principal feasts on the calendar for June?

A. *CALENDAR OF THE UNIVERSAL CHURCH*

June 2nd. *SS. Marcellinus and Peter*, martyrs; St. *Erasmus,* martyr bishop, one of the forty "auxiliary saints." Invoked against intestinal diseases.

June 4. *St. Francis Caracciolo,* founder of the Clerks Minor Regular.

June 5. *St. Boniface,* bishop and martyr, Apostle to Germany.

June 6. *St. Norbert,* bishop, and founder of the Order of the Premonstrants.

June 9. *SS. Primus and Felician,* brothers by blood and martyrdom.

June 10. *St. Margaret,* widow, and Queen of Scotland.

June 11. *St. Barnabas,* apostle, and companion to St. Paul.

June 12. *St. John of Facundus,* confessor.

June 14. *St. Basil the Great*, bishop and Doctor of the Church.

June 15. *SS. Modestus and Vitus,* martyred at the same time. St. Vitus (also called St. Guy) is invoked against St. Vitus' dance, lethargy, and the bites of animals.

June 18. *St. Ephrem,* deacon and doctor, called the "Cither of the Holy Spirit."

June 19. *St. Juliana Falconieri,* virgin.

June 20. *St. Silverius,* pope and martyr.

June 21. *St. Aloysius Gonzaga,* young Jesuit religious, and protector of the purity of youth.

June 22. *St. Paulinus,* Bishop of Nole.

June 24. *Nativity of St. John the Baptist,* precursor of our Lord, Patron of French Canadians.

June 25. *St. William,* abbot, founder of the Congregation of Hermits.

June 26. *SS. John and Paul,* Roman martyrs.

June 27. *Our Lady of Perpetual Help.*

June 28. *St. Ireneus,* Bishop of Lyons, martyr.

June 29. *SS. Peter and Paul,* apostles, called "the two pillars of the primitive Church." The Feast of the Holy See. Let us offer up a more fervent prayer today, then, for the Holy Father, as well as for the new priests to be ordained today.

June 30. *Commemoration of St. Paul,* apostle.

B. *FRANCISCAN CALENDAR*

June 1. *St. Angela of Merici,* Tertiary, foundress of the Ursulines.

June 2. *BB. Herculan,* Franciscan priest; *Felix,* Capuchin Brother; and *John Pelingotto,* Tertiary.

June 8. *BB. Baptista Varani, Isabelle of France, and Agnes of Bohemia,* virgins and Poor Clares.

June 9. *BB. Pacificus of Caredano, Andrew of Spello, and Lawrence,* Franciscans.

June 13. *St. Anthony of Padua,* Franciscan priest, the Evangelical Doctor, especially invoked for the finding of lost articles.

June 15. *Bl. Yolanda,* duchess of Poland, widow and Poor Clare; *Humilane and Paula Gambara,* widows and Tertiaries.

June 17. *St. Ives,* Tertiary priest and patron of lawyers.

June 23. *St. Joseph Cafasso,* Tertiary priest.

June 27. *BB. Guy of Cortona,* Franciscan priest, *and Benvenuto of Gubbio,* a Franciscan Brother invoked for deliverance from crop-destroying insects.

THE TIME AFTER PENTECOST

L 46—What great themes are expressed in the time after Pentecost?

The time after Pentecost is the last and longest part of the liturgical year. It runs from *Trinity Sunday* (the first Sunday after Pentecost) to the *First Sunday of Advent.* As we have said previously, its length varies in accordance with the date of Easter. It can run from *the 10th of May clear up to the 3rd of December.*

In his beautiful *Missal Vespéral,* Dom Gaspar Lefebvre gives a magnificent synthesis of this period of the liturgical year, which we reproduce here:

1. *Explanation of doctrine*: "Following the reign of the Father over the people of God, which is recalled by the Advent season; after that of the Son, which begins with his birth on Christmas and closes with his Ascension, and which recalls the season of Christmas and the Paschal season, the liturgy celebrates the reign of the Holy Spirit, which extends to the whole Church; is manifested starting with Pentecost and continuing to the end of the world; and is mentioned in the 24th and last Sunday after Pentecost. The Pope dominates the ecclesiastical hierarchy, and the Eucharist dominates the Sacraments. The reign of the Holy Spirit, therefore, is visibly manifested by the Church of Rome, from whose centre the Blessed Sacrament radiates. The Spirit is the soul vivifying the Church; Christ, hidden in the Host, is the heart, from whence the blood of grace circulates through the veins, via the channel of the sacraments, into all the members. St. Peter and his successors, with all the bishops, form the head, from whence proceed the nerve fibres commanding the whole body; and this

"body" is made up of all Christians. The sanctification of souls is ascribed to the Holy Spirit; who realizes, in the course of centuries, the entire life of the Saviour in his Mystical Body, the Church. The Mission of the Holy Spirit is to *teach* all things, bringing to mind all that Christ has said and *applying* the merits of his Passion to souls. The reign of the Holy Spirit is the extension of that of Christ, to which he gives a universality of time and place that was lacking in Palestine. For it is no longer the Saviour working alone in one spot of the globe and at a given time; but it is the Church, who, incorporated by virtue of the Holy Spirit in the Blessed Sacrament, constitutes a marvellous prolongation of the Incarnation—a Christ augmented by all our souls.

"The time after Pentecost is more especially consecrated to the cycle of the saints or the life of the Church. The Epistles and Gospels speak to us of the fruits of sanctity produced by the Holy Spirit in souls. And throughout this time, we are spectators of the magnificent flowering of saints which never ceases—in every century and in every clime—to reproduce the soul of Christ. Our souls, after having copied Christ himself, may continue to imitate him in his members—penetrated as they are with the life of their Head.

2. *Historical Background.* "Beginning with the feast of Pentecost which marked her birth, the Church down through the centuries has reproduced in its entirety, the life of Christ, whose Mystical Body she is.

"In infancy, Jesus was persecuted and obliged to flee into Egypt, during the slaughter of the Holy Innocents.—For four centuries, the Church was subject to the most violent persecution and was obliged to hide in the catacombs and in the wilderness.

"Jesus as a youth withdrew to Nazareth, and spent the greater part of his life in meditation and prayer.—The Church, starting with Constantine in the fourth century, knew a long period of peace. Everywhere cathedrals and abbeys arose, within whose walls the divine praises resounded, and wherein bishops and abbots, priests and religious, opposed the encroachments of heresy by means of study and indefatigable zeal.—Christ, the Divine Missionary sent by the Father to earth's far distant regions, began, at thirty, his apostolic career.—The Church, beginning with the sixteenth century, was obliged to resist the assaults of resurgent paganism; and spread Christ's Gospel in the recently discovered portions of the globe. And from her midst new militias and numerous legions of missionaries unceasingly arose, whom she sent throughout the whole world to preach the Good News.

"Christ brought his life to a close by his Sacrifice on Golgotha —soon followed by the triumph of the Resurrection.—The Church at the end of time, like Christ on the Cross, was to appear vanquished; but it would be she that would win the victory. 'The Body of Christ,' wrote St. Augustine, 'like the human body, was once young; but at the end of the world, will appear to men to be aged.' "

L 47—What should we do from a spiritual viewpoint, in the time after Pentecost?

"Christians who received divine life in Baptism at Easter, have as their duty during the course of the year, and particularly on Sunday, to nurture this divine life in the Eucharist and bring it to maturity. It is their duty to banish whatever of worldly or profane may have entered into their hearts. And above all, it is their duty to wait—with ardent longing—for the Lord's return." (Parsch.)

So shall we live now, from day to day, the mysteries we have recalled during the preceding liturgical seasons. We shall daily live our resurrected life.

Every Sunday is really a *"little Easter."* But, whereas the first Sundays after Pentecost stress the Easter theme, the last ones speak to us particularly of Christ's return and turn our eyes toward Heaven. But while waiting, and in order to rise glorious, we must fight. The theme of spiritual combat is presented every Sunday. Now to conquer and triumph, we have the Holy Eucharist—source of charity and guarantee of our resurrection. So we shall communicate at least every Sunday.

"With Advent and Lent, the Christian soul passed through the crucible of the purgative way. It has been initiated into the secrets of the illuminative way by all of Christ's mysteries, from his birth to his Ascension. At Pentecost, the Holy Spirit became its interior Master to teach it the divine science of union. From now on, the soul will live in a more intimate manner the mystery of the unitive way." (Dom Vandeur.)

L 48—Could you say a few words concerning the principal feasts of the time after Pentecost?

Among the principal movable feasts; i.e., those whose date varies with the date of Easter, we may note:

A. TRINITY SUNDAY

Celebrated the first Sunday after Pentecost, this feast opens the time after Pentecost. (The Paschal season having terminated the preceding Saturday, Ember Saturday, the last day of the Octave of Pentecost.

The Feast of the Holy Trinity owes its origin to the fact that the ordinations of Ember Saturday, which were celebrated at night, were prolonged until the following day, Sunday, which lacked a proper liturgy. As every Sunday of the year is consecrated to the Blessed Trinity, on the first Sunday of Pentecost, we celebrate a votive Mass composed in the seventh century in honour of the mystery of the Holy Trinity. *(Missal Vespéral.)*

This mystery sums up all that we know, all of the mysteries encountered:

1. It was the Father who sent his Son to redeem us.
2. It was the Son who reveals the Father and who directs us to him.
3. It is the Holy Spirit who unites men to the Father and Son.

And whatever the Church does, is done in the name of the Father, Son, and Holy Spirit.

It is this intimate life of the Trinity—the life of charity—in which we share. Trinity Sunday is thus a feast of adoration, of recollection, and likewise of thanksgiving. This day we renew the promises of our Baptism.

O Holy Trinity, make me live ever in your presence, and may I be one with my brothers; as you—Father, Son, and Holy Spirit—are one, among yourselves.

B. CORPUS CHRISTI OR THE FEAST OF THE BLESSED SACRAMENT

The austere framework of the liturgy of Holy Week not permitting of the solemn celebration of important feast days, the institution of the Eucharist is not observed in a manner befitting its importance, until after the close of the Paschal Season. Today, that is, the Thursday after Trinity Sunday, we commemorate one of Christ's greatest graces to us—the gift of himself in sacramental form, as the Bread of the Eucharist. It is at the same time Christ's royalty that we celebrate today. The proof is the millions of Catholics who, all over the globe, kneel in adoration to proclaim their faith in their Head, mysteriously present in the Sacred Host.

In most places, the Feast of Corpus Christi—or more precisely, the Feast of the Blessed Sacrament—is celebrated the Sunday within the octave (i.e. the Second Sunday after Pentecost.)

Our attitude during this day and throughout the octave will be that of thanksgiving and gratitude for the inestimable gift of the Holy Eucharist.

We shall assist in preparing the repository. We shall donate flowers, and adorn our dwellings—but more than all else, our hearts.

We shall profit by this eucharistic feast to make a little examination of conscience as to our relations with Jesus in the Blessed Sacrament:

Could not our Communions be more frequent? . . . More fervent? . . . Our Mass better lived? . . .

Could not our visits to the Blessed Sacrament be more numerous?

Are we enthusiastic and zealous in spreading devotion toward the Holy Eucharist?

In these days we shall read the *sixth chapter* of St. John's Gospel. . . . the Sequence of the Mass of the Feast: *Lauda Sion. . .*the *Pange lingua.*

C. THE FEAST OF THE SACRED HEART

The Friday following the octave of Corpus Christi, the Church observes the *Feast of the Sacred Heart.* This is the feast of Jesus' love for his Father and for us. This love inspired his every act and led him to the "folly of the Cross."

The destitution of the Crib, the thirty years of self-effacement in the workship at Nazareth, the painful labours contingent on the preaching of the Gospel, the ingratitude of the Jews, and finally the drama of Calvary—all this from love!

It is particularly on the Cross that Christ glorifies his Father and saves men, that the love of Jesus' heart is made manifest. The heart pierced by the lance is the symbol of this love which continues to the end.

But it is not Jesus alone who ought to love the Father and atone. It is ALL OF US. When Jesus died, it was to merit for us the strength to love with him and to make reparation with him. Now that is the very thing we forget! Men leave Jesus to love and to make reparation all alone. Thus they render useless, inoperative, Christ's reparation and love.

Let us make reparation for ourselves. Let us also atone for those who do not atone.

Let us atone first of all by regretting our sins, by accepting suffering, by imposing voluntary penances on ourselves, by together offering all our love at Mass, with Jesus and Mary, to the glory of God the Father.

We shall recite daily the *Litany of the Sacred Heart* and the *chapelet of the Sacred Heart.* Let us often repeat, "*Jesus meek and humble of heart, make my heart like unto Yours,*" etc.

If you have not already done so, you will want to enthrone the *Sacred Heart* in your home or room. Next, you will consecrate yourselves to this Divine Heart with all the members of your family.

We have drawn up for the use of "victim souls" (see page 198) a text for enthronement of the *Sacred Heart* in their office or room, and a formula of *consecration.*

We insert these two texts here, in the hope that under the Holy Spirit's influence, they may prove beneficial:

ENTHRONEMENT OF THE SACRED HEART
(In my room or office)

O Jesus, my God, my Saviour and my Perfect Model, I welcome You to my humble room.

I adore You with my whole being, and recognize You as my King. I enthrone You here in my room, in the place of honour; desiring thereby to express to You that I consider You the Guide and Master of my whole life. I introduce You here, O my Divine Friend, that I may dwell with You, work with You, suffer with You, pray with You, live with You, and die with You. I have made a place for You in my home, and near me, because I wish to be more closely united to You, in order to think, love, will, rule my life, and work more in accordance with Your spirit and plans.

Lord Jesus, my King and my Friend, great is my need for You! For deep down, I love You so little! I lose You so easily from sight! I speak to You so rarely...and when I do, I speak so often of myself! I work with so deficient a supernatural intention, with so much vanity and so much absorption with earth! My apostolate suffers from this! O my King of Love, O tender Lover of souls, You chose me as Your apostle, that I might go forth and bear abundant and lasting fruit. This is my dearest wish. Strengthen my resolution to win souls for You, especially souls for Your priesthood.

For these reasons, I have prepared for You here a residence and a throne. I would, with You, begin a new life—a life of love and fruitfulness.

I will sit down at my work table with Your picture before me, to work in Your presence. I will never enter my room or leave it without imploring Your blessing. Before taking up my pen, before opening a book, or doing any work, I will look up to You for aid and counsel. Before opening a letter or starting one, I will look up to You for light and Your consent. During my spiritual reading, study, or other occupations, I will turn toward You with trust, every time that I come across some obscure point or difficulty.

Here it is, before Your image, that I will come with my perplexities. Here, close to You, I will kneel when tempted or sad. Here it is that I will come for strength, solace, and comfort, instead of seeking these from people—or in the world's clamourous pleasures.

Is not Your Heart burning with love, surrounded by flames...Your Heart thorn-crowned and surmounted by a cross...just as it appeared to St. Margaret Mary...to remind me of the debt of gratitude I owe You, O my beloved Saviour? And does it not invite me to sacrifice myself in turn, that I may set on fire with divine love this world frozen over with selfishness and hate?

Yes, O Jesus, I promise it! You can count on me! And every night I will give You an accounting of my day.

O my Jesus, my King, remember that I am Your apostle entirely consecrated to Your service.... Remember that I am Your 'victim for priests.' Remember that on my sanctification depends the salvation of so many of my brothers. . . . Please help be to become holy! Have mercy on your poor child who is so weak, and draw me to Your Heart pierced by the lance. Remember the love that fills Your Divine Heart and wills to overflow in other hearts. Remember its sadness at lost souls. Forget my unworthiness and permit me to enter Your Heart—that burning furnace of charity. Let me dwell in it, transform myself in it, consume myself in it. Never permit the manual labour that I do, my secular occupations, work among others, or conversations with friends, to distract me from thoughts of You and from Your love. Never permit me to return to the wasted hours, and acts without merit and without fruit of the past. Fill me with Your life and spirit. Be the force and light of the words that I speak to my neighbour and of those I write. . . . Be the Guide and Commander of all that I do, wherever I may be or go.

O Jesus, I want to live and act so united to You, be in all things so dependent on You, that I may joyously repeat, "I live, I labour, I toil, I suffer, but no longer like a pagan, or a doubting Thomas, or an egoistical drone. No. I live, but it is no longer I that live! No longer am I my own guide; trusting in my own strength and wisdom. It is "Christ who lives in me." It is You, O Jesus, who live, suffer, and labour in me and through me. It is You who direct all and make all fruitful.

Since souls are instructed by the Word, but are saved through suffering; in order that my apostolate may bear fruit, I accept in advance all the crosses that You may see fit to send me:

The cross of ingratitude.
The cross of jealousy.
The cross of being misunderstood.
The cross of betrayal.
The cross of calumny.
The cross of failure.
The cross of being forsaken.
The cross of poverty.
The cross of physical or spiritual suffering.
The cross of separation from loved ones.
The cross of mortality.

I accept everything, even inactivity, to sustain the activity of Your priests.

O Mary, Queen of the clergy and my Mother, I give myself to Jesus through you! Form within me a "host" worthy of you, so that I may soon become a victim of love for priests.

St. Francis, Patron of Catholic Action, you who, though not a priest, had so exalted a concept of the priesthood; you who loved Christ to the point of having your hands, feet, and heart pierced; unite yourself to me, so that I may soon become like you—a furnace of love, sending forth light and warmth.... And may I ever remain true to my sublime vocation of victim. Like you, I would choose for my ambition the bringing of all souls to Heaven!

It is done. My sacrifice is accomplished, O Christ. Henceforth, You are the King and Master, not only of this room but of all who dwell therein. My home is Yours.

I abandon myself wholly to your good pleasure. Do with me what You will.

CONSECRATION TO THE SACRED HEART
OF A "VICTIM FOR PRIESTS"

O adorable Heart of Jesus, the most loving, the most generous of hearts! I, Your victim for priests, am filled with gratitude at the sight of all Your benefits and of my sublime vocation of victim—of one wholly devoted to Your dearest interests.

Today, together with all kindred souls, who, like me, devote and immolate themselves in the service of Your priests, I want through Mary—in their name and my own—to offer myself anew to You; to consecrate myself to You utterly and irrevocably. I want to be a Christian according to Your Heart. I want to employ all my strength to make men love You; and to win, if possible all hearts to You. Receive my heart, O Jesus; or rather, take it Yourself. Change it and purify it that it may be worthy of You! Make it gentle, humble, patient, faithful, and generous like Yours, setting it on fire with the flames of Your love. Hide it in Your Divine Heart, with all those hearts that love You and are consecrated to You. Never permit me to take it back!

Ah, it were better to die, than to sadden Your adorable Heart!

Yes, I give myself wholly to You! Here is my body; here is my blood. Take them! Here are my energies, my strength, my goods, my talents, and all that I possess. Take them, for all is Yours.... I know that such an offering implies many sacrifices and much suffering...but does it not take a soul to save a soul, out of the millions of periled souls? With the help of Your grace, I will never give up! It is above all through my Mass that I desire to transform my life and the lives of others by uniting my sacrifice with Yours.

Make divine all that is human in me. Unite to Your infinitely merciful Heart, my own heart, saddened at seeing You so little loved!

Transform my daily cross into a living crucifix; in such a way that it will be no longer I who live, but You living in me. Never permit my sufferings, pains, and afflictions to be lost. Gather up the fragments.... Just as the lowly drop of water is absorbed into the wine of the chalice, so let my life be transformed into Yours. Let my tiny crosses be intertwined with Your immense Cross; so that with You, I may save souls and merit for multitudes the eternal joys of Heaven.

Consecrate the joys and trials of my life; for devoid of union with You, they merit no recompense.

Transform me, "transubstantiate" me, so that as the bread becomes your Body at the Consecration and the wine your Blood; I, too, may be lost in You. It matters little that the "appearances" remain the same; it matters little that in the eyes of others, I seem the same as before. My state of life, my daily occupations, my work, my family, my neighbour—all these things are but the "species," the "appearances," of my life—appearances that may very well remain unchanged.... But the *substance* of my life—my soul, intelligence, will, and heart—"transubstantiate" them, totally transform them; so that You may think with my mind, love with my heart, will with my will, speak through my lips, and act through all my members. Yes, Heart of Jesus, always to love, honour, and serve You in the person of your priests, and of those persons You place on my path; and to be Yours forever—such is the desire of my heart for all eternity.

My beloved Mother Mary, Mother of the First Priest, and Queen of the clergy; obtain for me to remain pure, generous, submissive, and faithful to my engagements; so that every day I may become a little less unworthy of my sublime vocation of victim for priests.

THE MORE I AM A VICTIM, THE MORE THEY WILL BE PRIESTS!
THE LESS I AM A VICTIM, THE LESS THEY WILL BE PRIESTS!

Heart of Jesus, burning with love for us,
Set my heart on fire with love for You!

"Lord, may the burning and delicious ardour of your love, detach my soul from all creatures under heaven; that I may die for love of Your love—who for love of my love did deign to die." (St. Francis of Assisi.)

L 49—Please state in a few words the general theme for the Sundays after Pentecost.

Here, briefly, is the general theme as indicated in the Epistle or Gospel:

Third Sunday after Pentecost: God's mercy toward sinners.
Fourth Sunday: Trust in God despite temptation and danger.
Fifth Sunday: Harmonious relations with our neighbour.
Sixth Sunday: The food of the Baptized is the Holy Eucharist.
Seventh Sunday: The tree is known by its fruits.
Eighth Sunday: Our duty to live as children of God.
Ninth Sunday: Fidelity to grace.
Tenth Sunday: The need for humility.
Eleventh Sunday: God's mercy.
Twelfth Sunday: Brotherly love.
Thirteenth Sunday: The spirit of faith and the duty of gratitude.
Fourteenth Sunday: Only one Master.
Fifteenth Sunday: The life of faith and the happy result of a visit from Jesus.
Sixteenth Sunday: The first place in my heart for Jesus.
Seventeenth Sunday: Love of God and neighbour.
Eighteenth Sunday: Heaven and the grandeur of the divine power of the priest.
Nineteenth Sunday: The great obstacle to grace—sin.
Twentieth Sunday: Time prepares for eternity—Persevering prayer.
Twenty-first Sunday: Forgiveness.
Twenty-second Sunday: Justice toward God and the State.
Twenty-third Sunday: Supplication.
Twenty-fourth Sunday: The end of the world.

L 50—Please name the principal feasts on the July Calendar.

A. CALENDAR OF THE UNIVERSAL CHURCH

Jul. 1. *The Most Precious Blood.* This feast affords us an opportunity for renewing our eucharistic devotion. For this Precious Blood is not only the Blood which flowed from the Saviour's wounds, but also the Blood which every morning on our altars streams from the heart of the Lamb to purify the sin of the whole world. Let us likewise pray for vocations to the priesthood; for the greater the number of holy priests, the more efficacious will be the outpouring of this redeeming Blood on the earth.

Jul. 2. *The Visitation.* The Blessed Virgin Mary visits her cousin, Elisabeth. This is the feast of the Magnificat. Let us honour Mary in this mystery, by our own practice of the duty of charity toward our afflicted and suffering brothers and sisters. (i.e. Not by means of vain consolations, but by giving them Christ Jesus.)

Jul. 5. *St. Anthony Zaccaria,* founder of the clerks regular of St. Paul (or Barnabites).

Jul. 7. *SS. Cyril and Methodius,* bishops.

Jul. 10. *The Seven Holy Brothers,* sons of St. Felicita; also *SS. Rufina and Secunda,* virgins and martyrs.

Jul. 11. *St. Pius I,* pope and martyr.

Jul. 12. *St. John Gualbert,* abbot.

Jul. 15. *St. Henry,* emperor.

Jul. 16. *Our Lady of Mt. Carmel,* feast of the brown scapular.

Jul. 17. *St. Alexis,* confessor.

Jul. 18. *St. Camillus de Lellis,* founder of a congregation of clerks to serve the sick.

Jul. 19. *St. Vincent de Paul,* priest founder of the Lazarists and the Daughters of Charity.

Jul. 20. *St. Jerome Aemilion,* support of orphans, the poor, and the plague-stricken. *St. Margaret,* virgin and martyr, invoked for kidney ailments and by expectant mothers.

Jul. 21. *St. Praxedes,* virgin and martyr.

Jul. 22. *St. Mary Magdelene,* penitent.

Jul. 23. *St. Appollinarius*, bishop and martyr, companion of St. Peter.

Jul. 25. *St. James the Greater,* Apostle of our Lord. *St. Christopher,* martyr, invoked for a safe journey or voyage.

Jul. 26. *St. Anne,* Mother of the Blessed Virgin Mary, Patroness of the Province of Quebec.

Jul. 27. *St. Pantaleon,* martyr, invoked against tuberculosis.

Jul. 29. *St. Martha,* model of the active life.

B. FRANCISCAN CALENDAR

Jul. 4. *BB. Gregory and companions,* Franciscans and Tertiaries, martyred in China.

Jul. 8. *St. Elizabeth,* Queen of Portugal, widow, Tertiary.

Jul. 9. *The Holy Martyrs of Gorcum,* Franciscan martyrs.

Jul. 10. *BB. Emmanuel Ruiz and companions,* Franciscan martyrs.

Jul. 11. *St. Veronica Guiliani,* virgin and Poor Clare.

Jul. 13. *St. Francis Solano,* Franciscan priest, Apostle of Peru.

Jul. 14. *St. Bonaventure,* Franciscan cardinal, 8th Minister General of the Franciscan Order, Seraphic Doctor.

Jul. 15. *The Holy Sepulchre of our Lord,* Let us renew our devotion to our Saviour's Passion and pray for the missionaries in the Holy Land.

Jul. 21. *Bl. Angeline of Marsciano,* countess, widow, foundress of the Third Order Regular (cloistered).

Jul. 23. *St. Lawrence of Brindisi,* Capuchin priest.

Jul. 24. *BB. Cunegund, Petronilla, and Felicia,* virgins and Poor Clares.

Jul. 27. *Bl. Magdelene Martinengo,* virgin and Capuchin Poor Clare.

Jul. 30. *BB. Simon, Peter, and Archangel,* Franciscan priests.

Jul. 31. *St. Ignacius of Loyola,* Tertiary, founder of the Jesuits, author of the "Spiritual Exercises."

L 51—What are the principal feasts for the month of August?

A. CALENDAR OF THE UNIVERSAL CHURCH

Aug. 1. *St. Peter in Chains,* a feast venerating the chains of the Apostle Peter in prison.

Aug. 2. *St. Alphonsus Ligouri,* bishop and Doctor, founder of the Redemptorist Fathers.

Aug. 5. *Our Lady of the Snows,* feast of the dedication of the Basilica dedicated to her.

Aug. 6. *Transfiguration of our Lord,* before his three apostles, Peter, James, and John, on Mount Thabor.

Aug. 8. *St. Cyriacus,* deacon and martyr, invoked for diseases of the eyes and diabolical possession.

Aug. 10. *St. Lawrence,* martyr, one of the most glorious deacons of the Church of Rome.

Aug. 11. *SS. Tibertius and Susanna, martyrs.*

Aug. 13. *SS. Hippolyte and Cassian,* martyrs.

Aug. 14. *St. Eusebius,* Roman priest who combatted the Arian heresy.

Aug. 15. *The Assumption of the Blessed Virgin,* the feast celebrating our Lady's glorious ascension into Heaven with body and soul, following upon her death of love in the Lord. Let us pray Mary for the grace of a holy death like hers.

Aug. 16. *St. Joachim,* father of the Blessed Virgin.

Aug. 17. *St. Hyacinth,* Dominican religious.

Aug. 18. *St. Agapitus,* fifteen-year old martyr.

Aug. 19. *St. John Eudes,* founder of the Eudes Fathers and the Sisters of the Good Shepherd.

Aug. 20. *St. Bernard,* abbot, the "honey-tongued" Doctor, and great lover of devotion to Mary.

Aug. 22. *The Immaculate Heart of Mary,* a feast requested by Mary herself in her apparitions at Fatima. Let us renew our consecration.

Aug. 23. *St. Philip Benizi,* confessor. General of the Servite Order.

Aug. 24. *St. Bartholomew,* one of the twelve Apostles of our Lord.

Aug. 26. *St. Zephyrinus,* pope and martyr.

Aug. 28. *St. Augustine,* bishop, Doctor of the Church, the son of St. Monica.

Aug. 29. *The Beheading of St. John the Baptist,* Feast of the martyrdom of the Precursor of Christ.

Aug. 30. *St. Rose of Lima,* virgin [and Dominican Tertiary].

Aug. 31. *St. Raymond Nonnatus,* confessor, cardinal.

B. FRANCISCAN CALENDAR

Aug. 2. *The Portiuncula, or Feast of Our Lady of the Angels.* Great Pardon of the Portiuncula. All the faithful will want to gain this marvellous indulgence (which St. Francis obtained through Mary's intercession) in order to help sinners and the souls in Purgatory.

Aug. 4. *Our Father, St. Dominic,* founder of the Dominicans and friend of St. Francis. The first cordbearer.

Aug. 7. *BB. Agathangel of Vendome and Cassian of Nantes,* Capuchin martyrs; also *St. Gaetan*, Tertiary priest, founder of the Theatines, dubbed the "hunter of souls."

Aug. 9. *St. John Mary Vianney,* the holy Curé of Ars, Tertiary.

Aug. 12. *St. Clare of Assisi,* virgin, foundress of the "Poor Ladies" or Poor Clares; collaborator with St. Francis in the maintenance of poverty in the Franciscan Order.

Aug. 13. *BB. John and Vincent,* Franciscans, and *Bl. Novellon,* Tertiary.

Aug. 17. *St. Roch,* Tertiary, especially invoked in public calamities and epidemics.

Aug. 18. *BB. Beatrice of Sylva and Paula of Montaldi,* virgins and Poor Clares; also *St. Clare of Montefalco*, virgin and Tertiary.

Aug. 19. *St. Louis of Anjou,* bishop and confessor, Franciscan.

Aug. 21. *St. Jane Frances de Chantal,* widow and Tertiary, foundress of the Order of the Visitation.

Aug. 25. *St. Louis IX,* King of France, patron of the Brothers of the Third Order.

Aug. 26. *BB. Timothy of Montecchio,* Franciscan priest, and *Bernard of Offida,* Capuchin Brother.

Aug. 27. *The Seven Joys of Mary,* a feast particularly dear to the Franciscan family. *St. Joseph Calasanctius,* cordbearer.

L 52—What are the principal feasts on the calendar for September?

A. CALENDAR OF THE UNIVERSAL CHURCH

Sept. 1. *St. Giles* or *Aegidius,* abbot, and the *Twelve Holy Martyr Brothers.* St. Giles is invoked against panic, insanity, and nightmares.

Sept. 2. *St. Stephen,* first King and Apostle of Hungary.

Sept. 5. *St. Lawrence Justinian,* Bishop of Venice.

Sept. 8. *The Nativity of the Blessed Virgin Mary.* Let us rejoice and give thanks today to God for bestowing so great a benefit on earth.

Sept. 9. *St. Gorgon,* martyr officer.

Sept. 10. *St. Nicholas of Tolentino,* hermit of St. Augustine.

Sept. 11. *SS. Protus and Hyacinth,* two brother martyrs.

Sept. 12. *The Holy Name of Mary.* Let us reverence it and often invoke it.

Sept. 14. *The Exaltation of the Holy Cross,* by Heraclius, who by his victory rescued it from the hands of idolators.

Sept. 15. *The Seven Dolors.* Let us feel compassion for the sufferings which the Blessed Mother willed to accept and endure for us. What shall be our response to so loving a Mother?...

Sept. 16. *St. Cornelius,* pope and martyr, and *St. Cyprian,* Bishop of Carthage.

Sept. 19. *St. Januarius,* bishop, *and his companions,* marytrs.

Sept. 20. *St.* Eustache, martyred with his *companions.* He is especially invoked against temporal and eternal fire.

Sept. 21. *St. Matthew,* Apostle of our Lord and one of the four Evangelists.

Sept. 22. *St. Thomas of Villanova,* bishop, also *St. Maurice and his companions,* martyrs of the Thebian Legion.

Sept. 23. *St. Linus,* pope and martyr.

Sept. 24. *Our Lady of Mercy.*

Sept. 26. *St. John of Brebeuf and his companions,* martyrs, secondary patrons of Canada. *SS. Cyprian and Justine, martyrs.*

Sept. 27. *SS. Cosmos and Damian,* martyr physicians, mentioned in the Canon.

Sept. 28. *St. Wenceslaus, duke and martyr.*

Sept. 29. *Dedication of St. Michael the Archangel,* chief of the Angels who overthrew Lucifer.

Sept. 30. *St. Jerome,* priest and Doctor, the most famous translator of the Bible.

B. FRANCISCAN CALENDAR

Sept. 1. *BB. John of Perugia and Peter of Sasso-Ferrato,* Franciscan martyrs.

Sept. 2. *BB. John Francis Burte and Apollinarius Moral,* Franciscans, and *Severin Girault,* Third Order regular, all martyred in Paris.

Sept. 4. *St. Rosalia of Viterba,* virgin and Tertiary.

Sept. 5. *BB. Gentil of Mathelica and Thomas of Tolentino,* and *Raymond Lulle,* Tertiary and martyr.

Sept. 6. *BB. Liberat,* priest, *Santes* and *Peregrin,* Franciscan Brothers.

Sept. 9. *Bl. Seraphine Sforza,* widow and Poor Clare. *BB. Louise* and *Micheline,* widows, Tertiaries.

Sept. 10. *The Blessed Forty-five Martyrs of Japan,* Franciscan Tertiaries.

Sept. 11. *Bl. Bonaventure of Barcelona,* Franciscan Brother.

Sept. 17. *The Stigmata of St. Francis.* Christ impressed his divine wounds in Francis' body, to affirm to the world that the Poverello had achieved resemblance with Christ. Let us strive wholeheartedly to resemble Christ by imitating the virtues of the Saint of Assisi.

Sept. 18. *St. Joseph of Cupertino,* Franciscan priest, especially invoked for success in examinations.

Sept. 23. *Discovery of the body of St. Clare.*

Sept. 24. *St. Pacific,* Franciscan priest.

Sept. 25. *Bl. Francis Mary,* Franciscan priest.

Sept. 26. *BB. Lucy of Salerno, and Delphine of Glandeves,* virgins and Tertiaries.

Sept. 27. *St. Elzear,* count of Sabran, Tertiary, who practiced virginity in the married state.

Sept. 28. *BB. Bernadine of Feltre, John of Dukla and Francis of Calderola,* Franciscan priests.

L 53—What are the principal feasts for the month of October?

A. *CALENDAR OF THE UNIVERSAL CHURCH*

Oct. 1. *Guardian Angels.* Let us, like St. Francis, have a great devotion to the holy angels. Let us commend ourselves to these celestial spirits that they may "keep us in all our ways."

Oct. 3. *St. Thérèse of the Child Jesus.* The example of the Little Flower's devotion to the mission cause is so inspiring and at the same time so practical, that the Holy Father declared her to be "patroness of missionaries." Our prayers, sacrifices, and duty of state fulfilled, will thus prove fruitful for souls; provided our sacrifices are made in the spirit of St. Thérèse, who, without ever quitting her cloister, always did everything for love of God.

Oct. 5. *St. Placidus and his companions,* martyrs.

Oct. 6. *St. Bruno,* founder of the Chartreux monks.

Oct. 7. *The Most Holy Rosary.* Let us stir up our devotion toward the Blessed Virgin; and in response to her desire, recently expressed at Fatima, be faithful in daily recitation of the Rosary.

Oct. 9. *St. Denis,* bishop, martyred with his companions. Especially invoked against diabolic possession.

Oct. 11. *The Maternity of the Blessed Virgin Mary.* Let us be mindful on this beautiful day to offer our grateful prayers to the Blessed Mother. Why not make it a habit (if we have time) to recite the Little Office of the Blessed Virgin, or some other prayer in Mary's honour on her feast days?

Oct. 13. *St. Edward the Confessor,* King of England.

Oct. 15. *St. Teresa of Avila,* virgin, reformer of the Carmelites.

Oct. 16. *St. Hedwig,* widow, and duchess of Poland.

Oct. 17. *St. Margaret Mary Alacoque,* virgin, nun of the Visitation, confidant of the Sacred Heart, and protaganist of this devotion in the world.

Oct. 18. *St. Luke,* Evangelist and companion of the Apostle Paul. Called "Mary's historian," because he is the evangelist who wrote most about our Lady.

Oct. 24. *St. Raphael the Archangel,* whose name means, "God heals," was sent by the Lord to cure Tobias.

Oct. 28. *SS. Simon and Jude,* Apostles of our Lord.

B. *FRANCISCAN CALENDAR*

Oct. 1. *Bl. Francis of Pisaro,* Franciscan, and *Nicholas of Forca,* Tertiary.

Oct. 4. *St. Francis of Assisi,* deacon, and founder of the Three Orders: Franciscan, Poor Clares, and the Third Order. He is also the heavenly Patron of Catholic Action. Undoubtedly, every true child of St. Francis or militant of Catholic Action ought to observe this feast with special fervour—Mass, Communion, practical resolutions—in order to obtain from St. Francis all the graces necessary for his apostolic activity.

Oct. 6. *St. Mary Frances of the Five Wounds,* virgin of the Third Order, a "victim" for sinners.

Oct. 8. *St. Bridget,* widow and Tertiary, foundress of the Order of St. Saviour.

Oct. 10. *St. Daniel and his companions,* Franciscans, martyrs in Morocco; also *St. Francis of Borgia,* Tertiary, who became general of the Jesuits.

Oct. 12. *St. Seraphin.*

Oct. 19. *St. Peter of Alcantara,* priest, reformer of the Franciscans, author of a magnificent treatise on prayer. Two virtues are characteristic: piety and mortification—virtues which the Church has us pray for in the collect of the day.

Oct. 21. *BB. James of Strepa and Matthew of Girgenti,* Franciscan bishops.

Oct. 23. *Bl. Josephine Leroux,* virgin and Poor Clare, a martyr of the French Revolution.

Oct. 25. *BB. Christopher of Milan, Balthassier Ravascheiri,* and *Thomas of Florence,* Franciscan.

Oct. 26. *Bl. Bonaventure of Potenza,* Franciscan.

Oct. 27. *Bl. Contardo Ferrini,* Tertiary.

Oct. 30. *Bl. Angel of Acri,* Capuchin.

A PRAYER TO CHRIST THE KING

O Christ Jesus, I acknowledge you as universal King. All that has been made was created for you. Exercise over me all the rights that you have.

I renew my baptismal promises, renouncing Satan, his pomps and his works; and I promise to live as a good Christian. Especially do I pledge myself, by all the means in my power, to bring about the triumph of the rights of God and of your Church.

Divine Heart of Jesus, I consecrate all my poor actions to the cause of your Kingship; that all hearts may acknowledge you their Ruler and so establish the Kingdom of your peace in all the world. Amen.

A plenary indulgence is attached to the recitation of the PRAYER TO CHRIST THE KING, under the usual conditions: Confession, Communion, visit to a church and prayers for the intention of the Holy Father. (At least, one Our Father, Hail Mary, and Glory Be.)

The last Sunday in October
FEAST OF CHRIST THE KING

The aim of the liturgical year being, on the one hand, to glorify Christ—and through him the Blessed Trinity—and on the other, Christ's development in our souls, the *Feast of Christ the King* truly crowns the whole of the liturgical year now drawing to a close.

Gloriously reigning at the Father's right hand, Christ ought likewise to reign over peoples, families, and individuals. He ought to be King of our thoughts, our affections, and all our activity.

On this day let us often repeat this ejaculatory prayer, *"Lord, Your Kingdom come!"* And let us—beginning today—destroy whatever could impede his reign in our life.

L 54—What are the principal feasts on the calendar for November?

A. *CALENDAR OF THE UNIVERSAL CHURCH*:

Nov. 1. *All Saints.*—In this liturgical period, on the Feast of All Saints, the Church Triumphant comes to encourage us and assist us in the effort required for being ourselves placed in the ranks of the conquerors. Let us reread today's Epistle and Gospel, so as to live in such a way as to assure ourselves of "the victor's palm."

Nov. 2. *All Souls.* This day furnishes an auspicious occasion for recalling our duty toward the dead. Let us be eager to gain for them as many as possible of the plenary indulgences which the Church places at our disposal today for every visit to a church or public chapel; with the recitation each time of six Our Fathers, Hail Marys, and Glory Bes for the intentions of the Supreme Pontiff, and the usual conditions of Confession and Communion.

Nov. 5. *The Feast of the Holy Relics,* has as its purpose the veneration by the faithful of the remains of those Saints glorified by God and the Church. These visible remains (bones, ashes, clothing, or other objects used by those Saints now in Heaven) constitute for us a continual sermon; and a pressing invitation to fidelity, courage, and hope in time of trial. Moreover, these relics often bring us many graces, and even miracles, which God seems to attach to their use.

Nov. 9. *Dedication of the Archbasilica of the Holy Saviour.* This is one of the great Roman basilicas, known today under the title of the Lateran Basilica.

Nov. 15. *St. Albert the Great,* bishop and Doctor of the Church.

Nov. 16. *St. Gertrude,* virgin and Benedictine abbess; the first revealer of devotion to the Sacred Heart.

Nov. 17. *St. Gregory Thaumaturgus,* bishop.

Nov. 18. *Dedication of the Basilicas of SS. Peter and Paul* at Rome.

Nov. 21. *Presentation of the Blessed Virgin.* Following the example of our Lady, who unhesitatingly consecrated herself wholly to God's service—and that at an early age—let us offer ourselves to God, consecrating ourselves to him body and soul, if not by the vow of virginity, at least by the virtue of chastity, according to our state in life.

Nov. 22. *St. Cecilia,* virgin and martyr, mentioned in the Canon. She is the patroness of musicians, because of the angelic concerts she heard when she offered praise to the Lord.

Nov. 24. *St. John of the Cross,* Carmelite religious, Doctor of the Church, and reformer of Carmel, together with St. Teresa of Avila.

Nov. 25. *St. Catherine,* virgin and martyr. She is the patroness of Christian philosophers, students, orators, and advocates; because she converted many scholars by her learning and logic.

Nov. 30. *St. Andrew,* Apostle of our Lord, remarkable for his love of the Cross.

B. *FRANCISCAN CALENDAR*

Nov. 4. *St. Charles Borromeo,* bishop Tertiary. Cardinal protector of the Friars Minor.

Nov. 5. *Feast of the holy relics.*

Nov. 6. *BB. Margaret of Lorraine,* Poor Clare; and *Jane of Maille,* Tertiary. The latter is invoked against timidity and fear.

Nov. 7. *BB. Helen Enselmini, Margaret Colonna, and Mathia of Nazzarei,* virgins and Poor Clares.

Nov. 13. *St. Didacus,* patron of Franciscan Brothers, who by their prayers, sacrifices, and manual labour facilitate and make fruitful the ministry of Franciscan priests.

Nov. 16. *St. Agnes of Assisi,* virgin and Poor Clare; sister of St. Clare.

Nov. 17. *BB. Salome, Jeanne, Elizabeth the Good,* virgins, Poor Clare, and Tertiaries.

Nov. 19. *St. Elizabeth of Hungary,* Duchess of Thuringia, widow, Tertiary, patroness of Tertiary Sisters. Remarkable for her charity toward the poor and needy.

Nov. 26. *St. Leonard of Port Maurice,* Franciscan Priest; patron of preachers and missionaries in Catholic countries.

Nov. 27. *BB. Bernardine of Fossa and Humble of Bisiniano,* Franciscans.

Nov. 28. *St. James of the Marches,* Franciscan.

Nov. 29. *All Saints of the Franciscan Order.* Illumined and warmed by the virtues of its glorious Founder, the Franciscan Order has always been a glowing furnace of sanctity. In addition to the 374 saints and blesseds of the three Orders whom the Church has officially recognized, there is a multitude of disciples of St. Francis whose merits and sacrifices are known to God alone. That is why, in a single feast, the Church permits us to venerate and invoke them; so that following in their train, we may obtain the grace to be intrepid in the Lord's battles and fervent in his service.

BIBLIOGRAPHY

Dom Guéranger: L'Année liturgique.
Pius Parsch: Le Guide de l'Année liturgique.
Fr. Benjamin, O.F.M. Cap.: En Prière avec la Sainte Eglise.
J. Colomb, P.S.S.: Histoire sainte et Liturgie.
Dom Gaspar Lefebvre: Missel vespéral (etc.)

IT IS HARD

To be prudent.
To be altruistic.
To begin again.
To avoid routine.
To apologize.
To mollify an angry man.
To support success.
To think before one acts.
To face ridicule.
To forgive and forget.
To acknowledge a mistake.
To remain true to one's ideals.
To accept a merited rebuke.
To do wonders with little.
To believe that sunshine always follows rain—

But it's worth it!

A TEACHER'S PRAYER

Lord Jesus, Supreme Educator of souls, I thank you for having called me to this wonderful task of education.

Make me ever more worthy of the confidence shown me by parents, by entrusting to me what is dearest to them in this world—their children!

Teach me to treat these souls with the delicacy and infinite patience of your Holy Spirit.

Grant me your light, the better to read hearts; your perspicacity for discerning your work and penetrating your designs; your mercy, for forgiving and healing; your wisdom for counseling and directing the young lives entrusted to me.

May my actions be your actions, my hands, your hands; my lips, your lips; my life, your life; so that nothing may touch these children that is not divine, and that I may not impede your action in their souls.

Grant me not to deviate in my teaching from the great laws of your Redemption; never to forget that the one essential is for the Kingdom of Heaven to be preached to every man born into this world, and for it to be transmitted to my students in all its truth and beauty.

And to you, Mary, whom God gave to the Child Jesus as an educator, you to whom men in these recent times have given the beautiful title of "Our Lady of the Schools;" obtain for me your docility to the Holy Spirit and your submission to the divine will; so that I may always be able to recognize the Heavenly Father's plans for each of my pupils, and assist them in finding the place destined for them by your Beloved Son in the great task of the world's redemption. Amen.

THE MOST PLEASING, THE MOST USEFUL

GIVE ME a farthing while you are still alive. This pleases Me more, and will be more useful to you, than if you were to give me a mountain of gold heaped as high as Heaven.

A single tear shed out of love for My Passion or for your sins, pleases Me more and will be more useful to you, than shedding an ocean of tears for some good that you lack.

The support of one mortifying and injurious word out of love for Me, pleases Me more and will be more useful to you, than to break on your body all the rods cut from the forests of the whole world.

One poor man, stranger, or friendless soul received for love of Me, pleases Me more and will be more useful to you, than if you were to fast for seven years on bread and water.

If you forbear to judge, and interpret and accept with kindness all that you see and hear, this will please Me more and be more useful to you, than if you were rapt to the third Heaven.

Whenever you desire to obtain some benefit from Me by your prayer, let your prayer be for all as well as for yourself.

Out of love for My Passion, support with meekness all that you will have to suffer.

Everywhere and always, place your hope and trust in Me.

—Our Lord to St. Albert the Great.

INDEX

— A —

— B —

— D —

Printed at
FERNAND DION PRES[S]
3451 Masson St.
Montreal, Canada